Definitive
XML
Application
Development

ISBN 0-13-088902-4

90000

9 780130 889027

The Charles F. Goldfarb Definitive XML Series

Megginson
▌ Structuring XML Documents

McGrath
▌ XML by Example: Building E-commerce Applications

Floyd
▌ Building Web Sites with XML

Morgenthal and la Forge
▌ Enterprise Application Integration with XML and Java

McGrath
▌ XML Processing with Python

Cleaveland
▌ Program Generators with XML and Java

Holman
▌ Definitive XSLT and XPath

Walmsley
▌ Definitive XML Schema

Goldfarb and Prescod
▌ Charles F. Goldfarb's XML Handbook™ Fourth Edition

Garshol
▌ Definitive XML Application Development

Titles in this series are produced using XML, SGML, and/or XSL. XSL-FO documents are rendered into PDF by the *XEP Rendering Engine* from RenderX: www.renderx.com

About the Series Editor
Charles F. Goldfarb is the father of XML technology. He invented SGML, the Standard Generalized Markup Language on which both XML and HTML are based. You can find him on the Web at: www.xmlbooks.com

About the Series Logo
The rebus is an ancient literary tradition, dating from 16th century Picardy, and is especially appropriate to a series involving fine distinctions between markup and text, metadata and data. The logo is a rebus incorporating the series name within a stylized XML comment declaration.

Definitive XML Application Development

■ Lars Marius Garshol

Prentice Hall PTR, Upper Saddle River, NJ 07458
www.phptr.com

Library of Congress Cataloging-in-Publication Data

```
Garshol, Lars Marius
    Definitive XML application development / Lars Marius Garshol.
      p.cm -- (The definitve XML series from Charles F. Goldfarb)
    ISBN 0-13-088902-4
      1. XML (Document markup language) 2. Application software--Development.
  I. Title. II. Series.
  QA76.76.H94 G37 2001
  005.7'2--dc21                                                    2001032187
```

Editorial/Production Supervisor: *Dmitry Kirsanov*
Acquisitions Editor: *Mark L. Taub*
Editorial Assistant: *Sarah Hand*
Marketing Manager: *Bryan Gambrel*
Manufacturing Manager: *Maura Zaldivar*
Cover Design: *Anthony Gemmellaro*
Cover Design Director: *Jerry Votta*
Series Design: *Gail Cocker-Bogusz*

© 2002 Prentice Hall PTR
A division of Pearson Education, Inc.
Upper Saddle River, NJ 07458

Opinions expressed in this book are those of the Author and are not necessarily those of the Publisher or Series Editor.

Series logo by Dmitry Kirsanov and Charles F. Goldfarb, copyright © 2002 Charles F. Goldfarb.

Prentice Hall books are widely used by corporations and government agencies for training, marketing, and resale.

The publisher offers discounts on this book when ordered in bulk quantities. For more information, contact: Corporate Sales Department, Phone: 800–382–3419; Fax: 201–236–7141; Email: corpsales@prenhall.com; or write: Prentice Hall PTR, Corp. Sales Dept., One Lake Street, Upper Saddle River, NJ 07458.

Printed in the United States of America

10 9 8 7 6 5 4 3 2 1

ISBN 0–13–088902–4

Pearson Education LTD.
Pearson Education Australia PTY, Limited
Pearson Education Singapore, Pte. Ltd.
Pearson Education North Asia Ltd.
Pearson Education Canada, Ltd.
Pearson Educación de Mexico, S.A. de C.V.
Pearson Education—Japan
Pearson Education Malaysia, Pte. Ltd.

Overview

Contents

Foreword

You hold in your hand a developer's feast!

That's not just content-free praise, even if it is a bit over the top. Feast is an apt metaphor for a book that can meet the demanding requirements of properly teaching XML application development.

Consider the characteristics of this book:

- It is nutritious. It teaches fundamentals that you will retain and reuse for years to come. Instead of just paraphrasing the specs of the API *du jour*, the book equips you to learn and use it — and tomorrow's APIs — right from the source specifications.

- It has many courses. XML processing can be event-based (e.g., SAX), tree-based (e.g., DOM), declarative (e.g., XSLT), or a mix of them, and with many variations and views of the XML document and its data. A single processing paradigm can't hack it.

- It is a planned meal. The many different aspects of XML development are presented in the context of a coherent model of XML representation and processing. The book explains *when* and *why* to use different processing techniques — as well as *how*.

- It is tasty. You'd expect no less from a chef with the skills of Lars Marius Garshol, the developer who created the xmlproc validating XML parser, helped design SAX, and translated SAX to Python.

Now you can satisfy your appetite for XML development skills, with *Definitive XML Application Development*. It will help you become more proficient, more confident and — as with any good feast — well-rounded!

Charles F. Goldfarb
Saratoga, CA
March 19, 2002

Preface

This book was written to help you develop applications that use XML. It focuses on general principles and techniques, aiming to give you knowledge that will remain valuable even after the standards and tools described have evolved a few iterations further than they are today.

The text approaches XML by asking questions like: What problems is XML used to solve? What general approaches to these problems exist, and what tools support them? What other technologies is XML related to? How can XML be used with these other technologies? After reading the book you should, whenever you need to do something with XML, be able to think of several different ways of solving your problem and to choose the best of these.

Who is this book for?

This book is written for developers, and much of it requires knowledge of programming. In general, the reader is expected to have done enough object-oriented programming to know what a class or a method is. The chapters in the first part of the book, as well as the first two chapters on XSLT, do not require programming knowledge and could probably be useful to anyone who is familiar with XML.

This book is not an introduction to XML, as it assumes that you know what XML is and have some familiarity with its main features.

It does not assume that you are an expert, however, and will explain many of the subtler aspects of XML that have consequences for software development.

Although the book uses Python in the source code examples, knowing Python is not a prerequisite, since the book contains an Appendix A, "A lightning introduction to Python," on page 1054. Readers who are not familiar with Python are strongly encouraged to read this appendix before going on to the rest of the book.

What the book covers

The book begins with a look at XML from the point of view of software development, comparing it to other related technologies. Many of the subtler aspects of XML, the XML family of standards, as well as their relationship to software development are also examined. Much space is devoted to the principles of XML software development, using parsers, and the existing techniques for development.

Three chapters are dedicated to each of the two most important XML programming APIs: the SAX and the DOM. Two chapters are dedicated to XSLT. In addition to these standards, several lesser-known APIs, tools and technologies are described. Some are included because of their utility, others were meant to put the main technologies in perspective.

The last part of the book describes XML application design issues in more detail and provides some larger examples that present complete XML applications or toolkits.

In Appendix C, "Python XML packages," on page 1108 there is a description of various distributions of Python XML software and how to install each of these distributions. If you are new to XML processing with Python, it is probably a good idea to look over this appendix before starting to read the tool-related parts of the book. Installing the tools so that you have them available and can play around with them as you read may also be a good idea.

The programming language

Python is a very high-level programming language that is unusually well suited for information-centric program development, since it has excellent support for creation and manipulation of data structures. It is a simple language, in many ways similar to the more widespread languages, such as Java, C++, and Visual Basic, but easier to understand and use.

This means that even though you may not understand Python now, you will be able to learn it quickly. In general, I have found that developers need to study Python for two days in order to be able to contribute usefully to projects. And since Python has so much in common with other languages, you should be able to make use of what you learn even if you usually develop in other languages.

This book mainly uses Python in examples and does in fact have a general bent towards Python. Why this is so, and what is so interesting about Python, may not be immediately obvious to you, so this section explains what Python is and why it is so interesting. However, even though the book uses Python, it is intended to be useful to all XML programmers, regardless of what programming languages they know or want to do XML programming in.

What is it?

Python is a programming language. It has often been called a scripting language, but I think this is a little misleading. The image, the term "scripting language" evokes in me is of a simple little language, dynamically typed and easy to use for amateurs, unsuitable for large applications, not as powerful as a "real" programming language, and definitely slower.

Python, however, is very much a "real" programming language, but at the same time it has some of the characteristics of a scripting language. It is simple, it is very dynamic, it is easy to use for amateurs, and it is slower than compiled languages such as C++, Eiffel, and Common Lisp. At the same time, however, it is very powerful, certainly every bit as powerful as Java, if not more, and eminently suitable for large applications. Among the things that have been written in Python are CORBA ORBs, Web browsers, relational database engines, validating XML parsers, and a full XSLT engine.

I often describe it as "Perl done right," and Python does have a lot in common with Perl. It is a scripting-like language, very suitable for text processing and systems programming, with excellent operating system integration and with many of the same features.[1] Python is also like Perl in that it was created by a single person for his own needs (Guido van Rossum), it used to be distributed as a single widely-ported open source interpreter implementation (there are now more than one), it is closely connected to the Internet and Unix, etc., etc.

At the same time, Python has much in common with Java, in that it is dynamic (much more so than Java) and object-oriented, has exceptions, has a very similar package model, supports in-program documentation, and Python byte-code can also be transferred across a network and executed in a restricted environment.

I am something of a programming language freak and have done development in at least a dozen different programming languages, and studied many more. In my experience, Python stands out because it is so easy and natural to develop in, something that makes Python development just plain nice and fun. Returning to Java or C++ after doing Python development simply feels painful and awkward. I think this is because Python is so clean, simple, and predictable, with few surprises or restrictions and with a large set of ready-made and easy-to-use libraries. Paul Prescod[2] has said that "Python is a language that gets its tradeoffs exactly right", which sums it up pretty well.

A common denominator

Another reason for choosing Python is that no matter which programming language the reader is already used to, Python should be easy to pick up, at least well enough to read. The syntax is clear and simple,

---

1. In fact, Perl's object-oriented features are modeled on Python's object model.

2. Affectionately known as the "St. Paul" of Python evangelism.

and the concepts in the language are very similar to those of mainstream languages such as Java, C, C++, Visual Basic, and Perl. So Python should not be an obstacle for any reader. In fact, it has often been described as "executable pseudo-code," and you will see it used as pseudo-code in some parts of the book.

Furthermore, using Python does not limit us to a single platform. Python runs just as well on Unix as it does on Mac or Windows, or even on a Psion palmtop or a VMS machine.

Python can talk to anything

One of the most appealing aspects of Python is that it is very well integrated with the rest of the world. This means that choosing Python hardly ever shuts you off from some technology or system that you would like your programs to interact with. For example, Microsoft fans will quickly discover that the Windows version of Python can talk to COM objects, create COM servers, connect to ActiveX, DDE, the Win32 API, the Windows registry, MFC, Windows Scripting Host, ADO, ODBC, and so on and so forth. In other words, even though Python is highly portable, you don't have to give up anything under Windows just because you use Python.

Many people, however, prefer to use something other than Windows, such as the Mac. Python is technologically agnostic, so it allows these people to have their way as well. Python runs on Mac, and the Mac version can access the communications toolbox, the font manager, the speech manager, the sound manager, the QuickTime services, and so on.

Other people believe in Unix and would rather use Python there. Again, this is no problem: the Unix versions of Python fit very well into Unix, and there are bindings for things such as Qt, KDE, Gtk, GNOME, Irix and Solaris sound modules, special Linux APIs, etc.

Yet others would like to remain pure, platform-wise, and prefer a strictly operating system-independent platform such as Java. Python can accommodate these people too! Jython[1] is an implementation of Python written in 100% Java which lets you run Python programs inside the Java virtual machine. You can use this as an embedded scripting language for an application, or simply write Python programs with full access to the nice Java stuff such as Swing, JDBC, Jini, RMI, etc.

And of course, apart from the platform issues, most of us would like to be able to speak Internet protocols and connect to other independent technologies. Again, Python can help. There are several ways to connect Python with CORBA, a standardized relational database API (a JDBC for Python), lots of XML tools (of course), LDAP modules, and so on. And the interpreter comes with libraries supporting FTP, HTTP, gopher, NNTP, SMTP, IMAP, POP, HTML, URL parsing, and much more out of the box.

To put it another way, Python is buzzword-friendly and TLA-compatible.[2]

Python is a natural fit for XML programming

Whenever I have to write an XML program of some sort, I usually think of Python first as the programming language to write it in. There are several reasons for this, the most important being that Python is so easy and natural to program in and that it is very well suited for text processing. It is also very easy to build data structures in Python, something that is very important for XML processing.

Another thing is that for anything that involves moving information between different systems, Python is a natural choice, given that whatever these systems may be, Python can very likely talk to them.

Also, Python is highly suitable for the many little programs and scripts that you write to do the small but necessary tasks that usually appear during a project. Doing everything in Python makes it easy to

---

1. The interpreter formerly known as JPython.
2. Three-Letter Acronym. Often used as a synonym for technologies, since many of them have three-letter acronym.

turn prototypes into full programs, and it also means that whenever a little script has to be developed further, the full toolbox implemented for that application is already available to you.

Acknowledgments

A number of people have helped me in different ways with comments, suggestions, information, and critical feedback in various forms while I was writing this book. I am grateful to all of them, and this section lists those I can remember. Not all of their advice has been followed, so any errors and blemishes that remain can safely be assumed to be mine.

Marcus Brisenfeldt
>   For very useful comments on the XSLT chapters.

Marco Cimarosti
>   For enthusiastic and detailed criticism of the chapter on characters, and for many useful suggestions.

Fred L. Drake, Jr.
>   For his very close reading of the text and source code in this book, and his many perceptive comments on both. There is not a chapter in this book that has not had many errors removed thanks to his careful scrutiny of the text.

Lutz Ehrlich
>   For his many useful comments on the first review version of the book.

Tony Graham
>   For painstakingly accurate and extremely useful criticism of the chapter on characters.

Geir Ove Grønmo
>   For his encouragement at a stage when I was very doubtful about the merits of this book, and for his perceptive and useful comments

on the XSLT and architectural forms chapters, which caught many little mistakes and omissions in the text.

Rob W. W. Hooft

For detailed and highly useful criticism on all levels of the book, and especially for the many perceptive and useful comments on the example source code in the book.

Michael Kay

Before writing the XSLT chapters I read his book *XSLT Programmer's Reference*, which did much to improve my understanding of the subject, and taught me some tricks that are used in this book. The section on XSLT performance also owes much to his 2000–06–02 posting to the XSL mailing list.

The Java chapters were also much improved by his detailed and very useful review, pointing out several weak points in the text and providing information I did not have.

Sean McGrath

For reviewing the book and making many useful comments, especially terminological ones. The term "suspended data" was first suggested by him.

Evelyn Mitchell

For painstakingly reviewing the book on paper and mailing me the entire package afterwards. Also, for for her many useful reminders of my tendency to use terms without defining them first.

Brendan Murray

For very useful corrections and suggestions on the chapter on characters, and especially for correcting some of my widely shared (but wrong) ideas about the ISO 8859 series of character sets.

Steven Newcomb

For providing information on the current status of GroveMinder and Epremis.

Uche Ogbuji

For reviewing the XSLT chapters, pointing several minor mistakes and one big one, informing me of parts that were out of date, and explaining to me 4XSLT subtleties that I did not understand without help.

Thomas B. Passin

For tirelessly reviewing the book again and again as it was written and sending me much useful criticism on all levels from individual words to overall organization of the book.

Gary L. Peskin

For quick assistance with implementing one Xalan-J extension element I couldn't figure out how to implement.

Solveig Marie Stiberg Pettersen

For proofreading, for encouragement, and for making sure that I took a break from book-writing every now and then.

Preben Randhol

For providing information on the Unicode support in Ada95.

Boudewijn Rempt

For his very useful comments on the first version of the book that allowed me to see very clearly its effect on a model reader.

Niko Schmuck

For his many useful comments on the manuscript at various stages of its development, for his encouragement, and for liking brown cheese.

Marcel Schoch

For fearlessly pointing out what he did not understand, thus showing me very clearly the weak points in my text.

Sylvia Schwab
> For practical help in communicating with the publisher in the last phase of the writing. This was a real life-saver at the time.

Valeriy E. Ushakov
> For useful feedback on the chapter on characters.

Fred Yankowski
> For useful comments on the first review version.

I would also like to direct a special thanks to Alina Kirsanova and Dmitry Kirsanov, who did a fantastic job of copyediting, indexing, and typesetting the book. Dmitry's keen eye caught many errors small and great throughout the text, and he greatly improved the quality of the prose. There is hardly a page in the book that is not the better for their work, and for this I give them my heartfelt thanks.

Of course, I made changes after all these people read the text, and in so doing no doubt introduced new errors. The honour for these errors, as well as for those so subtly hidden that they escaped the eyes of all my reviewers, and even the Editor himself, I should like to reserve for myself. You will find the best of these listed on `http://www.garshol.priv.no/download/text/ph1/errata.html`. If you spot one that is not on the list already, I would like to hear about it.

In addition to the people who have helped me with the book, I would like to thank all those people who have used so much of their time to give us the standards and software this book discusses. This includes the SGML and XML families of standards, Web standards, character standards, XML software, and Python itself. Without the efforts of all these people over the past three decades, what is discussed in this book would not exist.

Uptodateness

The main problem with books about Internet technology is that the technology changes so quickly that books rapidly become dated. To help you decide whether the book is up to date or not, here is a list of the various standards and tools covered in this book, and the version of each that the book is based on.

The versions of tools and standards covered in this book

What	Version	Release date
DOM	2.0	2000–11–13
DOM	3.0	2000–11–14
Python	2.1	2001–05–05
Jython	2.1	2001–12–31
SAX	2.0	2000–10–16
Unicode	3.0	2000–02–01
XML	1.0 2nd ed.	2000–10–06
XML Infoset	1.0	2001–10–24
xmlproc	0.70	2000–05–11
4Suite	0.10.1	2001–01–15
PyXML package	0.7	2001–12–20
XSLT	1.0	1999–11–16
XSLT	1.1 WD	2000–12–12
XPath	1.0	1999–11–06
Pyxie	?	Not yet published
pysp	0.1	Not yet published
Sab-pyth	0.51	2000–12–18
XInclude	1.0 WD	2000–03–22
XBase	1.0 CR	2000–09–08
Sablotron	0.50	2000–12–29
xmlarch	0.30	Not yet published

In the table above, WD is used as an abbreviation for "Working Draft," and CR for "Candidate Recommendation," both meaning W3C specifications that are still work in progress.

Working with XML

- XML and data representation
- How XML is processed
- Views of documents
- Typical tasks
- Characters

Part One

This first part of the book introduces the concepts that are necessary to make full use of the techniques and tools presented in the following chapters.

XML and information systems

- Representing data digitally
- XML and digital data
- Information systems
- XML and information systems

T his book describes a method for representing data inside computers. As information flows through the processes that operate on it, its forms and representations change in subtle ways. These transformations are governed by patterns of rules usually called programs. Computers are information processing machines, and programs are essentially servants created to serve the needs of the information stored and processed in these machines. Programs exist to display data, to transform data, to move data from one location to another, and to let humans interact with data.

When creating information-centric applications, the many methods of representing data, XML being one among many, must be considered in relation to other methods and the needs of the information itself. Often, the information will be best served by flowing from one representation to another, as each representation best serves the purpose of one part of the system.

In this chapter we will consider how XML compares to other important methods of data representation, such as relational databases and object-oriented databases. This provides a basis for understanding how XML can be used profitably and at which points in a larger application data is best represented as XML. Later, we will look at how to write applications that read, process, and generate XML, and the various methods for doing this. Finally, we will consider how to use XML together with other information technologies in order to create useful applications.

1.1 | Representing data digitally

Today's computers are digital machines, which means that any information that is to be processed by them must be represented as a sequence of binary digits (zeroes and ones). This is slightly problematic because such sequences do not have any obvious meaning. To take one example, it is impossible to tell what the string `01001000011010010010001` actually means without knowing what rules were used to produce it.

To represent information digitally we use rules that define how to convert the information from the human understanding of it into strings of bits. A collection of such rules is known as a *notation* in this book, but often called a *data format* in ordinary computer terminology. Knowing the notation also allows us to go the other way and interpret the string back into human terms. A very common interpretation for binary strings is as numbers written in base 2, i.e. in the binary system. If this interpretation were applied to the binary string above it would yield the number 4745505. This might well be the correct interpretation, but it doesn't really tell us much or seem like a very useful interpretation without a context. One context might be: the number is the population of Denmark.[1]

Another common representation of digital information is the ASCII character encoding, where text is represented by assigning a number to each character that may occur in text, and every character is

---

1.   It is not, but it is a plausible context.

represented as its number written out in base 2 with 8 bits (or binary digits) per character. If we interpret the string above according to this ASCII notation,[1] we find that it spells out characters number 72, 105, and 33, in that order. These three characters together form the string `Hi!`. In other words, it is a greeting.

1.1.1 *Notations*

So far we have only considered the encoding of individual values or data items, such as strings and numbers, without any context for these to be interpreted in. In computing such values hardly ever appear in isolation, but are usually found in a larger context, a structured collection of data items. Imagine that a digital data stream is received by an application somehow, disregarding the transmission method for the moment. This means that a stream of binary digits will be pouring into the application, which must then somehow make sense of this stream of information. Doing so requires not only the ability to decode individual data items, but also to locate the boundaries of each item and put the items together into a coherent structure. The rules for how to interpret the stream in this higher-level sense are called a notation.[2] Notations can be made to represent very nearly anything at all, be it documents, databases, sound, images, or any other kind of data. Note that there are two main kinds of notations: character based and bit based. The first consisting of characters, just like text, the structure of the second being defined in terms of bits and bytes.

One notation is the textual notation, which applies the ASCII character encoding to entire data streams. This character based notation is simple and convenient and can be used to represent anything at all,

---

1.   The word *notation*, as used in this book, means what in ordinary terminology is meant by a *data format*.

2.   The term notation is used in this series to mean a set of rules for representing information in files. It is usually called a format, but since that term is somewhat vague we use the term notation here.

from novels through laundry lists to payroll information. However, its conceptual structure is not apparent in the text and so it cannot be processed automatically by software for purposes other than editing and display. To be able to perform most other tasks, a less general and more application-specific notation is needed.

An example may serve to make this discussion of data encoding and data formats clearer. Shown in Example 1–1 are the first 200 bytes of a digital data stream, with each byte in the stream interpreted as a base 2 number and displayed as a hexadecimal number, which is a common way of displaying raw binary data.

Example 1–1. An example data stream

```
46 72 6f 6d 3a 20 59 6f 75 72 20 66 72 69 65 6e 64 20 3c 66 72 69 65
6e 64 40 70 75 62 6c 69 63 2e 63 6f 6d 3e a0 54 6f 3a 20 4c 61 72 73
20 4d 61 72 69 75 73 20 47 61 72 73 68 6f 6c 20 3c 6c 61 72 73 67 61
40 67 61 72 73 68 6f 6c 2e 70 72 69 76 2e 6e 6f 3e a0 53 75 62 6a 65
63 74 3a 20 41 20 66 75 6e 6e 79 20 70 69 63 74 75 72 65 a0 4d 65 73
73 61 67 65 2d 49 44 3a 20 3c 35 30 33 32 35 42 41 32 38 42 30 39 33
34 38 32 31 41 35 37 46 30 30 38 30 35 46 42 37 46 43 32 35 30 31 45
36 36 42 35 45 40 6d 61 69 6c 2e 70 75 62 6c 69 63 2e 63 6f 6d 3e a0
44 61 74 65 3a 20 46 72 69 2c 20 38 20 4f 63 74
```

This binary dump doesn't make a lot of sense in the form it is shown here, but if we are told that it is a character based notation, things become much clearer. Interpreted as ASCII text, the first 200 bytes of the data stream look like Example 1–2.

Example 1–2. The data stream as ASCII

```
From: Your friend <friend@public.com>
To: Lars Marius Garshol <larsga@garshol.priv.no>
Subject: A funny picture
Message-ID: <50325BA28B0934821A57F00805FB7C@mail.public.com>
Date: Fri, 8 Oct
```

Suddenly, we see that the data stream is not just a text stream, but an email. Emails have a stricter and less general notation than plain text files, which is defined in Internet specifications, the relevant ones being RFCs 822 and 2045 to 2049. RFC stands for Request For Comments and RFCs are official Internet documents that can be found at `http://www.ietf.org/rfc/rfcXXXX.txt` and also at a huge number of mirror sites world-wide.

The email notation starts with a list of headers and continues with a body that holds the actual email contents. Example 1–2 shows the beginning of the headers. Each header is placed on a separate line, lines being separated by newline characters.[1] On each line, the name of the header field appears first, followed by a colon and a space and then the value of the header field. This enables us to locate individual data items in the email headers, and also to put them together into a larger structure where each data item has a name. Knowing the name of each header field, together with detailed knowledge of the email notation, also tells us how to decode the value in each field. This can sometimes be rather complex, such as in the case of the date.

Example 1–3 shows the entire set of headers for the email, together with an abbreviated body.

In order to be able to decode the body of the email we have to look at the `Content-type` header field, which tells us what data notation is used in the body. In this case, the field says `multipart/mixed`. This particular notation is defined by the Internet mail standard known as MIME (Multipurpose Internet Mail Extensions), defined in RFCs 2045 to 2049. It is used for emails that consist of several parts, called attachments. This means that the body consists of several data streams, each making up one attachment, separated by the boundary string also given in the `Content-type` field.

If we look closely at the body, we will see that it contains first a message to users using mail readers that are not MIME-aware, outside

---

1. The newline characters specified in RFC 822 are carriage return (ASCII 13) followed by line feed (ASCII 10).

Example 1–3. The entire email

```
From: Your friend <friend@public.com>
To: Lars Marius Garshol <larsga@garshol.priv.no>
Subject: A funny picture
Message-ID: <50325BA28B0934821A57805FB7C@mail.public.com>
Date: Fri, 8 Oct 1999 11:26:22 +0200
MIME-Version: 1.0
X-Mailer: Internet Mail Service (5.5.2448.0)
Content-Type: multipart/mixed; boundary="----_=_NextPart_000_01116F"
X-UIDL: 37ef28060000035b

   This is a MIME-encoded message. Parts or all of it may be
   unreadable if your software does not understand MIME. See RFC 2045
   for a definition of MIME.

----_=_NextPart_000_01116F
Content-type: text/plain

Hi Lars,

here is a funny picture.

----_=_NextPart_000_01BF116F
Content-type: image/gif; name="funny.gif"
Content-transfer-encoding: base64
Content-disposition: attachment; filename="funny.gif"


...
----_=_NextPart_000_01116F
```

of the first attachment. The first attachment has a form similar to the email itself, with headers and a body. In this case, the body is plain ASCII text, and requires no special treatment.

The second attachment, however, is a different matter. It contains a GIF image, encoded with the base64 encoding. This is a common encoding much used on the Internet for encoding binary data as text, so that it may be safely used with applications that only expect ordinary text.[1] In this case, after decoding the base64 data the application will

---

1.   It is defined in RFC 2045.

have another stream of digital information, this time in the GIF notation.

To be able to interpret and display the GIF image, the application must start from scratch again and locate the various fields inside the stream that makes up the image, decode them and use them to decode the rest of the stream. Exactly how this is done is not really relevant to this example, so we will skip this for now. Note that the GIF notation is a binary notation, which is both more efficient and harder to decode and understand than a text notation.

What we have just examined is a notation for email messages. It tells us how to decode a stream of digital information into a coherent data structure that makes sense to a human being. Inside the stream appear various data items and also new data streams, which are the contents of the two attachments. The individual data items have their own notations specified by the larger notation, as do the data streams.

1.1.2 *Data representation*

So far, we have only discussed the notation itself, but not what the application should do with the represented in it. The application needs to somehow store the information in the working memory, and to do this it must choose some *data representation*. The working memory of a computer is nothing but a huge array of bytes, just like the data stream, which means that the notation could well be used to represent the information inside a running program by simply storing the stream as-is in memory. However, notations are generally very awkward to use as the actual data representation in a program, since they are completely flat (being sequences of binary digits) and programs generally need to be able to traverse and modify the data. It is of course possible to do this using the external notation, but it is rather awkward, as Example 1–4 shows.

This implementation of the Email class uses the external email notation as the internal representation of emails inside the program. This is done by keeping the email as a string, so that values can be

Example 1–4. Using the external notation as internal representation

```
import string

class Email:
    """A class for encapsulating email messages and providing access
    to them."""

    def __init__(self, email):
        self._email = email

    def get_header(self, name):
        """Returns a list of the values of all instances of the
        header with the given name."""
        values = []
        pos = string.find(self._email, "\n" + name + ": ")
        while pos != -1:
            end = string.find(self._email, "\n", pos + 1)
            values.append(self._email[pos + len("\n" + name + ": ")
                                      : end])
            pos = string.find(self._email, "\n" + name + ":",
                              pos + 1)

        return values

    def add_header(self, name, value):
        "Inserts a header with the given name and value."
        pos = string.find(self._email, "\n\n")
        assert pos != -1

        self._email = self._email[ : pos + 1] + \
                      name + ": " + value + "\n" + \
                      self._email[pos + 1 : ]

    # ...
```

extracted from the string and the entire email can be modified by modifying the string. As should be obvious, this is both awkward and inefficient.

A much more natural representation would be to have a dictionary keyed on header names that maps to a list of values to represent the headers. The attachments could be represented as a list of attachment objects, where each attachment object holds a dictionary of header fields and a file-like object to represent the attachment contents. Further classes could also be defined to represent the values in the various fields (email addresses, dates, etc.). Such an implementation is shown in Example 1–5.

Example 1–5. Using a more natural representation

```
class Email:
    """A class for encapsulating email messages and providing access
    to them."""

    def __init__(self):
        self._headers = {}
        self._attach  = []

    def get_header(self, name):
        """Returns a list of the values of all instances of the
        header with the given name."""
        return self._headers[name]

    def add_header(self, name, value):
        "Inserts a header with the given name and value."
        try:
            self._headers[name].append(value)
        except KeyError:
            self._headers[name] = [value]

    # ...

class Attachment:
    """A class for encapsulating attachments in an email and
    providing access to them."""

    def __init__(self):
        self._headers = {}
        self._contents = None

    # ...
```

What we have done now is to design an internal data structure that is optimized for storing the information from the email in the working memory of a program.n Both the data stream and the data structure are digital, but they have very different properties. The data stream is a sequential stream of bytes[1] (defined by a notation), while the data structure is not necessarily contiguous in memory, has no specific order and is highly granular rather than flat as the data stream.

One thing that is important to understand is that while the data structure represents the original email data stream it does not do so fully. The data structure keeps only the information we consider essential (what is called the logical information), and throws away much information about what the original data stream looked like. One of the pieces of information we have lost is what boundary string was used between each attachment, or what the warning before the first attachment was. We can no longer recreate the original email!

This means that although the second representation is much more usable than the first, it carries a hidden cost: the loss of information that may at times be necessary. As we will see later, central XML specifications do the same, and this has both benefits and costs that one must be aware of. For if you do need to recreate the original data stream, you will need to solve this problem somehow, and the XML specifications and established practice will offer little or no help.

1.1.3   *Serialization and deserialization*

The problem with having the data in the working memory of the application is that once the application is shut down or the power to the machine is turned off, the contents of the working memory are lost. Also, the application cannot communicate its internal structures directly to other programs, since they are not allowed to access its

---

1.   The stream always consists of bytes, even it it may be character based.

memory.[1] Programs running on other computers will not be able to access the data at all.

Using a notation solves this problem, however, because it gives us a well-defined way of representing our data as a data stream. It does leave us with two problems, however, which are those of moving data back and forth between the notation and the internal data structure. The technical term for the process of writing a data structure out as such a binary stream is *serialization*. It is so called because the structure is turned into a flat stream, or series, of bytes. Once we have this stream of bytes, we can store it into a file on disk where it will persist even if the application is shut down or the power is turned off. The file can then be read by other applications. We can also transmit the stream across the network to another machine where other applications can access it.

In the example of the email program, for example, the email program will receive the email from a mail server and store it in memory in its internal data structures. It will then write this internal structure out to its database of emails, which can be organized in many different ways. Some programs simply put each email (using the original notation) in a separate file, while others use more sophisticated database-like approaches.

In general, we can say that data has two states: *live* and *suspended*. Live data is in the internal structure used by program and is being accessed and used by that program. Suspended data is serialized data in some notation that is either stored in a file or being transmitted across a network. Suspended data must be deserialized to be turned into live data so that it can actually be used by programs. The *deserialization* of character based notations is usually known as *parsing*, and a substantial branch of computer science is dedicated to the various

---

1.   Some operating systems do actually allow precisely this through a feature called shared-memory inter-process communication. It is relatively difficult to use and presents its own obstacles and problems, and is not much used. For the purposes of this discussion we will ignore it completely.

methods of parsing.[1] The vaguer term *loading* is also at times used as a synonym for deserialization.

It is not necessarily the case that each notation has a single data structure, and vice versa. In fact, usually each application supporting a notation will have its own data structure that is specific to it. In many cases applications will also support many notations.

Note that serialized (suspended) data need not be written to a file when it is stored. It can also be stored in a database (most database systems support storage of uninterpreted binary large objects, also known as *blobs*), as part of another file (as the email example showed) or in some other way. In fact, serialized data doesn't need to be stored at all, but can instead be transmitted across the network or to another process on the same machine.

1.1.4 *Data models*

Over the years, certain methods for structuring data have established themselves as useful general approaches to building data structures. When such a method is formalized by a specification of some kind it becomes a *data model*. A data model is perhaps easiest explained as a set of basic building blocks for creating data structures and a set of rules for how these can be combined.

One of the most widely used and best-defined data models is the relational model where data is organized into a table with horizontal rows, each containing a record, and vertical columns, representing fields. Each record contains information about a distinct entity, with individual values in each field. This is the data model used in comma-separated files and in relational databases. In relational databases some fields can also be references into other tables.

---

1. For more information, see "the Dragon book," as the classic book, *Compilers: Principles, Tools, and Techniques*, by Aho, Sethi, and Ullmann, is usually known.

Another common data model is the object-oriented one, where data consists of individual objects, each of which has a number of attributes associated with it. Attributes have a name and a value and can be primitive values or references to other objects. This model is used by object-oriented programming languages and databases.

Defining a data model that states how data must be structured has several benefits. First, it gives a framework for thinking about information design that can be very helpful for developers by providing a set of stereotypes or templates which can be applied to the problem at hand to yield a solution. Secondly, it allows general data processing frameworks (that is, databases) to be created that can be used to create many different kinds of applications. The prime example of such frameworks are relational databases.

At this point you may be wondering what the data model used by emails is, and the answer is that email specifications do not use any particular data model. Instead, they use a well-known formalism known as EBNF (Extended Backus-Naur Form) to formally specify the notation of emails, and leave the conceptual structure undefined. People tend to agree on what the structure is anyway, although they can occasionally disagree on details, some of which may be important.

To be able to use a data model, the application developer must represent the information in the application in terms of that data model. Doing so lets the application use the notations and data processing frameworks that are based on the data model. For example, to be able to represent the structure of emails in relational databases, the application must express the structure of the emails using the tabular data model. Table 1–1 shows the result of this translation.

As you can see, it was a relatively simple translation. The only real problem was how to represent the attachments. The solution used here was a bit simplistic, since the attachment headers are just strings. This means that their structure is not represented using the data model at all, so this isn't really a very good solution. The attachments should have their own (almost identical) tables, but for simplicity I did not do that here.

Table 1–1   Email as table

Field	Value	Order
From	Your friend <friend@public.com>	
To	Lars Marius Garshol <larsga@garshol.priv.no>	
Subject	A funny picture	
Message-ID	<50325BA28B0934821A57805FB7C@mail.public.com>	
Date	Fri, 8 Oct 1999 11:26:22 +0200	
MIME-Version	1.0	
X-Mailer	Internet Mail Service (5.5.2448.0)	
Content-type	multipart/mixed	
X-UIDL	37ef28060000035b	
Body	Content-type: text/plain Hi Lars, [...]	1
Body	Content-type: image/gif [...]	2

Representing information in the application using the data model of the underlying framework is usually easy, but sometimes awkward or even quite difficult. The relational model is especially strict and inflexible, which made it possible to describe it very precisely mathematically and develop a powerful set of mathematical abstractions and techniques for working with relational data. Due to this work, relational databases today are well understood, extremely reliable and scalable and may perhaps in fairness be called the greatest success of computer science so far. For all their power, however, they are not suitable for all applications, and this is one of the facts that motivated the development of alternative models, such as the object-oriented one.

Restricting the possible forms of data to a specific data model has another benefit: formal languages can be defined to describe the structure of the data in terms of the underlying data model. Using such languages, the data structure of an application can be described formally and precisely. Such a description is known as a *schema* and the languages as *schema languages*.[1] In the relational model, for example, a schema will define the tables used by an application, the type of each column in each table, and any cross-references between the tables.

Defining a schema for an application has the benefit that the framework can use it to automatically validate the data against the schema to ensure no invalid data is entered. With relational databases this means that you cannot put text in numeric columns, enter postal codes that are too long or too short, or insert a reference to a row in a table that does not exist (nor can you remove a row from one table if there are references to it from other tables).

1.1.5 *Summary*

Figure 1–1 shows how a live data structure inside an application can be serialized into a suspended sequential data stream which can then be sent over the network, passed to another application or written to

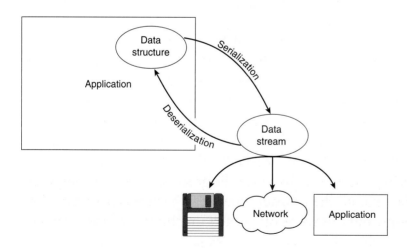

Figure 1–1   Summary of data representation terms

---

1.   Such languages are sometimes also referred to as schema definition languages, that is, languages used to define schemas.

disk. It also shows how the stream can be read back into the application to rebuild the internal data representation. Today, the representation will usually be defined as a set of classes, but programming languages that are not object-oriented have other ways of representing data. The internal data representation will be defined in terms of a data model, such as the relational or the object-oriented. The data stream will be written according to a notation of some kind, and the notation will also be based on a data model.

Initially, we discussed the notations of individual values and data items. It is worth noting that the notation of values is often shared between the external notations and the internal data representations. These mainly differ in the way they compose larger structures from collections of values and data items, and not so much in the notation of individual values.

1.2 | XML and digital data

XML is a markup language. Or, rather, it is a way of creating markup languages. What this means, in the terminology of the previous section, is that it is a data model with a standardized notation for serialization. With XML, the notation is what often receives the most attention, and many think that the notation actually *is* XML. This is partly because this is the only visible form XML data has, which makes it appear more real to many people than the conceptual data model.

As you will see in this book, however, it is the data model that is the most important part, and the syntax is just a method for storing XML and moving it from one place to another. There could also perfectly well be more than one XML syntax reflecting the same data model.[1] The important step when representing data as XML is in any case to

---

1.   And in fact there are. The Lisp community, for example, tends to use Lisp syntax to represent XML fragments inside their programs, often interleaved with source code.

express it in terms of the XML data model. So if we want to represent the email we saw earlier, we must model its structure using elements and attributes. And if we want, we can then represent that structure using an XML file.

One way to represent emails as XML is to use an element type to represent header fields (which we might call header, with further name and value element types for the header name and value) and then another element type for each attachment (which we might call attachment). The result might look like Example 1–6.

Example 1–6. An email in XML syntax

```
<email>
  <header>
    <name>To</name>
    <value>Lars Marius Garshol &lt;larsga@garshol.priv.no></value>
  </header>
  <header>
    <name>Subject</name>
    <value>A funny picture</value>
  </header>
  <header>
    <name>Message-ID</name>
    <value>&lt;50325BA28B0934821A57805FB7C@mail.public.com></value>
  </header>
  <header>
    <name>Date</name>
    <value>Fri, 8 Oct 1999 11:26:22 +0200</value>
  </header>
  <header>
    <name>MIME-Version</name>
    <value>1.0</value>
  </header>
  <header>
    <name>X-Mailer</name>
    <value>Internet Mail Service (5.5.2448.0)</value>
  </header>
  <header>
    <name>Content-Type</name>
    <value>multipart/mixed</value>
  </header>
```

```
<header>
  <name>X-UIDL</name>
  <value>37ef28060000035b</value>
</header>
<attachment>
  <header>
    <name>Content-type</name>
    <value>text/plain</value>
  </header>

Hi Lars,

here is a funny picture.

</attachment>

<attachment>
  <header>
    <name>Content-type</name>
    <value>image/gif; name="funny.gif"</value>
  </header>
  <header>
    <name>Content-transfer-encoding</name>
    <value>base64</value>
  </header>
  <header>
    <name>Content-disposition</name>
    <value>attachment; filename="funny.gif"</value>
  </header>

  ...
</attachment>

</email>
```

Clearly, this is exactly the same information as in the plain text notation, but expressed in a different notation, and using a formalized data model. This is just one of many possible translations into XML that could be used. For example, we might very well have used dedicated element types to represent some of the more important header fields, such as To and From.

One noteworthy aspect of the XML version of the data is that we have decided to keep the original notation of the individual values.

Many of the values have an internal structure that might well have been captured in XML, but to keep the complexity of the example down this was not done. The base64 encoding of the GIF image was also kept; it is convenient for XML because it encodes the binary data, which may contain illegal byte sequences according to XML's rules, using only characters which have no special meaning in XML and thus can safely be used.

This document (complete pieces of XML data is called *documents*) has a corresponding conceptual structure as dictated by the XML data model. This structure is what mathematicians would describe as a tree, which means that it consists of pieces called *nodes*, each having one parent and any number of children. Another way to describe it is to say that it is strictly hierarchical. The data model is described in more detail in 2.4.4, "Drawing the line," on page 74. Figure 1–2 shows the structure of our XML email document as the data model.

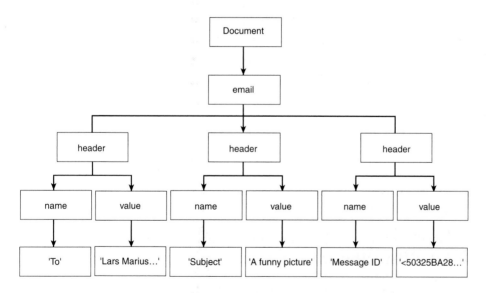

Figure 1–2   The conceptual document structure

What Figure 1–2 shows is the true structure of the XML document; the syntax is just its serialized form. In a way, one could say that this structure is what we meant, or had in mind, when we wrote the email XML document.

The diagram contains one node whose significance may not be immediately obvious. This is the "Document" node, which represents the entire XML document. Most systems that represent XML documents have something that is equivalent to this node. This is because it is convenient to have something that contains the entire document, where DTD information and information about what was before and after the document element can be stored. It is possible to make do without this node, however, and some systems do.

In addition to the syntax and the data model, there is a standardized API called the Document Object Model (the DOM), which defines one way of representing this structure using objects in a programming language. This means that how to represent XML documents inside programs has also been standardized. DOM implementations can read in XML documents and create the corresponding structure, and also write this structure back out in serialized form. The DOM is described in detail in Chapter 11, "DOM: an introduction," on page 396.

An application that wants to work with XML emails can use the DOM to access the contents of XML emails. However, that is much more awkward than using the `Email` class since it requires the application to work in terms of elements and attributes, rather than header fields and values. Because of this, it may be better to use the DOM to create an Email object, and then let the applications use that object instead.

1.3 | Information systems

An information system is a collection of information that is, in essence, a model of some aspects of the world. It is of interest to its users because it can answer questions about these aspects of the world. Before the advent of computerized information systems the only way to find out if, for example, a book was available in a library or lent out was to go and look at the shelf where the book ought to be. If it was not there, it would be assumed that someone was currently reading it. Today, however, librarians will consult the library information system to see whether the book is available or not, and only check the information from the system against external reality (the shelf) if the reader insists.

An information system need not be digital: A paper encyclopedia, for example, is an information system that can answer a large number of questions when consulted by a human. This book, however, is written strictly with digital information systems in mind. These are usually used to store information about the world external to the computer, but not always. One exception might be the registries that many computer systems maintain of installed software and configuration information for that software.

1.3.1 *Anatomy of classical information systems*

Any information system exists as part of a larger context in which the system plays a specific role. In the case of the library, the information system will be consulted and updated by the librarians. This will be its context, and the role it plays is something that can help answer questions such as "what books does the library have," "where can I find this book," "is this book available or not," and so on.

Figure 1–3 shows a diagrammatic outline of what the library information system might look like. In the center, there is a data store of some kind, most likely a relational database. Around it are several applications which all access the central data repository, without being aware of each other. These applications are used by three different groups of people: the librarians, the readers, and the system administrators. This is how classical information systems have generally been structured. There are some variations in the exact structure of the system, but in a broad outline, these are the features that most such systems have had.

In such systems, the basis of the entire system is the schema used to define the internal data representation in the data store. The schema

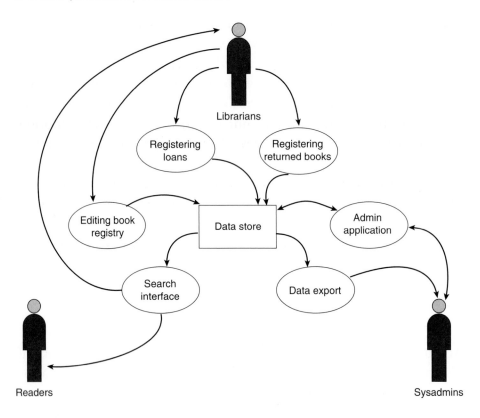

Figure 1–3   The anatomy of the library information system

defines how data is stored in the data store, and this determines how applications can access and work with the data. The schema defines the structure of the data and lays down constraints on it. For example, the schema might say that the book ID code must be unique, each row in the loan table must have valid book and reader ID codes, and so on. These rules are (usually) enforced by the data store, which means that even though there are many different applications, perhaps written by different people over a long period of time, one can be certain that none of the applications will violate these rules.

Another role played by the schema is that of documenting the structure of the data that the system manages as well as many of the assumptions made in the system design. Together with prose, the schema is very valuable as documentation, since it is concise, clear, and unambiguous.

It should also be noted that the schema plays a very important role in that it effectively defines the limits for what kinds of functionality can be supported by the applications in the system. For example, if the library information system does not record the Dewey classification code of each book, searching for books by their Dewey codes cannot be supported at all.

The information stored in a database is in a half-way state between liveness and suspendedness, not really being entirely in memory or entirely serialized. It should probably be considered to be live, since the application does not need to expend much effort to access the data and the data certainly are not serialized in the database. The data export application in Figure 1–3 would serialize information from the system into some kind of transport notation, whether for sending to other installations elsewhere or for backup purposes. Other than that, the library system does not really do any serialization or deserialization. It holds all its needed data internally and has little need for communication with the outside world, except through user interaction.

1.3.2 *Formality in information systems*

Digital information systems can usefully be divided into two categories: *formal* and *informal* systems. In formal systems the information follows strict rules, while informal systems are free-form. This division is not absolute, since systems can have varying degrees of formality, but a typical example of an informal information system might be a collection of word processor documents containing a list of the CDs available in a library in the form of prose.

Even though this collection of documents could be consulted by a human to find, for example, the number of songs in the CD collection, a computer would not be able to do the same, since it cannot read text and understand what it says. To enable a computer to answer this question, one would have to develop a formal information system to store the information in such a way that the computer, still without knowing what a song or a CD really is, could perform some simple operations that would result in the number of songs being counted.

Doing this, however, means formalizing the system and making it more rigid, which may be hard if the information in it has a very complex structure, or if that structure is poorly understood. Furthermore, a formal system will be harder to extend, since formal systems give much less flexibility in terms of how information is expressed. The benefit is much greater convenience in use through automation. For example, although a human might in theory count the songs on all the CDs in a library, that would require a large amount of manual work, while a properly designed digital information system could answer the question within seconds.

Quite often, an organization will start out with a highly formal system, such as one for books in a library. After the system has been in use for a while, the library starts stocking CDs in addition to books, but since CDs do not fit in the information system (the structure being too specifically directed towards books) the list of CDs is kept in simple text documents instead.

Eventually, this solution is bound to become insufficient to support the number of CDs that the library accumulates. To solve this, the original information system is extended with support for CDs, and the information in the text documents is migrated from the text documents to the larger system. From this point on, both CDs and books will be supported. Most large real-life information systems will at any point in their lifetime consist of a highly formal core with several smaller informal systems clustered around them. These informal systems will typically contain less data and often also be only temporary in nature. Some of them, however, will grow and eventually demand to be made more formal and need applications of their own.

One of the strengths of XML is that it supports this very well, since it can support both relatively informal and quite formal data. XML information systems also tend to be easier to set up initially and also to change later than their more formal competitors. XML is generally less formal and controlled than data in ordinary databases. With XML, checking validity is a separate operation, performed when necessary, and not something enforced by the data storage mechanism itself (except when an XML database with such functionality is used, which is relatively rare).

1.3.3 *Ontologies*

To be able to formalize the system, one really should design a schema that defines the structure, but before a schema can be made there are two steps that need to be taken. Often, these are taken without being explicitly thought through, and this may even work well, but it is still worth knowing about the steps.

The parts of the world that are considered within the scope of the information system are often called the *Universe of Discourse* (UoD) for that particular information system. The next step towards a schema is to analyze the UoD to find out what it consists of and which parts of it are considered interesting. In the example above, this would mean the CD collection of some library, and implicitly, only the music CDs (since we mentioned songs) and not the CD-ROMs with software and data.

This analysis would result in what is called an *ontology*, which means a theory of reality. Such a theory of reality might state that our particular UoD consists of CDs, artists, and songs. This is a pretty naive theory, though, as it omits many interesting aspects of the UoD. For example, artists can be individual people, such as Mariss Jansons and Peter Gabriel, but also groups of people, such as the Oslo Philharmonic Orchestra and Genesis. Some artists have released music both individually and as part of a group of people (for example, Peter Gabriel was a member of Genesis until 1975, but released solo albums after that).

Another, and even subtler problem arises when we try to count the songs in the CD collection, because we haven't decided what a song really is. For example, Peter Gabriel has released three different CDs that all contain a song titled *Biko*. Does this count as one song, or as three? The version on the album usually[1] known as *3* is the original studio version, the version on *Plays Live* is a live recording, and the version on *Shaking the Tree* is indistinguishable from the original studio version on *3*.

The complexity does not stop there, for these CDs are issued in slightly different versions in different countries, and records that were originally released as LPs are often re-released once on CD with poor quality and later remastered to much better quality. This produces CDs with identical titles and song listings, identical (or near-identical) covers, but with subtly different sounds.

Clearly, to be able to make a structured information system for something as messy as this, we need a theory of reality, an ontology that can tell us what is what. One such ontology already exists, and is known as IFLA FRBR, or Functional Requirements for Bibliographic Records, defined by the International Federation of Library Associations and Institutions. The specification can be found at `http://www.ifla.org/VII/s13/frbr/frbr.pdf`. This ontology deals with what it calls *creations* (not just music) and defines three main categories of creations:

manifestations

These are tangible creations that are either physical objects composed of atoms and molecules or digital objects consisting of bits and bytes. A CD and a track on a CD would both be manifestations, as would notes printed on paper.

performances

These are spatio-temporal creations, that is, creations that have taken place as events in space and time. A concert would be a typical example of a performance. If a performance is recorded somehow, that recording becomes a manifestation of the performance.[2]

---

1.   His first three albums have no titles.

2.   Note that the performance itself is not classified as a manifestation.

works

Works are the least tangible category of creations, being abstract creations. For example, if you think of a new melody, that becomes an abstract creation, and its existence will not be revealed until you either make a manifestation of it (by writing down the notes) or a performance of it (by humming it or singing it out loud).

With this ontology in hand, we can suddenly make sense of the confusion we suffered earlier. The question "How many songs are there?" was ill-posed, in the sense that we had not properly defined the term "song." Instead, we have three new terms, and occurrences of these we can count with confidence. So, *Biko* is a work, which has been performed in the studio and also live in concert. The three occurrences of the work are three different manifestations of two different performances of one work.[1]

1.3.4 *Information models*

With the ontology in place, we can start to make an *information model* for our UoD. The information model is a detailed conceptual model of all the information in the system, including all types of items[2] with their fields (or properties) and the relationships between them. For our example we could start by defining the item types CD, track, person, artist, and work (choosing to disregard performances) and then continue by defining the attributes of each and their relationships.

An information model differs from a schema in that the schema is defined in terms of a data model, while the information model is

---

1.   Note that this analysis completely disregards the fact that there are millions of copies of these CDs, and instead classifies all copies together. Most libraries would not be satisfied with this, and would want to keep track of the separate copies as well. This is a simple extension of the ontology, however, and presents no particular problems.

2.   It is difficult to know what term to use here. Class, entity, and object all have problematic connotations. The term 'item' is a compromise.

independent of any particular data model. In fact, part of the reason for making an information model is that the model is not plagued by the weaknesses of some data models, and this means that we can model the data more-or-less directly.[1] The information model is generally created either informally, using some undefined data model, or it is created using some formal modelling language. Among the possibilities are the Entity-Relationship (ER) language, Object Role Modeling (ORM), and Unified Modeling Language (UML). Some people also use the EXPRESS schema language, since it is so powerful that even though one doesn't plan to use EXPRESS in the system to be developed, EXPRESS can serve to define the information model.

Once all the item types, their attributes, and relationships were worked out and clearly defined, we would have an information model for the information system. This would not be something that could be used directly to generate programs or to configure software to manage the system for us, but would be a conceptual specification that could serve as documentation for the system. Typically, the developers of the software components in the system would use the information model as guidance when developing the components, and it would also be used to set up any central data repositories such as a database.

To make a schema for the system, the developers would need to select a schema language and express the information model in terms of the data model used by that schema language. This step often involves more than a simple reformulation of the information model, since changes may prove necessary for various kinds of performance reasons. Generally, the information model is designed to be easy to understand, while the schema must be designed to be efficient.

---

1. In a sense the information model could be described as a schema made using a perfect schema language that matches our needs exactly. This doesn't exist, of course, but we try to get as close as we can.

1.3.5 *Summary*

To briefly reiterate the terms introduced in this section, an information system is a model of a subset of the external world known as the Universe of Discourse. The basis for the model is an ontology, a theory of reality, based on which a conceptual information model describing the detailed structure of the system is created. The information model is then turned into a schema for the data model used by the system (or possibly more than one schema, if the system uses more than one data model).

1.4 | XML and information systems

The first thing to realize is that the arrival of XML does not mean that all information systems that are not based on XML become obsolete all of a sudden. In fact, the reality is very much the opposite; XML and classical information systems are complementary and can be used together. Classical information systems are classical because they are extraordinarily useful, and XML will not change that. What XML is likely to change is the amount of interoperability between information systems. In some cases, it will also change what such systems can do and how they are put together.

This section examines how XML can be used with information systems, particularly classical ones, but also how it makes it possible to create new kinds of applications and uses.

1.4.1 *XML in traditional information systems*

Traditional information systems follow the basic anatomy outlined in Figure 1–3, with a central data store around which applications are clustered which access it. The exact form of this data store may vary with the application, and the arrival of XML has a number of consequences for the data store.

1.4.1.1 XML files

The most obvious way of basing an information system on XML is to simply use a set of XML documents, stored as files in the file system, as the central data store. This approach has been much used in document-oriented systems and is implicitly assumed by the standard interfaces of many XML tools. These tools expect to be run from the command line and to be passed file names as arguments. The main benefit of this approach is that it requires no work at all to set it up, and any developer and user can understand it.

The first consequence of this approach is that now the XML documents in the file system become the primary representation of the information in the system. The applications in the cluster around this data store will generally take one or more XML documents and produce some output from it. Very often this will be HTML or some other publishing format. Any updates to the information in the system must be made to the XML files, since all other renditions of the information are derived from these files. To have the updates reflected in the published files, one simply runs the translating applications again.

In general, all applications that wish to make use of the information in the XML files will use an XML parser to read the information into its own internal data structure (see 2.3.2, "The parser model," on page 57). This process must be repeated every time an application is started, which may be very awkward if the volume of the information is large. Any application that wishes to change the information must first load in the documents, then change its internal structure and finally write the information back out in XML form so that other applications can access it.

When modifying the source XML documents in this way it is important to preserve all important aspects of the documents in the transformation. But just as in the email example this may be difficult, since the programs are operating on an internal representation of the XML documents rather than the external form of the documents. Since the internal representation contains less information than the original documents did, necessary information may have been lost. We will return to this problem (and the solutions to it) in more detail later.

Of course, updating shared information in this way will often be dangerous, since multiple applications may attempt to modify the same document at the same time, which can cause information to be lost or corrupted. Another problem is that although one can make a schema for the data in the form of a DTD or an *XML Schema definition*,[1] nothing prevents an application (or a user with a text editor) from modifying the XML files in a way that does not conform to the schema.

1.4.1.2   XML databases

Databases were invented to solve the problems with concurrent access to large volumes of information, and provide proven solutions to these problems. This makes them highly desirable for applications that either involve concurrent access or work with large volumes of data, and in fact also for many applications that do neither.

To use databases with XML one must implement the XML data model in a database and then use this to store the tree structure of the XML documents in the database. One approach to this is to use an existing database system, whether relational, object-oriented, or something else, and implement an XML storage system on top of it. (Note that this approach confuses the information model/data model distinction somewhat, since the data model of the database is now used to implement the XML data model.) Another approach is to develop a database specifically based on the XML data model. Such databases are

---

1. XML Schema definitions are schemas for XML documents that conform to the W3C Recommendation known as *XML Schema*. We call them XML Schema definitions in this book in order to distinguish between instances of XML Schema, and the general concept of schemas for XML documents. Note that the language defined in this specification is called XML Schema Definition Language (XSDL), though it is often referred to as "XML Schema."

often called *native XML databases*, since the XML data model is their only data model.

In both cases the solution has much in common with the "XML files" solution, the main difference being the location of the XML documents. The central data store still uses the XML data model and can also use the same kinds of schemas. When an application now wishes to use an XML document from the central data store, it will no longer load it into memory using a parser, but rather connect to the database. Once connected it will be presented with some API that represents the XML document inside the database and access the document information through this API (see 3.4, "Virtual documents," on page 92 for more information on this). This does away with the problems with large XML documents that do not fit in memory and take long to load, since documents are now not loaded at all and the database handles memory management transparently.

The manner in which the XML documents are updated is also changed completely, since the applications are in direct contact with a document that lives inside a database. To change a document, the application will make the change through the document API and then commit it to the database. The costly and risky operation of writing the document back out to disk is done away with; instead, the database updates its internal structure, taking care of any concurrency and data integrity issues.

The only disadvantage to this solution is that it takes longer to set up and requires more know-how. It may also be that the XML database solutions do not support all programming languages in the way that the "XML files" solution does. However, for large-scale projects, using files is generally not an option at all, making the choice obvious.

1.4.1.3 Traditional databases

However, it is definitely possible to use XML in an information system without having to use XML as the data model for the central data repository. Instead, the data store can use traditional databases and their data models, but map data back and forth between the database model and XML as needed. This has the advantage that existing systems can continue as they are today.

Imagine that the national library of some country decides one day that all libraries in the country must allow their users to search for the books they seek not only in the local libraries, but in all libraries in the country. The users should then be allowed to order any books not in the local library from other libraries and have them delivered to the local library to be picked up there.[1]

This means that the library information system in Figure 1–3 must add more applications. It must now be able to produce, at regular intervals, some report in serialized form that shows the updates to the local database since the last report. This report will be sent to the national library which will use it to prepare a report of nation-wide updates to be sent to all libraries in the country. This means that the system must also be able to receive a similar report from the national library that provides similar updates to the national database of books. Figure 1–4 shows the information system updated to handle this new situation.

This information system also uses XML, but in a less direct way than the other approaches discussed so far. However, for information systems with more traditional data, this may be a much better solution than putting all data into the XML data model, since traditional databases have much more convenient data models.

1.4.2 *Bridging information systems*

The discussion of information systems given so far in this chapter is based on the traditional view of a database system, where there is a clearly defined information system and the database itself at the heart of that information system. However, most organizations do not have just one information system. Most of them have lots of information systems, and these are usually isolated from one another. XML

---

1. In fact, Norwegian libraries have offered just such a service for many years.

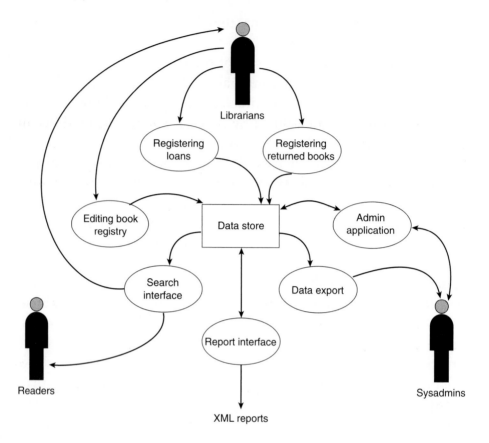

Figure 1–4   The library system with XML reporting

promises to solve this problem, by making it possible to build bridges between these systems. Or, to take an entirely different view of the same thing, XML does not require a central database, or even a clearly defined information system, and so it provides a completely different way of creating applications.

The XML equivalent of an information system is what is known as an XML application. An XML application consists of three things: an information model, an XML representation of the information model (often formalized in a DTD or schema definition) and all the programs that can work with data marked up according to the information model.

The result is that the traditional concept of one application or one information system does not apply to XML-based systems. With XML, the information becomes the focal point, and the software exists as a cloud of independent components and systems that interact with one another and accept or emit the XML-encoded data. How they interact with one another is not defined by XML at all, and many different arrangements are possible.

One example of this might be RSS (Rich Site Summary), which is a very simple XML application developed by Netscape for their my.netscape.com site. The idea behind this site was that it would allow Web site publishers to add simple news channels to their sites, which people could subscribe to through the my.netscape.com site. Each user would register and get a user name and password, and then subscribe to a selection of channels interest to them.

When logging into the site later, the user would be shown the current news from each channel he or she subscribed to. Effectively, this would be a personalized news system with content delivered by outside sources. The RSS DTD was developed to enable site publishers to mark up their news channels consisting of news items, each with a title and a link to some Web page with more information. (RSS is described in more detail in 6.4, "RSS: An example application," on page 149.)

This application quickly became a big hit with site owners and hundreds of RSS channels were established, something that caused others to start making more RSS client systems. Today you can also subscribe to RSS channels through my.userland.com, geekboys.org and you can get at least three dedicated RSS clients to use on your desktop.

Figure 1–5 shows a conceptual view of RSS as an information system. As can be seen, it incorporates the following software components:

- The publishing system of the site owner (manual or automated) that produces the site itself and the accompanying RSS document.
- The RSS subscription and publishing system of my.userland.com, developed with no knowledge at all of the site

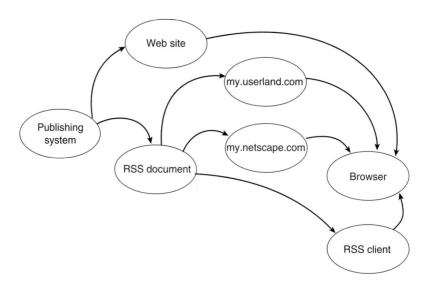

Figure 1–5   RSS as an information system

owner's publishing system, but which can still work with it, through the information provided by the RSS document. Effectively, the RSS document becomes an interface with unusually loose coupling.

- `my.netscape.com` has an equivalent system, developed independently of both `my.userland.com` and the site owner's system (www.geekboys.org is another example, and there are probably more).

- The RSS client running on the end-user's computer is yet another software component independent of the others. In a sense, the Web browser could also be described as part of the system, even though it doesn't understand RSS at all.

To summarize, XML applications do not need to be information systems in the traditional sense, but that they can be something that joins together previously separate information systems in new ways.

The XML
processing model

- XML history
- XML namespaces
- Documents and parsers
- The result of parsing

I n this chapter we look at how XML can be used in software development. This includes describing the XML data model, the various tools for working with XML, and the parts of the XML standards that are particularly relevant for developers. A number of non-obvious issues relating to development are also discussed.

2.1 | A bit of XML history

In XML, two previously separate computing cultures have come together, and the resulting family of specifications inevitably reflects this. Many features are provided more than once, and in some cases higher-level standards do not make full use of the features provided by lower-level standards, precisely because of this meeting of cultures. For this reason, there are things in the XML family of specifications that may seem puzzling to those who do not know its history, so this section presents a brief history of XML.

The history of XML starts in 1969, when Charles Goldfarb together with two other IBM researchers created a system for creating markup languages they called GML. This was an acronym for Generalized Markup Language (and also the initials of the three behind it). GML was much used inside IBM for text processing, and IBM even based large publishing projects and word processing systems on it. After GML had been in use for some years, there was interest in standardizing it, and eventually a process was started to make GML into an ISO standard. This work was led by Goldfarb and reached its first milestone in 1986 when SGML (Standard Generalized Markup Language) was first published as an ISO standard.

XML was later designed to be a subset of SGML[1] that would be easier to implement, without giving up too many useful features. The result is that SGML is a much larger language than XML, and generally differs from XML in the following ways:

flexibility

Via an SGML declaration, SGML applications can modify the SGML syntax, turn features on or off, modify the character set, and tweak SGML systems in other ways. With the corresponding SGML declaration, SGML systems can be told to follow the rules of XML, making it possible to process XML in SGML systems.

syntax

SGML allows a large number of variations in the syntax, mainly to make SGML easier to author by hand. The variations, for the most part, provide methods to express document constructs more concisely, such as by omitting tags, parts of tags, attribute names, etc. These variations make the SGML syntax extraordinarily complex, but are very handy for human authors.

---

1.   Or what is formally known as an *application profile*.

features

SGML has quite a few features that XML does not. SGML has many more attribute types than XML, it supports attributes of entities, it supports external entities as full documents (with DOCTYPE declarations) and so on.

When Tim Berners-Lee created the Web in the early 1990s, he based the notation for Web pages (HTML) loosely on SGML. In HTML 2.0, published as RFC 1866, this basis was made more formal, but by then current practice had diverged from correct SGML and this has still not changed. When the Web had become a success, the Web consisted of millions of documents, containing enormous amounts of useful information. Many people were concerned that these documents had very little formal structure, and so the information in them could not be extracted and made use of by software for purposes other than simple display.

Since SGML was designed for structuring documents and making it possible to process them automatically with software, and HTML was based on SGML, using SGML seemed an obvious solution. SGML is a big and complex language, however, and hardly any browser vendors had implemented even HTML according to specification. Furthermore, SGML generally requires the parser to read the DTD before it can parse the document itself, since elements may be omitted and inferred from the DTD, and there is no way to tell which elements are empty without reading the DTD[1].

In the summer of 1996 a W3C activity was started (largely due to Jon Bosak's initiative) to look at the use of SGML on the Web. This group quickly decided to make a subset of SGML optimized for the web and published its first working draft, titled *Extensible Markup Language*, in November 1996. Over the next year and a half XML as we know it today was defined and the final Recommendation was published in February 1998.

---

1.   Information on how to work with SGML in XML systems can be found in 24.2, "Creating XML from SGML," on page 954.

After the XML Recommendation had been published its users found quite a few little mistakes, ambiguities, and omissions in it. These were reported to the editors, who collected a list of corrections known as errata. When the number of errata passed 100 the editors created a new edition of the specification known as *Extensible Markup Language (XML) 1.0 (Second Edition)*. The new edition defined exactly the same language as the previous one, but was much clearer and also had fewer errors. In general, when checking the text of the XML Recommendation you should be careful to use the second edition. In some cases it may also be useful to compare it to the first edition to see what it said.

At the time of writing the W3C is working on a new version of XML known as XML 1.1 (earlier known as XML Blueberry). This version makes some changes to XML in the area of Unicode support, all of which are listed below. (Note that since this is work in progress, the actual decisions on these issues are not known, only what the issues are.)

- What characters are allowed in XML documents. For example, is character number 0 allowed?

- What characters are allowed as whitespace in XML documents. The issue here is whether the NEL (next line, U+0085) character used on some mainframe platforms should be allowed or not.

- What characters are allowed in names in XML documents. XML 1.0 was careful to only allow characters that belong in names, such as letters, digits, and so on, throughout all of Unicode. The problem is that as new characters are added to Unicode, the set of name characters needs to be extended to follow it. The issue is how to achieve this without creating a maintenance nightmare.

2.2 | An introduction to XML namespaces

Before we move on to look at parsers, this section presents an introduction to XML namespaces. An understanding of namespaces is necessary to understand most of the rest of the book, since namespaces are becoming a central part of XML and the XML family of specifications. Many of the APIs and technologies presented in this book are based on namespaces, and so it is necessary to be familiar with them in order to make full use of the rest of the book.

Note that throughout this chapter, and also the rest of the book, I will use many relatively advanced XML terms without defining them. If you find an XML term that you are not familiar with, consult Appendix B, "Glossary of terms," on page 1100.

2.2.1 *Why namespaces?*

The *XML Namespaces* specification is definitely the most controversial specification in the whole family of XML specifications, mainly because it changes one of the most fundamental parts of the XML data model: the structure of element-type and attribute names.

The purpose of namespaces is to allow developers to mix elements and attributes defined by different authorities, which may not be aware of one another, in a way that avoids name conflicts. For example, the W3C has defined several very general XML applications, such as XInclude. XInclude defines an element type which can be used in XML documents to refer to and include other files in the document. This functionality is the same as that provided by entities, but it works on the application level rather than on the syntactical level.

Namespaces enable the W3C to define such an element type and schema designers to use it,[1] with no fear of conflicts between the name

---

1. Note that I use the general term *schema* to refer to all kinds of schemas for XML documents, whether they be informal, DTDs, XML Schema

used by the W3C and names used in the local schema. This is done by making element-type names consist of two parts: a URI which identifies the namespace and a local name which is the ordinary XML element-type name. Through the domain name system, this enables people worldwide to define globally unique URIs for their namespaces, even if the local names may clash with other local names.

URI is an acronym for *Universal Resource Identifier*, and URIs can be of two kinds: URNs or URLs. URLs are Universal Resource Locators, which include the familiar Web addresses like `http://www.w3.org/` and `ftp://ftp.w3.org/`.

URNs, Universal Resource Names, are rather different creatures, and are rarely used compared to URLs. URNs are like public identifiers in that they are symbolic *names* for resources, rather than addresses that tell applications where to find the resources. A URN must be resolved into a URL before the resource it refers to can be retrieved. Syntactically, URNs begin with the `urn:` prefix, which tells applications that they are dealing with a URN rather than a URL. There can be several different URN schemes, just as there are several different URL schemes.

URNs, Universal Resource Names, are rather different creatures, and rare compared to URLs. URNs are unlike URLs in that they are symbolic *names* for resources, rather than addresses that tell applications where to find the resource. A URN must be resolved into a URL before the resource it refers to can be retrieved. Syntactically, URNs begin with the `urn:` prefix, which tells applications that they are dealing with a URN rather than a URL. There are several different URN schemes, just as there are several different URL schemes.[1]

---

definitions or written in some other schema language. The schema language defined by the W3C is always referred to as XSDL.

1.   Note that in strict web terminology, a URL can actually be a URN if it is a symbolic name for a resource that is intended to remain stable over a long period. Some web services (such as `purl.org`) enable users to define persistent URLs (like `http://purl.org/example!`) that are merely symbolic and resolve into the real URL. This allows the real URL to change without breaking links to the persistent URL, which is just updated. These

2.2.2   *The syntax of namespaces*

The most obvious way to add namespaces to XML would be by allowing documents to be written with the namespace URIs as part of the XML element-type and attribute names. This could have been done, for example, by putting curly braces around the URIs, as shown in Example 2–1.

Example 2–1. What XML namespaces might have looked like

```
<{http://www.w3.org/1999/xhtml}html>
  <{http://www.w3.org/1999/xhtml}head>
    <{http://www.w3.org/1999/xhtml}title>
    A minimal XHTML 1.0 document
    </{http://www.w3.org/1999/xhtml}title>
  </{http://www.w3.org/1999/xhtml}head>
  <{http://www.w3.org/1999/xhtml}body>
  </{http://www.w3.org/1999/xhtml}body>
</{http://www.w3.org/1999/xhtml}html>
```

The problem with this is that it is not conformant with XML 1.0 and that it is verbose and unwieldy in the extreme. To avoid these problems the concept of prefixes was introduced. A prefix, for example xhtml, is declared to map to the namespace URI, for example http://www.w3.org/1999/xhtml, and then combined with the name inside the namespace to form composite names like xhtml:title. Processors can use the prefix declaration to find the namespace URI.

Attributes are used to declare the namespace prefixes, using the reserved name prefix xmlns. The attribute xmlns:xhtml="http://www.w3.org/1999/xhtml" would declare the xhtml prefix to map to the XHTML namespace URI inside the element it appears on. Example 2–1 would then become Example 2–2 showing the correct XML namespace syntax.

URLs are considered to be URNs, even though they are not URNs syntactically.

Example 2–2. What XML namespaces actually look like

```
<html:html xmlns:html="http://www.w3.org/1999/xhtml">
  <html:head>
    <html:title>A minimal XHTML 1.0 document</html:title>
  </html:head>
  <html:body>
  </html:body>
</html:html>
```

More than one namespace can be declared at the same time, as long as they use different prefixes. When a document only uses a single namespace, using the prefixes all the time is unnecessary, and the XML Namespaces Recommendation has a concept of a *default namespace* which can be used. By declaring a namespace with no prefix, like so: xmlns="http://www.w3.org/1999/xhtml", all elements that do not have prefixes are automatically put into that namespace.

A namespace declaration is valid for the element the declaration attribute appears on, which means that if the declaration is not on the document element the declaration is not valid in the whole document. Also, a declaration on a child element that uses the same prefix will shadow the outer declaration. The default namespace can also be turned off by setting it to the empty URI. Example 2–3 demonstrates all this.

Example 2–3. A complex namespace example

```
<a xmlns="http://foo.org/1" xmlns:p2="http://foo.org/2">
  <p2:b/>
  <c/>
  <d xmlns="" xmlns:p2="http://foo.org/3">
    <p2:e/>
  </d>
</a>
```

Table 2–1 shows the namespace of each element in Example 2–3.

Table 2–1   The namespaces of the elements in Example 2–3

Element	Namespace	Explanation
a	`http://foo.org/1`	Is in the default namespace it declares.
b	`http://foo.org/2`	Is in the namespace of the `p2` prefix.
c	`http://foo.org/1`	Is also in the default namespace.
d	none	Has no prefix, and turns off the default namespace.
e	`http://foo.org/3`	Declaration of `p2` on the parent shadows the `p2` from the root element.

Attribute names can also use the name prefixes in the same way as element-type names. Note that an attribute with no prefix is *not* in the default namespace, nor does it automatically belong to the same namespace as the element it appears on. However, some XML specifications state that in their particular XML application, attributes with no namespace default to the namespace of their element. This difference between the general model and that used by specific applications can be a bit confusing, but it generally works well in practice.

2.2.3   *Consequences for the data model*

As a result of the introduction of namespaces into XML, the names of attribute and element types now consist of two parts: a namespace URI and a local name. The *local name* is the part after the colon, so called because it is local to the namespace. If the name has no namespace, there is no namespace URI, and this case is typically represented in programs by an empty string or `null/none/nil`.

A prefixed name is known as a *qualified name*, but the qualified name is just a convenient shorthand used in documents, and not part of the data model as such. The actual prefix used is a syntactical detail that most applications do not care about, and should not care about; what matters is the namespace URI and the local name. Applications that require a specific prefix are not playing by the rules and are re-introducing the very risk of name collisions that namespaces were supposed to remove.

The attributes that declare namespace prefixes are not considered attributes in the data model, and so most processing frameworks will hide these. One would think that the information in them is just another lexical detail, but many generic applications actually need this information, so the set of declared namespaces at any point in the document is considered part of the data model.

This is used to implement applications where qualified names can appear, for example, in attribute values. To be able to interpret the qualified names correctly, it is necessary for the application to know what namespace declarations are in effect at any given point in the document. Most applications will not care, but all generic processing frameworks have to provide this information if they wish to support such applications.

2.2.4   *What namespaces do*

A common misconception about namespaces is that the namespace URI refers to a schema that defines the semantics of the elements and attributes in that namespace. This is not really correct, however, since the decision on how to interpret the namespace URI was not taken until Christmas 2000. Before then, there had been two different schools of thought within the W3C, one of which held that a namespace URI was purely symbolic, just a name, while the second held that it should refer to a schema.

These two schools were both substantial in membership and very much convinced that the other side was wrong. A special mailing list was created to resolve the issue, and the debate eventually ran to well over 2000 email messages before the issue was resolved.

Before this decision was taken, the namespace URI had no meaning whatsoever other than to be a globally unique name. Now, however, it will become a reference to an XML document that contains metadata about the namespace. This metadata is likely to include a schema, but may also include much else.

2.3 | Documents and parsers

A complete piece of XML data, generally called a document, may be stored in many different forms and still remain an XML document. The form described in the XML 1.0 Recommendation is the default syntactical representation of XML documents when they are serialized. A serialized XML document found in the file system is generally expected to be self-contained. That is, all applications that implement XML properly should construct equivalent internal representations of this document after reading it, and all the information needed to do so should be provided in this file and other files referenced from it.

Newcomers to XML often want to change how documents are processed by doing things like declaring entities and setting their values from their program code or by parsing the content of certain elements with their own code so that they can, for example, include raw binary content in their XML documents, which would not follow the XML syntax and be rejected by a standard parser. Tricks like these have serious disadvantages in that they make the correct processing of the document depend on program code. This means that general XML tools like editors, validators, transformation engines, databases, query engines, and so on can't work with the data unless they are extended to support the same tricks. This isn't possible in general, and even if it were it would be very inconvenient.

This doesn't mean that XML cannot cater to these needs, only that it is very important not to go against the letter of the XML Recommendation, but instead do these things within the law, since this does not impact interoperability. In general, the way to do this kind of thing is to define element types and attributes which are given the desired meanings and behaviours.

Like most other general data processing frameworks, XML has a schema language, although the situation of XML is perhaps a bit unusual in that it actually has many schema languages. The schemas written in the schema language defined in the XML 1.0 Recommendation are called *Document Type Definition*s, or DTDs. In addition to DTDs, the W3C has defined a schema language called *XSDL*. There are also several other proposals for schema languages, the most popular of which seems to be RELAX-NG and Schematron. Both of these are described in more detail in Chapter 23, "Schemas," on page 892.

ISO, the organization that originally standardized SGML, is currently working on a standard called DSDL, which will contain a framework for describing different schema languages and creating validating processes using different schema languages. RELAX-NG and Schematron are both planned to become part of this standard. DSDL is currently under development, so no more is said about it in this book. See `http://xml.coverpages.org/dsdl.html` for more information.

Note, however, that in XML, DTDs are in a privileged position, in that they not only constrain the allowed structure of the XML documents that use them, but also modify their structure. The details of these modifications are presented in 2.4.2.1, "How the DTD affects the document," on page 69.

2.3.1 *Storing XML documents*

XML inherits its view of document storage and retrieval from SGML, but modifies it somewhat. Both views state that documents are stored as *entities*, which are any referenceable collections of characters. This means that an XML document can be in a file, on the Web, in a database, in a document management system, or just about anywhere else. Note that the document itself begins in an entity (called the *document entity*), as does the external subset.

Entities can be of two main kinds: internal and external. An *internal entity* is just a string, declared internally in the DTD. An *external entity*, however, is an external reference, usually to a file, but it can in principle refer to anything. Note that entities can also be *general entities*, which are used in documents, and *parameter entities*, which are used in DTDs. General entities have three main uses:

- providing mnemonic names for characters that may be difficult to type on some keyboards (such as `&Aring;`, ` `, and others used in HTML) and as an escape syntax for reserved characters (such as `&lt;` and the other entities predefined in XML);

- enabling XML documents (and DTDs) to be split into distinct parts for easier management. This book, for example, was written as a single SGML document with chapters in separate files, knitted together using entities;

- providing a macro functionality for frequently reused pieces of text.

The first and the last of these uses are usually accomplished with internal entities, while the second is done with external entities. SGML (and XML) standardizes two ways of specifying the location of an entity: system and public identifiers. In SGML, a system identifier has no standardized interpretation and it is up to each SGML system to decide how to interpret it. Nearly all interpret it as a file name, and in some cases also as a URL, and this works very well in practice. In the XML Recommendation, system identifiers are required to be URIs and their interpretation is standardized.

Public identifiers serve as symbolic names for entities and cannot be dereferenced directly, so that when a document is moved from one system to another (which means the system identifiers in the document may now point to resources that are not accessible from the second system), the public identifier can be used instead to find alternative ways of retrieving the entity.

The classical example of this is someone writing an HTML document on one system using SGML software, which requires the DTD, and then moving it to another system. These two systems are unlikely to have the HTML DTD installed in the same location on the local disks, so the public identifier of the HTML DTD can be used instead. The usual way to resolve public identifiers has been to use a catalog file which gives a mapping from the public identifier to the system identifier on a specific system. More details on catalog files and how to work with them are given in 10.3, "Working with entities," on page 380.

2.3.1.1 The Web context

Since XML is a W3C Recommendation, quite a bit of work has been done to make it fit naturally into the Web context. One of the things that have been done was hinted at above: the location of entities is specified using URIs. URIs are actually much more complex creatures than the common URL. The main thing that is forgotten is that in order to have proper URI support, applications must absolutize all relative URIs they come across, and they must do this correctly.

Doing this correctly is much more difficult than it sounds, since it means keeping information that developers tend to throw away. To take one example, a document may refer to a DTD in a different local directory, which then refers to an external parameter entity using a relative URI. In this case, the reference to the external parameter entity must be resolved against the URI of the DTD, which must then be known.

And if the document refers to the DTD using a relative URI, the application must have given the parser the full URI of the document. If the application just created an input stream and gave it to the parser, the parser does not have the information it needs to find the DTD and parsing will fail.

It is in order to deal with these issues that so many of the standards and APIs described in the rest of this book are so careful to provide mechanisms for passing on and remembering base URIs.

2.3.1.2 Notations and unparsed entities

The normal way to include non-SGML content in SGML documents was to put it in an external file and then define an entity for the file.

The entity would be associated with a formally declared notation, which tells the parser not to parse the entity (since it is not SGML or XML[1]). Such entities are called *unparsed entities*, since the parser will not read them at all. A typical declaration of an unparsed entity is shown in Example 2–4.

Example 2–4. How to declare an unparsed entity

```
<!NOTATION gif PUBLIC "-//CompuServe//Graphics Interchange
                       Format//EN">
<!ENTITY diagram SYSTEM "diagram.gif" NDATA gif>
```

Example 2–4 declares the notation `gif` and associates it with a public identifier that makes it clear to most humans who see it that the notation is the GIF image format defined by CompuServe. The entity `diagram` is then declared, and the last part makes it clear that this is not an XML entity, but rather a GIF entity (that is, an unparsed entity).

A document would then use an attribute of the type `ENTITY` or `ENTITIES` to actually refer to the entity, to let applications know where to find the file and, in a platform-independent way, tell them the notation of the file.

Notations can also be declared and used (with `NOTATION` attributes) to formally declare the syntax used inside an element and to declare the application which a processing instruction targets. These two uses are rare in XML.

2.3.2   *The parser model*

The XML 1.0 Recommendation assumes that when XML documents are processed, there will be two distinct pieces of software involved: the parser and the application. The parser is responsible for reading

---

1.   Well, it can be, even though it won't be parsed. This can actually be a convenient way of including literal XML and SGML content.

the raw bytes that make up the serialized XML document and creating from them some representation for the elements and attributes that make up the conceptual XML document. The application is the software that will take the document and use it to perform some task, whatever that task may be.

The job of the XML parser is clearly defined by the XML Recommendation and is essentially the same regardless of the application that uses it. This means that an XML parser can be written independently of the application and maintained as a self-contained reusable module. In fact, many such parsers are now available as modules that can be used by any application to read in XML documents. Much of this book is devoted to explaining how to use XML parsers to build applications.

Figure 2–1 shows a conceptual diagram of this model of XML processing.

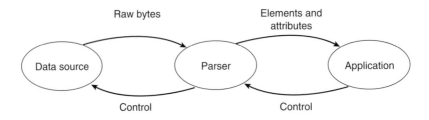

Figure 2–1   The basic XML processing model

As shown in Figure 2–1, the parser appears as an intermediary between the application and the data source, interpreting the document from the raw stream of bytes and passing it on to the application. Usually the parser will control the data source and read the physical document from it, but some parsers let the application read the data from the source and push it into the parser. Such parsers are known as *incremental parsers*, since they parse the document piece by piece as it is fed to them.

Parsing XML documents involves turning pairs of angle-bracketed tags into elements, resolving entity references, interpreting character references and CDATA marked sections, and sometimes also verifying the document structure against the declarations in a DTD. While XML is a relatively simple standard compared to many others, this task is not as simple as one might be tempted to think, and fully supporting the XML Recommendation[1] takes quite a bit of work and requires close attention to be paid to the text of the Recommendation.

Once the parser has done its work, the data is delivered to the application as elements, attributes, and pieces of text. The exact form of this interface can vary considerably, but somehow the application must take the information passed to it and make use of it. What data structures the application uses will vary, but most likely these will be objects that represent the kinds of things the application works with, which can be people, cars, books, or just about anything. The usual way to handle this is to write a small module that uses the information received from the parser to build this structure of application-specific objects, thus fully translating the XML document into the internal data structure.

Quite often this reading of the document will only be a minor part of a larger application, which means that the structure of the program will be similar to Figure 2–2.

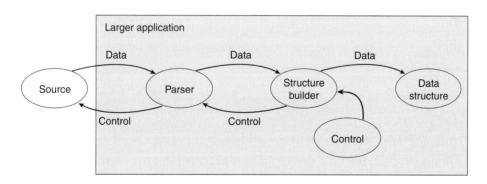

Figure 2–2   XML input to larger application

---

1. The full title is *Extensible Markup Language (XML) 1.0, W3C Recommendation 10-February-1998.*

There are many different alternatives for each of the interfaces here, and the interface between the structure builder and the larger application will almost always be different for every application. For the interface between the parser and the structure builder, there are two main alternatives: *event-based* and *tree-based*. These will be described further below in this chapter, and one part of the book is devoted to each kind of interface (Part Two, "Event-based processing," on page 138 and Part Three, "Tree-based processing," on page 394).

2.3.3   *What does a parser do?*

The parser receives a sequence of bytes from some data source, which can be a file, a blob in a database, a network connection, or something completely different. The first step the parser must take is to interpret the sequence of bytes into a sequence of characters. Strictly speaking, this is not the job of the parser and in many cases the parser will use functionality provided by its environment to do this. However, even if the environment provides the necessary functionality, the parser will have to set up the character converters, since only the parser knows the rules for deciding what character encoding the byte stream is in.

Also, many programming environments do not provide the necessary functionality, which means that in these cases the parser must do the conversion itself before it can begin its true task. How the translation from bytes to characters is done depends on the character encoding used, and it is a subtle process. More details on it are available in Chapter 5, "Characters — the atoms of text," on page 108. This process is illustrated in Figure 2–3.

Once this is done, the parser is ready to start interpreting the markup in the document. This interpretation is done by scanning through the characters one by one in sequence and reacting whenever the characters "<" or "&" are seen. Based on this scanning the parser will (for the example in Figure 2–3) produce this sequence of events:

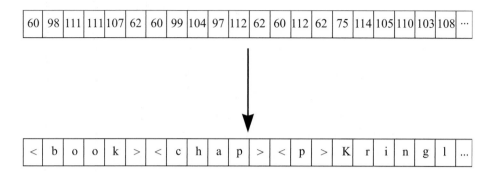

Figure 2–3 Mapping bytes to characters

- Start of element "book".
- Start of element "chap".
- Start of element "p".
- Text "Kringla heimsins — the round platter of earth ..."

Some parsers will pass the document contents on to the application as they go along, whereas others will use these events to build up the document tree structure (see Figure 2–4), and only pass the tree to the application when it is complete. This difference affects the way in which applications interact with the document they receive, and each way of receiving the document has its uses. These will be explored in depth later in the book.

The central thing common to all parsers is that their true work is one thing, and one thing only: to parse characters into elements and attributes. No interpretation whatsoever of the semantics of the document is done by the parser. This is the domain of the application, which is the code that you will write, and the domain that this book covers.

Strictly speaking the XML Recommendation does not only define what the parser has to do, but also goes two steps further. One is mentioned already: The specification tells the parser how to set up character conversions from non-Unicode encodings. The Recommendation also defines two reserved attributes: `xml:lang`, which can contain a language code specifying the language of the data in that element,

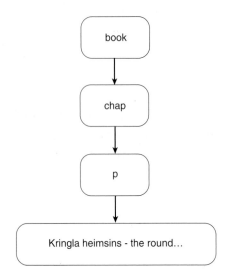

Figure 2–4   The document tree

and `xml:space`, giving information about whitespace processing. These have to be treated specially, so strictly speaking the XML Recommendation defines the behavior of an XML processor, which *mainly* consists of a parser. The XML Recommendation in fact consistently refers to the parser as an XML processor, precisely because of this.

2.3.3.1   The two kinds of parsers

As mentioned earlier, SGML requires the parser to read the DTD in order to be able to parse the document correctly, and since XML was to be used in a Web context it was necessary to remove this requirement. When parsing a document that has been downloaded from a remote site, it often does not make sense to validate the document if you cannot correct it in case anything is wrong. Furthermore, XML DTDs can be quite large. The DocBook DTD, for example, is about 500 Kb.

In order to support both parsers that read the DTD and those that do not, the XML Recommendation defines two different kinds of XML parsers: validating and non-validating ones.[1] The Recommendation allows non-validating parsers to omit certain steps in the parsing (without requiring the steps to be omitted), but requires validating parsers to perform absolutely all of them. Among the steps that non-validating parsers may omit is reading the external parts of the DTD.

However, the cost of this approach is that the exact contents and form of the document that are passed on to the application may vary with the parser it uses in ways that may be hard to predict. All validating parsers that conform to the Recommendation will produce identical results for all documents. This is not necessarily the case with non-validating parsers, however, since these may vary in exactly which steps they perform and which they do not. They may also produce results that differ from those produced by validating parsers.

In general, this can be understood in terms of which things the non-validating parsers are allowed *not* to do, and these are listed below.

- They are not required to read the parts of the DTD that are external to the document entity, generally called *the external subset*. Any parts of the *internal subset* (the declarations inside the DOCTYPE declaration) that they do read they must process and use in the same way as validating parsers.

- If the parser does not process external parameter entity references inside the internal subset it must stop reading the internal subset after the first external parameter reference that it does not read.[2] This is because the parameter entity may contain declarations that override those found later in the internal subset, and it is better that the parser ignore these declarations than use wrong values for them.

---

1. See Section 5.1 of the XML Recommendation.
2. Note that if the XML declaration has standalone='yes' the parser can keep reading the internal subset anyway, since this means that the external parameter entities do not contain any dangerous declarations (see Section 5.1, fourth paragraph, last sentence, but only in the second edition).

■ Non-validating parsers are allowed to skip external entities (general entities, that is, not just parameter entities). If it does, it must report the fact to the application. This is a rather serious concession since it means that non-validating parsers are allowed to skip what may turn out to be huge chunks of the document at will.

2.3.3.2   Conformance of documents

According to XML 1.0, there are two possible levels of conformance for documents: they can be well-formed, or they can be valid. An XML document is *well-formed* if all its entities follow the XML syntax rules, have correctly nested tags, and meet the formal well-formedness constraints given in the Recommendation.[1] The moment an XML parser discovers that the document is not well-formed, it is required to stop reporting data to the application. It is allowed to keep parsing to report more errors, but it cannot keep reporting data to the application.[2]

This draconian[3] treatment of errors was mandated to avoid repeating the experience of non-conformant HTML caused by lenient browsers. Today, implementing a parser that can read all the HTML that can be found on the Web and interpreting it in the same way as the Web browsers is extremely difficult.[4] Tim Bray, the editor of the XML Recommendation, claims that both Microsoft and Netscape wanted this behavior, probably because of their experiences with supporting HTML. It seems as though requiring such strict behavior has had the

---

1.   See the XML Recommendation, Section 2.1, first definition.

2.   See the XML Recommendation, Section 1.2, definition of "fatal error".

3.   *Draconian* is an adjective often used to describe inflexible or severe treatment of errors by software. It originates with the infamous ruler of ancient Athens named Draco, today mainly known for his extremely severe code of law.

4.   Jon S. von Tetzschner and Geir Ivarsøy, the primary developers of the Opera Web browser, once claimed that in the first couple of years of development they spent at least half their development time making the browser support bad HTML...

desired effect: there is hardly any non-conformant XML to be found on the Web today.

XML has another level of compliance beyond well-formedness. An XML document can be *valid* if it is well-formed, has a DTD, and conforms to the declarations in it.[1] This means that all valid XML documents are well-formed, while the opposite need not be true, and that no XML document can be valid without having a DTD. XML Namespaces introduces a different level of compliance beyond well-formedness. Such compliance is generally known as being *namespace-conformant*, although the XML Namespaces Recommendation does not define a formal term for this concept. XML Schema has yet another level of compliance, in that documents that conform to a schema are said to be *schema-valid*.

The Venn diagram[2] in Figure 2–5 shows the relationship between the different XML conformance levels. All XML documents are well-formed, since anything that is not well-formed, quite simply, is not an XML document. Some XML documents are also valid, nearly all are namespace-conformant,[3] quite a few are both and some are just valid or just namespace-conformant. In addition, some documents are schema-valid, and these are all namespace-conformant, but some are also valid.

The ideal XML document is valid, namespace-conformant, and schema-valid, all at the same time. This is of course only in the strictly formal sense of ideal, since we would also prefer our documents make sense, contain only true statements, and be complete in the sense that they contain all the information we want them to contain. To remain in this truly ideal state an XML document must constantly change to reflect changes in the external reality and perhaps also in its schema.

---

1. See the XML Recommendation, Section 2.9, third paragraph, last sentence.
2. This is a mathematical term for diagrams that use overlapping ovals to show the relationships between overlapping groups.
3. Documents that don't use XML namespaces are namespace-conformant as long as they don't use colons in their element-type or attribute names.

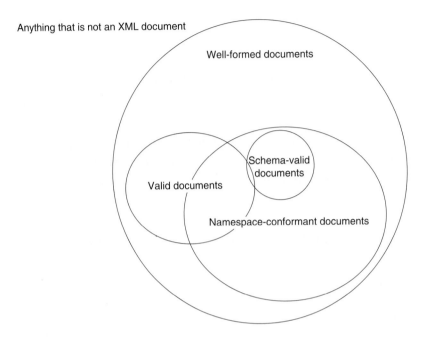

Figure 2–5   The various XML conformance levels

2.4 | The result of parsing

2.4.1 *Why use a parser?*

During the design of XML one of the design principles was based on the idea of a mythical person called the DPH (short for the Desperate Perl Hacker). This person was imagined to be faced with an XML document and a very tight deadline without knowing what XML was, and the goal was that he or she should still be able to extract the information from the document without having any XML software available. It is not obvious that this goal was fulfilled, but the final specification is rather close to having done so. The result is that when developing XML applications, many people are tempted to not use an XML parser (often because they think it is difficult to find one or learn how to use it) and instead try hacking together a simple XML reader themselves.

This is nearly always a bad idea, because:

- It is virtually guaranteed that there already exists an XML parser for the programming language you are using, whether that is Objective Caml, Haskell, Common Lisp, Eiffel, or Ruby, or something better-known.

- Actually making a full XML parser is quite a bit of work, even if you don't implement validation. Having written a parser in one of the most convenient programming languages available today (Python), I can promise you that learning to use someone else's parser is easier than writing your own.

  If you do decide to write your own full XML parser, that's great, and I hope you then make it available to others, whether commercially or as open source. (If you do make it available as open source, please let me know, so I can include it on my list of free XML software.)

- If you don't make a full XML parser and carefully develop it to match the word of the XML Recommendation, there will be differences between the language accepted by your XML reader and proper XML. This means that the software and users that provide XML to be read by your parser *will* come over time to create XML that differs from correct XML. This will inevitably impact interoperability, since anyone using a proper XML parser will have problems with some of the documents which nevertheless work "correctly" with your XML reader.

  Apparently, someone has already made an RSS application which does not use a proper XML parser, because there are quite a few RSS documents out there that use unescaped ampersands (&) in their URLs, something that causes proper XML parsers to reject the documents. Very likely this has happened because the document providers only tested their document with some non-conformant RSS application, if indeed they tested them at all.

2.4.2 *Logical and lexical information*

When the application reads the XML document through an XML parser, the XML parser creates an internal representation of the document. As mentioned earlier, this means that we will lose information about the original document. All the things that your application does not need to know about the document are hidden from it. Typical examples of this is the amount of whitespace inside tags, the order the attributes appeared in, whether empty elements appeared as empty-element tags or elements with start- and end-tags but no content, etc. This is of course a major relief to the application writer, who usually doesn't care about these things, but it can also be a source of difficulties, for what if the application needs to know something the parser has thrown away?

In general, parsers pass on the contents of the document and its structure omitting the details about how the document was represented externally, but agreeing on exactly what this means is harder than it may seem. Are comments a part of the document? Some think so, others do not. Is the XML declaration part of the document? Most would think not. And what about the DTD?

The most obviously necessary part of this information is what is called the *logical information*, as opposed to the much more rarely needed *lexical information*. This is roughly the difference between what is in a document and how the document was put together. All applications need to know *what* is in the document, but only a few care *how* it was represented. Logically it does not matter whether an "a" in the text reported to the application came from a literal a character in the document or whether it came from a character reference (a). And very few applications indeed care whether the reference was a or a.[1]

When you start really digging into it, the lexical information is quite substantial and complex. It includes things such as the entity structure

---

1. Or whether upper-case or lower-case letters were used in the hexadecimal number...

of the document (which parts come from which entities, and this includes entity references inside attribute values), whitespace inside tags (between element-type name and first attribute name, first attribute name and "=", and so on), comments, whitespace between the target and data of a processing instruction, which text came from CDATA marked sections, and so on and so forth ad nauseam.

Most parser writers, API designers, and programmers are only too happy to forget about these lexical details, but in some cases they really are needed. If the document is to be able to make a round-trip through the application and make it back out in a byte-by-byte identical form, or some approximation thereof, the application really needs all those finicky lexical details.

And when do you need to do this? Well, first of all, XML editors need this, since it would be a poor editor which, after editing a document consisting of several files, would save it as a single file, or which would strip out all comments. Some would also be unhappy about an editor not preserving whitespace in tags. In general, applications that take an XML document, modify it, and then replace the original with the modified version, must take care not to lose information that may in some sense be important to the user.

Exactly what matters to the user is of course dependent not just on the specific application, but also on the usage pattern of a particular application installation, which means this can be a rather complex question. In general, the more you preserve, the safer you are, but preserving more also means more work, making this a trade-off that can be difficult to get right.

2.4.2.1 How the DTD affects the document

An important part of what a parser is required to do (and this was not mentioned in the previous section) is to read the DTD and act on the declarations in it. As mentioned earlier, there are two classes of parsers: validating and non-validating, and only the validating parsers are required to read the entire DTD. In both cases, however, the parsers are required to use the information in the parts of the DTD that they have read to make certain modifications to the document contents before they present it to the application. These modifications include:

- If attributes have been declared with default or fixed values, the parser has to insert these values into all occurrences of the element type for which these attributes have been declared.

- For attributes declared to be of some type other than CDATA, the parser is also required to strip any leading and trailing whitespace and also reduce all whitespace between tokens in the attribute value to single space characters. This process is known as attribute value normalization, and is of course only done if the parser has actually read the attribute declarations at all.

  Putting the declarations in the internal subset before any parameter references will force all parsers to read and act on them, but this is generally impractical, since it requires the declarations to be repeated in all documents.

There is also another, rather subtle, point where the DTD influences how the document is passed to the application. In nearly all documents there are three kinds of whitespace:

- Whitespace that is significant to the application that will use the document. A typical example of this is whitespace that is used to format document content, such as in program source code included in the document. This whitespace is important for the correct presentation of the document and is really part of the content of the document.

- Whitespace that is only partly significant to the application that will use the document, but which occurs in character data. A typical example is whitespace in running text in a paragraph. All that matters to the application is where whitespace appears (so it can tell the words apart), but not the exact form of the whitespace (line breaks, tabs, or a number of spaces).

■ Whitespace that is insignificant to the application, which occurs inside an element that only contains other elements. One example of this might be an element that represents a data record and has one child element per field in the record. The field elements will typically each appear on a separate line, and the whitespace separating them is only there to make reading and editing of the markup as text easier (if the whitespace is indeed present at all).

To make it easier for applications to ignore insignificant whitespace validating parsers are required by the XML Recommendation to identify which character data in the document is whitespace of the last kind described above. All whitespace must be reported, but the last kind must somehow be singled out; the details of how to make the distinction clear to applications is left to the discretion of API designers. The other two cannot be told apart by a parser, and so it is left to the application to sort those out.

Because the contents of the DTD affect the contents of the document through the content transformations described above as well as by providing entity declarations and identifying ignorable whitespace, the exact contents of the document may differ with the XML parser you use, since not all XML parsers will read the external subset, and also with how you configure it (some parsers can be told whether to read the external subset or not).

Because of this, the XML declaration has the `standalone` declaration, which is in effect used to tell the parser whether reading the external subset will affect the document contents or not. The declaration can only be set to yes (that is, standalone) if reading the external subset will not cause default attribute values to be inserted or attribute values to be normalized, if the external subset does not contain declarations of entities used in the document and if no whitespace occurs in elements with only-element content.

This means that in practice, hardly any documents that have an external subset will be standalone unless they have been converted into standalone documents on purpose. Also, the XML Recommendation does not explicitly state what parsers are to do if the document is not standalone, but in many cases this will cause the parser to attempt to read the external subset. Others will take no notice of the standalone declaration at all. The end result is that the `standalone` declaration is not very useful in practice.

However, most processing frameworks allow some degree of control over whether the external subset is to be read or not, and using these features is usually the best way to handle this particular problem. Further chapters will show what features specific processing frameworks provide to deal with this.

If this section seems to have a lot of fine details about whitespace handling, it is because the DTD can affect it significantly. It may seem strange for the W3C to have attached such importance to whitespace in the XML recommendation, but remember that XML is used for presentation as well as processing, and whitespace plays a large role there.

2.4.3   *DTD information*

In addition to the distinction between logical and lexical information there is the DTD information issue. Most applications do not care about the DTD, since the details of the information model of the application have to be programmed directly into the application code anyway. This means that in a sense, the application already "knows" the DTD, and it certainly has no need to read it to see what it says.

Still, quite a few applications need to know the contents of the DTD to be able to do their job properly. One example might be DTD editors, which need to be able to read in a DTD to display it and allow users to edit it. Another example might be a generic application that merges together a set of separate XML documents. If any of these documents use `ID` attributes, it might be that two of these documents each use the same `ID`. In this case the application has to ensure that it doesn't just naively copy the documents together, since this would produce a document with two identical `ID` values. The only way to avoid this problem is to make the application access the DTD information to find out which attributes are ID, IDREF, and IDREFS attributes and then modify those that are in conflict (or modify all IDs in some systematic way), remembering to also update the IDREF and IDREFS attributes.

One of the difficulties with the DTD information is that it does not follow the XML data model, but requires a separate representation. Note that even though XSDL uses XML syntax it also needs a data representation of its own, so using XSDL does not make this problem much simpler. This makes the parser API more complex if it exposes the DTD, and because of this many parsers do not expose the DTD information, even though they have to have this information available in some form internally for their own use.

The distinction between logical and lexical information also makes sense for DTDs. Most DTD-aware applications only need to know the logical part of the DTD information, such as which element types were declared, what are their content models and attributes, etc. However, sometimes information about the representation of the DTD is needed, such as when you need to know which part of the DTD came from the internal subset and which from the external, or when you need to know the parameter entity structure, the comments in the DTD, or the exact amount of whitespace used to format element and attribute declarations.

To take one example, an application that converts DTDs into XML Schema definitions is relatively easy to write if one has a DTD parser that can parse a DTD into a convenient object structure. However, most real DTDs use parameter entities to declare shared attributes and parts of content models once, to later refer to these in the declarations that need these shared components.

The problem with this is that parameter entities are essentially a macro mechanism which operates on the lexical level. Thus, the parameter entity structure is not part of the logical information of a DTD. Also, there are many different ways to use parameter entities, and it is by no means obvious whether a parameter entity declaration contains an element-type name, a part of an element-type name, a part of a content model, a set of attributes, or even why it contains these things. That is, it's obvious to a human reader, but not to software.

The result is that for the XHTML DTD,[1] for example, a naive DTD to schema converter will produce a huge schema where the declarations of the attributes that are shared by all or groups of element declarations are repeated over and over. The natural way to handle this in an XML Schema definition would be to declare an `attributeGroup` that contains these shared attributes and then refer to it from each element declaration. Unfortunately, to be able to do this the converter has to either reverse-engineer the attribute declarations into groups based on heuristic rules or access the parameter entity declarations, which is not much easier.

2.4.4   *Drawing the line*

The XML 1.0 Recommendation only defines the syntax of XML documents, and leaves their conceptual structure undefined. This means that it is almost completely silent about how to draw the line between logical and lexical information, and also about what the parsed document actually looks like. In order to be able to properly define the APIs of parsers (which pass the parsed document on to their applications), the structure of XML databases (which store the logical document instead of its syntactical representation), and the behavior of query languages (which operate on structures representing documents), the conceptual structure of XML documents very much needs to be defined.

There is actually a W3C Recommendation that defines the abstract structure of XML documents, or, if you will, the XML data model. This Recommendation is called the XML Information Set, or just the Infoset. The Infoset defines a conceptual data model using a formalism of its own invention, where the atomic pieces that data structures are composed of are called *items*. This word was chosen since nodes, elements, attributes, entities, and objects were all used for other purposes

---

1.   XHTML is the XML version of HTML.

or had wrong connotations. Each item in the model has a number of named properties, all of which have values.

With the infoset we can split the information from the XML document into core infoset items and properties, peripheral[1] items and properties, and purely lexical information that is not part of the data model at all.

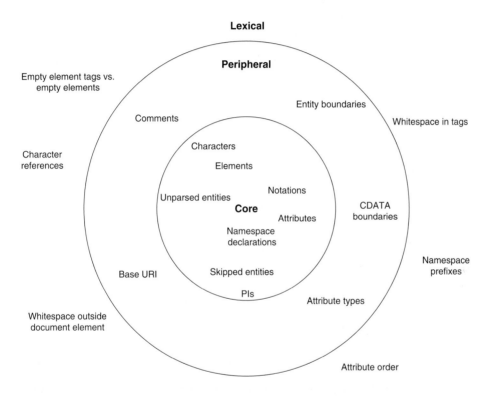

Figure 2–6   Lexical and logical information in XML documents

Figure 2–6 shows the different levels of lexical and logical information in XML documents according to the Infoset. The inner circle contains the true logical information, the next circle contains the boundary

---

1.   The final version of the infoset does not do this, but I still use these terms because they are so useful.

cases (termed "peripheral" properties and items in early Infoset drafts) and outside lie the items that are definitively lexical.

Example 2–5. An example XML document

```
<doc>
<p xmlns="http://www.w3.org/1999/xhtml">
We know that an ocean goes from <q>Norvasund</q> all the way to ...
</p>
</doc>
```

Example 2–5 shows an XML document, a part of which uses namespaces. Figure 2–7 shows the corresponding Infoset structure.

As you can see from the figure, the Infoset contains some properties that one might not expect. For example, both the document item and all element items have a `base uri` property, which contains the base URI of the entity from which they came, if it is known. Elements from external entities will have a different `base uri` property value.

The XML application XML Base, or XBase, defines an attribute `xml:base`, which can be used on any element to locally override the `base uri` property. It is inherited to all child elements, except those that come from external entities. XML Base is defined by the W3C and is a member of the XML family of specifications.

Two properties worthy of note are the `namespace name` and `local name` properties, which together make up the element-type name. As this implies, the Infoset takes an XML-with-namespaces view of XML. The namespace prefix was originally not part of the infoset at all, but has been introduced in later versions.

Two properties of element items that are not shown in the figure (to avoid cluttering it too much) are `declared namespaces` and `in-scope namespaces`. The first contains an unordered set of namespace prefixes and namespace URIs declared for the element, the second contains all namespace prefixes and URIs in scope for that element. The first property is always a subset of the second.

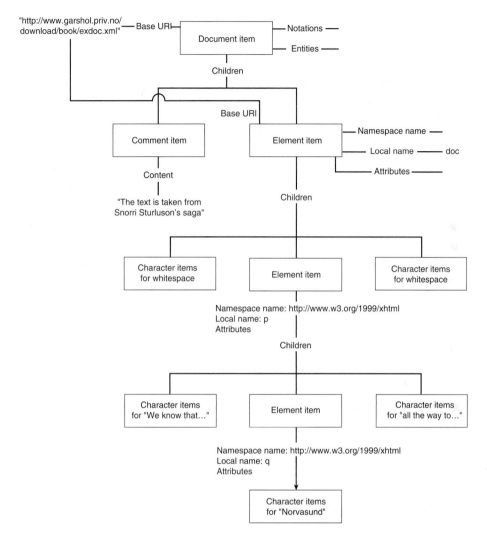

Figure 2–7   The Infoset of the document

Another thing that may seem strange about the Infoset is that there are no text items, only sequences of character items. The character items have two properties: the character number (in the Unicode character set) and whether the character should be considered ignorable whitespace or not.

The `notations` and `entities` properties on the document item are there because XML 1.0 requires that all notation declarations and unparsed entity declarations that the parser has read must be reported to the application. This requirement is there because if this information is not made available to the application, it will not be able to access the unparsed entities at all.

The Infoset does not require documents to be represented in exactly this way, only that all the information in the Infoset be made available somehow. Many of the APIs that you will see later in the book, even though they may be very different, conform to the Infoset. Others do not conform, because their designers have made a deliberate decision to only provide a simplified view of XML documents.

Views of documents

- The tree view
- The event view
- Virtual views
- Virtual documents

Chapter

3

As discussed in the previous chapter, the XML data model, or Infoset, can be represented in many different ways, all of which are valid representations of the same underlying model. This chapter explores some of the most common ways of creating and representing Infoset instances. Essentially, it provides a sneak preview of the subjects discussed in more detail in the rest of the book.

3.1 | Documents viewed as events

One of the ways XML documents can be viewed is as a sequence of structured tokens. These might be tokens representing a start-tag, a processing instruction, a piece of character data, an end-tag, and so on. Of the main ways to view a document, this view is decidedly the most low-level. Many important properties of the document, such as the tree structure, are still implicit in this view and must be inferred by anything that uses this view. In fact, the mapping from bytes to these structured tokens is the minimum of the job a parser must do.

Still, having an XML parser that can turn a serialized XML document into a sequence of such tokens is a long step forward from only having the sequence of bytes available. Since this view is very easy to implement and also very efficient, most parsers have such an interface. Higher-level interfaces, being less efficient and requiring more work to implement, are usually implemented on top of this event-based view.

Example 3–1. A document to be parsed

```
<book>
<chap id="first-chap">
<title>Saga of the Ynglings</title>
<p>
<q>Kringla heimsins</q>, the round plate of earth that mankind lives
on, is much cut into by the sea. [...]
</p>
</chap>
</book>
```

The document in Example 3–1, which is the famous beginning of Snorri Sturluson's *Saga of the Norwegian Kings*, could be parsed into the sequence of structured tokens shown below. For brevity, the ignorable whitespace has been ignored.

- Start of book element.
- Start of chap element with id attribute set to 'first-chap'.
- Start of title element.
- Characters 'Saga of the Ynglings'.
- End of title element.
- Start of p element.
- Start of q element.
- Characters 'Kringla Heimsins'.
- End of q element.

- Characters ', the round platter of earth...'.
- End of p element.
- End of chap element.
- End of book element.

There are two main ways in which this sequence of tokens could be communicated from the parser to the receiving application. In both, the application would first ask the parser to start parsing from some data source. The parser could then set up its internal state as necessary to continue and then return. The application would then resume control and call a function (or method) in the parser each time it needs another token. In pseudo-code, the application might take the form shown in Example 3–2.

Example 3–2. An example of how to use a pull parser

```
parser = Parser("file.xml")  # parser is initialized
while not parser.is_finished():
    token = parser.get_next_token()
    # act on information in token
```

A parser with this kind of interface is called a *pull parser*, because the application is pulling the information from the parser. An example of such a parser is shown in 22.1, "Pull APIs," on page 843.

Alternatively, the parser could retain control after the call that initializes it, keep parsing, and for each token call a function or method in the application to pass the token to the application. Each of these calls to the function or method provided by the applications would be considered an event (similar to event calls from a GUI framework to a GUI application). In this case, the pseudo-code for the application might be as shown in Example 3–3.

As can be seen, this kind of API is fundamentally the same as the pull API. The main difference is that the handling of the event tokens is detached from the code that starts the parsing, which can make the program harder to read, but also more flexible. In both cases, the heart

Example 3–3. An example of a basic event API

```
def event_handler(token):
    # act on information in token

parser = Parser()
parser.register_handler(event_handler)
parser.parse("file.xml")
```

of the application is the code that decides what kind of token has been received and acts on the information in the token. This code will usually be similar to that in Example 3–4.

Example 3–4. Dispatching on token types

```
def event_handler(token):
    if token.type == START_TAG:
        # handle start-tag
    elif token.type == END_TAG:
        # handle end-tag
    elif token.type == CHARACTERS:
        # handle characters
    # and so on
```

Note that the code inside this function could be copied out and appended to the code in Example 3–2, showing how strongly equivalent these two approaches are.

This kind of interface has a weakness in that when the parser creates the token, it knows the token type, but when the application resumes control, the information must be "rediscovered." This means that the parser will be putting its knowledge of the token type into a flag and let each and every application write the code to read the information back out from the flag and then jump to the right part of the application code.

The process of mapping from a particular piece of a document to the code that implements the application's reaction to that piece of the document is generally known as *dispatching*. In some processing

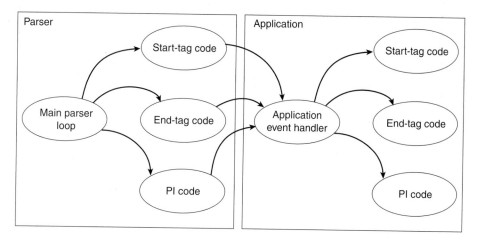

Figure 3–1   Event flow with single event handler

frameworks writing the dispatching code can be a lot of work, while in others one can use a special-purpose syntax to do it very easily.

The flow of control is shown in Figure 3–1, and as can be seen the application event handler must be rewritten for each application, and it is also inefficient as the code must enter a big `if`, `switch`, or `case` statement to branch out to the correct handler code again. This could be avoided if the parser interface were extended with one callback function or method for each kind of event, as shown in Figure 3–2.

Since this form of interface is superior both in performance and convenience, most parsers implement an interface of this kind. Also, since this allows for function or method signatures that are tailored to the specific event type, most interfaces of this type do away with the token objects and simply put the information in the event into the parameters of the callback function or method. Example 3–5 shows pseudo-code for the central loop of a parser written in this way. (Many XML parsers are in fact written in just this way.)

Note that this code has been lifted from the xmlproc XML parser and only slightly modified for readability. See the source of the `xml.parsers.xmlproc.xmlproc` module to compare this example with the real code.

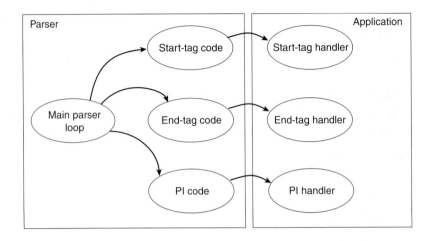

Figure 3–2   Event flow with multiple event handlers

How to write applications that use interfaces of this kind is what Part Two, "Event-based processing," on page 138 is all about.

3.1.1   *Generating output with events*

The fact that a document can be viewed as a sequence of events means that events can not only be used by a parser to transmit a document to an application, but they can also be used by an application to go the other way, that is to generate a document (as a sequence of bytes) for output from the program.

Traditionally, when moving a document from one application to another, the document is first serialized into a file. The file is then read by another process, which parses the document and builds its internal representation of the document. A common example of this might be a translation engine that translates an XML document from its source representation into an XML document with formatting semantics. (Several SGML and XML DTDs for formatted documents exist and these are much used to publish SGML and XML documents.) The formatting XML document could then be read by another engine that

Example 3–5. Pseudo-code for an XML parser

```
class XMLParser:

    # ...

    def do_parse(self):
        while self._pos < len(self._buffer):
            if self._buffer[self._pos] == '<':
                self._pos = self._pos + 1
                if self._buffer[self._pos] == '/':
                    self._parse_end_tag()
                elif self._buffer[self._pos] == '?':
                    self._parse_processing_instruction()
                elif self._buffer[self._pos] == '!':
                    # figure out whether it is a comment
                    # or a <!DOCTYPE
                else:
                    self._parse_start_tag()

            elif self._buffer[self._pos] == '&':
                self._pos = self._pos + 1
                if self._buffer[self._pos] == '#':
                    self._parse_char_ref()
                else:
                    self._parse_entity_ref()

            else:
                self._parse_character_data()

    def _parse_start_tag(self):
        # parse name and attributes, and see if it is
        # an empty-element tag

        self._event_handler.start_element(name, attrs)
        if empty_element_tag:
            self._event_handler.end_element(name)

    # ...
```

converts formatting XML documents into PDF documents. This is illustrated in Figure 3–3.

However, since the sequence of events completely describes the document, in many cases it may not be necessary for the application to serialize the document in order to give it to another application.

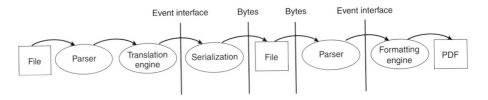

Figure 3–3   Using translation and formatting engines to produce PDF

Instead the application could just pass the events directly to the other application. Of course, this requires them to have a common event API and to be in the same process. This is often the case, as we'll see, and when it is, the result may be as shown in Figure 3–4.

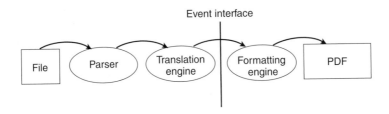

Figure 3–4   Efficient coupling of translation and formatting engines

Obviously, coupling the engines together in this way is much more efficient and convenient. It also retains the flexibility of the previous example, since the event interface cleanly separates the two engines.

3.2 | Documents viewed as trees

Apart from being viewed as a sequence of tokens or events, a document can also be seen as a complete tree structure with nodes representing elements, attributes, and data. This view is a higher-level one than the events/tokens view, in part because the containment structure of the document is now made explicit. Compared to event-based interfaces tree-views are fairly direct translations of the Infoset into software APIs.

However, creating this representation requires more work than simply generating a sequence of events or tokens, and so fewer parsers do this. Strictly speaking, building the tree structure is not something done by the parser, but rather by a separate entity called a *tree builder*. For simplicity it is common to call the entire thing a parser.

Quite often, the tree builder is a parser application that uses the event-based interface of the parser. In fact, there are also some stand-alone tools that only deal with document tree structures, but which can use event-based parsers to read documents into the tree structure. These are often slightly less convenient to use than the parsers that build a tree structure themselves, since they require two separate tools to be installed and integrated. Pseudo-code for an event-based tree builder is shown in Example 3–6.

Example 3–6. Pseudo-code for an event-based tree builder

```
class TreeBuilder(EventApplication):

    def __init__(self):
        self._tree = Tree()
        self._current = self._tree    # current containing node
        self._stack = []              # previous currents

    def get_tree(self):
        return self._tree

    def start_element(self, name, attrs):
        elem = ElementNode(name, attrs)
        self._current.add_child(elem)
        self._stack.append(self._current)
        self._current = elem

    def characters(self, characters):
        self._current.add_child(DataNode(characters))

    def end_element(self, name):
        self._current = self._stack.pop()

    # ...
```

Such a tree builder could typically build a tree structure from a file using a convenience function like the one shown in Example 3–7.

Example 3–7. Pseudo-code for building a tree

```
def load(sysid):
    builder = TreeBuilder()
    parser = Parser()
    parser.register_handler(builder)
    parser.parse(sysid)
    return builder.get_tree()
```

The main disadvantage of the tree view is that building a large object structure is usually expensive in any language. If the document is large, the resulting tree can easily become too large to fit in the working memory of the computer. Part of the problem is that the document inevitably becomes larger as a tree structure than it was as a serialized document, though the extent of this depends both on the implementation and the language it is written in.

So even if the tree view allows applications to pass documents from one to another, this is less efficient than using events and may not always be possible. Some tree implementations support building only parts of the tree at a time, which can solve the size problem, but this requires using a hybrid tree/event model to represent the document.

A major advantage of the tree view is that the entire document is available at the same time, and this makes it possible to modify the document while holding it in memory. This approach is both convenient and natural for programmers. After the tree has been modified it can be serialized again by traversing it and writing out the corresponding byte representation. One way to do this is to walk the tree and fire the corresponding events, which also means that even applications that require event input can easily be made to accept tree representations of documents. Working with the tree view of documents is described in more detail in Part Three, "Tree-based processing," on page 394.

In summary, the tree and event views of documents are equivalent, but each has its benefits. It is also easy to convert one view to the other.

However, when moving documents across interfaces between different parts of an application, one should use events, unless it is clear that the recipient will really need a tree (or the sender already has a tree). This is because event passing is much more efficient than tree-building, and one should not add costly operations to such interfaces unless necessary.

3.3 | Virtual views

So far we have talked only about views that present the source document as it actually is, but sometimes one might want to see the document in some other way. Typical examples of this might be when one wants to see the document with ignorable whitespace stripped or with XInclude inclusions performed. Allowing an application to receive such a virtual view of the document can make the application much easier to write.

There are many ways to achieve this, but an especially attractive approach is placing a filter between the XML parser and the application to translate from a real view to the desired virtual view. This approach is effective, transparent to the user and requires almost no changes to the application. A conceptual diagram of this is shown in Figure 3–5.

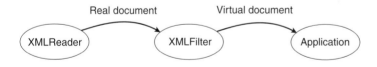

Figure 3–5   Using a filter to create a virtual view

Similarly to the real views, virtual views may be used not only when reading in a document, but also when it is being generated for output or when it is being transmitted between two applications. This becomes possible if the document is generated by firing the corresponding events, since this gives a convenient point at which to intercept and modify the document before it is passed on to its destination. The same can be done with tree representations, but this is generally harder and less efficient.

This technique will be discussed in more detail in 10.2, "Parser filters," on page 360.

3.4 | Virtual documents

Since the XML syntax and data model are separate, it is possible to represent data that is not in the XML syntax using the XML data model. This can have many different applications and can make it much easier to integrate non-XML data into XML applications. A simple example might be when one wants to turn a comma-separated (CSV) file into XML so that it can be converted to HTML using XML conversion tools.

One way to do this would be to write a CSV file reader that has the same interface as an XML parser, with the single difference that it can only read CSV files as input and always produces output in one fixed schema. The output would typically take the form of events, so that a generic tree builder could be used by those who wish to access the XML as a tree. It would make little sense to write a tree builder specifically for the CSV file reader.

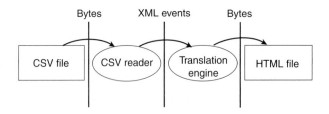

Figure 3–6   Using a filter to map CSV files into XML

If the filter were written with a standardized event-based interface, it could be used with any kind of XML application that supported that interface, as shown in Figure 3–6. This would allow CSV files to be processed exactly as though they were XML files. (An example implementation of this can be found in 25.1.1, "The CSV file reader," on page 973.)

Another benefit of the separation between the format and the model is that XML documents need not be serialized into the standardized notation. Instead, one can choose other, more specialized, notation when this is appropriate. One example might be a bit based notation that would use less space and could also be deserialized more efficiently than ordinary XML. The Wireless Application Protocol (WAP) environment, for example, uses a bit based XML notation to transmit XML documents to mobile phones, due to the strict constraints on transfer speed and memory capacity of these devices.

Another interesting application would be to store XML documents in compressed form to save space, which might be important for network transfers. One XML compression utility, known as XMill, uses several XML-specific techniques to achieve much better compression than, for example, the widely used ZIP archive notation. XMill can be found at `http://www.research.att.com/sw/tools/xmill/`. The researchers behind it are considering to make an event-based interface to XMill, which would make it very easy to add support for reading and producing XMill files to XML software. If the XMill reader could implement the same interface as XML parsers, applications that wished to support XMill files directly could then support this reader in addition to the XML parsers they already use.

A final benefit of the syntax/model separation is that XML documents do not in fact need to be serialized at all to be stored. As discussed earlier, XML databases store representations of XML documents that applications can access directly without having to parse them at all. These databases can have complex underlying storage structures, which need not be apparent to the applications that use these databases. One might, for example, store the conceptual structure of XML documents in relational databases.

Figure 3–7 shows what the XML document in Example 3–1 might look like when stored in a relational database. Except for the attributes (which would have to live in a separate table), such a table could

	A	B	C	D	E	F
1	nodeid	nodetype	nodename	nodevalue	parent	sibling_no
2	0	1				
3	1		2 book		0	1
4	2		2 chap		1	1
5	3		2 title		4	1
6	4		3	Saga of the Ynglings	5	1
7	5		2 p		4	2
8	6		2 q		7	1
9	7		3	Kringla Heimsins	8	1
10	8		3	, the round plate of earth that [...]	7	2
11						
12						

Figure 3–7   An XML document stored in an RDBMS

represent any XML documents. To connect to this document, one could use a mapping layer like the pseudo-code in Example 3–8.

Example 3–8. Mapping an RDBMS to an XML document

```
class XMLDatabase:

    def __init__(self, dbconn):
        self._dbconn = dbconn

    def get_document(self):
        row = get_first_row(self.dbconn,
                    "SELECT * FROM document WHERE parent is NULL")
        return Document(self._dbconn, row["nodeid"])

class Document:

    def __init__(self, dbconn, id):
        self._dbconn
        self._id = id

    def get_document_element(self):
        row = get_first_row(self._dbconn,
                    ("SELECT * FROM document WHERE parent=%d AND "
                     "nodetype='Element'")%
                     self._id)
        return Element(self._dbconn, row)
```

```
class Element:

    def __init__(self, dbconn, row):
        self._dbconn = dbconn
        self._id = row["nodeid"]
        self._gi = row["nodename"]
        self._parent = row["parent"]

    def get_parent(self):
        row = get_first_row(self._dbconn,
                            "SELECT * FROM document WHERE nodeid=%d" %
                            self._parent)
        return Element(self._dbconn, row)

    def get_children(self):
        children = []
        for row in get_all_rows(self._dbconn,
                            "SELECT * FROM document WHERE parent=%d" %
                            self._id):
            children.append(create_node(row))
```

This example is somewhat simplistic, of course, but it illustrates how it is possible in principle to create an XML document-view on data in a relational database, and also how XML documents can be represented in relational databases.

In addition to the tree-based interface, some databases also perform retrieval of documents in serialized form. Such databases are useful for searching and storage with locking semantics.

Common processing tasks

96

T his chapter describes the most common individual operations performed by XML applications and some the common problems encountered, together with suggestions for how to solve them. Most of the rest of the book is dedicated to how to implement programs that perform just these tasks. In general, information on each task is spread throughout the book under sections organized by technique rather than having specific sections assigned to each task.

4.1 | Serialization and deserialization

The simplest example of an XML processing task is perhaps when a traditional application uses XML as its external representation. One example of this is the open source Dia drawing program for Linux, which uses an XML notation to store Dia drawings. (See `http://www.lysator.liu.se/~alla/dia/` for information on Dia.) To use this notation Dia must be able to load XML documents from their serialized form into the internal data structures that Dia uses while a user is working on a drawing. While the user is working, Dia will be modifying the internal data structures, leaving the original document unmodified on the disk, until the user decides to save the drawing, whether to the same file or to a different file. At this point Dia must serialize its internal data structures into an XML document again, producing a sequence of bytes that can be written to the file.

Since the XML DTD used by Dia is unique to Dia, it makes sense to regard the drawings shown graphically by Dia as the primary version of the drawings, and the XML documents merely as drawings stored to disk. This is a view of XML documents that differs from that described in 2.3, "Documents and parsers," on page 53, and so different considerations apply. An application that modifies XML documents must be very careful to preserve the important aspects of those documents through the modification. In this case, however, only software is intended to see the documents, no users are ever expected to do so (except perhaps some curious individuals), so only the logical content matters, and lexical details can be disregarded, making the application much simpler.

Deserialization is the most common task of all, and there are very few XML applications that do not perform this job at all (even databases should support import of documents). Serialization is also very common, but decidedly less so than deserialization, since XML is often read in by an application without being written back out as XML, to be instead translated to some other form and perhaps not even written out at all.

4.2 | Transformation

Quite often one has information in one representation that needs to be converted to another for some reason. This might be to enable exchange with others, to be able to use it with a specific application, for presentation or for some other reason. The process of converting from one representation to another is called *tranformation*.

Transformation can be done by a standalone tool that takes one serialized document and transforms it to another serialized document, or it can be done with a filter, as described in the previous chapter. In both these cases the transformation itself is likely to be implemented in much the same way, and so a well-designed transformer could be written as a filter and made available both as a filter and as a standalone application.

Transformation can be done for several different reasons, some of the most common being:

- Publishing content from XML documents. This will generally involve conversion from XML to HTML, PDF or other rendition notations. When the structural information inherent in the XML documents is lost in such transformations they are called *down-conversions*.

- Creating XML documents from non-XML sources. This can be to convert legacy data into XML, to create XML in order to be able to use XML tools on the data, or for some other reason. Since the purpose has traditionally been to structure legacy documents, this is often called *up-conversion*.

- Creating data in some notation expected by specific applications. This is generally done because one wants non-XML application to be able to use the information in the XML documents. Such conversions do not have to lose information and so might perhaps be thought of as side-conversions.

- Generating XML in the XML form required by an application. Sometimes more than one XML application for the same purpose exists and one may want to be able to move data between these.

In general, such transformations may be faced with difficulties on four different levels:

- the notation level, e.g. when the target is XML and the source is a bit based notation of some kind, for example a Word document;

- the data model level, when one form uses a different underlying data model than the other does, for example, if one is an XML document and the other, a relational database;

- the information model level, when the source and target forms differ as to how they model the information and which parts of it they include, such as RSS and XMLNews; and

- the ontological level, when the two forms differ in their view of external reality and therefore organize information according to different principles.

The following sections introduce each of these levels in more detail.

4.2.1   *Notation differences*

Differences in syntax or notation often imply differences in data model, but need not do so. There is more than one possible notation for XML (consider XMill and the bit based WAP notation), but generally conversions between these can be done with reusable tools. Sometimes, however, the information is only available in a non-XML-based form, such as an RTF document, a DBF database file, an Excel spreadsheet, or some other notation.

In this latter case, getting documentation for the notation and writing software to read it can be a quite time-consuming task and require a substantial effort — but in general handling this is only a matter of effort and the problem can be solved. Also, quite often reusable software that can bridge the syntactical gap exists. Such software will often read the non-XML notation and produce some direct XML transformation of it, which can be useful as a starting point for further conversion.

4.2.2   *Differences in the data model*

Differences in the underlying data model can be slightly awkward, such as when the source data comes from a database and the target data is XML, since these data models are rather different. In such cases the information model of the data must effectively be translated from one data model to another, taking care to preserve all important aspects of the source data, and catering to differences in how things such as character encodings, references, missing values, and binary data are handled.

In general, handling differences of this kind is not too difficult, and can be worked around with a little ingenuity, which may perhaps involve inventing new conventions to deal with features missing in the target data model. For example, relational databases use foreign keys to refer from one table to another, a feature that is missing in XML. This can be handled by ignoring the problem (letting those who use the data find the connection from the source data) or by inserting the referred-to data directly rather than referring to it. A third possibility may be to create IDs and insert references to them in the generated XML.

4.2.3   *Differences in the information model*

Differences in the information model used, such as when mapping between the XML applications of two different genealogical databases, are on a higher level compared to notation and data model differences. On this level one is no longer dealing with the syntax or data model the information is represented in, so whether data comes from an XML source or some other source makes no difference at this level. In this sense this is no longer a purely XML-related problem, but a general problem that almost any kind of information system can run into.

Genealogical databases allow users to store information about the family relationships of groups of people. Such databases are often used by ordinary people interested in genealogy, generally to store information about their own family and its ancestors. They are also used by historians, anthropologists, and other kinds of researchers. A large number of such applications exists, and they do not all have the same features.

This can cause problems when converting from the data files of one database to those of another. What if one database supports divorces and multiple marriages and the other does not? Or if one supports adoption and the other does not[1]? In these cases, mapping between the different information models may be difficult, or even impossible, and important information may be lost in the conversion.

In general, the solutions to this problem are either to use specific conventions to indicate unsupported features when converting from a system that has a feature to another that does not. For example, the names of adopted children may have a " (*) " appended to indicate that they are adopted, if the program does not support it. Alternatively, one can just accept that not all information will survive the conversion and simply make the best of it.

4.2.4   *Ontological differences*

This level concerns the foundation from which the information model is built, and differences on this level can be very serious indeed. On this level any differences concern the underlying view of reality and what the information actually represents in the external world. If there are disagreements on this level, automated transformation is likely to be at best very difficult. To stay with the genealogical example, genealogical databases used by people who research their own genealogical history are generally based on the traditional western model of family relationships. This is not sufficient for anthropologists, however, since they often do research on ethnic groups that take rather different views of genealogy.[2]

---

1.   Not a very likely scenario, but useful for illustration.

2.   Many thanks to Boudewijn Rempt for suggesting this excellent example and pointing me to a good source of information on it. See

To take some examples, in the west, family descent is generally considered to follow the father-line. That is, when the king dies, his sons are the first in line to inherit the throne, which is known as patrilineal descent. However, other societies have followed different conventions, such as the Ashanti people of western Africa. In the Ashanti kingdom, matrilineal descent was practiced, which means that descent and inheritance followed the mother-line. In other words, when the king died, his sister's sons were the first in line to inherit the throne.[1]

These are not the only alternatives, however. For example, in many island societies arable land is very scarce and for an individual not being in a position to inherit, land may be a serious problem. Some societies have attempted to alleviate the problem by introducing so-called ambilineal descent. In this model, each person may choose whether to inherit from their father-line or mother-line. This increases the chances of being able to inherit land or other means of survival, such as important positions in society, although at some cost in terms of the complexity of family life.

Other societies have introduced further complexities, such as the concept known to anthropologists as moieties. Under this system, society is divided into separate groups (moieties) and members of one moiety are only allowed to marry members of a different moiety, reducing the chances of in-breeding. Another complexity is the clan system practiced in many tribal societies, where the nation is divided into a fixed number of clans. In general, the members of each clan are united by a special relationship to some powerful totemic spirit and clan boundaries may cross family boundaries in unpredictable ways.

---

http://www.umanitoba.ca/anthropology/tutor/ for more information.

1. The first British emissaries to the Ashanti kingdom learned this the hard way. Having had the King's sons educated in England in order to ensure that a British-friendly prince would be first in line to inherit the throne, they were unpleasantly surprised to discover that the King's sons were in fact not in line to inherit the throne at all!

Clearly, genealogy software developed to the western (patrilineal) model of descent will have serious problems with genealogical data from a society with completely different rules for genealogical descent. Problems of this kind can quite often be impossible to solve automatically, and many people feel that if e-commerce is to succeed, common ontological models need to be established. There are several efforts currently underway to establish common ontologies as a basis for e-commerce and to create mechanisms for interchange between them. The most important of these are perhaps IFLA FRBR, BizTalk, OASIS-Open, CommerceOne, and the WSDL/UDDI specifications.

4.3 | Validation

It is quite common for data-centric applications to receive data from sources that are not completely reliable with regards to the data they produce. The unreliable source may be human operators of some kind, whether they create the data or just enter it from other sources, or it may be untrusted software. In such cases it can be extremely useful to check the data against the information model of the application to see whether it is correct or not. This is generally known as validation in XML. As with transformation, this task has several levels, and becomes increasingly difficult to solve on higher levels.

When working with XML, the lowest level, the syntactical (or notation) level, is handled by the parser or the XML generator used. A parser will ensure that all syntactical problems in documents being read in are detected, and similarly, a good XML generator will ensure that it is impossible to generate XML documents that are not syntactically correct. Syntactical correctness is known as well-formedness in XML, and documents that are not well-formed will be rejected by XML parsers (as mentioned earlier). Syntactical correctness usually guarantees adherence to the data model, and in general, adherence to the data model is taken for granted and not verified.[1]

The next level, the information model level, is a bit more difficult since it is dependent on the specific application. However, with an XML DTD it is possible for a validating parser to ensure that the data follows the information model. On the other hand, XML DTDs are not very strong on constraints and so there will usually be many aspects of the information model which a validating parser cannot check. XSDL is a bit stronger on constraints than DTDs, but also has its limitations. More about this in Chapter 23, "Schemas," on page 892.

At the ontological level there are still more, and even more difficult, problems relating to whether the data really corresponds with the real world in the way that it is supposed to. For example, when a library database states that Ibsen wrote "Poison", how can any software possibly check whether this is correct or not? (In fact it is not correct; the author was Alexander Kielland.) Sometimes, it is possible for software to do some amount of verification against external reality, such as when validating a bookmark collection. Software can detect if the links actually refer to existing resources on the Web (mostly, at least), but it cannot control that the contents of the resource are still relevant for whoever made the bookmark.

4.4 | Modification

Sometimes one needs to modify an XML document automatically, for example by changing the data of an element, deleting a part of the document, or by adding a new element to it. In general, this will be done when the primary form of the data is stored as XML and updated automatically by software. An example of the latter might be an XML document containing a log, where one periodically needs to add new

---

1. It would be a paranoid XML application indeed that verified that each element was a child of the same element that was its parent!

log entries. In this kind of process the lexical information may suddenly become very important, since such applications may not always be allowed to remove this information from a document.

One example of this may be when a document made up from several subdocuments is stored in a document management system for editing. When users edit the compound document they will usually want to see the subdocuments at the same time as the master document, so the document management system will have to combine the documents into one document and then later reverse the process. In so doing it must take care to preserve the internal DTD subsets of each document, keep track of which parts of the document came from which subdocument and perhaps also make sure to preserve processing instructions, comments, CDATA marked sections, entity references, and character references.

In general, applications that store their data as XML should consider using an XML database solution rather than storing the data in files. This does away with the lexical problem entirely, since with XML databases there is no syntactical representation at all (as shown in Figure 3–7). In cases where this is not possible or desirable, solutions may involve raw string hacking in addition to using a full XML parser.

4.5 | Information extraction

Quite often an XML document is processed simply to extract information from it to use somewhere else. Examples of this kind of application are all kinds of searching on behalf of an end-user, when the information is needed by an application (such as an RSS client) or is pulled from several different documents to produce some kind of report.

Searching is likely to become an important application area in the future as more and more information can be found in XML form, and because of this the W3C is defining a query language called XML Query. This language is quite promising, and can not only query XML documents, but also traverse the results in various ways, and also built new XML documents as the query results. XML Query is likely to become a quite important specification in the future.

When extracting information from a document it is common to simply deserialize the document into some convenient application-specific object structure. This allows the application to easily extract the information it needs and use it directly, and in these cases extraction can be seen as a special case of deserialization. However, in some cases one may want to apply a different approach. The XPath language can be used to define pointers into a document that can be evaluated to produce either document fragments or single values. See Chapter 15, "XSLT: an introduction," on page 522 and especially 16.1, "XPath in detail," on page 565 for more information about XPath and how to use it.

Characters — the atoms of text

T his may seem like a strange chapter to find in a book on XML, but in fact, the subtle issue of characters and their digital representation is a very important subject (although sadly ignored), and it is especially important for XML. Character handling is a simple matter, even on a computer, if one only ever uses the letters A to Z without accents. However, most of the world does not do this, and even English-speaking computer users sometimes need to use accents in their text. The aim of this chapter is to help you understand the basic concepts of working with digital text and characters in general, and in XML in particular.

If you find that this chapter bores you, you can skip it without worrying about whether you will understand the remaining chapters. However, it is probably a good idea to read the first paragraphs of the section on XML and Unicode on page 128 anyway.

5.1 | Terminology

5.1.1 *What is a character?*

So, what is a character? Intuitively, most of us think of it as a letter, but when you start thinking about it, you quickly see that there are many more kinds of characters than just letters. There are also punctuation characters, digits, and maybe even whitespace characters. The symbols used by mathematicians are also usually considered characters, as are many other typographical symbols, such as the paragraph sign. Other languages and scripts also have different kinds of symbols that are considered characters.[1] Computers also use a class of characters known as control characters, which don't appear in printed text. (More about these below.) Given this variety of kinds and uses of characters, a better definition might be to say that characters are the atoms of which text is composed.

The XML Recommendation[2] defines a character to be "an atomic unit of text as specified by ISO/IEC 10646." In other words, it says what I said above, and then defers to ISO standard number 10646 for the actual definition. The SGML standard defines a character as "An atom of information with an individual meaning, defined by a character repertoire," and a character repertoire as "A set of characters that are used together." In both cases the meaning is the same: a character is an atom of text, as defined by some character standard. This, of course, leaves open the question of what should and should not be included in a character set, and this has been the subject of many heated debates.

In general, though, a character is an abstract concept, represented by a family of graphical shapes which share some commonality. This means that a bold "a", an italic "a", and a superscripted "a" are all the

---

1.   An interesting example is the Indic character Om, which is a symbol with religious significance, representing the sacred syllable "Om" much used in meditation. This character is included both in the Indic ISCII-91 character set as well as in Unicode (as U+0950).

2.   Section 2.2, first paragraph.

same character, although represented by slightly different shapes. When representing text, we usually want these to be seen as the same character, but with different formatting information attached to it. That is, we separate the levels of character representation and display. This clearly makes sense; just imagine what computing would be like if the strings "XML" and "**XML**" did not compare as equal, because one was bold and the other not.

For this reason it is usually most convenient to consider text to consist of abstract characters rather than graphical shapes or numbers. In other words, one should be aware that when working with text there are two different levels of interpretation: the level where one is dealing with bytes and the level where the bytes are interpreted into abstract characters. Well-designed text processing systems make this distinction clear, and I will try to do the same in the rest of the book.

5.1.2   *What is a character set?*

A *character set* is simply a set of characters distinguished from one another and gathered into some form of collection. Such a collection of characters can have many purposes and can take different forms, and in fact, not all of them have any relation to computers at all. For example, in eastern Asia, countries such as Japan, China, Taiwan, and South Korea have defined character sets which simply contain the characters children are supposed to learn in school. One example is the Japanese Gakūshū Kanji, which is the set of 1006 Chinese characters, known as *kanji* in Japan and *hanzi* in China, that Japanese children learn during their first six grades of school.

The character sets we are concerned with are mainly those defined for use with computers, which are known as *coded character sets*. These will typically give each character a number — known as its *code point* — and a name, as well as define how to encode the characters digitally. Sometimes they also deal with such things as identifying properties of each character and transformations between them, or define how to combine and display the characters.

5.2 | Digital text

We all know how to represent characters visually by drawing them, but the question of how to represent them digitally is a much more difficult one. To take one example, how would you represent the string "Hello!" as a sequence of binary digits? Abstraction is needed to strip away the uninteresting aspects of the string, and this is where character sets come to the rescue. As stated above, coded character sets assign numbers to each character in the set. Since we already know how to encode numbers digitally — as binary numbers — we can now encode characters, simply by representing them as the numbers they are assigned in the character set.

In this way, a string becomes a sequence of numbers, and by having special routines that interpret these sequences as strings we can successfully make them represent text. To display the text, all we need is a table of images with an entry for each character. Such a table is often known as a *font*, and each individual entry, a *glyph*. The mapping between characters and glyphs can in some cases be rather complex, and so I will not delve into that subject here. Comparing two strings can be done by storing the strings as arrays of numbers, and simply comparing them number by number.

The best-known and most important character set at the moment is probably the ASCII character set. Using a table of the ASCII character set, we can see that the string "Hello!" can be represented as a sequence of ASCII characters number 72, 101, 108, 108, 111, and 33. The only thing that then remains is to encode these numbers digitally, which could be done by saying that each character occupies a byte and thus making the string into an array of bytes.

5.2.1 *Character sets and encodings*

A major problem in internationalization work is that many people confuse the concept of a character set with that of a character encoding. The character set, as described above, is the collection of numbered characters. A *character encoding*, on the other hand, is how you map a sequence of character numbers into (or from) a sequence of binary digits. (Which was the last thing we did in the previous section.)

Since the encoding dictates how strings are represented, which is important for the speed and storage use of programs, the encoding usually has a major impact on the form of the character set. So when someone says that "ASCII is a 7-bit character set" that's a misunderstanding, but a very common and natural one. On the one hand, the ASCII character set is a collection of 128 characters, which has nothing to do with 7 bits. On the other hand, however, the ASCII character set is usually considered the same as the ASCII character encoding, which does use 7 bits, and the reason that there are 128 characters is exactly because this is the number of different characters you can express with 7 bits.

For character sets like ASCII and many others, the distinction between a character set and a character encoding is not really important, but it becomes very important the moment we start talking about Unicode (as we very soon will). The reason this is so important for Unicode is that Unicode has several different encodings of the same character set. And since Unicode is the character set of XML, this distinction is also important to us. Many of the oriental character standards also separate the notions of character sets and encodings, as does ISO 2022, and each character encoding supports a number of character sets.

5.2.2 *Character repertoires*

ISO and SGML character terminology includes the term *character repertoire*, which is similar, but not equivalent, to a coded character set. Some character standards, such as Unicode and ISO 6937, allow characters outside the base character set to be represented by using *combining characters*. This method represents characters outside the character set by combining characters from the character set. For example, ASCII might have used this method to represent "ê", which is not in ASCII, as "e^". Of course, special rules are needed to determine when one means "e^" and when one means "ê", but standards like Unicode and ISO 6937 provide this.

The character repertoire is then the set[1] of all characters that can be represented using the characters in the character set. For most character sets this is identical to the character set, but this is not the case for ISO 6937 and Unicode. In fact, strictly speaking, Unicode should not have included characters like "ê" at all since they can be represented using combining characters. The reason they are included anyway is to ensure backwards compatibility with existing character sets and software.

5.3 | Important character standards

Which character standards are important to you depends very much on where in the world you live and what languages you work with. The character standards used for western languages are important to all of us, however, because so many fundamental standards and tools are built on them. This section will therefore focus on the western character standards. Those who want to learn more are referred to *The SGML & XML Cookbook* by Rick Jelliffe in this series and *CJKV Information Processing* by Ken Lunde.

The most basic and most common character set today is ASCII, also known as US-ASCII, which defines the 26 characters needed for English (that is, A to Z) in upper and lower case, with punctuation and some control characters. Control characters are characters that were used for signals in wire communication and for control of display terminals. Examples of such characters that are still in use are the carriage return and line feed characters. One example of a character that is not is the "bell" character, which is number 7. No accented characters and no

---

1.   Here used in its strictly mathematical sense, as a collection.

non-English characters are included. 128 characters are defined altogether.

The result is a character set that suffices for English, but for hardly any other language in the world. For example, my own native language, Norwegian, can't be written with US-ASCII, since it uses three extra characters: æ, ø, and å. In Norwegian, these are considered to be separate characters and not modified forms of the other characters. In fact, using these with software can often be difficult even today because of the trouble with the various character set standards and how software relates to them. One area where this causes problems is email, since many Norwegians use the special characters in their names, but only ASCII characters are allowed in email headers.[1]

5.3.1   *ISO 8859*

There is an important ISO character set standard that extends ASCII for many of the languages in the world with a series of 256-character character sets. This standard is known as ISO 8859[2] and consists of a number of parts, each defining a character set. At the moment there are 14 parts; the most important of these, and the second most important character set today, is the one often known as ISO Latin 1 or just Latin 1, which is defined in ISO 8859–1 (that is, part 1 of the ISO 8859 standard).

ISO 8859–1 includes the 128 characters from ASCII, but adds 128 additional characters, thus requiring 8 bits. The additional characters are accented characters, certain special forms of punctuation, and some characters needed in other parts of Europe. Among these are the

---

1. Various schemes for encoding other character encodings in ASCII have been defined to work around this problem, so this is a truth with some modifications.

2. The full official name being *ISO/IEC 8859, Information technology — 8-bit single-byte coded graphic character sets.* Each of the parts also has its own name and year associated with it.

æ, ø, and å needed to write Norwegian. All the ISO 8859 character sets are identical to ASCII in the lower 128 characters (0 to 127), and reserve characters 128 to 159 for some extremely rare control characters from ISO 6429.

The ISO 8859 character set standards have been restricted to using 8 bits because this exactly corresponds to one byte on modern computers, and most computer systems (even today) assume that a character is represented by a single byte. This doesn't work for all languages, but allows computer systems to maintain backwards compatibility, so this outdated assumption has remained. Today it is beginning to be abandoned with the introduction of Unicode, but this is only progressing slowly.

ISO 8859–1 suffices for most Latin-based scripts, which means almost all the languages of North and South America, Western Europe and many other parts of the world, so it has become the dominant character set in the world at the moment. Like ASCII, it is encoded in 8 bits, but unlike ASCII, it needs the last of the 8 bits, something that occasionally causes trouble on the Internet, where many protocols and older software assume characters to be represented by only 7 bits.

ISO 8859 does not only consist of ISO 8859–1, however, but also has thirteen other character sets for different parts of the world, all of which are identical to ASCII in the lower 128 characters and then add 128 additional characters. The list below shows the different ISO 8859 character sets.

ISO 8859–1 (Latin alphabet no. 1)
> The Western European languages, but also Malaysian, Swahili, and Tagalog. For French, ISO 8859–15 below might be a better choice.

ISO 8859–2 (Latin alphabet no. 2)
> The Central European languages, such as Albanian, Czech, German, Hungarian, Polish, Romanian, Serbo-Croatian, Slovak, Slovene, and Swedish.

ISO 8859–3 (Latin alphabet no. 3)

The Southern European languages, such as Catalan, French, Galician, Italian, Maltese, and Turkish (although for Turkish 8859–9 is a better choice), and also Afrikaans.

ISO 8859–4 (Latin alphabet no. 4)

The Northern European languages, such as Danish, Estonian, Finnish, German, Greenlandic (that is, Inuit or Eskimoic), Sami (or Lappish), Latvian, Lithuanian, Norwegian, and Swedish. This character set has now been superseded by ISO 8859–10.

ISO 8859–5 (Latin/Cyrillic alphabet)

The Eastern European languages written with Cyrillic script, such as Bulgarian, Byelorussian, Macedonian, Russian, Serbian, and Ukrainian.

ISO 8859–6 (Latin/Arabic alphabet)

Arabic without accents. Farsi (or Persian) and Urdu are also written with Arabic script, but this character set lacks the extra characters needed for these languages.

ISO 8859–7 (Latin/Greek alphabet)

Modern Greek.

ISO 8859–8 (Latin/Hebrew alphabet)

Hebrew and Yiddish.

ISO 8859–9 (Latin alphabet no. 5)

Many Western European languages, but most importantly Turkish.

ISO 8859–10 (Latin alphabet no. 6)

Northern European languages, such as Danish, Estonian, Faeroese, Finnish, German, Inuit, Icelandic, Sami, Lithuanian, Norwegian, and Swedish. Note that the Norwegian Sami community has rejected this character set and uses a character set of their own design (known as Windows Sami 2) instead. Note also that one character needed for Latvian has been left out.

ISO 8859–11 (Latin/Thai alphabet)
Thai. (This character set is the same as the one known as TIS-620.)

ISO 8859–12
This character set does not yet exist. A character set for Indic scripts may appear as ISO 8859–12 in the future.

ISO 8859–13 (Latin alphabet no. 7)
The Baltic rim, that is, Latvian, Lithuanian, and Estonian.

ISO 8859–14 (Latin alphabet no. 8)
The Celtic languages, that is, Gaelic and Welsh.

ISO 8859–15 (Latin alphabet no. 9)
Western European languages. This character set modifies ISO 8859–1 to include the euro symbol (€), capital Y with diaeresis (Ÿ, strangely, 8859–1 only had the lower-case version of this) and some special characters needed for French, such as the oe ligature (œ).

ISO 8859–16
A character set for Romanian has been proposed as ISO 8859–16, although this seems to be controversial.

A very good source for more information on these character sets is Roman Czyborra's `http://czyborra.com/charsets/iso8859.html`.

5.3.2 *The problem with exchange*

The ISO 8859 collection of character sets solved the basic problem of enabling Norwegian, German, Russian, and Arabic users to write text in their native languages on their computers, and gave rise to the basic model that most computer systems follow today. In this model, each character is represented as a single byte (giving room for 256 different characters). When installing the operating system, the user configures the computer to use one such 256-character character set for all text. In most cases this character set will be ISO 8859–1, or some variant of it, but this depends on the selected language.

The exchange problem hinted at in the section title refers to what happens if one moves a text file from one computer that uses this model to another that uses the same model, but with a different default character set. This would happen, for example, if a text file is copied from a Linux machine to a Mac without converting the bytes representing characters. The default for Linux in Western Europe is ISO 8859–1, while the default for MacOS is MacRoman (a proprietary character set defined by Apple). A program wouldn't know that anything went wrong, but when seeing a byte with the number 248 ("ø" on the Linux machine) it would map this to a wrong abstract character, and display a wrong glyph, because character number 248 would be "¯" (macron) on a Mac.

The problem here is caused by people using different character sets, and, more importantly, files not being labeled with the character encodings used to encode the text in them. The Internet standards solve this problem by having special HTTP headers for specifying the character encoding, as well as declarations that can be inserted in HTML and XML documents. (For a description of how XML does this, see page 128.)

5.3.3 *Windows code pages*

Microsoft Windows uses the model with a user-configurable default character set described in the previous section. Most of these character sets (called *code pages*) are based on the corresponding ISO 8859 character sets, but Microsoft has taken advantage of the fact that the control characters between 128 and 159 are not needed in the PC environment and inserted extra characters there.

These extra characters include dashes, angle quotes, and other characters, often used in documents for presentational purposes. It is a problem that much software (and also many users) incorrectly label such documents as ISO 8859-x documents, even when they use characters that do not exist in these character sets.

More seriously still, many authors use HTML character references to refer to characters in the 128–159 range as if they were characters in the Windows code page. Unfortunately, many browsers have added extra code to display these characters accordingly.

5.3.4   *Unicode*

Unicode is the character set to end all character sets. In fact, what is usually referred to as Unicode is actually two parallel standards produced by two different standards bodies. One is ISO 10646, *Information technology — Universal Multiple-Octet Coded Character Set (UCS)*, produced by ISO, and the other is the Unicode standard, produced by the Unicode Consortium. These two standards define an identical set of characters, but they differ somewhat in what they provide around that set of characters, in terms of encodings, character properties and so on. However, this causes no problems in practice and this duality can for all practical purposes be disregarded.

The Unicode character set aims to include all characters in all languages and scripts, whether living or dead and whether natural or invented. In fact, it is also known as the Universal Character Set (UCS), and this is exactly what it aims to be: a character set that includes all characters that have ever been in use.

At the moment, this character set includes all of the ISO 8859 characters, Japanese, Korean, Vietnamese, Chinese, most of the Indic scripts and indeed all the major scripts used in the world today. A number of lesser-known scripts remain, as do some dead scripts, such as the Rongo-Rongo script used on Easter Island in antiquity, and some rarely-used characters. This includes, among other things, Japanese characters used to write place names as well as some Chinese ideographs (hanzi/kanji).

This completeness, and the fact that Unicode/ISO 10646 is the only character set to be so complete, is what makes Unicode a natural base standard for all kinds of standards that need to deal with text. It also means that Unicode is now a natural internal text encoding for most programs and operating systems. Unicode also serves as a natural reference database for characters. The syntax U+XXXX (where XXXX are four hexadecimal digits) is often used in writing to refer to Unicode characters by their code point.

For a long time all the characters in Unicode were given numbers below 65536, and this made many people believe that Unicode is a 16-bit character set, including at times the Unicode consortium itself. This, however, is not really the case, and numbers above 65536 have now been used. The fact is that Unicode as currently defined has 21 bits available, while the ISO 10646 standard speaks of the UCS as a four-byte, that is, 32-bit, character set. An important feature of Unicode is that the lower 256 characters of it are identical to the ISO 8859–1 character set.

The most obvious way to encode characters from a character set such as Unicode is to use 32 bits per character, but if you, like most computer users of the world, only need the lower 256 characters, and perhaps even just the lower 128, this is very wasteful as it quadruples the memory requirements from one byte per character to four bytes per character. Consequently, many different character encodings for Unicode have appeared employing various space-saving and backwards-compatible schemes, all of which have their uses and advantages. Table 5–1 lists the different Unicode encodings, and rough descriptions of each encoding are given below.

The UCS-2 encoding is the original Unicode encoding, and in it each Unicode character is represented as a 16-bit (2-byte) number that refers to the character's code point in Unicode. Originally, Unicode was intended to not assign any characters above U+FFFF. The alignment with ISO 10646 changed this, however, and so to be able to handle the characters above U+FFFF, UCS-2 had to be replaced with

Table 5–1   The Unicode encodings

Encoding	Type	Base size
UTF-7	variable-width	8 bits, only 7 of which are used
UTF-8	variable-width	8 bits
UTF-16	variable-width	16 bits
UTF-32	fixed-width	32 bits
UCS-2	fixed-width	16 bits
UCS-4	fixed-width	32 bits

UTF-16. UTF-16 extends UCS-2 with a system where a certain range of characters is interpreted in pairs of two 16-byte quantities to give the numerical value of one character outside the strict 2-byte range. These quantities are known as *surrogate pairs*. They are also sometimes called surrogate characters, but in truth they are artifacts of the UTF-16 encoding and not really characters at all. This range of characters is left empty in the character set, and is thus an example of an encoding influencing the character set. These characters really have no meaning in the other encodings, except for UTF-7, which also uses them. With the surrogate characters UTF-16 can represent the characters up to U+10FFFF, which is sufficient for the foreseeable future.

The UTF-8 encoding comes from the experimental Plan 9 operating system, where it was developed as an encoding of Unicode backwards-compatible with ASCII. It achieves this backwards compatibility by encoding ASCII as ASCII, which leaves the 8th bit for other purposes. In UTF-8, having the 8th bit set on a byte indicates that it is part of a sequence of bytes together representing a single character. The form of the first byte indicates the number of bytes used to encode that character. The full details about UTF-8 can be found in RFC 2279.

UCS-4 is like UCS-2, but with four bytes instead of two, enabling it to represent all of Unicode with no special tricks. UTF-32 is nearly identical to UCS-4, but with some very minor differences.[1] So of all the Unicode encodings, only UCS-2, UCS-4 and UTF-32 are really fixed-width encodings, and of those only UCS-4 and UTF-32 can encode the entire character set. The characters above 65536 are not in use yet and so UCS-2 can for the moment represent all assigned Unicode characters. This will change in the near future, however.

The UTF-7 encoding is rather different from the other Unicode encodings in that it is a modal encoding. This means that the encoding contains shift sequences that shifts the "mode" of the encoding, that is, it changes the interpretation of the following bytes. UTF-7 uses only 7 bits, so it can be safely used in email headers and other places where software might strip the 8th bit. It encodes letters, digits, and some few punctuation characters as themselves, but all characters outside this range have to be encoded differently. This is done by using a "+" character to start a base64-encoded section, which continues until a character outside the base64 character set is found, or a "-" is found which terminates the sequence explicitly.

5.3.4.1 The structure of the character set

A character set as huge as Unicode needs some high-level structure in order to make development of it feasible at all, and also to make it easier to navigate in for those making software and higher-level specifications. On the highest level, Unicode consists of 16 *planes*, each consisting of 65536 characters. The planes for which there are planned uses at the moment are:

The Basic Multilingual Plane (or BMP)
    This is the first plane, from U+0000 to U+FFFF.

---

1. See Unicode Technical Report 19 for a description of these. That explanation requires understanding of concepts not covered in this book, which is why I do not describe the differences here.

The Secondary Multilingual Plane (or SMP)
This is the second plane, from U+10000 to U+1FFFF, and is used for various extinct scripts as well as some notational systems.

The Supplementary Plane for CJK Ideographs (or SIP)
This is the third plane, from U+20000 to U+2FFFF, which is used for additional Chinese and Korean characters beyond those in the BMP.

The General Purpose Plane (or GPP)
This is plane number 14 (counting from zero), stretching from U+D0000 to U+DFFFF. The only "characters" planned to be placed here are the controversial language tags, intended to be used for indicating the language of text. This is something that many feel XML should be used for, rather than the character set, but apparently the Unicode and ISO working groups chose this approach to keep the IETF from adding language tags unilaterally to UTF-8.

Within each of these planes there are so-called sub-blocks, with names and ranges defined in the Unicode standard. Figure 5–1 shows a rough outline of these blocks in BMP, where some of the blocks have been merged to keep the diagram from becoming impossibly detailed.
Below are explained some of the terms used in Figure 5–1.

Symbols
Various kinds of symbols like mathematical symbols, currency symbols, and so on.

CJK
Short for "Chinese, Japanese, and Korean."

Yi
A little-known script used in China.

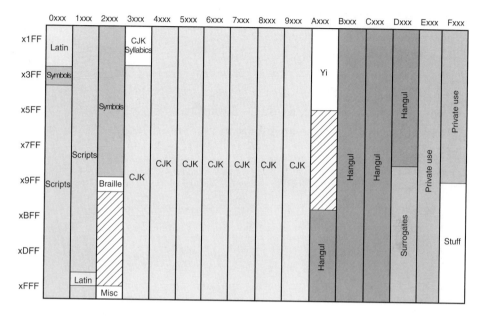

Figure 5–1 The BMP structure

Hangul
The Korean script.

Figure 5–2 shows the planned outline of the SMP, although it should be noted that at the time of writing this is only a planned layout that may change before the standard is finalized.

Below are explained some of the terms in Figure 5–2.

LTR/RTL
Short for "left-to-right scripts" and "right-to-left scripts."

Conlang
Short for "constructed languages," meaning invented and fictional scripts. One example might be the Deseret script invented by the Mormons for English.

Undeciph
Short for "undeciphered."

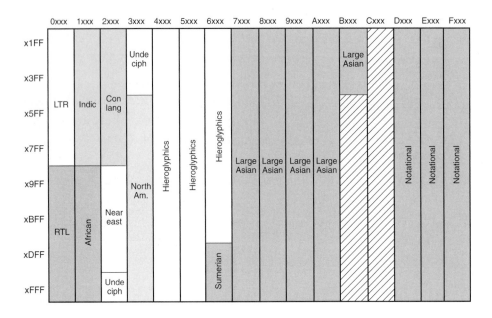

Figure 5–2   The SMP structure

5.3.4.2   Other things provided by Unicode

Unicode does not only define a character set and a collection of encodings for it, but also provides many useful algorithms and much useful data about the characters. The most obviously useful part is perhaps the Unicode character database, which contains information about the characters in the standard. This includes category information (separating characters into letters, numbers, punctuation, etc.), case mappings, names, information about which scripts use the characters, etc.

Unicode also has a well-defined display algorithm with rules for how to combine characters and also how to display bidirectional text. There are also algorithms for sorting and case folding and a recommendation on how to implement regular expressions for international text.

5.3.5 *Other character sets*

There is a plethora of other character sets than those described so far, many of which are no longer in use, but also some rather important ones that are still used. An important group of character sets is the 256-character character sets defined by Apple for the Macintosh. These are based on ASCII, but not on the ISO 8859 series. There are sets for Western European languages (MacRoman), Greek (MacGreek), and many other scripts.

Unicode is a relatively new standard, and the approach taken by the ISO 8859 series is useless for the Oriental languages which have tens of thousands of characters. This has led to the development of lots of oriental character sets and encodings. The most important of these character encodings are listed in Table 5–2. (The underlying character sets have been left out.)

Table 5–2 The most important Oriental character encodings

Name	*Language*	*Comment*
Shift-JIS	Japanese	
EUC-JP	Japanese	
ISO 2022-JP	Japanese	
EUC-KR	Korean	
ISO 2022-KR	Korean	
Johab	Korean	
Big 5	Chinese (Taiwan)	
EUC-TW	Chinese (Taiwan)	
GB 2312	Chinese (China)	should properly be called EUC-CN, now superseded by GBK
GBK	Chinese (China)	
ISCII	Indic languages	8-bit
VISCII	Vietnamese	8-bit

5.3.6 *XML and Unicode*

The XML definition of what a character is refers to the ISO 10646 definition of a character, and this is no accident, for XML uses the Unicode/ISO 10646 character set and, in the data model, XML documents are made up of abstract Unicode characters.[1] An XML document can be stored in other character encodings, but these must be mapped to Unicode before the document is parsed. Note that XML does not allow *all* Unicode characters to be used; it is very careful to disallow a lot of control characters as well as the surrogate code points.

To enable the XML parser to do the mapping from the encoding used in the XML document to Unicode, the encoding that is used must be indicated in the XML declaration. If there is no such indication, parsers must assume that the document is encoded with either UTF-8 or UTF-16. To find out which of these two character encodings is in use, the XML parser will look at the first two bytes and if they are either 0xFF and 0xFE or 0xFE and 0xFF it will assume that this is the Unicode Byte Order Mark, which is used in UTF-16 to tell whether the text has been encoded with the high byte first or the low byte first. (This is necessary because little-endian machines and high-endian machines will do this differently.) It will then assume that the encoding is UTF-16. If there is no Byte Order Mark in the first two bytes, the parser will look at the XML declaration at the beginning of the document to see what it says. If the XML declaration gives the name of the encoding, the parser will use that, and if not, it will assume that the encoding is UTF-8.

This means that if your document uses ISO 8859-x, ASCII, or any other ASCII-based 8-bit encoding without stating so, the parser will assume that you are in fact using UTF-8. If you have restricted yourself to the ASCII characters this will work fine, but if you use characters with a code point higher than 128, these will trigger the UTF-8 escaping rules, which means they will almost certainly be seen as illegal

---

1. XML is a bit schizophrenic as it doesn't really decide whether it is based on Unicode or on ISO 10646.

UTF-8 bit sequences and bring the parsing to a grinding halt. The solution is, of course, to insert the correct encoding declaration.

Another item worthy of note is that character references (such as `&#65;`) are always considered to refer to Unicode characters. The number of the character reference is the Unicode code point of the character referred to. This is regardless of the character encoding used for the specific document, which is a very good thing. It makes it easy to use some Unicode characters even in documents encoded with character sets which do not have these characters.

The XML Recommendation only requires parsers to support UTF-8 and UTF-16. In practice, parsers fall into three categories:

- Those which do not support Unicode. This will generally be because their programming environment makes it difficult to support Unicode. These parsers will generally either use ISO 8859–1 or just assume the default character set of the system (or some chaotic combination of both).

- Those which support Unicode, but make no special attempt to support many character encodings. These parsers will generally support UTF-8, UTF-16, and ISO 8859–1 (since it is so easy). Not supporting 8859–1 is rare in the extreme, and also rather pointless. Some will go further and support more of the 8859 series through conversion tables. Some parsers also have mechanisms by which applications can plug in support for more encodings.

- Those which support Unicode and lots of different encodings. These will generally support all the Unicode encodings listed above, the entire 8859 series, many oriental encodings and vendor encodings as well as lesser-known encodings like EBCDIC.

SGML is older than Unicode and is not based on it at all. Instead, SGML allows the user to specify what character set is used in the SGML declaration. This is done by a reference to a well-known character set, and allows SGML systems to support Unicode as well as other character sets in a controlled way.

5.4 | Characters in programming languages

Different programming languages handle characters in different ways, but nearly all provide special data types, syntax, and operations for dealing with text. The level of sophistication varies from C (where strings are arrays of numbers and the only special provision for them is a syntax for string and character literals) to languages like Java (which provides full internationalization) and Perl (which has very fancy text operations built into the core language).

5.4.1   *C*

As stated above, C has very primitive support for text since it doesn't really have a dedicated data type for characters, but lets the user freely mix characters and numbers. That is, there is no notion of abstract characters in C, only numbers which can be considered to be ASCII characters. However, there is a syntax for character literals (such as "c") that allows one to type characters directly in the source code and have them automatically translated to the right number.

However, this only works reliably for ASCII characters, since the C `char` data type is a signed byte (that goes from –128 to 127), so ISO 8859–1 characters outside the ASCII range will end up as negative numbers. This can be troublesome because comparison between a `char` value and the code point of a character cannot be performed directly if the code point is above 127. Also, a single character can end up occupying two bytes when it is converted to an `int`, due to C's rules for sign-extending data.

The language also supports string literals (such as "hello!"), and these work like arrays of characters. In addition to this, the standard libraries have functions for comparing and working with strings. (Note that not even string comparison is built-in to the language.) The result is that internationalized (or even ordinary!) string processing in C is an awkward affair.

In addition to the single-byte `char` data type, there is the `wchar_t` data type, which is a "wide character." The character set and encoding of these characters are not defined by the C standard, and different compilers interpret them differently. For example, Microsoft Visual C++ uses Unicode and UTF-16 (or possibly UCS-2), while GNU GCC uses Unicode and UCS-4. This is troublesome in that each application and reusable module has to invent its own mechanisms for handling multibyte text (that is, text that does not follow the "character is single byte" convention). This causes problems for XML parsers, for example, which must be reusable and return Unicode text to their client applications.

5.4.2   *C++*

C++ is very nearly a superset of C and adds object-orientation, a stricter type regime, and an enlarged standard library to C. In doing so it inherits all the mechanisms (and weaknesses) discussed above for C. In addition, C++ has standard string classes known as `std::string`, for 8-bit strings, and `std:wstring`, which is a container of `wchar_t` elements, and so subject to the same problems as the `wchar_t` type itself.

A large number of libraries for making it easier to deal with international text in C++ (and C) exist, one of the most important being ICU. ICU is a large library developed as an open source project run by IBM, which has support for lots and lots of internationalization issues such as calendars, character set conversion, date and time formatting, and much more. The ICU home page can be found at `http://oss.software.ibm.com/developerworks/opensource/icu/project/`.

5.4.3 *Java*

Java is similar to C in that it has character and string literal syntaxes, and in that characters are numbers. However, it is a much more modern language, and differs in that all characters in Java are Unicode characters and that strings consist of abstract characters. Character arrays use the UTF-16 encoding, but what strings use is effectively a matter private to the implementation of the `String` class. Also, the character type is a separate type in Java, although conversion between it and the numeric types is automatic, using Unicode code points for the mapping.

Another important difference is that strings in Java are objects with methods for comparison, examination of parts, and for extracting slices of the strings. Note that this means that simple `==` comparison for strings does not work in Java either, since this compares references rather than values. The result is rather ugly: one has to call the `equals` method instead.

One last, and very important, thing about Java and Unicode is that Java uses streams (and only streams) for input and output, whether to files or to the network, as well as to databases and other systems. These streams are of one of two types: either byte or character streams, and Java enforces a strict separation between the two. Byte streams are raw binary streams, but with character streams, one is receiving Unicode characters converted from whatever encoding the underlying byte stream used.

It's worth noting that on systems that use the "character is byte" model described above, Java will assume that input is in the platform default encoding unless explicitly told otherwise. This makes representing text, even international text, very easy and straightforward in Java. Developing XML tools in Java is also made much easier by this, since Unicode support is nearly entirely painless.

5.4.4 *Perl*

Starting with version 5.6 Perl supports Unicode. In Perl programs that say `use utf8;` all strings are Unicode strings. The internal encoding used is UTF-8, but this is invisible to the Perl programmer, since Perl strings consist of abstract characters rather than bytes. It also has support for converting text read from outside Perl into Unicode. The regular expression and other string processing features in Perl are all Unicode-aware, and their interpretation of character classes depends on the current locale.

5.4.5 Python

Python, like Perl, has good support for text, through the `string` type. It does not have a separate notion of characters, though, for a character is just a single-character string. Strings can appear as literals, be compared with ==, be cut up with slices, be added, built, measured for length, etc. Python also has a regular expression library for parsing.

Python version 2.0 is the first version of Python with Unicode support, and unlike Perl, it uses UTF-16 for strings internally, which makes many operations much easier to support. In version 2.0 Python has two different kinds of strings: old-style ASCII strings and new-style Unicode strings. If a string literal is prefixed with u, it becomes a Unicode string, and one can use \uXXXX escape sequences inside them, where the XXXX is a hexadecimal character number referring to a Unicode code point.

When performing an operation on both a normal string and a Unicode string, the result will be a Unicode string (so 'c' + u'c' will produce u'cc' rather than 'cc'). The concept of byte and character streams has also been introduced into Python 2.0, which means that proper international text processing is very easy in Python 2.0.

More details on Python 2.0's Unicode support are provided in A.5.8, "Unicode support," on page 1097.

5.4.6 Common Lisp

Common Lisp is the most important Lisp dialect in use today, together with Scheme. For those who do not know: It is a statically-scoped language with optional type declarations, that is usually compiled to native code and achieves performance comparable to that of C++ and usually much better than that of Java. It has an extremely flexible and extensible syntax and incorporates many advanced features found in no other programming language today.[1]

In Common Lisp characters belong to a special data type and conversion between characters and numbers must be done with special functions. This mapping is not defined in the standard to allow implementors greater freedom to choose, but many implementations use Unicode. Applications can usually use compile-time macros to test for the presence of Unicode support. (Interestingly, the ANSI Common Lisp standard predates the Unicode effort by two years, but still has better support for Unicode than many languages developed much later.)

Strings are also special objects, while still being arrays of characters, and the language supplies a large set of functions for comparing and working with them. Even basal operators like + are functions in Common Lisp, so in this sense the default comparison operators[2] can be used with strings.

5.4.7 *tcl*

The Tool Command Language, or tcl, is a scripting language that is often compared to Perl and Python, although it is often considered to be less structured than these. Its main features are a very simple and general syntax, easy integration with C programs, and a very simple and natural execution model. It has excellent support for string processing, just like Perl and Python.

---

1. One of these allows programs to update class definitions in running programs and have existing objects of that class modified to the new definition in a controlled way while the program runs.

2. Common Lisp has a richer set of comparators than do most other languages. In other words, the plural "operators" is not a typo.

Unicode is supported in tcl since version 8.1, using the UTF-8 encoding internally for all strings. This is invisible to tcl code, however, so tcl strings effectively consist of abstract characters. The language can convert back and forth between many different character encodings and has a concept of the default platform encoding (just like Java). The Tk GUI toolkit used by tcl also supports Unicode.

5.4.8 *Ada95*

Ada95 has an 8-bit type named `Character` which is defined to be interpreted as ISO 8859–1 code points. It also has a 16-bit type named `Wide_Character` which is defined to be interpreted as a Unicode code point. There are also a `String` type (array of `Character`) and a `Wide_String` type (array of `Wide_Character`). The `Wide_String` type effectively becomes UCS-2-encoded text by the letter of the standards. The result is that Ada95 has very good (but only partial) built-in support for Unicode.

5.5 | Further problems

The character standards discussed in the previous section only solve a small part of the internationalization problem, that of encoding international text digitally. Still remaining are the problems of case conversion, sorting, and display. Case conversion (that is, converting between upper- and lower-case characters) is highly language-specific, which means that contextual knowledge is needed to know how to turn "I" into a lower-case character. In most cases, the answer will be "i", but in Turkish it is actually "ı" (dotless i).

Similarly, sorting also depends on the language in use. In Norwegian, for example, "æ", "ø", and "å" are sorted after all other letters of the alphabet (in the order given above). In Dutch, the letter sequence "IJ" is considered a separate character and sometimes sorted after "I" and sometimes after "Z". In Hungarian, "sz" is considered a separate character, but sometimes occurs when a word ending in "s" is combined with a word beginning in "z" to form a composite word, in which case it is considered to be two different characters. The only way to separate these two cases is to use a Hungarian dictionary.

Finally, layout can be extremely tricky, since different scripts differ greatly in how they are displayed. European scripts are written left-to-right top-down, while Hebrew and Arabic are written right-to-left top-down (although numerals are written left-to-right), Japanese and Chinese can be written top-down left-to-right, i.e. in columns rather than rows, as can Mongolian. Other languages, such as many Indic languages, stack letters on top of each other on the line, or even arrange them in an order that differs from the reading order, technically known as the logical order.

In addition to this many languages have complicated composition rules. Arabic, for example, has four versions of each character, depending on whether the character is first, middle, or last in a sequence of continuous characters, or stands alone. Displaying software has to be aware of this and select the right glyph from its fonts to represent each character in a text.

In general, though, these problems are orthogonal to XML, so I will not delve deeper into them here, since the subject could provide enough material for an entire series of books. Those interested can consult the books mentioned earlier in this chapter, as well as the Unicode standard and Unicode technical reports 10 (sorting) and 21 (case mapping).

Event-based processing

138

Part Two

This part shows how to build applications that use event-based processing, teaches the related concepts and techniques, as well as introduces the main tools for event-based development. The main focus is on the SAX API, but other ways of doing event-based processing are also discussed.

Event-based processing

- Advantages and disadvantages
- Writing event-based applications
- Tools for event-based processing
- RSS: an example application

O f the main approaches to processing, the event-based approach is the most low-level, which is why it is covered first. The fact that it is the most low-level also means that it is more often implemented[1] than the other approaches, that it provides a good starting point for building higher-level abstractions, and that it is often not as convenient from a programming perspective. However, it is still a very good choice for many processing applications, as you'll see in this part of the book.

Another important aspect of event-based processing is that it is often useful in the design of general XML processing systems and in larger applications.

---

1. This argument is often known as the "worse is better" argument, after a famous (and excellent!) article by Richard Gabriel.

6.1 | Benefits and disadvantages

Compared to tree-based processing, event-based processing has several benefits to recommend it, such as:

Resource use
Event-based processing does not require much memory, since only a tiny piece of the document is seen at a time. Also, building a complete document tree requires the creation of large numbers of objects and much book-keeping to build the tree correctly. This is costly in terms of time as well as memory.

Convenience
When programs are written in terms of events they are often easier to formulate, especially when one only wants a subset of the information, and more resistant to changes in the positioning of elements than when they are written in terms of tree nodes. This does not hold in every case, however, and often depends on the granularity of events and the contextual information provided by the framework.

Simplicity
APIs are usually simpler than the alternatives, and so easier to learn (and implement!).

Practical for building data structures
Often an XML document is processed only to build an internal data representation, and in these cases event-based interfaces provide an excellent way to do this, since one does not have to build a big tree that's later thrown away. Another benefit is that many of the disadvantages of not having the full document available at all times disappear, since at the end of the process one will have a complete set of information, only not as a tree, but as an object structure.

However, there are not only benefits to event-based processing, and for some kinds of tasks, pure event-based processing is not the best way to write an application. The main disadvantages are:

Only a "peephole" view of the document

At any one point in time, you can only see a small piece of the complete document, which means that if the processing application needs information that appears elsewhere in the document, things can become difficult. It is always possible to solve this problem, but it can be awkward at times.

Another implication of this is that the application will need to keep track of relevant state on its own, since information in previous events is not a natural part of an event-based interface. Some things, such as the stack of open elements, the sibling number of each element, etc., may be provided by the framework, but often it is not.

Cannot modify the document

When you only want to modify a part of the document, iterating over the entire document with events may not be the best way to do it, especially if the document already is in some form of persistent storage and can be modified directly, without going through a complete read-in/write-out cycle.

Searching may be difficult

Certain kinds of search criteria, such as, "locate the first p element that appears after a table of 6 rows of 4 columns," may be more difficult to implement with an event-based interface.

Source may be difficult to understand

Event-based programs typically consist of a number of little pieces of code that are triggered by input events, each modifying the state of the application, and to understand how these pieces interact, it is usually necessary to understand the structure of the input — and even then, it can be difficult to understand the code. The main problem is that the order of events is not defined by the source code, but by the input.

In summary, pure event-based processing is good for building application-specific representations from XML input, for various kinds of filters, and for simpler kinds of translations. For more complex translations and for searching, tree-based processing is usually better. In some cases, hybrid solutions may be the best. These will be covered in 22.2, "Hybrid event/tree-based approaches," on page 851.

6.2 | Writing event-based applications

Writing an event-based processing application requires a somewhat unusual way of thinking which may be unfamiliar at first and often takes a while to get used to. The source of the problem is that the application must react to events that come to it in a certain order, and this order may not always be convenient. For example, you may need the contents of an element (for example, `person-name`), but in a typical event-based interface this information will be provided in three different events:

- Start of element: `person-name`.
- Data: "Lars Marius Garshol".
- End of element: `person-name`.

The problem is that in our application, we are first notified that the sought-after element begins, but we are not given its contents, since they have not appeared yet. Instead, we have to wait for the next event, which does not tell us that we are inside the desired element, so we must have made a note of that fact during the previous event.

In many event-based interfaces our problems may not even be over with this, since the data event may be split into several successive events, so we will need to accumulate data before the end of element event at last tells us that we have the complete data. This simple example shows several typical features of event-based applications, the main one being that the application needs to keep track of where in the document it is while it waits for all the desired information to appear in the event stream.

For this reason, event-based applications are best written as objects that can hold internal state while receiving events from the event source (which will usually be a parser). Implementing an application as an object will make it easier to have several instances of the application active at the same time, so that each will have a separate copy of the internal state variables in its object instance.

6.3 | Tools for event-based processing

The tools for writing event-based processing applications can roughly be divided into three groups:

- The native APIs of the XML parsers that provide an event-based API. These APIs generally expose the document information as events and provide some configuration possibilities, but usually provide little in the way of conveniences. The available parsers are listed in this section, and their APIs shown in the next chapter.
- SAX. This is the standard API for event-based XML processing. Like the parser APIs, it provides the document information, some support for configuration, but few utilities or conveniences for application developers. SAX is described in Chapter 8, "SAX: an introduction," on page 234, Chapter 9, "Using SAX," on page 268, and Chapter 10, "Advanced SAX," on page 338.
- Various processing frameworks building on the parsers and/or SAX. These frameworks are event-based, but make the document tree (either in full or in fragments) available to the processing application. Some of these frameworks are covered in 22.2, "Hybrid event/tree-based approaches," on page 851.

6.3.1 *What parsers are there?*

Most XML parsers have an event-based API as their lowest level of access, and quite a few only provide an event-based API and leave possible tree-building for others to implement on top of the parser. This section will provide an introduction to the various XML parsers available for Python programmers and also discuss the APIs of some of them.

Making an XML parser is by no means simple, and in the development of a parser, trade-offs have to be made between desirable features such as code size, speed, flexibility, feature-completeness, amount of information provided, quality of error messages, etc. The result is that there are a lot of different parsers out there, and the optimal choice of parser depends on the requirements of each specific project.

6.3.1.1 Python parsers

For Python programmers there are many different XML parsers available, and these can be divided into three main groups:

- the pure Python parsers,
- the C/C++ parsers,
- the Java parsers.

Of these, the C/C++ parsers are only available in the original Python interpreter implemented in C (often known as *CPython*), whereas the Java ones are only available in Jython. The pure Python parsers are available in both cases.

At the time of writing there are only two pure Python parsers available, xmllib and xmlproc. xmllib was written by Sjoerd Müllender, to be a part of the standard Python library together with the earlier sgmllib and htmllib. It is not a fully conformant parser, since it does not support Unicode, and does read the internal subset, to take one example, and this means that the transformations described in 2.4.2.1, "How the DTD affects the document," on page 69 are not performed. However, xmllib has a very convenient API and comes with the Python interpreter, so it can be very useful for simple scripting tasks. This parser does not validate or read external entities, but it does support namespaces.

The xmlproc parser was written by myself to provide Python with a full XML parser written in pure Python. It is not fully conformant,[1] but it supports Unicode and reads both the internal and external DTD subsets, can validate, and also supports namespaces. It has an API that provides full access to DTD information, and its DTD parser can be used independently of the rest of the parser. The DTD API is covered in 23.3, "DTD programming," on page 908. There are also some more advanced features regarding entities that are covered in 10.3, "Working with entities," on page 380. The xmlproc parser has a very object-oriented API, and many pythoners feel that it is a bit Java-like and not very pythonic.[2]

6.3.1.2 C/C++ parsers

The Python interpreter is written in C and has an internal API that can be used to write extension modules in C that behave in the same way as modules written in pure Python.[3] This makes it possible to write performance-critical code in C for greater speed, and also to make modules written in C available to Python code. This has been exploited to make some of the XML parsers written in C available as Python modules. At the moment four parsers written in C have been integrated:

1. It fails to be completely conformant since it does not check for some illegal characters, and allows elements to begin in one entity and end in another. These problems will probably be fixed as soon as I can find a way to do so that does not impact performance too much.

2. With which I can only agree. More convenient and pythonic APIs to it are available, though.

3. This interface is described in the *Extending and Embedding* and *Python/C API* sections of the documentation that comes with the Python distribution.

- expat,
- sgmlop,
- RXP,
- Xerces-C.

Unlike the pure Python parsers, these parsers must either be installed as platform-dependent binaries or compiled from source code, which requires a C compiler and the Python sources. The benefit is that they are faster than the pure Python parsers by a significant margin. See the benchmarks in 9.6.2, "Benchmarks," on page 334 to get an idea of the speed differences.

The best-known of these parsers is expat written by James Clark. It is much used in C/C++ programs, in Mozilla, in the Opera Web browser, as a Perl module, and in many other projects as well. It is fast, highly conformant, supports namespaces, but does not validate. It was originally adapted as a Python module by Jack Jansen and has since been updated, extended and modified by many others.

The sgmlop parser is a reimplementation of xmllib in C and was written by Fredrik Lundh with the specific purpose of serving as a Python module. So unlike the other two parsers, sgmlop is not a general C module adapted to Python, but natively written as a Python extension module. This is perhaps part of the reason why it is the fastest of the three. (It is also, like xmllib, not completely conformant.)

RXP was written by Richard Tobin as a general C parser, and unlike expat it can validate. It also supports namespaces, and is available as a part of the LTXML toolkit from the University of Edinburgh. Unlike most other parsers, RXP has a pull-interface that returns a stream of token objects rather than a tree-based or event-based interface. Because of this it is not described in this chapter, but left for 22.1.1, "RXP," on page 845.

The Xerces-C parser is maintained as part of the Apache Project, which also developes many other XML modules, including the widely used Xerces-J Java XML parser (see below). Xerces-C is written in C++, supports XML namespaces, Unicode, is highly portable, and is generally considered to be of good quality. It even implements a partial XML Schema validator. A wrapper module for the Xerces-C parser has been written by Jürgen Hermann, who calls the module Pirxx.

6.3.1.3 Java parsers

For those doing development in Jython there are two sets of parsers available: pure Python ones and Java ones. The Python parsers are substantially slower than the Java parsers in this environment, which makes it very tempting to use Java parsers. And in fact this may often be a good idea; they are (almost) as easy to use as the Python parsers, since the Jython interface to Java code is so natural as to be almost transparent.

The only real disadvantage to using Java parsers in Jython applications is that it ties the application to Jython and makes it impossible to run in CPython. However, in many cases this does not matter; if the application also uses Java-specific APIs like JDBC and Swing, it will be difficult to port anyway. It should also be noted that SAX, presented in Chapter 8, "SAX: an introduction," on page 234, solves this problem and enables applications to be parser-independent.

The most important Java parsers are described in depth in 19.2, "Java XML parsers," on page 707.

6.4 | RSS: An example application

This section introduces RSS, an XML application that will be used extensively as an example application throughout the book. We will also develop a toolkit for working with RSS in Chapter 26, "The RSS development kit," on page 994. Note that RSS was described earlier in 1.4, "XML and information systems," on page 33.

RSS (or Rich Site Summary) is a very simple XML application originally introduced by Netscape, for use with their my.netscape.com site. An RSS document defines a news channel and contains some metadata about the channel and a list of news items with links. This is the exact minimum of what is required to make a very simple news syndication service, which is what RSS is intended to enable.

RSS became popular very quickly and today there are thousands of RSS channels on the net. There are two main reasons for this. First, RSS is very simple, so users understand it quickly, and implementors have an easy job.[1] Second, RSS appeals to Web users as it makes it easier to keep track of news, and it appeals to Web publishers as it provides an easy way to attract more traffic.

Most people who have been on the net for a while have a set of sites that they come back to at intervals to see what has been updated. Some of these sites only provide links to other material (often known as weblogs), whereas others provide complete news articles, and still others are simply informational Web sites. In any case, the problem for readers and publishers alike is that these sites are updated at differing intervals, requiring the user to remember when to come back to a particular site.

Most of these sites provide a page where new news items and updates appear. The problem is that this page is published as HTML in a form that contains just the information needed to present the news visually, not in an abstract notation. This makes it very difficult to develop automated services that provide access to this information, since for every site added to the service, one needs to write software to interpret the HTML markup and extract the information. This can be both difficult and time-consuming, not to mention likely to break the moment a site changes its layout.

RSS solves this problem because it is abstract and can be processed automatically by software that actually understands the structure of the provided content. Thus, one can make dedicated clients that lets users aggregate news from a set of channels, remembers what the user has read already, and perhaps also filters out news that is known to not be interesting. In fact, such clients have been developed already, both as Web sites (my.netscape.com, www.geekboys.org, and my.user-

---

1.   This is another example of the worse-is-better paradox at work.

land.com) and as special-purpose clients that run on your local machine. Figure 6–1 shows a screenshot from the client developed with the RSS kit demonstrated in this book.

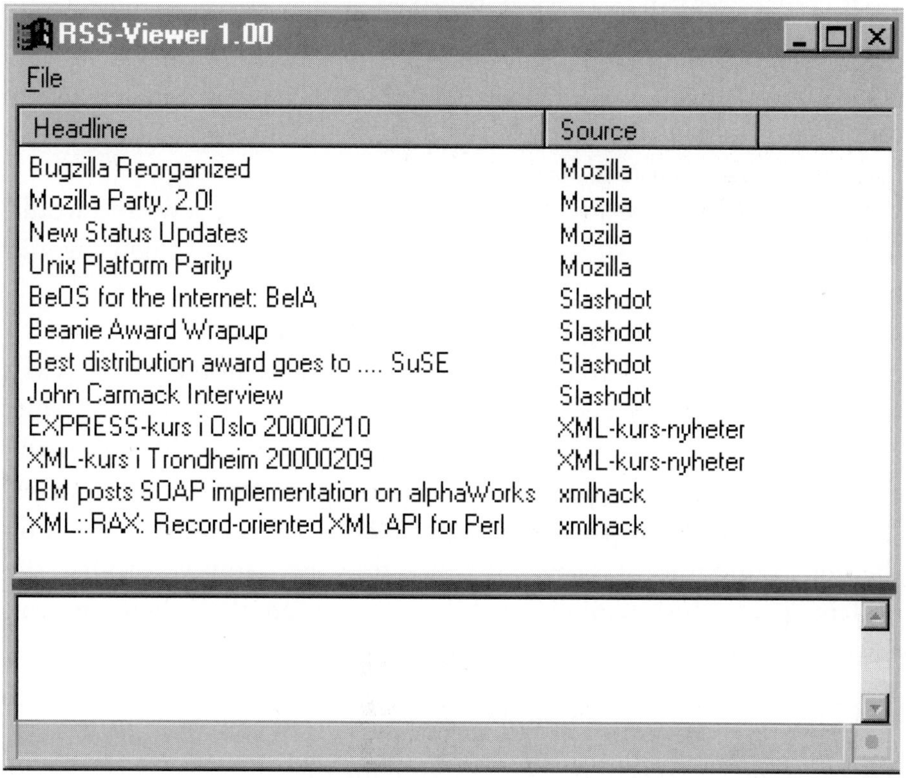

Figure 6–1   The news listing window of the RSS viewer

6.4.1   *Typical RSS usage*

Personally, I use RSS with the RSS viewer shown in Figure 6–1 to keep track of news. I get news items from sites like Slashdot, mozilla.org MozillaZine, xml.com, xmlhack.com, python.org, Tasty Bits from the Technology Front (tbtf), as well as interesting snippets from Robot Wisdom.

Every now and then, in a pause in my work, I tell the client to get new news items and it scans through the RSS documents of these sites, picking out the new items and adding them to the window shown above. I then remove the items that do not look interesting and start reading the ones that remain. Reading an item is done simply by selecting an item and telling the client to load it in my browser. The client then contacts my browser (using different methods depending on platform), loads the URL of the item in the browser, and removes it from the list of unread items.

I've found this to be a very easy way to keep track of news and would only wish that more sites did the same, so that reading news would become easier for me.

In addition to reading RSS news, I also publish an RSS channel. I maintain an index of free XML tools,[1] which is stored as an XML document and published by a set of Python scripts. These scripts automatically keep track of new tools and new versions of tools being added to the index and produce an HTML page with recent updates. Using the RSS kit, these scripts also produce an RSS channel containing the exact same information as the updates page. However, unlike the updates page, this channel can be shown by an RSS client or read through a personalized page on one of the RSS Web sites.

6.4.2   *The structure of RSS documents*

There are currently three versions of RSS: 0.9, 0.91, and 1.0. The two first versions were defined by Netscape, while 1.0 is being defined by a group of individuals. 0.9 is a subset of 0.91, with only the document element type different, while 1.0 makes quite a few changes, which are described in the following section. The difference between 0.9 and 0.91 is mainly that 0.91 adds a lot of metadata about the channel and also allows for descriptions of the channel and the individual news items. This section shows a subset of RSS 0.91. Version 1.0 differs from the

---

1.   Found at http://www.garshol.priv.no/download/xmltools/.

two previous versions in that it uses namespaces and is firmly based on RDF.[1]

Example 6–1 is a complete RSS document that is automatically produced for my Free XML tools site.

Example 6–1. An RSS document

```
<?xml version="1.0"?>
<!DOCTYPE rss PUBLIC "-//Netscape Communications//DTD RSS 0.91//EN"
            "http://my.netscape.com/publish/formats/rss-0.91.dtd">
<rss version="0.91">
  <channel>
    <title>Free XML tools</title>
    <link>http://www.garshol.priv.no/download/xmltools/</link>
    <description>An index of free XML tools.</description>
    <language>en</language>
    <managingEditor>larsga@garshol.priv.no</managingEditor>

    <item>
      <title>New product: tDOM.</title>
      <link>http://www.garshol.priv.no/.../tDOM.html</link>
    </item>

    <item>
      <title>New version of LotusXSL: 31.Aug.99.</title>
      <link>http://www.garshol.priv.no/.../LotusXSL.html</link>
      <description>Updated to 13.Aug.99 WDs, separate XPath and
      query packages, new extension architecture, thread safety,
      and much more.
      </description>
    </item>

    <item>
      <title>New product: 4XPath.</title>
      <link>http://www.garshol.priv.no/.../4XPath.html</link>
    </item>

    <!-- [...more items...] -->
  </channel>
</rss>
```

---

1.   RDF is a metadata framework intended by the W3C to be the basis of the new Semantic Web. It has an XML-based syntax, but a different data model.

As can be seen, RSS documents have a very simple structure. There are a few more element types than what is shown here and a few rules for where they can appear. The rest of this section gives an informal definition of RSS 0.91. An up to date definition can be found at `http://my.netscape.com/publish/formats/rss-spec-0.91.html`. Table 6–1 defines the meaning of all the RSS element types.

Table 6–1   The RSS 0.91 element types

Parent	Element type	Meaning
channel	title	Name of the channel, the one which people use to refer to it.
channel	link	The URL of the channel home page.
channel	description	A brief description of the channel.
channel	language	The language of the channel content. Allowed values are RFC 1766 language tags.
channel	image	A channel logo (see below for the child elements).
channel	copyright	The copyright statement of the channel.
channel	managingEditor	The email address of the person responsible for the channel contents.
channel	webMaster	The email address of the channel webmaster.
channel	rating	The PICS rating of the channel (see below).
channel	pubDate	The publication date for the channel contents.
channel	lastBuildDate	The date when the channel was last updated.
channel	docs	A URL that refers to the definition of the used format.

Table 6–1   The RSS 0.91 element types

Parent	Element type	Meaning
channel	textinput	The channel feedback form (see child elements below).
channel	skipDays	Days during which aggregators should not read the channel. Content is a sequence of day elements, containing English names of weekdays.
channel	skipHours	Hours (in GMT) during which aggregators should not read the channel. Content is a sequence of hour elements, containing numbers from 1 to 24.
channel	item	A news item in the channel (see below for child elements).
image	url	The URL of the channel logo image. Allowed notations are GIF, JPEG, and PNG.
image	title	A text to be used as a replacement for the image when the image cannot be shown.
image	link	The URL of the channel home page.
image	width	The width of the image in pixels.
image	height	The height of the image in pixels.
item	title	The title or headline of the news item.
item	link	The URL of the news item.
item	description	A synopsis of the news item.
textinput	title	The label of the submit button.
textinput	description	Explains the purpose of the textinput.
textinput	link	The URL the textinput contents are to be submitted to.
textinput	name	The name of the URL parameter the textinput contents are to use when submitted.

The recommended syntax for email addresses in RSS documents is: larsga@garshol.priv.no (Lars Marius Garshol). PICS is a system for rating Web content that can be used to filter out unwanted content such as violence, pornographic material, etc. See http://www.w3.org/PICS/ for more information.

In RSS documents, dates follow the RFC 822 date syntax: Sun, 26 Nov 2000 13:00:22 +0200.

Example 6–2 shows an informal DTD that defines the RSS structure. Element types that are not defined have #PCDATA content. Although the DTD requires elements to have a particular order, RSS does not. The DTD does this because it would be very difficult to describe the structure otherwise.

Example 6–2. A simplified RSS 0.91 DTD

```
<!ELEMENT rss (channel)>

<!ELEMENT channel (title, link, description, language, image?,
                   copyright?, managingEditor?, webMaster?, rating?,
                   pubDate?, lastBuildDate?, docs?, textinput?,
                   skipDays?, skipHours?, item+)>

<!ELEMENT image (title, url, link, width?, height?)>

<!ELEMENT item (title, link, description?)>

<!ELEMENT textinput (title, description, name, link)>

<!ELEMENT skipDays (day+)>
<!ELEMENT skipHours (hour+)>
```

6.4.3   *RSS 1.0*

As mentioned above, RSS 1.0 differs from the two previous versions in that it is not defined by Netscape, but by a group of volunteers, and that it uses namespaces and is firmly based on RDF. It also extends RSS with a concept of *modules*, which we will return to below. The

RSS 1.0 specification can be found at `http://purl.org/rss/ 1.0/spec`.

The parts of RSS that are found in version 0.9 are the same in RSS 1.0, although there are some additions. The first is that the document element is required to carry namespace declarations that declare the default namespace to be `http://purl.org/rss/1.0`, and the `rdf` prefix to map to `http://www.w3.org/1999/02/22-rdf-syntax-ns#`. The `image`, `item`, and `textinput` elements are now moved out of a `channel` element and made children of the document element.

The RSS components from RSS 0.91 are moved into a separate module, which uses the namespace `http://purl.org/rss/1.0/ modules/rss091/` and the fixed prefix `rss091`.[1] The RSS 1.0 specification allows definition of separate modules providing extra functionality to be added to RSS through the use of namespaces. This allows RSS to be extended for specific uses without causing the core specification to grow uncontrollably. RSS 1.0 has at the moment three modules: RSS 0.91 backwards compatibility, Dublin Core (metadata about resources), and Syndication. The RSS 1.0 Modules specification at `http://purl.org/rss/1.0/modules/` describes how new modules can be added. This book does not use any of the modules except for RSS 0.91, in order to keep examples to a manageable size.

The last addition of importance is that some RDF machinery has been added to the application, in the form of an `rdf:about` attribute on every container element. The container elements also have `inchannel` child elements that refer to the same URL as the `rdf:about` attribute on the `channel`. This is needed for RSS to be an RDF application.

Example 6–3 shows the RSS document in Example 6–1 converted to RSS 1.0.

---

1.   Fixed prefixes are generally not considered good practice. This may have been done to allow software that is not namespace-aware to support RSS 0.91.

Example 6–3. An RSS 1.0 document

```
<rdf:RDF xmlns="http://purl.org/rss/1.0/"
         xmlns:rss091="http://purl.org/rss/1.0/modules/rss091/"
         xmlns:rdf="http://www.w3.org/1999/02/22-rdf-syntax-ns#">

<channel rdf:about="rss091.rss">
  <title>Free XML tools</title>
  <link>http://www.garshol.priv.no/download/xmltools/</link>
  <description>An index of free XML tools.</description>
  <rss091:language>en</rss091:language>
  <rss091:managingEditor>larsga@garshol.priv.no
    </rss091:managingEditor>
</channel>

<item rdf:about="http://www.garshol.priv.no/.../tDOM.html">
  <inchannel rdf:resource="rss091.rss"/>
  <title>New product: tDOM.</title>
  <link>http://www.garshol.priv.no/.../tDOM.html</link>
</item>

<item rdf:about="http://www.garshol.priv.no/.../LotusXSL.html">
  <inchannel rdf:resource="rss091.rss"/>
  <title>New version of LotusXSL: 31.Aug.99.</title>
  <link>http://www.garshol.priv.no/.../LotusXSL.html</link>
  <description>Updated to 13.Aug.99 WDs, separate XPath and query
  packages, new extension architecture, thread safety, and much
  more.</description>
</item>

<item rdf:about="http://www.garshol.priv.no/.../4XPath.html">
  <inchannel rdf:resource="rss091.rss"/>
  <title>New product: 4XPath.</title>
  <link>http://www.garshol.priv.no/.../4XPath.html</link>
</item>
</rdf:RDF>
```

Using XML parsers

- xmlproc
- Pyexpat
- xmllib
- Working in Jython
- Choosing a parser

Chapter

7

T his chapter presents the XML parsers available to Python programmers and their native APIs, which are all event-based. It should be read with the understanding that most applications will not use these parsers directly, but rather use the parser-independent SAX API described in the next chapter. The parsers are described anyway because using them directly is sometimes useful, and in any case it is useful to have some knowledge of the parsers and their interfaces.

7.1 | xmlproc

This parser has a very straightforward object-oriented interface, and has been accused of being too Java-like and not sufficiently Pythonic. In the sense that it does not make full use of Python's features to provide all the conveniences that it could have provided, that is certainly true. As you'll find, however, the best way to use xmlproc is not through its native interface.

To make up for this lack of convenience, xmlproc provides many features that other parsers do not, and tries to be easy to integrate into other applications and frameworks. It is made up of several different modules in the `xml.parsers.xmlproc` package, each providing a separate part of the total functionality.

The heart of the xmlproc APIs is the `xml.parsers.xmlproc.xmlproc` module, containing the `XMLProcessor` class which is the actual XML parser. The general style of the xmlproc APIs is such that the application must be implemented as a set of event-handling objects which are registered with the parser and receive events from it. In addition to the XML parser itself, there are modules for namespace processing, validation, DTD parsing, DTD representation, and some additional utilities. These modules can all be used both with the parser and independently.

The namespace support is discussed in 7.1.5, "Namespace support in xmlproc," on page 188, while the DTD support is discussed in 23.3, "DTD programming," on page 908.

7.1.1   *Interface outline*

The basic structure of an xmlproc application is as shown in Figure 7–1, where the gray `XMLProcessor` object is the parser itself, while the other objects are implemented by the application developer.

The various objects here have their specific roles:

XMLProcessor
> This is the xmlproc parser. If you want validation you can use the `xmlval.XMLValidator` class instead.

Application
> This object receives all document events from parsing, such as notification of start- and end-tags, character data, etc.

ErrorHandler
> All error messages are passed to this object.

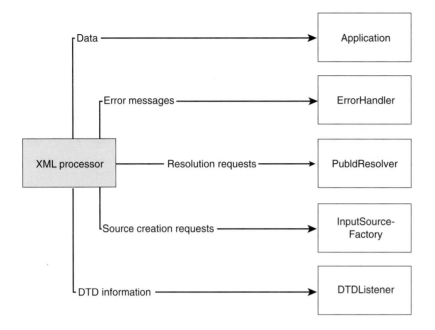

Figure 7–1   Outline of the xmlproc API

PubIdResolver

    This object is given the task of mapping public identifiers to system identifiers (and also remapping system identifiers), by whatever means it pleases. (Public and system identifiers were introduced in 2.3.1, "Storing XML documents," on page 54.)

InputSourceFactory

    The InputSourceFactory creates a file-like object from a system identifier, which can be used to implement support for new kinds of system identifiers.

DTDListener

    This object receives event callbacks from parsing a DTD, such as "element type declared", "attribute declared", etc. Since this handler deals with DTDs rather than document contents, it is not covered in this chapter, but left for 23.3, "DTD programming," on page 908.

So, to create an application, one implements the `Application` interface, instantiates a parser, gives it the `Application` object, and starts parsing. The code fragment in Example 7–1 shows an outline of this process.

Example 7–1. A basic xmlproc application

```
from xml.parsers.xmlproc import xmlproc

class MyApplication(xmlproc.Application):
    pass # Add some useful stuff here

p = xmlproc.XMLProcessor() # Use xmlval.XMLValidator
p.set_application(MyApplication())
p.parse_resource("foo.xml")
```

Note that strictly speaking `Application` is a class, since the Python language does not have a construct called interfaces. The word *interface* is used throughout this book in a way similar to how it is used in Java, that is, to signify a set of methods an object must implement to be able to play a specific role in an ensemble of objects. The reason for this is that Python's dynamic typing makes it possible for any class to implement the `Application` interface, without actually inheriting from the `Application` class, which in this sense becomes part documentation and part convenience, rather than a formal necessity to satisfy the type system of the language as it would be in Java.

To expand this example into an application that does something useful you must write the contents of the `MyApplication` class. How to do this is explained in 7.1.2.2, "The `Application` interface," on page 170.

7.1.2   *Interface reference*

This section presents a detailed reference of all the interfaces of xmlproc, interspersed with explanatory text and examples.

7.1.2.1 The parser

The main methods of the XMLProcessor and XMLValidator classes
are listed below. These are the methods needed to specify event receivers
for the parser and to control parsing.

set_application(app)
  Tells the parser which Application object to send document
  events to.

set_error_handler(err)
  Gives the parser a reference to the object that decides what to do
  with error messages.

set_inputsource_factory(isf)
  Tells the parser which InputSourceFactory object to use for
  creating file-like objects from system identifiers.

set_pubid_resolver(pubres)
  Tells the parser which PubIdResolver object to use for finding
  the system identifier of an entity from its public and system identifiers.

set_dtd_listener(dtd_listener)
  Tells the parser where to send DTD parse events. The
  dtd_listener object must implement the DTDConsumer interface,
  which is described in 23.3, "DTD programming," on page 908.

parse_resource(sysid, bufsize = 16384)
  Tells the parser to parse the resource with the given system identifier
  (sysid), which can be either a local file name or a URL. The
  bufsize parameter is optional, and holds the buffer size. If it is
  omitted the buffer size is set to 16 Kb.

deref()
  CPython 1.5 did not have full garbage collection, only reference
  counting, which meant that data structures with circular references

would never be released. (See A.5.6, "Memory management," on page 1094 for more details.) During parsing the parser creates circular data structures, so to release the memory allocated by the parser in Python versions that do not have full garbage collection it is necessary to call this method. Calling this method severes the circular references so that the objects are released. Once this method has been called the parser will no longer work.

set_error_language(lang)

Tells the parser which language to report errors in. lang must be an ISO 639 language identifier. If the language is not supported, a KeyError will be thrown. Currently supported are 'en' (English), 'no' (Norwegian), 'sv' (Swedish), and 'fr' (French).[1] Translations of the error messages in the xml.parsers. xmlproc.errors module to other languages will be received with gratitude.

The specification of ISO 639 can be found at http:// lcweb.loc.gov/standards/iso639-2/.

set_data_after_wf_error(stop)

According to the XML Recommendation, XML parsers are not allowed to pass document data to an application after a well-formedness error has occurred. (They are, however, allowed to continue parsing and passing error messages.) This is xmlproc's default behavior.

This method can be used to make xmlproc continue reporting data even in the face of well-formedness errors, since there may be applications (such as editors) which need this functionality.

Setting the argument to false makes xmlproc continue to report data events after errors.

---

1.   The Swedish translation was done by Marcus Brisenfeldt, the French by Alexandre Fayolle.

`set_read_external_subset(read)`

    Using this method, the non-validating parser can be told to read the external DTD subset and all external parameter entities. It will not do this by default. Note that the validating parser will ignore calls to this method.

    Setting the argument to `true` makes xmlproc read the external subset.

  In addition to these methods, xmlproc provides a number of methods that can be called during parsing to get document information. These are:

`get_current_sysid()`

    Returns the system identifier of the current entity. This means that if the parser is currently parsing an external entity the system identifier of this entity will be returned. If the parser is parsing the document entity the system identifier of this entity will be returned.

`get_offset()`

    Returns the current offset (number of characters) from the start of the current entity. All location information points to the beginning of the construct that triggered the current event.

`get_line()`

    Returns the current line number.

`get_column()`

    Returns the current column position on the current line.

`get_dtd()`

    Returns an object representing the DTD of the current document, as described in 23.3, "DTD programming," on page 908.

`get_elem_stack()`

    Returns the list that holds the parser's internal stack of the names of open elements. Note that this is the list used by the parser and not a copy, which means the application must *not* modify this list. It also means that the list is live and changes whenever the parser modifies it. Therefore all calls to this method return references to the same list object, making it only necessary to call the method once.

get_raw_construct()

This method returns the original source string that triggered the current callback event. A typical example may be `'<p id="example">'` during a call that represents this start-tag.

get_current_ent_stack()

This method returns a snapshot of the current stack of open entities, in the form of a list of (*entity name*, *entity sysid*) tuples. The list returned by this method is not live, unlike that returned by `get_elem_stack`.

In addition to reading the document from a URL or a file, xmlproc can do what is known as *incremental parsing*. This means that instead of giving the parser a source to read from, one feeds blocks of text into the parser, getting events out from the other end. In a sense the parser can be thought of as a grinder into which material is fed to generate output. A typical conversation with the incremental parsing API of xmlproc may look as shown in Example 7–2.

Example 7–2. Using xmlproc incrementally

```
p = XMLProcessor()
# configure parser
block = myfile.read(16384)
while block != "":
    p.feed(block)
    block = myfile.read(16384)
p.close()
```

This example starts by creating an instance of the xmlproc parser. Then it reads text in 16 Kb blocks from some file-like[1] object and feeds these blocks into the parser, which causes callbacks to be fired from the parser into the application. The application then executes whatever it has been implemented to do.

The methods of the incremental parsing interface are in the XMLProcessor class, and are listed below. Figure 7–2 is a state diagram showing how these methods can be used.

reset()

> Resets the parser after a call to close, making it ready to parse another document.

feed(text)

> Gives the parser a chunk of text, which it will parse. Incomplete syntactical constructs will be left in an internal buffer for subsequent calls.

close()

> Makes the parser process all remaining text in the internal buffer. After this call the parser will not be in a state to parse more documents until reset has been called.

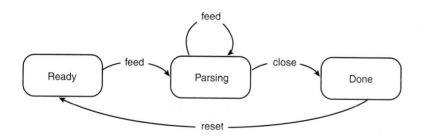

Figure 7–2   State diagram for xmlproc

---

1. A file-like object is the Python equivalent of a stream in Java or C++. It implements the same methods as a file object, but can provide text from a different source, such as a string or a database blob.

Figure 7–2 is a conceptual state diagram for xmlproc, showing how to use the incremental interface. Initially, when the parser is created, it is in the "Ready" state. In this state it is ready to start parsing a new document, but hasn't started yet. When `feed` is called for the first time, the parser jumps into the "Parsing" state, where it remains for all following `feed` calls, until finally `close` is called. When `close` is called, xmlproc finishes the document and jumps into the "Done" state, where it is finished with parsing, but not ready for another document yet. After `reset` has been called, it is back in the "Ready" state, and can parse another document.

7.1.2.2   The `Application` interface

The `Application` object is the main object that xmlproc applications must implement, since it is the one that receives all document information. The interface is based on callbacks to an external object. A default (empty) implementation of `Application` is provided in the `xml.parsers.xmlproc.xmlapp` module.

`set_locator(parser)`
> This method is called by the parser to give the application an object it can query to get the current position in the document. The `parser` parameter refers to the parser.

`doc_start()`
> Called when parsing begins, before any of the other data callbacks.

`doc_end()`
> Called at the end of the document, after all other data callbacks.

`handle_start_tag(name, attrs)`
> Called for each start-tag in the document. `name` is the name of the element type, and `attrs` is a dictionary of the element attributes.

`handle_end_tag(name)`
> Called by the parser for each end-tag in the document, `name` being the name of the element type.

`handle_data(data, start, end)`
> Called by the parser for all character data in the document, regardless of what form it takes (CDATA marked section, normal data, entity reference, etc.). The expression `data[start:end]` will give the actual contents. The parser does not do this itself for speed reasons, since in many cases the data may not be needed, and this approach will thus avoid unecessary string allocation and copying.
>
> Note that if you forget to slice the string, you will pass to your application a string that is most likely a 16 Kb block of XML markup with the real character data buried somewhere inside it.

`handle_ignorable_data(data, start, end)`
> Called by the parser for all character data in elements which do not have #PCDATA content. At the time of writing this method is only called during validating parsing, but in future releases the non-validating parser will also do so when it has sufficient DTD information (that is, when `set_read_external_subset(1)` has been called, or when the element type declarations have appeared in the internal subset).

`handle_pi(target, data)`
> Called for all processing instructions in the document. The `target` argument is the name of the PI target, and `data` is the PI data.

`handle_comment(data)`
> Called when the parser encounters a comment. The `data` argument is the contents of the comment.

`handle_doctype(root, pubid, sysid)`
> Called when the parser encounters the DOCTYPE declaration. The `root` argument is the name of the document element type, `pubid`

is the public identifier (or None if there was none) and sysid is the system identifier.

set_entity_info(xmlver, enc, sddecl)

Called when the parser encounters the XML declaration, or any text declarations in external entities. The xmlver argument is the XML version, enc is the contents of the encoding pseudo-attribute, and sddecl is the contents of the standalone declaration. Unspecified items will be set to None.

As the careful reader may have noticed the Application interface lumps in three lexical callbacks with the purely logical events (the last three in the list above). The lexical callbacks are included because they are often useful (especially the handle_doctype method) and they were all easy to implement with little impact on the logical interface.

The xmlproc parser comes with three ready-to-use implementations of the Application interface in the xml.parsers.xmlproc.utils module. These are:

ESISDocHandler

Produces ESIS output from the document events. ESIS, short for *Element Structure Information Set*, is a conceptual specification of the data model of SGML documents and can be thought of as an early version of the SGML equivalent of XML's Information Set. It is defined in *ISO 13673*, the SGML conformance testing standard, but can also be found in *The SGML Handbook* by Charles Goldfarb and Sean McGrath's *Parseme.1st* in this series.

This document handler produces the ESIS notation that was defined by James Clark for his NSGMLS SGML parser. For an online definition of the notation, see http://www.jclark.com/ sp/sgmlsout.htm. Or, you can simply try it out; the notation is really very simple.

Canonizer

Produces canonical XML output from the document events. Canonical XML is a subset of the ordinary XML syntax defined in such a way that logically equivalent documents will always have the exact same canonical XML document. This makes canonical XML very useful for comparing the outputs of various parsers to see whether they agree or not.

Note that this class does not produce canonical XML according to the W3C's upcoming Canonical XML specification, but instead uses James Clark's original canonical XML specification. Most likely an updated canonizer will be written at some stage.

`DocGenerator`
Produces an XML document from the document events, which, unlike the output from the `Canonizer`, is intended to be readable. The whitespace of the input document is not modified.

All of these classes have a constructor that accepts a file-like object as an optional parameter. The parameter defaults to standard output, i.e. `sys.stdout`.

7.1.2.3 A small example

Before we move on to explain the rest of the xmlproc interfaces, in this section we develop a small xmlproc application to make what has been said so far a little clearer. The application presented in this section simply reacts to parser events by printing out messages and does not really do anything useful. The source code is given in Example 7–3.

7.1.2.4 The `ErrorHandler` interface

Since a parser can be used in a variety of different contexts, it is impossible for the parser writer to know how to handle any errors that may arise. In modern programming languages, the common way to handle this is to raise an exception and let whoever called you take care of the problem in a way appropriate for the context you are being used in. This is an excellent approach that is much used by xmlproc in contexts other than parsing.

Example 7–3. A small xmlproc application

```python
from xml.parsers.xmlproc import xmlproc

class MyApplication(xmlproc.Application):

    def handle_start_tag(self, name, attrs):
        print "Element %s just started" % repr(name)

    def handle_end_tag(self, name):
        print "Element %s just ended" % repr(name)


p = xmlproc.XMLProcessor()
p.set_application(MyApplication())

p.feed("<doc>")
p.feed("This is some sample text, which doesn't get printed, since")
p.feed("there is no character data handler.")
p.feed("<p>Hmm. Previous text should also have been in a para.</p>")
p.feed("</doc>")
p.close()
```

The disadvantage to this approach is that in most languages (Common Lisp being an exception[1]) raising an exception means jumping out of the current execution context with no easy way to return to it. This means that a parser that raises an exception on an error will be unable to return to the point where the error occurred and continue parsing.

In general, xmlproc always attempts to recover from syntactical errors in ways that leave the parser able to continue parsing without causing new spurious errors. To this end there are quite a few places in the parsing code where xmlproc will first report an error and then try various tricks to get to a state where it expects to be able to continue parsing with no more errors. It does not succeed in all cases, but hopefully its handling of such cases will improve with time.

---

1.   Pun sort of inevitable rather than intended or unintended as such.

For this reason xmlproc uses a separate error handler object to which parsing errors are reported as method calls and where applications can decide what to do with them. Common actions are logging errors to a file, writing them to the console, showing them in dialog boxes, and raising exceptions (even though, or perhaps even because, this stops parsing). If no error handler is supplied, error messages are simply suppressed. A default implementation which does nothing is provided in the `xml.parsers.xmlproc.xmlapp` module. More information on how to write error handlers can be found in 9.5.2, "How to write an error handler," on page 319.

The methods of the `ErrorHandler` interface are:

`set_locator(locator)`

> This method is called by the parser to give the error handler a reference to the parser, from which it can read location information relevant to the received error messages.

`warning(message)`

> This method is called to give the error handler a texual message (in the `message` parameter) indicating a warning. This will be something that is not distinctly classified by the XML Recommendation as an error, but which the parser still finds worthy of attention.

`error(message)`

> Reports an error that is not classified by the XML Recommendation as a fatal error, such as a validity error.

`fatal(message)`

> Reports a fatal error to the application. Unless the parser has been told to behave otherwise (with the `set_data_after_wf_error` method) it will now stop passing data events to the application, in accordance with the XML Recommendation.

The xmlproc parser comes with three ready-to-use implementations of this interface in the `xml.parsers.xmlproc.utils` module. These are listed below, together with the signatures of their constructors.

`ErrorPrinter(level = 0, out = sys.stderr)`

> Prints out all error messages it receives to the file-like object `out`, filtering out some, depending on the value of `level`. Namely, a `level` of `0` or lower tells the error handler to print all messages, `1` tells it to not print warnings, `2` or means only print fatal errors.

`ErrorRaiser(level = 0)`

> Raises `XMLParseExceptions` on all errors that are above the `level` threshold. The threshold is interpreted in the same way as for `ErrorPrinter`.

`ErrorCounter()`

> Counts warnings, errors and fatal errors in the `warnings`, `errors`, and `fatals` attributes.

In general it is a very bad idea to develop applications (even one-off applications) that ignore error messages, since sooner or later you are bound to point the parser at a non-existent document or a document with errors in it, and be confused when the application does not work as expected but with no visible complaints. For this reason I strongly recommend that you always use an error handler in your programs. With `ErrorPrinter`later or `ErrorRaiser` only a single line is needed.

7.1.2.5 The `PubIdResolver` interface

The `PubIdResolver` is used by the parser to find the system identifier of an entity from its public and system identifiers. The default implementation provided in `xml.parsers.xmlproc.xmlapp` always returns the system identifier it is given. Applications can use this interface to control the resolution of public identifiers or to remap system identifiers. Both `PubIdResolver` and `InputSourceFactory` can be used to remap system identifiers, but this is the handler that should be used to do this. The reason is that the parser will think that the system identifier returned by the `PubIdResolver` is the one from which the entity is actually read, and the one against which relative system identifiers will

be resolved. It is also the system identifier that will be reported by the
`get_current_sysid` method.

PubIdResolver has three methods, one for each kind of entities
that might need public identifier resolution. The return value for all
three methods is the resolved system identifier of the entity. There are
three methods so that resolver implementations can tell the different
kinds of entities apart. This was motivated by the way the SGML Open
Catalogs work, but was considered to be generally useful and so
adopted for the API.

`resolve_entity_pubid(pubid, sysid)`
> This method resolves the public identifier of a general entity, and
> it is passed the public identifier (`pubid`) and system identifier
> (`sysid`) of the entity as found in the DTD. The public identifier
> may be None, but the system identifier can never be.

`resolve_doctype_pubid(pubid, sysid)`
> This is exactly like `resolve_entity_pubid`, except that it is called
> for the entity referenced by a DOCTYPE declaration, if there was one
> and if it referenced an external entity.

`resolve_pe_pubid(pubid, sysid)`
> Exactly like the previous two, but this time for parameter entities.

In the `xml.parsers.xmlproc.utils` module there is a reusable
implementation of this interface called `DictResolver`, which has a
constructor that accepts a dictionary mapping public identifiers to
system identifiers.

7.1.2.6 The InputSourceFactory interface

The `InputSourceFactory` is used by the parser to create file-like
objects from system identifiers. Its main purpose is to allow applications
to extend the parser with support for new kinds of system identifiers,
such as URNs, URLs that point to unusual resources such as database
blobs, documents in document management systems, etc.

The `InputSourceFactory` only has a single method:

`create_input_source(sysid)`

This method is passed a system identifier, as returned by the `PubIdResolver` or passed in from an application, and must return a file-like object opened for reading. The default implementation calls the built-in function `open` for files and uses `urllib` to access other system identifiers.

The files that are returned may be both byte and character streams. Byte streams are detected and converted to character streams. The only method that must be implemented by the file-like objects is `read`.

`InputSourceFactory` only has the default implementation, since I have been unable to think of any other implementations that would be generally useful. Martijn Faassen has written an `InputSource-Factory` for his Zope application which uses xmlproc to validate XML documents inside Zope. This `InputSourceFactory` understands references to Zope documents and can retrieve them using the internal Zope mechanisms.

Anyone wanting to cache commonly used remotely stored entities could do this by writing a caching `InputSourceFactory`. In theory, this could also be done by writing a `PubIdResolver`, but since that only returns a system identifier, it would have to return wrong identifiers in order to refer to locally cached versions, which could cause problems in several ways.

7.1.3 *An example application*

In this section we write a more complete xmlproc application (Examples 7–4 to 7–13). Our first real application will take an RSS document and translate it to HTML that is ready to be posted on the Web. We also implement an error handler that writes error messages to the standard error and inserts them in the generated HTML document, inside a PRE element. This may in some cases be useful, since it will make the generated document contain the error messages and clearly show that something went wrong (and even what).

In Example 7–4, we import xmlproc, and then declare two HTML templates that are used for HTML generation. These can be edited to modify the output of the script.

Example 7–4. An xmlproc application converting RSS to HTML (1 of 10)

```
"""
This application uses xmlproc to convert RSS documents to HTML.

$Id: xmlproc_rss2html.py,v 1.5 2001/08/19 19:27:41 larsga Exp $
"""

import sys
from xml.parsers.xmlproc import xmlproc, xmlapp

# --- Templates

top = \
"""
<!DOCTYPE HTML PUBLIC "-//W3C//DTD HTML 4.0 Transitional//EN">
<HTML>
<HEAD>
  <TITLE>%s</TITLE>
</HEAD>

<BODY>

<H1><A HREF="%s">%s</A></H1>
"""

bottom = \
"""
</UL>
<HR>

<ADDRESS>
Converted to HTML by xmlproc_rss2html.py.
</ADDRESS>

</BODY>
</HTML>
"""
```

The constructor in Example 7–5 creates a number of attributes that are used to keep track of information we need in the application. The _data attribute is used to accumulate character data, while _first_item is used to tell us whether the current item element is the first or not. (You'll see why this is interesting later.) The _title, _link, and _descr attributes are used to hold the values of the corresponding elements.

Example 7–5. An xmlproc application converting RSS to HTML (2 of 10)

```
# --- The converter

class RSS2HTML(xmlapp.Application):

    def __init__(self, out = None):
        xmlapp.Application.__init__(self)
        self._out = out or sys.stdout

        # tracking state
        self._data = ""
        self._first_item = 1

        self._title = None
        self._link = None
        self._descr = None
```

The _out attribute holds a file-like object to which the output is written. It is initialized from the optional out parameter to the constructor, and defaults to sys.stdout. Note how we use None in the method declaration, since the default values in the declaration are initialized when the module is loaded. This means that if anyone later changes sys.stdout and we refer to it in the method declaration, we will get the old value and things will not work as intended. Hence the use of None and the strange-looking out or sys.stdout.

The use of the or operator shown here provides a compact and very readable alternative to the use of if statements in some cases. In Python, the or operator will return the first of its operands which evaluates as true. The result is that in this case _out will be set to out if out is true, otherwise it will be set to sys.stdout. You'll see this little trick used throughout the book as it is so compact and readable.

Example 7–6. An xmlproc application converting RSS to HTML (3 of 10)

```
def handle_data(self, data, start, end):
    self._data = self._data + data[start : end]
```

The method in Example 7–6 receives character data events from the parser and accumulates the data passed to it in the _data attribute. Note that we accumulate rather than simply set _data to be data[start:end] because single runs of character data may be reported in more than one call to this method. Why this is so is explained in 8.3.2, "The ContentHandler interface," on page 248.

Example 7–7. An xmlproc application converting RSS to HTML (4 of 10)

```
def handle_start_tag(self, name, attrs):
    self._data = ""

    if name == "item":
        self._descr = "" # reset for this item
        if self._first_item:
            self._out.write(top % (self._title, self._link,
                            self._title))

            if self._descr:
                self._out.write("<p>%s</p>" % self._descr)
            self._out.write("\n<UL>\n")

        self._first_item = 0
```

At the beginning of each element we reset the _data so that it will always only contain data from the current element (Example 7–7). For each item, we also reset the description attribute, since items are not required to have a description and if we don't do this, items with no description will get the previous item's description. Also, if we are at the first item we write out the top of the page with the correct data.

This has to be done here, because this is the only place where we have all the information about the channel and know that we have all of it.

When we hit the end-tag of a title, link, or description element we simply copy its contents from the _data parameter to the correct attribute (Example 7–8). Then, when we hit the end of the item element, we write the item out with the correct info.

Example 7–8. An xmlproc application converting RSS to HTML (5 of 10)

```
def handle_end_tag(self, name):
    if name == "title":
        self._title = self._data

    elif name == "link":
        self._link = self._data

    elif name == "description":
        self._descr = self._data

    elif name == "item":
        self._out.write('  <li><a href="%s">%s</a> %s\n' %
                            (self._link, self._title, self._descr))
```

When we hit the end of the entire document we print out the bottom template and consider ourselves done with the translation (Example 7–9).

Example 7–9. An xmlproc application converting RSS to HTML (6 of 10)

```
def doc_end(self):
    self._out.write(bottom)
```

The error handler in Example 7–10 takes two file-like objects: one that the document is written to, and one that error messages are written to. All errors and warnings are written out using the internal __write method, which is given the error message and a label telling it what kind of message it is writing.

Example 7–10. An xmlproc application converting RSS to HTML (7 of 10)

```
# --- The error handler

class ErrorPrinter(xmlapp.ErrorHandler):
    "This handler simply prints error messages to standard error."

    def __init__(self, doc, out = None):
        self._out = out or sys.stderr
        self._doc = doc

    def warning(self,msg):
        self.__write("WARNING", msg)

    def error(self,msg):
        self.__write("ERROR", msg)

    def fatal(self,msg):
        self.__write("FATAL ERROR", msg)
```

The method in Example 7–11 creates a string representing the current location in the document and uses it, together with the label and the error message, to create the message that it will write out. Once this is done it writes to both the document and the error output.

Example 7–11. An xmlproc application converting RSS to HTML (8 of 10)

```
    def __write(self, label, msg):
        location = "%s:%d:%d" % (self._locator.get_current_sysid(),
                                 self._locator.get_line(),
                                 self._locator.get_column())
        msg = "%s: %s at %s\n" % (label, msg, location)
        self._out.write(msg)
        self._doc.write("<PRE>%s</PRE>" % msg)
```

The function in Example 7–12 actually does the conversion, given a system identifier and a file-like object. It does not close the file-like object because it can never know whether the calling code actually wants this done or not. The out argument might be sys.stdout, in which cases closing the file could have undesirable effects.

Example 7–12. An xmlproc application converting RSS to HTML (9 of 10)

```
# --- The driver

def convert(sysid, out):
    p = xmlproc.XMLProcessor()
    p.set_application(RSS2HTML(out))
    p.set_error_handler(ErrorPrinter(out))
    p.parse_resource(sysid)
```

Example 7–13. An xmlproc application converting RSS to HTML (10 of 10)

```
# --- The main program

sysid = sys.argv[1]
out   = open(sys.argv[2], "w")

convert(sysid, out)

out.close()
```

7.1.4   *Using xmlproc to validate documents*

In addition to being a module that can be used in XML applications, xmlproc also provides some general standalone applications which can be useful in their own right. These are the command-line parsers and the GUI wxValidator parser interface, which can parse XML documents and show their structure (as perceived by the parser!) as well as report on any errors. Seeing the structure as seen by the parser can be very useful in debugging, by verifying that the parser is interpreting the document the way you expect.

The command-line script xvcmd.py is used to invoke the validating parser. The structure of the command-line is roughly: [python] xvcmd.py [options] [urlstodocs], with the individual options explained below.

urlstodocs

Any arguments remaining after the below options will be interpreted as system identifiers of documents, and xvcmd will try to parse the documents they refer to.

-c catalog

This option will make xvcmd load and use the catalog file at cata-log. If this option is not specified, xvcmd will see if the environment variables XMLXCATALOG or XMLSOCATALOG are set (in that order) and use them instead. Catalog files are explained in 10.3.1, "Public identifiers and catalog files," on page 381.

-l language

This option will make xvcmd report errors in the specified language (which must be an ISO 639 language identifier). Currently support-ed are en (English), no (Norwegian bokmål), fr (French), and sv (Swedish).[1]

-o notation

Specifying this option will make xvcmd output the parsed document in the specified notation. e means ESIS output, x means canonical XML output, and n means ordinary, or normalized, XML output.

-n

This option makes xvcmd do namespace processing and report names as "URI local-part" in output. Namespace errors will also be detected.

--nowarn

This option will make xvcmd suppress warning messages, although errors will still be printed.

---

1. The error messages are stored in the xml.parsers.xmlproc.errors module, and translations of the messages to other languages are gratefully received for incorporation into future releases of the parser.

`--entstck`

> This option makes xvcmd print the stack of open entities whenever an error occurs. This can be very useful in tracking down errors that occur inside internal entities.

`--rawxml`

> This makes xvcmd print the original XML string that caused the error for all errors in the document. Can be useful in figuring out what the parser is complaining about in a document.

Example 7–14. Example input to xvcmd.py

```
<doc>
This is a simple sample document.
It even has a <?pi?> and an
<element with="an attribute"/>.
<!-- And, not to forget, a comment. -->
</doc>
```

The resulting output from running xvmcd.py with the document in Example 7–14 as input (with a command-line of `xvcmd.py -o n demo.xml`) is shown in Example 7–15.

Example 7–15. Example output from running xvcmd.py

```
xmlproc version 0.61dev

Parsing 'demo.xml'

E:demo.xml:2:6: Element 'doc' not declared
<doc>
This is a simple sample document.
It even has a <?pi ?> and an
E:demo.xml:5:31: Element 'element' not declared
<element with="an attribute"></element>.
</doc>
Parse complete, 2 error(s) and 0 warning(s)
```

In the output, the first two lines are a standard preamble, followed by a representation of the document. Lines beginning with E: are error messages, in this case resulting from the lack of a DTD (which means that the document is not valid). Note that the PI changes (whitespace is inserted between the target and the non-existent data), the empty element tag is turned into an element with start- and end-tags, and the comment disappears.

The xpcmd.py script performs the same function as xvcmd.py, except that it does not validate. It supports the exact same command-line options, except for the -c option, which does not make sense for a non-validating parser. It also has an additional option, --extsub, which makes it parse the external DTD subset and any external parameter entities.

The dtdcmd.py program provides a command-line interface to the DTD parser, which can be used to check the syntax of DTDs without having to attach them to a document. It accepts only a single argument: the system identifier of the DTD to be parsed.

In addition to these there is also the wxValidator program, which provides a GUI interface to xmlproc implemented using the wxPython windowing toolkit. wxPython is a Python module that provides access to the wxWindows GUI toolkit, which can be used both on Windows and Unix (and hopefully also the Mac with time).

The screenshot in Figure 7–3 shows what wxValidator looks like after having parsed the document in Example 7–16.

The upper text field takes the file name of the document to parse, while the second text field takes the file name of the catalog file to use when parsing. The drop-down list beside the "Parse" button chooses the language of error messages. The three check boxes control whether warnings are to be shown, whether output is to be shown and whether the document should be validated or not, respectively.

The screenshot in Figure 7–4 shows the result of parsing the same document, but this time with Norwegian error messages and with output on. The second window shows the result of parsing as rendered by the DocGenerator class mentioned above.

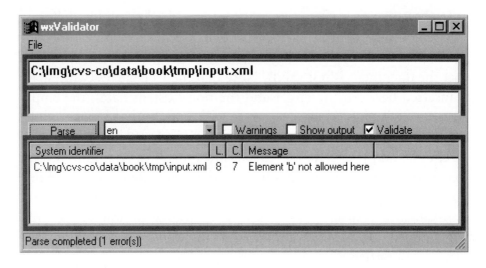

Figure 7–3   wxValidator after parsing a document

Example 7–16. Input document to wxValidator

```
<!DOCTYPE [
  <!ELEMENT doc (a, b)>
  <!ELEMENT a   (#PCDATA)>
  <!ELEMENT b   (#PCDATA)>
]>

<doc>
  <b/>
  <a/>
  <b/>
</doc>
```

7.1.5 *Namespace support in xmlproc*

At the moment xmlproc supports namespaces through extensions in
the `xml.parsers.xmlproc.namespace` module. Expanded names
are reported as `'namespace-uri local-name'` strings. To make
xmlproc do namespace processing follow the pseudo-code in
Example 7–17.

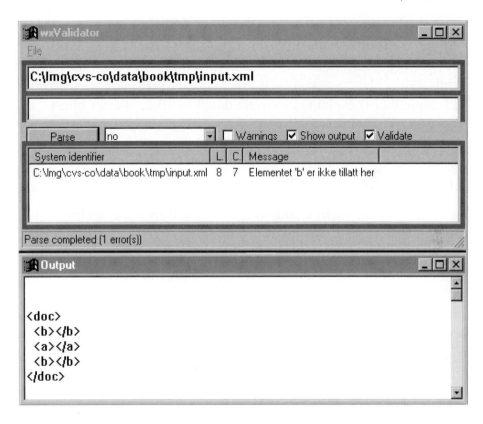

Figure 7–4   wxValidator after parsing a document with output

Example 7–17. How to make xmlproc do namespace processing

```
from xml.parsers.xmlproc import xmlproc, namespace

class MyApplication(xmlproc.Application):
    pass # implement usual interface

p = xmlproc.XMLProcessor()
ns = namespace.NamespaceFilter(p)
p.set_application(ns)
ns.set_application(MyApplication())
p.parse_resource("tst.xml")
```

Setting up parsing in this way installs the `NamespaceFilter` object between your application and the xmlproc parser, enabling it to perform namespace processing on the document before it is passed on to your application. The `NamespaceFilter` class is really a parser filter, a technique that is explained in more detail in 10.2, "Parser filters," on page 360.

7.1.6 *Pitfalls*

As far as I know, there is only one real pitfall in using xmlproc, and this will be removed as soon as possible. If any of your handlers raise an `IndexError`, this exception will be caught by xmlproc and cause its internal buffering to go haywire. The result will generally be that it will parse the end of the buffer more than once, which will cause it to complain about phantom end-tags that are not really there. If this happens to you, try searching for `IndexErrors` being raised by your code somewhere.

7.2 | Pyexpat

Pyexpat is an adaptation of the expat XML parser as a Python module, using the Python C API. As expat itself is written in C, Jack Jansen has written the C code necessary to load expat into Python and access it as though it were written in Python. This code has later been extended by Paul Prescod, Andrew Kuchling, and several others. So to client applications the fact that expat is not written in Python is very nearly invisible.

Pyexpat does not validate, does not read the external DTD subset, and by default does not read external entities, although it can be made to do so. It is also, like xmlproc, an incremental parser with support for namespaces. In Python 2.0, Pyexpat can read any character encoding Python can, while in Python 1.5, expat's own encoding support is used, and only UTF-16, UTF-8, and ISO 8859–1 are supported.

Pyexpat can be compiled to pass strings to the application encoded either as UTF-8 byte strings or as UTF-16 Unicode strings. In Python 1.5, UTF-8 strings are used, while in Python 2.0, UTF-16 strings are the default. Applications that expect ISO 8859–1 output will generally work fine with UTF-16, but be unpleasantly surprised when they receive UTF-8 output. For example, what was "é" in ISO 8859–1 input will turn into "Â\202" in UTF-8. The attribute `returns_unicode` on the parser object can be used to tell whether UTF-16 Unicode strings or UTF-8 byte strings are returned.

Caution
Note that Pyexpat has gone through quite a few changes in its interface and feature set. Quite a few of the things described in this section are only available with Pyexpat versions 2.30 and newer. Note that the `pyexpat` module has an attribute `__version__` which can be used to test which version you are using.

7.2.1   *The interface*

Pyexpat has a very simple interface, the main feature being the `ParserCreate` function, which usually takes no arguments (more on this below) and returns a parser object. This parser object is then used to parse actual documents by pushing pieces of the document into it, which causes Pyexpat to call registered handler functions to pass document events to the application.

Note that Pyexpat has over time used many different package names, which can cause some confusion when you look at older source code. Today, Pyexpat lives in the `xml.parsers.expat` module, and you should only use that package name when using Pyexpat directly.

To use the parser, follow these steps:

1. Create the parser with the `ParserCreate` function.
2. Register the handler functions on the parser with the attributes listed below.
3. Feed content into the parser with the `Parse` method.

4. Tell the parser that the document has ended with a final call to `Parse`.

The parser object only has a single method:

`Parse(text, final)`
>   This method makes Pyexpat parse the text in the `text` parameter (a string) and call the corresponding handler functions. As long as the `final` parameter is `0` Pyexpat does not require the document to be complete, but after the last block `Parse` must be called with `final` set to `1`, so that Pyexpat can check that the document is complete.
>
>   One usually pushes input blocks into `Parse` with `final` set to `0`, and then does a last push with an empty string and `1`, in order to make sure that Pyexpat finishes parsing.
>
>   Note that if an error occurs, Pyexpat will stop parsing and return `0`. If parsing is successful Pyexpat will return `1`.

`ParseFile(fileobj)`
>   Like `Parse`, except it is called only once, with a file-like object as the parameter. The entire document is read from the object, which need only have the `read` method.

The Pyexpat handler functions are attributes on the parser object, and Pyexpat applications are created by writing handler functions and then setting them as parser attributes. The available handlers are:

`StartElementHandler(name, attrs)`
>   This function is called for each start-tag in the document, with the element type name in `name` and the attributes as a dictionary in the `attrs` parameter. The dictionary maps attribute names to attribute values.

`EndElementHandler(name)`
>   This function is called for each end-tag in the document, with the element type name in `name`.

`CharacterDataHandler(data)`

 This function is called for each piece of character data in the document, with the character data in the `data` parameter as a string.

`ProcessingInstructionHandler(target, data)`

 This function is called for the processing instructions in the document, with the target in the `target` parameter as a string, and the PI data in the `data` parameter (also as a string).

 In addition to these handlers there are some more handlers for namespaces, lexical information, and external entities, which are described later. Following the XML Recommendation, Pyexpat stops parsing the moment it hits a well-formedness error. Because of this limitation, error information can be obtained by reading a number of attributes on the parser object rather than by receiving values passed to an error handler. These attributes are:

`ErrorCode`

 This attribute contains the error number of the current error, if any. (It contains 0 if there is no error.) A corresponding error message can be obtained by calling the `ErrorString(no)` function inside the `pyexpat` module with the error number as the argument.

`ErrorLineNumber`

 This attribute contains the line number of the document where the error occurred.

`ErrorColumnNumber`

 This attribute contains the column number of the line in the document where the error occurred.

`ErrorByteIndex`

 This attribute contains the byte offset of the first byte in the document where the error occurred, counted from the first byte of the document.

Note that the location information attributes can be read at any point during parsing, not just when errors have occurred.

7.2.2   *An example application*

As an example application we will use the RSS to HTML converter again, since it is by now well understood and allows for comparison with the xmlproc application.

One difference with xmlproc is that the most obvious way to write a Pyexpat application is as a set of functions. This has the problem that since the application needs to manage its internal state, there is no obvious place to put this, except as global variables in the module. It also has the disadvantage of not clearly showing the close relationship between the handler function and their state variables, and it means that only one application can be used at any given time, since different application instances would otherwise clobber one another's variables.

In Example 7–18, another approach has been chosen, where the application is written as a class, and methods are used as the handler functions. This is possible since the methods of an object are available as values (by leaving off the parentheses that signal a call) that are still bound to the object, and thus become functions with a fixed `self` parameter. (In Python terminology, they are known as *bound methods*.)

Interestingly, the application becomes almost identical to the xmlproc application when written in this way. The driver function is different, and there are some other small differences, but the applications themselves are almost the same.

Example 7–18. The Pyexpat RSS to HTML converter

```
"""
This application uses Pyexpat to convert RSS documents to HTML.
"""

import sys, codecs
from xml.parsers import expat
```

```
# --- Templates

top = \
"""
<!DOCTYPE HTML PUBLIC "-//W3C//DTD HTML 4.0 Transitional//EN">
<HTML>
<HEAD>
  <TITLE>%s</TITLE>
</HEAD>

<BODY>

<H1><A HREF="%s">%s</A></H1>
"""

bottom = \
"""
<HR>

<ADDRESS>
Converted to HTML by expat_rss2html.py.
</ADDRESS>

</BODY>
</HTML>
"""

# --- The converter

class RSS2HTML:

    def __init__(self, out = None):
        self._out = out or sys.stdout

        # tracking state
        self._data = ""
        self._first_item = 1

        self._title = None
        self._link = None
        self._descr = None
```

```
def start_tag(self, name, attrs):
    self._data = ""

    if name == "item":
        self._descr = None # reset for this item
        if self._first_item:
            self._out.write("\n<ul>\n")

        self._first_item = 0

def end_tag(self, name):
    if name == "title":
        self._title = self._data

    elif name == "link":
        self._link = self._data

    elif name == "descr":
        self._descr = self._data

    elif name == "channel":
        self._out.write(top % (self._title, self._link,
                               self._title))

        if self._descr != None:
            self._out.write("<p>%s</p>" % self._descr)


    elif name == "item":
        self._out.write('  <li><a href="%s">%s</a> %s\n' %
                        (self._link,self._title,self._descr or ""))

    elif name == "rss":
        self._out.write("</ul>\n")
        self._out.write(bottom)

def data_handler(self, data):
    self._data = self._data + data
```

```
# --- The driver

def convert(sysid, out):
    app = RSS2HTML(out)
    p = expat.ParserCreate()
    p.StartElementHandler = app.start_tag
    p.EndElementHandler = app.end_tag
    p.CharacterDataHandler = app.data_handler

    error = 0
    inf = open(sysid)
    buf = inf.read(16384)
    while buf != "":
        if p.Parse(buf, 0) != 1:
            error = 1
            break
        buf = inf.read(16384)

    inf.close()

    if error or p.Parse("", 1) != 1:
        print "ERROR: %s in %s:%s:%s" % \
                (expat.ErrorString(p.ErrorCode),
                 sysid, p.ErrorLineNumber, p.ErrorColumnNumber)

# --- The main program

sysid = sys.argv[1]
out   = codecs.open(sys.argv[2], "w", "iso-8859-1")

convert(sysid, out)

out.close()
```

7.2.3   *Dealing with encodings and namespaces*

As mentioned above, the ParserCreate(encoding = None, nssep = None) function is usually used with no arguments; Pyexpat can figure out the encoding of an XML document using the rules in the XML Recommendation (as described in 5.3.6, "XML and Unicode," on page 128). However, if the document is read from the Web or from some other source which knows the character encoding, this other source may override the usual default encoding (which is UTF-8). The encoding parameter can be used to tell Pyexpat explicitly which encoding to use in such circumstances.

As mentioned above, Pyexpat will use the encoding support in Python 2.0 to handle character encodings, so it can deal with any character encoding Python 2.0 can handle. This applies both to the encoding argument and to encodings declared in the XML document.

If the second argument is given, it must be a single character, and Pyexpat will turn on its namespace processing. When doing namespace processing Pyexpat will report expanded names as 'uri localname', and the separator character will be the character given in this parameter. I recommend to always use space, which is illegal in both URIs and XML names. It also makes it easy to split the uri and localname apart with the built-in string.split function.

When doing namespace processing, expat will suppress namespace declaration attributes. It will also use two extra handler functions, described in the list below.

StartNamespaceDeclHandler(prefix, uri)
> This function is called for each namespace declaration in the document, before the StartElementHandler call for the element on which the declaration appeared. The prefix argument holds the namespace prefix, and the uri argument holds the namespace URI.

EndNamespaceDeclHandler(prefix)
> This handler is called to signal the end of a namespace declaration when the element on which the namespace declaration appeared ends. It is called after the corresponding EndElementHandler event.

7.2.4 *Lexical and DTD information*

Pyexpat has some extra handler functions for reporting lexical information and DTD information. These are listed below. Most applications can just ignore these handlers, but in some cases they may be useful.

`CommentHandler(content)`

This function is called to report comments in the document. The `content` argument holds the contents of the comment.

`StartCdataSectionHandler()`

This function is called to report the beginning of a CDATA marked section. The contents of the marked section will be reported to the `CharacterDataHandler`.

`EndCdataSectionHandler()`

This function is called to signal the end of a CDATA marked section which has already been reported to the `StartCdataSection-Handler`.

`NotationDeclHandler(name, base, sysid, pubid)`

This handler is called to report the declaration of a notation in the internal DTD subset. The `name` parameter holds the name of the notation, `base` is the system identifier of the document, `sysid` is the system identifier of the notation, and `pubid` is the public identifier of the notation.

This handler (and the next) is present because the XML Recommendation requires all parsers to report this information to the application.

`UnparsedEntityDeclHandler(name, base, sysid, pubid, ndata)`

This handler is called to report the declaration of an unparsed entity. Here, `name` holds the name of the entity, `base` is the document system identifier, `sysid` is the system identifier of the entity, `pubid` is the public identifier, and `ndata` holds the name of the notation associated with the entity.

`NotStandaloneHandler()`

This handler is called when a document does not have the standalone declaration, but does have either an external subset or a reference to an external parameter entity. If this handler returns 0,

parsing will not continue and the parser will report an error. The
default handler returns 1.

`StartDoctypeDeclHandler(doctypeName)`
> This handler is called when the start of the DOCTYPE declaration is
> encountered. The `doctypeName` parameter holds the name of the
> document element.

`EndDoctypeDeclHandler()`
> This handler is called when both the internal and the external sub-
> sets of the DTD have been parsed.

`ExternalParsedEntityDeclHandler(name, base, sysid, pubid)`
> This is called for each declaration of an external parsed entity in
> the DTD. The `name` argument has the name of the entity, `base` is
> the base URI, the `sysid` is the system identifier that the entity
> should be resolved against, and `pubid` is the public identifier of the
> entity, if any.

`InternalParsedEntityDeclHandler(name, reptext, length)`
> Called for each declaration of an internal parsed entity in the DTD.
> The `name` argument has the name of the entity, `reptext` is its
> replacement text (that is, its value), and `length` has the length of
> the replacement text.

7.2.5 *Handling external entities*

The Pyexpat parser does not read external entities by default, and in
fact, a bit of programming is necessary to make it read them at all. This
is because expat does not have any functionality at all for reading input
from a data source. Instead, it requires you to push data into it in order
to get it to parse anything at all. Thus, expat cannot open an external

entity and read from it, but requires the application to do this and feed the contents back to expat.

When an external general entity is encountered by expat, it will call the `ExternalEntityRefHandler(context, base, sysid, pubid)` handler function. (In other words, this function is not called for the external subset or external parameter entities.) The `context` argument holds internal expat data that the application is just supposed to pass back to expat without looking at, and the `base` argument holds the system identifier that is used to resolve the `sysid` argument to an absolute URI. The `sysid` argument holds the URI of the entity, and the `pubid` holds its public identifier (or `None` if there is none).

When expat calls the handler function, the application must decide what to do. Generally, the application will want to read in the external entity. To do this it must resolve the location of the entity and start receiving text from the entity. To make expat parse the contents of the entity, a new parser object must be created by calling the `External-EntityParserCreate(context)` method on the existing parser object. The `context` argument must be the same as that received in the `ExternalEntityRefHandler` handler function.

The text must then be read from the entity and pushed into the new parser object with its `Parse` method. After the handler has returned, expat will continue parsing the parent entity. The handler must return `1` if the entity was parsed successfully, or `0` if there was a fatal error that should cause parsing to terminate. If there was an uncaught exception in the handler, parsing stops and the exception is passed back to Python.

If the application decides not to read the external entity, that is its own business, and Pyexpat does not care about it at all, nor is there any way to inform it of this fact.

Examples 7–19 to 7–21 contain a reusable implementation of external entity support for Pyexpat which you can use in your own applications if you wish. They also illustrate the concepts explained above.

Example 7–19. A general external entity implementation (1 of 3)

```
"""
How to implement external entity support for Pyexpat.
"""

import sys, urllib, urlparse
from xml.parsers import expat

# --- The application

class ExternalEntityHandling:

    def __init__(self, parser):
        self._parsers = [parser]
```

We need a reference to the parser in order to be able to create the special parser object that parses external entities (Example 7–19). We also need a stack of parser objects, since external entities can refer to further external entities.

The method in Example 7–20 simply creates the new parser, adds it to the stack, and then opens the external entity. Note that it uses `urlparse.urljoin` to produce an absolute URI from the `sysid`

Example 7–20. A general external entity implementation (2 of 3)

```
    def external_entity_handler(self, context, base, sysid, pubid):
        newp = self._parsers[-1].ExternalEntityParserCreate(context)
        self._parsers.append(newp)

        source = urllib.urlopen(urlparse.urljoin(base, sysid))
        buf = source.read(16384)
        while buf != "":
            if newp.Parse(buf, 0) != 1:
                return 0

            buf = source.read(16384)

        del self._parsers[-1]
        return 1
```

parameter. We also return 0 or 1 to Pyexpat to indicate whether the entity was parsed correctly or not.

It may seem strange that we put the new parser on the stack before moving on to feed data to it and then retrieve it from the stack before returning, but the reason we have the stack is because new calls to `external_entity_handler` will occur inside calls to `Parse` from this method (Example 7–21).

Example 7–21. A general external entity implementation (3 of 3)

```
# --- A test driver

def element_start(name, atts):
    print "Start:", name

def _test(sysid):
    p = expat.ParserCreate()
    p.SetBase(sysid) # necessary to tell expat the base URI
    app = ExternalEntityHandling(p)
    p.StartElementHandler = element_start
    p.ExternalEntityRefHandler = app.external_entity_handler

    error = 0
    inf = open(sysid)
    buf = inf.read(16384)
    while buf != "":
        if p.Parse(buf, 0) != 1:
            error = 1
            break
        buf = inf.read(16384)

    inf.close()

    if error or p.Parse("", 1) != 1:
        print "ERROR: %s in %s:%s:%s" % \
                (expat.ErrorString(p.ErrorCode), sysid,
                 p.ErrorLineNumber, p.ErrorColumnNumber)

if __name__ == "__main__":
    _test(sys.argv[1])
```

7.3 | xmllib

In version 2.0 of Python xmllib was deprecated, and developers are now recommended to use SAX instead. The main reason for this is that xmllib is not fully conformant with the specification, in ways that will be explained later. We still describe xmllib in this section, since it has an interface that is not much like the interfaces of most other XML parsers, making it an interesting example. This parser makes good use of Python's dynamic nature to create an interface that is both convenient and natural. It is implemented in the `xmllib` module that is part of the standard Python library, where the functionality is provided by the `XMLParser` class. Applications are written by subclassing the `XMLParser` class and overriding its methods. This effectively entwines the parser and the application in a single object, which is unlike the approach taken by xmlproc and Pyexpat.

The xmllib parser is implemented in the `XMLParser` class, and it expects applications to subclass that class and override methods and variables to tailor xmllib's behavior and at the same time implement the application itself. Thus, the interface exposed by xmllib serves several purposes: controlling and tailoring the behavior of the parser and receiving data from the parser. The correspondence between the different purposes and parts of the parser interface is not very systematic, but still rather intuitive.

The main parts of the interface are:

parser control methods
These are the methods used to control parsing, such as the `feed`, `close`, and `reset` methods of xmllib's incremental parsing interface. Like Pyexpat and xmlproc, xmllib is an incremental parser.

general methods
This interface consists of methods for general document events such as start of element, end of element, etc. It is most useful for writing applications that are independent of a specific schema, since

the interface described below handles schema-specific applications better.

mapping interface

This interface provides more convenient access to the parsed document than does the general interface which can be tailored to your specific application. This interface is in fact implemented by the default implementations of the methods in the general interface. More details on this below.

static DTD interface

This interface is made up of variables that can be preset by the application, to give the parser some of the information that may appear in the DTD, such as attribute default values and entity declarations.

The following sections will cover each of these parts of the interface in more detail.

7.3.1 *The parser control interface*

This is the interface through which the parsers environment controls the parsing process. Below is the list of methods that make up this interface.

`reset()`

Resets the parser, losing all unparsed text. Should be called after `close` has been called, to prepare the parser for a new document. (The `reset`, `feed`, and `close` methods have exactly the same semantics as in xmlproc.)

`feed(text)`

Pushes text to be parsed into the parser. It will parse the text as far as it can, and when it cannot continue any further it will leave the incomplete constructs in an internal buffer until the next call. The text block can be of any size.

`close()`

Forces all text left in the internal buffer to be parsed now. The parser will protest if any incomplete constructs are left at this stage or if the document is not properly terminated. This method can be overridden, but must then call the original.

`setnomoretags()`

Enter CDATA marked section mode, and stay in it for the rest of the document. This method allows XML documents that are not well-formed to be processed and should not be used.

`setliteral()`

Parse the rest of the contents of the current element as though it were inside a CDATA marked section. This method allows XML documents that not well-formed and interpretations of documents that disagree with the XML Recommendation, so it should not be used either.

`syntax_error(message)`

This method is called when syntax errors are encountered, and the `message` parameter holds a description of the problem. The default implementation raises `RuntimeError` (an exception built-in to Python), but can be overridden to let the parser continue after fatal errors.[1] Errors from which the parser cannot recover raise `Runtime-Error` without calling `syntax_error` at all.

---

1.   This is what the XML Recommendation calls well-formedness errors. It is possible to write a parser that can continue parsing after hitting such errors, even though this means that the document is not well-formed, and the Recommendation requires parsers to stop passing data to the application after finding such errors.

7.3.2 *The general interface*

The purpose of this interface is to pass information about document contents from the parser back to the application. To do this the interface has a set of general methods (listed below) and schema-independent applications can subclass `XMLParser` and override these to get the document information. Most of these methods are used for logical information, but some are also used for lexical information. Those used for logical information are:

`unknown_starttag(name, atts)`

This method is used to report start-tags. The `name` parameter contains the element type name and the `atts` parameter contains the attributes of the element as a dictionary. Note that the name of this method and the next derive from how they are intended to be used in the specialized interface of xmllib. This book presents a view of xmllib that differs somewhat from how it was intended to be used, but which makes xmllib useful for general applications as well.

`unknown_endtag(name)`

This method reports end-tags, and the `name` parameter holds the element type name.

`handle_data(data)`

This method is used to report character data back to the application. The data parameter holds the character data as a string. It is worth noting that CDATA marked sections will *not* be reported in this callback, but rather in the one below.

`handle_cdata(data)`

This method is used to report the contents of CDATA marked sections, and the contents will be in the `data` parameter as a string. This means that xmllib applications will be sensitive to whether content appeared in a CDATA marked section or literally. This can be worked around, however, simply by making your `handle_cdata` implementation call `handle_data`.

```
handle_proc(target, data)
```
This method is called for each processing instruction in the document. The `target` parameter holds the PI target, while the `data` parameter holds the PI data.

Using only this simple interface it is possible to make complete XML processing applications. The xmllib parser provides more functionality than this, but this is the core. Example 7–22 is a simple XML application that shows how to use xmllib:

Example 7–22. A simple xmllib application

```python
import xmllib

class EventPrinter(xmllib.XMLParser):

    def unknown_starttag(self, name, atts):
        print "Start of", name

    def handle_data(self, data):
        print "Data:", repr(data)

    def unknown_endtag(self, name):
        print "End of", name
```

Example 7–23 shows how this application can be used by loading it into the Python interpreter and using it interactively to parse a trivial XML document.

As a more meaningful and complete illustration, Examples 7–24 to 7–28 contain a simple xmllib application that counts the number of occurrences of each element type, each PI target, and the number of data blocks and their combined length.

The initializer (Example 7–24) merely calls xmllib's initializer (which is very important, parsing will fail otherwise) and sets up the internal state necessary to start collecting statistics.

Example 7–23. Interaction with xmllib

```
>>> parser = EventPrinter()
>>> parser.feed("<doc")
>>> parser.feed(">")
Start of doc
>>> parser.feed("This is some text.")
Data: 'This is some text.'
>>> parser.feed("This is a bit more.")
Data: 'This is a bit more.'
>>> parser.feed("<empty/>")
Start of empty
End of empty
>>> parser.feed("</doc>")
End of doc
>>> parser.feed("<!-- Error!")
>>> parser.close()
Traceback (innermost last):
  File "<stdin>", line 1, in ?
  File "C:\Python\Lib\xmllib.py", line 153, in close
    self.goahead(1)
  File "C:\Python\Lib\xmllib.py", line 365, in goahead
    self.syntax_error("bogus `%s'" % data)
  File "C:\Python\Lib\xmllib.py", line 748, in syntax_error
    raise RuntimeError, 'Syntax error at line %d: %s' % \
RuntimeError: Syntax error at line 1: bogus `<'
```

Example 7–24. An xmllib application that collects statistics about documents
(1 of 5)

```
import xmllib, sys

# --- The xmllib application

class StatsGatherer(xmllib.XMLParser):

    def __init__(self):
        xmllib.XMLParser.__init__(self) # initializes xmllib
        self._elems       = {}
        self._pis         = {}
        self._data_blocks = 0
        self._data_len    = 0
```

The event handler in Example 7–25 increases the count for the received element type by one, and if no such elements have appeared yet it sets the count to 1.

Example 7–25. An xmllib application that collects statistics about documents (2 of 5)

```
def unknown_starttag(self, name, atts):
    self._elems[name] = self._elems.get(name, 0) + 1
```

Because CDATA marked sections are reported in a separate callback and we do not want to distinguish them in any way, we simply reroute that callback to the ordinary handle_data callback (Example 7–26).

Example 7–26. An xmllib application that collects statistics about documents (3 of 5)

```
def handle_data(self, data):
    self._data_blocks = self._data_blocks + 1
    self._data_len = self._data_len + len(data)

def handle_cdata(self, data):
    self.handle_data(data)
```

The print_stats method (Example 7–27) prints the collected statistics. This method is not called by xmllib, but is called from the part of code that instantiates the parser and controls parsing.

Example 7–28 is the main program, which opens the file to read from, creates the parser, pushes the data into the parser and then, finally, prints the statistics.

7.3.3   *The specialized interface*

The interface described above is best suited for general applications like the document statistics example. When writing an application for

Example 7–27. An xmllib application that collects statistics about documents (4 of 5)

```
    def handle_proc(self, target, data):
        self._pis[target] = self._pis.get(target, 0) + 1
    def print_stats(self):
        print "Data blocks: %d" % self._data_blocks
        print "Data length: %d" % self._data_len
        print "\n---Elements"
        for pair in self._elems.items():
            print "%s: %d" % pair

        print "\n---PIs"
        for pair in self._pis.items():
            print "%s: %d" % pair
```

Example 7–28. An xmllib application that collects statistics about documents (5 of 5)

```
# --- Main program

inf = open(sys.argv[1])
p = StatsGatherer()
buf = inf.read(1024)
while buf != "":
    p.feed(buf)
    buf = inf.read(1024)
p.close()

p.print_stats()
```

a specific document type, the unknown_endtag method usually consists of a long list of if statements, each testing for a specific element type. With xmllib, there is an elegant way to avoid these if statements by using the elements dictionary.

The elements attribute of the XMLParser class maps element type names to functions handling the start and end-tags of the corresponding elements. The functions unknown_starttag and unknown_endtag will be called for elements which do not occur in the elements dictionary.

Note that the XMLParser's constructor will scan through all the methods defined on the object and attempt to build the elements dictionary itself, unless it exists when the constructor is called. Method names of the form start_foo will be assumed to be start-tag handlers for foo elements, while method names of the form end_foo are assumed to be end tag handlers for these elements. This process can be slow, so in some cases you may want to initialize the elements dictionary before calling the constructor, to avoid this.

Pseudo-code for a typical schema-specific application written using the general interface is shown in Example 7–29.

Example 7–29. Pseudo-code for a schema-specific application

```
class RSSApp(xmllib.XMLParser):

    # ...

    def unknown_endtag(self, name):
        if name == "item":
            self.handle_item()
        elif name == "title":
            self.handle_title()
        elif name == "link":
            self.handle_link()
        # ...
```

Usually, the actions for each element type will be so simple that there will not be separate methods for each, but I used methods in this case to make the example simpler. Example 7–30 shows pseudo-code for the same application written with the elements dictionary. (Note that xmllib was never intended to be used as in Example 7–29; this code was only written to explain how the specialized interface works.)

Using the elements dictionary does away completely with the need to implement the unknown_starttag and unknown_endtag methods. For this trivial example the difference is not so big, but in general this can be a significant improvement, as later examples will show. Note

Example 7–30. Pseudo-code for a schema-specific application (now using `elements`)

```
class RSSApp(xmllib.XMLParser):

    def __init__(self):
        self.elements = { "item"  : (None, self.handle_item),
                          "title" : (None, self.handle_title),
                          "link"  : (None, self.handle_link)   }
        xmllib.XMLParser.__init__(self)

    # ...
```

how we initialize the dictionary before calling the base constructor, to avoid the default setup process.

7.3.4 *An example application*

As an example of an xmllib application, this section describes a simple script that converts an RSS document with news items into an HTML document for publishing on the Web. Examples 7–31 to 7–39 make use of the `elements` dictionary, and a comparison with the exact same application implemented with xmlproc in a previous section should show the benefits of this approach (see Examples 7–4 to 7–13).

Example 7–31. RSS to HTML conversion application written with xmllib (1 of 9)

```
"""
This program converts an RSS document to an HTML document,
using xmllib.
"""

import xmllib

# --- Templates

top = \
"""
<!DOCTYPE HTML PUBLIC "-//W3C//DTD HTML 4.0 Transitional//EN">
```

```
<HTML>
<HEAD>
  <TITLE>%s</TITLE>
</HEAD>

<BODY>

<H1><A HREF="%s">%s</A></H1>
"""

bottom = \
"""
<HR>

<ADDRESS>
Converted to HTML by xmllib_rss2html.py.
</ADDRESS>

</BODY>
</HTML>
"""

# --- The converter

class RSS2HTML(xmllib.XMLParser):

    def __init__(self, out):
        self.elements = {
          "rss"         : (None,              self.end_rss),
          "channel"     : (None,              self.end_channel),
          "item"        : (self.start_item,   self.end_item),
          "title"       : (self.start_pcdata, self.end_title),
          "link"        : (self.start_pcdata, self.end_link),
          "description" : (self.start_pcdata, self.end_descr)
        }

        xmllib.XMLParser.__init__(self)
        self._out = out

        # state tracking variables
        self._data = ""
        self._item_count = 0

        self._title = None
        self._link = None
        self._descr = ''
```

In Example 7–4 we start declaring the application class, subclassing xmllib. XMLParser. The constructor takes a parameter out, which is a file-like object to which the output is written. The elements dictionary described above is set up with the requisite handler methods. Then the state-tracking attributes are declared: data is used for the contents of text blocks, item_count is used to count the number of items we have seen so far, and the three last attributes are used to hold information about a channel or item.

The two methods in Example 7–32 receive text data from the parser and store it in the data attribute for use by the other methods. Note how we override the handle_cdata method and make it call handle_data as explained earlier.

Example 7–32. RSS to HTML conversion application written with xmllib (2 of 9)

```
def handle_data(self, data):
    self._data = self._data + data

def handle_cdata(self, data):
    self.handle_data(data)
```

At the end of the title, link, and description elements, the application will have collected the element contents in the data attribute, and it can be moved over to the correct attribute so that it is ready for use when the containing element ends (Example 7–33).

Example 7–33. RSS to HTML conversion application written with xmllib (3 of 9)

```
def end_title(self):
    self._title = self._data

def end_link(self):
    self._link = self._data

def end_descr(self):
    self._descr = self._data
```

When the `channel` element ends we can take the title and link and
write out the contents of the top template, adding the description if
there was one (Example 7–34). Since we don't know where the `chan-
nel` element will actually end (this can be after the metadata, or after
all items[1]), and this method has to be called after the metadata, this
method is called from the `start_item` method in Example 7–35. (It
is never called directly by xmllib.)

Example 7–34. RSS to HTML conversion application written with xmllib (4 of 9)

```
def end_channel(self):
    self._out.write(top % (self._title, self._link, self._title))

    if self._descr != None:
        self._out.write("<p>%s</p>" % self._descr)
```

The method in Example 7–35 checks whether this is the first item,
and if so it calls `end_channel` and writes the start-tag for the `ul` element in the output (the list of items).

Example 7–35. RSS to HTML conversion application written with xmllib (5 of 9)

```
def start_item(self, atts):
    self._item_count = self._item_count + 1
    if self._item_count == 1:
        self.end_channel()
        self._out.write("\n<ul>\n")
```

The method in Example 7–36 handles the news items and is called
after each one to write out the HTML representation of the news item
from the information stored in the three data attributes.

---

1.   This is, strictly speaking, in violation of the DTD. However, RSS 0.9 did
     not have a DTD at all, and furthermore RSS practice has never been very
     strict, so making RSS applications somewhat lenient is generally a good
     idea.

Example 7–36. RSS to HTML conversion application written with xmllib (6 of 9)

```
def end_item(self):
    self._out.write('  <li><a href="%s">%s</a> %s\n' %
                    (self._link, self._title, self._descr))
    self._descr = ''
```

The method in Example 7–37 is called by xmllib on the start-tags for the `title`, `link`, and `description` elements to reset the `data` attribute before accumulating text in it. The fact that the same method is used for three different elements causes no problems at all; the method just appears three times in the `elements` dictionary.

Example 7–37. RSS to HTML conversion application written with xmllib (7 of 9)

```
def start_pcdata(self, atts):
    self._data = ""
```

The method in Example 7–38 is called when the document element ends; it closes the `ul` element and writes out the bottom template.

Example 7–38. RSS to HTML conversion application written with xmllib (8 of 9)

```
def end_rss(self):
    self._out.write("</ul>\n")
    self._out.write(bottom)
```

Example 7–39 is the main program, which takes two command-line arguments, opens file objects, calls `convert`, and closes the file objects afterwards.

Example 7–39. RSS to HTML conversion application written with xmllib (9 of 9)

```
# --- Conversion driver

def convert(inf, out):
    p = RSS2HTML(out)

    buf = inf.read(16384)
    while buf != "":
        p.feed(buf)
        buf = inf.read(16384)

    p.close()

# --- The main program

import sys

inf = open(sys.argv[1])
outf = open(sys.argv[2], "w")

convert(inf, outf)

inf.close()
outf.close()
```

7.3.5   *Handling lexical information*

In addition to the (almost) purely logical interface described so far, xmllib also provides some lexical information to the application, through the following callbacks:

`handle_xml(encoding, standalone)`
> This method is called for the XML declaration, and the `encoding` and `standalone` parameters contain the values of the corresponding pseudo-attributes of the XML declaration. If the attributes are not specified, their values will be `None` and `'no'`, respectively.

`handle_doctype(root, rawdata)`
> This method is called when the `DOCTYPE` declaration is encountered, and the `root` parameter contains the name of the document element

type, while the `rawdata` parameter contains the rest of the declaration after the document element type name. Note that this includes the entire internal DTD subset, if it is present.

`handle_charref(num)`
This method is called on character references, and the `num` parameter is a string that contains either the decimal number or a hexadecimal number preceded by "x", depending on what was in the document.

The default implementation resolves the character reference into a character and calls `handle_data` to pass it on to the application.

`unknown_entityref(name)`
This method is called on entity references for which the parser does not know the definition, and the `name` parameter contains the name of the referenced entity. For known entity references the contents of the entity are parsed.

7.3.6   *Advanced use*

7.3.6.1   Namespaces

The xmllib parser supports XML Namespaces and will process any namespace declarations in XML documents, reporting expanded names as strings of the form `'uri localname'`. This goes for both element type names and attribute names. The `elements` dictionary also works with expanded names and uses as keys the names of the same form (`'uri localname'`) as are reported through the general callback methods.

Nothing special is needed to turn on namespace processing; xmllib will automatically start resolving names once it sees namespace attributes. There is no way to turn off namespace processing, and the attributes that declare namespace prefixes will be stripped and not passed on to the application at all.

In addition to supporting expanded names for elements, the `XMLParser` class has a method `getnamespace()`, which returns a dictionary containing all the namespace prefixes currently in effect and their mappings to namespace URIs.

Example 7–40. Using EventPrinter with namespaces

```
>>> parser = EventPrinter()
>>> parser.feed("<doc xmlns='ns-uri'>")
Start of ns-uri doc
>>> parser.feed("<empty/>")
Start of ns-uri empty
End of ns-uri empty
>>> parser.feed("<html:p xmlns:html='html-uri'>")
Start of html-uri p
>>> parser.feed("This is an <html:tt>HTML</html:tt> example.")
Data: 'This is an '
Start of html-uri tt
Data: 'HTML'
End of html-uri tt
Data: ' example.'
>>> parser.feed("</html:p></doc>")
End of html-uri p
End of ns-uri doc
```

Example 7–40 demonstrates how to use the EventPrinter application shown on page 208 with a document that uses namespaces.

7.3.6.2 Entities

As stated earlier, xmllib does not read the DTD, so it doesn't know what entities are defined there. For applications that are tied to a specific DTD (and thus have a fixed set of entities) this can be handled by defining the entitydefs attribute of the parser object to be a dictionary mapping entities to entity values.

If these entity values contain markup, that markup will be correctly parsed by xmllib. However, since the entity values have to be strings, this technique can't be used to handle external entities (unless one maps the entity to an object that somehow loads in the external entity and provides a string-like interface to it).

7.3.6.3 sgmlop

The sgmlop parser is written in C and distributed both separately and as a part of the XML-SIG XML Package. It implements nearly the same interface as xmllib, but runs much faster since it is written in C. This parser lives in the `xml.parsers.sgmlop` module. With sgmlop, applications are not subclassed from the `XMLParser` class, but instead the `XMLParser` object is instantiated and the application is registered with the `register` method. Listed below are the methods sgmlop applications can implement.

`finish_starttag(name, attrs)`
    Called for start-tags, like `unknown_starttag` in xmllib.

`finish_endtag(name)`
    Called for end-tags, like `unknown_endtag` in xmllib.

`handle_proc(target, data)`
    Receives processing instructions.

`handle_data(data)`
    Receives character data.

`handle_cdata(data)`
    Receives CDATA marked sections.

`handle_comment(contents)`
    Receives comments.

`handle_charref(num)`
    Used identically to `handle_charref` in xmllib.

`handle_entityref(name)`
    The same as `unknown_entityref` in xmllib.

```
handle_special(contents)
```
   Called when the parser encounters the DOCTYPE declaration, passing it as the contents string.

   Examples 7–41 to 7–43 show the statistics application implemented using sgmlop.
   The major difference with the xmllib application is that we don't subclass the XMLParser class, but create a class with no base class instead (Example 7–41).

Example 7–41. The sgmlop statistics application (1 of 3)

```
import sgmlop, sys

# --- The sgmlop application

class StatsGatherer:

    def __init__(self):
        self._elems       = {}
        self._pis         = {}
        self._data_blocks = 0
        self._data_len    = 0
```

   Note how the method in Example 7–42 had to be renamed to finish_starttag.

Example 7–42. The sgmlop statistics application (2 of 3)

```
    def finish_starttag(self, name, atts):
        try:
            self._elems[name] = self._elems[name] + 1
        except KeyError:
            self._elems[name] = 1
```

   Since the application is no longer a subclass of the parser we must instantiate both, and use the register method to tell the parser where to send data (Example 7–43).

Example 7–43. The sgmlop statistics application (3 of 3)

```python
    def handle_data(self, data):
        self._data_blocks = self._data_blocks + 1
        self._data_len = self._data_len + len(data)

    def handle_cdata(self, data):
        self.handle_data(data)

    def handle_proc(self, target, data):
        try:
            self._pis[target] = self._pis[target] + 1
        except KeyError:
            self._pis[target] = 1

    def print_stats(self):
        print "Data blocks: %d" % self._data_blocks
        print "Data length: %d" % self._data_len
        print "\n---Elements"
        for pair in self._elems.items():
            print "%s: %d" % pair

        print "\n---PIs"
        for pair in self._pis.items():
            print "%s: %d" % pair

# --- Main program

inf = open(sys.argv[1])
p = sgmlop.XMLParser()
app = StatsGatherer()
p.register(app)
buf = inf.read(1024)
while buf != "":
    p.feed(buf)
    buf = inf.read(1024)
p.close()

app.print_stats()
```

7.3.6.4 DTD information

In order to make xmllib correctly insert attribute values and correctly interpret entity references within XML documents it is necessary to provide xmllib with the information programmatically, since xmllib does not parse the DTD, whether the external or the internal subset. (It should be noted that this is strictly in violation of the XML Recommendation, which requires even non-validating parsers to read the internal subset, precisely to gather this information.)

The `attributes` variable is a dictionary that maps element-type names to dictionaries that map attribute names either to `None` or to a default value. If an attribute dictionary exists for an element type, all attributes in the document that do not appear in the dictionary will be reported as illegal. (This can be used as a form of validation, to ensure that only allowed attributes appear.) Note that expanded names, of the form `'nsuri lname'`, can be used here as well.

The `entitydefs` variable maps entity names to their values (or, more formally correct, their replacement texts). This can be used to define entities in addition to those defined in the XML Recommendation. Note that any markup in these entity values will be parsed. External entities are not supported. This behavior is implemented by the default `handle_entityref` method.

With both these variables it is important to remember to not simply use the default dictionaries (which are shared between all `XMLParser` instances), but to create new ones for each particular application.

7.3.7 *Pitfalls*

The xmllib parser has a rather intuitive and easy-to-use interface, but there are still a couple of places where a user who does not know the interface in detail can go wrong. The most common problems are:

- Forgetting to call `XMLParser.__init__` in the constructor of the application class. This will typically result in an `AttributeError` that complains that the attribute `rawdata` does not exist inside the `feed` call, since this tries to add the fed text onto the `rawdata`, internal buffer, which is created by the constructor.

- Forgetting to override `handle_cdata`. This is likely to result in an application that works correctly for a while (potentially a long time) until someone uses a CDATA marked section in an input document and its contents are ignored, because the application expects all character data to be reported through `handle_data`.

- Trying to use xmllib 0.2 or 0.3 in JPython 1.1. This does not work because xmllib uses features in regular expressions that the regular expression module used by JPython does not support correctly. This causes an `IndexError` to be raised in the `parse_starttag` method with the message "group 7 is undefined".

  In Jython 2.0 this problem has been fixed.

- Modifying the `attributes` or `elements` dictionaries without creating new ones for each xmllib application object. This will cause all instances to share the same object, which can cause instances of different applications to share values. This can be especially serious for the `elements` dictionary, since it can cause the methods in the dictionary to be bound to the wrong object if two application objects are used at the same time.

7.4 | Xerces-C / Pirxx

The Pirxx module has a very simple interface: it only implements the SAX interface presented in the next chapter. This means that you don't need to learn a special interface for it, you can just use the interface you already know.

You can find out how to use Pirxx in SAX by looking at Table 8–1.

7.5 | Working in Jython

When writing XML applications for Jython the range of available parsers is different from that in CPython. One important thing to be aware of is that the pure-Python parsers work in both Jython and CPython. This means that for truly portable applications, they are the only alternatives. (Well, not really. SAX, presented in the next chapter, provides another alternative.)

However, working in Jython means that one has complete access to all Java libraries and applications, and this includes the Java XML parsers, of which there are quite a few. A major advantage to the Java XML parsers, compared to the pure Python ones, is that they are much faster, since they are written in Java. So for Jython applications, using Java parsers may be an attractive alternative. (A list of the various parsers appeared in 6.3.1.3, "Java parsers," on page 149.)

Examples 7–44 to 7–51 show an application that uses James Clark's XP parser to convert RSS documents to HTML. XP is an open source parser written in Java that is both very fast and highly conformant, and I expect it to be available from `http://www.jclark.com/xml/xp/` for a long time to come.

Example 7–44 is familiar. We import the needed classes and set up templates for the output. Note that the Java classes are imported as if they were ordinary Python classes.

The state tracking (Example 7–45) is nearly the same as for the xmlproc application, the main difference being the `resetData` method. This is used in the same way as the `data` attribute in the xmlproc application, to contain textual element content, but here we have to use a Java character array, because this is what XP passes to us. Jython distinguishes between Python lists and Java arrays, making this extra complexity necessary.

So in this case we will use a static character array and accumulate characters in it (using `charlength` to remember how many) and only convert the characters to a string when we need to.

Example 7–46 is nearly exactly the same as in the xmlproc application, the only difference being that we call `resetData` to reset our

Example 7–44. An RSS to HTML conversion implemented with XP (1 of 8)

```
"""
An example application using XP to convert RSS documents to HTML in
Jython.
"""

import sys, jarray

from java.lang import String
from com.jclark.xml.parse import EntityManagerImpl
from com.jclark.xml.parse.base import ParserImpl, ApplicationImpl

# --- Templates

top = \
"""
<!DOCTYPE HTML PUBLIC "-//W3C//DTD HTML 4.0 Transitional//EN">
<HTML>
<HEAD>
  <TITLE>%s</TITLE>
</HEAD>

<BODY>

<H1><A HREF="%s">%s</A></H1>
"""

bottom = \
"""
<HR>

<ADDRESS>
Converted to HTML by XP_rss2html.py.
</ADDRESS>

</BODY>
</HTML>
"""
```

buffer, and that XP passes an event object to us. We use the `getName` method to extract the element name from it.

Again, the method in Example 7–47 is nearly exactly the same as in the xmlproc application. The `getData` method is used to turn the internal buffer into a string.

Example 7–45. An RSS to HTML conversion implemented with XP (2 of 8)

```
# --- The converter

class RSS2HTML(ApplicationImpl):

    def __init__(self, out):
        self._out = out

        # tracking state
        self.resetData()
        self._first_item = 1

        self._title = None
        self._link = None
        self._descr = None

    def resetData(self):
        self._chararray = jarray.zeros(16384, "c")
        self._charlength = 0
```

Example 7–46. An RSS to HTML conversion implemented with XP (3 of 8)

```
    def startElement(self, event):
        self.resetData()

        if event.getName() == "item":
            self._descr = None # reset for this item
            if self._first_item:
                self._out.write("\n<ul>\n")

            self._first_item = 0
```

The `characterData` callback (Example 7–48) is called by XP to pass characters to it. We use the `copyChars` method of the event object to copy the characters into our buffer and update the buffer size. The `getData` method instantiates a string from the buffer and returns it.

Finally, we use the `endDocument` callback (Example 7–49) to finish the HTML page.

Example 7–47. An RSS to HTML conversion implemented with XP (4 of 8)

```
def endElement(self, event):
    name = event.getName()
    if name == "title":
        self._title = self.getData()

    elif name == "link":
        self._link = self.getData()

    elif name == "descr":
        self._descr = self.getData()

    elif name == "channel":
        self._out.write(top % (self._title, self._link,
                               self._title))

        if self._descr != None:
            self._out.write("<p>%s</p>" % self._descr)

    elif name == "item":
        self._out.write('  <li><a href="%s">%s</a> %s\n' %
                        (self._link, self._title, self._descr or ""))
```

Example 7–48. An RSS to HTML conversion implemented with XP (5 of 8)

```
def characterData(self, event):
    event.copyChars(self._chararray, self._charlength)
    self._charlength = self._charlength + event.getLength()

def getData(self):
    return String(self._chararray, 0, self._charlength)
```

Example 7–49. An RSS to HTML conversion implemented with XP (6 of 8)

```
def endDocument(self):
    self._out.write("</ul>\n")
    self._out.write(bottom)
```

Example 7–50 takes a file name and a file-like output object and performs the conversion. The `EntityManagerImpl` object is used to create an `OpenEntity` object, from which XP (in the form of the `ParserImpl` object) can read.

Example 7–50. An RSS to HTML conversion implemented with XP (7 of 8)

```
# --- The driver

def convert(sysid, out):
    em = EntityManagerImpl()
    doc_entity = em.openFile(sysid)

    p = ParserImpl()
    p.setApplication(RSS2HTML(out))
    p.parseDocument(doc_entity)
```

Example 7–51 is identical to the xmlproc application code.

Example 7–51. An RSS to HTML conversion implemented with XP (8 of 8)

```
# --- The main program

sysid = sys.argv[1]
out   = open(sys.argv[2], "w")

convert(sysid, out)

out.close()
```

As these examples should show, using Java XML parsers in Jython is hardly any different from using Python XML parsers in CPython. The main difference is in handling Java arrays (this is actually the main trouble with the Java/Python interface), which is slightly awkward, but if handled in the way shown in Examples 7–44 to 7–51, it contributes to higher performance.

7.6 | Choosing a parser

When writing an XML application, and having decided that an event-based interface to parsed XML documents is preferred, an important decision remains: which one? One can choose to use the native API of one of the parsers, but this has the disadvantage of tying the application to that single parser, so the choice is obviously an important one. An alternative to this choice can be to use the SAX API (described in the following chapter), which enables applications to remain completely parser-independent. However, this benefit comes at the price of some lost functionality. Many XML parsers have extra features that are not available when accessing them through SAX.

As a general rule, I would not recommend using the native parser APIs unless the application needs functionality that is not available through SAX. However, sometimes this *is* needed, and then one must choose the right parser. When choosing a parser there are many possible criteria that can be used, and their importance depends on the specific application. The criteria listed below are considered to be the main ones:

speed
   Different parsers have quite different performance, so the parser choice can affect the overall performance of your application.

conformance
   Different programmers may interpret the specifications differently, and not all parsers are 100% complete, so the same XML document may be interpreted differently by different parsers. That the parser chosen conforms to the XML Recommendation is important to avoid unpleasant surprises.

size
   The size of the parsers differ quite substantially, so this can be important for some applications.

error messages

Some parsers have only a single error message ("Syntax error") while others provide more detailed diagnostics, some have localizeable error messages, some are better at recovering from errors, etc. etc. For some applications, for example validators meant for end users, this may be important.

features

Parsers differ in what they support of external entities, validation, catalog files, namespaces, access to DTD information, access to lexical information, etc.

Table 7–1 briefly summarizes the various features of the XML parsers available to Python programmers. More details on the speed of various parsers are available in 9.6.2.2, "Native APIs," on page 336.

Table 7–1   XML parsers available in Python

Parser	Where	Fast	Validating	Conformant	Other
Pyexpat	CPython	yes	no	yes	
xmllib	(J/)CPython	no	no	no	convenient
sgmlop	CPython	yes	no	no	convenient
xmlproc	J/CPython	no	yes	mostly	flexible, feature-complete
Xerces	Jython	yes	yes	yes	slightly awkward, big, and complex
XP	Jython	yes	no	yes	slightly awkward
Æ2	Jython	yes	yes	yes	slightly awkward, unusually compact code

SAX: an introduction

- Background
- Introduction
- The SAX classes
- Examples

# Chapter 8

T his chapter begins the coverage of SAX interfaces that will be continued in the next two chapters. In this chapter only the background and history of SAX, as well as the most important interfaces, are covered. The next chapter will show more of the techniques for SAX programming, while the last chapter will cover more advanced topics and parts of the APIs.

8.1 | Background and history

As the XML Recommendation was being finished, the readers of the XML-DEV mailing list, including many people who had been active in creating the XML Recommendation, felt that there was something missing from the list of XML specifications planned at that time. There were a number of different XML parsers in Java available at that time, which all did more or less the same thing, and they all had very similar APIs. The previous chapter should show a similar situation rather clearly: the APIs of Pyexpat, xmlproc, XP and to some extent also xmllib, differ only in small details. For this reason it was decided to design a common API for XML parsers in Java to make it possible to write XML applications and utilities that do not depend on a specific XML parser, but instead are able to work with all parsers.

The W3C was at that time busily working on the Document Object Model (DOM) (see Part Three, "Tree-based processing," on page 394), which could in a sense have filled this role. However, the XML-DEV participants felt that in addition to the DOM something simpler and more lower-level was needed. Also, the XML-DEV participants were impatient for something that could be used immediately, and were disinclined to wait for the DOM. (The DOM was not finished until 5 months after SAX.)

The need for something like SAX had started to make itself felt in the summer of 1997, and suggestions for a common API had surfaced with regular intervals after that. Various suggestions had floated around, as had the name XAPI-J. In the end David Megginson simply stepped forward in January 1998 and nominated himself as chairperson of the design process. He structured the discussion by posting a set of questions to the list, each in a separate email, and the ensuing discussion was long and highly productive. Among the participants were parser writers, specification editors, XML application developers, and many others.

The interface was gradually refined, through proposals from David and counter-proposals from various list readers, and eventually a design was chosen and an implementation done by David Megginson. This was debugged and refined in several stages, and finally frozen on 11 May 1998. During the discussions, the name "Simple API for XML," or SAX, was eventually chosen, after a long and hard debate and a vote among the list members. The main implementors of XML parsers, such as Megginson himself, James Clark, Tim Bray, and several others, very quickly implemented SAX drivers for their parsers. The result was that when IBM, Oracle, Sun, and the Apache XML Project later released XML parsers they also implemented SAX drivers for their parsers. Today, nearly all Java XML parsers implement SAX.

Interoperability between these parsers has been good, right from the beginning. In fact, when Peter Murray-Rust (one of the two initial maintainers of the XML-DEV list) added SAX support to Jumbo, the first XML browser, after the release of SAX, he created a menu where the user could choose which XML parser to use.

The design and subsequent adoption of SAX is something almost unknown in the history of XML: a specification designed by a set of volunteers with no formal organization and later almost universally adopted by individuals and corporations alike. Today SAX has been ported to Python and Perl, a port to C++ is being discussed, and SAX version 2.0 has been completed. (More about SAX 2.0 later.)

Most of the general discussion of SAX in this book applies to both versions 1.0 and 2.0, while the interfaces shown are those of SAX 2.0, which, in some cases, are identical to those of SAX 1.0. Comments that are specific to SAX 1.0 will be labeled as such.

Note that David Megginson maintains the official SAX site at `http://www.megginson.com/SAX/`.

8.2 | Introduction

The role that SAX now plays in the collection of XML specifications is as a simple low-level common API for XML parsers, and like the interfaces we looked at in the previous chapter, it is event-based. SAX has consciously been designed to be light-weight, simple, and low-level and hardly any concessions to ease of use have been made in the design. Because of this, it is almost trivial to add support for it to most parsers, and the performance impact is usually negligible. The result is that today SAX is supported by nearly all XML parsers in the languages to which SAX has been ported.

In the family of XML specifications, however, SAX also plays another role that is not as well known. In nearly all applications SAX has now become the API that sits between the code that does nothing but parse and anything built on top of this, regardless of whether that is another general processing system or an end-user application. This means that SAX now serves as a common API to the point in a system where XML data enters the system.

Because of this SAX is the de facto standard for event-based representations of XML documents. In other words, SAX can be used to pass documents between applications, to generate XML documents from non-XML sources and enter them into applications, and, in short, wherever XML document contents need to be represented. Later chapters will illustrate the consequences of this in more depth.

In essence, the SAX application model consists of three parts: an XML parser, a SAX driver for that parser, and the application developed by the user. The relationships between these parts are shown in Figure 8–1.

Figure 8–1   A model of SAX applications

As the figure shows, not only does the parser pass information to the application, but the application also sets parameters on the parser and starts parsing.

This model is similar to the basic XML processing model we saw in Figure 2–1; the only thing that is really new is the appearance of a SAX driver between the parser and the application. This driver encapsulates the parser and presents an implementation of the SAX API to the application, while in reality the parser itself may have a rather different interface.[1] One benefit of this approach is that if the parser developer does not provide a SAX interface, anyone can write a driver for that

---

1.   Today, many parsers implement the SAX API directly, rather than use a driver approach.

parser and thus use it in SAX applications anyway. This is in fact what David Megginson did when he released a sample package of SAX drivers, including one for MSXML, the Microsoft XML parser.

8.2.1 *What SAX does*

SAX provides a low-level basic API to an XML parser and only that; it hardly makes any concessions to convenience at all. Instead, the guiding principle behind the design is that SAX should be as low-level and lightweight as possible, allowing more convenient APIs, or processing frameworks, to be built on top of it. The benefit of this approach is that it allows such frameworks to be built in a parser-independent fashion, and allows for more than one such framework to be built on top of this parser-independent layer, which means developers can try out different ideas of how to build frameworks. At the same time it minimizes the amount of work necessary for parser writers.

Another reason to build SAX this way is that it enables SAX to be the common API for event-based representation of XML documents, as described earlier. This could be used in moving them from the parser to the application, when transmitting documents between applications, and when writing out the document. To enable such uses, a framework must not incur undue performance costs and must not require applications to implement anything that is not really necessary.

Both the Python and Java versions of SAX have been designed with this in mind, while the Perl version of SAX was built with a focus on convenience. This means that the Perl version of SAX cannot be used in to transmit documents in this way, but also that it is much more convenient to use. Python programmers who want something similar should look at saxtracker, described in 8.4.1, "RSS to HTML converter," on page 258, and eventdom, described in 22.2.2, "eventdom," on page 877.

SAX 1.0 provides access to all logical information about a document as described in the XML 1.0 Recommendation, as well as customization of external entity resolution and complete parser independence. Before very long, however, it was realized that this was not enough. Further requirements included:

- access to most of the lexical information about a document,
- access to all logical information about the DTD of a document, as well as some of its lexical information,
- support for namespaces,
- support for standardized extensibility.

To meet these requirements, SAX 2.0 was defined by more or less the same group of people that defined SAX 1.0, still led by David Megginson. SAX 2.0 adds support for namespaces and extensibility, but support for the lexical and DTD parts of the API proved rather more difficult to reach consensus on. Due to this problem, the lexical and DTD support was separated out into a package called SAX 2.0-ext, using the core support for standardized extensibility. This meant that they could be used with the SAX 2.0 core without modifying it, and without being part of it. (You'll see how later.)

Since SAX 1.0 is now effectively obsolete, this book uses SAX 2.0 exclusively, but, as mentioned earlier, nearly all of the general comments apply equally to both versions.

8.2.2   *SAX parsers*

At the moment there are quite a few SAX 2.0 parsers available to Python programmers. Table 8–1 gives a quick overview of those available at the time of writing. It is likely that this list will be extended with time, so it may no longer be complete by the time you read this.

The `drv_javasax` driver makes Java SAX parsers available to Jython programs through the Python SAX interface. It is essentially a wrapper around the Java SAX API. SP is an SGML parser, more information on which you can find in 24.2.1, "SP," on page 955.

Table 8–1   SAX 2.0 parser drivers in Python

Parser	*Driver*	*Distribution*
Pyexpat	`xml.sax.expatreader`	with Python 2.0
xmlproc	`xml.sax.drivers2.drv_xmlproc`	with xmlproc (and PyXML)
Java SAX	`xml.sax.drivers2.drv_javasax`	PyXML
Pirxx	`pirxx`	`pirxx`
SP	`xml.saxtools.drivers.drv_pysp`	SP

8.2.3   *An overview of SAX*

A SAX application can consist of many different objects, some of them written by the parser developer and some by the application developer. Figure 8–2 shows the main objects that can be involved in a SAX application, with the objects supplied by the parser developer filled with gray. (The support for lexical and DTD information mentioned above has been left out from this diagram.)

The ellipses in this figure do not necessarily represent individual objects, but rather *roles* (or responsibilities). That is, each ellipse represents an interface with a certain responsibility, but in actual applications a single object may implement more than one interface. The interfaces should be thought of as distinct roles that objects may play in an application.

XMLReader
>   This is the parser driver, which provides the interface to the parser. It has methods to start parsing, set handlers, and configure the parser. The XMLReader interface is an instance of the design pattern known as Adapter.[1]

---

1.   The best book on design patterns is *Design Patterns*, by Gamma, Helm, Johnson, and Vlissides, published by Addison-Wesley in 1994 (ISBN 0–201–63361–2).

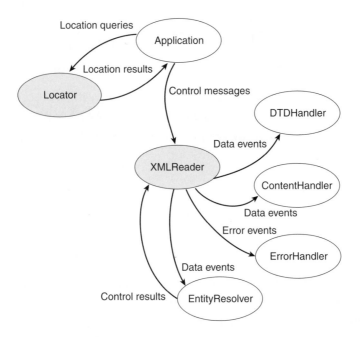

Figure 8–2   A model of SAX applications

Application

This is not an object in the same way as the other ellipses are, it is simply meant to represent the parts of your application that are not SAX objects. (There is no SAX interface or class named `Application`.) This is typically the code that starts parsing, registers handlers, and makes use of the information from SAX objects.

ContentHandler

This is the main handler in SAX, the one that receives document content events, and the one most often used. All logical document content is reported to this handler. In SAX 1.0 the corresponding handler was called `DocumentHandler`.

ErrorHandler

This handler receives notification of errors and decides what to do with them. It can handle the errors in whatever way it pleases. It may ignore them, print them to the console, create dialog boxes, or even stop parsing by throwing an exception.

EntityResolver

This object is used by the parser to map external entity references onto data sources from which the parser can read document content. This can be useful to control how the parser accesses document storage.

Locator

This object, if present, can tell you the current location in the document. You can only trust this object to return correct information during event calls. This object is usually the same as the XMLReader object.

DTDHandler

This handler is notified of notation declarations and declarations of unparsed entities in the parts of the DTD seen by the parser. It is not useful unless your application actually uses these features.[1] Support for this handler is required in SAX because it is required by the XML Recommendation that XML parsers make this information available to applications.[2]

8.2.4   *A very simple example*

Before we go into the details of the SAX interface, this section demonstrates a very simple example, one that counts the number of elements in a document. The application takes the file name of the document from the command line.

---

1.   Unparsed entities are an SGML feature intended to be used for referencing non-SGML files from SGML documents. A typical usage would be for including images in documents.

2.   See the XML Recommendation, Sections 4 (third paragraph), 4.7 (last paragraph), and 4.4.6.

Example 8–1. A very simple SAX application

```
from xml.sax import parse, handler
import sys

# --- ContentHandler

class ExampleApp(handler.ContentHandler):

    def __init__(self):
        self._count = 0

    def startElement(self, name, attrs):
        self._count = self._count + 1

    def endDocument(self):
        print "There were ", self._count, " elements."

# --- Main program

parse(sys.argv[1], ExampleApp())
```

To read Example 8–1, it is best to start at the bottom, under the "Main program" comment. Here a function in the SAX package (described in 8.3.5, "The xml.sax module," on page 256) is used to parse the file given in the command-line argument, passing events to our ContentHandler.

The actual application is implemented by a simple ContentHandler, which counts the number of times the startElement method is called. Finally, when endDocument is called, it prints the number of elements found. The whole process of counting is driven by the parser, which calls the methods of the handler as it parses the document.

8.3 | The SAX classes

This section, together with 10.1, "The advanced parts of the API," on page 339 and 10.2, "Parser filters," on page 360, describes the entire SAX 2.0 API. This section covers the core SAX 2.0 API, while the other two sections describe the more advanced parts of the API. The SAX 2.0 API lives in the `xml.sax` package in Python. The Java version is described in Chapter 19, "SAX in Java," on page 704.

The Python version of SAX 2.0 is divided into the following modules:

`xml.sax`

This module holds convenience functions for starting parsing as well as a bootstrap function for creating parsers.

`xml.sax._exceptions`

This module holds the SAX exception classes.

`xml.sax.expatreader`

This module holds the SAX driver for the Pyexpat parser. It is mentioned here because it is the only driver that is distributed with Python 2.0.

`xml.sax.handler`

This module holds the base classes of the SAX handlers and the symbolic constants for the extension properties and features.

`xml.sax.saxutils`

This module holds various utilities useful for working with SAX.

`xml.sax.xmlreader`

This module holds the `XMLReader` class and related classes.

`xml.sax.drivers2`

This package holds various drivers for parsers other than Pyexpat. It is not distributed with Python 2.0, but comes with the PyXML package.

The following sections describe the main interfaces and classes contained in these modules in more detail.

8.3.1   *The* XMLReader *interface*

The XMLReader object represents the parser, although in many cases it may only be a wrapper around the actual parser. Note that the XMLReader object does not have to really be an XML parser; it can be anything that is capable of producing SAX events from some data source. This can be something that walks a document tree to produce output events, a parser of some notation other than XML that maps this notation to XML, an object that reads from a database, and so on.

The XMLReader interface allows the application to set handlers, set parameters for the parsing, and start parsing. The name has been chosen because SAX 1.0 already used the name Parser and to emphasize that the object does not really need to be a parser, as long as it can emit SAX events.

parse(source)

This method makes the parser start parsing and does not return until the entire document has been parsed or parsing has been terminated because of errors. Effectively, nearly all that happens in a SAX application is driven from this method, which is where the controlling loop will be for as long as the document is being parsed.

The source argument is used by the parser to find out where to read the document from. It can be either a string (filename or URL) or an InputSource object. (The InputSource class is described in 10.1.3, "The InputSource class," on page 341.) The method may raise IOError or SAXException exceptions. The application is allowed to call the method more than once on the same parser instance, but it is not allowed to call it while a parse is in progress.

To parse more than one document at the same time, for example in different threads, the application can create two separate XMLReader instances, one for each document.

setContentHandler(handler)

This method registers a ContentHandler with the parser, which means that during parsing the parser will send document events to the given object. A parser can only have one ContentHandler instance attached to it, but it is allowed to change handlers during parsing. If no `ContentHandler` is registered, document events will be silently ignored.

Applications that want more than one `ContentHandler` to receive events during the same parse can register a single `ContentHandler` instance that propagates events to all the other instances.

setErrorHandler(handler)

This method registers the `ErrorHandler` with the parser, and works exactly like `setContentHandler`. If no error handler is registered, any error will cause parsing to terminate.

setDTDHandler(handler)

This method registers the `DTDHandler` with the parser, and works exactly like `setContentHandler`. If no handler is registered, these events are silently ignored.

setEntityResolver(resolver)

This method registers the `EntityResolver` with the parser, and works exactly like `setContentHandler`. If no resolver is registered, the parser will use its own mechanisms for resolving public and system identifiers.

setLocale(locale)

This method allows applications to tell the parser which locale it is operating in. This is mainly useful for getting error messages in the right language. The `locale` argument must hold a two-letter ISO 639 language code as a string. This means that to get English error messages one must use `'en'` and to get Norwegian ones, `'no'`. The ISO 639 standard can be found at `http://lcweb.loc.gov/standards/iso639-2/`.

At the time of writing, the only parser supporting this is xmlproc, but when using Java XML parsers with SAX, the argument will be passed through to the Java SAX driver, which may or may not support this. Parsers which do not support this method or the requested locale will raise a `SAXException`.

`getContentHandler()`
> Returns the current `ContentHandler`.

`getErrorHandler()`
> Returns the current `ErrorHandler`.

`getDTDHandler()`
> Returns the current `DTDHandler`.

`getEntityResolver()`
> Returns the current `EntityResolver`.

In addition to these methods there are the methods that provide extensibility support. These are described below in 10.1.7, "SAX 2.0 extensibility support," on page 346.

8.3.2   *The* `ContentHandler` *interface*

This is the main class and the one you will be spending the most time on when writing SAX applications. The `ContentHandler` is the object that receives document content from the parser and does something useful with it. All the other SAX classes are really only supporting classes for getting the right information into this class and dealing with problems that may prevent the information from getting to the `ContentHandler`.

When writing a SAX application you can implement a `ContentHandler` in one of two ways:

- You can subclass `ContentHandler` and provide implementations of the methods you need. `ContentHandler` has empty implementations of all methods and so events you don't implement will be ignored.

- You can write your own class which implements all the methods in the ContentHandler interface. Since Python does not have static typing, this will work fine as long as all the methods are present and have the signatures that SAX expects.

The ContentHandler methods are:

startDocument()

This method is called when parsing begins, before any of the other methods in the ContentHandler, except setDocumentLocator. It simply signals that parsing has begun, and is mainly useful for initialization.

In many simple applications this method isn't really necessary, since in such applications you can usually do whatever initialization you want before you call parse. However, when writing application-independent ContentHandler components, this method may be useful to initialize the component in a way that is independent of the environment it is used in.

endDocument()

This is startDocument's twin that is called when parsing ends after the whole document has been parsed, and that is the last method called during a parse. It is even less used than startDocument, but with standalone ContentHandlers it can be very useful for book-keeping, for example for checking the provided information for completeness and ensuring that all references inside a document actually pointed to something that appeared in the document.

startElement(name, attrs)

This method is called to notify the application that now another element begins, so it is effectively called every time the parser sees a start-tag. The name parameter contains the element type name and the attrs parameter contains the attributes as an instance of the Attributes class, described in 8.3.3, "The Attributes interface," on page 253.

This event, and its twin `endElement`, are the application's only source of information about the element structure of the document, so it is crucial for SAX applications. The `startElement` and `endElement` calls will appear in pairs, mirroring the occurrences of start- and end-tags in the document.

Empty elements are reported as a `startElement` call immediately followed by a corresponding `endElement` call. This means that it is impossible to distinguish '`<elem></elem>`' from '`<elem/>`' when using SAX. This is, however, as it should be, since this is a lexical distinction that has nothing to do with the logical document content. In fact, the Infoset does not even include this distinction as an optional information item.

It should be noted that in namespace mode SAX uses `startElementNS` and `endElementNS` rather than `startElement` and `endElement`. The namespace support is rather complex, however, so it is not described until 10.1.8, "SAX 2.0 and namespaces," on page 351.

`endElement(name)`

This method notifies the application of the end of an element, and must match a previous `startElement` event. The attributes and content of the element are not available during this call, but have been made available through previous calls, so if the application needs this information at this point it must have recorded it from the previous calls.

This style of programming is inconvenient, but is a consequence of the low-level design approach chosen for SAX. However, there are various ways of dealing with this problem; some of them are described in 9.2.1, "Acting after the event," on page 274.

`characters(data)`

This method is called to notify the application of character data in the document. The XML Recommendation requires all whitespace in the document to be reported to the application,[1] so all whitespace in the document will be included in these calls.[2] The content of the characters event can be found in the `data` string.

There is one strange thing about `characters` that is very important to remember: The character data inside an element may be reported in more than one `characters` call, even though it might appear as a continuous piece of character data in the document. This splitting will usually happen when text pieces have entity references, CDATA marked sections, character references, or comments in them.

It can also happen for other reasons, however. Most XML parsers keep an internal buffer of characters from which they read the document. In most cases, if parsers reach the end of the buffer while reading character data they will just report the data they have seen so far, and then refill the buffer from their data source, repeating the process on that buffer.

This means that SAX applications which rely on character data to arrive in a single piece can work perfectly for long periods of time, before suddenly unexpectedly missing out pieces of data. This will almost certainly happen silently, with no error message, so it is very important to be aware of this problem. There are also ways around this problem, which will be presented in the next chapters.

`ignorableWhitespace(data)`

This method is nearly the same as `characters` and is also called for character data. Some parsers will call this method for the contents of elements that they know (by reading the DTD) can only have elements and whitespace inside them. (This was described in more detail in 2.4.2.1, "How the DTD affects the document," on page 69.)

---

1.   See the XML Recommendation, Section 2.10, second paragraph.

2.   It is worth noting that according to the XML Information Set, the whitespace outside the document element is *not* considered part of the document, and thus is not reported.

The XML Recommendation requires validating parsers to report such whitespace in a way that distinguishes it from other kinds of character data,[1] so SAX has a dedicated method for this content. This makes it easy for the vast majority of applications that do not need this information to ignore it, avoiding expensive checks to see which element the characters belong to.

It is worth noting, however, that not all parsers use this method. The driver for the validating parser in xmlproc does this, as do many of the Java parsers. Some non-validating parsers also call this method, but they can of course do so only to the extent that they have read the DTD's subsets.

`processingInstruction(target, data)`

This method is called for each processing instruction in the document. The `target` parameter contains the PI target name (the name that appears before the first whitespace inside the PI) and the `data` parameter contains the rest of the PI.

`setDocumentLocator(locator)`

This method is called before parsing begins (and before `start-Document`), if the parser provides location information. In this case, the `locator` parameter will contain an object implementing the `Locator` interface (described in 10.1.6, "The `Locator` interface," on page 345). This object can be used to get the current position in the document during parsing. If this method is not called it means that no location information is available.

`skippedEntity(name)`

This method is called for external general entities that are not parsed by the parser. They may be skipped because the parser never reads external entities, because it has been configured not to do so, or because it has not read the entity declaration, which may have

---

1.   See the XML Recommendation, Section 2.10, second paragraph.

appeared in the external DTD subset. The `name` parameter contains the name of the skipped entity.

There is no callback method for comments in the `ContentHandler` interface, since SAX considers comments to be lexical details that do not belong in the `ContentHandler`.

8.3.3 *The* `Attributes` *interface*

The `Attributes` class is used to pass collections of attribute values to applications in the `startElement` event. In a sense, this could be said to be a breach of the otherwise purely event-based mode of SAX, but for reasons of efficiency and practicality it was decided to make the start of an element a single event. It is in any case hard to envision any real benefits from having one method call per attribute on the start-tag.

It is worth noting that SAX allows parsers to reuse a single `Attributes` instance across different `startElement` calls in order to avoid costly reinstantiation. This means that `Attributes` instances that have been stored away by the application for later use may stop returning the correct values once the `startElement` call they arrived on has ended. To safely store `Attributes` instances, it is necessary to call their `copy` method to obtain stable copies.

The methods of the `Attributes` interface are given below. Note that they are rather different from those of Java SAX.

`getLength()`
    Returns the number of attributes in the list.

`getValue(name)`
    Returns the value of the attribute with name `name`. If it does not exist, the `KeyError` exception will be raised. If it exists, the value will be a string.

getNames()

> Returns a list of the names of all the attributes that appeared on the element.

getType(name)

> Returns the attribute type of the attribute with the given name. The type is one of 'CDATA', 'ID', 'IDREF', 'IDREFS', 'NMTOKEN', 'NMTOKENS', 'ENTITY', 'ENTITIES', or 'NOTATION', and is always in upper case. Enumerated attribute types that are not notation types will be reported as 'NMTOKEN'.
>
> It is important to be aware that not all parsers will read the external DTD subset, so some parsers may not know the attribute type of all attributes. For attributes for which the attribute type is unknown, the parser will return 'CDATA'.

In addition to the methods inherited from Java SAX, Python Attributes instances can also be treated like a Python dictionary. This means that the familiar keys, has_key, values, items, copy, and get methods will work as they would with a dictionary mapping attribute names to values. Note also that the interface has some additional methods that are only meaningful in namespace mode. These are listed in 10.1.8, "SAX 2.0 and namespaces," on page 351.

In addition, the len function will return the number of attributes, and the index syntax will map attribute names to values. This means that for printing the name-value pairs in an Attributes instance, all the methods shown in Example 8–2 will work.

8.3.4   *The* ErrorHandler *interface*

The ErrorHandler object is used by the parser to report problems back to the application. Every time the parser finds a problem in the document it will call a method on the provided ErrorHandler object. Problems can range from warnings about potential problems through non-fatal errors (usually validity errors) to fatal errors (usually a well-formedness error). The design of the SAX ErrorHandler class is very

Example 8–2. Using the `Attributes` object

```
# using items
for (name, value) in attrs.items():
    print name, "=", value

# using keys
for name in attrs.keys():
    print name, "=", attrs[name]

# using Attributes methods
for name in attrs.getNames():
    print name, "=", attrs.getValue(name)
```

similar to the corresponding class in the xmlproc API, for the simple reason that the xmlproc design was strongly influenced by the design of SAX.

One might perhaps expect parsers to raise exceptions when they encountered problems, but in most programming languages this would mean losing the original execution context and make it impossible for the application to continue after the problem report. For this reason the `ErrorHandler` interface was designed to allow applications to make this decision themselves. However, parsers are allowed to stop parsing after reporting a fatal error.

It is worth noting that the XML Recommendation explicitly forbids parsers to continue passing document data to the application after a well-formedness error.[1] Also, in the face of well-formedness errors many parsers, among them expat, will refuse to continue parsing. Others will continue, but stop passing data events and only pass error events, while still others can be configured to keep passing data events for those applications that need this facility.

What to do with the error information passed to the `ErrorHandler` is up to the application. It can choose to ignore them, print them to `sys.stderr`, write them to a file, or display them in a GUI. More

---

1.　See the XML Recommendation, Section 1.2, the definition of "fatal error".

information about how to use error handlers is given in 9.5.2, "How to write an error handler," on page 319.

The `ErrorHandler` methods are:

`warning(exc)`

> This method is called to inform the application of a potential problem, something that the XML Recommendation may consider an error only "for interoperability,"[1] potentially troublesome DTD declarations, or perhaps use of obsolete and no-longer supported syntaxes.
>
> The exc parameter will hold a `SAXException` object (described in 10.1.1, "The `SAXException` exception," on page 339), which can be queried for information. The application can also `raise` the object and thus end parsing.

`error(exc)`

> This method is called to inform the application of a non-fatal error, such as a validity error. The exc parameter holds a `SAXException`.

`fatalError(exc)`

> This method is called to inform the application of a fatal error, such as a well-formedness error or a failure to find the document. The exc parameter holds a `SAXException`.

8.3.5 *The* `xml.sax` *module*

This module holds three useful functions, which can be used to start applications:

`parse(source, c_handler, e_handler = None)`

> Calling this function makes SAX create the default parser, register the given `ContentHandler`, and start parsing the given document. The source argument is a string or an `InputSource`, just as with

---

1.   Defined in Section 1.2 of the XML Recommendation.

the `parse` method of the `XMLReader`. If an `ErrorHandler` is given as the optional third argument, that too will be registered before parsing begins.

`parseString(string, c_handler, e_handler = None)`
This is exactly the same as `parse`, except that it parses the given `string` parameter as an XML document.

`make_parser(parser_list = [])`
This function will create and return an `XMLReader` object. If the `parser_list` is given, it must be a list of the module names of SAX 2.0 drivers. The function will then attempt to instantiate each driver and return the first it manages to instantiate. If it can't instantiate any of the given parsers (or if none are given), it will instantiate the default, which is expat.

The default parser can be overridden in CPython by setting the environment variable `PY_SAX_PARSER` to the module name of the wanted driver. In Jython this can be done via the `python.xml.sax.parser` property. This value can also be a comma-separated list of module names.

A third possibility is to modify the value of the `default_parser_list` variable in the `xml.sax` module directly.

The parser list that results from all this will begin with the contents of `parser_list` followed by the parsers specified in `PY_SAX_PARSER` and finally with Pyexpat as the last fallback.

Note that both `parse` and `parseString` use `make_parser` to create the parser they use, which means that any SAX application that uses one of these three functions to create its parser can be influenced in its choice of parser in the same way.

8.4 | Two example applications

This section contains two complete SAX applications that are included in order to help the reader organize the understanding of the APIs presented so far. In addition to these examples, the following chapter holds many more examples.

8.4.1   *RSS to HTML converter*

Example 8–3 shows the by now very familiar RSS to HTML converter, this time written using SAX. It is included mostly for comparison with the other implementations of this utility in the previous chapter, and there is nothing really new about this implementation.

Example 8–3. The SAX RSS to HTML converter

```
import sys, codecs
from xml.sax import handler, parse

# --- Templates

top = \
"""
<!DOCTYPE HTML PUBLIC "-//W3C//DTD HTML 4.0 Transitional//EN">
<HTML>
<HEAD>
  <TITLE>%s</TITLE>
</HEAD>

<BODY>
<A HREF="%s"><H1>%s</H1></A>
"""
```

```
bottom = \
"""
<HR>

<ADDRESS>
Converted to HTML using SAX 2.0.
</ADDRESS>

</BODY>
</HTML>
"""


# --- ContentHandler

class RSS2HTMLHandler(handler.ContentHandler):

    def __init__(self, out = None):
        self._out = out or sys.stdout

        # tracking state
        self._data = ""
        self._first_item = 1
        self._top_done = 0

        self._title = None
        self._link = None
        self._descr = None

    def startElement(self, name, attrs):
        self._data = ""

        if (not self._top_done) and \
           (name == "item" or name == "image"):
            self._out.write(top % (self._title, self._link,
                                   self._title))

            if self._descr != None:
                self._out.write("<p>%s</p>" % self._descr)

            self._top_done = 1
        elif name == "item":
            self._descr = None # reset for this item
            if self._first_item:
                self._out.write("\n<ul>\n")

            self._first_item = 0
```

```
    def endElement(self, name):
        if name == "title":
            self._title = self._data

        elif name == "link":
            self._link = self._data
        elif name == "description":
            self._descr = self._data

        elif name == "item":
            self._out.write('  <li><a href="%s">%s</a> %s\n' %
                        (self._link, self._title, self._descr or ""))

    def endDocument(self):
        self._out.write("</ul>\n")
        self._out.write(bottom)

    def characters(self, chars):
        self._data = self._data + chars

# --- Conversion function

def htmlconv(infile, out):
    outf = codecs.open(out, "w", "iso-8859-1")
    parse(infile, RSS2HTMLHandler(outf))
    outf.close()

# --- Main program

if __name__ == "__main__":
    import sys
    htmlconv(sys.argv[1], sys.argv[2])
```

8.4.2   *Statistics collector*

This section describes a SAX application that gathers statistics about
an XML document. It counts the number of occurrences of each element type, attribute, and processing instruction target, as well as the
average length of each attribute. In Examples 8–4 to 8–6, the complete
source code of the application is presented.

Example 8–4 is the SAX `ContentHandler`, which collects the information about the document. As can be seen, for each element it increases the count of its type, and then does the same with each of the attribute instances on that element. The handling of processing instructions is similar. The `report` method is called by the application to print the collected statistics.

Example 8–4. A SAX statistics collector (1 of 3)

```
# This application processes documents to gather statistical
# information about them.

import sys
import operator

from xml.sax import parse, handler

# ====== SAX APPLICATION

# --- ContentHandler

class StatsHandler(handler.ContentHandler):

    def __init__(self):
        self._elems       = {}
        self._attrs       = {}
        self._attrlengths = {}
        self._pis         = {}
        self._pilengths   = {}

    def startElement(self, name, attrs):
        self._elems[name] = self._elems.get(name, 0) + 1
        for (aname, value) in attrs.items():
            self._attrs[(name, aname)] = \
                self._attrs.get((name, aname), 0) + 1
            self._attrlengths[(name, aname)] = \
                self._attrlengths.get((name, aname), 0) + len(value)

    def processingInstruction(self, target, data):
        self._pis[target] = self._pis.get(target, 0) + 1
        self._pilengths[target] = \
                        self._pilengths.get(target, 0) + len(data)
```

```
def report(self):
    print "===== DOCUMENT REPORT"
    print
    print "---ELEMENT TYPES"
    print "%20s    %5s" % ("Type", "Count")
    for (name, count) in self._elems.items():
        print "%20s    %5s" % (name, count)
    print

    print "---ATTRIBUTES"
    attrs = self._attrs.keys()
    attrs.sort()
    format = "%20s    %20s    %5s    %5s"
    print format % ("Element","Attribute","Occur","Avgln")
    for (ename, aname) in attrs:
        count = self._attrs[(ename, aname)]
        print format % (ename, aname, count,
                        self._attrlengths[(ename, aname)] / count)
    print

    print "---PI TARGETS"
    print "%20s    %5s" % ("Type", "Count")
    for (name, count) in self._pis.items():
        print "%20s    %5s" % (name, count)
    print
```

Example 8–5 is the error handler of the application, which simply counts the number of errors of each kind and produces a report of these numbers.

Example 8–7 shows the output after running the application on a simple RSS document.

8.5 | Python SAX utilities

In addition to the core SAX API covered in the previous section, Python SAX has another module (xml.sax.saxutils) which contains various utilities that make life easier for the SAX developer. Among these, there are two functions listed below.

Example 8–5. A SAX statistics collector (2 of 3)

```
# --- ErrorHandler

class CountErrors:

    def __init__(self):
        self._warnings = 0
        self._errors   = 0
        self._fatals   = 0

    def error(self, exception):
        self._errors = self._errors + 1

    def fatalError(self, exception):
        self._fatals = self._fatals + 1

    def warning(self, exception):
        self._warnings = self._warnings + 1

    def report(self):
        print "---ERRORS"
        print "Warnings      ",self._warnings
        print "Errors        ",self._errors
        print "Fatal errors",self._fatals
        print
```

Example 8–6. A SAX statistics collector (3 of 3)

```
# --- Main program

stats = StatsHandler()
errors = CountErrors()

p = parse(sys.argv[1], stats, errors)

stats.report()
errors.report()
```

escape(data, entities = {})
>   Escapes all occurrences of &, <, and > with the predefined XML entities for these characters. The entities argument can hold a dictionary mapping additional characters to replacement values.

Example 8–7. The output of running the stats application

```
===== DOCUMENT REPORT

---ELEMENT TYPES
                Type      Count
                 rss          1
             channel          1
               title          4
         description          2
                link          4
                item          3


---ATTRIBUTES
            Element                  Attribute     Occur      AvgLn
                rss                    version         1          4

---PI TARGETS
                Type      Count

---ERRORS
Warnings     0
Errors       0
Fatal errors 0
```

This function is very useful when writing XML output, since it handles the troublesome business of escaping illegal characters.

`prepare_input_source(source, base = '')`
  Returns an `InputSource` object (see 10.1.3, "The `InputSource` class," on page 341) that has a byte stream that can be read from. The `source` argument can be a string holding a file name or a URI, a file-like object, or an `InputSource` object. The `base` argument holds the base URI against which the `source` will be resolved if it is a string holding a relative path or URI.

  This function is generally used by `XMLReader` implementations to interpret the argument to the `parse` method.

8.5.1 *The* XMLGenerator *class*

The XMLGenerator class is a ContentHandler implementation that uses the events it receives to write an XML document corresponding to those events to a file-like object. This can be used to write SAX event streams to file and also as a utility for generating XML documents.

The only method that is different from those of ContentHandler is the constructor:

```
XMLGenerator(out = sys.stdout,
   encoding = 'iso-8859-1')
```
Creates an XMLGenerator object that writes to the out parameter. The encoding argument is what will appear in the XML declaration it produces.

With this class it becomes trivial to write a SAX application that reads in an XML document and writes it back out in normalized form. That is, it writes out another document that is logically equivalent, but not necessarily lexically equivalent. The source code is given in Example 8–8.

Example 8–8. An XML normalizer

```
import sys
from xml.sax import parse, saxutils

parse(sys.argv[1], saxutils.XMLGenerator())
```

Example 8–9 shows an example XML document that will be processed with this normalization application.

When this program is run on this document, it produces the output shown in Example 8–10, which is equivalent logically, but different lexically rather. This is because the parser (and the SAX interface) has hidden all the lexical information from the XMLGenerator.

Example 8–9. Input to the normalizer

```
<doc version    = '1.0'
     other-attr = '2.0'>
<![CDATA[Simon & Schuster]]>

This should become an '&#65;'.
</doc>
```

Example 8–10. Output from the normalizer

```
<?xml version="1.0" encoding="iso-8859-1"?>
<doc version="1.0" other-attr="2.0">
Simon &amp; Schuster

This should become an 'A'.
</doc>
```

Using SAX

- An introduction to XBEL

- Thinking in SAX

- Application-specific data representations

- Some example applications

- Tips and tricks

- Speed

T his chapter explains in more detail how to use the parts of SAX that you have learned so far to write SAX applications. It explains the techniques that can be used and the different ways to structure SAX applications, and also covers issues such as error handling and performance. Before we move on to this, however, the next section introduces XBEL, an XML application that will be used in examples throughout the book, just like RSS.

9.1 | An introduction to XBEL

The idea for XBEL comes from Mark Hammond, who one day posted an email to the Python XML-SIG suggesting that it might be a useful learning exercise to develop an XML DTD for storing Microsoft Internet Explorer bookmarks in XML. He was quickly joined by other members of the XML-SIG who extended the concept to cover all browsers and, under the leadership of Fred L. Drake, Jr., developed a fully documented and well-considered XML DTD.

Software for conversions between the XBEL DTD and the different file formats of various browsers was quickly developed, and Fred Drake even adopted XBEL as the native bookmark notation of the Grail Web browser (which is written in pure Python). The main application area of XBEL is exchange of bookmarks between different browsers. Using XBEL one can convert back and forth between bookmark files from MSIE, Netscape, Opera, and Lynx.

Another interesting way to use XBEL is to maintain a set of links in an XBEL document (which may well be hand-written; XBEL is easy to author manually). This document can then be automatically converted into HTML as part of the site. However, it can also be converted into bookmark files for the various browsers, something that allows users to load the bookmarks into their own bookmark collections. This can be an interesting addition to a link collection Web site or to a talk on a specific topic that includes a large number of URLs. (An XBEL document with all the URLs given in this book can be found on the CD-ROM at `data/xbel/book-urls.xml`.)

9.1.1 *The structure of XBEL documents*

Example 9–1 shows a short hand-written XBEL document. Hand-written XBEL documents differ from their auto-generated counterparts in that they often contain descriptions and that they hardly ever contain the `added`, `visited`, and `modified` attributes on folders and URLs. These attributes give the time at which the actions were last performed on a node (where node is a common term for bookmarks and folders).

Example 9–1 shows nearly all of XBEL, except for the already mentioned attributes, the `id` attribute on nodes, and some minor extra element types, which are listed below:

`separator`

    This element type is used to indicate separators like those supported by Netscape bookmarks. It has no contents, no attributes and can appear anywhere nodes can.

Example 9–1. An example XBEL document

```
<xbel>
<title>My bookmark collection</title>
<desc>
This is my example collection of bookmarks.
</desc>

<bookmark href="http://www.yahoo.com/">
  <title>Yahoo!</title>
  <desc>From here you can find anything.</desc>
</bookmark>

<folder>
  <title>XML</title>
  <bookmark href="http://www.oasis-open.org/cover/">
    <title>The SGML/XML Web Pages</title>
    <desc>From here you can find anything about XML and SGML.</desc>
  </bookmark>
</folder>
</xbel>
```

alias

> This element type is a symbolic reference to another bookmark or folder, also as supported by Netscape. The symbolic reference is exactly similar to Unix file system soft links, and includes the referenced bookmark or folder as though it had appeared directly. The reference is defined by the `ref` attribute of the element, which refers to the `id` of the bookmark or folder.
>
> The `alias` elements can appear anywhere nodes can.

info

> This element type can appear inside the `xbel`, `folder`, and `bookmark` elements after the `title` element and is merely a container for the `metadata` element explained below.

metadata

> The `metadata` element type is included as a means of providing XBEL with a mechanism for controlled extension. In the DTD `metadata` is declared to be empty and to have an attribute named

`owner`. This attribute is intended to contain a URI which distinguishes whoever defined the semantics of the contents of the element.

Those who extend XBEL are allowed to add content and new attributes to the element type, and the XBEL report states that namespaces should be used to distinguish these.

Example 9–2 is the XBEL 1.0 DTD, with some of the comments removed or trimmed, since some of the explanations have already appeared above.

Example 9–2. The XBEL DTD

```
<!-- This is the XML Bookmarks Exchange Language, version 1.0.
     It should be used with the formal public identifier:

     +//IDN python.org//DTD XML Bookmark Exchange Language 1.0//EN//XML

     One valid system identifier at which this DTD will remain
     available is:

     http://www.python.org/topics/xml/dtds/xbel-1.0.dtd
     -->

<!-- Customization entities.  Define these before "including"
     this DTD to create "subclassed" DTDs.
     -->
<!ENTITY % local.node.att  "">
<!ENTITY % local.url.att   "">
<!ENTITY % local.nodes.mix "">

<!ENTITY % node.att      "id       ID    #IMPLIED
                          added    CDATA #IMPLIED
                          %local.node.att;">

<!ENTITY % url.att       "href     CDATA #REQUIRED
                          visited  CDATA #IMPLIED
                          modified CDATA #IMPLIED
                          %local.url.att;">

<!ENTITY % nodes.mix     "bookmark|folder|alias|separator
                          %local.nodes.mix;">
```

```
<!ELEMENT xbel (title?, info?, desc?, (%nodes.mix;)*)>
<!ATTLIST xbel
          %node.att;
          version   CDATA       #FIXED "1.0"
>
<!ELEMENT title      (#PCDATA)>

<!--================== Info ====================================-->

<!ELEMENT info (metadata+)>

<!ELEMENT metadata EMPTY>
<!ATTLIST metadata
          owner     CDATA       #REQUIRED
>

<!--================== Folder ==================================-->

<!ELEMENT folder    (title?, info?, desc?, (%nodes.mix;)*)>
<!ATTLIST folder
          %node.att;
          folded    (yes|no)    'yes'
>

<!--================== Bookmark ================================-->

<!ELEMENT bookmark (title?, info?, desc?)>
<!ATTLIST bookmark
          %node.att;
          %url.att;
>

<!ELEMENT desc       (#PCDATA)>

<!--================== Separator ===============================-->

<!ELEMENT separator EMPTY>

<!--================== Alias ===================================-->

<!ELEMENT alias EMPTY>
<!ATTLIST alias
          ref       IDREF       #REQUIRED
>
```

XBEL has its own Web site at `http://pyxml.source-forge.net/topics/xml/xbel/`, which contains more information about it.

9.2 | Thinking in SAX

9.2.1 *Acting after the event*

Writing SAX applications can be a bit difficult at first, because it requires a mind-set that is rather different from that of most programmers today. This is because SAX is such a primitive event-based API and because it provides no information beyond the current event. This means that your code has to wait until SAX has made all the information you need available; it can't start acting on the contents of an element before it has all been made available. To take an example: When converting an RSS document to HTML, one may want to make an H1 element from the channel title. The first solution that occurs to many is to put the necessary code in the startElement method, but this doesn't work, because the sequence of events may be as shown below:

- `startElement('title', ...)`
- `characters('AT')`
- `characters('&')`
- `characters('T newsflash')`
- `endElement('title')`

As you can see, the program can't do anything in the startElement method, since the element contents are not available yet. And as shown above, it can't really do anything in the characters method either, since it doesn't know whether it has received all the element contents yet. There may always be another characters call before the end of the element. So the place to act is in the `endElement` event, when all information about the element has been received.

There is a problem with this as well, however, because in the `endElement` event, the element contents are no longer available. This means that the program has to record the element contents while it is in the `characters` event. And in fact there is yet another problem: knowing that the element is a title element isn't enough, since we don't want to create `H1` elements for the item titles. We need to know that the immediate parent is the `channel` element.

This illustrates two important things about event-driven programming: the need for state tracking and the principle of only acting after all necessary information has arrived.

9.2.2 *Tracking state*

What information from the event stream needs to be tracked varies with the application, since different XML applications have different structures and the needs of client applications vary with the structure. Typically, the structure one needs to track is context information (which elements are we inside now) and data values (character data or attribute values) that will be needed at a later stage.

9.2.2.1 An example application

The application shown in Examples 9–3 to 9–10 converts XBEL documents to HTML and does quite a bit of state tracking. It generates HTML documents where the outermost folders are mapped to level 2 headings and folders at the next level are mapped to level 3 headings. The bookmarks themselves are mapped to unordered lists of links, and folders at levels below the second level generate a bolded list item and start a new list for their own contents.

Example 9–3 should be familiar by now: it imports SAX and declares the top and bottom templates as needed by the HTML-generating code further down.

Example 9–3. An XBEL to HTML converter (1 of 8)

```
# This script converts XBEL bookmark collections to Web pages, using
# application-specific state tracking.

import codecs
from xml.sax import handler, parse

# --- Templates

top = \
"""
<!DOCTYPE HTML PUBLIC \"-//W3C//DTD HTML 4.0 Transitional//EN\">
<HTML>
<HEAD>
  <TITLE>%s</TITLE>
</HEAD>

<BODY>
<H1>%s</H1>
"""

bottom = \
"""
<HR>

<ADDRESS>
Converted by xbel2html.py, using SAX.
</ADDRESS>

</BODY>
</HTML>
"""
```

Example 9–4 is the SAX handler class, and all its state-tracking mechanisms are declared in the constructor. _out is the file object to which the generated HTML is written. _inside is used to keep track of what element we are currently inside. The constants inside the class are the acceptable values of this variable.

_contents is used for the contents of elements with text contents, _url to hold the URLs of bookmarks, and _folder_level to count the folder level we are currently at.

Example 9–4. An XBEL to HTML converter (2 of 8)

```
# --- ContentHandler

class XBELHandler(handler.ContentHandler):

    ROOT        = 0
    FOLDER      = 1
    BOOKMARK    = 2
    NONE        = 3

    def __init__(self, out):
        self._out = out
        self._inside = XBELHandler.NONE # what context are we in?
        self._contents = ""
        self._url = None
        self._folder_level = 0
        self._ul_started = 0
```

_ul_started is perhaps the most complex variable; it is used to keep track of whether we are currently inside a UL list or not in the generated output. This makes it possible to ensure that all generated LI items will appear inside a UL list.

Example 9–5. An XBEL to HTML converter (3 of 8)

```
    def startElement(self, name, attrs):
        self._contents = ""

        if name == "xbel":
            self._inside = XBELHandler.ROOT
        elif name == "folder":
            self._inside = XBELHandler.FOLDER
            self._folder_level = self._folder_level + 1
        elif name == "bookmark":
            self._inside = XBELHandler.BOOKMARK
            self._url = attrs["href"]
```

The startElement method (Example 9–5) resets the _contents variable to make sure that the contents of this element are not mixed up with those of the previous element. It also updates the _inside variable and records bookmark URLs when necessary. The folder level count is increased when we enter `folder` elements.

The method in Example 9–6 simply accumulates textual content whenever we are inside a folder or bookmark element. This is really only used for accumulating `title` and `desc` contents, so it could perhaps be restricted more with an extra flag. (This would make it a little bit faster, but we are not really concerned with performance here, so we let it be.)

Example 9–6. An XBEL to HTML converter (4 of 8)

```
def characters(self, data):
    if self._inside != XBELHandler.NONE:
        self._contents = self._contents + data
```

In the `endElement` method (Example 9–7) we know that `title` can occur in one of three contexts: as the title of the entire bookmark collection (in which case we write out the template with the title), of a bookmark, or of a folder. In the latter two cases we write out the bookmark or start the folder.

The only kind of description that is handled is a description of the entire bookmark collection. Ideally the method in Example 9–8 should also handle descriptions of folders and bookmarks, but I've chosen to leave that out for simplicity.

Example 9–9 ensures that we write out the bottom template as well.

9.2.2.2 Reusable state trackers

In the previous application, a large part of the code was dedicated to maintaining state information, and it's clear that much of this machinery could be generalized and made reusable simply by keeping track of the general element structure of the document. That is, it is not really necessary to do state tracking in a way that is specific to XBEL, since most of the application-specific information could be inferred from the element structure of the document. Writing a

Example 9–7. An XBEL to HTML converter (5 of 8)

```
def endElement(self, name):
    if name == "title":
        if self._inside == XBELHandler.ROOT:
            self._out.write(top %
                            (self._contents, self._contents))

        elif self._inside == XBELHandler.BOOKMARK:
            if not self._ul_started:
                self._out.write("<ul>\n")
                self._ul_started = 1
            self._out.write('<li><a href="%s">%s</a> \n' %
                            (self._url, self._contents))

        elif self._inside == XBELHandler.FOLDER:
            if self._ul_started == 1:
                self._out.write("</ul>\n")
                self._ul_started = 0

            if self._folder_level == 1:
                self._out.write("<h2>%s</h2>\n" %self._contents)
            elif self._folder_level == 2:
                self._out.write("<h3>%s</h3>\n" %self._contents)
            else:
                if not self._ul_started:
                    self._out.write("<ul>\n")
                self._out.write("<li><b>%s</b>\n" %
                                self._contents)

            self._ul_started = 0
```

Example 9–8. An XBEL to HTML converter (6 of 8)

```
    elif name == "desc":
        if self._inside == XBELHandler.ROOT:
            self._out.write("<p>%s</p>" % self._contents)

    if name == "folder" or name == "bookmark":
        self._inside = XBELHandler.NONE

    if name == "folder":
        self._out.write("</ul>\n")
        self._folder_level = self._folder_level - 1
```

Example 9–9. An XBEL to HTML converter (7 of 8)

```
def endDocument(self):
    self._out.write(bottom)
```

Example 9–10. An XBEL to HTML converter (8 of 8)

```
# --- Main program

import sys

outf = codecs.open(sys.argv[2], "w", "iso-8859-1")
parse(sys.argv[1], XBELHandler(outf))
```

generalized `ContentHandler` that keeps track of the element structure is a simple thing to do.

Also, the example application was made more complex by weaving HTML generation together with structure interpretation. A better design is possible by factoring out HTML generation into a separate object. Doing a redesign along these lines would give us an application that is split into three parts as shown in Figure 9–1.

Figure 9–1   Structure of the second XBEL to HTML example

This redesign gives us a much cleaner implementation where more than one output notation is easily supportable, and where we can reuse the state tracking part in other applications. So even though there is more code in Examples 9–11 to 9–17, the code is more flexible and easier to maintain, so it will save us work in later examples.

The top part of the script is unchanged, so it's not repeated here.

Example 9–11 is the state tracker class, in a fairly simple edition. It maintains a stack of the open elements as a list and also keeps track of the contents of the current element, provided the element is found in the _keep_contents_of dictionary.

Example 9–11. Redesigned XBEL to HTML converter (1 of 7)

```
# --- State tracker

class SAXTracker(handler.ContentHandler):

    def __init__(self, keep_contents_of = []):
        self._elemstack = []
        self._contents = ""

        self._keep_contents_of = {}
        for element in keep_contents_of:
            self._keep_contents_of[element] = 1

    def startElement(self, name, attrs):
        self._contents = ""
        self._elemstack.append(name)

    def characters(self, data):
        if self._keep_contents_of.has_key(self._elemstack[-1]):
            self._contents = self._contents + data

    def endElement(self, name):
        del self._elemstack[-1]
```

The XBELHandler (Example 9–12) is now much simplified, and only needs to initialize the SAXTracker and keep a reference to the generator object. The only state that is maintained by the handler is the URL of a bookmark. This could have been avoided by keeping attributes on the stack as well, but this was skipped in order to make the state tracker simpler.

Had we maintained an attribute stack, the method in Example 9–13 would not have been needed at all, since all it does is record the URLs of bookmarks and defer to the SAXTracker implementation of startElement.

Example 9–12. Redesigned XBEL to HTML converter (2 of 7)

```
# --- ContentHandler

class XBELHandler(SAXTracker):

    def __init__(self, out):
        SAXTracker.__init__(self, ["title", "desc"])
        self._out = out # a generator object, not a file object
        self._url = None
```

Example 9–13. Redesigned XBEL to HTML converter (3 of 7)

```
    def startElement(self, name, attrs):
        if name == "bookmark":
            self._url = attrs["href"]

        SAXTracker.startElement(self, name, attrs)
```

The endElement method (Example 9–14) is now the real meat of the program and has been much simplified by the rewrite. Now it simply uses the element structure to call out to the generator with the correct parameters and the generator does the rest of the work.

Example 9–14. Redesigned XBEL to HTML converter (4 of 7)

```
    def endElement(self, name):
        SAXTracker.endElement(self, name)

        if name == "title":
            if self._elemstack[-1] == "xbel":
                self._out.top(self._contents)
            elif self._elemstack[-1] == "bookmark":
                self._out.bookmark(self._contents, self._url)
            elif self._elemstack[-1] == "folder":
                self._out.start_folder(self._contents)

        elif name == "desc" and self._elemstack[-1] == "xbel":
            self._out.description(self._contents)

        elif name == "folder":
            self._out.end_folder()
```

Example 9–15. Redesigned XBEL to HTML converter (5 of 7)

```
def endDocument(self):
    self._out.bottom()
```

The method in Example 9–15 is nearly unchanged, and now simply defers to the generator, telling it to finish the file it is generating.

The `HTMLGenerator` (Example 9–16) now cleanly encapsulates the HTML-generating code from the previous application. The code is nearly unchanged, but is now much clearer in intent, easier to change and more clearly separated from the rest of the program. In addition, it is perfectly possible to imagine generator implementations that generate XSL Formatting Objects or LaTeX code, or some other format entirely.

The main program (Example 9–17) is nearly unchanged, except that the `XBELHandler` is now given a `HTMLGenerator` object instead of a file-like object.

9.3 | Application-specific data representations

As the previous implementation showed, maintaining a separation between decoding the element structure of the XML document and performing the functionality of your application can give much cleaner code. Behind this realization a deeper insight is lurking: most XML documents really have two structures at different levels, the structure that follows the data model, made up of of elements and attributes, and the underlying information model of the application itself.

In the case of XBEL the real data obviously consists of folders and bookmarks, not elements and attributes, and in a sense, splitting the application into `XBELHandler` and `HTMLGenerator` reflects this. However, if we were to write another XBEL example that performed something different from conversion to another notation (say, an XBEL bookmark collection editor), it wouldn't be obvious how to reuse code

Example 9–16. Redesigned XBEL to HTML converter (6 of 7)

```
# --- HTMLGenerator

class HTMLGenerator:

    def __init__(self, out):
        self._out = out
        self._ul_started = 0
        self._folder_level = 0

    def top(self, title):
        self._out.write(html_top % (title, title))

    def start_folder(self, title):
        self._folder_level = self._folder_level + 1

        if self._ul_started == 1:
            self._out.write("</ul>\n")
            self._ul_started = 0

        if self._folder_level == 1:
            self._out.write("<h2>%s</h2>\n" % title)
        elif self._folder_level == 2:
            self._out.write("<h3>%s</h3>\n" % title)
        else:
            self._out.write("<li><b>%s</b>\n" % title)

        self._ul_started = 0

    def end_folder(self):
        self._out.write("</ul>\n")
        self._folder_level = self._folder_level - 1

    def bookmark(self, title, url):
        if not self._ul_started:
            self._out.write("<ul>\n")
            self._ul_started = 1
        self._out.write('<li><a href="%s">%s</a> \n' % (url, title))

    def description(self, text):
        self._out.write("<p>%s</p>" % text)

    def bottom(self):
        self._out.write(html_btm)
```

Example 9–17. Redesigned XBEL to HTML converter (7 of 7)

```
# --- Main program

import sys

outf = codecs.open(sys.argv[2], "w", "iso-8859-1")
parse(sys.argv[1], XBELHandler(HTMLGenerator(outf)))
```

from the previous application, since the code is so geared towards producing output.

What would be really useful in a case like this would be a module that could build an XBEL-specific data structure for use by any XBEL application. This make first two parts of the previous example reusable, leaving only the HTML generation to be implemented specifically for that application. Similarly, the code would be useful for an XBEL editor, conversion programs for browser bookmark formats, and most other kinds of XBEL applications one could imagine.

The structure of the XBEL to HTML converter would then be as shown in Figure 9–2. The state tracker could be used in all SAX applications, while the representation builder and XBEL representation could be used in any XBEL application. For example, the XBEL editor mentioned earlier could be built using these two components.

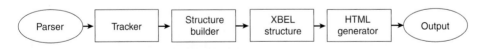

Figure 9–2   Structure of the third XBEL to HTML converter

There is another benefit to this structure: now we are independent of the source notation used in our XBEL applications. Since representation building is now separated from the resulting representation, we can have one representation builder per input notation.

Figure 9–3 gives an overview of some possible XBEL components and how they can be composed to create XBEL applications. A few of these components will actually be given as examples in this book.

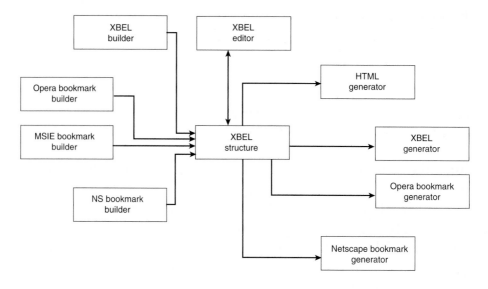

Figure 9–3   A suite of XBEL components

9.3.1   *XBEL data representation*

In this section we create a set of Python classes designed to represent instances of the XBEL information model. In general, what is wanted from such modules is the represent itself, utilities for creating it from the XML representation, and utilities for regenerating the XML representation. This and the two following sections will create a module known as xbellib that has this functionality.[1]

Example 9–18 gives the source code of the classes that represent the XBEL information model.

---

1.   Note that in order to be able to present the module as three separate examples I had to split it into three files: xbellib_model, xbellib_builder, and xbellib_dumper, which are merged into a single module using import statements in the real xbellib.py.

Example 9–18. The XBEL information model

```python
# A set of Python classes for representing XBEL documents.

class NodeWithTitle:
    """Common abstract base class for xbel, folder and bookmark
    elements."""

    def __init__(self, id = None, title = None, desc = None):
        self._id    = id
        self._title = title
        self._desc = desc
        self._added = None

    def get_id(self):
        return self._id

    def set_id(self, id):
        self._id = id

    def get_title(self):
        return self._title

    def set_title(self, title):
        self._title = title

    def get_desc(self):
        return self._desc

    def set_desc(self, desc):
        self._desc = desc

    def get_added(self):
        return self._added

    def set_added(self, added):
        self._added = added

class NodeWithChildren(NodeWithTitle):
    "Common abstract base class for xbel and folder elements."

    def __init__(self, id = None, title = None, desc = None):
        NodeWithTitle.__init__(self, id, title, desc)
        self._nodes = []

    def get_nodes(self):
        return self._nodes
```

```
    def add_node(self, node):
        self._nodes.append(node)

class BookmarkCollection(NodeWithChildren):
    "Represents an entire XBEL document."

class Folder(NodeWithChildren):
    "Represents a folder element."

    def __init__(self, id = None, title = None, desc = None):
        NodeWithChildren.__init__(self, id, title, desc)
        self._folded = 1

    def is_folded(self):
        return self._folded

    def set_is_folded(self, folded):
        self._folded = folded

class Bookmark(NodeWithTitle):
    "Represents a bookmark element."

    def __init__(self, url, id = None, title = None, desc = None):
        NodeWithTitle.__init__(self, id, title, desc)
        self._url = url
        self._visited = None
        self._modified = None

    def get_url(self):
        return self._url

    def set_url(self, url):
        self._url = url

    def get_visited(self):
        return self._visited

    def set_visited(self, visited):
        self._visited = visited

    def get_modified(self):
        return self._modified

    def set_modified(self, modified):
        self._modified = modified
```

```
class Separator:
    "Represents separator elements."

class Alias:
    "Represents alias elements."

    def __init__(self, ref_node = None):
        self._ref_node = ref_node

    def get_ref_node(self):
        return self._ref_node

    def set_ref_node(self, ref_node):
        self._ref_node = ref_node
```

This code is relatively straightforward; it is worth noting, however, that although they also represent nodes, Separator and Alias do not inherit from NodeWithTitle. This means that there is no common base class for all nodes, but since Python does not have static typing this does not matter.

9.3.2   *The XBEL representation builder*

Now that we have defined our object representation, we are ready to create a SAX application which can turn XML documents into instances of the object representation. The source code to this representation builder is given in Examples 9–19 to 9–24.

In Example 9–19, we initialize the structures used to build the XBEL object structure. The first one is the BookmarkCollection object itself. The second is an internal attribute (self._current) used to hold the current node at any point in the document. The self._stack attribute is used to hold a stack of currently open container nodes, so that we can restore the correct value of self._current when we leave this node.

The self._nodes_by_id dictionary maps the IDs we have seen to the corresponding node objects. The self._aliases tuple holds the alias nodes we have seen so far, together with the IDs they referred to. When we have parsed the entire document we can use these two structures to insert the correct references into all the alias nodes.

Example 9–19. An XBEL representation builder (1 of 6)

```
# A SAX application that can build XBEL objects from XML documents.

from xml.sax import parse, handler
from saxtracker import SAXTracker # this is the SAXTracker class,
                                  # moved out into its own module.
from xbellib_model import *

# --- The SAX application

class XBELHandler(SAXTracker):

    def __init__(self):
        SAXTracker.__init__(self, ["title", "desc"])
        self._bookmarks = BookmarkCollection()
        self._current = self._bookmarks
        self._stack = []
        self._nodes_by_id = {}
        self._aliases = []
```

The method in 9–20 is called by the code that started parsing, after parsing has been completed, in order to retrieve the structure built by the structure builder.

Example 9–20. An XBEL representation builder (2 of 6)

```
    def get_structure(self):
        return self._bookmarks
```

Whenever we encounter the start-tag of a node (Example 9–21), the first if statement in this method creates the corresponding node object. If there is interesting information in attributes, this is recorded on the node. Note that the alias element is handled somewhat differently.

Example 9–21. An XBEL representation builder (3 of 6)

```
def startElement(self, name, attrs):
    SAXTracker.startElement(self, name, attrs)

    node = None
    if name == "folder":
        node = Folder(attrs.get("id"))
        if attrs.has_key("folded"):
            node.set_is_folded(attrs["folded"] == "yes")
    elif name == "bookmark":
        node = Bookmark(attrs["href"], attrs.get("id"))
        node.set_added(attrs.get("added"))
        node.set_visited(attrs.get("visited"))
    elif name == "separator":
        node = Separator()
    elif name == "alias":
        node = Alias()
        self._aliases.append((node, attrs["ref"]))

    if node:
        self._current.add_node(node)
        self._stack.append(self._current)
        self._current = node

    if (name == "folder" or name == "bookmark") and \
       attrs.has_key("id"):
        self._nodes_by_id[attrs["id"]] = node
```

When the node has been created we add it to the current container (in the second `if`), push the container onto the stack and set this node as the current node.

Finally, in the third `if`, we check whether the current node is a folder or a bookmark with an ID, and if so, we record a mapping from the ID to the node.

The `endElement` (Example 9–22) becomes unusually much simpler than the `startElement` handler in this application. All we have to do is to set titles and descriptions on the current node for those that have such things. In addition, we pop the new current container from the stack whenever we hit the end-tag of a node element.

Example 9–22. An XBEL representation builder (4 of 6)

```
def endElement(self, name):
    SAXTracker.endElement(self, name)

    if name == "title":
        self._current.set_title(self._contents)
    elif name == "desc":
        self._current.set_desc(self._contents)

    elif name in ("folder", "bookmark", "separator", "alias"):
        self._current = self._stack.pop()
```

Finally, when we reach the end of the document (Example 9–23), we go through all the alias references we have seen and set the correct references. This has to be done at the end of the document in order to handle references to nodes that appear later in the document.

Example 9–23. An XBEL representation builder (5 of 6)

```
def endDocument(self):
    for (alias, ref) in self._aliases:
        alias.set_ref_node(self._nodes_by_id.get(ref))
```

At last, we provide a simple utility method (Example 9–24) to make it easier to turn XBEL documents into object structures, effectively hiding how the loading is done.

Example 9–24. An XBEL representation builder (6 of 6)

```
# --- utility functions

def load_xbel(filename, error_handler = None):
    handler = XBELHandler()
    parse(filename, handler, error_handler)
    return handler.get_structure()
```

9.3.3   *The XBEL serializer*

The missing piece of functionality that we initially described as necessary is generation of an XBEL document from the object representation. Since the object representation is relatively simple, this is a rather straightforward job. The source is given in Example 9–25.

Example 9–25. An XBEL document serializer

```
# A function for writing out XBEL objects as documents.

from xbellib_model import *

def serialize(xbel, out):
    out.write("<xbel>\n")
    _serialize_title(xbel, out)
    _serialize_nodes(xbel.get_nodes(), out, 1)
    out.write("</xbel>\n")

def _serialize_title(node, out, indent = "  "):
    if node.get_title():
        out.write("%s<title>%s</title>\n" %
                  (indent, node.get_title()))
    if node.get_desc():
        out.write("%s<desc>%s</desc>\n" %
                  (indent, node.get_desc()))

def _serialize_nodes(nodes, out, level):
    indent = "  " * level

    for node in nodes:
        if isinstance(node, Folder):
            if node.get_id():
                id = ' id="%s"' % node.get_id()
            out.write('%s<folder folded="%s"%s>\n' %
              (indent, {1 : "yes", 0 : "no"}[node.is_folded()], id))
            _serialize_title(node, out, "  " * (level + 1))
            out.write('\n')
            _serialize_nodes(node.get_nodes(), out, level + 1)
            out.write('%s</folder>\n\n' % indent)
```

```
    elif isinstance(node, Bookmark):
        out.write('%s<bookmark href="%s"' %
                    (indent, node.get_url()))
        if node.get_id():
            out.write(' id="%s"' % node.get_id())
        if node.get_added():
            out.write(' added="%s"' % node.get_added())
        if node.get_visited():
            out.write(' visited="%s"' % node.get_visited())
        out.write(">\n")

        _serialize_title(node, out, "  " * (level + 1))
        out.write('%s</bookmark>\n' % indent)

    elif isinstance(node, Separator):
        out.write("%s<separator/>\n" % indent)

    elif isinstance(node, Alias):
        out.write('%s<alias ref="%s"/>\n' %
                    (indent, node.get_ref_node().get_id()))
```

This serializer is mostly straightforward, but it has a weakness in that it uses isinstance to find out what kind of node it is looking at. This ties the serializer to a particular implementation, which may not always be desirable. To solve this, the representation interface should be extended with node type information in some form.

9.3.4   *The XBEL to HTML converter*

Now that we have implemented the different parts of the xbellib module, writing an XBEL to HTML converter is much easier than it was for the original that we did back in 9.2.2.1, "An example application," on page 275. The source of the converter based on xbellib is given in Example 9–26.

Once we have converters capable of building XBEL object representations from bookmark formats of various browsers, this application could easily be expanded to support those formats as source formats in addition to XBEL itself. Doing this extension is left as an exercise for the reader.

Example 9–26. The XBEL to HTML converter based on `xbellib`

```
# This script converts XBEL bookmark collections to Web pages, using
# xbellib.

import xbellib, codecs

# --- Templates

top = \
"""
<!DOCTYPE HTML PUBLIC \"-//W3C//DTD HTML 4.0 Transitional//EN\">
<HTML>
<HEAD>
  <TITLE>%s</TITLE>
</HEAD>

<BODY>
<H1>%s</H1>
"""

bottom = \
"""
<HR>

<ADDRESS>
Converted by xbel2html.py, using xbellib.
</ADDRESS>

</BODY>
</HTML>
"""

# --- HTML generator

def convert(infile, outfile):
    xbel = xbellib.load_xbel(infile)
    outf = codecs.open(outfile, "w", "iso-8859-1")
    title = xbel.get_title() or "Bookmark collection"
    outf.write(top % (title, title))
    if xbel.get_desc():
        outf.write("<p>%s</p>\n" % xbel.get_desc())

    convert_nodes(xbel.get_nodes(), outf, 1)

    outf.write(bottom)
    outf.close()
```

```
def convert_nodes(nodes, outf, level):
    bookmarks = filter(lambda node:
                       isinstance(node, xbellib.Bookmark), nodes)
    folders   = filter(lambda node:
                       isinstance(node, xbellib.Folder), nodes)

    if bookmarks and level < 4:
        outf.write("<ul>\n")
        for bookmark in bookmarks:
            outf.write('  <li><a href="%s">%s</a> %s\n' %
                       (bookmark.get_url(),
                        bookmark.get_title() or bookmark.get_url(),
                        bookmark.get_desc() or ""))
        outf.write("</ul>\n")

    if folders and level < 4:
        for folder in folders:
            outf.write("<h%d>%s</h%d>" %
                       (level + 1, folder.get_title(), level + 1))
            if folder.get_desc():
                outf.write("<p>%s</p>\n" % folder.get_desc())
            convert_nodes(folder.get_nodes(), outf, level + 1)

    if level > 3 and nodes:
        outf.write("<ul>\n")
        for node in bookmarks + folders:
            if isinstance(node, xbellib.Bookmark):
                outf.write('  <li><a href="%s">%s</a> %s\n' %
                           (node.get_url(),
                            node.get_title() or node.get_url(),
                            node.get_desc() or ""))
            elif isinstance(node, xbellib.Folder):
                outf.write('  <li><b>%s</b> %s\n' %
                           (node.get_title(), node.get_desc() or ""))
                convert_nodes(node.get_nodes(), outf, level + 1)

        outf.write("</ul>\n")


# --- Main program

import sys
convert(sys.argv[1], sys.argv[2])
```

9.4 | Example applications

This section presents some further examples of SAX applications in order to cover more kinds of applications than those shown so far.

9.4.1   *The RSS to HTML converter revisited*

This section revisits the RSS to HTML converter shown in 8.4.1, "RSS to HTML converter," on page 258. One might think that writing this converter using the SAXTracker utility would be easier, but this isn't really the case. Through the use of the internal attributes _title, _link, and _descr the converter avoids the need for the element stack, and accumulation of character data is done easily. However, what the converter *does* spend some effort on is copying the accumulated character data from the _data attribute into the attributes dedicated to each element. If one were to support all the RSS 0.91 element types, the amount of code dedicated entirely to this would be quite substantial.

The code that does this copying is fairly predictable, which leads us to think that perhaps SAXTracker could be improved to do this for us. And in fact, it can very easily be. Python has the built-in functions getattr and setattr, which can use names represented as strings to access the attributes of an object. With these functions we can change the SAXTracker keep_contents_of dictionary into a dictionary named field_elements, which maps element type names to object attributes. The SAXTracker will copy the contents of the element into the corresponding attribute on the application object.

The version of the tracker shown in Example 9–27 is implemented in a way that would be very advanced and difficult to achieve in languages like Java and C++. In Python, however, it turns out to be very simple and straightforward, thanks to Python's dynamic features. Armed with this new and improved SAXTracker we can rewrite the RSS to HTML converter to make use of it, as shown in Examples 9–28 to 9–32.

Example 9–27. The improved `SAXTracker`

```
from xml.sax import handler

# --- State tracker

class SAXTracker(handler.ContentHandler):

    def __init__(self, field_elements = {}):
        self._elemstack = []
        self._contents = ""
        self._field_elements = field_elements

    def startElement(self, name, attrs):
        if self._field_elements.has_key(name):
            setattr(self, self._field_elements[name], "")
        self._elemstack.append(name)

    def characters(self, chars):
        if self._field_elements.has_key(self._elemstack[-1]):
            parent = self._elemstack[-1]
            attr   = self._field_elements[parent]
            setattr(self, attr, getattr(self, attr) + chars)

    def endElement(self, name):
        del self._elemstack[-1]
```

Example 9–28 remains pretty much the same, the main difference being that we now import the `SAXTracker` class.

In Example 9–29 we set up the tracker, telling it to map the three important RSS field elements to the same object attributes that the first RSS to HTML converter used. Note how much of the state-tracking machinery disappears, since the tracker object now does all tracking and copying for us.

The `startElement` method has not really changed (Example 9–30). We no longer reset the `_data` attribute, and we call out to `SAXTracker`, but the method still does the same thing. Note that we take care to reset the `_descr` attribute, since some `item` elements may not have descriptions.

Example 9–28. The RSS to HTML converter, using `SAXTracker` (1 of 5)

```
import sys, codecs
from saxtracker2 import SAXTracker
from xml.sax import parse

# --- Templates

top = \
"""
<!DOCTYPE HTML PUBLIC "-//W3C//DTD HTML 4.0 Transitional//EN">
<HTML>
<HEAD>
  <TITLE>%s</TITLE>
</HEAD>

<BODY>
<A HREF="%s"><H1>%s</H1></A>
"""

bottom = \
"""
<HR>

<ADDRESS>
Converted to HTML using SAX 2.0.
</ADDRESS>

</BODY>
</HTML>
"""
```

Example 9–29. The RSS to HTML converter, using `SAXTracker` (2 of 5)

```
# --- ContentHandler

class RSS2HTMLHandler(SAXTracker):

    def __init__(self, out = None):
        SAXTracker.__init__(self, {"title" : "_title",
                                   "link" : "_link",
                                   "description" : "_descr"})
        self._out = out or sys.stdout

        # tracking state
        self._first_item = 1
```

Example 9–30. The RSS to HTML converter, using `SAXTracker` (3 of 5)

```
def startElement(self, name, attrs):
    if name == "item":
        self._descr = None # reset for this item
        if self._first_item:
            self._out.write("\n<ul>\n")

        self._first_item = 0

    SAXTracker.startElement(self, name, attrs)
```

The copying from _data to the element-specific attributes is replaced with a call to `SAXTracker` (Example 9–31), which now does all this tedious work for us. Which is what we wanted to achieve by writing the improved `SAXTracker` in the first place.

The rest (Example 9–32) is also unchanged.

Example 9–31. The RSS to HTML converter, using `SAXTracker` (4 of 5)

```
def endElement(self, name):
    SAXTracker.endElement(self, name)

    if name == "channel":
        self._out.write(top % (self._title, self._link,
                               self._title))

        if self._descr != None:
            self._out.write("<p>%s</p>" % self._descr)

    elif name == "item":
        self._out.write('  <li><a href="%s">%s</a> %s\n' %
                        (self._link, self._title, self._descr or ""))
```

9.4.2   *An XML generator*

The XBEL serializer in Example 9–25 produced its XML output by writing strings to a file-like object. This creates code that is often a little awkward to read and write, particularly because it can be awkward to write out optional attributes and because one needs to look at the string

Example 9–32. The RSS to HTML converter, using SAXTracker (5 of 5)

```
    def endDocument(self):
        self._out.write("</ul>\n")
        self._out.write(bottom)

# --- Conversion function

def htmlconv(infile, out):
    outf = codecs.open(out, "w", "iso-8859-1")
    parse(infile, RSS2HTMLHandler(outf))
    outf.close()
```

templates to figure out what is happening. It also has the weakness that
if we want to use this XML for something inside our application, we
have to parse it again, which is both awkward and wasteful. A better
way to do this is to transmit the document directly inside the program
using SAX events.

In this section we write an XML generator that presents a simple
and easy-to-use API to its clients, and which can produce output as a
string, to a file, or as a sequence of SAX events. This simplifies our
serializer, and at the same time allows it to be used in more than one
way. The serializer will be used in later examples, such as Examples 10–29 to 10–35 and 26–6 to 26–9, to produce XML output that
can be used in several ways.

The idea is that it should be possible to use the API in the way shown
in the interpreter dialog in Example 9–33.

Example 9–33. Using the XML generator

```
>>> import xmlgen
>>> gen = xmlgen.string_writer()
>>> gen.startElement('item')
>>> gen.fieldElement('title', 'New XML generator released!')
>>> gen.fieldElement('link',  'http://www.somewhere.org/')
>>> gen.endElement()
>>> print gen.get_string_value()
<item><title>New XML generator released!</title>
<link>http://www.somewhere.org/</link></item>
```

(Note that the last line has been split to make the example readable.)
Example 9–34 lists the source of the XML generator module.

Example 9–34. An API for generating XML output

```
"""
An XML-generating module with an easy-to-use API.
"""

import cStringIO
from xml.sax.xmlreader import AttributesImpl
from xml.sax.saxutils import XMLGenerator

# --- The XML writer class

class XMLWriter:

    def __init__(self, cont_handler):
        self._cont_handler = cont_handler
        self._elemstack = []

    def startDocument(self):
        self._cont_handler.startDocument()

    def endDocument(self):
        self._cont_handler.endDocument()

    def startElement(self, name, attrs = {}):
        self._elemstack.append(name)
        self._cont_handler.startElement(name, AttributesImpl(attrs))

    def characters(self, chars):
        self._cont_handler.characters(chars)

    def endElement(self, name = None):
        self._cont_handler.endElement(name or self._elemstack[-1])
        del self._elemstack[-1]

    def processingInstruction(self, target, data):
        self._cont_handler.processingInstruction(target, data)

    def emptyElement(self, name, attrs = {}):
        self.startElement(name, attrs)
        self.endElement()
```

```
    def fieldElement(self, name, content, attrs = {}):
        self.startElement(name, attrs)
        self.characters(content)
        self.endElement()


    def fieldElementOptional(self, name, content, attrs = {}):
        if content:
            self.startElement(name, attrs)
            self.characters(content)
            self.endElement()

    # output generation control

    def close(self):
        if hasattr(self, "_fileobj"):
            self._fileobj.close()

    # retrievers

    def get_string_value(self):
        return self._string.getvalue()

    # contenthandler control

    def setContentHandler(self, handler):
        self._cont_handler = handler

# --- The namespace-aware XML writer class

class XMLWriterNS(XMLWriter):

    def __init__(self, cont_handler, default_ns):
        self._cont_handler = cont_handler
        self._default_ns = default_ns
        self._elemstack = []

    def startElement(self, name, attrs = {}):
        self._elemstack.append(name)
        # process attrs first!
        self._cont_handler.startElement((default_ns, name), name,
                                        AttributesImpl(attrs))

    def endElement(self, name = None):
        name = name or self._elemstack[-1]
        self._cont_handler.endElement((default_ns, name), name)
        del self._elemstack[-1]
```

```
# --- Convenience creation functions

def file_writer(filename):
    return fileobj_writer(open(filename, "w"))

def string_generator():
    out = cStringIO.StringIO()
    xmlgen = XMLWriter(XMLGenerator(out))
    xmlgen._string = out
    return xmlgen

def fileobj_writer(fileobj):
    xmlgen = XMLWriter(XMLGenerator(fileobj))
    xmlgen._fileobj = fileobj
    return xmlgen

def sax_writer(cont_handler, lex_handler = None):
    return XMLWriter(cont_handler)
```

Using this generator module we can rewrite the XBEL serializer as shown in Example 9–35.

Example 9–35. The improved XBEL serializer

```
# A function for writing out XBEL objects as documents.

from xbellib_model import *
import xmlgen

def serialize(xbel, out):
    serialize_to_generator(xbel, xmlgen.fileobj_writer(out))

def serialize_to_generator(xbel, gen):
    gen.startElement("xbel")
    _serialize_title(xbel, gen)
    _serialize_nodes(xbel.get_nodes(), gen)
    gen.endElement()

def _serialize_title(node, gen):
    gen.fieldElementOptional("title", node.get_title())
    gen.fieldElementOptional("descr", node.get_descr())
```

```
def _serialize_nodes(nodes, gen):
    for node in nodes:
        if isinstance(node, Folder):
            attrs = {}
            if node.get_id():
                attrs["id"] = node.get_id()
            attrs["folded"] = {1 : "yes",0 : "no"}[node.is_folded()]
            xmlgen.startElement("folder", attrs)
            _serialize_title(node, gen)
            _serialize_nodes(node.get_nodes(), gen)
            xmlgen.endElement()

        elif isinstance(node, Bookmark):
            attrs = {"url" : node.get_url()}
            if node.get_id():
                attrs["id"] = node.get_id()
            if node.get_added():
                attrs["added"] = node.get_added()
            if node.get_visited():
                attrs["visited"] = node.get_visited()
            xmlgen.startElement("bookmark", attrs)

            _serialize_title(node, gen)
            xmlgen.endElement()

        elif isinstance(node, Separator):
            xmlgen.emptyElement("separator")

        elif isinstance(node, Alias):
            xmlgen.emptyElement("alias",
                            {"ref" : node.get_ref_node().get_id()})
```

9.4.3   *A document example*

So far we have concerned ourselves only with simple data-oriented
XML applications like RSS and XBEL. This section demonstrates an
application that can convert Shakespeare's plays (as published in XML
by Jon Bosak) to HTML, as an example of a more complex and document-like application. It should be noted that this is a very simple
application compared to most real document-oriented applications,
but here we just want a simple example.

9.4.3.1   The document structure

The structure of the plays in Bosak's collection is relatively simple, as is the document structure of most works of fiction. In general, it can be considered to consist of two parts: the front matter and the play itself. The fragment in Example 9–36 illustrates the front matter.

Example 9–36. Example of the front matter of a play

```
<PLAY>
<TITLE>The Tragedy of Hamlet, Prince of Denmark</TITLE>

<FM>
<P>ASCII text placed in the public domain by Moby Lexical Tools,
1992.</P>
<P>SGML markup by Jon Bosak, 1992-1994.</P>
<P>XML version by Jon Bosak, 1996-1999.</P>
<P>The XML markup in this version is Copyright &#169; 1999 Jon
Bosak. This work may freely be distributed on condition that it
not be modified or altered in any way.</P>
</FM>

<PERSONAE>
<TITLE>Dramatis Personae</TITLE>

<PERSONA>CLAUDIUS, king of Denmark. </PERSONA>
<PERSONA>HAMLET, son to the late, and nephew to the present
king.</PERSONA>
<PERSONA>POLONIUS, lord chamberlain. </PERSONA>
<PERSONA>HORATIO, friend to Hamlet.</PERSONA>
<PERSONA>LAERTES, son to Polonius.</PERSONA>
<PERSONA>LUCIANUS, nephew to the king.</PERSONA>

<PGROUP>
<PERSONA>VOLTIMAND</PERSONA>
<PERSONA>CORNELIUS</PERSONA>
<PERSONA>ROSENCRANTZ</PERSONA>
<PERSONA>GUILDENSTERN</PERSONA>
<PERSONA>OSRIC</PERSONA>
<GRPDESCR>courtiers.</GRPDESCR>
</PGROUP>
```

As the excerpt in Example 9–36 shows, the front matter is relatively simple in structure. The main difficulty is that PERSONA elements can appear both alone and in groups, and the groups have a description that appears at the very end.

Example 9–37. Example from the body of a play (1 of 3)

```
<ACT><TITLE>ACT I</TITLE>

<SCENE><TITLE>SCENE I.   Elsinore. A platform before the
castle.</TITLE>
<STAGEDIR>FRANCISCO at his post. Enter to him BERNARDO</STAGEDIR>

<SPEECH>
<SPEAKER>BERNARDO</SPEAKER>
<LINE>Who's there?</LINE>
</SPEECH>

<SPEECH>
<SPEAKER>FRANCISCO</SPEAKER>
<LINE>Nay, answer me: stand, and unfold yourself.</LINE>
</SPEECH>

<SPEECH>
<SPEAKER>BERNARDO</SPEAKER>
<LINE>Long live the king!</LINE>
</SPEECH>

<SPEECH>
<SPEAKER>FRANCISCO</SPEAKER>
<LINE>Bernardo?</LINE>
</SPEECH>

<SPEECH>
<SPEAKER>BERNARDO</SPEAKER>
<LINE>He.</LINE>
</SPEECH>
```

As the excerpt in Example 9–37 shows, the play has ACT and SCENE containers, each adorned with a TITLE. The SCENEs consist of SPEECHes, each having SPEAKERs and LINEs. The main complication is the STAGEDIR elements, which can appear outside SPEECHes, inside

SPEECHes and inside LINEs. Example 9–38 shows a STAGEDIR appearing inside a LINE.

Example 9–38. Example from the body of a play (2 of 3)

```
<SPEECH>
<SPEAKER>HAMLET</SPEAKER>
<LINE>Indeed, upon my sword, indeed.</LINE>
</SPEECH>

<SPEECH>
<SPEAKER>Ghost</SPEAKER>
<LINE><STAGEDIR>Beneath</STAGEDIR>  Swear.</LINE>
</SPEECH>

<SPEECH>
<SPEAKER>HAMLET</SPEAKER>
<LINE>Ah, ha, boy! say'st thou so? art thou there,</LINE>
<LINE>truepenny?</LINE>
<LINE>Come on--you hear this fellow in the cellarage--</LINE>
<LINE>Consent to swear.</LINE>
</SPEECH>

<SPEECH>
<SPEAKER>HORATIO</SPEAKER>
<LINE>Propose the oath, my lord.</LINE>
</SPEECH>
```

There is also some additional structure that needs to be handled. Before and immediately inside the ACTs there may appear PROLOGUE and EPILOGUE elements, which some of the plays have. In Example 9–39, there are examples of both. Some plays also have an INDUCTion before the first ACT. One example of this is also shown in Example 9–39.

9.4.3.2 The application

In the application in Examples 9–40 to 9–48, I have taken the simplest possible approach to the problems presented by the conversion. The result is that the order of elements is not changed at all, so the applica-

Example 9–39. Example from the body of a play (3 of 3)

```
<PROLOGUE><TITLE>PROLOGUE</TITLE>
<SPEECH>
<SPEAKER></SPEAKER>
<LINE>Two households, both alike in dignity,</LINE>
<LINE>In fair Verona, where we lay our scene,</LINE>
<LINE>From ancient grudge break to new mutiny,</LINE>
<LINE>Where civil blood makes civil hands unclean.</LINE>

<EPILOGUE><TITLE>EPILOGUE</TITLE>
<STAGEDIR>Spoken by a Dancer</STAGEDIR>
<SPEECH>
<SPEAKER></SPEAKER>
<LINE>First my fear; then my courtesy; last my speech.</LINE>
<LINE>My fear is, your displeasure; my courtesy, my duty;</LINE>
<LINE>and my speech, to beg your pardons. If you look</LINE>
<LINE>for a good speech now, you undo me: for what I have</LINE>
<LINE>to say is of mine own making; and what indeed I</LINE>
<LINE>should say will, I doubt, prove mine own marring.</LINE>

<INDUCT><TITLE>INDUCTION</TITLE>
<STAGEDIR>Warkworth. Before the castle</STAGEDIR>
<STAGEDIR>Enter RUMOUR, painted full of tongues</STAGEDIR>
<SPEECH>
<SPEAKER>RUMOUR</SPEAKER>
<LINE>Open your ears; for which of you will stop</LINE>
<LINE>The vent of hearing when loud Rumour speaks?</LINE>
```

tion requires little state tracking beyond what the original `SAXTracker` utility provides. This has simplified the application quite substantially. If we were to do a transformation that reordered the contents in any way, however, this conversion would be very difficult to write using SAX and it would have been better to use some different method.

Again we import the needed classes and define our templates (Example 9–40). Note that this time the top template contains a reference to a CSS stylesheet. This is used to simplify the HTML that the application needs to produce and to make the application more flexible. When the output uses CSS there is no need to rewrite the application merely to change the colors or the layout of the output. Instead, the stylesheet can be modified. The stylesheet that is used will be shown at the end, together with screenshots.

Example 9–40. SAX application for converting the plays to HTML (1 of 9)

```
import sys
from saxtracker import SAXTracker
from xml.sax import handler, parse

# --- Templates

top = \
"""
<!DOCTYPE HTML PUBLIC "-//W3C//DTD HTML 4.0 Transitional//EN">
<HTML>
<HEAD>
  <TITLE>%s</TITLE>
  <LINK REL=stylesheet HREF="play.css" TYPE="text/css">
</HEAD>

<BODY>

<H1>%s</H1>
"""

bottom = \
"""
<HR>

<ADDRESS>
Converted from Jon Bosak's XML to HTML with SAX.
</ADDRESS>

</BODY>
</HTML>
"""
```

Note also that this time we use the original SAX tracker, rather than the one with object attribute mapping, since we only need to handle one element at a time in this application.

We write our ContentHandler as a SAXTracker application (Example 9–41), and list the elements that may contain text. The elements listed above are all the elements that may contain character data apart from some very minor elements that I have decided to ignore. As usual, the ContentHandler takes a file-like object as a parameter.

Example 9–41. SAX application for converting the plays to HTML (2 of 9)

```
# --- The ContentHandler

class PlayToHtmlHandler(SAXTracker):

    def __init__(self, out = None):
        SAXTracker.__init__(self, ["TITLE", "P", "PERSONA",
                                   "GRPDESCR", "SPEAKER", "LINE",
                                   "STAGEDIR"])
        self._out = out or sys.stdout
```

Example 9–42. SAX application for converting the plays to HTML (3 of 9)

```
    def startElement(self, name, attrs):
        # front matter

        if name == "FM":
            self._out.write("<h2>Front matter</h2>\n")

        elif name == "PERSONAE":
            self._out.write("<h2>Dramatis personae</h2>\n")
            self._out.write("<ul>")

        elif name == "PGROUP":
            self._out.write("<li>")

        # play

        elif name == "PROLOGUE":
            self._out.write("<h2>Prologue</h2>\n")

        elif name == "EPILOGUE":
            self._out.write("<h2>Epilogue</h2>\n")

        SAXTracker.startElement(self, name, attrs)
```

The startElement method (Example 9–42) is used mainly to produce headings for the element types that start sections with fixed titles. Note that the list of PERSONAE is placed within an ordinary HTML UL element. Note also that PGROUP elements are handled by placing all the persons listed in them in a single list item, so the PGROUP

Example 9–43. SAX application for converting the plays to HTML (4 of 9)

```
def endElement(self, name):
    SAXTracker.endElement(self, name)

    # front matter

    if name == "TITLE" and self._elemstack[-1] == "PLAY":
        self._out.write(top % (self._contents, self._contents))

    elif name == "P":
        self._out.write("<p>%s</p>\n" % self._contents)
```

element is used to start the list item. This avoids the need to check whether a PERSONA is the first in the group.

As usual, the endElement method (Example 9–43) is where the real work is done. The title of the play is handled simply, by checking for the end of a TITLE element that has a PLAY element as its parent. This triggers writing out the top template. The Ps of the FM element are also easy to handle.

The PERSONA elements immediately inside the PERSONAE element are handled by creating an LI element for each (Example 9–44). Those inside a PGROUP we simply write out, followed by a comma, so that the GRPDESCR will finish off the list item. Once we hit the end of a PERSONAE element we know that there are no more PERSONAs to come, and close the UL list that we started in startElement.

Example 9–44. SAX application for converting the plays to HTML (5 of 9)

```
    elif name == "PERSONA":
        if self._elemstack[-1] == "PERSONAE":
            self._out.write("<li>%s</li>\n" % self._contents)
        else: # group
            self._out.write(self._contents + ", ")

    elif name == "GRPDESCR":
        self._out.write(self._contents + "</li>\n")

    elif name == "PERSONAE":
        self._out.write("</ul>\n")
```

The contents of the play are surprisingly simple to handle (Example 9–45). We create H2 and H3 elements for the TITLEs, and paragraphs for the SPEAKER, LINE, and STAGEDIR elements. Each P has its own class so the CSS stylesheet rules have some way of telling the different kinds of paragraphs apart. Note that this solution will in some cases nest P elements in the output. Luckily, browsers can handle that.

Example 9–45. SAX application for converting the plays to HTML (6 of 9)

```
# play

elif name == "TITLE" and \
    (self._elemstack[-1] in ("ACT", "INDUCT")):
    self._out.write("<h2>%s</h2>" % self._contents)

elif name == "TITLE" and self._elemstack[-1] == "SCENE":
    self._out.write("<h3>%s</h3>" % self._contents)

elif name == "SPEAKER" and \
    self._elemstack[-2] not in ("EPILOGUE", "PROLOGUE"):
    self._out.write("<p class=speaker>%s:</p>\n" %
                    self._contents)

elif name == "LINE":
    self._out.write("<p class=line>%s</p>" % self._contents)

elif name == "STAGEDIR":
    self._out.write("<p class=stagedir>%s</p>" %
                    self._contents)

self._contents = ""
```

We could have handled STAGEDIR elements inside running text on a single line by checking the parent and creating I elements for them instead of P elements. This would have made browsers render the STAGEDIR contents on the same line as the rest of the LINE. The handling of the LINE elements would also have to be changed so that the I element could be created inside the P resulting from the LINE.

It would have been the best to let the startElement start the P and to output the self._contents before entering STAGEDIR elements.

The `endElement` handler for the `LINE` could then print the `self._contents` and close the `P`.

Example 9–46. SAX application for converting the plays to HTML (7 of 9)

```
def endDocument(self):
    self._out.write(bottom)
```

In Example 9–46, we simply use the end of the document to write out the bottom template.

Example 9–47. SAX application for converting the plays to HTML (8 of 9)

```
# --- Conversion function

def convert(infile, out):
    if sys.hexversion > 0x2000000:
        import codecs
        outf = codecs.open(out, "w", "iso-8859-1")
    else:
        outf = open(out, "w")

    parse(infile, PlayToHtmlHandler(outf))
    outf.close()
```

The Shakespeare's plays contain non-ASCII characters, something that causes problems when we try to write them out to ordinary Python files in Python 2.0. To avoid this we use the `codecs` module to do proper conversion from Unicode to the encoding we want to use (Example 9–47).

Example 9–48. SAX application for converting the plays to HTML (9 of 9)

```
# --- Main program

if __name__ == "__main__":
    convert(sys.argv[1] , sys.argv[2])
```

When displayed with the CSS stylesheet shown in Example 9–49 the converted plays look as in the screenshots in Figures 9–4 and 9–5.

Example 9–49. The CSS stylesheet

```
/*
    Stylesheet for the HTML version of the play.
*/

H1, H2, H3 {
  font-family: Verdana, Arial, Helvetica, sans-serif;
  color: navy;
  font-weight: bold;
}

H1 {
  text-align: center;
  margin-top: 24pt;
  margin-bottom: 24pt;
  font-size: 220%;
}

H2 {
  margin-top: 12pt;
  margin-bottom: 12pt;
  font-size: 170%;
}

P.speaker {
  color: navy;
  font-weight: bold;
  margin-bottom: 3pt
}

P.stagedir {
  font-style: italic;
  margin-left: 36pt;
}

P.line {
  margin-top: 3pt;
  margin-left: 36pt;
  margin-bottom: 0pt;
}
```

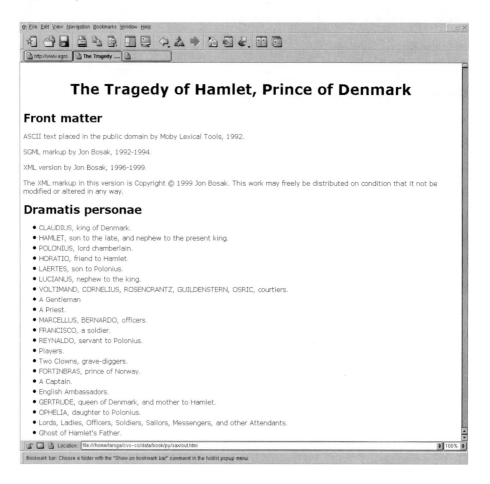

Figure 9–4   Screenshot of *Hamlet* front matter

It may seem strange that this application does not use either a generator interface or an object representation in the way that we did for the XBEL example. However, document-oriented applications generally have such complex structures that these approaches tend not to work very well for them. We could have made such an interface for an application as simple as this, but in more realistic document examples this would not have been very useful.

Figure 9–5   Screenshot of Hamlet content

Another thing that may seem strange is that this example produces HTML output that is not well-formed XHTML, but instead makes use of SGML-specific shortcuts, such as not quoting the attributes. The reason for this is that the only real gain in using XML syntax rather than SGML syntax is that there are more tools for processing XML than for processing SGML. And who would want to process the HTML output from this conversion, as long as the original XML is available?

9.5 | Tips and tricks

9.5.1 *Pitfalls in SAX programming*

When programming SAX applications there is a number of little details in the way SAX is defined (and the way XML parsers work) that can cause problems for naively implemented applications. This section points out these pitfalls, so that you can avoid them in your own code.

- The splitting of `characters` and `ignorableWhitespace` events. This has been mentioned several times already, so I will be brief here, but do remember to enable your code to handle character data that is split up and reported in more than one event. Code that cannot handle this will, sooner or later, silently misbehave.

- The fact that `Attributes` instances are not guaranteed to return the same values after the `startElement` method call with which they arrived has returned. If `Attributes` instances are stored away by the application, this can cause `Attributes` instances to return values that seem impossible. Use the `copy` method to make copies of the `Attributes` objects.

- When there is a container element type that has a number of field elements as children (like `item` with `title` and `link` in RSS), it is common to have a set of attributes on the `Content-Handler` class to store these field values in. You must then remember to reset these attributes on the start-tag of the container element. Otherwise, if one container element lacks a field it will get the value stored in the attribute from the previous container element.

- When an element type may have mixed content, that is, when it may contain both character data and elements, SAX applications often pick up only the last part of the character data inside that element. To give an example, the `title` element of most document applications may have mixed content. A SAX application that creates a table of contents for such a document may have the titles of some parts of the document truncated to the last part if it does not cater to this possibility.

Typically, the application will accumulate character data when `self._elemstack[-1] == 'title'`, or some similar condition, holds. When the title is, say, The `<ic>Content-Handler</ic>` interface, the application will pick up only `' interface'`. One simple solution may be to change the condition to `'title' in self._elemstack`, as well as to change the code that resets the attribute in which the character data is accumulated.

9.5.2 *How to write an error handler*

Writing error handlers can often be difficult, since it is hard to predict what kinds of errors can occur and in what kinds of contexts the code will be used. Error handling is also a subject for which there is little traditional wisdom to use for guidance, and few tutorials cover the subject at all. However, there are some general guidelines and tips that could make it easier to make the right decisions.

The first thing to remember is that silently ignoring real errors is the worst thing one can do. If an error has occurred it is important to discover this as close to the source of the error as possible, and if one subsystem silently recovers, the error will not be discovered until later, possibly much later. At that stage it will be difficult to discover where things went wrong and much time may be wasted searching for the source of the error. So, in general, never ignore an error unless you *know* you can safely do it.

The second most important consideration is to not make error handling so rigid that the application becomes awkward to use. For example, displaying a single dialog box for each parsing error is not a good idea if there can be many such errors. The user will then have to OK his/her way through every single dialog box before being able to continue working. Similarly, applications and libraries should not disallow actions merely because the programmer felt uneasy about them.

It is quite possible that some user will find a good use for these actions, in which case it would not be a good idea to disallow them.

In general there are two different situations in which error handling is implemented: when the deployment context is known and when it is not. The deployment context is not known when you make a general utility that is designed to be embedded in many different kinds of applications, such as an XML parser. It is known when you make an application with a GUI, or a tool that is run from the command line, or any application that is in some way standalone.

When usage context is not known the main considerations are to give client applications flexibility, to make as much error information available as possible and not to hide errors. The two main ways to do this are to have an error handler object, as in SAX, that receives notification when execution should not be interrupted, or to use exceptions when it should. The more information you can provide about the error, the better. Also, the more abstract that information is, that is, the more error codes or other kinds of formal cause identifiers it has, the better.

When the usage context is known the main consideration is to help the user decide what to do. Has the user done something wrong? Is there a configuration problem? Is it a network or system/disk failure of some kind? Is it a bug? Also, what should the user do about it? The more you can help the user to understand the cause of the problem, the better. Another important point to consider is what your application can usefully tell the user and what it can give the system administrator or application developer. Tracebacks? Internal state? Offending input, whether from documents or from other kinds of data? The date/time at which the problem occurred? Log excerpts?

9.5.3   Using SAX in Jython

Doing SAX development in Jython is not very different from doing it in CPython. Essentially, there are two choices of SAX drivers:

```
xml.sax.drivers2.drv_javasax
```
If you have a Java SAX 2.0 parser installed, you may use this driver. It will be much faster than using xmlproc.

```
xml.sax.drivers2.drv_xmlproc
```
If you want to use xmlproc that is fully possible, but it is really only recommended if you wish to use some features that are specific to xmlproc.

The Jython driver is a bit unusual in that its constructor takes an argument that can be either the class name of a Java `XMLReader` or an instance of a Java `XMLReader` class. If the argument is not given, the driver will attempt to use the `org.xml.sax.Driver` system property to find the class name of a parser.

Example 9–50 shows the source code of a trivial program that uses the Jython driver with the Xerces SAX driver to output a normalized XML document.

Example 9–50. Using the Jython driver

```
import sys
from xml.sax.saxutils import XMLGenerator
from xml.sax.drivers2 import drv_javasax

p = drv_javasax.create_parser("org.apache.xerces.parsers.SAXParser")
p.setContentHandler(XMLGenerator())
p.parse(sys.argv[1])
```

An alternative way to achieve the same result is to set the `python.xml.sax.parser` property to `xml.sax.drivers2.drv_javasax`, and `org.xml.sax.Driver` to `org.apache.xerces.parsers.SAXParser`. Then `xml.sax.make_parser` will return the Jython driver, and the Jython driver will use the Xerces SAX parser. The same code will then work just as well in CPython.

9.6 | Speed

The first rule of performance improvement is very simple: don't! Improving performance often takes a lot of time, introduces new bugs, and tends to create code that is harder to read and maintain. So unless performance is so bad that it is somehow a problem in itself, don't bother!

Having said that, it should be noted that performance is a notoriously difficult area to discuss, and a major part of the reason for this is that there is no such thing as a general metric for performance. This may sound surprising, but the fact is that how fast a piece of hardware or software is will depend on what it is used for. For this reason benchmarks should be viewed with deep suspicion since there is no guarantee that what a benchmark measures is what you want.

One example of this is that ordinary Intel Pentium processors are very fast (compared to the next example) at general-purpose computing. The special-purpose Shark processor is slow at general-purpose computing, but about 100 times faster on computing Fourier transformations, since it has dedicated hardware for such computations.[1] The result is that the Pentium will run XML parsers much faster than the Shark, but the Shark will run signals processing software much faster than the Pentium. So none of these processors can really be said to be the fastest for all purposes.

An extremely important rule of thumb that is closely related to this is that the performance enhancement from a given improvement depends on how often the improved part is used. This means that if you improve a part of your program that is rarely executed, the improvement will yield little overall benefit. This rule is known as *Amdahl's Law*, after Gene Amdahl, who first stated it, and it is absolutely central to any optimization work. We will keep coming back to this rule in the following sections.

---

1.   Fourier transformations are much used in signals processing, which often needs to be done in real time, hence the interest in computing them quickly.

9.6.1 *Optimizing code*

In general there are two levels that affect performance of the code: the overall architecture and the detailed implementation. The overall architecture is the most important, because if bad performance is designed into the very structure of the tool, only a redesign can remove it. The choice of processing approach belongs in this category: building a document tree and traversing it is as good as guaranteed to always be slower than pure event-based processing. Sometimes, however, there is no other way than to build the document tree, or convenience may be more important than speed, so we often do it anyway.

The second level, that of the detailed code structure, is easier to affect, and on this level the performance of the application is to some extent a function of how much effort has been invested in its optimization. If lots of effort is spent on it, the performance is almost bound to improve, but never more than the overall design allows.

To write fast code, the main requirement is to have an understanding of the performance model of the framework the code is written in. This means both the programming language and the libraries that are used by the application. In general, such an understanding comes from knowledge of how hardware, operating systems and programming languages work, as well as of the implementation of the framework. Experience is also necessary.

One of the reasons why C and C++ are considered to be so fast is that they have very predictable performance models (especially C). A language like Python, on the other hand, is harder to predict, since it is further removed from the hardware. Common Lisp is perhaps the most difficult language of all in this respect, since tiny changes in type declarations or low-level code structure can dramatically change the code that the compiler produces. In most languages, however, the performance model is relatively simple, but it must always be learned.

When working on optimizing code, it is easy to introduce improvements that break subtle cases which the slower version of the code got right. To guard against such errors, automated testing tools, such as unit tests and regression tests can be extremely valuable and save much time. For more information, see `http://www.junit.org/junit/ doc/testinfected/testing.htm` or Chapter 6 of *The Practice of Programming* by Brian Kernighan and Rob Pike.

Another useful tip is that heavy optimization of a piece of code can often make it both longer and much more convoluted, so that it becomes hard to see what it really does. In these cases it may be useful to keep the original short and readable version in a comment so that readers of the code could see what the optimized code does.

In general, when optimizing code, the first thing to do is to study the code to see where improvements will have the most impact. A simple, but contrived, example may illustrate this.

Example 9–51. A pointless function

```
def fun():
    for x in range(1000):
        fx = x ** 3 + 2 * x ** 2 + (-50) * x + 3

        for y in range(1000):
            fx = y ** 3 + 2 * y ** 2 + (-50) * y + 3
```

The code in Example 9–51 simply calculates a simple polynomial function 1,001,000 times. On my laptop, Python runs this function in about 2.8 seconds. However, using Horner's rule we can optimize the polynomial, and if we use this technique on only the uppermost polynomial we get the version shown in Example 9–52.

Example 9–52. A faster, but still pointless function

```
def fun():
    for x in range(1000):
        fx = 3 + x * (-50 + x * (2 + x))

        for y in range(1000):
            fx = y ** 3 + 2 * y ** 2 + (-50) * y + 3
```

This optimization buys us nothing at all. In fact, the inaccuracy of the measurement completely obscures the effect; this function clocks in at an average of 2.9 seconds over 10 tries. So, what if we optimize the second polynomial, and revert the change of the first? Then the average execution time suddenly drops to 1.9 seconds. Why? We made the exact same change, and only to a different line. Because the second line is executed 1,000,000 times and the first is executed only 1000 times. If it takes `t1` seconds to execute the first line and `t2` seconds to execute the second, the total execution time is `t1 * 1000 + t2 * 1,000,000`. Obviously, changes to `t1` will have nearly no effect, while changes to `t2` will have a huge effect.

So when optimizing, the trick is to find the lines that are executed very often, but which can be speeded up. If actions performed less often are slowed down to speed these lines up, the result is still likely to be an overall performance improvement. The primary tool to find out where a program is spending its time is known as a *code profiler*. Python has one in the `profile` module, and since its section in the Python library documentation is so good I will not speak about it here.

9.6.1.1 How to optimize Python code

One thing that distinguishes Python from many other languages is that referring to a name (variable, function, module, class, etc.) is not free. Inside a function, referring to a local name is much faster than referring to a global name, since the former is a mere array lookup, while the latter is a hashtable lookup. So when a function uses a global name many times, or when a method uses a class attribute, copying the value into a local variable and using that instead may speed the function up substantially.

Also, creating instance objects and calling methods and functions is generally slow in Python. Using built-in objects such as lists and dictionaries is faster, but still not fast. In performance-critical parts of an application, it may be worthwhile to avoid these when they are not strictly necessary.

In general, adding extra tests for cases that can be optimized tends to slow the code down, since variable lookup and extra byte-code execution are relatively expensive in Python. So for this to be worth the extra work, the savings must be relatively large.

Since Python itself is so slow, built-in functions will generally beat code that you write every time. Combinations of `filter`, `reduce`, `map`, `string.join`, `string.translate`, `string.split`, and the `array` module can often lead to surprising speedups.

A little more information on this can be found in the Python FAQ at `http://www.python.org/doc/FAQ.html#4.7`.

9.6.1.2 How to optimize SAX applications

In general, SAX applications are as fast as their `startElement`, `endElement`, and `characters` methods. These are by far the most often called methods, so any optimization efforts should start here. In general, the following aspects of each method should be considered:

- Actions that are performed for all element types. These should be kept to the absolute minimum and blood-optimized, and if one can find ways to avoid performing actions for all element types then by all means use those ways.

- Element type dispatch, that is, branching out to the correct handling of each element type. This is performed for every element type and should be optimized as much as possible. The important thing is to make it fast for the most common element types. The other element types are not as important.

  In general there are two ways to do this: if you use a big `if` block with one `elif` for each element type, make sure that the tests are ordered by frequency of occurrence in the documents. Also, make sure that the tests are fast by adjusting the order of boolean expressions. That is, make it `fast and slow`, not `slow and fast`, since if the first expression fails, the second one is never executed.

The other way to do dispatch is to use a dispatch table. A dispatch table is a dictionary that maps element types to handler methods. This does away with the `if` statement entirely, making all methods equally fast. The cost is that it introduces an extra method call. Dispatch tables are generally good when there are many common element types.

  ▪ Handling the most common element types. This should be as fast as possible, since this code will be executed the most often.

9.6.1.3 Optimizing the plays application

With these guidelines in hand, let us do a benchmark of the application that converts Shakespeare's plays to HTML and try to improve it. The benchmark is performed by calling the `convert` function once for each play and measuring the time needed to convert all 37 plays. The original version shown in Examples 9–40 to 9–48 did this in 21.5 seconds on my laptop.[1] With all the functionality commented out, except for the calls to the `SAXTracker` and handling the `LINE`s, it takes 16.5 seconds. So realistically we can only shave about 25% off the total time needed to run the conversion.

Generally, the fact that we can only hope to optimize away at most 25 percent of the total running time would in most cases mean that we should not try to do it at all. In this section we do it anyway to illustrate some of the different possible approaches to such an optimization. To get a more realistic example we would have had to have a much more complex application, so complex as to make it unusable as an example.

Following the guidelines from the previous section we look at the XML source of hamlet.xml to see what element types are the most common. Running the SAX statistics from 8.4, "Two example applications," on page 258 we get the output shown in Example 9–53.

---

1. No information about the laptop is provided, since all we need to judge our optimizations are relative improvements.

Example 9–53. Statistics from hamlet.xml

```
===== DOCUMENT REPORT

---ELEMENT TYPES
Total number: 16

           Type name      Occur
         (None, 'ACT')        5
          (None, 'FM')        1
     (None, 'GRPDESCR')       2
         (None, 'LINE')    4014
            (None, 'P')        4
      (None, 'PERSONA')      26
     (None, 'PERSONAE')       1
       (None, 'PGROUP')       2
         (None, 'PLAY')        1
     (None, 'PLAYSUBT')       1
        (None, 'SCENE')      20
      (None, 'SCNDESCR')       1
       (None, 'SPEAKER')    1150
        (None, 'SPEECH')    1138
      (None, 'STAGEDIR')     243
         (None, 'TITLE')      27
Total: 6636
```

The output clearly shows that LINE is the most important element type (2 out of 3 elements are LINEs), but that SPEAKER and SPEECH are also important, and that STAGEDIR may have some influence. Armed with this information and the guidelines from the previous section, we take a look at the startElement and endElement methods of the plays application.

The improved version shown in Examples 9–54 and 9–55 runs at 19 seconds, which means that we have realized nearly all of the potential we could expect to realize. So we stop there.

It quickly becomes apparent that the startElement method is not doing anything with these four element types, but the entire set of comparisons is performed anyway. We fix this by adding a dictionary of the four common element types, so if the current element is one of these we call the SAXTracker and return, as shown in Example 9–54.

Another thing to consider is that each time we write to the file object, we access it as `self._out.write`. This costs us in that we must first look up the `_out` attribute in our own object and then the `write` attribute on the `_out` object. By copying the method from the file-like object to ourselves in the constructor, we save one lookup. (The method remains bound to the file-like object, so the meaning is the same.) All `self._out.write` calls now change to `self._write` calls.

Example 9–54. Optimized version of the play converter (1 of 2)

```
cutoff = {"SPEECH" : 1, "SPEAKER" : 1, "STAGEDIR" : 1, "LINE" : 1}

class PlayToHtmlHandler(SAXTracker):

    def __init__(self, out = None):
        SAXTracker.__init__(self, ["TITLE", "P", "PERSONA",
                                   "GRPDESCR", "SPEAKER", "LINE",
                                   "STAGEDIR"])
        self._write = (out or sys.stdout).write

    def startElement(self, name, attrs):
        if cutoff.has_key(name):
            SAXTracker.startElement(self, name, attrs)
            return

        # the rest of the method is unchanged
```

Similarly, the big `if` test in the `endElement` method is not handling the most common element types first. Also, for the SPEECH element we go through all the tests. So we rearrange the order and insert an empty branch for the SPEECH element near the top so that we don't waste any time on it (Example 9–55).

As an alternative to manually tuning the structure of the `if` statements that do the dispatching, we could try a completely different approach: a dispatch table. By providing a method for each element type we wish to handle and then creating a dictionary that maps element type names to methods, we could avoid the big `if` statements

Example 9–55. Optimized version of the play converter (2 of 2)

```
def endElement(self, name):
    SAXTracker.endElement(self, name)

    if name == "LINE":
        self._write("<p class=line>%s</p>" % self._contents)

    elif name == "SPEECH":
        pass

    elif name == "SPEAKER" and \
         self._elemstack[-2] not in ("EPILOGUE", "PROLOGUE"):
            self._write("<p class=speaker>%s:</p>\n"
                        % self._contents)

    elif name == "STAGEDIR":
        self._write("<p class=stagedir>%s</p>" % self._contents)

    elif name == "TITLE":
        if self._elemstack[-1] == "SCENE":
            self._write("<h3>%s</h3>" % self._contents)

        elif self._elemstack[-1] == "ACT" or \
             self._elemstack[-1] == "INDUCT":
            self._write("<h2>%s</h2>" % self._contents)

        elif self._elemstack[-1] == "PLAY":
            self._write(top % (self._contents, self._contents))

    elif name == "P":
        self._write("<p>%s</p>\n" % self._contents)

    elif name == "PERSONA":
        if self._elemstack[-1] == "PERSONAE":
            self._write("<li>%s</li>\n" % self._contents)
        else: # group
            self._write(self._contents + ", ")

    elif name == "GRPDESCR":
        self._write(self._contents + "</li>\n")

    elif name == "PERSONAE":
        self._write("</ul>\n")

    self._contents = ""
```

completely. With this approach, the ContentHandler becomes as shown in Examples 9–56 to 9–59.

We use the SAXTracker (Example 9–56) almost as before, changing only the control structure that is used to connect the right element type names with the right actions. Note also that we use two dispatch tables, one for startElement and another for endElement.

Example 9–56. The play to HTML converter using dispatch tables (1 of 4)

```
# --- The ContentHandler

class PlayToHtmlHandler(SAXTracker):

    def __init__(self, out = None):
        SAXTracker.__init__(self, ["TITLE", "P", "PERSONA",
                                   "GRPDESCR", "SPEAKER", "LINE",
                                   "STAGEDIR"])
        self._out = out or sys.stdout

        self._start_dispatch = {"FM"       : self.start_FM,
                                "PERSONAE" : self.start_PERSONAE,
                                "PGROUP"   : self.start_PGROUP,
                                "PROLOGUE" : self.start_PROLOGUE,
                                "EPILOGUE" : self.start_EPILOGUE,
                                "LINE"     : self.noop,
                                "SPEECH"   : self.noop,
                                "SPEAKER"  : self.noop,
                                "STAGEDIR" : self.noop }

        self._end_dispatch = {"LINE"     : self.end_LINE,
                              "SPEAKER"  : self.end_SPEAKER,
                              "STAGEDIR" : self.end_STAGEDIR,
                              "TITLE"    : self.end_TITLE,
                              "P"        : self.end_P,
                              "PERSONA"  : self.end_PERSONA,
                              "GRPDESCR" : self.end_GRPDESCR,
                              "PERSONAE" : self.end_PERSONAE}
```

The startElement method now looks up the correct handler method in the dispatch table and then calls it (Example 9–57). The line that does this may look a little strange. What happens is that Python first evaluates the expression before the argument list and then calls the resulting value (which must of course be a callable object). Instead of trying to look up the method, assign it to a local variable, test if the value is None and then call it, we do this directly and catch the resulting KeyError if any. This is faster when the most common case is that the lookup succeeds.

Example 9–57. The play to HTML converter using dispatch tables (2 of 4)

```
def startElement(self, name, attrs):
    try:
        self._start_dispatch[name] ()
    except KeyError:
        pass

    SAXTracker.startElement(self, name, attrs)

def endElement(self, name):
    SAXTracker.endElement(self, name)

    try:
        self._end_dispatch[name] ()
    except KeyError:
        pass

    self._contents = ""

def endDocument(self):
    self._out.write(bottom)
```

To ensure that the most common case really *is* that the lookup succeeds, the noop method (which does nothing) has been added and the four most common element types map to this in the start dispatch table.

Example 9–58 is a simple rewrite of the original code with the contents of the if branches turned into method bodies, but otherwise left unchanged. None of the branches themselves has to be changed in any way, and the reason for this is that no local variables are used, only object attributes.

Example 9–58. The play to HTML converter using dispatch tables (3 of 4)

```python
# --- start element handlers

# front matter

def start_FM(self):
    self._out.write("<h2>Front matter</h2>\n")

def start_PERSONAE(self):
    self._out.write("<h2>Dramatis personae</h2>\n")
    self._out.write("<ul>")

def start_PGROUP(self):
    self._out.write("<li>")

def start_PROLOGUE(self):
    self._out.write("<h2>Prologue</h2>\n")

def start_EPILOGUE(self):
    self._out.write("<h2>Epilogue</h2>\n")

# --- end element handlers

def end_LINE(self):
    self._out.write("<p class=line>%s</p>" % self._contents)

def end_SPEAKER(self):
    if self._elemstack[-2] != "EPILOGUE" and \
        self._elemstack[-2] != "PROLOGUE":
        self._out.write("<p class=speaker>%s:</p>\n" %
                        self._contents)

def end_STAGEDIR(self):
    self._out.write("<p class=stagedir>%s</p>" % self._contents)

def end_TITLE(self):
    if self._elemstack[-1] == "SCENE":
        self._out.write("<h3>%s</h3>" % self._contents)

    elif self._elemstack[-1] == "ACT" or \
         self._elemstack[-1] == "INDUCT":
        self._out.write("<h2>%s</h2>" % self._contents)

    elif self._elemstack[-1] == "PLAY":
        self._out.write(top % (self._contents, self._contents))
```

```
def end_P(self):
    self._out.write("<p>%s</p>\n" % self._contents)

def end_PERSONA(self):
    if self._elemstack[-1] == "PERSONAE":
        self._out.write("<li>%s</li>\n" % self._contents)
    else: # group
        self._out.write(self._contents + ", ")

def end_GRPDESCR(self):
    self._out.write(self._contents + "</li>\n")

def end_PERSONAE(self):
    self._out.write("</ul>\n")
```

One final optimization is to make noop a function written in C rather than a Python function (Example 9–59). This makes it much faster to call, and saves us quite a bit of overhead.

Example 9–59. The play to HTML converter using dispatch tables (4 of 4)

```
import os
noop = os.getcwd
```

The version with dispatch tables clocked in at 25 seconds without the noop method, and used 21 seconds with the noop method. Again, the conclusion is that the main costs are not in the application, but in XML parsing.

9.6.2 *Benchmarks*

Even though it is, as I wrote above, impossible to measure performance in general, this section presents some benchmarks of the Python XML parsers. These benchmarks should not be taken as absolutes, but rather as a general guide to the approximate costs of various approaches. This information is mainly valuable in comparison with the other benchmarks provided in this book, especially when it comes to choosing the general approach to take in a processing application.

All the tests were run on the laptop I used during the final part of the work on this book, a Pentium III 850 MHz with 256 Mb of RAM, running Python 2.0 under RedHat Linux 7.0.

9.6.2.1 The test documents

Since the performance of XML processing frameworks will to some extent depend on the document in question, four different documents have been used:

Othello

> This is Shakespeare's play *Othello*, taken from Jon Bosak's collection of Shakespeare plays. It is 243 Kb in size and has a relatively simple structure, somewhere in between a document and a data file. Running the SAX statistics application on it (described in 8.4, "Two example applications," on page 258) tells us that it uses 14 element types, with altogether 6194 element instances, no attributes, and no processing instructions.

XSLT-WD

> This is the 1999–07–09 working draft of the XSLT specification. It is 179 Kb in size and is structured like a document, with much running text. It uses much more entity references and CDATA marked sections than most documents do. It has 66 element types, with 2243 instances, 391 attributes, and no processing instructions.

xmltools

> This is a topic map of my XML tools Web site serialized to the standard XML syntax of topic maps.[1] The result is a very data-like

---

1. Topic maps are a very interesting new ISO standard for representing information structures. See `http://www.topicmap.com/` for more information.

document with much markup and heavy use of attributes. It is 269 Kb in size and has 8 element types with 5112 instances, 4292 attributes, and no processing instructions.

airports.rdf

This is David Megginson's airports.rdf, an RDF document containing the full names, codes, and coordinates of a number of airports in the world. It is 804 Kb in size and very data-like, with much markup, heavy use of namespaces and attributes. It has 8 element types, with 16702 instances, 2963 attributes, and no processing instructions.

9.6.2.2   Native APIs

Table 9–1 shows the results of parsing each of the test documents 10 times with different XML parsers. The documents were all parsed with empty applications.

Table 9–1   Benchmark results for native parser APIs

Parser	Othello	WD-XSLT	xmltools	airports.rdf
xmlproc	1.3	0.6	1.8	4.3
xmlproc (validating)	2.3	1.6	—	—
Pyexpat	0.11	0.07	0.14	0.39
xmllib	1.8	0.7	1.8	5.8
sgmlop	0.09	0.04	0.1	0.27
RXP				

All numbers in the table represent time measured in seconds.

9.6.2.3 SAX driver overhead

Table 9–2 shows the results obtained by running each of the test documents 10 times using the SAX drivers for different parsers, again with empty applications.

Table 9–2   Benchmark results for SAX drivers

Parser	Othello	WD-XSLT	xmltools	airports.rdf
Pyexpat	0.22	0.1	0.24	0.7
xmlproc	1.9	0.8	2.4	6.1

Advanced SAX

- Advanced parts of the API

- Parser filters

- Working with entities

- Mapping non-XML data to XML

I n this chapter we go deeper into the subject of SAX, covering both the more advanced parts of the API as well as some of the more sophisticated ways of using it.

10.1 | The advanced parts of the API

As mentioned earlier, we did not cover the entire SAX API in 8.3, "The SAX classes," on page 244, but left the more advanced parts for later. This section (together with the next one) covers the parts of the API not yet discussed.

10.1.1 *The* SAXException *exception*

SAXException is used to encapsulate SAX errors and warnings, and contains information about the problem. A SAXException does not contain much information, however, and is mainly intended for general errors and not parsing errors. For parsing errors, the `SAXParse-Exception` (see the next section), which contains location information, is used.

In general, SAX applications should only raise exceptions derived from the `SAXException` class, since these are the only exceptions SAX parsers and SAX-using applications will expect. If other kinds of exceptions need to be passed out, they can be wrapped in the `SAX-Exception`, to be raised within the application and pass out through the parser to the application.

In Java, methods must declare what exceptions they may throw, which is very useful as it helps developers control their exception handling. In the Java version of SAX only two kinds of exceptions *can* be raised, since only the `SAXException` is declared on the various SAX methods. The first kind is of course the `SAXException` and its descendants. However, some exceptions can be raised nearly anywhere, and in order to keep these from becoming a real nuisance (in the sense that they must be *declared* everywhere), any exception classes derived from `RuntimeException` do not need to be declared. The Jython `Exception` class is derived from `RuntimeException`, which means that Jython code can freely raise whatever exceptions it wishes, making interaction with Java SAX code much easier.

The `SAXException` methods are:

`__init__(msg, exception)`
> This is the `SAXException` constructor that creates an instance of it. The `msg` parameter must hold a string error message, while the `exception` can be either `None` or an exception to be embedded.

`getException()`
> Returns the embedded exception, or `None` if there is none.

`getMessage()`
> Returns the error message associated with this exception.

10.1.2 *The* SAXParseException *exception*

SAXParseException is used to report parsing errors to the application. It is a subclass of SAXException, and extends it by providing location information. An application which receives such an object can either read information from it or reraise it. Note that location information will only be available from this exception if the parser supports this.

The SAXParseException methods are those of SAXException, with the following additions:

getPublicId()
> Returns the public identifier of the entity where the problem occurred, or None if the public identifier is not known.

getSystemId()
> Returns the system identifier of the entity where the problem occurred, or None if the system identifier is not known. If the system identifier was given as a relative file name, it is possible that the parser will return it as an absolute file name, or even as an absolute file URL.

getLineNumber()
> Returns the number of the line where the problem occurred (within the entity where the problem occurred), as an integer. If the parser does not support this method, -1 is returned.

getColumnNumber()
> Returns the number of the column on the line where the problem occurred (within the entity where the problem occurred), as an integer. If the parser does not support this method, -1 is returned.

10.1.3 *The* InputSource *class*

This class is defined in the xml.sax.xmlreader module, and actually serves as an interface with a default implementation in the same class. It represents a source from which parsers can read a document and is used to conveniently collect all the different information a parser may need to get the contents of a document in a single object. It is used in two places in SAX: as an argument to the `XMLReader.parse` method and as a return value from the `EntityResolver.resolveEntity` method.

The class collects the pieces of information listed below, some of which may be empty, that is, `None`. In general, an XML parser that wants to read an XML document will try the different attributes in the order they are listed below, using the first that is present.

- A character stream. In Python, this will be a file-like object that returns Unicode strings when read from, just like the file-like objects provided by the `codecs` module. This should not be used in Python 1.5, since there is no such thing as a character stream there.
- A byte stream. In Python, this will be a file-like object that returns ordinary byte strings when read from.
- A system identifier, that is, a URI.

The `InputSource` class methods do not have any built-in smarts, but only return exactly the information that was put into the `Input-Source` object. To resolve the information in an `InputSource` instance so that it has at least a byte stream that can be read from, the `prepare_input_source` function of the `xml.sax.saxutils` module can be used.

The `InputSource` class has the methods listed below.

`__init__(sysid = None)`
   The constructor takes an optional parameter that holds the system identifier of the entity.

`getSystemId()`
   Returns the system identifier (that is, URI or file name) from which the entity can be read, or `None` if it is not known.

`setSystemId(sysid)`
> This method is used to set the system identifier.

`getPublicId()`
> Returns the public identifier of the entity, or None if it does not have any.

`setPublicId(pubid)`
> Sets the public identifier.

`getByteStream()`
> Returns a file-like object from which the entity can be read, or None if this is not available. Note that such objects return uninterpreted characters, requiring the parser to do the conversion to Unicode on its own.

`setByteStream(stream)`
> Sets the file-like object.

`getEncoding()`
> Returns the name of the character encoding used in the data returned by the file-like object.

`setEncoding(encoding)`
> Sets the encoding name.

`getCharacterStream()`
> Returns a Unicode file object that returns Unicode strings rather than byte strings.

`setCharacterStream(stream)`
> Sets a character stream from which the parser can read. To create a Unicode file object instead of an ordinary file object, see the built-in codecs module which has functionality for this.

10.1.4 *The* EntityResolver *interface*

Applications can use this handler to control how parsers resolve external entity references. This can be very useful when it is hard to reference entities directly or when entities are not available through normal URLs. (More about this in 10.3, "Working with entities," on page 380.) The handler has only one method:

resolveEntity(pubid, sysid)

> This method is called for every external entity reference in the document, with the public and system identifiers in the pubid and sysid parameters. It must return either an InputSource object or the system identifier as a string.
>
> The default action if no resolver is registered is simply to return the sysid parameter.

10.1.5 *The* DTDHandler *interface*

The name of this handler may give the impression that it provides information about the DTD. It does do this, but only providing the information necessary to work with unparsed entities. (Unparsed entities are described in 2.3.1.2, "Notations and unparsed entities," on page 56.) This information consists of notation declarations and the unparsed entity declarations themselves. A handler that provides more information about the DTD can be found in 10.1.10, "The DeclHandler interface," on page 358.

The DTDHandler has two methods, one for notations and one for unparsed entities:

notationDecl(name, publicId, systemId)

> This method is called to inform the application of the declaration of a notation. All parameters are strings, but both the publicId and the systemId can be None if no identifiers were given in the declaration.

`unparsedEntityDecl(name, publicId, systemId, ndata)`
> This method is called to inform the application of the declaration of an unparsed entity. All parameters are strings, but the `systemId` can be `None` if no identifier was given in the declaration. The `ndata` parameter holds the name of the associated notation.

Example 10–1. A document with unparsed entities

```
<!DOCTYPE doc [
  <!NOTATION gif PUBLIC "-//CompuServe Graphics Interchange
                         Format//EN">
  <!ENTITY image SYSTEM "image.gif" NDATA gif>
]>

<doc>
  <img src="image"//>
</doc>
```

When Example 10–1 is parsed with a SAX parser, the `notationDecl` method will be called with the arguments (`'gif'`, `'-//CompuServe Graphics Interchange Format//EN'`, `None`), and the `unparsedEntityDecl` method will be called with the arguments (`'image'`, `None`, `'image.gif'`, `'gif'`).

10.1.6 *The* Locator *interface*

This interface provides the functionality necessary to find the exact location of the original XML string within the document that caused the current `ContentHandler` event. Note that the locator passed from the `XMLReader` to the `ContentHandler` with the `setDocument-Locator` method is only guaranteed to give valid results during `ContentHandler` callbacks. The values returned will of course also change with each method call. Applications that wish to store the location of an event after returning from the callback method can use the `Location` class described below, after the list of methods.

Not all parsers provide this functionality, and they are not required to do so.

`getPublicId()`

Returns the public identifier of the current entity, or `None` if it is not known.

`getSystemId()`

Returns the system identifier of the current entity, or `None` if it is not known. It would not be known if the application passed in an `InputSource` instance without a system identifier.

`getLineNumber()`

Returns the number of the line on which the event began. If it is not known `-1` will be returned.

`getColumnNumber()`

Returns the number of the column on the line where the event began. If it is not known `-1` will be returned.

The `xml.saxtools.utils` module contains an implementation of this interface, called `Location`, whose constructor accepts only one argument: another `Locator`. It then copies all the information that locator can provide and stores it internally, so that it may be reused later.

10.1.7 *SAX 2.0 extensibility support*

As mentioned earlier, SAX 2.0 provides mechanisms for controlled extension through the concepts of properties and features. Properties are named values on the `XMLReader` which can be retrieved and set, while features are named capabilities that can be turned off and on. SAX 2.0 defines some properties and features, but allows anyone to define their own ones in addition to the core set.

The feature and property names take the form of URIs in the same way as namespace names, but these URIs are not intended to refer to anything. Many of the participants in the design discussion wanted a syntax similar to that of Java packages, that is, `org.xml.sax.properties.foo` rather than `http://xml.org/sax/properties/foo`. This was turned down on the grounds that it would mean that only those who own domains could define SAX properties and features, while the use of URIs enables anyone who has a Web site to define properties and features.

In general, property and feature names should be assumed to be compared using ordinary string comparison. This means that although technically, URI comparison requires more that simple string comparison, one should not expect all SAX implementations to do this the right way.

Some SAX 2.0 features have recommended default values, but in many cases the state of a feature is a property of the SAX driver being used, and cannot be changed at all. For example, the validation feature cannot be turned on if the XML parser used by the driver does not support this. Also, SAX implementations are not required to support, or even recognize, any features or properties at all.

The set of core features defined by SAX 2.0 is:

`http://xml.org/sax/features/namespaces`
> This feature is used to control whether namespace processing is performed or not. The default is that it is not (in Python; in Java the default is that it is), but in the cases where namespace processing is wanted it it can be turned on with this feature. The details of how namespace processing works are given in the next section.

`http://xml.org/sax/features/namespace-prefixes`
> This feature controls whether or not qualified names and namespace declaration attributes are reported. The default is that they are not reported.

`http://xml.org/sax/features/string-interning`

This feature controls whether or not names are interned. In any XML document, there are lots and lots of names and comparison of names is an operation performed very often by most XML applications. Python (and Java) both have a built-in operation called `intern` that will take any string and enter it in a global table of interned strings. This means that two calls to `intern` with the same string value will return the same object. That is, the objects will compare as equal with the `is` operator in Python and with `==` in Java.

This has the benefit that string comparisons and dictionary lookup are a bit faster, since strings can be compared with pointer comparison (a single machine code operation) rather than string value comparison (lots of operations). In Python, this means that the `is` operator can be used to compare strings. In Java, it means that strings can be compared using `==` rather than the `equals` method, which is more convenient and also much faster.

Another benefit is that when the SAX output is used to build a DOM tree, interned strings will save memory, since nodes will share the strings rather than each node having its own copy. In Java, all decent parsers will do interning, but with this feature applications can ensure that strings are also entered in the JVMs string table, so that applications can intern its strings in the same table.

In Python, this feature is mainly useful for checking whether the parser is doing interning or not. None of the Python parsers allow the value of this feature to be changed, and the speed benefit for Python parsers is much less than it is for Java parsers.

`http://xml.org/sax/features/validation`

This feature is used to control whether validation is performed or not. The default is whatever the driver decides it is, but it will generally be that validation is not performed.

`http://xml.org/sax/features/external-general-`
    `entities`
    This feature is used to control whether external entities are read or not. Note that it only applies to general entities, not parameter entities, which are controlled by the next feature.

`http://xml.org/sax/features/external-parameter-`
    `entities`
    This feature is used to control whether external parameter entities are read or not, including the external subset. If this property is true, the external subset will be read.

The state of each feature and property can be queried and set with the methods below:

`getFeature(name)`
    Returns the state of the feature with the given name. Note that only two possible values are allowed: `true` and `false`. These do not exist as Python values, but whatever this method returns should only be interpreted as `true` or `false`.
    If the feature is not recognized, the `XMLReader` will raise a `SAXNotRecognizedException`. If it is recognized, but not supported, it will raise `SAXNotSupportedException`, or possibly return `false` and refuse all requests to turn it on.

`setFeature(name, state)`
    This method is used to control the state of the named feature. The `XMLReader` will raise `SAXNotSupportedException` if it does not support the requested state. Note that this will also happen if the method is called during parsing and the feature is read-only during parsing. (All the core features are read-only during parsing.)

`getProperty(name)`
    Returns the current value of the named property, raising the same exceptions as `getFeature` in the same situations.

```
setProperty(name, value)
```
Sets the value of the named property, provided that the property can be changed. The same exceptions are raised in the same cases as for `setFeature`.

The set of core properties defined by SAX 2.0 is listed below:

```
http://xml.org/sax/properties/lexical-handler
```
This property contains the `LexicalHandler` callback handler. The property is used instead of `setLexicalHandler` and `getLexicalHandler` methods since the `LexicalHandler` is not part of core SAX 2.0. This is described in 10.1.9, "The `Lexical-Handler` interface," on page 356.

```
http://xml.org/sax/properties/declaration-handler
```
This property contains the `DeclHandler` callback handler in the same way as with the `LexicalHandler`. The `DeclHandler` is described in 10.1.10, "The `DeclHandler` interface," on page 358.

```
http://xml.org/sax/properties/dom-node
```
For parsers that are really DOM tree walkers, this property will return the DOM node that caused the current event. No other parsers will support this property. Note that before parsing starts, this property can be used to set the starting node.

```
http://xml.org/sax/properties/xml-string
```
During parsing this property contains the original string that caused the current event. This can be used by applications that wish to get information about the detailed lexical representation of the document.

It should be expected that many SAX drivers will provide features and properties that are specific to them and the functionality that they provide. At the moment, however, not too many drivers have been developed in Python, primarily because the person supposed to do so has been busy writing this book. In any case, below is a list of the properties and features defined by SAX drivers so far.

`http://garshol.priv.no/symbolic/properties/catalogs`
> A list of file names and URIs referring to catalog files that the parser should read and take into account. (Catalog files are described in 10.3, "Working with entities," on page 380.) At the moment only implemented by `drv_pysp`, but the driver for xmlproc is likely to follow very soon.

`http://garshol.priv.no/symbolic/properties/driver-version`
> The version of the SAX driver as a string. At the moment only implemented by `drv_pysp`, but the drivers for xmlproc and Pyexpat are likely to follow very soon.

`http://garshol.priv.no/symbolic/properties/parser-version`
> The version of the XML parser used by the SAX driver as a string. At the moment only implemented by `drv_pysp`, but the drivers for xmlproc and Pyexpat are likely to follow very soon.

10.1.8 *SAX 2.0 and namespaces*

The main difference between SAX 1.0 and SAX 2.0 is the support for XML namespaces. The change is much more dramatic than it may sound at first because namespaces change the representation of two of the most fundamental parts of XML, element-type and attribute names, from being simple strings to being compound objects with three attributes. The three attributes of expanded names are the namespace URI, the local name, and the original qualified (or raw) name that appeared in the document. For `xhtml:p` the namespace URI would be `http://www.w3.org/1999/xhtml` (given the appropriate namespace declarations, of course), the local name would be `p`, and the qualified name would be the original `xhtml:p` string.

Expanding the API to support both views of names at the same time proved to be very difficult both in the Java version and in the Python version, and in both cases countless emails were written before consensus was reached. Due in part to the differences between the languages, different solutions were chosen in each language.

In Java, the signatures of the element events are `startElement(nsuri, lname, qname, attrs)` and `endElement(nsuri, lname, qname)`. In namespace mode, the two first attributes will always have values, while `qname` may or may not. In XML 1.0 mode `qname` is guaranteed to have a value, while the others may or may not be empty strings.

In Python, there are two different sets of element event methods; the `startElement` and `endElement` methods that you have already learned are called by the parser in non-namespace mode. In namespace mode the methods `startElementNS` and `endElementNS` are used instead. The signatures of these methods are given below, together with some extra methods related to namespace support.

`startElementNS(name, qname, attrs)`
> The name parameter holds the expanded name of the element type as `(namespaceURI, localname)` tuple, while the `qname` parameter holds the qualified name. For elements which have no namespace the `namespaceURI` will be `None`. The `attrs` parameter holds an `Attributes` instance.
>
> The separation of the three components of expanded names into two separate objects, a tuple and a string, reflects the fact that two of these components make up the name proper, while the third one is a lexical detail. Thus, the `name` parameter can be treated as the name itself and be stored in dictionaries, compared with other names, and so on, while the `qname` parameter merely contains additional information for those who want it. Including the qualified name in the tuple would have made comparisons very awkward.
>
> Note that SAX parsers are not required to provide the `qname` value, and some of them, like Pyexpat, are in fact unable to.

`endElementNS(name, qname)`
  The parameters here are the same as for the corresponding `startElementNS` event.

`startPrefixMapping(prefix, uri)`
  This method is called for every namespace declaration in the document to signal the beginning of a region of the document in which the given namespace prefix is mapped to the given namespace URI. This is primarily used to interpret namespace prefixes used in document content.

  The method is called before the `startElementNS` event of the element on which the corresponding declaration appears. Note that there is no guaranteed order in which this event will be triggered for namespace prefixes declared on the same element. Note also that there will never be any calls for the `xml` prefix, since that is predeclared and can never change.

  For the default namespace, the `prefix` argument will be `None`.

`endPrefixMapping(prefix)`
  Signals the end of the scope of a namespace declaration. The method is called after the `endElementNS` event of the element on which the declaration appears. Note that there is no guaranteed order in which this event will be triggered for namespace prefixes declared on the same element, nor is there any guarantee that the order will be the same as for the corresponding `startPrefixMapping` events.

In namespace mode, the interface of the `Attributes` object is the same as in non-namespace mode, but the object has more methods than those that were listed in 8.3.3, "The `Attributes` interface," on page 253. Also, attribute names are no longer represented as strings, but as `(nsuri, localname)` tuples. The additional methods are listed below.

`getValueByQName(self, qname)`

> Returns the value of the attribute that had the given qualified name in the source document. If the attribute did not exist, or if the parser does not provide prefix information, `KeyError` will be raised.

`getNameByQName(qname)`

> Returns the name of the attribute with the given qualified name or raises `KeyError` if prefixes are not available or if the attribute does not exist.

`getQNameByName(name)`

> Returns the qualified name of the attribute with the given name, or raises `KeyError` if the attribute does not exist.

`getQNames()`

> Returns a list of the qualified names of all the attributes of the element. If namespace prefixes are not available the list will be empty.

Example 10–2 shows a variation of the familiar RSS to HTML converter for RSS 1.0, this time using namespaces.

Example 10–2. An RSS 1.0 to HTML converter

```
import sys
from xml.sax import handler, make_parser

# --- Templates

top = \
"""
<!DOCTYPE HTML PUBLIC "-//W3C//DTD HTML 4.0 Transitional//EN">
<HTML>
<HEAD>
  <TITLE>%s</TITLE>
</HEAD>

<BODY>
<A HREF="%s"><H1>%s</H1></A>
"""
```

```
bottom = \
"""
<HR>
<ADDRESS>
Converted to HTML using SAX 2.0.
</ADDRESS>
</BODY>
</HTML>
"""


# --- ContentHandler

rssns = "http://purl.org/rss/1.0/"

class RSS2HTMLHandler(handler.ContentHandler):

    def __init__(self, out = None):
        self._out = out or sys.stdout

        # tracking state
        self._data = ""
        self._first_item = 1
        self._top_done = 0

        self._title = None
        self._link = None
        self._descr = None

    def startElementNS(self, name, qname, attrs):
        self._data = ""

        if (not self._top_done) and \
            (name == (rssns, "item") or name == (rssns, "image")):
            self._out.write(top % (self._title, self._link,
                                    self._title))

            if self._descr != None:
                self._out.write("<p>%s</p>" % self._descr)

            self._top_done = 1

        elif name == (rssns, "item"):
            self._descr = None # reset for this item
            if self._first_item:
                self._out.write("\n<ul>\n")

            self._first_item = 0
```

```
    def endElementNS(self, name, qname):
        if name == (rssns, "title"):
            self._title = self._data

        elif name == (rssns, "link"):
            self._link = self._data

        elif name == (rssns, "description"):
            self._descr = self._data

        elif name == (rssns, "item"):
            self._out.write('  <li><a href="%s">%s</a> %s\n' %
                            (self._link, self._title, self._descr or ""))

    def endDocument(self):
        self._out.write("</ul>\n")
        self._out.write(bottom)

    def characters(self, chars):
        self._data = self._data + chars

# --- Conversion function

def htmlconv(infile, outfile):
    outf = open(outfile, "w")
    parser = make_parser()
    parser.setContentHandler(RSS2HTMLHandler(outf))
    parser.setFeature(handler.feature_namespaces, 1)
    parser.parse(infile)
    outf.close()

# --- Main program

if __name__ == "__main__":
    import sys
    htmlconv(sys.argv[1], sys.argv[2])
```

10.1.9 *The* LexicalHandler *interface*

The LexicalHandler interface is not part of the SAX 2.0 core, and SAX implementations are not required to support it. The handler only provides lexical information about the document, and to be fully understood, this information must be interpreted together with that provided by the `ContentHandler`.

The `LexicalHandler` and the `DeclHandler` presented in the following section were originally intended to be part of SAX 2.0, but there were substantial disagreements over what form they should take, and consensus on their design proved hard to reach. In consequence, they were separated out into a package of their own, known as SAX 2.0-ext, and only finished much later. At the time of writing no Python SAX drivers support them, but by the time you read this, xmlproc and Pyexpat are likely to support both.

The `LexicalHandler` is registered with XML readers through the `setProperty` method. It has the methods listed below.

`comment(content)`

Called for comments anywhere in the document, which includes the DTD, if the parser reads that. To see where in the document the comment appears, this event must be seen in connection with other events of the `ContentHandler`, `DeclHandler`, and this handler. The `content` parameter holds the contents of the comment as a string.

`startDTD(name, public_id, system_id)`

Called when the DOCTYPE declaration is encountered. The `name` parameter holds the name of the document element type, and the `public_id` and `system_id` are the public and system identifiers of the DTD. Both will be `None` if not given in the document. If the `DeclHandler` is supported, this event will be immediately followed by DTD events. A `startEntity` event will be reported before declaration events from the external DTD subset are reported, and this can be used to infer from which DTD subset declarations derive.

`endDTD()`

Signals that the reading of DTD declarations has been completed. Anyone calling `startDTD` must also call this method.

`startEntity(name)`

Signals the beginning of an entity. This event, and the `endEntity` event, together provide information about the entity structure of documents. The `name` parameter is the name of the entity, which will begin with `'%'` if it is a parameter entity, and will be `'[dtd]'` if it is the external DTD subset. There is no `startEntity` call for the document entity.

`endEntity(name)`

Reports the end of an entity, and works just like the `startEntity` event.

`startCDATA()`

Signals the start of the CDATA marked section. Any character data reported to the `ContentHandler` after this event and before the corresponding `endCDATA` will be known to come from a CDATA marked section.

`endCDATA()`

Signals the end of a CDATA marked section.

This handler is not as useful as many of the others, but still has some legitimate uses. It may, for example, be used to implement document transformations that preserve more of the lexical representation of the original document than would otherwise be possible. Another very important feature of the handler is that it provides access to the information in the DOCTYPE declaration, thus making it possible to implement, for example, a validating parser filter.

10.1.10 *The* `DeclHandler` *interface*

The `DeclHandler` interface provides information about the declarations in the DTD, except those reported to the `DTDHandler`. Like `LexicalHandler`, it is not part of the SAX core and support for it is optional. Only logical information about the DTD is provided through this handler, but if supported, the LexicalHandler may provide supplementary lexical information.

Note that, since XML 1.0 only allows one declaration of each element type,[1] SAX only reports the first of these. Similarly, since it allows any number of re-declarations of attributes, general entities, and parameter entities, but ignores all but the first, only the first declaration of each is reported.[2]

attributeDecl(elem_name, attr_name, type,
    value_def, value)

Used to report a single attribute declaration in an ATTLIST. The elem_name parameter is the element-type name, attr_name is the attribute name.

The type parameter will be one of 'CDATA', 'ID', 'IDREF', 'IDREFS', 'NMTOKEN', 'NMTOKENS', 'ENTITY', 'ENTITIES', or 'NOTATION', or, if it is an enumerated attribute, it will be a list of the tokens in the enumeration.

The value_def parameter is a string holding the default declaration of the attribute, which may be '#IMPLIED', '#REQUIRED', '#FIXED', or None.

The value parameter is a string holding the attribute's default value, or None if it has none.

elementDecl(elem_name, content_model)

Reports element declarations, with the name of the element type in the elem_name parameter. The content_model parameter holds the content model of the element type. It will be 'EMPTY' for empty element types, 'ANY' for element types with ANY content, and a tuple of the form (separator, tokens, modified) otherwise. The tuple will represent the outermost parenthesis of the declaration, with the separator used in separator, the list of

---

1. See the XML Recommendation, Section 3.2, para 5.

2. See the XML Recommendation, Section 3.3, last para before 3.3.1; Section 4.2, last para before 4.2.1.

tokens in `tokens` and the modifier `'+'`, `'*'`, `'?'`, or `None` in `modifier`. The list of tokens will contain either strings representing element-type names or, for sub-parentheses, new tuples of the same form.

Thus, the `content_model` for `(foo)+` will be `(None, ['foo'], '+')`, that for `(foo | bar | baz)?` will be `('|', ['foo', 'bar', 'baz'], '?')`, while `(foo, (bar | baz))` will be represented as `(',', ['foo', ('|', ['bar', 'baz'], None)], None)`.

`internalEntityDecl(name, value)`
> Used to report internal entity declarations. The `name` parameter is the name of the entity, beginning with `'%'` if it is a parameter entity, while `value` is the replacement text of the entity as a string.

`externalEntityDecl(name, public_id, system_id)`
> Reports parsed entity declarations, since unparsed ones are reported to the `DTDHandler`. The `name` parameter is the name of the entity, beginning with `'%'` if it is a parameter entity, while `public_id` and `system_id` are the public and system identifiers, respectively. If not given, the `public_id` will be `None`.

For more about schemas, DTDs, and what this handler can be used for, see Chapter 23, "Schemas," on page 892.

10.2 | Parser filters

In the external environment, XML documents often have a different form from what would be the most convenient form for our software. The traditional way of dealing with this has been to do the so-called pre-processing by running a program that converts the file (or files) into a new set of files that more closely match the input we would like to see. The pre-processed set of documents is then loaded into the software. This is a rather awkward way of doing things, however, and in components that are intended to be reusable in many different contexts, it may not be acceptable at all.

Another way of hiding the difference between the desired and real form of an XML document is to present to the application a virtual view of the document (as discussed in 3.3, "Virtual views," on page 91). One way of doing this can be to insert, between the XML parser and the application, some code that changes what the application sees. In SAX terminology this is known as a *parser filter*. Figure 10–1 shows what this looks like conceptually.

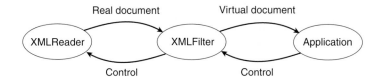

Figure 10–1   Outline of an application with a filter

As the diagram shows, the filter presents a parser-like interface to the application, allowing the application to configure it and set it up for parsing. At the same time, the filter presents an application-like interface to the parser, configures it and receives data from it. The data received by the filter is modified and passed on to the application in the desired form. It is of course also possible to chain together several filters to achieve a combined effect.

The great benefit of this method is that it allows us to modify the XML document seen by an application in a way that is completely independent of the application. The application does not know that a filter is involved at all, so the technique can be used with all kinds of applications, even if they have not been developed to use filters at all.

Parser filters are a powerful and simple mechanism that somehow feels very attractive for many developers, much like regular expressions. And as with regular expressions, one is often tempted to use them beyond what they are really suitable for. Ideally, a parser filter should be relatively simple, and developers should be suspicious of too long filter chains, as these can be hard to maintain and debug.

One immediately attractive application of parser filters is to use them for conversions from one DTD to another. This approach can make it easy to enable an application that accepts documents conforming to a certain DTD also accept other similar DTDs. Whether this really is a good solution depends on the nature and structure of the application. To use a mapping filter in front of a structure builder, for example, makes little sense, since it would be more efficient to simply develop a structure builder directly for the variant DTD.[1] Mapping parser filters can still be useful, mainly in cases where the application has no structure builder or where it is hard to adapt it to accept different input DTDs.

A very good way of using parser filters is for presenting virtual views of the structure of a document that are not specific to one schema, but are general and can be used by any application. Examples of such filters may be filters that implement very general XML applications (like XInclude or XBase) or which do very general transformations (filtering by namespace, mapping attributes to elements, etc.). Reuse of views between applications is not easy otherwise, since different applications have different structure builders, if they use structure builders at all.

Examples of general virtual views may be:

- a view where some attributes have been inherited onto children that do not have them from parents where they are really specified (an example of such a filter can be found in 10.2.3, "The attribute inheritance filter," on page 370),

- a view where one DTD has been mapped to another using a general mechanism such as architectural forms (see Chapter 18, "Architectural forms," on page 692),

---

1. If one wants to separate the processes of XML interpretation and object generation, the traditional factory and builder patterns are better alternatives than parser filters.

- a view where a set of elements have been filtered out, perhaps based on their namespace.

10.2.1 *Developing filters*

Ideally, filter development should happen within a filter development framework with dedicated features for developing filter-based applications. Such a framework might provide features like sharing of resources (e.g., locators), entity managers, element stacks, and so on. It should also have features for easy assembly of configurations of filter components for use in applications.

The MDSAX framework written in Java used to provide this, but development of this framework has been discontinued. David Brownell's XML Utilities (also written in Java), which is still being maintained, does provide some of these features. In keeping with its principle of being low-level and the smallest common denominator, SAX 2.0 does not provide such a framework. However, it does provide a common interface for filters and a convenience base class for filters. This increases the chances that separately developed filters may interoperate and also eases filter development in the absence of supporting frameworks.

10.2.1.1 SAX filter classes

SAX provides a general interface that all parser filters should conform to. This is the `XMLFilterBase` interface in the `xml.sax.saxutils` module, which extends `XMLReader`, adding the operations listed below.

`__init__(parent = None)`
   The constructor takes an optional `parent` argument, which is the event source that the filter will receive events from. This can be an `XMLReader` or another `XMLFilter`, which will receive events from either an `XMLReader` or yet another `XMLFilter`.

`setParent(parent)`
> This method allows the parent to be set after the filter has been instantiated.

`getParent()`
> This method allows applications to retrieve the parent. What purpose this would serve is not clear, but for reasons of symmetry and because it may turn out to be useful, the method is available.

In general, applications will use filters by first instantiating an `XMLReader`, and then building a stack of `XMLFilter` instances that receive events from one another. The application will then register handlers on the topmost filter and use that filter as though it were a parser. One way to see this is that the upper filter is an `XMLReader` with added functionality.

Figure 10–2 shows such a stack of filters, with the `XMLReader` at the bottom. The arrows show a request from the application to the topmost filter (this might be a `parse` method call, or perhaps a `getProperty` method call). The request is echoed down the stack to the `XMLReader`, from where the responses come back up (provided there is a response). In some cases one of the filters may decide that "this call is for me" and not pass the request on further down. For example, this may happen if `getProperty` is called for a property that is specific to the service the filter provides.

The responsibility of a filter is to propagate control requests from the entity above it (which may be the application or another filter) to its parent, and also to pass events the other way. SAX 2.0 provides a convenience base class (the `XMLFilterBase`, in `xml.sax.saxutils` just mentioned) which does just this. This allows filter implementors to extend it and override only those methods where the filter is performing additional work.

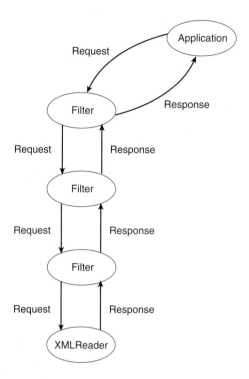

Figure 10–2   A stack of SAX 2.0 parser filters

10.2.1.2 Guidelines for filter writers

To make a filter as reusable as possible it should be written as a self-contained component with clear interfaces to the outside world. Ideally it should not depend on anything other than SAX and present a configuration interface to the outside world, but nothing else. This also implies that a filter shouldn't modify anything in the environment around it, but only pass on a modified event stream. The benefit of not depending on the environment and not modifying it is that this decreases the chances that the filter may be unsuitable for a specific deployment context.

In general, filters that aim to be reusable should present a configuration interface to its environment, much like Unix commands accept command-line options that modify how they work. It is most convenient for the client software if this interface is presented as a set of methods, but any methods added beyond the methods of the `XMLFilter` interface will not be accessible to the application if the filter is wrapped by another filter.

This can be solved by using the features and properties model of the `XMLReader`, most likely by defining new features and properties specific to the filter. However, whether such features and properties make sense or not when the filter is wrapped by another may be difficult to decide. In general, it is safest to define both specific methods and features/properties.

The `getFeature` and `getProperty` methods of filters should provide the correct values if the filter knows them, and otherwise pass the request on further down the stack. The `setFeature` and `setProperty` methods are more difficult, however. The filter should record the settings that it needs, and reject those that it cannot accept. The difficulty is whether or not the values should be passed on further down the stack. What the correct action is will generally depend on both the filter and the feature or property in question. Some general rules can be established, however:

- If you catch a value and use it, and then pass the value further down the stack, make sure to catch any `SAXNotRecognized-Exceptions`, since the value *has* been recognized.

- If you do not pass the value on, you should be certain that only you could possibly make any use of this value. Remember, if someone else needs this value, but cannot get it, they will be in an awkward position.

- If you do pass the value on, be sure to handle any `SAXNot-SupportedExceptions` correctly. It may be that these exceptions should be ignored, or that they should be passed on and the value passed down should be discarded. What you should never do is record the value and then let someone further down raise a `SAXNotSupportedException`, since this is bound to confuse client software.

10.2.2 *The character joiner filter*

This example filter (Examples 10–3 to 10–5) joins consecutive SAX characters events together into single events, in order to solve the problem with split characters events described on 8.3.2, "The `Con-tentHandler` interface," on page 248.

Example 10–3 is the configuration interface that the filter presents to the application. It allows the application to control where the filter receives events from, and lets it configure the functionality of the filter. In this case it consists of allowing the application to decide whether or not processing instructions should cause characters events to be split. (The default is that they should not.)

Example 10–3. The character joiner filter (1 of 3)

```
# This parser filter joins consecutive 'characters' events together
# into single events.

from xml.sax.saxutils import XMLFilterBase

feature_split_on_pis = \
  "http://garshol.priv.no/symbolic/sax/cjf/split-on-pis"

class CharactersJoinFilter(XMLFilterBase):

    # configuration

    def __init__(self, parent = None):
        XMLFilterBase.__init__(self, parent)
        self._contents = ""
        self._split_on_pis = 0

    def set_split_on_pis(self, split):
        """Controls whether the filter allows PI occurrences to
        split characters events."""
        self._split_on_pis = split
```

The `feature_split_on_pis` constant is used by the methods shown in Example 10–4.

Example 10–4. The character joiner filter (2 of 3)

```
# features / properties

def getFeature(self, name):
    if name == feature_split_on_pis:
        return self._split_on_pis
    return self._parent.getFeature(name)

def setFeature(self, name, state):
    if name == feature_split_on_pis:
        self._split_on_pis = state
    self._parent.setFeature(name, state)
```

Here we define `getFeature` and `setFeature` methods for the filter that duplicate the functionality of the configuration methods above. I've defined a URL in the `garshol.priv.no` domain, since this is a domain owned by myself, using a reserved area of its Web namespace (`symbolic/`).

Example 10–5 stores up any characters received in the internal `_contents` buffer and passes them on, emptying the buffer as soon as an element starts or ends. If `_split_on_pis` is set, PIs will also cause this behavior.

Note that this filter may cause character data from different entities to be reported in a single `characters` call. If this happens, applications that use location information will be deceived as the events passed to the application will give the impression that all the character data came from a single entity, when in fact it did not. In cases where this is a problem one should not use this filter at all.

When the document shown in Example 10–6 is processed by a SAX parser, the most likely result is:

- `startElement('doc', ...)`
- `characters('Char')`
- `characters('a')`
- `characters('cters.')`
- `processingInstruction('pi', 'target')`

Example 10–5. The character joiner filter (3 of 3)

```
# events

def characters(self, content):
    self._contents = self._contents + content

def startElement(self, name, attrs):
    if self._contents:
        self._cont_handler.characters(self._contents)
        self._contents = ""
    self._cont_handler.startElement(name, attrs)

def endElement(self, name):
    if self._contents:
        self._cont_handler.characters(self._contents)
        self._contents = ""
    self._cont_handler.endElement(name)


def processingInstruction(self, target, data):
    if self._split_on_pis and self._contents:
        self._cont_handler.characters(self._contents)
        self._contents = ""
    self._cont_handler.processingInstruction(target, data)
```

Example 10–6. An example document

```
<doc>Char&#97;cters.<?pi target?> More chars.</doc>
```

- ▣ `characters(' More chars.')`
- ▣ `endElement('doc')`

When using the `CharactersJoinFilter` with default settings, this
will be what the application receives:

- ▣ `startElement('doc', ...)`
- ▣ `processingInstruction('pi', 'target')`
- ▣ `characters('Characters. More chars.')`
- ▣ `endElement('doc')`

When the split on PIs option is set, the result will be as follows:

- `startElement('doc', ...)`
- `characters('Characters.')`
- `processingInstruction('pi', 'target')`
- `characters(' More chars.')`
- `endElement('doc')`

Example 10–7 is a pseudo-code showing how to use this filter in an application.

Example 10–7. Using the filter in an application

```
import sys
from xml.sax import make_parser
from cjf_filter import CharactersJoinFilter

class MyApplication:
    # implementation omitted

filter = CharactersJoinFilter(make_parser())
filter.setContentHandler(MyApplication())
filter.parse(sys.argv[1])
```

This code will create the filter and give to it a parser to use as a parent. The filter is then used as if it were a parser, and uses the parser it has been given to make this simulation effective. The application does not need to know that a filter is involved at all, but merely does what it would do in any case.

10.2.3 *The attribute inheritance filter*

This example filter inherits attribute values from parent elements onto child elements. This functionality is useful for XML applications which specify that implementations are to behave as if certain attributes really were inherited. The application can configure which attributes are to be inherited, since in most cases only some of the attributes are to be inherited.

The XML Recommendation defines two attributes, `xml:lang` and `xml:space`, whose values apply to all the descendant elements of the elements the attributes appear on. The only exception to this rule is if one of the descendant elements also specifies the attribute. Example 10–8 attempts to motivate this rule.

Example 10–8. Example of an inherited attribute

```
<p xml:lang="en">
Inside this paragraph, <em>everything</em> is in English,
<span xml:lang="no">men det er ikke dette</span>.
</p>
```

In the example, the content of the em element is obviously in English, while the content of the span element is not. (It's Norwegian, and says "but this is not.") This is precisely the behavior that the parser filter in Examples 10–9 and 10–10 implements.

Example 10–9. A parser filter for attribute inheritance (1 of 2)

```
# This filter inherits selected attributes from parent elements
# onto their children.

from xml.sax.saxutils import XMLFilterBase
from xml.sax.xmlreader import AttributesImpl

class MutableAttributesImpl(AttributesImpl):

    def __init__(self, attrs):
        localattrs = {}
        for (k, v) in attrs.items():
            localattrs[k] = v
        AttributesImpl.__init__(self, localattrs)

    def __setitem__(self, key, value):
        self._attrs[key] = value
```

The MutableAttributesImpl class (Example 10–9) is implemented because the filter needs an Attributes class that allows the attributes to be modified. Since the parameter to the constructor is an Attributes instance (and thus non-modifiable), its contents must be copied into a local dictionary to allow the MutableAttributesImpl to do its job.

Example 10–10. A parser filter for attribute inheritance (2 of 2)

```
class AttributeInheritanceFilter(XMLFilterBase):

    # initialization

    def __init__(self, parent, inherited):
        XMLFilterBase.__init__(self, parent)
        self._inherited = inherited # dict w/inherited attrs as keys
        self._attstack = [{}]

    # events

    def startElement(self, name, attrs):
        inherit = self._attstack[-1].copy()
        for inherited in self._inherited.keys():
            if attrs.has_key(inherited):
                inherit[inherited] = attrs[inherited]

        attrs = MutableAttributesImpl(attrs)
        for (k, v) in self._attstack[-1].items():
            if not attrs.has_key(k):
                attrs[k] = v

        self._cont_handler.startElement(name, attrs)
        self._attstack.append(inherit)

    def endElement(self, name):
        del self._attstack[-1]
        self._cont_handler.endElement(name)
```

The filter itself (Example 10–10) is relatively simple. It maintains a stack of inherited attributes, and for each new element it takes a copy of the topmost entry, adds whatever new attributes there are to it and pushes it onto the stack. First making the copy and then adding the new attributes has the side effect that locally defined values will override inherited ones. Then it creates a mutable attribute list, sets the inherited attributes on that, and passes it to the application.

Example 10–11. Input to the inheritance filter

```
<doc xml:base="root">
  <tst/>
  <tst xml:base="tst">
    <tst/>
  </tst>
</doc>
```

If the document in Example 10–11 is read in through the inheritance filter and the filter is told to inherit the xml:base attribute, the result will be as though the document in Example 10–12 has been read in.

Example 10–12. Corresponding output from the inheritance filter

```
<doc xml:base="root">
  <tst xml:base="root"/>
  <tst xml:base="tst">
    <tst xml:base="tst"/>
  </tst>
</doc>
```

10.2.4 *The XInclude filter*

XInclude is an alternative to external entities in that it can be used to pull other resources into a document. Inclusions are specified by using an include element from the XInclude namespace. This element type uses an href attribute to refer to the resource that is to be included. The parse attribute can be used to control how the resource referred to by the href attribute is to be included. The list below describes the alternatives:

`xml`

This value indicates that the resource should be parsed as an XML document, and the results inserted. The resource may in turn contain further XIncludes.

`text`

This value indicates that the contents of the resource should be included in the document as text.

The default value is `xml`.

One of the benefits of XInclude is that it does not require an entity to be first declared in the DTD and then used in the document. Instead, definition and use appear in the same place. Another benefit is that XInclude processing happens after parsing, which makes it easier for applications that wish to do so to retain the storage structure of the documents that would in many cases be lost if entities were used. Still another benefit is that the schema or DTD can control where XInclude elements may appear, something that is not possible with entities.

At the time of writing, no parsers support XInclude directly, something that makes it desirable to write a parser filter that supports it. This makes it possible to use XInclude with any parser that supports SAX 2.0 (Examples 10–13 to 10–23).

Example 10–13 is trivial: documentation string, import statements, and a declaration of the XInclude namespace URI. Declaring the URI in this way makes it easily visible to those who read the source, easy to change, and accessible to client code.

Example 10–14 is the filter class itself. The constructor takes two parameters: a parent object and a callable object that, when called, returns an object that can be used as a parent. This is necessary because the filter needs to allocate a new parser to parse included XML documents. This approach allows client code to give the filter a function that will return an event source of the right class and with the right configuration.

The `_xinclude` attribute holds the name of the XInclude element as it is represented by SAX 2.0. The `_locator` holds a reference to the

Example 10–13. Source code of the XInclude filter (1 of 11)

```
"""
An XInclude implementation written as a SAX 2.0 parser filter. The
implementation follows the 2000-03-22 working draft.

Spec: <URL: http://www.w3.org/TR/2000/WD-xinclude-20000322 >

$Id: xinclude.py,v 1.4 2001/08/19 19:27:41 larsga Exp $
"""

import urlparse, urllib

from xml.sax.handler import feature_namespaces
from xml.sax._exceptions import SAXNotSupportedException
from xml.sax._exceptions import SAXException
from xml.sax.saxutils import XMLFilterBase

# --- Global attributes

xinclude_ns = "http://www.w3.org/1999/XML/xinclude"
```

Example 10–14. Source code of the XInclude filter (2 of 11)

```
# --- The filter

class XIncludeFilter(XMLFilterBase):

    def __init__(self, parent, parent_factory):
        """The parent_factory is a callable object that, when
        called, returns an object that can be used as a parent event
        source for the filter."""
        XMLFilterBase.__init__(self, parent)
        self._factory   = parent_factory
        self._xinclude  = (xinclude_ns, "include")
        self._locator   = None
        self._stack     = []
        self._open_uris = []

        parent.setFeature(feature_namespaces, 1)
```

`Locator` object, which is necessary to be able to get the current system identifier, so that relative system identifiers can be correctly absolutized.

The _stack attribute is where locators and parents are stored away when a new parser is created when a new document is included. This allows the filter to process arbitrarily deep inclusions and still return to the original state. The _open_uris attribute holds a list of the system identifiers of documents that are currently being read from. This allows the filter to detect inclusion loops.

Note that we tell our parent that we need namespace processing by turning it on. If this is for some reason not supported by our parent, instantiation of the filter will fail. This is necessary because the filter depends on namespace processing to be able to reliably detect XInclude elements.

The filter intercepts the setDocumentLocator call (Example 10–15) so that it can store the locator for its own use, and then passes the locator on to the registered ContentHandler.

Example 10–15. Source code of the XInclude filter (3 of 11)

```
# SAX 2.0 methods

def setDocumentLocator(self, locator):
    self._locator = locator
    self._cont_handler.setDocumentLocator(locator)
```

The setFeature call is also intercepted (Example 10–16), so that the filter can make sure that the application does not attempt to turn off namespace processing. All other feature requests are passed on to the parent.

Example 10–16. Source code of the XInclude filter (4 of 11)

```
def setFeature(self, feature, state):
    if feature == feature_namespaces and not state:
        raise SAXNotSupportedException(
            "XInclude processing requires namespace processing")

    self._parent.setFeature(feature, state)
```

The startDocument event is intercepted (Example 10–17) because the filter needs to ensure that a locator has been made available. Without the locator it will be impossible to absolutize relative URLs correctly. Also, since startDocument and endDocument will be fired for each included document, the filter takes care to ensure that they will be passed on to the application only when they refer to the root document. The filter also makes a note of the current system identifier, so that it can detect any attempts to include the root document.

Example 10–17. Source code of the XInclude filter (5 of 11)

```
def startDocument(self):
    if self._locator == None:
        raise SAXException("Locator support is required.")

    if self._stack == []: # only report the first...
        self._open_uris.append(self._locator.getSystemId())
        self._cont_handler.startDocument()

def endDocument(self):
    if self._stack == []: # only report the last...
        self._cont_handler.endDocument()
```

The startElement handler checks whether the new element is an XInclude element, and if not just passes it on (Example 10–18). If it is an XInclude element, the URL is retrieved from it and absolutized against the current base URL. Then, the content of the parse attribute is retrieved, with 'xml' as the default. Actually performing the include is deferred to internal methods defined further down.

Note that the start of the XInclude element is never passed on to the application. This makes the included contents effectively replace the element in the eyes of the application.

The method in Example 10–19 ensures that the XInclude end element event is not passed on to the application.

Example 10–20 shows the internal methods of the filter, which are not intended to be called from the outside. The _resolve_abso-lute_uri method uses the standard urlparse module of the Python

Example 10–18. Source code of the XInclude filter (6 of 11)

```python
def startElementNS(self, name, qname, attrs):
    if name == self._xinclude:
        try:
            url = self._resolve_absolute_uri(
                                        attrs[(None, "href")])
        except KeyError, e:
            self._report_error("The XInclude href attribute is "
                               "required.")
            return

        parse = attrs.get((None, "parse"), "xml")
        if parse == "text":
            self._read_text_from_uri(url)
        elif parse == "xml":
            self._read_xml_from_uri(url)
        else:
            self._report_error("Unknown XInclude parse value " +
                               repr(parse))

    else:
        self._cont_handler.startElementNS(name, qname, attrs)
```

Example 10–19. Source code of the XInclude filter (7 of 11)

```python
def endElementNS(self, name, qname):
    if name != self._xinclude:
        self._cont_handler.endElementNS(name, qname)
```

Example 10–20. Source code of the XInclude filter (8 of 11)

```python
# XIncludeFilter methods

def _resolve_absolute_uri(self, uri):
    return urlparse.urljoin(self._locator.getSystemId(), uri)

def _read_text_from_uri(self, uri):
    inf = urllib.urlopen(uri)
    buf = inf.read(16384)
    while buf != "":
        self._cont_handler.characters(buf)
        buf = inf.read(16384)
    inf.close()
```

interpreter to create an absolute URL from the current URL and the one given in the `href` attribute.

The `_read_text_from_uri` method uses the standard module `urlopen` to open the URL and read the text contents from it. The contents are then just pumped into the `characters` event of the application without further ado. This works because the `characters` method receives parsed characters, which means that entity and character references are already resolved, so there is no need to escape special characters.

Strictly speaking, the text should have been checked for characters that may not appear anywhere in XML documents, but for simplicity this is skipped.

Since we have no idea what client applications may wish to do with XInclude errors we report them to the error handler we have been given (Example 10–21). This ensures that no errors are ignored and that applications are free to handle the errors as they wish. We use `SAXParse-Exception` in order to provide location information to applications.

Example 10–21. Source code of the XInclude filter (9 of 11)

```
def _report_error(self, message):
    self._err_handler.error(SAXParseException(message, None,
                                              self._locator))
```

It would have been better if we could somehow inform applications that our errors were XInclude errors rather than XML parsing errors. This would perhaps have been best achieved by creating an `XInclude-Error` exception class that could be embedded in the `SAXParse-Exception`. This has been omitted for simplicity, however.

The method in Example 10–22 is the heart of the XInclude filter, and perhaps also the one that contains the most subtleties. The first thing it does is verify that it has not already opened the document referred to, so that inclusion loops are avoided. Once that has been made clear, the current parent and locator are put on the stack, and the URI is included on the stack of open URIs.

Example 10–22. Source code of the XInclude filter (10 of 11)

```
def _read_xml_from_uri(self, uri):
    if uri in self._open_uris:
        self._report_error("XInclude inclusion loop detected! "
                           "Bad reference to %s." % repr(uri))
        return

    self._stack.append((self._parent, self._locator))
    self._open_uris.append(uri)

    self._locator = None # to make sure that it is reset
    self._parent = self._factory()
    self._parent.setContentHandler(self)
    self._parent.setErrorHandler(self)
    self._parent.setEntityResolver(self)
    self._parent.setDTDHandler(self)
    self._parent.setFeature(feature_namespaces, 1)
    self._parent.parse(uri)

    (self._parent, self._locator) = self._stack[-1]
    del self._stack[-1]
    del self._open_uris[-1]
```

Then, a new parent is created, handlers are registered, and the new parent is told to parse the included document. Once parsing ends, the stacked parent and locator are popped off the stack and the open URI is popped from its stack. The net result is that this method does not change the state of the filter at all, the only effect it has is the event calls that are passed from the new parent through itself to the application.

The filter also includes a brief test program (Example 10–23) that sets up the filter with a `ContentHandler` that produces text output to the screen and starts parsing. This serves as an example of how to use the filter, but it is also useful for testing the filter.

10.3 | Working with entities

Most people think of XML documents as text files that contain XML markup, but this is only the most common way to use the concepts in

Example 10–23. Source code of the XInclude filter (11 of 11)

```
# --- Test program

if __name__ == "__main__":

    import sys
    from xml.sax.saxutils import XMLGenerator
    from xml.sax import make_parser

    f = XIncludeFilter(make_parser(), make_parser)
    f.setContentHandler(ContentGenerator())
    f.parse(sys.argv[1])
```

the XML Recommendation. In fact, an XML document as described by the XML Recommendation is an *entity* that contains markup, where an entity can be any kind of referenceable collection of characters. This means that an XML document can perfectly well be stored as a blob in a database, a resource on the Internet, or any other kind of collection of characters that is referenceable. What is more, an XML document need not consist of only a single entity, but can be composed of a tree of such entities that include one another.

One of SAX's strengths is that it lets you control how SAX parsers resolve entity references, and this can be used to implement cases such as those listed above. The key to all this, of course, is the `Entity-Resolver` interface.

10.3.1 *Public identifiers and catalog files*

Quite often XML and SGML documents refer to entities that are well-known and may have arrived on the local system separately from the referring document. A prime example of this would be the DTD for HTML 4.01, which many users have downloaded on their own, and which also comes with some SGML applications. On some operating system distributions, such as the Debian distribution of Linux, this DTD is actually installed with the operating system.

In such cases it might be useful to be able to refer to the entity by name rather than by its location, which may well change when the document is moved to another site. This is what public identifiers do: they provide well-known names for entities so that documents can refer to the entities they need by name if they want. However, this mechanism isn't very useful unless there is a general way to tell applications where to find entities with specific public identifiers. This is what catalog files do. In their simplest form, they describe how to map public identifiers to system identifiers (that is, file names or URLs).

There are two main kinds of catalog files. One is SGML Open Catalogs, defined by the SGML Open consortium, which is now called OASIS. The definition of the SGML Open Catalog notation can be found in *OASIS Technical Resolution 9401:1997* at `http://www.oasis-open.org/html/a401.htm`. These catalog files have a simple text notation that is not based on SGML or XML at all. In addition to this, John Cowan has made a proposal for an XML syntax for catalog files, called XML Catalog. The XML Catalog proposal can be found at `http://www.ccil.org/~cowan/XML/XCatalog.html`. These two proposals have the exact same semantics, and it is only the syntax that is different.

SGML Open catalogs are supported by nearly all SGML tools, as well as by some XML tools, although still rather few. XML Catalogs are supported by some XML tools (about as many as SGML Open Catalogs), but they are not supported by any SGML tools.

10.3.1.1 Catalog file formats

Example 10–24 shows an SGML Open Catalog file that contains mappings from the public identifiers for XHTML, RSS, and XBEL to local copies of those DTDs. Text fragments between double hyphens are just comments. The BASE entry gives the base system identifier against which all relative system identifiers in the catalog are resolved. If the BASE entry is omitted, the system identifier of the catalog file itself is used as the base. Example 10–25 shows an XML Catalog with identical meaning.

Example 10–24. An SGML Open Catalog

```
BASE "c:\my documents\xml\"

-- XHTML 1.0 --

PUBLIC "-//W3C//DTD XHTML 1.0 Strict//EN"
       "xhtml\xhtml1-strict.dtd"
PUBLIC "-//W3C//DTD XHTML 1.0 Transitional//EN"
       "xhtml\xhtml1-transitional.dtd"
PUBLIC "-//W3C//DTD XHTML 1.0 Frameset//EN"
       "xhtml\xhtml1-frameset.dtd">

-- RSS --

PUBLIC "-//Netscape Communications//DTD RSS 0.91//EN"
       "rss-0.91.dtd">

-- XBEL --

PUBLIC "+//IDN python.org//DTD XML Bookmark Exchange
        Language 1.0//EN//XML"
       "xbel-1.0.dtd">
```

Note that the data which appears outside the elements is considered comments.

In addition to what is shown in the examples above, SGML Open Catalogs and XML Catalogs support more entry types. These are described below.

SYSTEM sysid1 sysid2

Entries of this type specify that occurrences of sysid1 are to be mapped to sysid2. This can be used, for example, to map online references to local references.

The equivalent XML Catalog entry would be <Remap SystemId="sysid1" HRef="sysid2"/>.

DELEGATE prefix sysid

This type of entry tells the catalog processors that all public identifiers that begin with prefix are to be resolved using the rules in the catalog at sysid.

Example 10–25. An example of an XML Catalog

```
<XMLCatalog>
  <Base HRef="c:\my documents\xml\"/>

  XHTML

  <Map PublicId = '-//W3C//DTD XHTML 1.0 Strict//EN'
       HRef = 'xhtml\\xhtml1-strict.dtd' />
  <Map PublicId = '-//W3C//DTD XHTML 1.0 Transitional//EN'
       HRef = 'xhtml\\xhtml1-transitional.dtd' />
  <Map PublicId = '-//W3C//DTD XHTML 1.0 Frameset//EN'
       HRef = 'xhtml\\xhtml1-frameset.dtd' />

  RSS

  <Map PublicId = '-//Netscape Communications//DTD RSS 0.91//EN'
       HRef = 'rss-0.91.dtd' />

  XBEL

  <Map PublicId = '+//IDN python.org//DTD XML Bookmark Exchange
                   Language 1.0//EN//XML'
       HRef = 'xbel-1.0.dtd' />

</XMLCatalog>
```

The equivalent XML Catalog entry would be `<Delegate PublicId="prefix" HRef="sysid"/>`.

`CATALOG sysid`

This entry loads the catalog at `sysid`, making the catalog processor use the entries in that catalog also.

The equivalent XML Catalog entry would be `<Extend HRef="sysid"/>`.

`DOCUMENT sysid`

This entry is used by command-line parser interfaces to tell what document to parse if none were specified on the command line. This entry type has no equivalent in XML Catalogs.

These types of entries are less frequently used, but can be very useful in some cases.

10.3.1.2 The xmlproc catalog file APIs

Of the XML parsers available in Python, only xmlproc supports catalog files. However, its catalog APIs are so flexible that they can be used with any of the parsers. The central part of the API is the `Catalog-Manager` class (found in the `xml.parsers.xmlproc.catalog` module), which is used to hold parsed catalog files and resolve public and system identifiers against the catalog information. The interface methods are shown below.

`__init__(self, error_handler = None)`
> The constructor creates an empty `CatalogManager` instance. Before it can be used for anything, the instance must load in a catalog file. The `error_handler` parameter can hold a reference to an `ErrorHandler` object, using the interface described in 7.1.2.4, "The `ErrorHandler` interface," on page 173. If no error handler is provided, the manager will create a handler that does nothing for itself.

`set_error_handler(err)`
> This method allows applications to change the error handler.

`set_parser_factory(factory)`
> This method is used to give the catalog manager a factory it can use to create catalog file parsers to parse catalog files. This factory will be used when catalog files are loaded as well as to read further catalog files referred to from the main one. The factory must have a single method `make_parser(sysid)` that returns a parser object.
>
> If no factory is set, the manager will use a default factory that only creates parsers for SGML Open catalogs.

`parse_catalog(sysid)`

Calling this method makes the manager parse the catalog file referred to and store its information internally.

`get_public_ids()`

This method returns a list of all the public identifiers mentioned in the catalog itself and in any delegates or other catalogs loaded from the catalog. (All referenced catalogs are loaded immediately during parsing, even DELEGATEs.)

`get_document_sysid()`

This method returns the value of the DOCUMENT entry if there was one.

`remap_sysid(sysid)`

Given a system identifier, this method returns the correct system identifier to use after remapping according to the SYSTEM entries in the catalog.

`resolve_sysid(pubid, sysid)`

This method will resolve the public and system identifier pair and return the correct system identifier as specified by the catalog, taking SYSTEM entries into account. Note that pubid can be None in the case where no public identifier was given.

The interpreter interaction in Example 10–26 shows the use of this class. (The `demo-cat` file contains the SGML Open Catalog file shown in the example in the previous section.)

Note how the system identifier is remapped to itself, since there were no SYSTEM entries in the catalog.

In addition to the `CatalogManager`, the `xml.parsers.xml-proc.catalog` module also contains xml.parsers.xmlproc.catalog a number of other useful classes, listed below.

`CatalogParser`

A catalog file parser with an event-based API.

Example 10–26. Interaction with the `CatalogManager`

```
>>> from xml.parsers.xmlproc import catalog
>>> cm = catalog.CatalogManager()
>>> cm.parse_catalog(r"c:\minedo~1\temp\demo-cat")
>>> cm.get_public_ids()
['-//W3C//DTD XHTML 1.0 Strict//EN',
 '-//W3C//DTD XHTML 1.0 Frameset//EN', ...]
>>> cm.remap_sysid("http://www.w3.org/TR/1998/REC-xml-19980210.xml")
'http://www.w3.org/TR/1998/REC-xml-19980210.xml'
>>> cm.resolve_sysid("-//W3C//DTD XHTML 1.0 Strict//EN",
... "xhtml.dtd")
'c:\\my documents\\xml\\xhtml\\xhtml1-strict.dtd'
>>> cm.resolve_sysid(None, "xhtml.dtd")
'xhtml.dtd'
>>>
```

`xmlproc_catalog`

An xmlproc `PubIdResolver` that can read a catalog and use it to resolve public identifiers for the xmlproc parser.

To learn how to use these classes, see the xmlproc documentation.

The XML Catalog support that xmlproc provides is in the `xml.parsers.xmlproc.xcatalog` module and consists of an XML Catalog parser that conforms to the same API as the SGML Open Catalog parser. The module also has two parser factories that can create XML Catalog parsers. One of these factories will use file name endings to decide which kind of parser to create.

10.3.2 *Using the SAX* `EntityResolver`

As described above, the xmlproc catalog APIs can be used to add support for catalog files to other XML parsers. The SAX 2.0 `Entity-Resolver` provides an easy way to do this. Example 10–27 shows an `EntityResolver` implementation that uses the xmlproc APIs to implement catalog support. The class is available in the `xml.parsers.xmlproc.catalog` module.

Example 10–27. Catalog support for SAX parsers

```
class SAX_catalog:

    def __init__(self, sysid, pf):
        self._catalog = CatalogManager()
        self._catalog.set_parser_factory(pf)
        self._catalog.parse_catalog(sysid)

    def resolveEntity(self, pubid, sysid):
        return self._catalog.resolve_sysid(pubid, sysid)
```

10.4 | Mapping non-XML data to XML

With SAX, it is easy to make XML applications read non-XML data as if it really were XML. All one needs to do is to give the application an XMLReader implementation that can read the data and map it to XML. In this section we develop an XMLReader that can read emails and map them to XML. (See Example 1–3 for an example of an email.)

The XMLReader will create XML documents following the very simple structure outlined in Example 10–28.

Example 10–28. Outline of XML mail structure

```
<email>
  <headers>
    <from>...</from>
    <to>...</to>
    <subject>...</subject>
    <header name="...">...</header>
    ...
  </headers>

  <body>
  ...
  </body>
</email>
```

In the generated XML we single out three header fields (from, to, and subject) and use the generic header elements for the rest, with the field name in the name attribute. The body element type holds the email body with no additional markup of any kind.

Examples 10–29 to 10–35 show a SAX XMLReader implementation that reads emails and outputs XML in the form shown in Example 10–28.

The XMLReader is built on top of the rfc822 module in the standard Python library, which contains a parser for emails (Example 10–29). All our XMLReader will do is to use this to map emails to XML using SAX. The header_elements map the email header names to element type names and the mail_namespace contains the namespace URI of the generated XML.

Example 10–29. A SAX XMLReader for emails (1 of 7)

```
import rfc822
from xml.sax.xmlreader import XMLReader, AttributesImpl
from xml.sax.handler import feature_namespaces
from xml.sax.saxutils import prepare_input_source, XMLGenerator
from xmlgen import XMLWriter, XMLWriterNS

try:
    import codecs
    use_unicode = 1
except ImportError:
    use_unicode = 0 # assume Python 1.5.2

# --- Constants

header_elements = {"from"    : "from",
                   "subject" : "subject",
                   "to"      : "to"       }

mail_namespace = "http://garshol.priv.no/symbolic/sax/mail/0.1"
```

The MailParser class (Example 10–30) allows applications to turn off or on whether it should deliver namespace-aware XML or not, using the standard getFeature and setFeature methods. Note that we do not implement the methods to get and set handlers, since these are implemented by the XMLReader base class.

Example 10–30. A SAX XMLReader for emails (2 of 7)

```
# --- The XMLReader

class MailParser(XMLReader):

    def __init__(self):
        XMLReader.__init__(self)
        self._namespaces = 0

    def getFeature(self, name):
        if name == feature_namespaces:
            return self._namespaces

        raise SAXNotRecognizedException(("Feature '%s' not "
                                         "recognized") % name)

    def setFeature(self, name, state):
        if name == feature_namespaces:
            self._namespaces = state
            return

        raise SAXNotRecognizedException(("Feature '%s' not "
                                         "recognized") % name)
```

If namespaces are to be supported we use the namespace-aware version of the generator (Example 10–31). Note how we declare mail_namespace as the default namespace of the document.

Example 10–31. A SAX XMLReader for emails (3 of 7)

```
    def parse(self, source):
        if self._namespaces:
            writer = XMLWriterNS(self._cont_handler, mail_namespace)
        else:
            writer = XMLWriter(self._cont_handler)
```

Example 10–32. A SAX `XMLReader` for emails (4 of 7)

```
source = prepare_input_source(source)
if use_unicode:
    (enc, dec, Reader, Writer) = codecs.lookup("iso-8859-1")
    stream = Reader(source.getByteStream())
else:
    stream = source.getByteStream()
```

In Example 10–32, we set up the necessary state variables before going on to generate the XML that represents the email. As noted earlier, we use the `prepare_input_source` function to interpret the argument. Note how we use the `codecs` module to create a character stream.

The generation of the headers is relatively straightforward (Example 10–33). We create the email parser, loop over its headers and call the event methods on the `ContentHandler`. Note how we are careful to provide a qualified name that maps to the expanded name in the `AttributesImpl` instance generated when namespace processing is on.

Example 10–33. A SAX `XMLReader` for emails (5 of 7)

```
writer.startDocument()
writer.startElement("email")
writer.startElement("headers")

message = rfc822.Message(stream)
for header in message.keys():
    if header_elements.has_key(header):
        elem = header_elements[header]
        attrs = {}
    else:
        elem = "header"
        attrs = {"name" : header}

    writer.fieldElement(elem, message[header], attrs)
    writer.characters("\n")

writer.endElement("headers")
```

Example 10–34. A SAX XMLReader for emails (6 of 7)

```
message.rewindbody()

body = stream.read()
print type(body)
writer.fieldElement("body", body)

writer.endElement("email")
writer.endDocument()
```

Finally, we ask the parser to rewind the file-like object to the start of the email body and generate the XML for the body (Example 10–34).

Example 10–35. A SAX XMLReader for emails (7 of 7)

```
if __name__ == "__main__":
    import sys
    p = MailParser()
    p.setContentHandler(XMLGenerator())
    p.parse(sys.argv[1])
```

When the example email in Example 1–3 is run through this XMLReader using the XMLGenerator as the ContentHandler, the output shown in Example 10–36 is produced.

Example 10–36. The email mapped to XML

```
<?xml version="1.0" encoding="iso-8859-1"?>
<email><headers><subject>A funny picture</subject>
<header name="x-mailer">Internet Mail Service (5.5.2448.0)</header>
<header name="content-type">multipart/mixed; boundary="----_=_
NextPart_000_01BF116F.31810180"</header>
<header name="message-id">&lt;50325BA28B0934821A57805FB7C
@mail.public.com&gt;</header>
<header name="x-uidl">37ef28060000035b</header>
<header name="date">Fri, 8 Oct 1999 11:26:22 +0200</header>
<header name="mime-version">1.0</header>
<from>Your friend &lt;friend@public.com&gt;</from>
<to>Lars Marius Garshol &lt;larsga@garshol.priv.no&gt;</to>
<header name="received">by mail with Internet Mail Service
(5.5.2448.0) id &lt;QW2FW41H&gt;; Fri, 8 Oct 1999 11:26:26
+0200</header>
</headers><body>
  This is a MIME-encoded message. Parts or all of it may be
  unreadable if your software does not understand MIME.

----_=_NextPart_000_01BF116F.31810180
Content-type: text/plain

Hi Lars,

here is a funny image.

----_=_NextPart_000_01BF116F.31810180
Content-type: image/gif; name="funny.gif"
Content-transfer-encoding: base64
Content-disposition: attachment; filename="funny.gif"

UEsDBBQAAAAIAHKmWCwhHUlOSWoARGpnAQAHABEAYXBhLnhtbFVUDQAHmIp5PEAIezy
5b15c9tWti/6v6rrHdBM5YjqUNRaOdndts5Vu9Mdn+sML3ZO33OdlAskQQkRCbABUEO
9VvDHgCQlJ10vT9ei3tiEdjY49arHp7/591ykdxkVZ2XxYvB6fhkkGTFtJzlxeWLQV6
+eTp0engP8/3957/4S/fvXz7Pg9/lZT5MnnzP2/efvVNMqC/qY//xrJkNknf7e0ny/A9
1dv/SYpJvUoG//HJ6etnfxrQez8n6ATf0gdF/Wx2/WJw1TSrZ8fHt7e34+4+u8qtOivBl
U9tVWjXlKiuSfPZiMMEmi10fdtGmyapDMrp8V6+Ukq14M3mQ3WYEPnjd5s8j6OL1b0xSy
Y3lCr+rJ+QV1UzRVOVtPn1Ot0pTJ9/fNVVVk8P6a3rs3/+eZ1crko6zqt7oM3r4q6SRc
ucro43JR62udKHWOtqvz5eP8bpmdv73K64T+P5qnbk7j5FVyuc5qfn6fzMrioEmKLJs
F05w/PxYOnp+vELHx8Egx7YzMvz0Kl3RtvA21dm0OVrxwnhT8E5b2gYli/zyqimwlk0
...

----_=_NextPart_000_01BF116F.31810180
</body></email>
```

Tree-based processing

- The DOM
- qp_xml
- Groves

Part Three

In this part we introduce tree-based processing and show how to write applications using this approach. The coverage of the DOM tree API takes most of the part, but other APIs are also covered.

DOM: an introduction

396

Chapter

11

This chapter introduces the tree-based approach to processing in general, as well as the DOM API, which is the standardized tree processing API.

11.1 | Tree-based processing

Of the main approaches to processing, most developers find tree-based processing the most obvious and easiest to understand. In fact, many think that there is no other way, and are surprised to learn that there are other ways of developing processing applications. Tree-based processing probably seems so natural because it presents the document as an object structure that can be traversed and modified directly. That is, it gives an impression of the document as something that can be "seen" and "touched," almost as if it were a physical object.

It is not to be denied that this form of processing has clear advantages, as having the tree directly available tends to make applications less contorted and more natural, because there is no need for state tracking.

397

Also, because the driving loop during processing will be in the processing code, the code becomes easier to read than event-based code often is. Another important difference is that unlike the event-based processing methods, a tree-based processing method can allow client code to modify the document, since the complete document is held in the document representation at all times.

The main disadvantage of tree-based processing is performance. The first problem is that if the document is big, it will require a lot of memory to represent. The DOM objects are relatively heavy-weight, so it is not at all unusual for a document to require 10 times as much memory in a DOM representation as the unprocessed document does on disk. Because of this documents can in some cases be too big for the physical memory of the computer. Documents of 100 Mb are by no means unheard of, and even today few computers can spare 1 Gb of memory for a single application.

The second problem is that building a tree to represent the document requires a large number of objects to be instantiated, especially for the DOM. Creating objects is usually a relatively costly operation in any language, and compared to event-based APIs that are usually much lower-level, this can result in a big performance hit for tree-based APIs.

Finally, a last problem is that in the tree-based approach, the application has to locate the information it needs in the tree itself. With the event-based approach, the information comes to the application instead. This makes tree-based applications much more sensitive to variations in the exact structure of the document. Also, the presence of lexical information, which appears as extra nodes and nodes of extra types, is much harder to handle for tree-based applications than for event-based applications. This is mainly because in event-based applications, lexical information is generally reported as a separate set of events, making it easy to ignore.

11.2 | Getting to know DOM

In versions 4.x of their Web browsers, Microsoft and Netscape added the ability for scripts to modify the contents of downloaded pages inside the browser, in order to allow for various kinds of interactivity. This capability was known as *Dynamic HTML* and allowed scripts to modify both the documents themselves and their style information. Unfortunately, the implementations were not compatible, and the W3C realized that a common specification was needed. At the same time it realized that this specification should not cover just the HTML functionality of these browsers, but also the (then) upcoming new XML language. The result was a specification that was developed quickly and a little out of sync with the rest of the XML family of specifications, and this has caused some complications.

Among the goals of the DOM design process were that it should be language- and platform-independent and that it should be possible to use it to navigate, create and modify documents. In addition, it was also intended to be useful for editors, so the model includes some of the lexical information needed by editors. Designers have been careful to make the DOM support as many kinds of usage contexts as possible, which has led to some restrictions that may seem strange to those who don't know the thinking behind them. The restrictions and their rationales will be explained in the text as we meet them.

The base part of the DOM is the so-called DOM level 1 core, which is able to describe most parts of XML documents. The DOM level 1 also consists of the level 1 HTML interfaces, which extend the core with HTML-specific classes for HTML element types. The DOM level 1 provides complete access to the logical information in the XML document and all the information required by the XML Recommendation. It is not namespace-aware, however, and because of this it does not provide all the information required by the Infoset. There is functionality for navigating the tree as well as for modifying most aspects of it. Also, there is quite substantial support for lexical information, although much of this is optional.

One problematic thing about the DOM as currently defined is that it does not address creating DOM trees from XML documents stored in files, so this basic operation is specific to each DOM implementation. After a DOM tree has been created, however, everything should be interoperable. That is, until you want to write the document back to a file, which must also be done in an implementation-specific way. Note, however, that a new version of the DOM that addresses this need is under development.

The DOM level 2 adds namespace-awareness to the core DOM, and also provides some extra modules. These have functionality for stylesheets, traversal, events, and ranges. The DOM level 2 is covered in 13.3, "DOM level 2," on page 475. The W3C is currently working on the DOM level 3, which currently exists as a set of working drafts. This development is discussed briefly in 13.4, "Future directions for DOM," on page 492.

11.2.1 *The Python DOMs*

The first Python DOM implementation was developed by Stefane Fermigier, and later taken over by the Python XML-SIG, more specifically Andrew M. Kuchling. Parallel to this, a company called Fourthought developed an implementation they called 4DOM, and for quite some time Python developers had two implementations to choose between. The one by the XML-SIG was called PyDOM, while Fourthought's was called 4DOM. After a while it was decided to discontinue development of PyDOM and for the XML-SIG to adopt 4DOM as its DOM implementation. This has now been done, and so today it is best to avoid PyDOM, especially since it uses a different interface than what 4DOM does.

Later, Paul Prescod developed minidom, a small and incomplete, but lightweight, DOM implementation. This implementation was later included in the Python 2.0 distribution (since it was much smaller than the rather large 4DOM) and is described in 13.1.2, "minidom," on page 472. In addition to minidom there is javadom, which wraps Java DOM implementations in the same interface as 4DOM and minidom. This makes it possible to write applications based on the Python DOMs and then use them with the Java DOMs when running in Jython, which is faster. The javadom implementation is covered in 13.1.1, "Using Java DOMs," on page 469.

4DOM implements the complete DOM level 1, both core and HTML. It also implements the core DOM level 2 as well as the traversal part of the level 2 DOM. The old PyDOM only implemented the DOM level 1 core. 4DOM will be used in the examples throughout the book, since PyDOM is effectively dead now. In minidom, parts of both the DOM level 1 and level 2 are implemented, although it leaves out some parts of the interfaces; javadom only implements the DOM level 1.

Fourthought has developed a large suite of Python tools for XML processing, of which 4DOM is but a piece in a larger puzzle. This suite is called 4Suite and also contains a DOM implementation known as DbDom, which stores the document in an object-oriented database. The database used is 4ODS, which is also a part of the 4Suite. This DOM implementation allows XML applications to store their XML documents in an object database and access them through a DOM interface. Because this tool was released so close to the deadline of this book it is not described here, unfortunately.

The 4Suite toolkit also contains two DOM implementations used by the XPath and XSLT implementations therein, known as pDomlette and cDomlette. Both are small, read-only DOM implementations optimized for use with the XPath and XSLT implementations; pDomlette is written in Python, while cDomlette is written in C.

11.2.2 *The specification language*

The DOM is specified in an API definition language called *IDL*, which is short for Interface Definition Language. IDL comes from the OMG (Object Management Group), which is a huge industry consortium dedicated to distributed object technology. The OMG's main specification is CORBA (Component Object Request Broker Architecture). CORBA is a standard for writing objects that communicate with each other transparently, regardless of which process or machine they are in, what language they are written in, or what operating system they run under. A good place to learn more about it is Steve Vinoski and Michi Henning's *Advanced CORBA Programming with C++*, which has a home page at `http://www.awl.com/cseng/titles/0-201-37927-9`.

To make this possible, CORBA needs a language-independent way of describing APIs, and this is what IDL is. The DOM had the same requirements as CORBA did with regards to system and location independence, so the W3C decided to define the DOM interfaces in IDL. In addition to the language independence benefits, this allows the interfaces to be automatically mapped to most programming languages using IDL compilers.

IDL was created mainly for use with languages like C and C++, and because of this IDL describes interfaces based on the abstractions that these languages provide. This makes it fit easily with Java, which is a very similar language, but it doesn't fit as well with a much more dynamic language like Python. So if the DOM interfaces do not seem very Pythonic to you, this is probably the reason. In order to compensate for some of these differences, the interfaces have been slightly adapted for use in Python. (These adaptations will be pointed out as we meet them.)

In IDL, interfaces consist of attributes and methods, just like in Python. IDL methods are mapped to Python methods with the same name and parameters. Attributes, however, are a bit more complex. Each IDL attribute is mapped to an attribute of the same name, but also to get and set methods. The interpreter dialog in Example 11–1 illustrates how the value of the attribute `answer` can be accessed on an instance of the imaginary `Question` interface.

There has been much discussion over whether DOM attributes are best represented as Python attributes or get/set-methods, and the conclusion has been that Python attributes are the right way to represent these attributes. However, the get/set-methods are retained since they

Example 11–1. Accessing IDL attributes

```
>>> question
<Question instance at 0079147C>
>>> question.answer
42
>>> question._get_answer()
42
>>> question._set_answer(43)
Traceback (most recent call last):
  File "<stdin>", line 1, in ?
PermissionDeniedError: You do not have sufficient privileges.
>>> question.answer = 42
Traceback (most recent call last):
  File "<stdin>", line 1, in ?
PermissionDeniedError: You do not have sufficient privileges.
```

are required by the IDL mapping and since they are usually somewhat faster than the attribute access. You are recommended to only use the attribute forms, however.

11.2.3 *The basic DOM model*

In a sense, the DOM presents two different interfaces at the same time, one generic API where everything in a document is an instance of the Node class, and another where everything in a document is an instance of some subclass of Node. In practice all objects are instances of some Node subclass, but code can use them as though they were Node instances, so both views exist at the same time. Nearly everything that can be done with a DOM tree can be done through the methods that the Node class exposes.

The more specialized interface has been added because it is easier to understand and more convenient to use. The "flat" Node-based interface is there because in some statically typed languages, it is costly to cast objects from one type to another, so the DOM uses a design that enables developers to avoid this entirely. This double view is less useful in a language like Python, where types are a property of values rather than of variables, making casting unnecessary. However, this design can have benefits in Python as well, since in some cases it removes the need to check the specific type of a node to perform an operation. The commonality forced on the API by the Node interface can also make some very general operations much easier to implement.

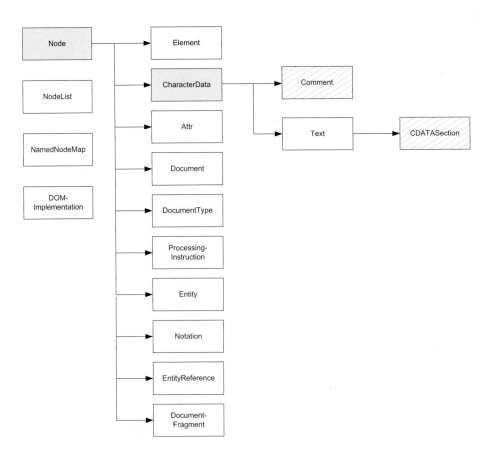

Figure 11–1   Inheritance hierarchy of the DOM interfaces

Figure 11–1 shows the inheritance hierarchy of the DOM interfaces. As you can see, all the interfaces except DOMImplementation, NodeList, and NamedNodeMap inherit from the Node interface. All those interfaces represent constructs that may occur in XML documents, except for `Document`, which represents the entire document and serves as the root of the tree.

Note that abstract interfaces (of which there will never be instances) are shaded gray, while interfaces that only represent lexical information are hatched.

The `NodeList` and `NamedNodeMap` interfaces are not described in this chapter, since in Python these are better used as if they were Python lists and dictionaries. Chapter 20, "DOM in Java," on page 754 describes these interfaces.

Note that DOM gets the names of some of the interfaces wrong in the sense that they clash with established SGML and XML terminology. The name of the `Text` interface, for example, is really a mistake since in SGML terminology, the entire document with markup and character data consists of nothing but text. In fact, text is the common term for markup and character data. So this interface should really have been called `CharacterData`, while if any interface should have been called `Text` it is probably the one that is now called `Node`.

11.3 | A DOM overview

11.3.1 *A quick introduction*

When we load the document in Example 11–2 into a DOM tree, the result is an object structure like the one shown in Figure 11–2.

The topmost object, which acts as the root of the whole tree, is the `Document` object. This object contains some references to more information about the document (the DOM implementation, the DTD, and so on), and also has methods for creating new objects that can be put into the tree.

In the `documentElement` attribute of the `Document` object we find the document element of the tree. In this case this is the `doc` element, represented by an `Element` object. This attribute is accessible as `documentElement` and also through the `_get_documentElement` method.

Example 11–2. A sample XML document

```
<doc>
This is a simple sample document.
It even has a <?pi?> and an
<element with="an attribute"/>.
</doc>
```

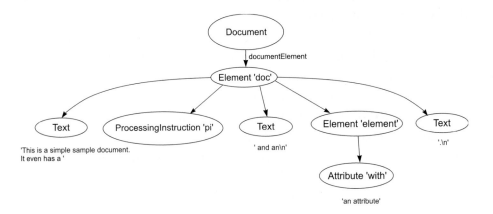

Figure 11–2   A DOM tree of Example 11–2

The Element object has a tagName attribute, which holds the element-type name, in this case 'doc'. It also has a childNodes attribute, which holds the list of child nodes. The first child node is the text immediately inside the doc element, represented by a Text object. The Text object has a value attribute, in which its contents can be found.

The next child node is a ProcessingInstruction object, which represents the processing instruction. It has a target attribute, in which we find the target name 'pi'. (If the processing instruction had had any data, it would have been in the data attribute.) After this node follows another Text node, representing the data between the processing instruction and the following element.

The next node is another Element node, this time representing the element element. This differs from the previous Element node by the fact that it has an attribute. The attribute is represented by an

`Attribute` node available from the `Element` node through the `getAttributeNode` method.

11.3.2 *The flat API*

In the flat view of the API, everything is a node (that is, an instance of the `Node` class), including the document itself. The `Node` interface has three main attributes: `nodeName`, `nodeValue`, and `nodeType`, which can usually tell you the most important things about any node. The exact meaning of `nodeName` and `nodeValue` vary with the node type, as shown in Table 11–1.

Table 11–1   The DOM node types

Node type	*nodeName*	*nodeValue*
`Element`	element-type name	None
`Attr`	attribute name	attribute value
`Text`	`'#text'`	text content
`CDATASection`	`'#cdata-section'`	text content
`EntityReference`	entity name	None
`Entity`	entity name	None
`ProcessingInstruction`	PI target	PI data
`Comment`	`'#comment'`	text content
`Document`	`'#document'`	None
`DocumentType`	document element name	None
`DocumentFragment`	`'#document-fragment'`	None
`Notation`	`'#notation'`	None

As can be seen, the logic behind the `nodeName` attribute is that either it is given the natural name of the node (as in the cases of elements and attributes), or it is given a name derived from the node type and prefixed with "#" to avoid clashes with user-defined names. Similarly, the `nodeValue` is the content of the node, when the node type has something that can naturally be considered content, and `None` otherwise.

Note that the `nodeName` attribute is read-only. This may seem strange, but for some node types it does not make sense to change the node name. Also, DOM designers expected that in some DOM implementations, e.g. those dedicated to specific XML applications such as MathML and SVG, each element type would be implemented by a different class, and most programming languages do not allow objects to change their class. The designers thus chose the safe route and made the attribute read-only.

As for the `nodeType` attribute, this is defined as an enumeration in the original IDL, and in Python this becomes an integer (with suitable constants defined in the DOM module). The `nodeType` is also read-only, because in most (if not all) implementations different classes are used to implement the different node types.

In addition to these three main data attributes, all DOM nodes have a number of tree attributes used for navigating around the tree. These are:

`parentNode`
    The parent of this node. For the `Document`, `DocumentFragment`, and `Attr`, this will be `None`, since these have no parent.

`childNodes`
    The children of this node. In the original IDL this is specified as a `NodeList`, but in the Python implementations `NodeLists` can be used as if they were ordinary list objects.

`firstChild`
    The first of the node's children, or `None`.

`lastChild`
    The last of the node's children, or `None`.

previousSibling
> The node immediately preceding this node in the child list of the parent, or None.

nextSibling
> The node immediately following this node in the child list of the parent, or None.

Finally, there are two attributes which are used for special purposes, and these are attributes (which holds the attributes of elements, since there was nowhere else to put them) and ownerDocument (which holds the Document to which the node belongs; for Document nodes, the value is None).

11.3.2.1 Walking the tree

Example 11–3 shows the result of loading the example document in Example 11–2 into 4DOM and walking around the resulting tree in the Python interpreter. How to load documents from files is explained in 12.1.2, "Loading an XML document," on page 438.

Example 11–3. Walking a DOM tree in the interpreter

```
>>> doc
<XML Document at 8763212>
>>> doc.nodeName
'#document'
>>> doc.nodeType
9
>>> ch = doc.childNodes
>>> ch
<NodeList at 8752556: [<DocumentType Node at 8720284: Name = '' with
0 entities and 0 notations>, <Element Node at 12205756: Name = 'doc'
with 0 attributes and 5 children>]>
>>> root = doc.documentElement
>>> root.nodeName
u'doc'
>>> root.nodeType
1
```

```
>>> ch = root.childNodes
>>> ch
<NodeList at 12193100: [<Text Node at ba0cdc: data = '\0xaThis is a
simple sa...'>, <Processing Instruction at 8498828: target = 'pi',
data = ''>, <Text Node at 81cdfc: data = ' and an\0xa'>, <Element
Node at 8491580: Name = 'element' with 1 attributes and 0 children>,
<Text Node at 85320c: data = '.\0xa'>]>
>>> txt = ch[0]
>>> txt.nodeName
'#text'
>>> txt.nodeType
3
>>> txt.nodeValue
u'\012This is a simple sample document.\012It even has a '
>>> pi = ch[1]
>>> pi.nodeName
'#processing-instruction'
>>> pi.nodeValue
u''
>>> pi.nodeType
7
>>> elm = ch[3]
>>> elm.nodeName
u'element'
>>> elm.attributes
<NamedNodeMap at 8491420: {u'with': <Attribute Node at 8736108:
Name = "with", Value = "an attribute">}>
>>> att = elm.attributes["with"]
>>> att.nodeName
u'with'
>>> att.nodeValue
u'an attribute'
```

This example listing mainly illustrates what was said in the previous section, but there are a couple of new things worthy of note. One of these is that in 4DOM, the value returned by childNodes is not a straight Python list, but rather a NodeList implementation done as part of 4DOM, which behaves as a normal Python list. In 4DOM the NodeList implementation also implements the extra methods specified by the DOM, while minidom does not do this and represents NodeLists as Python lists. You are recommended to only use them as if they were ordinary Python lists, which is also the most practical way to use them.

11.3.2.2 The Node methods

The Node interface, as noted earlier, is the base interface for all interfaces representing document constructs. And as mentioned earlier, it is possible to navigate through the DOM tree using nothing but the attributes defined on the Node interface. This interface has some methods as well, however, and these are mainly useful for modifying the tree. Many of these methods are operations on the child list and assume that the node operated on is of a type that is allowed to have children. If it is not, an exception will be raised.

insertBefore(newChild, neighbourChild)
> This method inserts a new child (newChild) before an existing child (neighbourChild) in the child list of this object. If neighbourChild is None, the new child will be inserted as the last child in the list. If neighbourChild is not in the child list, an exception will be raised.

replaceChild(newChild, oldChild)
> Replaces the oldChild node with newChild, returning oldChild. If oldChild is not in the child list, an exception will be raised.

removeChild(oldChild)
> Removes oldChild from the child list of the node and returns it. If oldChild is not in the child list, an exception will be raised.

appendChild(newChild)
> Adds newChild to the end of the child list of the node.

hasChildNodes()
> A convenience method that returns true if the node has children, and false otherwise. It can safely be called on all node types.

```
cloneNode(deep)
```
> Returns a copy of the node with all the node data except for the parent reference. Also, unless `deep` is `true`, the children will not be copied. If it is `true`, all descendants will be copied recursively. Note that the attributes of elements will also be cloned, even though they are not considered children. This method is safe to call on all node types.

11.3.2.3 Modifying the tree

Using the methods above and the methods on the `Node` interface it is possible to modify a DOM tree in much the same way one would do in an XML editor. Certain aspects of the tree remain fixed, and to access these, one needs the detailed interface described below. Example 11–4 uses the flat API and the factory methods on the `Document` object to modify the document we used in Example 11–3, continuing from where we left off there.

In Example 11–4 we could have cloned the existing nodes with `cloneNode` to create the new nodes. This was not done, because then we would have been unable to change the names of the element and processing instruction nodes. The `Document` methods were used instead, since they allow the node names to be specified.

Example 11–4. Modifying a DOM tree

```
>>> txt = doc.createTextNode("Now there is even more text.\n")
>>> pi = doc.createProcessingInstruction("second", "pi")
>>> elm = doc.createElement("p")
>>> elm.appendChild(txt)
<Text Node at 8781136: data = 'Now there is...'>
>>> elm.appendChild(pi)
<Processing Instruction at 8781728: target = 'second', data = 'pi'>
>>> root.appendChild(elm)
<Element Node at 8655888: Name = 'p' with 0 attributes and
2 children>
```

When serialized back to an XML document, the modified document looks like in Example 11–5.

Example 11–5. The modified DOM document

```
<doc>
This is a simple sample document.
It even has a <?pi ?> and an
<element with='an attribute'/>.
<p>Now there is even more text.
<?second pi?></p></doc>
```

Note how the first PI was changed when serialized back. A space was inserted after the PI target, since the serializer expected there to be data after the target. This representation is logically equivalent to that in Example 11–3. This is confirmed by the Infoset, which does not make any distinction between these cases at all.

11.4 | Fundamental DOM interfaces

So far we have only seen the flat API based on the Node interface. This API can be very convenient when one does not care about the types of the nodes. It also tends to be more efficient in traditional statically typed languages. In these languages, access to properties other than those declared on the Node interface requires subverting the type system somehow, and "casting" a node reference into some more specific type. Python and other dynamically typed languages don't have this problem, since with dynamic typing the type follows the value rather than the variable that refers to it, so one can access any property of a node, provided that the node in question actually has that property.

The downside is of course that the compiler cannot verify before the program is run that it will never attempt an operation on a value that the value does not allow because it is of wrong type. It could be argued that, strictly speaking, most statically typed languages do not have this guarantee either, since it is possible to override the type system through "casts" and similar operations. Languages in which programs that pass the compiler are guaranteed to be type-safe are known as strongly typed. (Neither C++ nor Java are strongly typed.[1])

The result is that in Python and other dynamically typed languages we can freely mix the flat and inheritance-based APIs as long as we know that the operations we use are supported on the objects we perform them on. This contributes to making DOM programming in Python more convenient than in Java. More convenient syntax for working with the NodeList and NamedNodeMap interfaces also helps.

The fundamental DOM interfaces are the interfaces that are shared between the XML and HTML parts of the DOM, and they are the most important interfaces in the DOM. Most applications will never need any other interfaces (except for the processing instruction interface).

11.4.1 *The* Document *interface*

This interface is a very important one, not just because it is the root of the DOM tree, but also because it is the one that is used to create new DOM nodes programmatically. In addition to this, it holds references to DTD information and meta-information about the DOM implementation. The Document node serves an additional purpose by being a container for any processing instructions and comments outside the document element. These will be held in its child list together with the document element.

The attributes on the Document interface are listed below.

---

1. A more serious problem is the performance hit taken by dynamically typed languages, as implementations have to constantly verify that the program is not doing something illegal, instead of being able to simply assume that it cannot do anything illegal, after this is guaranteed by the compile-time checks done by the compiler. (Statically typed languages only need to perform this check at the points where programmer does type casts, hence the expensiveness of this operation.)

doctype
> The `doctype` attribute holds a reference to a `DocumentType` node if the document has an associated DTD, and is `None` otherwise. The attribute is read-only, which means that the application cannot change the the DTD of a `Document`.

implementation
> The `implementation` attribute holds a reference to a `DOMImplementation` object that represents the DOM implementation used by this particular `Document` instance. The `DOMImplementation` object can be queried for information about the implementation. The attribute is read-only, unsurprisingly.

documentElement
> This attribute holds the `Element` object that represents the document element of the document. This node also appears in the `childNodes` attribute of the document, but is repeated here in order to make it easier to access. This attribute is also read-only.

Note that since the document may have PIs and comments outside the document element, the `childNodes` attribute may hold nodes representing them as well, not just the document element node.

In addition to these attributes, the `Document` interface has a number of methods for creating other objects, as well as a method with a weak querying capability. These methods are listed below.

createElement(name)
> Creates a new `Element` object with the given element type name.

createDocumentFragment()
> Creates an empty `DocumentFragment` object. This interface is described in 11.4.5, "The `DocumentFragment` interface," on page 423.

createTextNode(data)
> Creates a new `Text` object with the given string as content.

`createComment(data)`
  Creates a new `Comment` object with the given string as content.

`createCDATASection(data)`
  Creates a new `CDATASection` object with the given string as content. Note that this is exactly the same as creating a `Text` object, except that it will be serialized differently. When possible, the `createTextNode` method should be used instead, as explained in 11.6.1, "The `CDATASection` interface," on page 427.

`createProcessingInstruction(target, data)`
  Creates a new `ProcessingInstruction` object with the given target and data.

`createAttribute(name)`
  Creates a new `Attr` object with the given name and an empty string as its value.

`createEntityReference(name)`
  Creates a new `EntityReference` object, referring to the entity with the given name.

`getElementsByTagName(name)`
  Traverses the descendants of the node in document order and returns a list of all element nodes with the given element-type name. Note that the special name `'*'` matches all element types.

With these methods and the flattened API it is possible to create nearly all aspects of documents programmatically, although there are some minor exceptions. There is one very important thing missing in both parts of the API, however: the ability to create `Document` instances. In fact, how to create a `Document` node is not defined by DOM level 1, so all implementations have their specific ways of doing this. With minidom, you can just import `xml.dom.minidom` and then instantiate the `Document` class in that module. How to do this for 4DOM is explained in 12.1.1, "Creating an empty document," on page 436.

11.4.2 *The* Element *interface*

Together with Document and Text, Element is one of the three most important interfaces in the DOM. Its interface is almost entirely dedicated to handling the attributes of the element. The Element interface has only one attribute (tagName), which contains the element-type name and is identical to nodeName. Note that the name is not really a very good one, since the XML specification calls this the element-type name, as does the SGML standard. (The Infoset has no term for it, since it takes a namespace view of XML.) The tagName is read-only, for the same reasons as the nodeName attribute.

The methods of the interface are listed below:

getAttribute(name)

Returns the value of the named attribute as a string. If the attribute does not exist, an empty string is returned. This makes it impossible to detect whether the attribute is present or not using this method. Instead, the getAttributeNode method below must be used for this.

setAttribute(name, value)

Sets the value of the named attribute. If the attribute doesn't exist already, it is created. If it exists, it is simply overwritten.

removeAttribute(name)

Removes the named attribute. If the attribute does not exist, no special action is taken.

getAttributeNode(name)

Returns the Attr object that holds the attribute with the given name. If the attribute is not specified, None is returned.

setAttributeNode(attr)

Inserts the attribute node on the element (note that attr must be an Attr instance). If the attribute already exists, it is replaced.

`removeAttributeNode(attr)`

Removes the given attribute (`attr` must be an `Attr` instance) from the element.

`getElementsByTagName(name)`

Just like on `Document`, this method traverses the descendants of the element in document order and returns a list of those with the given element type name. The special element-type name `'*'` matches all elements.

`normalize()`

When a document is loaded from a file or when it is created by modifying the tree, one can easily end up with a tree where data is split into `Text` nodes that are adjacent to each other. This can be awkward when working with the tree, so calling this method causes all adjacent `Text` nodes below the element to be merged. This is intended to solve that problem, but note that `CDATASection` nodes are not considered `Text` nodes and will not be merged. For this reason, using this method to merge split text nodes is *not* recommended. For more about this, see 11.6.1, "The `CDATASection` interface," on page 427.

11.4.3 *The* `CharacterData`, `Text`, *and* `Comment` *interfaces*

In the DOM, the `Text` and `Comment` interfaces are sub-interfaces of an interface called `CharacterData`, which is a common interface for nodes that contain strings. A DOM tree can't actually hold `CharacterData` nodes; all nodes must belong to one of its sub-interfaces. The DOM defines this interface only to simplify the DOM API.

Note that these nodes represent the character data of a document after it has been parsed. Characters that were escaped with character references and entity references in the source document will all be represented as plain text in these nodes. So when setting the value of a `Text` node, be aware that setting it to `'Donald Duck & Co'` is equivalent to writing `'Donald Duck &amp; Co'` in a source document. In fact, it is not possible to build a DOM tree that is serialized back to a document containing an unescaped `'&'` character. The only way to do this is to write your own serializer, since such a document would not be well-formed, and it would be a poor DOM implementation that lets applications produce documents that are not well-formed.

The `CharacterData` interface has only two attributes:

`data`
> This attribute holds the character data of the node and is identical to `nodeValue`.

`length`
> This attribute holds the number of characters in the node contents. The term *characters* used here is not entirely accurate since the DOM specification assumes that all character data in a DOM tree will be represented in the UTF-16 encoding, where some characters can be represented as two surrogate code units. What the `length` attribute counts is 16-bit code units, rather than true characters.[1]
>
> This attribute is read-only, since it does not make sense to change the length of the text without changing the text itself.

In addition to these attributes, the interface has a number of methods for working with the data contents of the node. These are listed below. (Note that all the offsets given in the list below start from 0.)

`substringData(offset, count)`
> This method returns a piece of the data held in the node, starting at `offset` and including `count` characters from that point on. If `data` were a Python string, the same effect could be achieved with Python slicing in this way: `data[offset : offset + count]`.

---

1. This decision makes it very awkward to use other encodings, such as UTF-8 (used in Perl) and UTF-32, in the DOM.

If the indexes given go outside the string boundaries, an exception is raised.

`appendData(newdata)`

Appends the given string to the character data in the node.

`insertData(offset, newdata)`

Inserts the given string in the node data at `offset`. This is equivalent to setting the `data` attribute to `data[ : offset] + newdata + data[offset : ]` in Python.

`deleteData(offset, count)`

The indexes work as with `substringData`, but instead of returning the substring, this method removes it from the node data. This is equivalent to setting the `data` attribute to `data[ : offset] + data[offset + count : ]` in Python.

`replaceData(offset, count, newdata)`

This method replaces the data in the substring with the given string. The replaced string does not have to be the same size as the new data. This is equivalent to setting the `data` attribute to `data[ : offset] + newdata + data[offset + count : ]` in Python.

Example 11–6 shows how the above operations work, as well as how to do the same operations with the Python slice syntax, where possible.

The `Comment` interface has no additional methods or attributes beyond those in the `CharacterData` interface, but it is still a separate sub-interface with a special value for the `nodeType` attribute.

The `Text` interface adds one additional method, the `splitText(offset)` method, which splits the `Text` node at the given offset. The data of the original node is shortened, and a new node with the remaining data is returned.

Example 11–6. How to do DOM `CharacterData` slicing

```
>>> txt = doc.createTextNode("example text")
>>> txt.substringData(8, 4)
'text'
>>> txt.data[8 : 12]
'text'
>>> txt.appendData(".")
>>> txt
<Text node 'example text.'>
>>> txt.data + "."
'example text.'
>>> txt.insertData(0, "The ")
>>> txt
<Text node 'The example text.'>
>>> txt.data[ : 0] + "The " + txt.data[0 : ]
'The example text.'
>>> txt.deleteData(11, 6)
>>> txt
<Text node 'The example'>
>>> txt.data[ : 11] + txt.data[11 + 6 : ]
'The example'
>>> txt.replaceData(4, 7, "node.")
>>> txt
<Text node 'The node.'>
>>> txt.data[ : 4] + "node." + txt.data[4 + 7 : ]
```

11.4.4 *The attribute interface*

The `Attr` interface represents an attribute value assignment on an element. As such its function is rather intuitive, but the way the DOM views the position of attributes in the document tree is rather surprising to most people. Attributes are not considered children of the element, which makes sense, since otherwise they would have to show up in the `childNodes` list. It also means that the element cannot be the parent of the attributes. And since attributes are not considered to be in the child list at all, they have no siblings either, so `parentNode`, `previousSibling`, and `nextSibling` are all `None` for `Attr` nodes.

This is not what most people expect, but once you stop to think about it, this is the solution that makes the most sense. This view of the element/attribute relationship is not unique to the DOM. The Infoset takes a similar view, as does traditional SGML thinking.

The `Attr` interface does not have any additional methods, but it does have three extra attributes, which are listed below.

name
> This is the name of the attribute (just like `nodeName`).

specified
> This is a boolean property that indicates whether this attribute has been explicitly specified (in the document or by DOM creation code), in which case it is `true`, or whether it has been inferred from default or `#FIXED` declarations in the DTD. The property is read-only.
>
> In general, this property can not be trusted to have the correct value. Most DOM implementations are built on SAX, and since SAX does not provide this information, such DOM implementations cannot have it either. Providing this information requires close integration with the parser. This information is, in any case, purely lexical and of little practical value.

value
> This is the value of the attribute, identical to `nodeValue`.

Note that the DOM specification states that attributes that are defaulted from the DTD must behave differently than other attributes. For example, when removed by calls to `removeAttribute` or `removeAttributeNode`, the calls succeed, but the attributes pop back into existence immediately. Note also that attempts to change attributes that are `#FIXED` in the DTD will fail with an exception. Few DOM implementations provide this kind of DTD awareness, but it is still good style to avoid operations that go against the DTD of the document.

Note also that attribute nodes have children, contrary to what you might expect. This allows the DOM to represent the entity structure of attributes in a controlled way. The only kinds of child nodes allowed in attributes are `Text` and `EntityReference` nodes. Note, however, that very few, if any, DOM implementations will create `Entity-`

Reference nodes, even if there were entity references in the source document. `EntityReference` nodes in attributes are especially rare, and it is only in extreme cases that this feature is useful at all.

11.4.5 *The* `DocumentFragment` *interface*

The `DocumentFragment` interface is, as the name says, intended to represent fragments of documents, rather than entire documents. If you want to represent the result of searching the document, of cutting out a part of the document, or simply some other part (or parts) of the document, you can use `DocumentFragment`. The interface extends the `Node` interface, adding no attributes or methods. `Document-Fragment` nodes are simply containers for their children and serve no other purpose.

The contents of `DocumentFragment`s are somewhat less restricted than those of `Document`s. `Document`s must have exactly one element child, but fragments may have zero, one or more element children. This allows fragments to represents regions of a document that are not necessarily contiguous.

When a `DocumentFragment` node is inserted into the node list of another node, what happens is that its children are inserted in its place.

11.4.6 *The* `DOMImplementation` *interface*

The `DOMImplementation` interface can be used to find out which DOM features a particular DOM implementation supports. There is no standard way to create a `DOMImplementation` instance, so the only reliable way to get hold of one is through the `implementation` attribute on the `Document` interface.

The interface has only one method, `hasFeature(feature, version)`, which returns `true` if a feature is supported and `false` otherwise. Both `feature` and `version` parameters are strings. The `version` parameter is `'1.0'` for level 1 and `'2.0'` for level 2. If it is

None, `true` will be returned if the implementation supports any version at all. Table 11–2 shows the possible values for `feature`.

Unfortunately, implementations of the `hasFeature` method are rather poor in most DOM implementations. Many will fail to return `true` for many of the features that they support.

Table 11–2   The features of the DOM

Feature	*Meaning*
XML	The DOM core
HTML	The HTML module
Views	The views module (level 2)
StyleSheets	The stylesheets module (level 2)
CSS	The CSS module (level 2)
CSS2	The extended interfaces of the CSS module (level 2)
Events	The events module (level 2)
UIEvents	The user interface events module (level 2)
MouseEvents	The mouse events module (level 2)
MutationEvents	The mutation events module (level 2)
HTMLEvents	The HTML events module (level 2)
Traversal	The traversal module (level 2)
Range	The range module (level 2)

A table that shows which DOM implementations support which features can be found on page 477.

11.5 | A simple example application

Example 11–7 implements the by now familiar RSS to HTML converter, which makes for an interesting comparison with the SAX implementation in Example 8–3. Note that it makes the simplifying assumption that the DOM implementation will not create CDATA marked section nodes or entity reference nodes. (These node types are described in the next section.)

Comparing this implementation with the SAX implementation, it is easy to see that this implementation is much easier to read, since the flow of control is entirely within the readable code, making the order of actions immediately obvious, unlike the SAX implementation.

Example 11–7. RSS to HTML converter using the DOM

```
import sys
from xml.dom.minidom import parse        # We use minidom

# --- Templates

top = \
"""
<!DOCTYPE HTML PUBLIC "-//W3C//DTD HTML 4.0 Transitional//EN">
<HTML>
<HEAD>
  <TITLE>%s</TITLE>
</HEAD>

<BODY>
"""

bottom = \
"""
<HR>

<ADDRESS>
Converted to HTML by rss2html.py.
</ADDRESS>

</BODY>
</HTML>
"""
```

```python
# --- The converter

def conv2html(root, out = None):
    out = out or sys.stdout
    title = data(root.getElementsByTagName("title")[0])
    link = data(root.getElementsByTagName("link")[0])
    channel = root.getElementsByTagName("channel")[0]
    descr = channel.getElementsByTagName("description")
    if descr != []:
        descr = data(descr[0])
    else:
        descr = None

    out.write(top % title)
    out.write('<h1><a href="%s">%s</a></h1>\n' % (link, title))
    if descr:
        out.write('<p>%s</p>\n\n' % descr)

    out.write("<ul>\n")
    for item in root.getElementsByTagName("item"):
        convitem(item, out)
    out.write("</ul>\n")

    out.write(bottom)

def convitem(item, out):
    title = data(item.getElementsByTagName("title")[0])
    link = data(item.getElementsByTagName("link")[0])
    descr = item.getElementsByTagName("description")
    if descr != []:
        descr = data(descr[0])
    else:
        descr = ""

    out.write('  <li><a href="%s">%s</a> %s\n' %
              (link, title, descr))

# --- Utilities

def data(element):
    return element.firstChild.nodeValue

# --- Main program

doc = parse(sys.argv[1])
root = doc.documentElement
conv2html(root)
```

Note that this example is very fragile, for two reasons. The first one is its poor implementation of the `data` utility function. The implementation in this example will fail if the data inside an element is split over several nodes, for example because the data arrived in more than one SAX `characters` call. In addition, the code will fail with tracebacks if some of the elements are missing. Both these problems will be solved in later examples when we introduce a module of reusable utility functions.

11.6 | Extended DOM interfaces

The DOM specification describes the interfaces in this section as extended interfaces. The reason it singles them out is that they are only used for XML and never used for the HTML part of the DOM. Another thing that makes these interfaces special is that most of them are of purely lexical significance, which means that most DOM implementations will not create them when reading from a file. Also, when instances of these lexical interfaces are found in the DOM tree, they complicate matters for processing software.

11.6.1 *The* CDATASection *interface*

In the DOM, pieces of character data that originally came from CDATA marked sections have an interface of their own, separate from the Text interface used for ordinary character data in the document. This distinction is purely lexical, and isn't something that normal applications care about. This is also why the SAX core does not make this distinction, or even make the information available at all. The Infoset makes the distinction optional for exactly the same reason.

The CDATASection interface extends the Text interface, but does not add any attributes or methods. This interface basically serves two purposes: indicating which parts of a document originally came from CDATA marked sections and enabling applications to indicate that upon serialization, specific pieces of data should be written out as CDATA marked sections.

This double representation for character data nodes means that for applications that work with DOM trees and look for character data it is not sufficient to look for nodes with a node type of TEXT_NODE; they must also look for nodes with a node type of CDATA_SECTION_NODE.

Another problem is that when retrieving the contents of an element, you need to be aware of the fact that the element contents could be split by a CDATA marked section. For example, the document in Example 11–8 will have a different DOM representation from the document in Example 11–9, even though the logical contents of these two documents are identical.

Example 11–8.

```
<doc>
Simon &amp; Schuster
</doc>
```

Example 11–9.

```
<doc>
<![CDATA[Simon & Schuster]]>
</doc>
```

In the first case, the children of the doc element can either be a single text node or multiple text nodes, if it were built from a SAX parser which split the characters events. Most likely it would be three text nodes, one for the data before the entity reference, one for the entity text, and one for the remaining data. In the second case, assuming the DOM implementation created CDATA nodes, it would be at least three nodes: whitespace text node, CDATA node, and final whitespace text node, but it could be more if the parser split the events due to buffering.

However, the most interesting problem is that if Example 11–9 *did* have a CDATA node, a call to normalize would join all the nodes into one in the first example, but leave three distinct nodes in the second case, since `normalize` doesn't merge `CDATA` and text nodes. This problem means that `normalize` is effectively useless, and other means should be used to extract complete data from a DOM tree.

In general, few DOM implementations create `CDATA` nodes when building from source documents (none of the Python ones do), and you are not advised to create any when building DOM trees yourself unless you have very specific requirements that only `CDATA` nodes can meet.

My personal opinion is that having the `CDATASection` interface in the DOM at all is a design mistake. Having an `isCData` attribute on the `Text` interface would have made things easier for the overwhelming majority of applications that do not need this information, while at the same time the information would be available to the applications that need it.

11.6.2 *The* `DocumentType` *interface*

DOM level 1 provides exactly the same DTD information as does SAX 1.0 (notations and unparsed entities), and for exactly the same reason: the XML 1.0 Recommendation requires this information to be provided to applications. In addition, DOM level 1 also provides information about external general entities, since this is needed for the `EntityReference` nodes. However, in DOM level 1 all interfaces and attributes dealing with the DTD are read-only.

The `DocumentType` interface extends the `Node` interface, and adds the three attributes listed below.

name
   This is the name of the document element in the document type.

entities
   This is a `NamedNodeMap` (which in Python simply means a dictionary) that maps entity names to their corresponding `Entity` objects.

notations
>   This is also a `NamedNodeMap` (again a dictionary) that maps notation names to their corresponding `Notation` objects.

Note that not all DOM implementations make this information available at all; 4DOM and javadom do, but minidom does not.

11.6.3 *The* `Notation` *interface*

This interface represents a notation declared in the DTD, and adds two new attributes to those defined on `Node`. Note that the notation name is only available through the `nodeName` attribute.

publicId
>   This attribute holds the public identifier of the notation, or `None` if none were specified.

systemId
>   This attribute holds the system identifier of the notation, or `None` if none were specified. Note that the XML Recommendation requires that at least one of these be specified, and allows both to be specified.[1]

11.6.4 *The* `Entity` *interface*

This interface is used to represent external general entities and unparsed entities in an XML document. This represents not the entity declaration in the DTD or the entity reference in the document, but rather the entity itself — that is, the file or Web resource or whatever, containing XML markup. This means that if the entity has been expanded by an XML processor, the `childNodes` property will contain the children of the entity. Contrary to what you might expect it is not used to rep-

---

1.   See the XML Recommendation, Section 4.7, production 82.

resent the document entity, only external references from a DOM tree, and `Entity` instances are only accessible through the `DocumentType` interface.

The `nodeName` attribute is the only attribute that holds the name of the entity. In DOM level 1, `Entity` instances and their subnodes are read-only.

The attributes of the `Entity` interface are listed below.

`publicId`
>   This is the public identifier of the entity, or `None` if it was not specified.

`systemId`
>   This is the system identifier of the entity, or `None` if it was not specified.

`notationName`
>   This is the name of the notation associated with the entity, or `None` if the entity was a parsed entity.

11.6.5 *The* `EntityReference` *interface*

This interface is used to represent entity references in the contents of a document. Instances of it appear as children of elements and attributes. The contents of the entity referred to by the entity reference are available as the list of children. Note that all the children and their descendants are read-only. If the DOM tree has an `Entity` object corresponding to the `EntityReference` object, the child node lists of these objects will be shared. `EntityReference` extends `Node`, but does not add any additional declarations.

Having `EntityReference` nodes in the document can be troublesome, because to get all the children of the parent, you must remember to filter out `EntityReference` nodes but include all their descendants. This can be rather awkward, and it can be hard to remember in all cases the complications that `EntityReference` nodes can cause. For this reason applications should not create `EntityReference` nodes unless they have very good cause to do so.

Note that most DOM implementations do not make lexical information such as the entity structure of the document available and will not create `EntityReference` nodes. In most cases this is a good thing, because it avoids all the problems discussed above.

11.6.6 *The* `ProcessingInstruction` *interface*

Instances of this interface represent processing instructions in the document contents. The target and data of the processing instruction are available through the normal `Node` attributes, but the interface also declares two extra attributes through which these are available.

`target`
     The target of the processing instruction.

`data`
     The data of the processing instruction.

All DOM implementations will provide processing instruction nodes when building from XML documents. Note that processing instructions can appear as children of `Document` and `Element`, and that they can have the same `nodeName` as `Element` nodes. This means that when searching for a specific element type, it is not sufficient to test for its `nodeName`, but its `nodeType` must also be tested.

Using DOM

N ow that you have been introduced to the various DOM interfaces, this chapter will show you how to use DOM to develop applications. It starts by showing how to do some of the most common tasks in such applications, and then moves on to develop a number of applications in order to show how to use the DOM in practice.

12.1 | Creating DOM trees

There are two main ways to create a DOM tree: by loading a serialized document from a file or by writing code that creates the tree. To create a tree from a source other than an XML document, you must start with an empty `Document` node. This section shows how to create the empty document and load a document from a file with 4DOM.

12.1.1 *Creating an empty document*

This operation is straightforward with most DOM implementations, and generally just requires consulting the API documentation for the implementation of the Document interface. Usually, one can create Document instances by simply instantiating the class that implements this interface. In some cases the constructor for this class requires references to particular objects, or it may even be private to the implementation. (This latter problem cannot occur in Python, though.) In these cases there is usually a utility class which has a method for doing the creation.

With 4DOM, Document creation is easy. The Document interface is implemented in the xml.dom.Document module, and Example 12–1 shows how it can be instantiated.

Example 12–1. How to create a 4DOM Document

```
>>> from xml.dom import Document
>>> doc = Document.Document(None)
>>> root = doc.createElement("sample")
>>> doc.appendChild(root)
<Element Node at 8109648: Name = 'sample' with 0 attributes and
0 children>
>>> root.appendChild(doc.createTextNode("This is a sample "
... "document\n")
<Text Node at 8073120: data = 'This is a sample d...'>
>>> elm = doc.createElement("p")
>>> elm.appendChild(doc.createTextNode("With two elements."))
<Text Node at 8104928: data = 'With two elements.'>
>>> attr = doc.createAttribute("xml:lang")
>>> attr._set_value("en")
>>> elm.setAttributeNode(attr)
>>> root.appendChild(elm)
<Element Node at 8078512: Name = 'p' with 1 attributes and
1 children>
```

The None argument to the Document constructor is there because the 4DOM implementation wants a reference to a DocumentType object. If you don't want to give it one, you can just pass None as in this example.

In this example, the only part that is specific to 4DOM is the creation of the document node; after that everything is common to all the Python DOMs. To use the same code with minidom, it is only necessary to change how the Document node is created. This is done by importing xml.dom.minidom and instantiating the Document class therein with no arguments.

Example 12–2 shows how the document just created would look when serialized.

Example 12–2. The example document serialized

```
<sample>This is a sample document
<p xml:lang='en'>With two elements.</p></sample>
```

When using Jython it is no more difficult to create a DOM tree, since its integration with Java code is so smooth. Example 12–3 shows how to create a Document node in the Xerces DOM implementation.

Example 12–3. How to create a Document with Xerces

```
Jython 1.1 on java1.2.2 (JIT: symcjit)
Copyright (C) 1997-1999 Corporation for National Research Initiat...
>>> from org.apache.xerces.dom import DocumentImpl
>>> doc = DocumentImpl()
>>> root = doc.createElement("doc")
>>> doc.appendChild(root)
[doc: null]
>>> doc
[#document: null]
```

The section on javadom (13.1.1, "Using Java DOMs," on page 469) demonstrates how to use the Java DOM implementations in Jython with exactly the same interface as 4DOM. The only differences are document creation and serialization.

12.1.2 *Loading an XML document*

4DOM provides good support for document loading through its `Reader` architecture, which ensures that all the different DOM implementations in the 4Suite collection have the same interface. The `Reader` interface is implemented by any piece of 4Suite which is able to build a DOM tree. This interface has the methods listed below.

`__init__(validate=0, keepAllWs=0, catName=None)`
    Creates the reader and sets it up ready to load XML documents. If the `validate` argument is `true`, the `Reader` will use a validating parser. If `keepAllWs` is `false`, ignorable whitespace will not be included in the tree.[1] The `catName` parameter holds the file name of a catalog file which will be parsed and used when resolving entity references. (This requires xmlproc to be installed, since it is implemented using xmlproc's catalog support.)

`fromStream(stream, ownerDocument = None)`
    Loads the document from the file-like object `stream` and returns the `Document` node. The `ownerDocument` argument, if given, will be used as the `Document` node and will thus serve as both container and factory for the loaded document.

`releaseNode(node)`
    Used in Python versions without garbage collection to break cyclic references in the sub-tree beneath a node.

4Suite has a number of implementations of this interface, all of which are listed below.

`xml.dom.ext.reader.Sax.Reader`
    This reader is part of 4DOM and uses SAX 1.0 to load documents.

---

1. In practice, this is any character data reported using the `ignorable-Whitespace` SAX event.

`xml.dom.ext.reader.Sax2.Reader`
>   This reader is part of 4DOM and uses an old version of SAX 2.0
>   to load documents. This version of SAX 2.0 is supported by the
>   PyXML package for backwards compatibility, so this reader works
>   just fine.

`xml.dom.ext.reader.HtmlLib.Reader`
>   This reader is part of 4DOM and builds an HTML DOM using
>   Python's sgmllib module. It does not accept any arguments to its
>   constructor, nor does it support `releaseNode`.

`Ft.Lib.pDomlette.SaxReader`
>   This reader is part of 4XSLT and pDomlette, and builds a
>   pDomlette DOM tree using the same SAX 2.0 version as 4DOM.

`Ft.Lib.cDomlette.RawExpatReader`
>   This reader is part of 4XSLT and cDomlette, and builds a
>   cDomlette tree using Pyexpat.

12.2 | DOM serialization

Quite often, an application reads an XML document into a DOM tree,
makes some modifications, and then writes the whole thing back out
to disk. The DOM specification has no functionality to support this,
but more or less all implementations do. Another quite common use
case is when an application wishes to write out information as an XML
document and finds it difficult to do this serially through SAX events.
In these cases creating a DOM tree and then serializing it can be very
effective.

4DOM supports this through the `xml.dom.ext` module, which has
two functions for writing a DOM tree to a file-like object. These are
described below.

```
Print(root, stream = sys.stdout)
```
This function simply writes out the DOM tree as it is, without making any changes to it at all. It supports CDATA marked sections, comments, as well as the DOCTYPE declaration with contents.

```
PrettyPrint(root, stream = sys.stdout,
    indent = ' ', width = 80,
    preserveElements = None)
```
This function writes out the DOM tree, but in a prettier way than its plain cousin. The optional parameters allow applications to customize what is used for indentation (the number of spaces or tabs), the width of the generated XML, as well as which element types do not get whitespace inserted inside them.

The interpreter dialog in Example 12–4 shows the creation of a DOM document that contains no whitespace for formatting the markup at all. It is then written out to standard out using both Print and PrettyPrint. In the first case, the entire document is written out on a single line, but in the second case, it is nicely indented.

12.2.1 *Non-XML serialization*

In some cases, an application may wish to store its data using the XML data model, but finds traditional XML serialization and parsing too slow. In these cases, "automatic" serialization of the objects in the DOM tree may be a useful alternative. Many modern programming languages can serialize an object structure into a byte stream and recreate the serialized objects, without requiring any code to be added to the objects to support this.

Python supports this through its pickle module, which can serialize nearly all kinds of objects and values into either a character based or a bit based notation. The bit based notation is slightly faster, but the character based notation is human-readable (with some effort) and can be useful in debugging. Note that the cPickle module is a C implementation of the same mechanism with the same notation and

Example 12–4. Serializing DOM trees with 4DOM

```
>>> from xml.dom import Document
>>> doc = Document.Document(None)
>>> doc.appendChild(doc.createElement("root"))
<Element Node at 8109584: Name = 'root' with 0 attributes and
0 children>
>>> root = doc.documentElement
>>> root.appendChild(doc.createElement("empty"))
<Element Node at 8119072: Name = 'empty' with 0 attributes and
0 children>
>>> p = doc.createElement("p")
>>> p.appendChild(doc.createTextNode("A bit of text."))
<Text Node at 8117472: data = 'A bit of text.'>
>>> from xml.dom import ext
>>> ext.Print(doc)
<root><empty/><p>A bit of text.</p></root>
>>> ext.PrettyPrint(doc)

<root>
  <empty/>
  <p>A bit of text.</p>
</root>
>>>
```

interface, but much faster than the `pickle` module, which is written in Python.

Java has supported a similar mechanism (known as Java serialization) since JDK 1.1, but requires all serialized objects to support a specific interface. This means that to make it possible to use object serialization with a DOM implementation, that implementation must have been written explicitly with support for object serialization. As far as I have been able to see, none of the Java DOM implementations support this.

The interpreter dialog in Example 12–5 shows loading of an RSS document into a DOM tree, its subsequent pickling (serialization into a pickle file), followed by its unpickling.

The pickle notation is portable across platforms as well as across interpreter versions. However, the notation has changed 3 times so far (we are at version 1.3) and even though new versions of the module support older file notations, the opposite is not true. Another potential problem is that class definitions are not saved with the objects, which

Example 12–5. Pickling and unpickling DOM trees

```
>>> import cPickle
>>> from xml.dom.ext.reader.Sax2 import Reader
>>> doc = Reader().fromStream(open("tools.rss"))
>>> outf = open("tools.pickle", "wb")
>>> cPickle.dump(doc, outf, 1)
>>> outf.close()
>>> doc = None
>>> inf = open("tools.pickle", "rb")
>>> doc = cPickle.load(inf)
>>> inf.close()
>>> doc
<XML Document at 8805968>
>>> doc.documentElement
<Element Node at 8808976: Name = 'rss' with 1 attributes and
9 children>
>>> doc.documentElement.childNodes
<NodeList at 8809056: [<Text Node at 8809296: data = '\n '>,
<Element Node at 8809696: Name = 'channel' with 0 attributes and
7 children>, <Text Node at 8830240: data = '\n '>, <Element Node
at 8830592: Name =  'item' with 0 attributes and 5 children>,
<Text Node at 8845152: data = '\n'>, <Element Node at 8845488:
Name = 'item' with 0 attributes and 5 children>, <Text Node
at 8852560: data = '\n '>, <Element Node at 8852896: Name = 'item'
with 0 attributes and 7 children>, <Text Node at 8873792: data =
'\n'>]>
>>>
```

means that if the pickled classes were updated, the objects may no longer work after unpickling.

However, it is easy to use the ordinary XML serialization support in the DOM implementation to dump the pickled objects out as XML. This makes it possible to go via XML to move the pickled objects to older interpreter versions or new versions of the DOM implementation.

12.3 | Some examples

12.3.1 *Modifying an RSS document*

In order to show how to use DOM for loading, modifying, and serializing XML documents, Examples 12–6 to 12–10 will read in an RSS document, insert a new news item at the top and then write the modified document back to its original file. Note that this is something that could also be done with SAX, but in a more awkward way. You would have to read in the document and write it back out again directly, inserting the new item in the process. More complex examples would be even more awkward to do with SAX.

Example 12–6. Inserting an item into an RSS document (1 of 5)

```
from xml.dom import ext
from xml.dom.ext.reader.Sax2 import Reader

ELEMENT_NODE = 1
```

In Example 12–6, we import the parts of 4DOM necessary to read in an XML document and write it back out. We also define a constant for the element node type, rather than try to access it in the Node class defined in xml.dom.Node in 4DOM, since that is rather awkward.

The function in Example 12–7 takes the document node and the data fields that go into the new news item and creates a new item element object to hold the data. Text nodes with '\n' in them are created and inserted to make the generated XML look a bit nicer; without them everything would end up on a single line, which would be rather hard to read.

The function in Example 12–8 takes the document node and the item element and inserts the item element in the right place. This is done by scanning through the list of the children of the document element. The for loop stops either when there are no more children or when an element with the name item is found.

Example 12–7. Inserting an item into an RSS document (2 of 5)

```
def create_item(doc, title, link, desc = None):
    item = doc.createElement("item")
    item.appendChild(doc.createTextNode("\n"))

    title_elm = doc.createElement("title")
    title_elm.appendChild(doc.createTextNode(title))
    item.appendChild(title_elm)
    item.appendChild(doc.createTextNode("\n"))

    link_elm = doc.createElement("link")
    link_elm.appendChild(doc.createTextNode(link))
    item.appendChild(link_elm)
    item.appendChild(doc.createTextNode("\n"))

    if desc:
        desc_elm = doc.createElement("desc")
        desc_elm.appendChild(doc.createTextNode(desc))
        item.appendChild(desc_elm)
        item.appendChild(doc.createTextNode("\n"))

    return item
```

Example 12–8. Inserting an item into an RSS document (3 of 5)

```
def insert_item(doc, item):
    # find out where to insert the new item
    first_item = None
    root = doc.documentElement
    for child in root.childNodes:
        if child.nodeType == ELEMENT_NODE and \
           child.nodeName == "item":
            first_item = child
            break

    # here, first_item is
    # either the first item element in the document
    # or None if there are no item elements in the document

    if first_item:
        root.insertBefore(item, first_item)
        root.insertBefore(doc.createTextNode("\n\n"), first_item)
    else:
        root.appendChild(item)
```

The second part of the code inserts the new node before the old one, if an old one was found (it could be that the document had no items yet), or at the end if no items were found. A couple of newlines are also inserted to separate the new item from the old ones.

Example 12–9. Inserting an item into an RSS document (4 of 5)

```
def add_item(filename, title, link, desc = None):
    doc = Reader().fromStream(open(filename))
    item = create_item(doc, title, link, desc)
    insert_item(doc, item)

    outf = open(filename, "w")
    ext.Print(doc, outf)
    outf.close()
```

The function in Example 12–9 takes a file name and the item fields, loads the document, creates the new item, inserts it, and writes the document back to the file.

Example 12–10. Inserting an item into an RSS document (5 of 5)

```
if __name__ == "__main__":
    import sys
    add_item(sys.argv[1], "New item!", "http://www.garshol.priv.no")
```

With this in hand we can process the RSS document in Example 12–11.

If we call the add_item function with the file name of this document and give it the title 'New version of 4DOM: 0.10.0' and the link 'http://www.garshol.priv.no/.../4DOM.html', the result would be the document in Example 12–12.

Note how the XML declaration and the DOCTYPE declaration have both disappeared. Neither of them ever made it into the tree, since SAX 1.0 (which we used here, as 4DOM does not support 2.0 yet), does not report them to its applications, and thus they were not

Example 12–11. An RSS document to operate on

```
<?xml version="1.0"?>
<!DOCTYPE rss PUBLIC "-//Netscape Communications//DTD RSS 0.91//EN"
            "http://my.netscape.com/publish/formats/rss-0.91.dtd">
<rss version='0.91'>
  <channel>
    <title>Free XML tools</title>
    <link>http://www.garshol.priv.no/download/xmltools/</link>
    <description>An index of free XML tools.</description>
  </channel>

  <item>
    <title>New product: tDOM.</title>
    <link>http://www.garshol.priv.no/.../tDOM.html</link>
  </item>

  <item>
    <title>New version of LotusXSL: 31.Aug.99.</title>
    <link>http://www.garshol.priv.no/.../LotusXSL.html</link>
    <description>Updated to 13.Aug.99 WDs, separate XPath and
    query packages, new extension architecture, thread safety,
    and much more.</description>
  </item>
</rss>
```

regenerated by the serializer. All other lexical information that is not retained by both SAX 1.0 and the DOM implementation will also be stripped out, such as comments. Note also how the new item is not indented in the way the others are, since we did not add the necessary whitespace to achieve this.

So, having tried the function we can conclude that it has a number of weaknesses:

■ Lexical information, and in particular the DOCTYPE declaration, is lost, because it is never read into the tree. The problem with the DOCTYPE can be worked around by explicitly inserting it. This is a bit awkward, but worth it if you really care about having it in your documents. Alternatively, a DOM implementation that supports SAX 2.0 can be used with a SAX driver that provides the necessary information.

Example 12–12. The modified RSS document

```
<rss version='0.91'>
  <channel>
    <title>Free XML tools</title>
    <link>http://www.garshol.priv.no/download/xmltools/</link>
    <description>An index of free XML tools.</description>
  </channel>

    <item>
<title>New version of 4DOM: 0.10.0</title>
<link>http://www.garshol.priv.no/.../4DOM.html</link>
</item>

<item>
    <title>New product: tDOM.</title>
    <link>http://www.garshol.priv.no/.../tDOM.html</link>
  </item>

  <item>
    <title>New version of LotusXSL: 31.Aug.99.</title>
    <link>http://www.garshol.priv.no/.../LotusXSL.html</link>
    <description>Updated to 13.Aug.99 WDs, separate XPath and
    query packages, new extension architecture, thread safety,
    and much more.</description>
  </item>
</rss>
```

- This is a lot of code to write to achieve very little. Other similar operations will require no less code, and it will be hard to reuse any code from this example. This is by far the most serious problem, and it indicates that some better approach should be found. As stated earlier, this better solution is to implement this operation in terms of an RSS-specific object structure. In fact, with such a structure, the entire loading, modification, and serialization can be written in three lines. (Doing so is left as an exercise for the reader. An RSS object structure is defined in 26.1, "The RSS object structure," on page 996.)

12.3.2 *XBEL to HTML conversion*

In this section we return to the XBEL to HTML conversion example that was shown earlier in 9.2.2.1, "An example application," on page 275. The conversion developed here is comparable to the first example in that section, but is more robust and produces higher-quality output.

However, our previous example (the RSS to HTML converter in 11.5, "A simple example application," on page 424) showed how difficult it can be both to find the elements one wants to work with and to extract their contents. These are very general operations, however, so we will develop a small collection of convenience functions to help us with this. These will all live in the `domutils` module; their signatures are shown below:

`find_first_child(parent, type, name)`
 This function iterates over the children of the `parent` node, returning the first node whose `nodeType` and `nodeName` match the `type` and `name` arguments. If none is found, `None` is returned.

`find_first_elem(parent, name)`
 This function does the same as `find_first_child`, but only for elements. This actually shortens the code quite a bit, since one doesn't have to add `ELEMENT_NODE` as a parameter everywhere.

`data(parent, alternative = None)`
 This function extracts the character data content of the `parent` and returns it as a string. If the `parent` parameter is `None`, the `alternative` is returned; this makes it much easier to use the function together with `find_first_child` and `find_first_child` when no node is found.

 Note that the function is not recursive, which means it will only look at character data nodes that are immediate children of the `parent` node.

```
predicate(nodetype, nodename)
```

This function is a rather unusual one, and very Pythonic. Given a node type and node name (much like the `find_first_child` function above), it returns a function that will return `true` for nodes that match these characteristics and `false` for all others. This is useful because Python has a built-in function `filter` that takes a predicate function and a list as parameters, and returns a new list with only those list members for which the predicate function returned `true`.

The `predicate` function is designed to be used in just this way: to conveniently filter out a set of nodes from a nodelist. This capability is very useful in extracting information from the DOM.

Example 12–13 shows how to use these functions.

Example 12–13. Using the `domutils`

```
>>> parent
<Element Node at 8733202: Name = 'folder' with 0 attributes and
5 children>
>>> ch = parent._get_childNodes()
>>> ch
<NodeList at 8720336: [<Text Node at 8742272: data = '   '>,
<Element Node at 8741536: Name = 'desc' with 0 attributes and
1 children>, <Text Node at 8747888: data = '\n   '>, <Element Node
at 8747056: Name = 'folder' with 0 attributes and 9 children>,
<Text Node at 8828928: data = '\n'>]>
>>> find_first_child(parent, ELEMENT_NODE, "desc")
<Element Node at 8741536: Name = 'desc' with 0 attributes and
1 children>
>>> find_first_elem(parent, "title")
>>> data(find_first_elem(parent, "desc"))
'Demo bookmarks'
>>> data(find_first_elem(parent, "title"), "<no title>")
'<no title>'
>>> p = predicate(ELEMENT_NODE, "folder")
>>> p
<function <lambda> at 86f810>
>>> desc = ch[1]
>>> folder = ch[-2]
>>> desc
```

```
<Element Node at 8741536: Name = 'desc' with 0 attributes and
1 children>
>>> folder
<Element Node at 8747056: Name = 'folder' with 0 attributes and
9 children>
>>> p(desc)
0
>>> p(folder)
1
>>> filter(p, ch)
[<Element Node at 8747056: Name = 'folder' with 0 attributes and
9 children>]
```

An implementation of the `domutils` module is shown in Example 12–14.

Example 12–14. The `domutils` module

```
import string

ELEMENT_NODE                   = 1
ATTRIBUTE_NODE                 = 2
TEXT_NODE                      = 3
CDATA_SECTION_NODE             = 4
ENTITY_REFERENCE_NODE          = 5
ENTITY_NODE                    = 6
PROCESSING_INSTRUCTION_NODE    = 7
COMMENT_NODE                   = 8
DOCUMENT_NODE                  = 9
DOCUMENT_TYPE_NODE             = 10
DOCUMENT_FRAGMENT_NODE         = 11
NOTATION_NODE                  = 12

def find_first_child(parent, type, name):
    for child in parent._get_childNodes():
        if child._get_nodeType() == type and \
           child._get_nodeName() == name:
            return child

def find_first_elem(parent, name):
    for child in parent._get_childNodes():
        if child._get_nodeType() == ELEMENT_NODE and \
           child._get_nodeName() == name:
            return child
```

```
def data(parent, alternative = None):
    if parent == None: return alternative

    content = []
    for child in parent._get_childNodes():
        if child._get_nodeType() == TEXT_NODE or \
            child._get_nodeType() == CDATA_SECTION_NODE:
              content.append(child._get_nodeValue())

    return string.join(content, "")

def recursive_data(parent, alternative = None):
    if parent == None: return alternative

    content = []
    for child in parent._get_childNodes():
        type = child._get_nodeType()
        if type == TEXT_NODE or type == CDATA_SECTION_NODE:
            content.append(child._get_nodeValue())
        elif type == ELEMENT_NODE:
            content.append(recursive_data(child))

    return string.join(content, "")

def predicate(nodetype, nodename):
    return lambda node, type = nodetype, name = nodename: \
                    (node._get_nodeType() == type and
                     node._get_nodeName() == name)

def type_predicate(nodetype):
    return lambda node, type = nodetype:
            node._get_nodeType() == type
```

Note that the module uses methods instead of attributes to access the DOM attributes. This is done because this is faster and we program a general utility that should be efficient. We also redeclare the DOM constants for the various node types so that applications that use the domutils module do not have to get these from a specific DOM implementation, which would increase their dependency on that implementation.

Using this library, it is much easier to write the XBEL to HTML converter than otherwise, as Examples 12–15 to 12–20 show.

Example 12–15 is familiar: we import the necessary modules (including `domutils`) and define the templates. The node type constants are loaded from `domutils`, which allows us to use them directly and avoid dependency on a specific implementation.

Example 12–15. A DOM-based XBEL to HTML converter (1 of 6)

```
import sys, string, codecs
from domutils import *
from xml.dom.ext.reader.Sax2 import Reader

# --- Templates

top = \
"""
<!DOCTYPE HTML PUBLIC \"-//W3C//DTD HTML 4.0 Transitional//EN\">
<HTML>
<HEAD>
  <TITLE>%s</TITLE>
</HEAD>

<BODY>
<H1>%s</H1>
"""

bottom = \
"""
<HR>

<ADDRESS>
Converted by xbel2html.py using the DOM.
</ADDRESS>

</BODY>
</HTML>
"""
```

The function in Example 12–16 is relatively straightforward. It takes a `bookmark` element and a file-like object, and writes out the bookmark as an HTML list item to the file-like object. First the contents of the `title` and `desc` elements are extracted. Note how the `alternative` argument of data is used to ensure that the variables will hold something useful.

Example 12–16. A DOM-based XBEL to HTML converter (2 of 6)

```
# --- Conversion functions

def convert_bookmark(bookmark, out):
    title = data(find_first_elem(bookmark, "title"), "<no title>")
    desc = data(find_first_elem(bookmark, "desc"), "")
    url = bookmark.getAttribute("href")

    out.write('  <li><a href="%s">%s</a> %s\n' % (url, title, desc))
```

The URL of the bookmark is extracted from the href attribute, and then the bookmark is written out using a template.

The function in Example 12–17 performs more-or-less the same task for folder elements. It first picks out the title, then writes it out and finally calls the function shown below to write out the children of the folder. The level argument tells the function on which folder nesting level it is. The folders on the first three levels get heading elements for their titles, while the folders below that only get their titles printed in bold.

Example 12–17. A DOM-based XBEL to HTML converter (3 of 6)

```
def convert_folder(folder, level, out):
    title = data(find_first_elem(folder, "title"), "<no title>")
    if level < 4:
        out.write("<h%d>%s</h%d>\n" % (level, title, level))
    else:
        out.write("  <li><b>%s</b>\n"  % title)
    convert_folder_contents(folder, level, out)
```

The function in Example 12–18 is a bit complex because of its handling of folder nesting. The first thing it does is collecting all bookmark and folder child elements into two separate lists. Then, it starts a list if there are bookmarks in the folder, or if we are past the third nesting level and there are folders in the folder. In other words, it starts a list if there will be list items in the folder.

Example 12–18. A DOM-based XBEL to HTML converter (4 of 6)

```
def convert_folder_contents(folder, level, out):
    bookmarks = filter(predicate(ELEMENT_NODE, "bookmark"),
                       folder.childNodes)

    folders = filter(predicate(ELEMENT_NODE, "folder"),
                     folder.childNodes)

    if len(bookmarks) > 0 or (level >= 3 and len(folders) > 0):
        out.write("<ul>\n")

    for bookmark in bookmarks:
        convert_bookmark(bookmark, out)

    if not (level >= 3 and len(folders) > 0) and \
       len(bookmarks) > 0:
        out.write("</ul>\n")

    for folder in folders:
        convert_folder(folder, level + 1, out)

    if level >= 3 and len(folders) > 0:
        out.write("</ul>\n")
```

First, all the `bookmark` children are written out. Then, if there will be no more list items and we have opened the list, the list is closed. Then, the folders are written out, and finally the list is closed if it is still open.

Finally, we get to the function that runs the entire conversion (Example 12–19). It takes a document node and a file-like output object and writes the converted document out to the file. It starts by writing out the top template with the bookmark file title. It then finds the description, if there is one, and writes it out. Finally, the folders and bookmarks on the top level are written out and the bottom template is written out.

Example 12–19. A DOM-based XBEL to HTML converter (5 of 6)

```
def convert(doc, out = None):
    out = out or sys.stdout

    root = doc.documentElement
    title = data(find_first_elem(root, "title"), "Bookmarks")
    out.write(top % (title, title))

    desc = find_first_elem(root, "desc")
    if desc:
        out.write("<p>%s</p>\n" % data(desc))

    convert_folder_contents(root, 0, out)

    out.write(bottom)
```

Example 12–20. A DOM-based XBEL to HTML converter (6 of 6)

```
outf = codecs.open(sys.argv[2], "w", "iso-8859-1")
convert(Reader().fromStream(open(sys.argv[1])), outf)
```

This application compares relatively favorably with the first SAX version of the same program. It is a little shorter, a little easier to read, and it produces a slightly better output. However, it is much slower than the SAX version and requires much more memory. XBEL documents, however, are not likely to be of such sizes that the lower performance could matter. The approach taken in the second SAX version with a separate generator object could have been used to advantage in the DOM version as well. However, the xbellib module is the best solution, and when using that solution, DOM is not really needed at all.

12.3.3 *Shakespeare revisited*

Here we revisit the Shakespeare's plays application for which we implemented a SAX XML to HTML converter in 9.4.3, "A document example," on page 305. In this section we implement the same converter, this time using DOM instead of SAX (Examples 12–21 and 12–22).

Example 12–21. Converting plays to HTML using DOM (1 of 2)

```
import sys, string
from xml.dom.minidom import parse
from domutils import *

ELEM = ELEMENT_NODE
# (This alias lets us keep lines short that would otherwise have to
# be broken across several lines, and would have made this example
# a lot less readable. Important in a book where the source must be
# readable.)

# --- Templates

top = \
"""
<!DOCTYPE HTML PUBLIC "-//W3C//DTD HTML 4.0 Transitional//EN">
<HTML>
<HEAD>
  <TITLE>%s</TITLE>
  <LINK REL=stylesheet HREF="play.css" TYPE="text/css">
</HEAD>

<BODY>

<H1>%s</H1>
"""

bottom = \
"""
<HR>

<ADDRESS>
Converted from Jon Bosak's XML to HTML with the DOM.
</ADDRESS>

</BODY>
</HTML>
"""
```

```
# --- Conversion functions

def convert(doc, out = None):
    out = out or sys.stdout

    play = doc.documentElement
    title = data(find_first_elem(play, "TITLE"),"[untitled]")
    out.write(top % (title, title))

    _convert_front_matter(find_first_elem(play, "FM"), out)
    _convert_personae(find_first_elem(play, "PERSONAE"), out)

    for act in filter(predicate(ELEM, "ACT"), play.childNodes):
        _convert_act(act, out)

    out.write(bottom)

def _convert_front_matter(fm, out):
    if fm == None:
        return

    out.write("<h2>Front matter</h2>\n")
    for p in filter(predicate(ELEM, "P"), fm.childNodes):
        out.write("<p>%s</p>\n" % data(p))

def _convert_personae(personae, out):
    if personae == None:
        return

    out.write("<h2>%s</h2>" %
            data(find_first_elem(personae, "TITLE"),
                "Dramatis Personae"))

    out.write("<ul>\n")

    for item in filter(type_predicate(ELEM), personae.childNodes):
        if item.nodeName == "PERSONA":
            out.write("  <li>%s</li>\n" % data(item))
        elif item.nodeName == "PGROUP":
            elems = filter(type_predicate(ELEM), item.childNodes)
            out.write("  <li>%s</li>\n" %
                    string.join(map(data, elems), ", "))

    out.write("</ul>\n")
```

```
def _convert_act(act, out):
    out.write("<h2>%s</h2>\n" % data(find_first_elem(act, "TITLE")))

    _convert_content(find_first_elem(act, "PROLOGUE"), out)

    for scene in filter(predicate(ELEM, "SCENE"), act.childNodes):
        _convert_content(scene, out)

    _convert_content(find_first_elem(act, "EPILOGUE"), out)
```

Note that the structural similarity between prologues, epilogues, and scenes allows us to use _convert_content to convert all of these to HTML.

12.3.4 *Using DOM for serialization*

In this section, we reuse the xbellib module from 9.3.1, "XBEL data representation," on page 286, creating a serializer for the object structure using DOM instead of writing directly to a file (Example 12–23).

This example works, but has a number of weaknesses compared to the more straightforward approach of writing to a file or generating a stream of SAX events:

- It is relatively complex, somewhat awkward, and requires quite a bit of code.
- It depends on a specific DOM implementation being installed.
- It is slow and requires a lot of memory.

In general, DOM is not the appropriate tool to use for serializing object structures. It is mainly useful for serialization when it is difficult to generate the output sequentially, but this quite simply does not happen when serializing well-designed object structures.

Example 12–22. Converting plays to HTML using DOM (2 of 2)

```
def _convert_content(container, out):
    if container == None:
        return

    out.write("<h3>%s</h3>\n" %
              data(find_first_elem(container, "TITLE"),
                   container.nodeName))

    for elem in filter(type_predicate(ELEM),
                       container.childNodes):

        if elem.nodeName == "SPEECH":
            out.write("<p class=speaker>%s</p>\n" %
                      data(find_first_elem(elem, "SPEAKER")))

            for line in filter(predicate(ELEM, "LINE"),
                               elem.childNodes):
                out.write("<p class=line>")

                for item in line.childNodes:
                    if item.nodeType == TEXT_NODE:
                        out.write(item.nodeValue)
                    elif item.nodeType == ELEM and \
                        item.nodeName == "STAGEDIR":
                        out.write("<i>%s</i>" % data(item))
                out.write("</p>\n")

        elif elem.nodeName == "STAGEDIR":
            out.write("<p class=stagedir>%s</p>\n" % data(elem))

# --- Main program

if len(sys.argv) == 3:
    outf = open(sys.argv[2], "w")
else:
    outf = sys.stdout

convert(parse(sys.argv[1]), outf)
```

Example 12–23. Serialization using DOM

```python
import xbellib

def xbel2dom(xbel, doc):
    """This function takes an XBEL structure and a DOM Document Node
    and creates a DOM tree reflecting the XBEL object structure."""

    doc.appendChild(doc.createElement("xbel"))
    root = doc.documentElement

    if xbel.get_title():
        title = doc.createElement("title")
        title.appendChild(doc.createTextNode(xbel.get_title()))
        root.appendChild(title)

    if xbel.get_desc():
        desc = doc.createElement("desc")
        desc.appendChild(doc.createTextNode(xbel.get_desc()))
        root.appendChild(desc)

    for child in xbel.get_nodes():
        root.appendChild(create_node(child, doc))

def create_node(node, doc):
    if isinstance(node, xbellib.Bookmark) or \
       isinstance(node, xbellib.Folder):

        if isinstance(node, xbellib.Bookmark):
            elem = doc.createElement("bookmark")
            elem.setAttribute("href", node.get_url())
        else:
            elem = doc.createElement("folder")

        if node.get_title():
            title = doc.createElement("title")
            title.appendChild(doc.createTextNode(node.get_title()))
            elem.appendChild(title)

        if node.get_desc():
            desc = doc.createElement("desc")
            desc.appendChild(doc.createTextNode(node.get_desc()))
            elem.appendChild(desc)

        if isinstance(node, xbellib.Folder):
            for child in node.get_nodes():
                elem.appendChild(create_node(child, doc))
```

```
            return elem

    elif isinstance(node, xbellib.Separator):
        return doc.createElement("separator")

    elif isinstance(node, xbellib.Alias):
        return create_node(node.get_ref_node(), doc)

    else:
        raise ValueError("Node of unknown type encountered! %s" %
                          node)
def serialize_4DOM(xbel, filename):
    from xml.dom import ext, Document

    doc = Document.Document(None)
    xbel2dom(xbel, doc)

    outf = open(filename, "w")
    ext.Print(doc, outf)
    outf.close()

if __name__ == "__main__":
    import sys
    serialize_4DOM(xbellib.load_xbel(sys.argv[1]), sys.argv[2])
```

12.4 | An example: a tree walker

In Examples 12–24 to 12–30, we create a SAX 2.0 XMLReader that
takes a node in a DOM tree and traverses over the sub-tree beneath it,
firing SAX 2.0 events as it goes. This can be used to turn a DOM tree
into a sequence of SAX events, useful, for example, when an application
expects SAX input and you already have a DOM tree.

  Example 12–24 is very simple. We load in the SAX modules, since
we use many of their classes. We also redefine the node type constants
to be independent of a specific implementation.

  The _processing attribute (Example 12–25) is used as a flag to
tell us whether we are currently walking the tree or not. We use this

Example 12–24. A DOM to SAX converter (1 of 7)

```
"""A DOM walker that fires SAX events, written as a SAX 2.0
XMLReader.

$Id: dom2sax.py,v 1.5 2001/08/19 19:27:40 larsga Exp $
"""

from xml.sax.saxutils import XMLGenerator
from xml.sax.xmlreader import *
from xml.sax.handler import *
from xml.sax._exceptions import *

# --- Useful constants

ELEMENT_NODE                  = 1
ATTRIBUTE_NODE                = 2
TEXT_NODE                     = 3
CDATA_SECTION_NODE            = 4
ENTITY_REFERENCE_NODE         = 5
ENTITY_NODE                   = 6
PROCESSING_INSTRUCTION_NODE   = 7
COMMENT_NODE                  = 8
DOCUMENT_NODE                 = 9
DOCUMENT_TYPE_NODE            = 10
DOCUMENT_FRAGMENT_NODE        = 11
NOTATION_NODE                 = 12
```

to prevent properties that are read-only during processing from being modified.

Example 12–25. A DOM to SAX converter (2 of 7)

```
# --- The walker

class DOMReader(XMLReader):

    def __init__(self, node = None):
        XMLReader.__init__(self)
        self._node = node
        self._processing = 0
```

The DOMReader class implements the XMLReader interface, and inherits the code for getting and setting features and handlers from XMLReader (Example 12–26). It supports the dom-node SAX property, so that applications can set the node to traverse from (either with setProperty or in the constructor). During walking, setting the node is not allowed. However, the current node can be retrieved during walking.

Example 12–26. A DOM to SAX converter (3 of 7)

```
# --- XMLReader methods

def getProperty(self, name):
    if name == property_dom_node:
        return self._node

    raise SAXNotRecognizedException(
                    "Property '%s' not recognized" % name)

def setProperty(self, name, value):
    if name == property_dom_node:
        if self._processing:
            raise SAXNotSupportedException("The DOM node cannot"
                            " be changed during processing")

        self._node = value
        return

    raise SAXNotRecognizedException(
                    "Property '%s' not recognized" % name)
```

The parse method ignores its source argument, sets the processing flag, and calls an internal method to process the start node (Example 12–27). Note that it also fires the startDocument and endDocument events. Care is taken to reset the processing flag after processing is finished, even if it failed.

Example 12–28 is the main method of the module, where things really happen. The method carefully ensures that whenever a ContentHandler event is fired, self._node will refer to the current node.

Example 12–27. A DOM to SAX converter (4 of 7)

```
def parse(self, source):
    self._processing = 1
    try:
        self._cont_handler.startDocument()
        self._process_node(self._node)
    finally:
        self._cont_handler.endDocument()
        self._processing = 0
```

Example 12–28. A DOM to SAX converter (5 of 7)

```
# --- Internal methods

def _process_node(self, node):
    old = self._node
    self._node = node
    type = node._get_nodeType()
    name = node._get_nodeName()

    if type == ELEMENT_NODE:
        self._cont_handler.startElement(name,
                        DOMAttributes(node._get_attributes()))

        for ch in  node._get_childNodes():
            self._process_node(ch)

        self._node = node
        self._cont_handler.endElement(name)

    elif type == TEXT_NODE or type == CDATA_SECTION_NODE:
        self._cont_handler.characters(node._get_nodeValue())

    elif type == PROCESSING_INSTRUCTION_NODE:
        self._cont_handler.processingInstruction(
                                name, node._get_nodeValue())

    elif type == DOCUMENT_NODE or type ==DOCUMENT_FRAGMENT_NODE:
        for ch in  node._get_childNodes():
            self._process_node(ch)

    elif type < 1 or type > 12:
        self._err_handler.warning(SAXException(
                        "Unknown node type: " + str(node)))
    self._node = old
```

Note how self._node is updated after having been set by child nodes before the endElement event is called.

The method uses the nodeType attribute to tell what kind of event to fire and does element nodes first, based on the assumption that these will be the most common (followed by text nodes). Children are handled recursively, by looping over the child list and calling _process_node for each child.

Note also that CDATA nodes are supported, and that warnings are triggered for nodes that are of unknown types.

The class in Example 12–29 is used to adapt NamedNodeMap instances containing Attr objects to the SAX Attributes interface. This is mostly straightforward, but attribute type information is not available, so 'CDATA' is always returned.

Example 12–29. A DOM to SAX converter (6 of 7)

```
# --- DOMAttributes

class DOMAttributes:

    def __init__(self, map):
        self._map = map

    def getLength(self):
        return len(self._map)

    def getType(self, name):
        return "CDATA"

    def getValue(self, name):
        return self._map[name]._get_nodeValue()

    def getValueByQName(self, qname):
        return self._map[qname]._get_nodeValue()

    def getNameByQName(self, qname):
        raise NotImplementedError("Not yet implemented!")

    def getQNameByName(self, name):
        raise NotImplementedError("Not yet implemented!")
```

```
    def getNames(self):
        return self._map.keys()

    def getQNames(self):
        return self._map.keys()

    def __len__(self):
        return len(self._map)

    def __getitem__(self, name):
        return self._map[name]._get_nodeValue()

    def keys(self):
        return self._map.keys()

    def has_key(self, name):
        return self._map.has_key(name)

    def get(self, name, alternative=None):
        return self._map.get(name, alternative)

    def copy(self):
        return self.__class__(self._map)

    def items(self):
        items = []
        for (name, attr) in self._map.items():
            items.append((name, attr._get_nodeValue()))
        return items

    def values(self):
        values = []
        for attr in self._map.values():
            values.append(attr._get_nodeValue())
        return values
```

Example 12–30 is a test driver that loads a document from file and writes it back by firing events from it into an XMLGenerator. This is useful for testing, and also shows how to use the module. Note how javadom is used if the script is run in Jython.

Example 12–30. A DOM to SAX converter (7 of 7)

```
# --- Test

if __name__ == "__main__":
    import sys
    if sys.platform[ : 4] == "java":
        import javadom
        doc = javadom.XercesDomImplementation(). \
                buildDocumentFile(sys.argv[1])
    else:
        from xml.dom.ext.reader.Sax2 import Reader
        doc = Reader().fromStream(open(sys.argv[1]))

    from xml.sax import saxutils
    walker = DOMReader(doc)
    walker.setContentHandler(XMLGenerator(open("out.xml", "w")))
    walker.parse(doc)
```

Advanced DOM

I n this chapter we cover more advanced subjects related to
the DOM, such as more DOM implementations, the HTML
part of the DOM, and performance issues.

13.1 | Other DOM implementations

This section introduces DOM implementations other than 4DOM,
showing how to create empty documents and load and parse documents
with them.

13.1.1 *Using Java DOMs*

The fact that the DOM specification is written in terms of OMG IDL
has caused a small problem, namely that IDL declarations are mapped
differently to Java and Python, in part because these two languages are
different and have different naming conventions. To take one example,

IDL attributes are mapped to attributes and get/set-methods in Python, but only to methods in Java. The get/set methods are also named differently. A read-only attribute named `foo` will be mapped to a method named `_get_foo` in Python, but in Java this becomes `getFoo`. A further difference is that the Python DOM implementations of `NodeList` and `NamedNodeMap` are extended to make these emulate Python lists and dictionaries.

This is problematic in the sense that it is often desirable to make Python XML application that work in both CPython and Jython, but which use Java DOMs in Jython. This is desirable because the Java implementations are faster and require less memory. When the interfaces are different, however, this is not possible.

In the XML-SIG package there is a module named javadom (which lives in the `xml.dom.javadom` package), which contains the necessary code to enable you to use the Java DOM implementations through the same interface as 4DOM and minidom. The interface used to create the first `Document` node and to load a DOM tree from a document is different from 4DOM and minidom, but in all other respects the interfaces are the same.

In fact, javadom is not a real DOM implementation; it only consists of implementations of all the DOM interfaces which simply wrap the underlying Java DOM objects in a Python DOM interface. In addition to the DOM interfaces, the javadom module contains one class for each Java DOM implementation it supports. This class can be used to create empty `Document` nodes and to load XML documents from strings, files, and URLs.

In Table 13–1 is shown what Java DOM implementations javadom supports.

The DOM implementation classes support the methods listed below:

```
createDocument()
```
This creates an empty `Document` node and returns it.

Table 13–1   DOM implementations supported by javadom

Implementation class	*DOM implementation*
SunDomImplementation	Sun's Java Project X
XercesDomImplementation	The Apache project's Xerces-J
BrownellDomImplementation	David Brownell's DOM2
IndelvDomImplementation	Indelv Inc.'s DOM
SxpDomImplementation	The Silfide project's DOM
OpenXmlImplementation	Assaf Arkin's OpenXML DOM
TidyDomImplementation	Andy Quick's JTidy DOM (see 24.1.1.3)

buildDocumentString(xmlstring)

This method parses the XML document contained in the xml-string string and returns the Document node.

buildDocumentFile(filename)

This method parses the XML document from the named file and returns the Document node.

buildDocumentUrl(url)

Downloads the XML document at the given URL and parses it, returning the Document node.

In general, javadom contains one class for each DOM interface. The class has an internal attribute named _impl, which contains a reference to the corresponding node in the Java DOM implementation. All the methods in the class are implemented in terms of calls to the methods in this node. The wrapper nodes are created lazily (that is, as they are needed), which makes loading much more efficient.

The interpreter dialog in Example 13–1 should show how easy it is to use javadom when you know 4DOM or minidom.

Example 13–1. How to use javadom

```
>>> from xml.dom import javadom
>>> impl = javadom.XercesDomImplementation()
>>> doc = impl.createDocument()
>>> doc
<Document with no root>
>>> root = doc.createElement("root")
>>> doc.appendChild(root)
<Element 'root' with 0 attributes and 0 children>
>>> doc.documentElement
<Element 'root' with 0 attributes and 0 children>
>>> doc.nodeName
'#document'
>>> i = doc._impl
>>> i
[#document: null]
>>> i.__class__
<jclass org.apache.xerces.dom.DocumentImpl at 735385559>
>>> doc = impl.buildDocumentString("<doc><p>Hi!</p>"
                                   "<p>Testing!</p></doc>")
>>> doc
<Document with root 'doc'>
>>> root = doc.documentElement
>>> root
<Element 'doc' with 0 attributes and 2 children>
>>> ch = root.childNodes
>>> ch
<NodeList [ <Element 'p' with 0 attributes and 1 children>,
<Element 'p' with 0 attributes and 1 children> ]>
```

13.1.2 *minidom*

The DOM implementation called minidom was developed by Paul Prescod with the aim of being as compact as possible. At the moment, the sources are only 15 Kb (477 lines). This implementation is now distributed with Python 2.0 as `xml.dom.minidom`; it lives in the `minidom` module and has a very simple module-level interface which is listed below:

```
Document()
```
This is the implementation of the Document interface. Document nodes can be instantiated directly and the constructor needs no arguments.

```
parse(stream_or_filename, parser = None,
    bufsize = 16364)
```
The parse function takes either a file-like object or a file name and creates the DOM tree from it. The DOM tree is returned by the function. The parser argument can be a SAX 2.0 parser driver, or None, in which case make_parser will be used to create one. The bufsize argument gives the buffer size to use.

```
parseString(document, parser = None)
```
Parses the document contained in the document string. The parser parameter can be a SAX 2.0 parser or None.

Serialization is also supported by minidom through the undocumented writexml(writer) method, which takes a file-like object as its only argument and writes the node itself and the sub-tree beneath it out as XML. The interpreter dialog in Example 13–2 illustrates this.

Example 13–2. Using minidom

```
Python 2.0 (#1, Oct 16 2000, 18:10:03)
[GCC 2.95.2 19991024 (release)] on linux2
Type "copyright", "credits" or "license" for more information.
>>> from xml.dom import minidom
>>> doc = minidom.Document()
>>> doc.appendChild(doc.createElement("doc"))
<DOM Element: doc at 136086692>
>>> root = doc.documentElement
>>> root.appendChild(doc.createTextNode("Hello!"))
<DOM Text node "Hello!">
>>> from StringIO import StringIO
>>> outf = StringIO()
>>> doc.writexml(outf)
>>> outf.getvalue()
'<doc>Hello!</doc>'
```

The following interfaces are implemented by minidom: `Document`, `Element`, `Attr`, `ProcessingInstruction`, `Text`, `Comment`. `NodeLists` are Python lists and `NamedNodeMaps` are dictionaries.

13.2 | The HTML part of the DOM

As mentioned earlier, the DOM not only supports XML, but also supports HTML documents. The HTML support consists of extensions to the core DOM, something that is possible since HTML is an SGML application, and thus has a very similar data model to that of XML. The extensions generally take the form of new interfaces for each HTML element type, which add properties to represent the attributes of these elements. In addition to this, there are some supporting interfaces and an `HTMLDocument` interface extending the core `Document` interface.

In general, HTML documents can just as well be represented in the core DOM, but the HTML part of the DOM is more convenient to work with. Another difference is that SGML HTML (as opposed to XHTML) uses case-insensitive element-type and attribute names, so the HTML DOM returns such names in canonical upper-cased form.

The convenience attributes that have been added to the HTML interfaces make them far easier to use for HTML generation than the generic interfaces, as Example 13–3 should illustrate.

The only Python DOM implementation that supports the HTML part of the DOM is 4DOM, which was used in Example 13–3. 4DOM allows HTML documents to be loaded using the `Reader` architecture, which was described in 12.1.2, "Loading an XML document," on page 438.

Example 13–3. Generating HTML

```
>>> from xml.dom.html import HTMLDocument
>>> doc = HTMLDocument.HTMLDocument()
>>> doc.title = "An HTML example"
>>> body = doc.body
>>> body
<Element Node at 8193440: Name = 'BODY' with 0 attributes and
0 children>
>>> body.appendChild(doc.createElement("h1"))
<Element Node at 8212368: Name = 'H1' with   attributes and
0 children>
>>> h1 = body.childNodes[0]
>>> h1.appendChild(doc.createTextNode("An HTML example document"))
<Text Node at 7d5b80: data = 'An HTML example docu...'>
>>> from xml.dom import ext
>>> ext.PrettyPrint(doc)

<HTML>
  <HEAD>
    <TITLE>An HTML example</TITLE>
  </HEAD>
  <BODY>
    <H1>An HTML example document</H1>
  </BODY>
</HTML>
```

13.3 | DOM level 2

DOM level 2 is a substantially larger specification than DOM level 1 and adds many new features to it, both in separate modules and by extending the existing interfaces from level 1. The main extensions to DOM level 1 are support for XML namespaces, for DocumentType and Document object creation, and for moving nodes between DOM documents.

DOM level 2 also has a number of new modules with additional functionality. These are:

Views

This module contains an abstract definition of a concept for defining views on documents, but doesn't actually define any such views. It has been included in the specification as a placeholder for the Views module that will actually appear in DOM level 3 specification. A placeholder was needed because there are a few places in DOM level 2 where view interfaces are referred to, and something was needed for them to refer to.

StyleSheets

This is a general module for representing stylesheets independently of any specific style language. It contains only a few very general interfaces and does not go into the internals of stylesheets at all. The only things it supports are metadata about stylesheets and interfaces to link them into documents.

CSS

This module is rather large and holds everything needed to represent, modify, and build CSS level 2 stylesheets.

Events

This module provides access to user-interface and document modification events as well as support for canceling such events.

Traversal

This module contains interfaces that can be used to walk a DOM tree and filter out those parts of the tree that the walker will see.

Ranges

The range module can be used to represent a range (that is, a consecutive region of content) in a document. This is mainly useful for implementations with a user-interface where the user can select a range of the document.

Not all these DOM modules are useful in all contexts and not all are much implemented either, and so I only cover the traversal module here, which is the only one I consider to be sufficiently useful in general.

Table 13–2 shows which parts of the DOM are implemented by which DOM implementations. Note that javadom only supports those parts of the DOM that are both wrapped in javadom and available in the underlying DOM implementation.

Table 13–2   Implementations of DOM modules

DOM	XML	HTML	Views	CSS	Events	Traversal	Range
PyDOM	yes (level 1)	no	no	no	no	no	no
4DOM	yes	yes	no	no	no	yes	no
minidom	mostly	no	no	no	no	no	no
javadom	yes (level 1)	no	no	no	no	no	no
Sun	yes (level 1[†])	no	no	no	no	no	no
Xerces	yes	no	no	no	no	no	no
DOM2	yes	no	no	no	no	no	no
Indelv	yes	no	no	no	no	no	no
SXP	yes	no	no	no	no	no	no
OpenXML	yes	no	no	no	no	no	no

[†] Implements an old DOM level 2 draft.

13.3.1 *DOM namespace support*

The namespace support in DOM level 2 has been introduced by adding new attributes and methods, which means that methods for namespace-aware and non-namespace aware access to the document tree coexist in the same interfaces. This means that it is possible to use both namespace and non-namespace access to the same document in the same application, but this is not recommended.

Expanded names are represented by giving the `Node` interface three new attributes `namespaceURI`, `prefix`, and `localname`. The result is that the name of an attribute or element type is represented in three different parts:

`namespaceURI`

> This holds the URI of the namespace, for example `http://www.w3.org/TR/REC-html40` for HTML 4.0 documents. If the node has no namespace, the value will be `None`, as it will be for all nodes that are not elements or attributes.

`localName`

> This holds the second part of the name, the local part, that is, the name after the prefix, which might be, for example, `body` in an HTML document.

`prefix`

> This holds the prefix used in the serialized form of an element or attribute, for example `html`. If the node doesn't have a namespace (or isn't an attribute or an element), the value will be `None`.

`tagName/nodeName`

> This holds the unprocessed name of the element, for example `html:body`. Note that the prefix is included here, which ensures that the value is the same as it would have been in DOM level 1.

Expanded names need to be represented not just in the attributes of nodes, but also when passed as parameters to DOM methods. For this reason, for each DOM level 1 method which accepts an element-type or attribute name, level 2 adds a new namespace-aware method with "NS" appended to the name.

These methods all work in exactly the same way as their namespace-unaware cousins, except that they are namespace-aware. The full list of such methods is:

- `Document.createElementNS(namespaceURI, lname)`
- `Document.createAttributeNS(namespaceURI, lname)`

- `Document.getElementsByTagNameNS(namespaceURI, lname)`

- `NamedNodeMap.getNamedItemNS(namespaceURI, lname)`

- `NamedNodeMap.setNamedItemNS(node)`

- `NamedNodeMap.removeNamedItemNS(namespaceURI, lname)`

- `Element.getAttributeNS(namespaceURI, lname)`

- `Element.setAttributeNS(namespaceURI, lname, value)`

- `Element.removeAttributeNS(namespaceURI, lname)`

- `Element.getAttributeNodeNS(namespaceURI, lname)`

- `Element.setAttributeNodeNS(attr)`

- `Element.getElementsByTagNameNS(attr)`

13.3.2 *Other level 2 core extensions*

13.3.2.1 Object creation

In addition to the namespace support, level 2 of the DOM extends level 1 in other ways. The most important addition is the two new methods on the `DOMImplementation` interface for creating `Document-Type` and `Document` nodes. These are important as they provide a standardized way of creating nodes of these types, but unfortunately this does not really solve the problem, since to be able to create new document types and documents, one must have a `DOMImplementation` object, and there is no standardized way for creating these.

The underlying problem is that the DOM specification uses CORBA IDL, which in itself provides no mechanisms for creating objects that implement the IDL interfaces. Instead, two main mechanisms are provided for getting hold of instances of CORBA interfaces: creating them locally and using a naming service to find important local or remote objects by name. When creating objects locally there can quite legitimately be several local implementations of the same interface, making a standard solution next to impossible.

The result is that we are left with having to resort to non-standard means of creating documents in each specific DOM implementation. Interestingly, Sun's JAXP specification aims at solving this problem for Java, but unfortunately this has not been widely implemented. For Python there is no solution at the moment.

In any case, the two new methods are:

`createDocumentType(qName, publicId, systemId,`
`    internalSubset)`

> This creates a new and empty `DocumentType` node. The `qName` parameter holds the qualified name of the document element. The `publicId` and `systemId` parameters hold the public and system identifiers. The `internalSubset` method holds the internal subset of the DTD as a string.
>
> The new node will be empty, since this method is meant to be equivalent to inserting a `DOCTYPE` declaration in the document.

`createDocument(namespaceURI, qualifiedName,`
`    doctype)`

> This creates a new `Document` node with a document element that has the name given by the `namespaceURI` and `qualifiedName` parameters. A document type can be given in the `doctype` parameter. Both `doctype` and `namespaceURI` can be `None`.

13.3.2.2 Getting elements by ID

In XML, attributes declared with the type ID can be used to uniquely identify elements in a document, and other specifications such as XSLT and XPointer can use this feature to locate an element by its ID. Naturally, this makes it important that the DOM support this, and DOM level 2 adds this support through the new `getElementById(id)` method on the `Document` interface.

This method accepts an element ID and returns the corresponding Element node, or None if no element has the given ID. Note that to do this, the underlying DOM implementation has to be aware that an attribute used in the document has been declared with the type ID in the DTD. SAX (and many parsers) expose the necessary information, but the DOM itself does not, so getElementById can't be expected to work for documents created with the DOM. In theory, it is of course possible for the DOM to read the DTD if a DOCTYPE declaration is inserted, but I doubt that many implementations do this.

13.3.2.3 Moving nodes between documents

In DOM, nodes (except documents and DTDs) can only exist within the context of an owning Document. This means that it is not accepted to move nodes that belong to one document directly into another document. The reason for this is that the two documents may be from different implementations which may not be compatible. For example, one may be an in-memory implementation while the other may be a database implementation. DOM level 1 had no standard solution for this, but level 2 adds the importNode(node, deep) method on the Document interface to support this.

Calling this method on a document and giving it the node to be imported will cause the node (and all its descendants, if deep is set to true) to be copied. The copies will have the ownerDocument attribute set to the document into which the nodes are being imported. After this operation the nodes can be inserted into their new owner document with the usual node insertion methods.

Example 13–4 demonstrates both the wrong and the right ways to move nodes between documents.

13.3.2.4 New Node methods

DOM level 2 adds two new methods to the Node interface: normalize and supports. The normalize method performs the same operation as the normalize method specified on the Element interface in DOM

Example 13–4. Mixing DOM documents

```
>>> from xml.dom import Document
>>> doc = Document.Document(None)
>>> doc2 = Document.Document(None)
>>> doc.appendChild(doc2.createElement('doc'))
Traceback (innermost last):
  File "<stdin>", line 1, in ?
  File "C:\Program Files\Python\xml\dom\Document.py", line 259,
  in appendChild
    self._4dom_addSingle(newChild)
  File "C:\Program Files\Python\xml\dom\Document.py", line 251,
  in _4dom_addSingle
    self._4dom_validateNode(node)
  File "C:\Program Files\Python\xml\dom\Node.py", line 382,
  in _4dom_validateNode
    raise DOMException(WRONG_DOCUMENT_ERR)
xml.dom.DOMException: DOM Error Code 4:
>>> root = doc.importNode(doc2.createElement("doc"), 1)
>>> doc.appendChild(root)
<Element Node at 8183376: Name = 'doc' with 0 attributes and
0 children>
```

level 1 (see page 417), that is, it joins together adjacent Text nodes in the sub-tree below the node.

The supports method is the same as the method with the same name on the DOMImplementation interface; it simply returns what the method on the DOM implementation of the owner document would have returned. (See page 423 for a description of this method.)

13.3.2.5 New DocumentType attributes

DOM level 2 adds three new read-only attributes on the DocumentType interface: publicId, systemId, and internalSubset. The publicId and systemId attributes hold the public and system identifiers of the DTD. The internalSubset attribute holds the entire internal subset of the document as a string. Note that with these three attributes DocumentType objects represent both the DOCTYPE declaration in the owner document and the contents of the DTD referred to by that declaration.

A consequence of this is that the `DocumentType` object is not really independent of the owner document. This is because the information in these three properties is all taken from the `DOCTYPE` declaration in the document. This dependence is not, however, something new in DOM level 2, since the logical contents of a DTD depend on the values of the parameter entities used in that DTD, and these can be controlled from the internal subset of a document.

13.3.3 *Traversal*

The traversal module of the DOM is intended to allow applications to define virtual views of documents and traverse over these. This feature is in a sense similar to using SAX filters and is rather simple to understand and use. It is less powerful than SAX filters, since it cannot change the traversed document, only filter it.

The DOM specification uses the term *physical view* to describe the view of the document as it really is, and the term *logical view* to describe a view of the document created by filters. This distinction has nothing to do with the lexical/logical distinction described in 2.4.2, "Logical and lexical information," on page 68. For this reason I have chosen not to follow the DOM terminology in this section, but refer to the created view as the *virtual view*.

The functionality of the traversal module is centered around three concepts:

- *filters*, which decide which nodes are part of the virtual view and which are not,
- *iterators*, which present a linear (flat) view of the tree, and
- *walkers*, which present a full tree view.

Both iterators and walkers apply filters to the document to produce a virtual view.

13.3.3.1 The NodeFilter interface

Filters are used to control which parts of the node set are seen by the iterators and walkers, and are implemented by the application developer. DOM does not provide any filter implementations. While traversing, iterators, and walkers will always ask their associated filter (if any) whether to return a node, and will ignore it if told so by the filter.

A nice thing about the separation between the filters and the iterators/walkers is that filter implementations have no need to know anything about the set of nodes that is traversed or the traversal order. This makes it much easier to implement general and reusable filters.

With iterators, filters can only tell the iterator whether to include or skip a particular node at a time, but with walkers, a filter can also tell the walker to reject a node, which means that the node and all its children are skipped.

In DOM level 2, filters must implement the NodeFilter interface. This interface has no attributes, and only a single method:

acceptNode(node)

This method takes a node as the parameter and decides whether or not to include it in the view. The method returns an integer code, indicating whether the node is accepted (FILTER_ACCEPT, 1), rejected (FILTER_REJECT, 2), or skipped (FILTER_SKIP, 3).

Accepted nodes will be returned by both iterators and walkers. Skipped nodes will be omitted by both iterators and walkers, although both will consider their children. For iterators, rejected and skipped nodes are treated the same way, but for walkers, rejected nodes differ in that their children will also be rejected.

In Java, the NodeFilter interface is found in the org.w3c.dom.traversal package. In 4DOM it is found in the xml.dom module, but since it only has one method there is no need to actually us the 4DOM class as the base class. The other traversal interfaces are in the same package. In both Java and Python the constants are found as static attributes in the NodeFilter.

Filters can modify the document they are filtering, but it is considered bad practice to do so. The whole intention of the traversal interfaces is that filters only be used for deciding whether to include nodes or not. However, it is impossible for traversal implementations to keep filters from modifying the DOM structure.

13.3.3.1.1   A filter example

Sometimes XML applications are defined in such a way that it makes sense to act on only the parts of documents that belong to the namespace of the application. A typical example is all kinds of applications that have a controlled extension mechanism which allows elements from other namespaces to be used in the documents. These will usually state that these extension elements are to be ignored by applications that do not understand them.

Example 13–5 shows a NodeFilter implementation which takes a dictionary of accepted namespaces as a parameter to the constructor,

Example 13–5. A DOM traversal namespace filter

```
class NamespaceNodeFilter:

    FILTER_ACCEPT   = 1
    FILTER_SKIP     = 3

    ELEMENT_NODE    = 1
    ATTRIBUTE_NODE = 2

    def __init__(self, namespaces = []):
        self._namespaces = {}
        for namespace in namespaces:
            self._namespaces[namespace] = 1

    def acceptNode(self, node):
        if (node.nodeType != NamespaceNodeFilter.ELEMENT_NODE and
            node.nodeType != NamespaceNodeFilter.ATTRIBUTE_NODE) or\
            self._namespaces.has_key(node.namespaceURI):
            return FILTER_ACCEPT
        else:
            return FILTER_SKIP     # don't reject children
```

and only accepts element and attribute nodes in those namespaces, skipping all other elements and attributes. Other kinds of nodes are passed through.

Note that if you wish to accept nodes that do not belong to a namespace you can do this by putting the namespace `None` into the dictionary.

Note that this example does not import any DOM modules to get the constants, but re-declares them instead, avoiding dependency on any specific DOM implementation. Similarly, the filter is not a subclass of `NodeFilter`, since this is not needed in Python and not doing it again avoids the dependency.

13.3.3.2 The `NodeIterator` interface

Iterators present a set of nodes in a linear sequence, allowing clients to move backwards and forwards in the sequence. The set of nodes iterated over can be any kind of node collection, but DOM level 2 defines only one iterator, which iterates over the nodes in a document sub-tree in document order.

The current position of an iterator is always *between* two nodes (or before the first or after the last), and moving one step in either direction causes the neighboring node on that side to be returned. Figure 13–1 shows an example of an iterator pointing into a sequence of nodes.

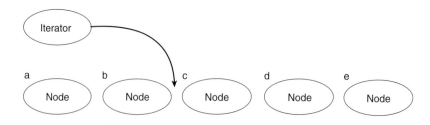

Figure 13–1   A `NodeIterator` pointing into a node set

In this situation, the iterator is pointing between two nodes; moving it forward would cause it to return the node labeled "c", and moving it backwards would cause it to return the node labeled "b". Because of this, a DOM iterator does not have a current node, just a current position.

Iterators consider the sequence they iterate over to be live, so that any changes to the underlying node set while the iterator is active may cause changes in what the iterator returns. This means that if, in Figure 13–1, we insert a new node "f" between "c" and "d", the iterator will return it after "c" and before "d".

The `NodeIterator` interface has three attributes, all of which are read-only and set on creation of the `NodeIterator` object:

`whatToShow`
> This attribute is used to filter what node types to show by node type. It is a bit complex, so the details are given below.

`filter`
> This attribute holds the `NodeFilter` used to filter what the `NodeIterator` shows. If it is `None`, there is no filter and all nodes are shown (except those screened by the other attributes).

`expandEntityReferences`
> If this attribute is set to `false`, `EntityReference` nodes and their children will be skipped. If it is `true`, `EntityReference` nodes and their children will be included. This is sub-optimal, because applications are more likely to want to be able to just ignore the `EntityReference` nodes, but see their children. Unfortunately, this behavior is not possible to implement for walkers using filters, since walkers will not hide the fact that the children of an `EntityReference` node do not appear in the child list of the `EntityReference`'s parent.

Together, these three attributes determine what the iterator will show and what it will skip. The `expandEntityReferences` attribute is checked first, and then the `whatToShow` attribute is applied to what passed the first attribute, and finally the `filter` is called on what has progressed so far. Effectively, this means that the filter only gets to see what the other two attributes allow through, and the iterator itself will only show what all three attributes agree to let through.

The `whatToShow` attribute is used to filter nodes by their node type and is really a bit mask. That is, it is a number that is interpreted bit by bit. What this means is that you can use it to accept nodes of any combination of types. To do this, a number of flags are defined in the `NodeFilter` interface. Their names should be self-explanatory; they include: `SHOW_ALL`, `SHOW_ELEMENT`, `SHOW_ATTRIBUTE`, `SHOW_TEXT`, `SHOW_CDATA_SECTION`, `SHOW_ENTITY_REFERENCE`, `SHOW_ENTITY`, `SHOW_PROCESSING_INSTRUCTION`, `SHOW_COMMENT`, `SHOW_DOCUMENT`, `SHOW_DOCUMENT_TYPE`, `SHOW_DOCUMENT_FRAGMENT`, and `SHOW_NO-TATION`.

To show nodes of all types, use `SHOW_ALL` to show nodes of one type, set `whatToShow` to one of the other values. To show nodes of a combination of types, use bit-wise or operation (|) to combine the values of several flags. For example, to show text and CDATA nodes, do `whatToShow = SHOW_TEXT | SHOW_CDATA_SECTION`.

The attributes control what the iterator shows, but the methods are what does the actual job of iterating and returning nodes to the application. The methods are:

`nextNode()`

This returns the next node in the sequence iterated over, and moves the iterator to the next node in the set.

`previousNode()`

This returns the previous node in the set, and moves the iterator to the previous node in the set.

`detach()`

This method makes the iterator release whatever resources it is holding onto and invalidates it, so that further calls will raise exceptions. This ensures that any allocated node lists are freed, but isn't really a very useful method in a Python environment, so 4DOM doesn't implement it.

13.3.3.3 The `TreeWalker` interface

As mentioned earlier, tree walkers are like iterators except that they present more directions of movement than only forwards and backwards. This means that the client can use the `TreeWalker` to walk the tree in any combination of directions. The `TreeWalker` also differs from the `NodeIterator` in that it has a current node at all times, and any movement causes it to jump to a new current node.

The interfaces are also similar. The `TreeWalker` interface has the same `whatToShow`, `filter`, and `expandEntityReferences` attributes with the same semantics as `NodeIterator`.

However, `TreeWalker` has one additional attribute:

`currentNode`
  This read-only attribute holds the node the `TreeWalker` currently points to.

The main part of the `TreeWalker` interface is made up of all the navigation method used to move around the tree. These all return the new current node or `None` if there are no more nodes in the desired direction of movement. If there are no more nodes, the current node is unchanged by the call. The available methods are:

`parentNode()`
  Moves to the nearest visible ancestor.

`firstChild()`
  Moves to the first child.

`lastChild()`
  Moves to the last child.

`previousSibling()`
  Moves to the nearest visible sibling before the current node.

`nextSibling()`
  Moves to the nearest visible sibling after the current node.

`previousNode()`
> Moves to the previous node in document order.

`nextNode()`
> Moves to the next node in document order.

13.3.3.4 The `DocumentTraversal` interface

The `DocumentTraversal` interface contains the methods used to create iterators and walkers, so it is used as the factory for creating these objects. Unfortunately, this object is subject to the same chicken-and-egg creation problems that we discussed in the context of the core DOM on page 469.

This means that there are no portable means of creating the `DocumentTraversal` object, so 4DOM skips it altogether and instead implements constructors directly on `NodeIterator` and `TreeWalker`. `NodeFilter` creation is not catered for by the DOM specification, since filters are intended to be implemented by developers.

The `DocumentTraversal` has only two methods:

`createNodeIterator(root, whatToShow, filter, expandEntityReferences)`
> This method creates and returns a `NodeIterator` object which iterates over the nodes in the sub-tree under the `root` node in document order. Initially, the iterator will be positioned before the `root` node. The `whatToShow`, `filter`, and `expandEntityReferences` parameters are used to initialize the parameters of the same names in the iterator.

`createTreeWalker(root, whatToShow, filter, expandEntityReferences)`
> Creates and returns a `TreeWalker` object with the `root` node as the start node. The walker will not be able to move higher up in the tree than the `root` node. The `whatToShow`, `filter`, and `expandEntityReferences` parameters are used to initialize the parameters of the same names in the iterator.

In 4DOM, this interface isn't implemented. Instead, the Node-
Iterator and TreeWalker classes in the xml.dom package can be
instantiated directly, using the constructor signatures shown above in
the DocumentTraversal definition.

13.3.3.5 Conclusion

This section may not have made it entirely clear where and how to
make use of the DOM traversal interfaces, and part of the reason for
this is that they have no obvious uses. In my opinion, the utility of the
traversal module is quite limited. Iterators can be used when one wants
to visit nodes in document order or when one does not care about the
order. The tree structure is a bit tricky to infer from this sequence of
nodes, so when iterators are used, one should either not care about the
structure, or be willing to figure it out by looking at each node.

Walkers seem to have very few uses since all they do is filter out parts
of the tree in ways that you could very easily re-implement when
needed. Implementing your own walkers to present a view of the tree
where nodes have been moved slightly (for example, by removing all
traces of entity reference nodes and "lifting up" their children) might
be interesting, however.

Filters, on the other hand, have many possible uses, mostly in
generic frameworks, but in some cases in specific applications as well.
They can be used separately from iterators and walkers, and can therefore be used even when other parts of the traversal framework are not
used. In fact, filters are so easy to implement separately that the DOM
implementation used does not need to support traversal at all.

So the conclusion is: Use iterators when you want to visit nodes in
document order or any order, and implement your own walkers to
present views of the document that are modified beyond what a filter
allows. Use filters whenever they seem useful, even if you don't use the
rest of the traversal module.

13.4 | Future directions for DOM

Work has begun on DOM level 3 specification, which at the moment consists of the following Working Drafts:

core

Updates the DOM core specification, adding many new attributes and methods to the existing interfaces.

content models and load and save

Divided into two parts: content models and load/save. The content models part contains interfaces that represent the declarations in DTDs and XML Schema definitions and extends the core interfaces to connect them with the core document model. The load/save part contains interfaces for loading XML documents into DOM trees and for writing the trees back out as documents.

views and formatting

Contains both general interfaces for representing any kinds of views on a DOM tree and specialized interfaces for representing a formatted view of a document. Provides detailed information about exactly where each piece of the document is displayed.

events

Contains new interfaces and events extending those already in DOM level 2. The main additions are events for keyboard activity and interfaces for creating groups of related listeners.

These additions essentially complete the DOM specification as it was originally planned, by adding DTD representation and support for loading and saving DOM trees. In fact, it goes far beyond the original ideas, creating a huge specification. DOM level 2 was several hundred pages, and it looks like level 3 will add another hundred pages at least.

The most useful parts seem to be the content models (really DTDs and XML Schema) part and the load/save part. The content models part finally enables DOM implementations to represent DTDs and at the same time looks like it will support XML Schema. The load/save part will make this functionality portable across DOM implementations, and at the same time provide more control over it.

For example, it may be that the DOM level 3 load/save specification will allow applications to control whether or not CDATASection nodes will be created during loading. It also seems likely that it will become possible to control whether EntityReference nodes will be created or not. The interfaces defined by the load/save specification are very similar to the SAX 2.0 interfaces, although they have different names. Properties and features are merged into the property concept and property names are not URIs.

How the DOM will be extended after level 3, and whether it will be extended at all, is not known. There have been discussions of specialized DOMs for MathML and SVG, but so far nothing concrete has emerged.

More details about DOM level 3 are not given here, since the specifications are quite new, and by the time they are finalized they are likely to look quite different.

13.5 | DOM performance

This chapter presents the result of a number of informal benchmarks of various DOM operations. As noted in 9.6, "Speed," on page 322, performance is notoriously difficult to measure, having no absolute metric, so these results should be regarded only as rough indications of performance.

All the tests were run on the same computer as the previous SAX performance tests.

13.5.1 *Loading XML documents*

This is perhaps the most important speed aspect of any DOM implementation, since most applications that use DOM will start by loading XML documents from disk.

13.5.1.1 Results

The documents from 9.6.2.1, "The test documents," on page 335 were each run five times through the Python script in Example 13–6, which basically loads DOM tree from file and prints the time it took to do so.

Example 13–6. A benchmark script for DOM loading

```
import time, sys
from xml.dom.ext.reader.Sax2 import Reader

start = time.clock()
doc = Reader().fromStream(open(sys.argv[1]))
used = time.clock() - start
print "Elapsed:", used
```

Table 13–3 shows the results. Numbers are given with two most significant digits only, since the measurement is too inaccurate for any more digits to be meaningful. Note that the javadom results are essentially benchmarks of the Java DOMs, since javadom does nothing more than call out to the Java DOM builder and wrap the result in a single `Document` object. The documents used to test loading times are described in 9.6.2.1, "The test documents," on page 335.

The results in Table 13–3 contain a number of interesting results. To make them easier to comprehend, we divide them into Python DOMs, C DOMs, Java DOMs, and pickled DOMs. The C and Java DOMs seem to operate at much the same speeds, both of which are much higher than the speed of the Python and pickled DOMs, by a factor of about 10. This in itself is interesting. There are also some

Table 13–3   Results of the DOM loading benchmark

Implementation	Othello	XSLT-WD	xmltools	airports
4DOM with Pyexpat	17	5.9	21	61
4DOM with xmlproc	18	6.3	22	64
minidom with Pyexpat	2.5	1.3	3.1	11
pDomlette	2.5	0.97	2.7	8.3
cDomlette	0.24	0.12	0.32	1.1
javadom with Sun DOM	0.26	0.16	0.31	0.65
javadom with Xerces	0.28	0.28	0.23	0.39
javadom with Indelv DOM	0.27	0.21	0.26	0.62
Pickled minidom	2.7	1.4	3.4	10

interesting variations among the Java DOMs, which seem to be fast on some documents and slow on others.

Pickling does not seem to be very interesting for minidom, since results are much the same as with ordinary XML parsing. Since pickling is much more awkward, there isn't much point in it, as there is only a microscopic speed gain.

Among the Python DOMs, it seems clear that both pDomlette and minidom are much faster than 4DOM, at least by a factor of 5.

13.5.2 *Serialization*

Writing DOM trees back to XML documents is a less common operation than reading documents, but it is still common enough to warrant a benchmark of its own. This benchmark uses the same documents as the loading benchmark and measures the time it takes to write an XML document to disk from an in-memory structure. The results in Table 13–4 are the average of 5 tries.

The first thing to notice is that 4DOM serialization is slow and that it could probably be speeded up quite a bit. Strangely, the Pretty-

Table 13–4   Results of the DOM serialization benchmark

Implementation	Othello	XSLT-WD	xmltools	airports
4DOM with `Print`	7.1	3.2		24
4DOM with `PrettyPrint`	6.1	2.7		21
minidom with `writexml`	1.1	0.67		4
minidom with `cPickle`	3.1	1.9	4.6	15

`Print` method is consistently faster than `Print`, so one might as well use that. Also, minidom seems to be very fast at serialization. Pickling minidom seems to be about three times slower than using the `writexml` method, making it thoroughly unattractive. Pickling 4DOM was not possible at the time of writing, and the bug was not fixed by the time this book went to press. Only one time for serialization of the xmltools document is given, since the other attempts ran out of memory and crashed.

Table 13–5 shows the time needed for combined serialization and deserialization round-trips for the different serialization alternatives.

Table 13–5   Results of the DOM round-trip benchmark

Implementation	Othello	XSLT-WD	xmltools	airports
4DOM with Pyexpat & `PrettyPrint`	23.1	8.6		82
minidom with `writexml`	3.6	3.2		15
minidom with `cPickle`	5.8	3.3	8	25

The conclusion seems rather clear: minidom is much faster than 4DOM, and pickling is slower for minidom than using the ordinary XML representation.

13.5.3 *Memory use*

Another important aspect of performance that you should have some idea about is the memory use of the various DOM implementations. This benchmark, with its results shown in Table 13–6, uses the same documents as the loading and serialization benchmarks, and measures the size difference of the Python process before the document is loaded and after it has been loaded.

Table 13–6   Memory use of DOM implementations

Implementation	Othello	XSLT-WD	xmltools	airports
4DOM	32 Mb	12 Mb	41 Mb	95 Mb
minidom	9.2 Mb	5.2 Mb	12 Mb	36 Mb
pDomlette	12 Mb	4 Mb	12 Mb	36 Mb
cDomlette	2.7 Mb	1.1 Mb	3.1 Mb	8.3 Mb

The conclusions from this exercise are rather surprising: minidom uses on average roughly a third of the memory 4DOM uses, and pDomlette uses about the same amount. In 4DOM, documents seem to become about 100 times larger when in memory, while in minidom and pDomlette they seem to increase only by a factor of 30. Clearly, there are definite limits on the sizes of the documents which the Python DOM implementations can hold.

cDomlette, however, uses far less memory than any of the other implementations. On average, documents seem to increase in size by a factor of about 10, while memory use seems to be around a third of that of minidom and pDomlette.

Other tree-based APIs

- qp_xml
- Groves

There are some interesting alternative tree-based XML APIs that compete with DOM, and this chapter looks at two of them. The first one is intended as a faster and less memory-intensive alternative, while the second one is more ambitious, being in effect an alternative data model to XML. A third tree-based API is described in 22.2.1, "Pyxie," on page 853.

14.1 | qp_xml

qp_xml is a small Python module written by Greg Stein that uses Pyexpat to build a minimal XML document tree. The name is an abbreviation of "Quick Parsing for XML," and this is exactly what it is. Trees are built very fast in qp_xml since hardly any work is being done in Python code, and at the same time it is very simple and easy to use.

A downside of qp_xml is that it throws away a lot of information about an XML document. All lexical information is lost, and even some logical information (notably PIs) is discarded, but the advantage is that the resulting model is extremely simple and builds fast.

Example 14–1. A sample document

```
<doc>
This is a <em>simple</em> document, about to be loaded into
<keyword>qp_xml</keyword>.
</doc>
```

The way the qp_xml model handles children and character data is a bit unusual, but in many ways more convenient than the more straightforward DOM solution. Figure 14–1 shows how the document in Example 14–1 would look when loaded into qp_xml.

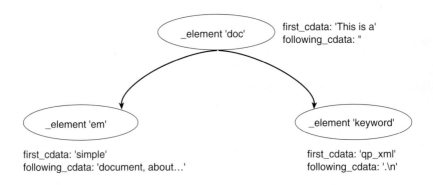

Figure 14–1   The sample document in qp_xml

The unusual part of how qp_xml models XML documents is in its handling of character data pieces versus elements. The `children` attribute of the `_element` class holds only the child elements of that element, but not the character data. Instead, the character data before the first child element is in the attribute `first_cdata` (for the document element in the example, this is `'This is a '`), then the contents of that element are held by the object representing that element, and the character data after the first child element and before the second (or before the end of the parent element) is found in the child element's `following_cdata` attribute (in our example this is ' document, about...').

This means that the character data of an element with child elements is held in the element itself and also one piece in each of the children. This makes it slightly awkward to retrieve, but luckily the qp_xml _element class has a method that returns the character data of an element.

One disadvantage of qp_xml is that it is read-only. The API does not have specific support for modifying the tree, and doing so requires a bit of care, especially in maintaining the character data dispersed throughout the document tree. So for applications that need to modify the tree, qp_xml is not really recommended.

14.1.1 *The qp_xml API*

The qp_xml module has a very simple API that is quickly learned. It consists of three parts: the loader class, the tree structure, and some useful functions for working with the tree. The loader class is named `Parser` and supports the method shown below:

`parse(input)`
> This method makes the parser parse `input` and return the root of the resulting tree. The `input` parameter can be either a string containing an XML document or a file-like object from which an XML document can be read. If parsing fails, the tree is deleted and a `qp_xml.error` exception is raised.
>
> The `parse` method can be called more than once, since the `Parser` object resets itself for each call.

The tree API is also rather simple, consisting of instances of a single class, `_element`. Instances of this class contain the relevant information about themselves in the following attributes:

name
> Contains the element-type name, or the qualified name in namespace terminology.

ns
> Contains the namespace URI of the namespace the element belongs to, if any. If the element does not belong to a namespace, the value is an empty string.

children
> Contains a list of the child elements, if any. Any character data in the element will be in the `first_cdata` attribute of the element and the `following_cdata` attributes of its children.

attrs
> Contains the attributes of the element, in a dictionary that maps attribute names to values.

first_cdata
> Contains any character data that appeared inside the element, up to the first child element.

following_cdata
> Contains the character data in the document immediately following the element itself, as described above.

lang
> Contains the value of the `xml:lang` attribute, if the element itself or one of its parents had a value for this attribute. (The value is inherited to children until overridden.)

In addition to these attributes, the `_element` class has two methods:

textof()
> Returns the character data of the element, which does not include that of child elements.

find(name, ns = '')

> This method finds the first child element with the given element-type name (and namespace name, if given).

This API makes it possible to quickly load and work with XML documents, in much the same way as with DOM. The interpreter dialog in Example 14–2 shows how this can be done.

Example 14–2. Using qp_xml

```
>>> from xml.utils import qp_xml
>>> p = qp_xml.Parser()
>>> root = p.parse("<doc>\nThis is a <em>simple</em> document,
about to be loaded into\n<keyword>qp_xml</keyword>\n</doc>")
>>> root
<xml.utils.qp_xml._element instance at 79c450>
>>> root.name
'doc'
>>> root.children
[<xml.utils.qp_xml._element instance at 79c5f0>,
 <xml.utils.qp_xml._element instance at 79d4e0>]
>>> root.following_cdata
' '
>>> root.attrs
{}
>>> root.first_cdata
'\012This is a '
>>> ch = root.children[0]
>>> ch.name
'em'
>>> ch.first_cdata
'simple'
>>> ch.following_cdata
' document, about to be loaded into\012'
>>> ch.children
[]
>>> root.textof()
'\012This is a  document, about to be loaded into\012\012'
>>> root.find("keyword")
<xml.utils.qp_xml._element instance at 79b620>
>>>
```

The module also contains some useful functions that are listed below.

```
dump(outf, root)
```
Writes the qp_xml tree passed in the `tree` argument as XML to the file-like object `outf`.

```
_clean_tree(elem)
```
Removes all circular references in the element `elem` and its children.

14.1.2 *An example application*

Example 14–3 shows the source code for the RSS to HTML converter, now implemented with qp_xml. Since very similar utilities are used, it is similar to the DOM example, but a little simpler and quite a bit faster.

14.1.3 *Performance*

This informal benchmark was performed on the same machine as the other benchmarks in this book, and used the by now familiar set of documents described in 9.6.2.1, "The test documents," on page 335. Table 14–1 shows (in the columns from left to right) the time needed to load a qp_xml tree from an XML document (averaged over five attempts), the memory used by each tree, and the serialization time using `cPickle` (also averaged over five attempts).

Table 14–1 Performance results for qp_xml

	Othello	*XSLT-WD*	*xmltools*	*airports*
Parsing time	1.3	0.6	1.2	3.8
Memory use	3.5M	1.5M	3.8M	9.8M
Serialization time	0.39	0.15		1.7
cPickle load time	0.51	0.18	0.49	1.5
cPickle dump time	0.37	0.14	0.43	1.2

Example 14–3. A qp_xml RSS to HTML converter

```python
import sys, codecs
from xml.utils import qp_xml

# --- Templates

top = \
"""
<!DOCTYPE HTML PUBLIC "-//W3C//DTD HTML 4.0 Transitional//EN">
<HTML>
<HEAD>
  <TITLE>%s</TITLE>
</HEAD>

<BODY>
"""

bottom = \
"""
<HR>

<ADDRESS>
Converted to HTML by rss2html.py.
</ADDRESS>

</BODY>
</HTML>
"""

# --- Utilities

def find_first_element(parent, name):
    for child in parent.children:
        if child.name == name:
            return child

# --- The converter

def conv2html(root, out = None):
    out = out or sys.stdout

    channel = find_first_element(root, "channel")
    title = find_first_element(channel, "title").textof()
    link = find_first_element(channel, "link").textof()
    descr = find_first_element(channel, "description")
```

```
    if descr != None:
        descr = descr.textof()
    else:
        descr = None

    out.write(top % title)
    out.write('<h1><a href="%s">%s</a></h1>\n' % (link, title))
    if descr:
        out.write('<p>%s</p>\n\n' % descr)

    out.write("<ul>\n")
    for child in root.children + channel.children:
        if child.name == "item":
            convitem(child, out)
    out.write("</ul>\n")

    out.write(bottom)

def convitem(item, out):
    title = find_first_element(item, "title").textof()
    link = find_first_element(item, "link").textof()
    descr = find_first_element(item, "description")
    if descr != None:
        descr = descr.textof()
    else:
        descr = ""

    out.write('  <li><a href="%s">%s</a> %s\n' %
              (link, title, descr))

# --- Main program

parser = qp_xml.Parser()
outf = codecs.open(sys.argv[2], "w", "iso-8859-1")
doc = parser.parse(open(sys.argv[1]))
conv2html(doc, outf)
```

These results compare very favorably with the DOM loading benchmarks presented in 13.5.1, "Loading XML documents," on page 494. Performance seems to be at least 10 times that of 4DOM, but only about a fourth of the Java DOMs. Memory size seems to be about a tenth of 4DOM's as well, and about a third of minidom's, which makes it comparable to that of cDomlette. This makes qp_xml a useful alternative to the DOMs in cases where performance and memory footprint really matter. Using cPickle seems to be a little faster than storing the data as XML, but probably not enough to justify the extra hassle.

14.2 | Groves

14.2.1 *What groves are*

As mentioned earlier, XML was defined in two steps: first the syntax and then the data model. The history of SGML was similar, in that the SGML standard itself only defined the syntax. Later, when the DSSSL (a stylesheet standard similar to XSLT and XSL) and HyTime (a linking and multimedia standard) ISO standards were being developed, the committees working on them discovered that they had slightly different ideas about the data model of SGML documents.

This made the need for defining a common data model apparent. At the same time it was recognized that for a linking language like HyTime to be able to link to data objects, it would need a data model for these objects, whether they are SGML documents or something completely different. To this end, the HyTime committee defined a data model they called *groves*. This data model is based on nodes with properties, and the values of some of these properties can be references to other nodes. This enables groves to represent any kind of graph and, essentially, any kind of data at all. The data model has some fundamental things in common with that of object-oriented languages, but there are also some important differences.

The grove model is defined in the HyTime ISO standard, which also contains a grove definition for SGML documents and another one for text files. This essentially serves as a formal definition of the SGML data model, and is the basis for both the HyTime standard and the DSSSL standard. The Infoset Recommendation for XML is similar to groves, but only accomplishes a subset of what groves do, since it is specific to XML.

The grove model contains something called *property sets*, which are essentially schemas for groves. They define the classes of grove nodes, properties of nodes in each class with their data types, and other constraints. Property sets also support something called *grove plans* which divide the property sets into modules. A class of nodes can have some properties in one module and some in another. Applications can then choose which modules they want to enable and which they do not. This can be used, for example, to effectively filter out lexical details that an application is not interested in.

A property set assigns types to each property of the nodes in the grove, although these differ somewhat from the types most of us are used to. Some of these types are familiar ones, such as char, string, strlist (list of strings), integer, intlist (list of integers), boolean, and so on. There are also types for node references, lists of node references, as well as lists of references to named nodes (these are similar to ordered dictionaries or hashtables).

Property sets also support other kinds of metadata about properties beyond the relatively traditional types discussed so far. This metadata provides extra information about the role played by various properties. The most important information is perhaps the distinction between what is called *sub-nodal properties* (references to contained nodes) and references that do not imply containment. For example, the reference from an element instance to its attributes is sub-nodal, since the element clearly contains the attributes. However, the reference from the element to the element type definition in the DTD is not sub-nodal, since the element does not contain its own definition.

Property sets contain more definitions similar to the concept of sub-nodal properties. One example of this is that each class can have one "children" property, which contains its children. For elements, this is the list of contained nodes (excluding the attributes). Classes that have no "children" property can have a "data" property, which holds the data carried by that class. The difference between "children" and "data" is that a "children" property holds child nodes, while a "data" property holds primitive values.

This extra metadata makes groves much more useful than they would otherwise be. The benefit lies in that application software can exploit it to perform general operations on groves whose property sets they have no pre-programmed knowledge of. For example, even though a grove is a general graph with references in all directions, it becomes a tree if only sub-nodal references are followed. Similarly, the content of any node can be extracted by using the children and data properties.

In addition to the properties defined by each property set, all nodes in any grove have a set of predefined properties known as the *intrinsic properties*. These properties are made possible by the extra metadata discussed above, and some of them are listed below.

parent
> If a node has found as the value of a "children" property of another node, the other node becomes its parent. So elements are the parents of their children, but not of their attributes, which have no parent.

origin
> This is like parent, but for the sub-nodal properties rather than for "children" properties. So an element is the origin of its attributes and also of its children.

grvroot
> This is the root of the entire grove, which could also have been found by walking up the tree along the origin references. The grove root has no origin.

treeroot
> This is similar to the grvroot property, but refers to the node found by following the parent properties of all ancestors rather than the origin properties. The treeroot has no parent, but may have an origin.

14.2.2 *What groves can be used for*

The primary use for groves as they are defined in the HyTime standard is for addressing, that is, determining what links point to.[1] HyTime has addressing mechanisms that are defined in terms of groves, so HyTime can address into any kind of grove, regardless of what it represents. As mentioned above, the standard incorporates a property set for SGML documents, but anyone can define new property sets for any kind of data.

To take one example, one might consider creating a property set for Excel spreadsheets. This might have a root node of the `Spreadsheet` class, which would contain a named node list of `Worksheet` nodes. The worksheet nodes would contain `Cell` nodes, which could have values or formulas. Using this simple property set, one could create SGML documents with hyperlinks to worksheets, cells, or ranges of cells in Excel spreadsheets in a controlled way.

The XML family of specifications does not have this capability, since it only has XPointer for addressing into XML documents. There has been much heated debate about whether or not the W3C should do something about this. So far, nothing has been done, and this does not seem to be a priority at the W3C.

However, once you have a grove representing an SGML document, it can well be used for other purposes than just addressing, since the grove is a fully interconnected tree structure much like the DOM. One purpose groves can be put to is document processing, just like with DOM. Groves, however, have no formal API, and no features for modifying groves have been defined. On the other hand, they are easily mapped to an API and using them for extracting information can be very practical.

---

1. Hypertext is really based on two things: *linking* and *addressing*. Linking is the act of asserting links, that is, saying that "these points in the information universe are related in this way." Addressing means defining just where those points are really located.

14.2.3 *Grove software*

Unfortunately, there isn't as much grove software out there as one would wish, and, strangely, much of it is written in Python. The following software packages contain grove implementations:

Jade
> This is James Clark's DSSSL Engine (hence the name), which implements the SGML grove as the basis for the stylesheet language. It is not a general grove implementation, though, as it only implements the SGML property set.

GPS
> This is Geir Ove Grønmo's general grove implementation written entirely in Python. It implements the XML property set on top of the Python SAX API, and also implements a general API for writing grove builders. GPS is open source under the GNU GPL license.

GroveMinder
> GroveMinder is a commercial application written by Peter Newcomb at Epremis. GroveMinder is a general grove implementation written in C++ which implements groves for SGML, Word documents, and Excel documents. It also has a general grove builder API, like GPS. GroveMinder groves can also be accessed from Python.
>
> Epremis is actively continuing development of GroveMinder, so if you are interested in groves it may be a good idea to have a look at this software. Their Web page is at `http://www.epremis.com/`.

14.2.4 *The GPS implementation*

The GPS grove implementation is interesting as an example, since it demonstrates many of the features that a grove system can and should have. (GroveMinder is even more full-featured, but since it is a commercial product I will not describe it here.) The main features of GPS are listed below:

- Full support for property sets. GPS can load a property set from an XML document and uses it actively in representing the grove. The grove can also be validated against the property set as it is being built and modified.

- Very general support for management of grove nodes, which means that a grove can be built using grove managers that perform validation, persistent storage, etc.

- Support for modifying a grove with grove plans.

- Support for traversing a grove with walkers and visitors.

- Support for building groves, according to the XML property set described below, from XML documents, using SAX.

- Support for storing groves in the ZODB object database.

- Automatic support for intrinsic properties.

14.2.5 *An example property set*

The GPS grove engine comes with a property set for XML documents, defined by Geir Ove Grønmo, based on the standard property set for SGML documents. This property set has five classes: `sgmldoc`, `element`, `attasgn`, `pi`, and `chars`. This means that it can represent an XML document with elements, attributes, PIs and characters, but nothing more.

The `sgmldoc` class represents the entire XML document, much like the `Document` interface of the DOM. It has three properties:

prolog

This is a nodelist of `pi` nodes which contains the processing instructions that may appear before the document element. Comments, whitespace, and the DOCTYPE declaration are all discarded.

docelem

This property contains the document element, as a node of the `element` class.

epilog
>   This is another nodelist of `pi` nodes, containing the processing instructions that appeared after the document element.

The `element` class represents elements in the document, and has the following properties:

gi
>   This is the generic identifier of the element, as it is called in SGML terminology. It is the name of the element type as a string.

id
>   This is the value of the `ID` attribute of the element, if it has an `ID`.

atts
>   This property contains the attributes of the element. The attributes are represented as a named node list (which GPS represents as a Python dictionary) of `attasgn` nodes.

content
>   This property contains the content of the element, something that the DOM calls the children of the element. The content is represented as a nodelist of `chars`, `element`, and `pi` nodes.

The `attasgn` class is equivalent to the `Attr` interface of the DOM, and represents an attribute assignment. This means that it holds both the attribute name and its value. It has the following properties:

name
>   Contains the name of the attribute.

value
>   Contains the value of the attribute.

The `pi` class represents processing instructions and only has the two obvious properties: `target` and `data`, each containing strings.

The chars class represents character data in the document and has only one property, value. This property contains the textual content of the class.

Example 14–4 contains an interpreter dialog showing how to use the saxgrove module.

Example 14–4. Loading an XML document into GPS

```
>>> import saxgrove
>>> doc = saxgrove.sload(r"\minedo~1\cvs-co\data\book\py\tools.rss")
>>> doc
<groves.StrictGroveNode class=sgmldoc>
>>> doc.get_properties()
('prolog', 'docelem', 'epilog')
>>> doc["epilog"]
[]
>>> doc["prolog"]
[]
>>> root = doc["docelem"]
>>> root
<groves.StrictGroveNode class=element>
>>> root["gi"]
'rss'
>>> root["id"]
>>> root["parent"]
<groves.StrictGroveNode class=sgmldoc>
>>> a = root["atts"]
>>> a
{'version': <groves.StrictGroveNode class=attasgn>}
>>> v = a["version"]
>>> v
<groves.StrictGroveNode class=attasgn>
>>> v["value"]
'0.91'
>>> v["name"]
'version'
>>> v["implied"]
>>> root["content"]
[<groves.StrictGroveNode class=chars>,
<groves.StrictGroveNode class=element>,
<groves.StrictGroveNode class=chars>,
<groves.StrictGroveNode class=element>,
<groves.StrictGroveNode class=chars>,
<groves.StrictGroveNode class=element>,
```

```
<groves.StrictGroveNode class=chars>,
<groves.StrictGroveNode class=element>,
<groves.StrictGroveNode class=chars>]
>>> channel = root["content"][1]
>>> channel
<groves.StrictGroveNode class=element>
>>> channel["gi"]
'channel'
>>> channel["content"]
[<groves.StrictGroveNode class=chars>,
<groves.StrictGroveNode class=element>,
<groves.StrictGroveNode class=chars>,
<groves.StrictGroveNode class=element>,
<groves.StrictGroveNode class=chars>,
<groves.StrictGroveNode class=element>,
<groves.StrictGroveNode class=chars>]
>>> title = channel["content"][1]
>>> title["gi"]
'title'
>>> title["content"]
[<groves.StrictGroveNode class=chars>]
>>> title["content"]
[<groves.StrictGroveNode class=chars>]
>>> title["content"][0]["value"]
'Free XML tools'
```

14.2.6 *Using groves*

Examples 14–5 to 14–7 show the by now very familiar RSS to HTML conversion application, this time written using GPS. It implements much the same convenience functions as does the DOM example in 12.3.2, "XBEL to HTML conversion," on page 448. Because of this, the GPS example is very similar to the DOM example, and the only real difference is in how the tree is built and how the convenience functions are defined.

As usual, we import the necessary modules and define our templates (Example 14–5).

The functions in Example 14–6 are nearly the same convenience functions as in the DOM example, except that find_first_child has now become find_first_instance, which seemed to fit better

Example 14–5. RSS to HTML conversion using GPS (1 of 3)

```
import sys, string
import saxgrove

# --- Templates

top = \
"""
<!DOCTYPE HTML PUBLIC "-//W3C//DTD HTML 4.0 Transitional//EN">
<HTML>
<HEAD>
  <TITLE>%s</TITLE>
</HEAD>

<BODY>

<H1><A HREF="%s">%s</A></H1>
"""

bottom = \
"""
<HR>

<ADDRESS>
Converted to HTML using GPS.
</ADDRESS>

</BODY>
</HTML>
"""
```

with its function in GPS. (It only finds element instances now, not nodes of any type.)

Example 14–7 shows the conversion drivers. One noteworthy aspect of this converter is that it will handle item elements found in channel as well as those found directly inside the rss element. Note also that when a link is missing, a data URL (see RFC 2397) is created. This data URL will, when dereferenced, turn out to contain itself, so that any attempts to follow such links in a browser will result in an empty screen containing the text "Missing link!". Unfortunately, only Netscape supports data URLs.

Example 14–6. RSS to HTML conversion using GPS (2 of 3)

```
# --- Utility functions

def predicate(gi):
    return lambda node, gi=gi: node.get_class_name() == "element" \
                               and node["gi"] == gi

def find_first_instance(parent, name):
    for child in parent["content"]:
        if child.get_class_name() == "element" and \
           child["gi"] == name:
            return child

def data(element, alternative = None):
    if not element:
        return alternative

    data = []
    for child in element["content"]:
        if child.get_class_name() == "chars":
            data.append(child["value"])
    return string.join(data, "")
```

Example 14–7. RSS to HTML conversion using GPS (3 of 3)

```
# --- Converter

def convert_item(item, out):
    title = data(find_first_instance(item, "title"), "<no title>")
    link = data(find_first_instance(item, "link"),
                "data:,Missing%20link!")
    descr = data(find_first_instance(item, "description"), "")
    out.write('  <li><a href="%s">%s</a> %s\n' %
              (title, link, descr))

def convert(doc, out = None):
    out = out or sys.stdout

    rss = doc["docelem"]
    channel = find_first_instance(rss, "channel")
    title = data(find_first_instance(channel, "title"),
                 "<no title>")
    link = data(find_first_instance(channel, "link"),
                "data:,Missing%20link!")
    descr = data(find_first_instance(channel, "description"))
```

```
    out.write(top % (title, link, title))
    if descr: out.write("<p>%s</p>\n" % descr)
    out.write("<ul>\n")

    for item in filter(predicate("item"),
                       rss["content"] + channel["content"]):
        convert_item(item, out)

    out.write("</ul>\n")
    out.write(bottom)

def convert_file(filename, out = None):
    convert(saxgrove.sload(filename), out or sys.stdout)
```

Declarative processing

Part Four

This part shows how you can create XML processing software without doing any programming at all, through the declarative approach. Several ways of doing this are presented, but the focus is on XPath and XSLT. One chapter is dedicated to integrating XPath and XSLT processors into applications.

XSLT: an introduction

- Declarative processing

- XSLT background

- Introduction to XSLT

- Some XSLT examples

Chapter

15

This part of the book is dedicated to approaches to XML processing that are very different from those we have seen so far: the declarative processing systems. The next three chapters cover XSLT and XPath, while the fourth describes another system known as architectural forms.

15.1 | Declarative processing

Declarative processing is rather different from both event-based and tree-based processing in that it is not based on traditional programming at all. Instead, with declarative processing, the developer declares what the result of processing should be and the declarative processing system will then deliver this. The core difference between this approach and programming is that a program specifies *how* a process should produce a result, whereas the declarative approach is to specify *what* the result should be.

This may sound impossibly optimistic, but consider the example of SQL, the query language for relational databases. In SQL, if we want to know how much each customer has spent on orders, we just say so and the details of figuring out the result are left to the query engine of the RDBMS.

Example 15–1. A sample SQL statement

```
select customer_name, sum(amount)
from customer, order
where customer_id = order_id
group by customer_name;
```

To execute Example 15–1, the query engine has to join together data from two different tables, traverse over the data set while collecting results, and sum the contents of the `amount` field in groups of records. The SQL statement, however, does not describe how to do this; instead it just says what we would like to see.

Another example of a declarative (or at least near-declarative) programming system is the Prolog language for logic programming. In Prolog, a program is a database of facts and rules, where facts are simple statements of fact ("Lars is the son of Knut," "Knut is the son of Edvin"), and rules describe how to infer new facts from those given ("A is the grandfather of B if there is a C such that B is the son of C and C is the son of A"). In Prolog, programs are built from these two kinds of components and nothing else, making Prolog a declarative language.[1]

Using the extremely simple Prolog program in Example 15–2, if we ask a Prolog interpreter whether `grandfatherof(lars, edvin)`, it will respond YES, since it can infer this with the given rule from the two `fatherof` facts given.

---

1. Or at least very nearly. There are features in Prolog not discussed here that depart from the pure declarative model.

Example 15–2. A sample Prolog rule database

```
fatherof(lars, knut).
fatherof(knut, edvin).
grandfatherof(A, B) :- fatherof(A, C), fatherof(C, B).
```

The advantage of the declarative approach is that it is much simpler for the developer, who can forget about the tedious details of how to produce the result, and instead focus on specifying exactly what the desired result is. Of course, this puts the burden of figuring out what to do on the declarative processing system, which thus requires much more effort to develop. Generally, declarative systems are domain-specific, since this makes it much easier to anticipate the features developers may want.

Another problem is that declarative computing systems tend to have strict limits on what they can do, since in a declarative system there is usually no way to implement new features. Doing so would require you to specify the *how*, and that wasn't supposed to be possible. Some very general systems, like Prolog, are so complete that most tasks can be accomplished with them, but for something more restricted, like SQL, it is impossible to develop extensions using the declarative language. This means that when using a declarative system one is usually limited to the features supported by that system, and if something that is not supported by the system is needed to produce the desired result, the developer is faced with the choice of either using some other processing framework or not achieving the result completely.

Quite often, when translating XML documents to HTML, only very simple rules are needed for much of the process, such as "replace para elements with p elements," "replace emph elements with em elements," etc. It would be very simple to develop a processing system that could accept declarations of this form and map source documents to output documents. This would be a very simple declarative XML processing system. It would also be a bit too simple to be of much use, which is why it hasn't been implemented.

This book will only cover two declarative XML processing systems: XSLT and architectural forms. XSLT is by far the best-known of these, and will be covered in the rest of this chapter and the next. Architectural forms will be covered in Chapter 18, "Architectural forms," on page 692.

15.2 | XSLT background

The origins of XSLT lie with DSSSL, an ISO-standardized stylesheet language for SGML.[1] DSSSL is a feature-rich language that supports online display of SGML documents (for example in SGML browsers), translation to publishing notations, and SGML-to-SGML translation. DSSSL is partly declarative, but also relies on Scheme, one of the two main Lisp dialects currently in use, to provide some features.[2]

When work on XML began in earnest in 1996, the XML Working Group of the World Wide Web Consortium envisioned a three-stage development process, where the three stages were XML itself, hyper-linking support, and stylesheet support. The first stage would define XML itself, the second would create a linking standard (called XLL) that would allow XML browsers and other software to recognize hyperlinks in XML documents, and the third would create a stylesheet language (called XSL) for displaying XML documents in browsers.

In the end, of course, the XML effort turned out to encompass rather more than these three stages, but this was the initial vision. At this point, the plan was to create a subset of DSSSL for use with XML, just as XML itself is a subset of SGML. A first attempt at such a subset was even defined, and given the name DSSSL-O. This idea was later abandoned, and the first XSL proposal used XML syntax and did not at all resemble the Scheme-based DSSSL.

---

1.   The definition of DSSSL can be found in ISO/IEC 10179:1996.

2.   During the writing of this book, the Jade DSSSL engine was used to convert it to RTF and PDF for review reading.

In the initial working drafts, XSL was defined in two clearly separated parts: an XML application for representing rendered documents and an XML application for XML-to-XML translation. The idea was that to display an XML document in a browser or convert it to a rendering notation, one would do an XML-to-XML translation from the source document to a corresponding document in the rendering application.

However, it soon turned out that all implementations of XSL implemented only one of the two parts, usually the XML-to-XML translation part (called the transformation part). Because of this, the two parts were divided into two specifications. The formatting application is now called Extensible Style Language (XSL) and is now nothing but a DTD for documents with formatting. The translation part is called XSL Transformations (XSLT) and mainly supports XML-to-XML translations. (There are also some features for XML-to-HTML and XML-to-text translations.)

Note that despite the name change the confusion has persisted, and it is quite common for XSLT to be referred to as XSL, while XSL is often called XSLFO to distinguish it from XSLT. In this book I use the terms as defined above.

15.2.1 *A quick overview*

Although XSLT was designed to support XML to XSL translations, it can also do translations to any other XML application. Since HTML through its common ancestry in SGML is very similar to XML, XSLT can also do translations to HTML, and there is specific support for this in the specification. In addition to this, XSLT supports translation to text, which, at least in theory, opens the possibility of conversion to plain text documents and also character based notations like TEX/LATEX and groff.

As mentioned above, XSLT stylesheets are written in XML, but in certain places where terseness is important they use an embedded syntax called XPath. This compromise between XML-based and non-XML-based syntax has helped to make XSLT much more readable (and writable!) than it would otherwise have been. XPath is an expression language that is used not only by XSLT, but also by XPointer, for several different purposes, to which we will return below. There is nothing in XPath that particularly binds it to either XSLT or XPointer, so it can be used separately from both. It gets its name from the fact that the language has clear similarities with the directory path syntax used by DOS/Windows and Unix. In this it is also similar to the directory path syntax of URLs. This chapter and the next also cover XPath.

The main thing an XPath expression can do is to be compared with a node in a document to decide whether the expression matches or not. This is used in XSLT stylesheets to describe to which nodes in the document the different rules in the stylesheet apply. It can also be used in processing frameworks to state which nodes in a document a handler object or function is supposed to handle. That is, it can be used to solve the dispatch problem we saw in event-based programs, where much code is devoted to triggering the right actions at the right time. With XPath, you can simply say: this function is called for the nodes that match this expression.

An interesting fact about XSLT is that despite being declarative it is so powerful that it is what computer scientists call *Turing-complete*.[1] This means that XSLT can in theory compute anything that a full programming language can. In practice the stylesheets for many of these tasks may be very awkward, and the input and output may require rather esoteric representation, but it is fully possible.[2] In fact, someone has already written an XSLT stylesheet that can place N queens on a

---

1. No formal proof of this exists, but the XSLT community generally agrees that this is the case.

2. Note that this is a very important point: XSLT stylesheets can perform any computation, *provided that the input is represented in a way that the stylesheets can access it in the right way*. In practice there are many things one might want to do that are impossible because the stylesheets cannot access the necessary information in the right way.

chessboard of N by N squares so that no queen can hit any of the others.[1]

In addition to matching, XPath expressions can be used to select a set of nodes given a starting node. This is what XPointer does, starting from the root node and selecting a part of the document. XPointer is used in linking, so that XML links can link to points inside other documents and not just to whole documents. This is also useful in XSLT and in processing.

Another thing XPath can do is to compute values from the contents of XML documents. This can be done in a number of different ways, and XPath can in fact be surprisingly useful for this kind of thing. We will return to this use later.

Note that even though both XSLT itself and XPath are declarative, most XSLT and XPath implementations can be extended in traditional programming languages. This is done by writing additional XPath functions and integrating them with the XSLT engine.

15.2.2 *Usage contexts for XSL and XSLT*

When XSL (and XSLT with it) was initially conceived of, it was intended to be used in browsers as a display mechanism for XML. However, XSL and XSLT have taken a long time to design and have both become large and complex specifications. The result is that browser implementors have been hesitant to adopt them. Today, only Microsoft Internet Explorer supports XSLT, and the current versions only implement an older draft of the specification. Mozilla (also known as Netscape 6) is likely to follow soon. What the developers of Opera

---

1. This is known as the *N*-queens problem. It is not especially difficult to implement, but it is fairly good as a test of the expressive power of a programming language. Note that it is rather difficult to implement efficiently, since the number of possible solutions for each N is $N!$. This number very quickly grows to grotesque size. For $N = 20$ it is a number with 18 digits, and after that the number of digits in fact grows faster than N itself.

will do is as yet unclear, although most likely they will eventually implement XSLT. None of the browsers supports any version of XSL, and instead rely on translation to HTML for presentation. Whether they will support XSL in the future is still unclear.

There are, however, a number of freely available XSLT and XSL implementations available outside Web browsers and in many different programming languages (see the next section for an overview). The XSLT implementations are usually general-purpose XSLT engines with APIs that allow them to be used in nearly any context. Some commercial implementations are only available as command-line tools, but this is mainly a question of packaging rather than of design.

This means that XSLT engines can be used to do ordinary conversions on the command line, but that they can also be embedded in various applications. For this reason they have been much used to convert XML to HTML for Web publishing. This has been done both offline and by integrating an XSLT engine in server-side applications to do the conversion on the fly. Several frameworks have been developed to support on-the-fly conversion in Web servers, the best known of which is probably Cocoon by the Apache project.

The current XSL implementations are all converters from XSL documents to some rendered notation. Most of them can convert to PDF, and one implementation, written in TEX, can convert to anything that TEX can convert to. XSL implementations for graphical display do not yet exist. (Although MSIE supports XSLT, it does so by allowing incoming XML documents to be transformed to HTML, which it then displays; there is no XSL support.)

15.2.3 *An overview of XSL and XSLT implementations*

At the moment there is only one XSLT implementation in Python. This is 4XSLT, developed by Fourthought. 4XSLT is built on top of 4DOM and 4XPath and implements the entire XSLT specification. It cannot be used with Jython, since the XPath parser it uses is written in C. The APIs of 4XSLT are described in 17.1.1, "Using 4XSLT," on page 641.

A number of XSLT implementations exist in Java, all of which are of course available in Jython. I only describe the open source ones here, since those are the most interesting.

XT

XT was written by James Clark, who also wrote the XSLT specification. (And, incidentally, the DSSSL specification, as well as its first implementation.) XT is, at the time of writing, the fastest XSLT implementation in Java and is highly conformant, although less complete than the others.

James Clark has made it clear that he does not intend to continue developing XT, given the number of good alternatives. A group of volunteers have taken over maintenance and run the site `http://4xt.org` dedicated to XT.

Saxon

Saxon originally began as a processing framework for XML, written by Michael Kay to support his own projects. It grew to include a full XSLT implementation and is now a very full-featured XSLT implementation with a number of useful extensions. The processing framework is still present, and can be used together with the XSLT engine.

Xalan-J

Xalan is an XSLT engine that started its life as LotusXSL, written by Scott Boag of IBM alphaWorks. It was later donated to the Apache XML Project where it is now being developed further. At the time of writing, Xalan is a little slower than XT and Saxon, full-featured, and relatively stable.

Sun XSLT Compiler

This is an XSLT engine that runs XSLT stylesheets by compiling them into Java source code that is then compiled to Java byte-code and run. The purpose of this is to make execution faster.

In addition to these Java XSLT implementations, there are a number of C++ implementations, which are listed below.

Sablotron

This XSLT implementation is being developed in C++ by a company known as The Ginger Alliance. The processor is not yet complete, but relatively high-performant. It has recently become popular through the creation of interfaces to it from many scripting languages, Python and Perl among them.

Xalan-C

This XSLT engine is a cousin of Xalan-J, and is also being developed as part of the Apache XML Project. It is not yet complete.

Transformiix

This XSLT processor was initially written by Keith Visco and is now being developed as part of the Mozilla browser project, into which it is incorporated.

XSLTC

Another XSLT compiler. This one is written by Olivier Gerardin and is based on Transformiix. It generates C++ code, which is then compiled. At the time of writing this implementation is only experimental.

There are also some XSL implementations available today.

FOP

This is an XSL-to-PDF converter written in Java as part of the Apache XML Project. It was originally started by James Tauber (in Python), but has since been donated to the Apache project. It is incomplete, but also has some support for SVG.

Passive TEX

> This is an XSL implementation based on TEX, written by Sebastian Rahtz. It can produce output in any notation that TEX can produce output in, and the output quality is generally very good.

REXP

> Another XSL-to-PDF converter written in Java by the University of Genoa. This project started from the FOP sources, but they have developed them separately in a different direction.

15.2.4 *XPath: uses and implementations*

XPath is rarely used on its own, but it is used by several processing frameworks for event dispatching and node selection. One framework that uses it is eventdom, described in 22.2.2, "eventdom," on page 877. It is also used (often slightly extended) by several systems as a query language for XML databases. Tamino, by Software AG, is one database that uses XPath in this way. It has also been used in other W3C specifications for various purposes.

All XSLT engines contain XPath implementations by necessity, but few of these have been separated from the XSLT engines to be used standalone. However, some tree-based processing systems and DOM implementations also provide XPath implementations. At the moment there are two XPath implementations in Python:

PyXPath

> PyXPath was written by Dieter Maurer and implements most of XPath. It can parse XPath expressions into objects and use these to select nodes in a PyDOM tree, as well as match and evaluate XPath expressions against a tree.

4XPath

> 4XPath was written by Fourthought, just like 4DOM. It can also parse expressions into objects and evaluate, select, and match against a 4DOM tree. 4XPath uses an XPath parser written in C, so it

cannot be used in Jython. Recently, Martin von Löwis has created a replacement parser written in pure Python; it has not yet been integrated, but this is likely to happen soon.

PyXPath is used by eventdom (see 22.2.2, "eventdom," on page 877), although this is likely to change, while 4XPath is used by 4XSLT (17.1.1, "Using 4XSLT," on page 641).

15.3 | Introducing XSLT

15.3.1 *XSLT processing model*

An XSLT processor takes two inputs: the XML document to be transformed and the XSLT stylesheet that describes the transformation, the output being another XML document. This processing model is illustrated by Figure 15–1. The input and the output need not be files, and the XSLT specification emphasizes this by calling the input document the *source tree* and the output document the *result tree*.

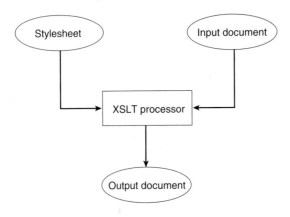

Figure 15–1   XSLT processing model

Referring to the input and output as the source and result trees also emphasizes another aspect of the translation: an XSLT processor

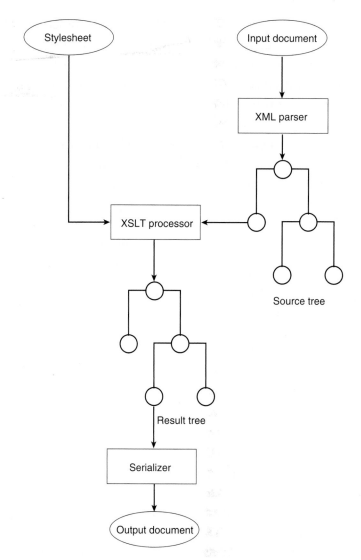

Figure 15–2   The processing model in more detail

operates on the logical structure of the document, as defined by the XSLT data model. This model is explained in more detail below.

Figure 15–2 illustrates this point, by showing how, when used from the command line to work with files, an XSLT processor uses an XML parser to create the source tree and a serializer to write out the result tree. This means that in many cases, XSLT processors will be based on technologies already described in this book. For example, the 4XSLT processor uses any installed XML parser supporting SAX 1.0 to create a 4DOM tree, which it will then operate on. The output will be in the form of a SAX-like event stream which is usually serialized to a file by 4XSLT.

XSLT can, as mentioned earlier, also produce HTML and text output, and given this, it may sound a little strange to speak of a result tree, since the output is thus not required to be well-formed XML. It is best to consider the result tree as something similar to the `Document-Fragment`[1] of the DOM, which must follow the XML data model, but which may also take certain liberties. Output escaping (for characters like "<" and "&") may also be turned off, and certain elements in HTML may be serialized in ways that are not conformant with XML, but this is the business of the serializer. In other words, that the output may not be well-formed XML is mainly an issue for the serializer, and much less so for the result tree.

15.3.2 *XSLT and XPath data models*

The XPath data model, which XSLT slightly extends, is a node-based model very similar to the grove, DOM, and Infoset models already described, but with some interesting differences. As in the DOM, all nodes have types and values, and some also have names. The values are formally known as *string-values* and the names as *expanded-names*, and both are key aspects of the model. All nodes, except for the root node, have a parent. In the XSLT model all nodes have a base URI, just as in the Infoset. Another difference in the XSLT model is the whitespace stripping described in 16.2.2.5, "Controlling whitespace in the output," on page 597.

The data model has seven types of nodes, described below.

---

1.   See 11.4.5, "The `DocumentFragment` interface," on page 423.

The root node

Each document has a single root node, which serves the exact same purpose as the DOM `Document` node, the Infoset Document Information Item and the `sgmldoc` class of groves. It has a list of child nodes (comments, PIs, and one element), but no name. Its string value is all the character data in the document.

In XSLT, the root node can have the same types of children as an element can. This is because the result tree might not be well-formed XML, and because the processor may be processing a document fragment. XSLT also adds a mapping from unparsed entity names to the corresponding system identifiers.

Element nodes

Elements have names (the element-type names), which are pairs consisting of their namespace URIs and the local names, children, attributes, and, possibly, a unique ID. The ID, if present, will come from an attribute declared to be of the `ID` type. The string value is all the character data found inside the element and its descendants.

Attribute nodes

Attributes have names, just like elements, but no children; the string value is the attribute value. The element an attribute appears on is its parent, even though the attribute is not a child of the element. This is different from both the DOM and the grove model; whether it differs from the current Infoset Working Draft is debatable, although I would say that it does.

Namespace nodes

Like the Infoset, the XPath data model contains namespace nodes. Such a node has the expanded name whose namespace URI is null and whose local name is the namespace prefix used in the declaration. Note that namespace nodes represent the namespace prefixes in effect on each element and not just the namespace declarations in the document. An element will have one namespace node per declaration it carries, as well as nodes for those declarations that are inherited from its parents.

Namespace nodes have a parent, which is the element they belong to, and a string value, which is the namespace URI.

Processing instruction nodes

These nodes have names where the namespace URI is null and the local name the PI target name, while the string value of a node is the PI data.

Comment nodes

These have no name, and the string value is their content.

Text nodes

Character data, CDATA marked sections, and character references are all represented by text nodes.[1] Unlike in SAX and DOM, text nodes never occur next to one another in the tree, but are always merged. If an element contains character data, a CDATA marked section, and more character data, but nothing else, this element will have a single text node child. This is very convenient, in that it makes the interpretation of XPath expressions much more straightforward and independent of the lexical details of a document.

Text nodes have no names and their string values are their character data.

15.3.3 *XSLT basics*

XSLT stylesheets consist of template rules that are instantiated to create the result tree. XSLT processing is done by traversing the source tree node by node in document order. For each node, the most important

---

1.   Like their close relations, the TextNodes of the DOM, XPath text nodes are misnamed. They should really be called data nodes, or character data nodes.

of the matching template rules is fired,[1] and this causes a result tree fragment to be instantiated. The result tree fragment is then inserted into the already accumulated tree. If requested by the template, the children of the node will also be processed.

All XSLT stylesheets have three default template rules defined, which are used if no other templates match. (This is why all nodes are matched by at least one rule.) The first rule handles elements and simply removes the element, but processes its contents. Processing instructions and comments are removed by the second rule. Character data, however, is copied through by the third rule. This means that the result of processing an XML document with an empty stylesheet is to remove all the markup and leave only the character data.

In XSLT template rules, the markup that is created when the template is instantiated appears literally. This means that in XSLT stylesheets, XSLT elements and result tree elements appear interspersed with one another. XSLT uses namespaces to ensure that XSLT elements and result tree elements can always be told apart. Only elements that are in the XSLT namespace will be interpreted as XSLT elements, while all elements outside of XSLT namespace will be considered result tree elements, even if the local part of the element name matches the name of an XSLT element type.

Below, I will follow the notation used by the XSLT specification and use the `xsl` namespace prefix when referring to XSLT element types. This is done to make it easier to see what I am referring to. The `xsl` prefix in itself has no meaning, however, and a stylesheet can use any prefix it likes for XSLT elements as long as that prefix is mapped to the XSLT namespace.

The document element of an XSLT stylesheet is `xsl:stylesheet`, and this element is not required to have any contents. So Example 15–3 is a minimal valid XSLT stylesheet that will process any XML document

---

1. There always is one, due to the default rules built-in to XSLT. The rules for deciding which rules are most important are described in 16.2.4, "Conflict resolution: precedence," on page 599.

by removing all the markup in it, but preserve the character data. (Note that there is an alternative way to write stylesheets that do not have the `xsl:stylesheet` element as the document element. This is described in 16.2.5, "Single-template stylesheets," on page 601.)

Example 15–3. A minimal XSLT stylesheet

```
<xsl:stylesheet xmlns:xsl="http://www.w3.org/1999/XSL/Transform"
                version="1.0">
</xsl:stylesheet>
```

This stylesheet does nothing but declare the XSLT namespace and set the required `version` attribute to the correct version number. Note that the `version` attribute does not have a namespace. XSLT attributes on XSLT elements are not required to have a namespace; instead, their namespace defaults to the XSLT namespace. Note that if you forget the namespace declaration or mistype the namespace URI the XSLT processor will not recognize your XSLT statements and ignore the entire stylesheet.

Figure 15–3 shows a rough conceptual model of the structure of XSLT stylesheets. The root is the `xsl:stylesheet` element, and inside this we find the *top-level element types*. These are various kinds of declarations and the template rules. When I later describe an element type as being a top-level element type, it means that it has to be a child of the `xsl:stylesheet` element, and not a descendant, as shown here.

Inside the template rules we find the element types that are allowed as template contents, and these can also be divided into two categories: *XSLT instructions* and *literal result elements*. XSLT instructions are element types defined as part of XSLT which can be used inside templates to control how output is produced. Literal result elements are non-XSLT elements which are part of the output from the template.

As Figure 15–3 shows, most instructions have template content, which means that they can contain the same things as templates themselves can. This also applies to literal result elements.

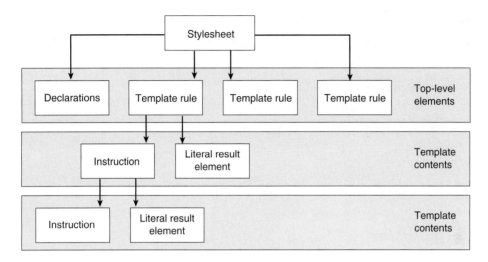

Figure 15–3   The structure of XSLT stylesheets

15.3.3.1 Writing template rules

Template rules are defined using the `xsl:template` element, which must appear directly inside the `xsl:stylesheet` element type. The `match` attribute of the element contains an XPath expression that defines which nodes in the source tree the template applies to. The expression in Example 15–4, `rss`, will match all elements of the type `rss`.

The stylesheet in Example 15–4 has a single template rule that applies to all elements of the type `rss`. Inside it are a number of elements not in the XSLT namespace, and these will all be instantiated in the result tree.

When this XSLT stylesheet is run on the RSS document in Example 15–5, the single rule will match the `rss` document element type. This will cause the HTML elements in the template to be instantiated. However, since the template does not say explicitly that the children of the `rss` element are to be processed, this is not done. The reason is that the XSLT engine needs to know where in the result tree the results of processing the children will be inserted. The result is that the output

Example 15–4. An XSLT stylesheet with a single rule

```
<xsl:stylesheet xmlns:xsl="http://www.w3.org/1999/XSL/Transform"
                version="1.0">

  <xsl:template match="rss">
    <html>
    <head>
      <title>RSS output</title>
    </head>

    <body>
    [...insert document contents here...]
    </body>
    </html>
  </xsl:template>

</xsl:stylesheet>
```

Example 15–5. An example RSS input document

```
<rss version='0.91'>
  <channel>
    <title>Free XML tools</title>
    <link>http://www.garshol.priv.no/download/xmltools/</link>
    <description>An index of free XML tools.</description>
  </channel>

    <item>
      <title>New product: tDOM.</title>
      <link>http://www.garshol.priv.no/.../tDOM.html</link>
    </item>

    <item>
      <title>New version of LotusXSL: 31.Aug.99.</title>
      <link>http://www.garshol.priv.no/.../LotusXSL.html</link>
      <description>Updated to 13.Aug.99 WDs, separate XPath and
      query packages, new extension architecture, thread safety,
      and much more.</description>
    </item>
</rss>
```

will consist only of the contents of the single template rule, as shown in Example 15–6.

Example 15–6. Output of the first XSLT stylesheet

```
<html>
<head>
  <title>RSS output</title>
</head>

<body>
[...insert document contents here...]
</body>
</html>
```

The main obstacle to continuing to improve this stylesheet is that we do not know how to tell the XSLT engine where to insert the results of processing the children of the document element. The xsl:apply-templates element does just this. It tells the XSLT engine which nodes to process (the default being all the children of the current node) and where to insert the results of that processing. With this in hand, we can extend the stylesheet to support more of RSS and produce a more useful output (Examples 15–7 to 15–10).

Example 15–7. A simple XSLT stylesheet for RSS (1 of 4)

```
<xsl:stylesheet xmlns:xsl="http://www.w3.org/1999/XSL/Transform"
                version="1.0">

  <xsl:template match="rss">
    <html>
    <head>
      <title>RSS output</title>
    </head>

    <body>
    <h1>RSS output</h1>
    <ul>
    <xsl:apply-templates/>
    </ul>
    </body>
    </html>
  </xsl:template>
```

We can now tell the XSLT engine where to continue processing, but we still do not know enough to handle this situation really well. Just inside the body element in the output we would like to put the title of the RSS channel, preferably inside an h1, but the title is not available to us at that stage. We could solve that by creating a new template rule for the title element type that would create an h1 element for its contents. We could also make template rules for item element types that would create li elements for them.

However, we wouldn't know where to create the ul element that would need to go around the li elements. Creating it in the root template as in Example 15–7 would solve the problem, but then the use of xsl:apply-templates would cause the heading to be created inside the ul element, which we do not want. The item elements cannot create one ul element for each item, and we cannot create a ul start-tag for the first item and the end-tag for the last.

A solution to this problem will be shown later, but for now we simply use a hard-coded title and move on to process the items (Example 15–8).

Example 15–8. A simple XSLT stylesheet for RSS (2 of 4)

```
<xsl:template match="item">
  <li><xsl:apply-templates/></li>
</xsl:template>
```

This rule creates an li result element for each item source element, leaving the handling of the child elements to the template rules for those elements.

The rule in Example 15–9 ensures that the title element inside an item will be converted to an HTML a element in the output. The default stylesheet rule will copy the data into the a element. In the href attribute we have used what is known as an *attribute value template*. These are XPath expressions written inside curly brackets, and their string value is inserted in the result tree. So in this case we insert the data in the link sibling element.

Example 15–9. A simple XSLT stylesheet for RSS (3 of 4)

```
<xsl:template match="title">
  <a href="{../link}"><xsl:apply-templates/></a>
</xsl:template>
```

The last template rule in Example 15–10 filters out the contents of the `channel` element, since the default stylesheet rule would otherwise copy the data of that element into the result tree, where we do not want them. Similarly, inside the `item` element there is the `link` element, whose contents we have already included in the previous template, so we filter that out as well. (The XPath expression `channel | link` matches all elements that are either of the type `channel` or of the type `link`.)

Example 15–10. A simple XSLT stylesheet for RSS (4 of 4)

```
<xsl:template match="channel | link">
</xsl:template>

</xsl:stylesheet>
```

Running the stylesheet from Examples 15–7 to 15–10 on the input RSS document we saw earlier produces the output shown in Example 15–11.

Apart from the problem with the title (and other channel metadata), this example shows clearly how easy it is to write XSLT stylesheets. Compared to the SAX and DOM versions of the same conversion program the XSLT stylesheet is much easier to write and understand and does not even require programming skills.

However, being essentially event-driven, the stylesheet suffers to some degree from the same problem as many SAX programs: the logic of the conversion is spread out all over the stylesheet. To make sense of it, some knowledge of the expected input is necessary. We will soon see how other features allow us to reduce the impact of this problem.

Example 15–11. Result of running the stylesheet above

```
<html><head>
<title>RSS output</title></head><body><h1>RSS output</h1><ul>

  <li>
    <a href='http://www.garshol.priv.no/.../4DOM.html'>New version
    of 4DOM: 0.10.0</a>
  </li>

  <li>
    <a href='http://www.garshol.priv.no/.../tDOM.html'>New product:
    tDOM.</a>
  </li>

  <li>
    <a href='http://www.garshol.priv.no/.../LotusXSL.html'>New
    version of LotusXSL: 31.Aug.99.</a>

    Updated to 13.Aug.99 WDs, separate XPath
    and query packages, new extension architecture, thread safety,
    and much more.
  </li>
</ul></body></html>
```

15.3.3.2 The `xsl:value-of` instruction

The `xsl:value-of` element is the solution to the title problem that plagued us in the above example. This instruction allows you to specify an XPath expression and have its string value inserted in the result tree. This means that instead of writing little template rules to convert child elements correctly, one can pull the data out of the child element and insert it directly in the template of the parent element. This makes for simpler, more efficient, and much more readable stylesheets.

The stylesheet in Example 15–12 is simpler than the previous one, and at the same time it produces higher-quality output. Note the use of the `select` attribute on the `xsl:apply-templates` element in the rule for the `rss` element. This means that templates will only be applied to elements that match the given XPath expression. This enables us to leave out the "blocking" rule for the `channel` element type, since the metadata elements inside `channel` will now never be processed.

Example 15–12. The example again, now with `xsl:value-of`

```
<xsl:stylesheet xmlns:xsl="http://www.w3.org/1999/XSL/Transform"
                version="1.0">

  <xsl:template match="rss">
    <html>
    <head>
      <title><xsl:value-of select="channel/title"/></title>
      <!-- 'channel/title' means select the channel child of the
           current element and then its title child. -->
     </head>

    <body>
    <h1><a href="{channel/link}">
        <xsl:value-of select="channel/title"/>
      </a></h1>
    <ul>
    <xsl:apply-templates select="item"/>
    </ul>
    </body>
    </html>
  </xsl:template>

  <xsl:template match="item">
    <li><a href="{link}"><xsl:value-of select="title"/></a>
        <xsl:value-of select="description"/></li>
  </xsl:template>

</xsl:stylesheet>
```

Note also how we do an `xsl:value-of` for the `item` description, even though the description is optional. If the description is not there, the expression will evaluate to an empty string, which is harmless in that position. We could not do the same with the `channel` description, since that needs a surrounding `p` element in the output and we wouldn't want to leave an empty paragraph for channels that have no description.

Note that while `xsl:value-of` is a powerful and very useful instruction, it has a disadvantage in that it places certain restrictions on the values that it inserts. In particular, these values cannot contain markup, so that the RSS titles, for example, cannot contain emphasized phrases. To support this, we would have to use `xsl:apply-tem-plates`.

15.3.4 *Some more useful XSLT instructions*

15.3.4.1 Conditionals

In the case of the `channel` description above, the ideal solution would be to have some way of including a `p` element with the description only if there actually is a `description` element inside `channel`. This is exactly what the `xsl:if` element offers. It has a required attribute `test` that contains an XPath expression. If this expression evaluates as `true`, the contents of the `xsl:if` element are instantiated into the result tree.

Example 15–13. An example of `xsl:if` use

```
<xsl:if test="channel/description">
<p><xsl:value-of select="channel/description"/></p>
</xsl:if>
```

The contents of Example 15–13 could have been inserted in between the `h1` and `ul` elements of the `rss` template and would then generate a description paragraph only when the `channel` actually has a `description` child.

The `xsl:if` instruction is useful for testing whether to include a part of a template or not, but it has no means of specifying alternatives. This is provided by the `xsl:choose` element, which can have any number of `xsl:when` elements that specify alternatives. The `xsl:when` children are tried in the order they appear, and the first one that matches is instantiated. There can optionally be an `xsl:otherwise` element at the end of the `xsl:choose` element, and if no `xsl:when` elements match, that element will be instantiated. If none of the `xsl:whens` match and there is no `xsl:otherwise`, nothing is instantiated.

Example 15–14. An example of `xsl:choose`

```
<xsl:choose>
  <xsl:when test="channel/managingEditor">
    <p>Editor: <xsl:value-of select="channel/managingEditor"/></p>
  </xsl:when>

  <xsl:when test="channel/webMaster">
    <p>Webmaster: <xsl:value-of select="channel/webMaster"/></p>
  </xsl:when>

  <xsl:otherwise>
  <p>No contact information.</p>
  </xsl:otherwise>
</xsl:choose>
```

Example 15–14 could be used to add contact information for the channel to the HTML output. One HTML paragraph would be produced, with the managing editor (if one was specified), or with the webmaster (if there was no managing editor, but the webmaster was specified), or, as a last resort, with a statement that no contact information was available.

15.3.4.2 Iteration

In the template for the `rss` element, we create a nearly complete HTML document, where the main contents are the contents of the `ul` list. Those contents are created by calling `xsl:apply-templates` with `select` set to `item`. However, there is only one template in the entire stylesheet that can match `item` nodes, so what we are effectively saying is: for each `item` child, instantiate the contents of the `item` template.

This is a relatively common situation, so XSLT has an element type that captures it, called `xsl:for-each`. It selects a set of nodes with an XPath expression in its `select` attribute and then instantiates its contents once for each node selected by that expression. This allows us to rewrite the XSLT stylesheet for RSS into one that only uses a single template, as shown in Example 15–15.

Example 15–15. An XSLT stylesheet for RSS with only a single template rule

```
<xsl:stylesheet xmlns:xsl="http://www.w3.org/1999/XSL/Transform"
                version="1.0">

  <xsl:template match="rss">
    <html>
    <head>
      <title><xsl:value-of select="channel/title"/></title>
    </head>

    <body>
    <h1><xsl:value-of select="channel/title"/></h1>

    <ul>
    <xsl:for-each select="item">
      <li><a href="{link}"><xsl:value-of select="title"/></a>
          <xsl:value-of select="description"/></li>
    </xsl:for-each>
    </ul>
    </body>
    </html>
  </xsl:template>

</xsl:stylesheet>
```

The XPath expressions inside the item don't have to change, because the XPath context changes inside the xsl:for-each element. Each time the contents of the element are instantiated, the context node is set to the node in the node-set that caused the instantiation. This means that the XPath expressions inside the xsl:for-each instruction will select nodes relative to the item that is currently being processed.

Thus, xsl:for-each brings an issue to the surface that we have so far avoided: the concept of the context node. XPath expressions are evaluated relative to a context node, and inside each XSLT template rule, this is the node that caused the instantiation of the rule. This, however, changes once we introduce xsl:for-each, for inside it the context node is the node that caused the contents of the xsl:for-each instruction to be instantiated.

Using Figure 15–4 for illustration, we will trace the execution of the stylesheet in the previous example. When we enter the template rule,

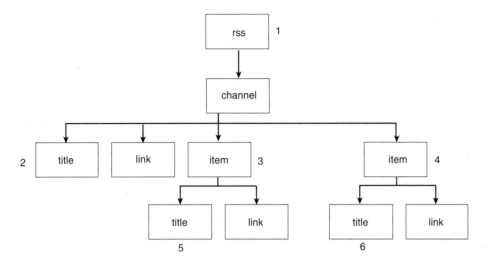

Figure 15–4   An RSS document

the context node is the node marked as "1" in the diagram. This means that the XPath expression used in the first xsl:value-of will select the node marked as "2", and insert the character data inside it. The xsl:for-each will then be executed and select first the node marked as "3", and then the node marked as "4". When node "3" is selected, the contents of the instruction are instantiated, causing the first xsl:value-of to select the node marked as "5". When node "4" is selected, the contents of the instruction are instantiated, causing the first xsl:value-of to select the node marked as "6".

The XPath context is discussed in more detail in 16.1.1, "The context," on page 566.

15.3.4.3 Sorting

When processing nodes in the document, the methods presented so far will all process the nodes in document order. Sometimes one would rather process the nodes in an order based on the contents of the document. XSLT provides explicit support for this, through the xsl:sort element type which can be used as a child element inside `xsl:apply-templates` and `xsl:for-each`.

The `select` attribute of the `xsl:sort` element type contains an XPath expression that is applied to each node in the set to be processed (the context being the node as the context node and the full node-set as the context node list). The string value of the XPath expression is used as the sort key. Several `xsl:sort` elements can be specified to provide alternative sort keys for the cases where the first sort keys are equal.

For example, when converting an XBEL document into HTML, one might want to sort the bookmarks inside each folder so that they appear in the resulting HTML output in alphabetical order. The template in Example 15–16 shows how `xsl:sort` can be used to do this.

Example 15–16. Using `xsl:sort` with `xsl:apply-templates`

```
<xsl:template match="xbel/folder">
  <h2><xsl:value-of select="title"/></h2>

  <ul>
    <xsl:apply-templates select="bookmark">
      <xsl:sort select="title"/>
    </xsl:apply-templates>
  </ul>
</xsl:template>
```

If a secondary sort key is needed, this could be specified by adding a second `xsl:sort` element after the first. Another variation is that in this case we might want to use `xsl:for-each` instead of `xsl:apply-templates`, since we want to treat all the nodes that are processed the same way.

With `xsl:for-each`, much the same `xsl:sort` syntax is used as with `xsl:apply-templates`, but here it is slightly more complex since the template appears inside the element together with the `xsl:sort` element. For this reason, XSLT requires that the `xsl:sort` element must appear before the template contents.

Example 15–17. Using `xsl:sort` with `xsl:for-each`

```
<xsl:template match="xbel/folder">
  <h2><xsl:value-of select="title"/></h2>

  <ul>
    <xsl:for-each select="bookmark">
      <xsl:sort select="title"/>

      <li><a href="{@href}"><xsl:value-of select="title"/></a></li>
      <!-- '@href' is the href attribute of the current element -->
    </xsl:for-each>
  </ul>
</xsl:template>
```

The default behavior of `xsl:sort` is to sort the values into ascending lexical order. If the `order` attribute is set to `'descending'`, the order will be descending instead. However, if you are sorting numbers, lexical order will not do, as it will reorder `['1', '2', '10']` to `['1', '10', '2']`, since it sorts by character rather than numeric value. To override this, the `data-type` attribute can be set to `'number'`. XSLT also allows XSLT engines to support other values using qualified names for these, to avoid collisions with later versions of the standard, but does not specify any.

The mechanisms presented so far leave one crucial aspect of sorting unresolved, however. Numerical order is universally dictated by mathematics, but not so for lexical order, which is culturally dependent. One example is that in Norwegian, "aa" is considered to be an equivalent form of the letter "å", which is the last letter in the Norwegian alphabet.[1] An additional complexity is that "aa" can occur in foreign names such as "Transvaal" in which case the "aa" is actually considered to be two a's in succession. The cases of the Dutch "ij" (which is considered a separate letter and more-or-less equivalent to "y") and the Hungarian "sz" are similar. As for the Chinese characters, there are

---

1. So being named Aaberg does not guarantee that you will appear first in any alphabetical order; quite the contrary.

several different ways to sort these,[1] which is natural, given that there are thousands of them.

The `lang` attribute can be used to specify the language of the values to be sorted, so that the XSLT engine can apply the correct algorithm. If no value is supplied, the specification states that "the language should be determined from the system environment," which basically means that the engine should use the platform default. To the best of my knowledge, no XSLT engine performs lexical sorting by any other means than sorting characters using their Unicode code points.

More information on sorting is available in Rick Jelliffe's *The SGML/XML cookbook*, also in this series, and in *Unicode Technical Report #10*. Also, *The Unicode Standard* has information on this. In addition to the Unicode Technical Report, there is *ISO 14561*, which is an ISO standard for international sorting.

15.3.5 *Processing modes*

Quite often, you might want to process a part of the input document more than once, typically to present different views of the same information. The most common example of this is the table of contents in a manual or book. This is produced by first processing the entire document once, extracting the headings, and afterwards processing it again, this time producing the contents. XSLT provides explicit support for this through the mode feature, which allows one set of templates to be defined for the table of contents mode and another set for normal processing. The document can then be processed first in the table of contents mode, using that set of templates, and afterwards again in normal mode.

A template rule is placed in a mode by setting the value of the `mode` attribute on the `xsl:template` element to the name of the mode. The name must be a qualified name. The `mode` attribute on

---

1.   Some common examples being by pronunciation, by the number of strokes, by corner complexity, by radical (component), etc.

`xsl:apply-templates` can then be used to specify what mode is to be used. If the attribute is not specified, the default nameless mode is assumed in both cases.

Example 15–18. Pseudo-code demonstrating the use of modes

```
<xsl:template match="Book">
  <h1><xsl:value-of select="title"/></h1>

  <h2>Table of contents</h2>
  <ul>
  <xsl:apply-templates mode="toc"/>
  </ul>

  <xsl:apply-templates/>
</xsl:template>

<!-- ToC processing -->

<xsl:template match="Part" mode="toc">
  <li><a href="..."><xsl:value-of select="title"/></a>
    <ul><xsl:apply-templates mode="toc"/></ul>
  </li>
</xsl:template>

<xsl:template match="Chapter" mode="toc">
  <li><a href="..."><xsl:value-of select="title"/></a></li>
</xsl:template>

<!-- Ordinary processing -->

<xsl:template match="Part">
  <h2><xsl:value-of select="title"/></h2>

  <xsl:apply-templates/>
</xsl:template>
```

Example 15–18 processes an imaginary DTD for books producing both a table of contents and the content of the book itself. The contents of the `Book` element are processed twice: first, from the `xsl:apply-templates` element in the `toc` mode, and second, from the second `xsl:apply-templates` element without using any mode. The template rules in the `toc` mode create the table of contents, while the rules outside it create the book contents.

15.3.6 *Useful bits and pieces*

15.3.6.1 Number formatting

Quite often, especially in document processing, one needs to generate numbers from the document contents. A representative example of this is generating section numbers for the section headings in a large document, such as this book. XSLT provides support for this through the `xsl:number` element type. This element generates numbers in two steps: first a list of numbers is produced, and then the list is converted to a string, which is then inserted.

The easiest way to generate a list of numbers is to use the `value` attribute. If this is present, it is evaluated as an XPath expression and the result converted to a number, which makes up a list of one number. Alternatively, the `level`, `count`, and `from` attributes can be used to generate a list of numbers.

If the `level` attribute is set to `multiple`, the ancestor nodes (including the context node) that match the XPath expression in the `count` attribute are selected. If the `from` attribute is specified, the selection stops when a node is found that matches the XPath pattern in the attribute (that node is not included). These nodes are placed into a list in the order they were found. A number is then generated for each node in the list by counting the number of preceding sibling nodes that match the `count` pattern and adding one.

This instruction is perfect for generating hierarchical numbers such as those used to label the sections in this book. With it, it is easy to select all elements of certain types and count the number of elements of the same type before them on the same level. This is typically what one wants to do with chapters, sections, subsections, and so on.

In addition to the `multiple` value of `level` there is also `single`, which does the same as `multiple`, except that it stops once the first node is found. The default value is `single`. The last alternative is `any`, which finds the first node before the context node in document order that matches the count pattern and counts the number of occurrences before it (adding one, of course). Note that any excludes attributes and namespace nodes.

Once we have the list of numbers, we are ready to convert it to a string. The main instrument in doing so is the format attribute. This is a kind of a template that describes how to convert the list into a string. The template consists of tokens and separator characters. Numbers and characters are considered tokens, while everything else is considered separators. So the string ' 1.1.1' is considered to consist of the following, shown as a pseudo-Python list: [' ', <token 1>, '.', <token 1>, '.', <token 1>, '.'].

There are many different kinds of tokens, each of which generates a different sequence of strings. The list below shows the different kinds of tokens (slightly simplified):

1

Generates the sequence 1, 2, 3, 4, ...

01

Generates the sequence 01, 02, 03, ..., 09, 10, 11, ..., 99, 100, 101, ... The more zeroes you put in front of the final 1, the more zeroes you get in the output.

A

Generates the sequence A, B, C, D, E, F, G, H, ..., Z, AA, AB, AC, ...

a

Generates the sequence a, b, c, d, e, f, g, h, ..., z, aa, ab, ac, ...

I

Generates the sequence I, II, III, IV, V, VI, VII, VIII, IX, X, ...

i

Generates the sequence i, ii, iii, iv, v, vi, vii, viii, ix, x, ...

Example 15–19 numbers the LI elements in an OL list using lower-case Roman numerals.

Example 15–19. Roman numbering of LI elements

```
<xsl:template match="LI">
  <xsl:number count  = 'LI'
              level  = 'any'
              from   = 'OL'
              format = 'i. '/><xsl:value-of select="."/>
</xsl:template>
```

Note the use of the from attribute above, to ensure that only the LI elements inside the current OL list are counted. Without it, all the preceding LI elements in the entire document would have been counted.

Example 15–20 numbers subsections in a book in a way similar to what was done for this book.

Example 15–20. Numbering subsections

```
<xsl:template match="subsection/title">
  <xsl:number count  = 'chapter | section | subsection'
              level  = 'multiple'
              format = '1.1.1. '/></xsl:value-of select="."/>
</xsl:template>
```

What has been presented here is how xsl:number works for English. There are various features in XSLT for controlling what language's conventions it is supposed to use and how to make the best use of those, but they are omitted for brevity.

XSLT also supports a second method for formatting numbers, through the format-number function. That is rather complex, however, and so is not explained in this book. See Section 12.3 of the XSLT Recommendation to find out how it works.

15.3.7 *Some pitfalls*

A common problem many XSLT stylesheet writers run into is that sometimes their output only consists of the character data in the input document and nothing else. This is generally a symptom indicating that the stylesheet has been ignored by the XSLT processor, and the most common reasons for this are:

- getting the XSLT namespace URI wrong on the document element, or omitting it altogether,

- specifying as the stylesheet some XML document that is not an XSLT stylesheet (for example because the stylesheet and the source document have been exchanged on the command line), or,

- mistyping the namespace URI of the namespace used in the input document in such a way that the application's namespace URI as given in the input document and in the stylesheet does not match.

15.4 | Two complete XSLT examples

To help you organize all the information presented in the previous sections, we now go through a complete XML to HTML conversion example, before exploring XSLT and XPath in more depth.

15.4.1 *XBEL to HTML conversion*

The XBEL to HTML conversion (Examples 15–21 to 15–26) is an interesting example because it is recursive, in that we need to treat the `folder` element types differently on different levels. This, together with the lack of a container element for the first level of nodes, makes this example challenging in a way that the others are not.

Example 15–21. An XBEL to HTML converter (1 of 6)

```
<xsl:stylesheet xmlns:xsl="http://www.w3.org/1999/XSL/Transform"
                version="1.0">

  <xsl:template match = "xbel">
    <html>
    <head>
      <title>
        <xsl:choose>
          <xsl:when test="title">
            <xsl:value-of select="title"/>
          </xsl:when>
          <xsl:otherwise>
            Bookmark collection
          </xsl:otherwise>
        </xsl:choose>
      </title>
    </head>

    <body>
    <h1>
        <xsl:choose>
          <xsl:when test="title">
            <xsl:value-of select="title"/>
          </xsl:when>
          <xsl:otherwise>
            Bookmark collection
          </xsl:otherwise>
        </xsl:choose>
    </h1>
```

We start out with the document element, and create a normal HTML header for it (Example 15–21). Note the way we check for a `title` element, and provide a substitute if necessary. According to the DTD, `title` is not required, which is why we do this.

The rest of the template for the document element inserts a description, if there is one. It then inserts a list of bookmarks, provided there are any. And finally, the folders are inserted, followed by a footer (Example 15–22). Note the use of `select` to separate `bookmarks` and `folders` from one another. We could also have used `xsl:for-each`, but this would have required repeating the `bookmark` template many

Example 15–22. An XBEL to HTML converter (2 of 6)

```
<xsl:if test = "desc">
  <p><xsl:value-of select = "desc"/></p>
</xsl:if>

<xsl:if test="bookmark">
  <ul>
    <xsl:apply-templates select = "bookmark"/>
  </ul>
</xsl:if>

<xsl:apply-templates select = "folder"/>

<hr/>

<address>
Converted to HTML from XBEL by xbel2html.xslt.
</address>

</body>
</html>
</xsl:template>
```

times. Using `xsl:for-each` for folders would have made more sense, but would result in a very long template rule. Also, we would have to use `xsl:apply-templates` sooner or later to handle unlimited levels of recursion.

The template rule in Example 15–23 is used for bookmarks wherever they occur. They are turned into list items that link to the bookmarked URL. The description is included, and evaluates to an empty string if it is not present.

Example 15–23. An XBEL to HTML converter (3 of 6)

```
<xsl:template match="bookmark">
  <li><a href="{@href}"><xsl:value-of select="title"/></a>
      <xsl:value-of select = "desc"/></li>
</xsl:template>
```

The rule in Example 15–24 is used for `folders` on the level directly inside the `xbel` element. These get H2 headers for their `titles` as well as descriptions with their own paragraphs. Bookmarks are handled in the same way as above. Finally, folders are included.

Example 15–24. An XBEL to HTML converter (4 of 6)

```
<xsl:template match="xbel / folder">
  <h2><xsl:value-of select="title"/></h2>
  <xsl:if test = "desc">
    <p><xsl:value-of select = "desc"/></p>
  </xsl:if>

  <xsl:if test="bookmark">
    <ul>
      <xsl:apply-templates select = "bookmark"/>
    </ul>
  </xsl:if>

  <xsl:apply-templates select = "folder"/>
</xsl:template>
```

The template rule in Example 15–25 is used for `folders` on the next level. Note how we use the boolean `or` operator in the boolean `test`. This is necessary because at this stage we wish to include both folders and bookmarks in the list.

Example 15–25. An XBEL to HTML converter (5 of 6)

```
<xsl:template match="xbel / folder / folder">
  <h3><xsl:value-of select="title"/></h3>
  <xsl:if test = "desc">
    <p><xsl:value-of select = "desc"/></p>
  </xsl:if>

  <xsl:if test="bookmark or folder">
    <ul>
      <xsl:apply-templates select = "folder | bookmark"/>
    </ul>
  </xsl:if>
</xsl:template>
```

The final template rule in Example 15–26 handles folders with more than 1 `folder` parent. This level we could not have handled using the `xbel / folder / ... / folder` expression because it cannot handle arbitrarily many levels. These folders are turned into list elements, and they also handle bookmarks and folders as list elements, like the previous example.

Example 15–26. An XBEL to HTML converter (6 of 6)

```
<xsl:template match="folder [ count(ancestor::folder) > 1 ] ">
  <li><b><xsl:value-of select="title"/></b>
    <xsl:value-of select = "desc"/>

    <xsl:if test="bookmark or folder">
      <ul>
        <xsl:apply-templates select = "folder | bookmark"/>
      </ul>
    </xsl:if>
  </li>
</xsl:template>

</xsl:stylesheet>
```

The following chapter will present all you need to know to understand the XPath expression used in this last template rule.

XSLT in more detail

- XPath in more detail

- More advanced uses of XSLT

- More advanced XSLT examples

- XSLT performance

Chapter
16

I n order to make full use of XSLT, it is necessary to fully understand XPath, since many operations are impossible to perform without using XPath expressions that are more complex than those we have seen so far. The first section of this chapter covers XPath in more detail in order to give you this understanding. Once XPath has been fully described we move on to the more advanced ways of using XSLT.

16.1 | XPath in detail

XPath has two syntaxes: an abbreviated syntax and an unabbreviated syntax. Any XPath expression can be written using the unabbreviated syntax, and this syntax is very systematic, as it makes the connection between the syntactical form of an expression and its meaning immediately clear. However, the most common XPath expressions use only a very small part of these capabilities, and these expressions are longer than they need to be. Because of this XPath also has the abbreviated syntax, which provides alternative shorter forms for these common expressions. Thus, every abbreviated XPath expression has an equivalent unabbreviated expression, but the reverse does not hold.

The examples that you have so far seen have, without exception, used the abbreviated syntax, and only a small part of it. This section and the next will describe the unabbreviated syntax and then explain the abbreviated syntax in terms of the unabbreviated one. However, before we can move on to the syntax itself, certain fundamental issues need to be discussed, such as the XPath context and the axis system.

16.1.1 *The context*

XPath is explicitly designed to be able to fulfill at least three different purposes in XSLT (node matching, node selection, and value computation) as well as to be used in XPointer and in various kinds of processing frameworks. To make this as easy as possible, there is a formalized concept of the context in which an XPath expression is evaluated. The context concept in XPath is very similar to the concept of a current directory and a set of environment variable assignments in operating systems like Unix and Windows. An XPath context consists of a context node (which is like the current directory), but it also contains several other things, which we will return to later.

XPath has two kinds of location paths: relative and absolute. The absolute paths are interpreted relative to the root node and the relative ones relative to the context node. Again, this is very similar to directory paths (as well as to URLs). However, this is only of interest when XPath is used for selection. When used for matching (as in XSLT template rule selectors), XPath expressions are evaluated without a specific context node. Instead, the formal definition states that they match a node if there exists a context node that makes the expression select the node. In practice, you can often forget about the context node when using XPath for matching, and instead use an intuitive notion of what the expression does and does not match.

In addition to the context node, an XPath context consists of:

the context position

This is the number of the context node in a list of nodes. Exactly what makes up this list of nodes will depend on the context in which XPath is used.

the context size

This is the number of nodes in the same list of nodes.

a set of variable bindings

These are variables just like in programming languages, and they can be used in XPath expressions in a similar way. How the values are bound is not defined by XPath.

a set of function bindings

These are functions like those in ordinary programming languages. XPath defines a core set of functions, but allows it to be extended, and XSLT and XPointer both exploit this by adding functions specific to those languages.

a set of namespace declarations

These are used to expand any namespace prefixes used in the XPath expression. Again, XPath does not specify where the declarations come from.

This is actually not the full story, since XSLT introduces the additional concepts of the *current node* and the *current node list*. Whenever an XPath expression is evaluated, its context node is taken from the XSLT current node, and its context node list, from the XSLT current node list. So, the rules given in 15.3.4.2, "Iteration," on page 549 for the context node in fact control the assignment of the XSLT current node.

The main significance of the distinction between the current node and the context node is that the context node may change during the evaluation of an XPath expression (according to rules that will be explained later), while the current node will remain constant. As will be shown later, there are ways to exploit this.

16.1.2 *Location paths*

16.1.2.1 The axis system

When navigating around a directory structure there are two obvious directions one can move in: upwards (from a node to its parent) and downwards (from a node to one of its children). Directory paths use the special name .. to move upwards (nothing else is needed, since there is only one parent[1]), while all other names point downwards. XML documents, however, are much more complex than directory structures, and one consequence of this is that you may want to move in more than one way when navigating an XML document. XPath formalizes this through the concept of axes.

XPath offers thirteen different axes of movement, but some of these are variants of each other, and so the number of truly different axes is around seven. The nodes on an axis in most cases have a specific order, which is the document order (or the opposite of document order, if the axis is what is called a *reverse axis*).

Figure 16–1 shows which nodes are included in which order in the various axes, when the context node is the grayed item element.

The axes are:

child
>   Along this axis we find the children of the context node. Recall that attributes are not considered to be children of an element, so they are not found along this axis. In the diagram, this axis contains the elements title, link, and description, in that order.

descendant
>   This axis contains the descendants of the context node, that is, the children of the context node, the children's children, the children's children's children, and so on. These appear in document order, which means in this case the title element, the 'Blah' text node,

---

1.   Well, usually. With soft links Unix directories can have more than one parent. The directory path syntax ignores that, however.

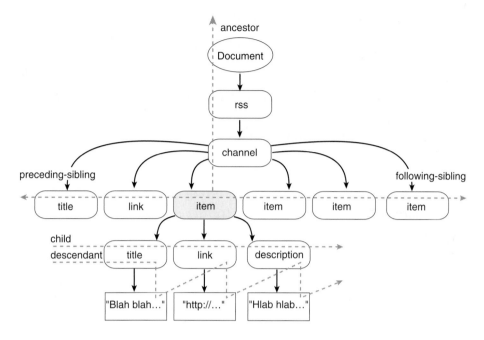

Figure 16–1   The different XPath axes

the link element, the 'http://' text node, the description element, and the 'Hlab' text node, in that order.

parent
    This axis contains the parent of the context node, if it has one. Note that it does not contain the parent of the parent, so this axis always has one or zero nodes. In Figure 16–1 this is the channel element.

ancestor
    This axis contains the parent and the ancestors of the parent, provided there is a parent. This goes all the way to the root node.

    This axis is a reverse axis, which means that nodes occur in reverse document order. This is rather intuitive when you think about it, since this means that the parent will be the first node, its parent the second, and the root node the final node.

In the diagram, this axis would contain the `channel` and `rss` elements, as well as the `Document` node, in that order.

`following-sibling`

    Along this axis are the siblings of the context node that appear after it in the list of children. In this case that would be the three `item` elements after the context node.

`preceding-sibling`

    This is the opposite of `following-sibling`, the siblings that appeared before the context node (or the elder siblings). This is also a reverse axis. In this case it would contain the `link` and `title` elements, in that order.

`following`

    This axis contains all the nodes of the document that occur after the context node in document order, except for descendants, ancestors, and attributes. That is, the axis only contains the nodes after this node and outside it. In our diagram, that would be the three `item` elements after the context node.

`preceding`

    This is the opposite of `following` and contains the nodes before the context node, except ancestors, descendants, and attributes. This is a reverse axis. In the diagram, it would contain the `link` and `title` elements, in that order. It differs from the `preceding-sibling` axis in that it would also contain any descendants of those two elements.

`attribute`

    Here are the attributes of the context node, in no particular order. Unless the context node is an element node, this axis will be empty, as it would be in our diagram, since the `item` element does not have any attributes.

`namespace`

> This axis contains the namespace nodes of the context node. This means that all the namespace declarations currently in scope are found along this axis, in no particular order. This axis is very rarely used.

`self`

> This axis contains the context node itself and nothing else. It is mainly useful in defining suitable expansions for the abbreviated syntax, so you can generally forget about this axis.

`descendant-or-self`

> This axis contains the context node and its descendants. Like the `self` axis, it is mainly useful to define expansions for the abbreviated syntax.

`ancestor-or-self`

> This is like `descendant-or-self`, except with ancestors instead of descendants.

Using this axis system, it becomes straightforward to use the rest of XPath to move around in a document to locate specific nodes or sets of nodes in a general way. The cost is the verbosity caused by constantly having to repeat the axis name, but the abbreviated syntax handles this problem.

16.1.2.2 Location steps

The addressing part of the HyTime standard talks about location ladders, and for addressing that is a rather good image. XPath location paths are put together from individual steps, and the evaluation process walks from step to step, thus traversing the document to end up at the desired nodes. In XPath, we can can point the ladder with the axes, and with the steps we can climb it one step at a time. We are even allowed to change the direction of the ladder for each step by specifying a different axis for that step.

Each XPath location step takes this form: `axis-spec::nodetest-predicates`. The first part is the axis specifier, which is the name of the axis. This defines the axis along which the second part, the node test, is applied. The node test can be simply the name of the nodes that will be selected. So the location step `child::p` will select the p children of the context node. Note that it will select *all* p children, not just one. The special name `*` selects all nodes regardless of name.

However, this will only work for element nodes, so it is possible to test for the type of the node using `comment()`, `text()`, or `processing-instruction()`, all of which match all nodes of their respective types. Comment and text nodes have no names, but PIs have a target (used as the node name in the XSLT data model) and one may often wish to select on this. To support this, there is a second form, where the target name is given in the node test, like so: `processing-instruction('target')`.

This makes it possible to do things like `child::text()`, which will select all text children of the context node. There is also a node type test `node()`, which will select any node of any type; `child::node()` will thus select all children of the context node.

To refine the selection beyond what a node test can do, a list of predicates can be appended. A predicate is simply a boolean expression contained in `[ ]` brackets. Nodes for which the expression is `true` are selected, and those for which it is not are excluded. Note that the predicate is evaluated with the node it is applied to as the context node. Expressions are explained below in 16.1.3, "XPath expressions," on page 574.

The last style rule in Examples 15–21 to 15–26, `folder [ count(ancestor::folder) > 1 ]`, uses a predicate to express the fact that it should only match folders with more than one `folder` parent. Note that it is possible to use several predicates in sequence, as in `folder [count(ancestor::folder) > 1] [child::desc]`, which only selects folders with more than one `folder` parent and at least one `desc` child.

16.1.2.3 Building a location path

When an XPath location path is evaluated, it has an initial context node in the context where the evaluation happens. How this node is defined is irrelevant for XPath, but it might be the current node under processing in a processing framework, or the element on which an attribute with an XPath value occurs in an XML document.

When doing location, evaluation starts with the context node and then evaluates the first step, returning a set of nodes. The evaluation then uses each of these nodes as the context node and evaluates the next location step with this as the starting point. The result is the union of all the node sets produced by this, and the process continues for each location step. Location steps are turned into location paths by concatenating the steps with ' / ' characters between each step. If the location path begins with a ' / ', it is an absolute location path which begins from the root node.

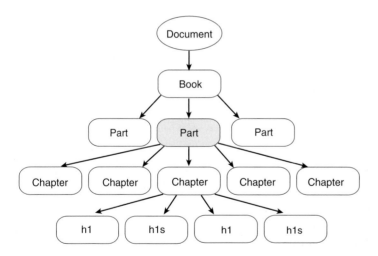

Figure 16–2   An example document

In the example document represented in Figure 16–2, the gray Part element is the context node. Below, a number of XPath expressions evaluated with this context are listed, along with those parts of the document that they select.

- The expression `child::Chapter` will select all five children of the `Part` element, in document order.

- The expression `child::Chapter/child::h1` will select first all five `Chapter` elements, and then all `h1` children of these, which in this case will be only the two ones found under the third `Chapter`. The resulting node set will only be the two `h1` elements, again in document order.

- `parent::*` will select the `Book` element.

- `parent::*/child::Part` will select all three `Part` nodes.

- `self::*` will select the context node itself.

- `preceding-sibling::*` will select the `Part` element on the left-hand side of the context node.

- `following-sibling::*` will select the `Part` element on the right-hand side of the context node.

- `ancestor::*` will select the `Book` element and the document node, in that order.

- `preceding::*` will select the first `Part` element, but not the `Book` element, and the document node, since those are both ancestors.

- `following::*` will select the last `Part` element, the `Book` element, and the document node, in that order.

16.1.3 *XPath expressions*

So far, only relatively simple uses of XPath have been shown, but XPath can do much more than this. The key to making full use of XPath is in the expression language. This can be used to compute values as well as to further refine selection and matching expressions. XPath expressions can evaluate to values of four types:

node sets

> These are collections of nodes without duplicates and with no defined internal order. Note that single nodes are represented as node sets with only a single node.

boolean

> This is the familiar true/false type we know from programming.

number

> These are floating-point numbers (which includes integers as a special case).

string

> These are strings as we know them from programming. Note that XPath strings are strings that consist of abstract Unicode characters. This differs from the definition used by the DOM, where strings consist of 16-bit units in the UTF-16 encoding. The difference is of course only detectable for characters outside the BMP, since those are the only ones that need more than one 16-bit unit in UTF-16.

Values in XPath that are not nodes or node sets can be created from variable references, literals, or function calls. Inserting literals is done in the same way as in programming languages; `true` is true, `false` is false, `5` is 5, and `'Hi!'` is the string "Hi!". Strings can also be written inside double quotes, as in `"Hi!"`.

In expressions, XPath supports all the familiar operators such as `+`, `-`, `*`, `=` (equals, not assignment, which does not exist), `!=` (does not equal), `<=`, `and`, `or`, etc. Division is done with the `div` operator, and `mod` computes the remainder after a division (and not modulo, as one might expect). This means that `5 + 5`, `true or false`, `'ab' <= 'ba'`, and `5 != 6` are all legal XPath expressions.

Note that it is possible to create booleans, numbers, and strings from node sets with the functions that are built-in to XPath, and this is why these types are there at all. In general it is easy to convert between the different types, and in many cases XPath does implicit type conversions based on how expressions are used. Note also that XPath does not have a null value like Python and Java do.

Below is a list of all functions defined by XPath:

`boolean(object)`
This function converts its argument to a boolean value. Numbers are converted to `true`, except for zero and `NaN` (a numerical value meaning not-a-number). Node sets and strings are converted to `true`, unless they are empty.

`ceiling(number)`
Converts decimal numbers to integers by returning the nearest larger integer.

`concat(string, string, string*)`
Returns the concatenation of its arguments. (The function must have at least two arguments. The * means zero or more repetitions, just like in content models and regular expressions.)

`count(node-set)`
Returns the number of nodes in the node set. This is a very useful function, because it can be used to test for the number of nodes that match an XPath expression. For example, `count(child::foo) < 5` is only `true` if the context node has fewer than five `foo` child elements.

`false()`
Returns `false`.

`floor(number)`
Converts decimal numbers to integers by returning the nearest smaller integer.

`id(ID)`
Returns the node in the same document as the context node with the given ID. The function is really more complex than this, but

the full details are omitted for brevity. See Section 4.1 of the XPath Recommendation to learn more.

`lang(string)`

Returns `true` if the value of the `xml:lang` attribute for the context node after inheriting from its ancestors is the given string. If the context node has no such value, the function returns `false`.

`last()`

This returns the context size from the expression context. What the context size is and how it is set is explained in 16.1.3.3, "Understanding the context list and position," on page 581.

`local-name(node-set)`

This function sorts the nodes in the node set in document order and returns the name of the first node.[1] For an element or attribute, this will be the local part of its name.

`name(node-set)`

Returns the name of the first node (in document order). If the node is an element or attribute, the name returned is its qualified name. This function returns the same as `local-name` except for elements and attributes.

`namespace-uri(node-set)`

Returns the namespace URI of the first node (in document order). If it has no namespace, an empty string is returned.

`normalize-space(string)`

Removes leading and trailing whitespace and replaces sequences of whitespace characters by a single space. Thus, `normalize-space(a)` is equivalent to `string.join(string.split(a), " ")` in Python.

---

1. What the name of a node is was explained in the section on the XPath data model, 15.3.2, "XSLT and XPath data models," on page 536.

`not(boolean)`

>   Returns the opposite of its argument, after having converted it to a boolean.

`number(object)`

>   Converts its argument to a number. Strings are interpreted as numeric literals, and those which do not contain valid numbers become NaN. `true` becomes 1 and `false` becomes 0. Node sets are converted to strings with the `string` function and then converted as strings.

`position()`

>   This returns the context position. This can be used to check whether the node is the first in its list of siblings, the last, or if it has any other specific position.

`round(number)`

>   Converts decimal numbers to integers by traditional rounding.

`starts-with(string, string)`

>   Returns `true` if the first string begins with the second, otherwise it returns `false`. Thus, `starts-with(a, b)` is equivalent to `a[ : len(b)] == b` in Python.

`string(obj)`

>   Converts the argument to a string and returns the string. For node sets, the result is the node value of the first node (in document order). For numbers and booleans, the result is what one would expect.

`substring(string, number, number?)`

>   Returns the substring of the string argument from the position specified by the second argument to the position specified by the third (which defaults to positive infinity). If the second argument is negative, it counts as 0. If the third argument is larger than the string length, the rest of the string is included.

Thus, `substring(a, b, c)` is equivalent to `a[b : c]` in Python, except when one of b or c are negative or larger than the string size.

`substring-after(string, string)`
Returns the part of the first string after the first occurrence of the second. If the first string does not contain the second, an empty string is returned. Thus, `substring-after(a, b)` is equivalent to `a[string.find(a, b) + len(b) : ]` in Python, except when b is not found in a.

`substring-before(string, string)`
Returns the part of the first string before the first occurrence of the second. If the first string does not contain the second, an empty string is returned. Thus, `substring-before(a, b)` is equivalent to `a[ : string.find(a, b)]` in Python, except when b is not found in a.

`sum(node-set)`
Calls `number` on each node in the node set and returns the sum.

`string-length(string?)`
Returns the number of characters in the string. If the argument is omitted, it defaults to the context node converted to a string with the `string` function.

`translate(string, string, string)`
This function is used to map occurrences of some characters to other characters. This can be used to do simple case conversion as well as some other useful operations. For each character in the first string, the function locates its first occurrence in the second string, and replaces it with the character at the same position in the third string. Characters that are not found are not changed. Characters that have no equivalent in the third string are removed. For example, `translate('Abc', 'abcdef', 'ABCDEF')` evaluates to `'ABC'`.

Thus, `translate(a, b, c)` is equivalent to `string.translate(a, string.maketrans(b[ : len(c)], c), b[len(c) : ])` in Python.

`true()`
    Returns `true`.

With this knowledge it is possible to use XPath to evaluate values such as numbers and strings and to create predicate expressions as described earlier. For example, in an RSS to HTML XSLT stylesheet we may want to single out news item in our own channel that originate with the Slashdot news site. This can be done with a selector like this: `item / title [ substring(self::node(), 0, 14) = 'via Slashdot: ']`.

16.1.3.1 The | operator

XPath has the | operator which can be used between two XPath expressions to produce the union of their results. This can be used both in selection and matching. For example, `foo | bar` selects both the `foo` and `bar` children of the context node, while matching all `foo` and `bar` elements in the document.

When testing an XPath expression for truth, `foo | bar` will be `true` if there are any `foo` or `bar` children of the context node. In this case the boolean `or` operator can be used with the exact same effect, since it will be `true` if any `foo` or `bar` elements are found. Note that this does *not* apply when selecting or matching, since `or` always produces a boolean result, while | produces a node-set result.

16.1.3.2 Referring to variables

XPath itself does not define any XPath variables, nor does it define how variables are assigned values. XSLT has mechanisms for this that we will encounter later, and many XPath implementations and processing frameworks which use XPath have their own ways of doing this.

Variable names in XPath are XML qnames, so they follow the same rules as XML element-type and attribute names.

Variables are referred to in expressions by prepending the variable name with $. Thus, `$foo` is an XPath expression that evaluates to the value of the `foo` variable in the XPath context.

16.1.3.3 Understanding the context list and position

How the context list and position are defined in XSLT and XPath may not be immediately clear. In practice, XPath provides some of the rules for how these are determined, while XSLT provides others. The expressions in XPath predicates are, as hinted at earlier, evaluated in a context different from that of the containing XPath expression. The first predicate is applied to the node list selected by the node test, the rest, to the same node list filtered by the predicates to their left. For each node in the list, the predicate is evaluated in a new context, consisting of that node as the context node and the list as the context node list.

This means that `child::folder [position() = last()]` will be evaluated by first selecting all `folder` children of the context node. The context node list will then be set to this list of nodes, the predicate applied to each in turn, and only the last node accepted.

As to how to evaluate the expression `position()`, however, XPath is silent, since this depends on the context of the entire expression, and XPath cannot define that. It is left to XSLT to define how this is interpreted. There are three main situations:

- Template rules for the root node have the current node list set to the root node.
- Other template rules have the current node list set to the list of nodes selected by the `xsl:apply-templates` instruction currently being evaluated. This defaults to the children of the current node, but can be overridden using the `select` attribute. The order of the nodes will be the document order, unless `xsl:sort` is used.

- The contents of `xsl:for-each` instructions have the current node list set to the nodes selected by the `select` attribute, in document order, unless `xsl:sort` is used.

Example 16–1 may illustrate this.

Example 16–1. Finding the context position

```
<xsl:stylesheet xmlns:xsl="http://www.w3.org/1999/XSL/Transform"
                version="1.0">

  <xsl:template match = "doc">
    <xsl:apply-templates/>
    <xsl:apply-templates select = "p"/>
  </xsl:template>

  <xsl:template match = "p">
    <xsl:value-of select="position()"/>
  </xsl:template>

</xsl:stylesheet>
```

In this example all `p` children of the `doc` element will be processed twice, once for each `xsl:apply-templates` instruction. The first time, their position in the list of all `doc` children will be printed; the second time, their position in the list of `p` elements that are children of the `doc` element will be printed.

16.1.3.4 Some examples

Examples below demonstrate some ways to use XPath expressions to express various kinds of conditions.

- `section [lang("no")]` selects all `section` children that are in Norwegian.
- `para [attribute::type = 'warning']` selects all `para` children that contain warnings.

- `concat(firstname, ' ', surname)` actually produces a string value. It selects the `firstname` and `surname` children and takes the string values of the first of each. Then the first name, a space, and the surname are concatenated into a new string in that order.

- `item / title [starts-with(self::node(), "via Slashdot: ")]` selects all `title` elements inside `item` children whose contents begin with the string `'via Slashdot: '`. Note that the `starts-with` function is given the context node, since, as noted earlier, predicates are evaluated with the node they test as the context node. Note also that the node is converted to a string as if with an implicit call to the `string` function.

- `section[count(ancestors::section) > 3]` matches all sections that are on the fourth section level or lower.

- `li[position() = 1]` selects the first `li` child.

- `li[position() = last()]` selects the last `li` child.

16.1.4 *Abbreviated syntax*

The abbreviated syntax is actually rather simple, and is easiest to explain in terms of how it expands to to the unabbreviated syntax. The simplest abbreviation it allows is to omit the axis specifier, which then defaults to the `child` axis, so that the expression `foo` simply means `child::foo`. This explains how `foo` selectors we have seen on XSLT template rules work: as long as there is a parent node from which the node can be selected, it will match. (Thanks to the document node, there always is a parent for these nodes.[1])

Another abbreviation is that the token `@` can be used to mean the `attribute` axis. This means that `@foo` will select the `foo` attribute of the context node. There is also an abbreviation for the context node,

---

1. Figuring out why the document node, which has no parent, does not pose any problems for this rule is left as an exercise for the reader.

. expanding to `self::node()`, and for the parent of the context node, `..` expanding to `parent::node`.

There is also an abbreviated way to test the context position, in that any predicate expression that results in a numeric value will be compared with the context position. Thus, `[x]` is an abbreviation for `[position() = x]`, where `x` can be anything that produces a numeric value. Thus, `chapter[16]` selects the sixteenth `chapter` child of the context node, while `chapter[last()]` selects the last chapter and `chapter[last() - 1]` selects the penultimate chapter. (Note that `chapter[16]` would not select this chapter,[1] since it is the second child of its `part` parent.)

The most complex abbreviation is the token `//`, which expands to `/descendant-or-self::node()/`. Since this expansion begins with `/`, this means that `//para` will select any `para` elements in the same document as the context node. The expression has this effect since it will select relative to the root node. To select the `para` descendants of the current node, `.//para` can be used, which expands to `self::node()/descendant-or-self::node()/para`.

As the last example above shows, these abbreviations do not need to be used alone, but can be used as part of larger XPath expressions. For example, `/book/part[4]/chapter[2]` would select this chapter in this book.

16.2 | Advanced XSLT topics

Now that you have understood the basics of XSLT and have a good grasp on XPath, we are ready to go into the more advanced parts of XSLT. As noted earlier, XSLT, like most declarative languages, is a large language with many features, because it is impossible or very awkward to implement missing features using the basic features of the language. For this reason, there is much more to learn about XSLT

---

1.   In the SGML document that makes up the manuscript of this book.

than there is about SAX or DOM. Of course, part of the reason is also that SAX and DOM are used in a programming language you already know; it is only the APIs and techniques you need to learn.

16.2.1 *Creating elements and attributes*

In addition to creating nodes in the output tree by writing them directly in template rules so that they are copied to the output, XSLT has element types which can be used to create nodes in the output tree. These are `xsl:element`, `xsl:attribute`, `xsl:attribute-set`, `xsl:text`, `xsl:comment`, and `xsl:processing-instruction`.

An `xsl:attribute` instruction may occur before other kinds of children inside both literal result elements and `xsl:element` instructions. In both cases, the `xsl:attribute` instruction causes an attribute to be added to the element node in the result tree. The `name` attribute holds the name of the attribute (it is an attribute value template), and the content holds the value of the attribute. Literal result elements inside the `xsl:attribute` element will either cause an error or be ignored.

Often, several attributes may be used together as a collection to achieve a specific purpose. For example, when creating HTML output, you may want to set `valign="top" border="0" cellpadding="0" cellspacing="0"` for all TH and TD elements in a table. XSLT makes this easier through the concept of named attribute sets, which can be declared with the `xsl:attribute-set` element type that must occur at the top level of the stylesheet. The element type has two attributes: `name`, which is required and gives the name of the set, and `use-attribute-sets`, which contains a whitespace-separated list of attribute sets to merge with the declared one. The content is a set of `xsl:attribute` elements that declare the attributes in the set.

Note that the XPath expressions in the `xsl:attribute` elements inside an `xsl:attribute-set` are evaluated in the context where the set is used, rather than in the context where it is declared. This means that the XPath expressions can refer to source tree nodes relative to the node that caused the instantiation of the attribute set.

To create an attribute set named `html-table-cell`, we can use a declaration like the one in Example 16–2.

Example 16–2. An XSLT attribute set

```
<xsl:attribute-set name = "html-table-cell">
   <xsl:attribute name = "valign">top</xsl:attribute>
   <xsl:attribute name = "align">left</xsl:attribute>
   <xsl:attribute name = "cellpadding">0</xsl:attribute>
   <xsl:attribute name = "cellspacing">0</xsl:attribute>
</xsl:attribute-set>
```

Note that attribute sets can be referenced both from `xsl:element` elements (see below) and from ordinary literal result elements. In the latter case, this is done through the `xsl:use-attribute-sets` attribute.

The `xsl:element` element type creates output elements, with the element-type name given in its required `name` attribute, which holds an attribute value template. The contents of the element can be both `xsl:attribute` elements and ordinary template contents. The `use-attribute-sets` attribute can be used to reference attribute sets.

Using these mechanisms we can make a template rule that creates an HTML table from the `items` in an RSS document, as shown in Example 16–3.

Note that this example uses both `xsl:element` and literal result elements in order to show that these are equivalent.

The main benefit of `xsl:attribute-set` is convenience and readability, as it allows a set of attributes to be created once and then reused in many different places. The main benefit of `xsl:element` and `xsl:attribute` is that their `name` attributes are attribute value templates, which means that the names of the created nodes can be set dynamically by the stylesheets. If you don't need to set the names dynamically, you should normally not use these instructions, since they

Example 16–3. A table of `items`

```
<xsl:template match="channel">
  [...title, link, description, etc...]

  <table>
    <xsl:for-each select="item">
      <tr>
      <xsl:element name="th" use-attribute-sets="html-table-cell">
      <a href="{link}"><xsl:value-of select="title"/></a>
      </xsl:element>
      <td xsl:use-attribute-sets="html-table-cell">
      <xsl:value-of select="description"/>
      </td>
      </tr>
    </xsl:for-each>
  </table>
</xsl:template>
```

bloat the stylesheet and are harder to read (as Example 16–3 should demonstrate).

There is also an `xsl:text` instruction that may be useful for creating text output where you wish to control whitespace or output escaping. It simply contains the text node that will be copied into the result tree. How to use it to influence whitespace and output escaping is explained in 16.2.2, "Output methods," on page 590.

16.2.1.1 Creating comments

If you want to create comments in the result tree, there is only one reliable way to do it: with the `xsl:comment` instruction. Since many XML parsers do not pass comments on to their applications (and since SAX2 has relegated this to a little-used extension), many XSLT engines will never see comments in your stylesheet. Also, when you use `xsl:comment`, you can use other XSLT instructions inside it to create its contents dynamically.

The `xsl:comment` instruction has no attributes, and its content is a template that is instantiated. Nodes other than text nodes are not allowed in the content and will either cause an error or be ignored.

Similarly with the string `'--'`, which will either result in an error or cause whitespace to be inserted so that it becomes `'- -'` instead.

Comments in the output are generally useful for only a few purposes:

- Comments can contain information to potential readers of the document source. A comment might, for example, say that the document is automatically generated by an XSLT stylesheet to be found in such and such a place, or present similar information.

- Comments can be used for debugging purposes. You can insert comments in the beginning (and sometimes also the end) of your templates to see what content in your output comes from what templates.

- Comments can also be used to escape `script` and `style` content in HTML output. The HTML output method knows that it should not escape reserved characters in these elements, but it does not in any way protect the contents against older browsers which may not understand these elements. To do that, it may be useful to wrap the entire contents in an `xsl:comment`.

Example 16–4 demonstrates this (note that the `foo:*` functions are invented by me for this example only).

Example 16–4. Generating a comment in an XSLT stylesheet

```
<xsl:comment>
This document was generated from the XML document at
<xsl:value-of select = "foo:source-uri()" /> using the stylesheet
<xsl:value-of select = "foo:style-uri()" />.  Please do not modify
this document, but modify the source or the stylesheet instead.
</xsl:comment>
```

This might, for example, result in the output as in Example 16–5.

Example 16–5. Comment output from the XSLT stylesheet

```
<!--
This document was generated from the XML document at
/home/acme/projects/foo/sources/set-a.xml using the stylesheet
/home/acme/projects/foo/sources/to-html.xslt. Please do not modify
this document, but modify the source or the stylesheet instead.
-->
```

16.2.1.2 Creating processing instructions

Processing instructions in templates are not copied to the output, which means that the only way to create them is with the `xsl:processing-instruction` instruction. The instruction has a single required attribute: `name`, which is the PI target. This is an attribute value template, and it must result in a valid PI target name, which means that it cannot begin with the letters `xml` in any combination of upper- and lower-case. This means that it cannot be used to create an XML declaration; but as long as `xsl:output` can do this, it would have been an inappropriate use of the instruction anyway.

The content of the element is a template that is instantiated to create the PI data. Note that it cannot contain the string `'?>'`. If it does, the processor will either signal an error or replace it with `'? >'`.

Example 16–6 creates an `xsl-stylesheet` processing instruction in the output, so that browsers and other software know where to find a stylesheet to display the document. This is may often be useful for displaying the results of XML to XML translations.

Example 16–6. Creating a processing instruction

```
<xsl:processing-instruction name="xsl-stylesheet">
  href="<xsl:value-of select = "$stylesheet" />" type="text/xsl"
</xsl:processing-instruction>
```

Example 16–6 may look a little strange, since it contains what one usually finds inside a start-tag (attribute assignments) in character data and with an XSLT instruction (`xsl:value-of`) inside it. That is a necessary consequence of what the instruction does, however. The example might result in the output shown in Example 16–7.

Example 16–7. Example of an `xslt-stylesheet` PI

```
<?xsl-stylesheet href="xbel2html.xslt" type="text/xsl"?>
```

Note that some whitespace has been removed in the example output to make it more legible. It should really have a ' `\n` ' between the target and the beginning of the data, as well as ' `\n`' between the data and the terminating ' `?>`'.

16.2.2 *Output methods*

As stated earlier, XSLT is primarily intended for XML-to-XML translation, but it also supports translation to other formats. One might think that translation to other formats is possible with what we have learned already, but in fact it is generally not. XSLT by default assumes that the output will be well-formed XML, and although it will not require a document element, it will escape all characters that have special meaning in XML. This means that although you can output, for example, LaTeX from your stylesheets, any occurrences of & or < will be escaped by the XSLT processor into `&amp;` or `&lt;`.

To avoid this problem, XSLT provides the `xsl:output` element type, which can be used to control how the XSLT processor serializes the result tree. You can think of this element as configuring the serializer component shown in Figure 15–2. The `xsl:output` element type has the following attributes:

`method`

> This attribute can have one of three values: `xml`, `html`, or `text`. Values with qualified names are also allowed as extensions. The default value is `xml`, unless the name of the document element type

of the output is `html` (and has no namespace), in which case it is `html`.

version

> This attribute specifies the version of the output notation that this stylesheet uses. For XML, the only possible value at the time of writing is 1.0. For HTML, it can be any HTML version; the default is 4.0. Until more versions of HTML are defined, the `version` attribute is unlikely to make any difference to the resulting output. This attribute is ignored for text output.

indent

> This can be `yes` or `no` and controls whether the XSLT processor should insert whitespace to make the output nicely indented. This attribute is ignored when the output method is `text`.

encoding

> This is the name of the character encoding to use when writing out the result tree. It must be a name from the IANA charset registry[1] or start with `x-`. However, since XSLT uses Unicode internally, it is possible for there to be characters in the result tree that cannot be expressed in the output encoding (which may be an 8-bit character encoding). In this case, the XML and HTML output methods will represent these characters using character or (for HTML) entity references. In the text output method, there is no such alternative, so this is considered an error.

media-type

> This is the MIME media type of the output. MIME media types are used by email and HTTP to specify the notation of a resource. This attribute is not used by the serializing process directly, but can be passed on to other software in the environment around it. One

---

1. See `http://www.isi.edu/in-notes/iana/assignments/character-sets`.

possibility is that when XSLT is used by a Web server to dynamically create output in response to request, this value can go into the HTTP header returned by the server.

The attribute defaults to `text/xml` with the XML output method, `text/html` with the HTML method, and `text/plain` with the text method. This attribute can be used with any output methods to override the defaults.

16.2.2.1 The XML output method

The `xsl:output` element type supports more attributes than those given above, but the attributes that only apply to the XML output method are listed below. Two of these attributes also apply to the HTML output method and are repeated there.

`omit-xml-declaration`

Must be `yes` or `no` and specifies whether or not the XML document should have an XML declaration. The output will contain an XML declaration with both a version pseudo-attribute and an encoding declaration unless this attribute is set to `yes`.

`standalone`

Must be `yes` or `no` and makes the serializer include a standalone pseudo-attribute in the XML declaration. Note that if this attribute is not specified, no standalone attribute is generated. Omitting this attribute makes the outputted XML declaration work both for document entities and external general entities. (These were explained in 2.3.1, "Storing XML documents," on page 54.)

The XSLT Recommendation seems to imply that if `omit-xml-declaration` is set to `yes` and `standalone` is specified, the value of `standalone` should be ignored and no XML declaration output.

`doctype-system`

Specifying this attribute causes a `DOCTYPE` declaration to be inserted in the output document with the system identifier set to the given value. The declaration will appear immediately before the document element. The name of the document element type given in the DOCTYPE declaration will be the name of the actual document element type in the output document.

doctype-public

> If doctype-system is specified, specifying this attribute will cause the DOCTYPE declaration to use the PUBLIC form of the declaration and the value of this attribute as the public identifier. If this attribute is not specified, the declaration will take the SYSTEM form. If the doctype-system attribute is not specified, this attribute will be ignored.

cdata-section-elements

> A whitespace-separated list of the qualified names of element types whose contents should be output inside CDATA marked sections. This has no effect on the logical contents of the output document, but those who wish to control this lexical aspect of the output document can use this attribute to do so.

Note that you cannot expect the XSLT serializer to respect other parts of the lexical representation of your document than those controllable using the above attributes. For example, the order of attributes in the output document cannot be predicted, while any sequences of whitespace inside tags (tags, not elements!) are likely to be replaced by single spaces.

16.2.2.2 The HTML output method

The HTML output method is very useful for producing HTML output, since it understands HTML and can avoid several subtle issues that may cause problems for browsers. Those issues are listed below.

- Empty elements will be output as start-tags without end-tags. For HTML 4.0, this means area, base, basefont, br, col, frame, hr, img, input, isindex, link, meta, and param. The reason for this rule is that HTML is an SGML application, and many older browsers do not handle the empty-element tag syntax, or the presence of end-tags for these elements, correctly.

- The script and style elements, which can contain JavaScript and CSS style rules, should have escaping disabled. This is because in JavaScript, < is the less-than operator, or it can be part of a string literal, and many browsers do not recognize this correctly if it appears as an entity reference. There are similar issues for CSS, where it can appear in string literals.

- The '<' characters in attribute values will not be escaped, since not all browsers handle this correctly.

- HTML attribute values that contain URLs will be escaped using the URL %-escape syntax. Note that this syntax requires that the URLs be UTF-8-encoded before escaping, which may not be supported correctly by all Web servers.

- PIs will be terminated with > rather than ?>.

- The output encoding will be declared using the META element type, as required by HTML.

Note that doctype-system and doctype-public are supported for HTML as well as for XML. The only difference is that in HTML, a DOCTYPE declaration will be output even if only doctype-public is specified.

Note that we had to escape the less-than sign in the JavaScript and to use the empty-element syntax for the br element to make the XML parser in the XSLT processor accept the document.

Example 16–8 will give the output shown in Example 16–9, which means that the JavaScript will not work and that strange things may happen to the br element.

If we insert an xsl:output element with method set to html and encoding set to iso-8859-1, we will instead get the result as in Example 16–10.

Example 16–8. An example of HTML output

```
<xsl:stylesheet xmlns:xsl="http://www.w3.org/1999/XSL/Transform"
                version="1.0">

  <xsl:template match = "/">
    <title>An example HTML document</title>

    <script>
    if (1 &lt; 2)
        document.write("You have an old browser!");
    </script>

    <p>
    This is just a simple document.<br/>
    Wow! A second line!
    </p>
  </xsl:template>

</xsl:stylesheet>
```

Example 16–9. Output from XML method

```
<?xml version="1.0" encoding="utf-8"?>
<title>An example HTML document</title><script>
    if (1 &lt; 2)
        document.write("You have an old browser!");
    </script><p>
    This is just a simple document.<br/>
    Wow! A second line!
    </p>
```

16.2.2.3 The text output method

The text output method is much simpler than the other two, since the output notation is so much simpler. All text nodes in the result tree are written out, but all other nodes are ignored. No special characters will be escaped in any way. If the output contains characters that cannot

Example 16–10. Output with HTML method

```
<meta http-equiv="Content-type" content="text/html;
                                    charset=iso-8859-1">
<title>An example HTML document</title>
<script>
    if (1 < 2)
        document.write("You have an old browser!");
    </script>
<p>
    This is just a simple document.<br>
    Wow! A second line!
    </p>
```

be expressed in the output encoding, the XSLT processor should[1] signal an error.

Note, however, that in some cases the whitespace rules of XSLT may cause text documents to look rather strange, and it may be very difficult to use some text formats as output without a preprocessing stage.

16.2.2.4 Controlling output escaping

In addition to the control over output escaping provided by the HTML and text output methods, XSLT provides a `disable-output-escaping` attribute on the `xsl:text` and `xsl:value-of` elements. This attribute can be set to `yes`, meaning that output escaping is disabled, and `no`, meaning that it is enabled.

This attribute can be used with both HTML and XML output methods, but is ignored for the text method, since that does not have any means for escaping anyway. Note that it can only be used when creating text nodes; any attempt at using it to create comment contents, processing instruction contents, or attribute values will result in an error.

---

1.   This is the term used by the XSLT Recommendation, and no formal definition of what it means is provided.

16.2.2.5 Controlling whitespace in the output

Whitespace in the result tree is contributed from two sources: the stylesheet and the source tree. In both cases, text nodes containing only whitespace are stripped from the documents before processing starts. Only two things can save a node from being stripped out:

- The inherited value of the `xml:space` attribute is `preserve`.
- In the stylesheet, the element-type name is `xsl:text`, or, in the document, the element is not one of those specified to have their contents stripped through the use of the `xsl:strip-space` element. (The default is that no elements in the source tree are stripped.)

The `xsl:strip-space` element type is a top-level element type and has a required attribute `elements` which specifies which element types should have their contents stripped. This attribute contains a whitespace-separated list of the following kinds of tokens: qualified element-type names, *, meaning all elements, and `prefix:*`, meaning all elements in the given namespace.

Note that there is an opposite `xsl:preserve-space` element type, also with an `elements` attribute with the same values, which defines the element types for which space is to be preserved. This element is mainly useful when it is easier to list the elements for which space is to be preserved than the opposite. The rules for XSLT stylesheets can thus be specified as stripping * and preserving `xsl:text`.

Example 16–11 shows a stylesheet that will copy the source tree of Example 16–12 through to the result tree unmodified.

When this document is processed with the given stylesheet, the result is as shown in Example 16–13, an exact copy of the input, except that an XML declaration has been added. This is because all whitespace is stripped from the stylesheet template, but none is stripped from the source tree.

If we then add the following element to the stylesheet at the top level, `<xsl:strip-space elements = "*"/>`, the result becomes

Example 16–11. An XSLT identity transform presenting whitespace

```
<xsl:stylesheet xmlns:xsl="http://www.w3.org/1999/XSL/Transform"
                version="1.0">

  <xsl:template match = "doc | title | p">
    <xsl:copy>
      <xsl:apply-templates/>
    </xsl:copy>
  </xsl:template>

</xsl:stylesheet>
```

Example 16–12. Input to the whitespace example

```
<doc>
  <title>Hello!</title>
  <p>
This is a bit of text.
  </p>
</doc>
```

Example 16–13. The output from the whitespace example

```
<?xml version="1.0" encoding="utf-8"?>
<doc>
  <title>Hello!</title>
  <p>
This is a bit of text.
  </p>
</doc>
```

Example 16–14. Modified output

```
<?xml version="1.0" encoding="utf-8"?>
<doc><title>Hello!</title><p>
This is a bit of text.
  </p></doc>
```

instead as shown in Example 16–14, since all whitespace nodes that can be stripped are.

As you can see, the only text nodes that are kept are those in the title and p elements, since they contain non-whitespace characters.

16.2.3 *Combining stylesheets*

Sometimes you may want to create stylesheets that consist of more than one file. This may be because you have made libraries of useful template rules, or because you have different stylesheets that handle different modules of your XML application, or it may be because your stylesheet is simply so big that it is awkward to maintain as a single file.

Whatever the reason, XSLT offers you two element types for combining stylesheets: xsl:include and xsl:import. These two have the same effect, except that with xsl:import, the imported definitions and template rules have lower precedence than the existing ones. The precedence rules are explained in the next section.

The effect of including another stylesheet is exactly the same as if the stylesheet had appeared literally instead of the xsl:include element. This means that they are in fact equivalent to entity references, except that the included stylesheet is not syntactically restricted in the way that external general entities are.

Both xsl:include and xsl:import must appear as top-level elements in the stylesheet, and xsl:import elements must appear before any other element inside the xsl:stylesheet element. There are no such restrictions on xsl:include elements.

16.2.4 *Conflict resolution: precedence*

Any languages that, like XSLT, use selectors to decide which of the many rules to apply to each node in the document tree, need some mechanism to decide what to do when more than one selector matches the same node. In XSLT, the rules are relatively simple: templates are sorted first by import precedence, and then by priority for those that have the same import precedence.

The import precedence rules for XSLT are actually rather complex. In general they imply that if stylesheet A is imported before B, then A and all stylesheets imported by it take precedence over B and all stylesheets imported by it. The general rule is to create an import tree and then traverse that tree to decide the precedences. For example, suppose that stylesheet A imports stylesheets B and C (in that order), and that B imports D and E (in that order) while C imports F. This would give the import tree shown in Figure 16–3.

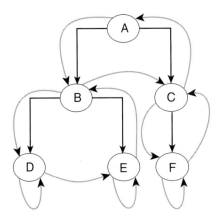

Figure 16–3   An XSLT import tree

In this tree, a stylesheet that occurs before another in what mathematicians call a pre-order traversal of the tree has lower priority. This order is defined by the gray arrows in the above figure. If you make a list of the nodes in the tree in the order you reach them by following the arrows, *but don't include the nodes until the second time you reach them,* you get the following order: D, E, B, F, C, A. And there you have the stylesheets in increasing order of import precedence.

The priority of a template rule can be set directly with the `priority` attribute of the `xsl:template` element type, in which case that priority value is used. If it is not set using this attribute, a so-called *default priority* is calculated instead. There are four possible default priorities:

- When the pattern is of the form `qname`, `@qname`, `child::qname`, `attribute::qname`, or `processing-instruction('name')`, the priority is 0.

  This means that the most common kinds of patterns, those that simply test for a specific element type, attribute, or processing instruction target, all have priority 0.

- Patterns of the form `prefix:*`, `@prefix:*`, `child::prefix:*`, or `attribute::prefix:*` have the priority –0.25.

  This means that patterns that simply test for an element or attribute in a particular namespace (disregarding the local name) have lower priority than the normal patterns. This makes sense, since they are less specific.

- Patterns that simply test for a specific node type (possibly using the `child` or `attribute` axes) have priority –0.5. This is also reasonable, since these are the least specific patterns possible with XPath.

- All other patterns have priority 0.5, which means that any pattern that uses several steps gets priority 0.5. This also makes sense, since these are (usually) more specific than the other patterns. However, it does mean that `foo / bar` is less specific than `baz / foo / bar` although they have the same priority.

Note that if two templates with the same priority match the same node, this is considered an error. The XSLT processor can then choose to either report the error or use the template that occurred last in the stylesheet.

16.2.5 *Single-template stylesheets*

It is possible to create XSLT stylesheets that consist of a single template rule, which essentially means using XSLT as a fancy template language. Such stylesheets are created by making the document element a literal result element and then specifying a template inside this literal result element. The context node inside this template will be the root element of the source tree.

For example, the RSS to HTML stylesheet that only used a single rule, shown in Example 15–15, could be rewritten differently, as Example 16–15 demonstrates.

Example 16–15. Alternate form of a single-rule stylesheet

```
<html xmlns:xsl="http://www.w3.org/1999/XSL/Transform"
      xsl:version="1.0">

  <head>
    <title><xsl:value-of select="rss/channel/title"/></title>
  </head>

  <body>
  <h1><xsl:value-of select="rss/channel/title"/></h1>

  <ul>
  <xsl:for-each select="rss/item">
    <li><a href="{link}"><xsl:value-of select="title"/></a>
        <xsl:value-of select="description"/></li>
  </xsl:for-each>
  </ul>
  </body>

</html>
```

Note how all the selectors in the template except those inside the `xsl:for-each` have `rss/` prepended. This is because they now select relative to the root node rather than the `rss` element. The single template rule has an implicit `match = "/"` on it.

16.2.6 *Variables, result tree fragments, and named templates*

XSLT has a concept of variables that is connected to the way they are used in XPath. It is possible to set the values of variables in XSLT and then refer to them in XPath expressions as shown in the previous chapter. XSLT provides two means of setting the values of variables: parameters and variables. Variables can be bound both at the top level of the stylesheet and inside templates, using the `xsl:variable` element type. If bound at the top level, the variable is global and visible everywhere. If bound in a template, the variable is only visible inside the `xsl:variable` element. Variable bindings can be nested and can shadow each other.

Parameters are intended to be passed to the stylesheet by external means. The most common alternatives are using command-line parameters or through the API of the XSLT engine when embedding it in another application. Parameters can be given default values using the `xsl:param` element type, which must occur at the top level.

The `xsl:param` and `xsl:variable` element types have the same structure. The only difference between them is that `xsl:param` declarations may be overridden by externally set values. There are two ways to set the value of a variable: using the `select` attribute or with a template inside the declaration. The `select` attribute contains an XPath expression, and the variable is set to the value the expression evaluates to.

Example 16–16. Using `xsl:variable`

```
<xsl:variable name="new-products"
              select='preceding::product[@new="yes"] |
                      following::product[@new="yes"]'>
  <h2>Index of new products</h2>
  <ul>
    <xsl:apply-templates select="$new-products" mode="new-index"/>
  </ul>

  <h2>New products</h2>

  <xsl:apply-templates select="$new-products" mode="new-list"/>
</xsl:variable>
```

Example 16–16 shows how `xsl:variable` can be used. The `xsl:variable` instruction first does an expensive search through the entire document for all new products, and then binds the resulting node set to the variable `new-products`. Inside the instruction, that node set is then processed once to create an index of the new products, and then processed again to create a full list.

This use of `xsl:variable` can improve performance, since the expensive XPath expression is only evaluated once. If there are thousands of products and only 10–20 new ones, this can result in significant speedups. Another benefit is that the big and ugly XPath expression does not have to be repeated twice.

Of course, any kind of XPath value can be bound to a variable in this way, including strings, numbers, and booleans. If the `select` attribute of the `xsl:variable` element is omitted, the template contents of the element will be instantiated and bound to the variable. In this case the value will be of the *result tree fragment* type, which we have not discussed so far. This is a type that XSLT adds to XPath, and it is not mentioned in the XPath specification. Result tree fragments are like source tree nodes in that they represent parts of an XML document, but differ in that they are part of the result tree and in that the only operations that are allowed on them are those that are allowed on strings. This means that the `/`, `//`, and `[ ]` operators are not allowed on result tree fragments.

The main use of result tree fragments is to copy them into the result tree with `xsl:copy-of`. This instruction contains a `select` attribute with an XPath expression and causes its value to be copied into the tree. It can copy both result tree fragments and ordinary source tree nodes. This can be useful for output pieces that need to be repeated, perhaps with tiny variations, in several places. There is also another use for them, which is discussed below.

Another use of variables and parameters, as well as of result tree fragments, is for *named templates*. These are ordinary `xsl:templates`, but with a name in the `name` attribute. These do not need to have `match` attributes (although they may), since they are primarily intended to be used as something similar to functions in ordinary programming languages. With the `xsl:call-template` instruction, it is possible to call a named template and have it instantiated. Examples 16–17 and 16–18 show how to use named templates.

Note that just as with `xsl:variable` and `xsl:param`, `xsl:with-param` can drop the `select` attribute and instead contain a template that makes the value a result tree fragment.

In Example 16–17, we create two indexes, one of vendors and one of products. Since these indexes have very similar structure, we use the named template below to actually generate them. The template takes two parameters: `what` and `elements`.

Example 16–17. How to use named templates (1 of 2)

```
<xsl:stylesheet xmlns:xsl="http://www.w3.org/1999/XSL/Transform"
                version="1.0">

  <xsl:template match="SOFTLIST">
    <xsl:call-template name="index-table">
      <xsl:with-param name="what"     select='"Vendors"'/>
      <xsl:with-param name="elements" select="VENDOR"/>
    </xsl:call-template>

    <xsl:call-template name="index-table">
      <xsl:with-param name="what"     select='"Products"'/>
      <xsl:with-param name="elements" select="PRODUCT"/>
    </xsl:call-template>

  </xsl:template>
```

In the named template in Example 16–18, we define the default values for the parameters and then move on to the template contents. We use the contents of the `what` variable in the heading. We iterate over the node set in the `elements` variable with `xsl:for-each`, to create a list item for each element. This is of course only possible if both PRODUCT and VENDOR elements have NAME and URL child elements.

Example 16–18. How to use named templates (2 of 2)

```
<xsl:template name="index-table">
  <xsl:param name="what"      select='"Index"'/>
  <xsl:param name="elements" select='/..'/>

  <h2><xsl:value-of select="$what"/></h2>
  <ul>
     <xsl:for-each select="$elements">
       <li><a href="{URL}"><xsl:value-of select="NAME"/></a></li>
     </xsl:for-each>
  </ul>
</xsl:template>

</xsl:stylesheet>
```

16.2.7 *Extra XPath functions*

XSLT defines some very useful XPath functions that are only available within XSLT. Some of them are relatively simple, and these are listed below. The more complex functions are explained in separate sections further down.

current()

Returns the XSLT current node. This can be used to access the XSLT current node in XPath expressions even when the evaluation of the XPath expression has caused the XPath context node to change.

unparsed-entity-uri(string)

This function takes the name of an unparsed entity and returns the URI of the entity as a string.

generate-id(node-set?)

This function generates a unique ID value for the first node (in document order) in the node set passed as the argument. If the argument is omitted, it defaults to the context node. The ID must consist of ASCII letters and digits and begin with a letter. This means that it will be an XML name, and can be used as an HTML anchor name.

The XSLT Recommendation does not specify how the ID is generated, but it must be different from all other IDs generated by this function during a single run. It must also be the same for the same node during the same run.

`system-property(string)`

This function is used to get information about the environment the stylesheet is run in, and the argument must be a qualified name. If the system property is unknown to the XSLT processor, it will return the empty string.

The XSLT Recommendation defines three system properties which must be recognized by all XSLT processors:

`xsl:version`

A string that contains the version number of XSLT implemented by the processor.

`xsl:vendor`

A string identifying whoever made the XSLT processor.

`xsl:vendor-url`

A URL that identifies the maker of the XSLT processor. This will generally be the URL of the maker's home page.

If we process the XML document in Example 16–19 with the stylesheet from Example 16–20 using 4XSLT, we get the output as in Example 16–21.

The output in Example 16–21 shows the values that Fourthought has defined for the `xsl:vendor` and `xsl:vendor-url` properties. 4XSLT generates the IDs of the various nodes prepending the string `'id'` to the value returned by calling the built-in Python function `id` on the node objects.

Example 16–19. Input to the functions stylesheet

```
<doc>
  <elem1/>
  <elem2/>
</doc>
```

Example 16–20. The functions stylesheet

```
<xsl:stylesheet xmlns:xsl="http://www.w3.org/1999/XSL/Transform"
                version="1.0">

  <xsl:template match = "doc">
    Version: <xsl:value-of select =
                          "system-property('xsl:version')"/>
    Vendor: <xsl:value-of select =
                          "system-property('xsl:vendor')"/>
    Vendor URL: <xsl:value-of select =
                          "system-property('xsl:vendor-url')"/>

    doc: <xsl:value-of select = "generate-id(.)" />
    doc: <xsl:value-of select = "generate-id(current())" />
    elem1: <xsl:value-of select = "generate-id(elem1)" />
    elem2: <xsl:value-of select = "generate-id(elem2)" />
    elem1: <xsl:value-of select = "generate-id(*)" />
  </xsl:template>

</xsl:stylesheet>
```

Example 16–21. Output from the functions stylesheet

```
Version: 1.0
Vendor: Fourthought Inc.
Vendor URL: http://4suite.org

doc: id9195472
doc: id9195472
elem1: id9217248
elem2: id9262208
elem1: id9217248
```

16.2.7.1 The document function

The document function allows XSLT stylesheets to process other XML documents in addition to the one they were requested to process. This can be useful, for example, to follow references in one document to subdocuments. The function works by taking a URI reference as a string and returning a node set that represents the XML document referred to by the string. How this operation is performed varies depending on what arguments the function is given.

The function's signature is document(object, node-set?). If object is a string, that string is taken as the URI, and other types are converted to strings in the usual manner, except for node sets. These generate a string per node, and document will return the union of the node sets of the documents they refer to.

If the XSLT processor for some reason can't retrieve the document referred to, it will either report an error or return an empty node set.

The document function can, for example, be used to make a stylesheet support the XInclude specification that we saw earlier in 10.2.4, "The XInclude filter," on page 373. The template rule given in Example 16–22 will follow all XInclude references.

Example 16–22. A template rule that supports XInclude

```
<!-- We assume that the 'xi' namespace prefix has been declared -->
<xsl:template match = "child::* [ @xi:href ]">
  <xsl:apply-templates select = "document(@xi:href)" />
</xsl:template>
```

This template rule works by matching any element that has an XInclude href attribute, and then applying the templates in the stylesheet on the document referred to by this attribute. This template can be used to add XInclude support to stylesheets, either by copying the template into them or through import/inclusion.

16.2.8 *Keys and cross-references*

Keys are a feature of XSLT that can be used to efficiently find nodes in a document which contain specific values. This can be used to handle cross-references, look up particular nodes, and for many other things. A stylesheet uses keys by declaring a set of named keys at the top level of the stylesheet using the xsl:key element. These declarations can be thought of as declaring indexes on the nodes in a document (like in a database) or as creating Python dictionaries of nodes keyed on particular values.

The xsl:key element type has three required attributes: name, match, and use. The name attribute gives the name of the key (or the index, or the dictionary). The match attribute contains an XPath expression; the nodes in the document that match this expression will be entered into this key (indexed or inserted into the dictionary) under the value computed from the use attribute. The use attribute contains an XPath expression that is evaluated with the matched node as the context node and used to compute the key value.

The key creation algorithm is shown as Python pseudo-code in Example 16–23, with one difference. The pseudo-code maps each key value to a single node, while in XSLT each key value can map to several nodes.

Example 16–23. Pseudo code for key compilation

```
use = CompileXPathExpression(attr["use"])
key = {}
for node in document.match(attr["match"]):
  value = use.evaluate(Context(node))
  if type(value) == node_set_type:
    for value_node in value:
      key[string(value_node)] = node
  else:
    key[string(value)] = node

document.add_key(attr["name"], key)
```

Once the keys have been declared, the template rules in the stylesheet can use the `key` function to look up the nodes with a given key value in a given key. The function has the following signature: `key(key-name, key-value)` and returns a node set containing the nodes that matched the value. The `key-name` must be a qname string, giving the name of the key. The `key-value` is the value to look up. Note that this can be a node set, and if it is, the result is the union of the sets returned by calling `key` with the string value of each of the nodes in the set.

The XSLT stylesheet fragment in Example 16–24 handles `alias` elements in XBEL documents by inserting the referenced elements directly in the place where the `alias` element occurred.

Example 16–24.

```
<xsl:key name = "id" match = "folder | bookmark" use="@id" />

<xsl:template match = "alias">
  <xsl:apply-templates select = "key('id', @ref)" />
</xsl:template>
```

The example works by defining a key named `id` which contains all `folder` and `bookmark` elements indexed on their `id` attributes. The template rule then applies the already defined template rules (which presumably handle `folders` and `bookmarks` correctly) to the element with the key value it finds in the `ref` attribute of the `alias` element.

16.2.9 *Messages*

XSLT provides a mechanism that allows template rules to send messages to whoever runs the XSLT processor. Who this person is and how the messages are passed on from the XSLT processor is not defined by the XSLT Recommendation. Possible ways of passing on messages are printing them on standard out, writing them to a log file, or displaying them in a dialog box.

Messages are sent using the `xsl:message` instruction. It has a `terminate` attribute, which can be either `yes` or `no`; if it is set to `yes`, the processor will terminate after sending the message. This instruction can be used both for error messages and for debug printouts to help the developer figure out what is happening inside during execution of a stylesheet.

The content of the `xsl:message` is a template that is the message value. How this content is interpreted is entirely up to each XSLT processor. It would be perfectly permissible for a processor to define its own namespace which stylesheets could use to control the display of messages.

Using `xsl:message`, we can extend the `alias`-handling stylesheet fragment in Example 16–24 to complain if an `alias` element refers to an ID that does not exist in the document as Example 16–25 demonstrates.

Example 16–25. Creating an error message for missing references

```
<xsl:key name = "id" match = "folder | bookmark" use="@id" />

<xsl:template match = "alias">
  <xsl:variable name = "refnode" select = "key('id', @ref)" />

  <xsl:choose>
    <xsl:when test="not($refnode)">
      <xsl:message>
      Alias element referred to non-existent ID
      <xsl:value-of select = "@href"/>.
      </xsl:message>
    </xsl:when>
    <xsl:otherwise>
      <xsl:apply-templates select = "$refnode" />
    </xsl:otherwise>
  </xsl:choose>
</xsl:template>
```

If the set of nodes matched by the key is empty, this template rule will emit a message. If it is not empty, the nodes will be processed. Note that this means that the rule will be perfectly happy if more than one node is matched. This can be avoided by using the `count` function: `not(count($refnode) = 1).`

16.2.10 *XSLT extensions and fallback*

As we have already seen in numerous examples, XSLT has been designed with the purpose to be extended by implementors, and this also applies to control element types. Anyone can define new XSLT control element types, provided that these element types have a namespace that distinguishes them from XSLT element types and result tree elements. XSLT implementors can then provide support for extension element types as they wish with no fear of naming conflicts with other vendors or future versions of the standard. XSLT also has features for dealing with unsupported extension element types and functions, which will be discussed below.

Most of the XSLT implementations today have defined both extension element types and functions for the convenience of their users. It is likely that the most useful of these will find their way into future versions of the XSLT Recommendation.

In order to identify extension elements as instructions, as opposed to literal result elements (which is the default interpretation of non-XSLT elements), their namespace must be defined as an extension namespace. This is done using the `extension-element-prefixes` attribute of the `xsl:stylesheet` element, or the `xsl:extension-element-prefixes` attribute of any non-XSLT element. This attribute contains a whitespace-separated list of namespace prefixes that map to extension elements. This attribute applies inside the element that bears it, but does not apply to any included or imported stylesheets.

This mechanism is not really needed for the processors which support these extension element types, but it is needed so that processors that do not support them can recognize them for what they are. This is useful because XSLT provides mechanisms that allow stylesheets to discover if extension element types are not supported and to specify alternative implementations that do not use these extensions.

The simplest mechanism is the element-available(qname) function, which returns false for extension and XSLT elements which are not supported. This can be used in conditions to specify what the processor must do if there is no support for the element type. Example 16–26 shows an instance of this.

Example 16–26. Testing for support for an extension element type

```
<xsl:stylesheet xmlns:xsl="http://www.w3.org/1999/XSL/Transform"
                xmlns:foo="http://foo.org/xslt/extensions"
                extension-element-prefixes="foo"
                version="1.0">

  <xsl:template match = "/">
    <xsl:choose>
      <xsl:when test = "not(element-available('foo:bar'))">
        <xsl:message terminate="yes">
        Sorry, support for the foo:bar element required to run this
        stylesheet. Try using the XSLT processor from foo.org
        instead!
        </xsl:message>
      </xsl:when>
      <xsl:otherwise>
        [...proceed to use the foo:bar instruction for something
        useful...]
      </xsl:otherwise>
    </xsl:choose>
  </xsl:template>

</xsl:stylesheet>
```

A more complicated mechanism is the fallback system. If an XSLT processor encounters an extension element type it does not recognize, it must scan the element for xsl:fallback children. If no such elements exist, an error must be signaled. If any fallback elements are found, they are instantiated in the order they appear. When not in fallback mode, xsl:fallback elements are just ignored.

Example 16–27 is equivalent to Example 16–26 that used the element-available function to test for support.

Example 16–27. Using fallback instead of `element-available`

```
<xsl:stylesheet xmlns:xsl="http://www.w3.org/1999/XSL/Transform"
                xmlns:foo="http://foo.org/xslt/extensions"
                extension-element-prefixes="foo"
                version="1.0">

  <xsl:template match = "/">
    <foo:bar really-useful-attribute = "baz">
      [...proceed to use the foo:bar instruction for something
      useful...]

      <xsl:fallback>
        <xsl:message terminate="yes">
        Sorry, support for the foo:bar element required to run this
        stylesheet. Try using the XSLT processor from foo.org
        instead!
        </xsl:message>
      </xsl:fallback>
    </foo:bar>
  </xsl:template>

</xsl:stylesheet>
```

Extension XPath functions are also allowed, but must have an associated namespace. Whenever an XSLT processor finds a call to a function with a name that contains a colon, it assumes that this is the qualified name of an extension function. If an unsupported extension function is found in an expression, the XSLT processor will signal an error.

Just as with extension element types, there is a function to test for support for extension functions: `function-available(name)`. It returns `true` for supported extension and XSLT functions and `false` for others.

16.2.11 *Producing XSLT stylesheets as output*

It may in some cases be convenient to create XSLT stylesheets that produce other XSLT stylesheets as output. One of the things this can be used for is automatic generation of stylesheets from higher-level documents that describe some kind of mapping in very general terms. Another possibility is implementing XSLT extension element types by processing an XSLT stylesheet in a way that effectively translates the extension element types into macros.

A fundamental problem with this, however, is that the elements that are output from the XSLT stylesheet have to be in the XSLT namespace. This is problematic because any elements in the XSLT namespace will be interpreted as XSLT instructions, and not as literal result elements. This can be solved by using some other namespace than the XSLT namespace for these elements, and then declaring this namespace to be an alias for the XSLT namespace. This will have the effect of outputting the elements in the not-XSLT-namespace as elements in the proper XSLT namespace.

Let's say that we want to implement an XSLT extension element that lets us abbreviate awkward constructs of the type shown in Example 16–28, which we have encountered many times already.

Example 16–28. A common XSLT fragment

```
<xsl:if test="description">
  <p>
    <xsl:value-of select="description"/>
  </p>
</xsl:if>
```

Using an element of our invention, which we will call `output-if`, this could be written as in Example 16–29.

Example 16–29. A shorter version of fragment

```
<lmgxsl:output-if select="description" wrap-in="p"/>
```

In order to implement this using XSLT, we have to process the XSLT stylesheet that uses this extension into another XSLT stylesheet that uses no extensions at all. This can be done by simply copying everything in the stylesheet except for this element type, which we map into an instruction of the original form. The stylesheet in Examples 16–30 to 16–32 does this.

The first template (Example 16–30) does nothing but copy the source tree directly through to the result tree unchanged. Note that we have declared three namespaces: the XSLT namespace, that of the extension element type, and a namespace for the XSLT elements that are to go into the result tree.

Example 16–30. An XSLT-to-XSLT stylesheet (1 of 3)

```
<xsl:stylesheet xmlns:xsl="http://www.w3.org/1999/XSL/Transform"
          xmlns:lmgxsl="http://garshol.priv.no/symbolic/xslt-ext"
          xmlns:xslout="http://www.w3.org/1999/XSL/TransformOutput"
          version="1.0">

  <xsl:template match="@*|node()">
    <xsl:copy>
    <xsl:apply-templates select="@*|node()"/>
    </xsl:copy>
  </xsl:template>
```

In Example 16–31, we map output-if elements into a combination of ordinary XSLT instructions and literal result elements. To do this, we must use a strange mix of XSLT instructions to be interpreted directly and XSLT instructions to be output as literal result elements. The namespaces are used to tell these apart.

Example 16–31. An XSLT-to-XSLT stylesheet (2 of 3)

```
  <xsl:template match="lmgxsl:output-if">
    <xslout:if test="{@select}">
      <xsl:element name="{@wrap-in}">
        <xslout:value-of select="{@select}"/>
      </xsl:element>
    </xslout:if>
  </xsl:template>
```

The xsl:namespace-alias element type in Example 16–32 solves a crucial problem with this stylesheet. Without this element, the xslout elements would be output using the namespace URI http://www.w3.org/1999/XSL/TransformOutput. Here, however, we say that this is just an alias for the ordinary XSLT namespace, so in the result tree, the xslout namespace is replaced with the xsl namespace. (Note that to indicate the default namespace, the token #default can be used, in both attributes.)

Example 16–32. An XSLT-to-XSLT stylesheet (3 of 3)

```
<xsl:namespace-alias stylesheet-prefix="xslout"
                     result-prefix="xsl"/>

</xsl:stylesheet>
```

With this stylesheet, we can take a stylesheet that uses the extension, such as the nonsensical one in Example 16–33, and produce a proper XSLT stylesheet, such as the one in Example 16–34.

Example 16–33. An extended XSLT stylesheet

```
<xsl:stylesheet xmlns:xsl="http://www.w3.org/1999/XSL/Transform"
            xmlns:lmgxsl="http://garshol.priv.no/symbolic/xslt-ext"
            version="1.0">

  <xsl:template match = "item">
    <lmgxsl:output-if select="description" wrap-in="p"/>
  </xsl:template>

</xsl:stylesheet>
```

16.3 | Advanced XSLT examples

We have now covered a large set of advanced XSLT and XPath functionality, so it is time to consolidate this knowledge by using it in some

Example 16–34. Processed XSLT stylesheet

```
<?xml version='1.0' encoding='UTF-8'?>
<xsl:stylesheet version='1.0'
            xmlns:lmgxsl='http://garshol.priv.no/symbolic/xslt-ext'
            xmlns:xsl='http://www.w3.org/1999/XSL/Transform'>

  <xsl:template match='item'>
    <xsl:if test='description'
            xmlns:xsl='http://www.w3.org/1999/XSL/Transform'>
    <p><xsl:value-of select='description'/></p></xsl:if>
  </xsl:template>

</xsl:stylesheet>
```

larger examples. This section provides two examples that use some of the techniques discussed above.

16.3.1 *Converting Shakespeare's plays to HTML*

Examples 16–35 to 16–45 show how to use XSLT with XML that has a more document-like structure, as opposed to the more data-oriented examples given so far.

As usual, the first rule is the rule for the document element type (Example 16–35). This creates the usual HTML wrapper, and like the previous Shakespeare converter in Examples 12–21 and 12–22, uses a CSS stylesheet to style the output. The only notable feature is the generation of the table of contents, using the toc mode (which is defined below, at the end of the stylesheet). Note also how the ACT elements are selected to avoid processing the other content in the play. This would have copied the data outside the ACTs during toc processing, and to avoid this, we would otherwise have had to make "blocking" empty template rules.

The P elements in the FM element, which appear immediately after the play's title, are simply converted to HTML paragraphs (Example 16–36).

Example 16–35. Play to HTML converter (1 of 11)

```
<xsl:stylesheet xmlns:xsl="http://www.w3.org/1999/XSL/Transform"
                version="1.0">

  <xsl:template match = "PLAY">
    <html>
    <head>
      <title><xsl:value-of select = "TITLE"/></title>
      <link rel="stylesheet" href="play.css" type="text/css"/>
    </head>

    <body>
    <h1><xsl:value-of select = "TITLE"/></h1>
    <h2>Table of contents</h2>
    <ul>
    <xsl:apply-templates mode="toc" select="ACT"/>
    </ul>

    <xsl:apply-templates/>

    <hr/>
    <address>
    Converted to HTML from Jon Bosak's XML by play2html.xslt.
    </address>
    </body>
    </html>
  </xsl:template>
```

Example 16–36. Play to HTML converter (2 of 11)

```
  <xsl:template match = "P">
    <p><xsl:apply-templates/></p>
  </xsl:template>
```

The dramatis personae is also easy to handle with the rule in Example 16–37. Note how we use `xsl:apply-templates` here, since it would be awkward to handle these two different cases with an `xsl:for-each` instruction.

The PERSONA elements are mapped to list items, as are the PGROUP elements (Example 16–38). Inside the PGROUP, we can use xsl:for-

Example 16–37. Play to HTML converter (3 of 11)

```
<xsl:template match = "PERSONAE">
  <h2><xsl:value-of select = "TITLE"/></h2>

  <ul>
    <xsl:apply-templates select = "PERSONA | PGROUP"/>
  </ul>
</xsl:template>
```

Example 16–38. Play to HTML converter (4 of 11)

```
<xsl:template match = "PERSONA">
  <li><xsl:apply-templates/></li>
</xsl:template>

<xsl:template match = "PGROUP">
  <li><xsl:for-each select="PERSONA">
      <xsl:apply-templates/>
    </xsl:for-each>, <xsl:value-of select = "GRPDESCR"/>
  </li>
</xsl:template>
```

each, since there is only one case to handle. The GRPDESCR is inserted at the end, using xsl:value-of.

For the act title, we create an H2 heading (Example 16–39). However, in order to be able to link to the act from the table of contents, we need to create a label with the NAME attribute of the A element. We use the prefix act and then generate a number from the number of acts before this one. This gives the first act the label act0, then act1, etc. Note that we have to go up to the ACT element from the TITLE to be able to select its preceding siblings before we can count them.

Example 16–39. Play to HTML converter (5 of 11)

```
<xsl:template match = "ACT/TITLE">
  <h2><a name="act{count(parent::*/preceding-sibling::ACT)}">
    <xsl:apply-templates/>
  </a></h2>
</xsl:template>
```

PROLOGUEs, EPILOGUEs, and INDUCTs all have their titles turned into H2 headings (Example 16–40). We do not create labels here, since we leave these out of the table of contents.

Example 16–40. Play to HTML converter (6 of 11)

```
<xsl:template match = "PROLOGUE/TITLE | EPILOGUE/TITLE |
                       INDUCT/TITLE">
  <h2><xsl:apply-templates/></h2>
</xsl:template>
```

SCENEs, being on the next level, have their titles turned into H3 headings (Example 16–41). We create labels for these as well, since they are also in the table of contents. In this case, we cannot use the preceding-siblings axis, since some of the preceding scenes may be in other acts, which makes them cousins rather than siblings. Had we done that, the first scene in each act would have been scene0, the second scene1, and so on. To avoid this, we use the preceding axis, since all earlier nodes lie along this axis, regardless of their position in the hierarchy. Because of this, we do not have to go up to the parent before following the preceding axis, even if we start from the TITLE.

Example 16–41. Play to HTML converter (7 of 11)

```
<xsl:template match = "SCENE/TITLE">
  <h3><a name="scene{count(preceding::SCENE)}">
       <xsl:apply-templates/></a></h3>
</xsl:template>
```

SPEAKERs and LINEs each get HTML paragraphs, although with different classes, so that the CSS stylesheet can tell them apart (Example 16–42).

Example 16–42. Play to HTML converter (8 of 11)

```
<xsl:template match = "SPEAKER">
  <p class="speaker"><xsl:apply-templates/></p>
</xsl:template>

<xsl:template match = "LINE">
  <p class="line"><xsl:apply-templates/></p>
</xsl:template>
```

In Example 16–43, we easily handle the case of STAGEDIRs inside LINEs by mapping them to the HTML SPAN elements. These element types are used for generic containers that do not require their own paragraph, which is perfect for our purposes. The SPAN elements are given a class so that the CSS stylesheet can handle them.

Example 16–43. Play to HTML converter (9 of 11)

```
<xsl:template match = "LINE / STAGEDIR">
  <span class="stagedir"><xsl:apply-templates/></span>
</xsl:template>

<xsl:template match = "STAGEDIR">
  <p class="stagedir"><xsl:apply-templates/></p>
</xsl:template>

</xsl:stylesheet>
```

Example 16–44 is the template rule for processing acts in the table of contents mode. It creates links to the internal labels produced by the main rules above using the same XPath expression. When processing the scenes (Example 16–45), they are selected (so that we avoid all other content) and the mode attribute is used again. If we had not given the mode name here, processing would have been done using the rules in the nameless default mode.

Example 16–44. Play to HTML converter (10 of 11)

```
<!-- Table of contents mode -->

<xsl:template match = "ACT" mode="toc">
  <li><a href="#act{count(preceding-sibling::ACT)}">
      <xsl:value-of select="TITLE"/>
    </a>
    <ul>
      <xsl:apply-templates mode="toc" select="SCENE"/>
    </ul>
  </li>
</xsl:template>
```

Example 16–45. Play to HTML converter (11 of 11)

```
<xsl:template match = "SCENE" mode="toc">
  <li><a href="#scene{count(preceding::SCENE)}">
    <xsl:value-of select="TITLE"/>
  </a></li>
</xsl:template>
```

16.3.2 *The rfc-index example*

The RFCs are a collection of documents published by the Internet Engineering Task Force (IETF). These documents started very informally in the early days of the Arpanet, but have since become a means of distributing Internet standards, proposals, guidelines, and various other kinds of information. Quite a few of the RFCs are also humorous.

In my work I often need to reference these documents, but unfortunately there are few proper indexes of RFCs, and since they now number almost 3000, having a proper index could make it much easier to find what I am looking for. So to keep track of the RFCs I have created an XML document where I enter information about RFCs as I find it.

The document has a rather simple structure. It begins with a list of RFC mirrors, each consisting of two URL pieces: the prefix before the RFC number in the URL and the suffix after. This allows me to use RFC numbers to create links to each RFC document. The rest of the document is a list of named categories, each of which contains the RFCs in it. The RFCs have various metadata such as title, nickname (short version of title), authors, publication date, keywords, and name of the standard defined in the RFC.

The DTD to this document is given in Example 16–46.

Example 16–46. The RFC index DTD

```
<!ELEMENT rfc-index (sites, category+)>

<!ELEMENT sites      (site+)>
<!ELEMENT site       (prefix, suffix)>
<!ELEMENT prefix     (#PCDATA)>
<!ELEMENT suffix     (#PCDATA)>

<!ELEMENT category   (name, rfc+)>
<!ELEMENT name       (#PCDATA)>

<!ELEMENT rfc        (number, title?, author*, date?, nickname?,
                      keywords?, standard?)>

<!ELEMENT number     (#PCDATA)>
<!ELEMENT title      (#PCDATA)>
<!ELEMENT nickname   (#PCDATA)>
<!ELEMENT author     (#PCDATA)>
<!ELEMENT date       (#PCDATA)>
<!ELEMENT standard   (#PCDATA)>

<!ELEMENT keywords   (keyword+)>
<!ELEMENT keyword    (#PCDATA)>

<!ATTLIST rfc   obsoleted-by CDATA #IMPLIED
                obsoletes    CDATA #IMPLIED>
```

16.3.2.1 Index to HTML conversion

Now I would like to process this index into an HTML document that has indexes of the RFCs by number, keyword, standard, author, and category. The stylesheet in Examples 16–47 to 16–53 does this.

In Example 16–47, we define the URL prefix and suffix of the RFC site that we wish to link to. This is defined as an XSLT parameter that can be overridden from the outside, defaulting to the first site listed in the source document.

Example 16–47. The RFC index to HTML stylesheet (1 of 7)

```
<xsl:stylesheet xmlns:xsl="http://www.w3.org/1999/XSL/Transform"
                version="1.0">

  <xsl:template match="rfc-index">
    <xsl:param name="prefix"
               select="string(sites / site / prefix)"/>

    <xsl:param name="suffix"
               select="string(sites / site / suffix)"/>
```

Example 16–48 is simple literal content, creating the top of the document, with internal links to each of the indexes, in order to make it easier to access them.

Example 16–48. The RFC index to HTML stylesheet (2 of 7)

```
<html>
  <head><title>An index of RFCs</title></head>

  <body>
  <h1>An index of RFCs</h1>

  <p><a href="#by-number">by number</a> |
     <a href="#by-standard">by standard</a> |
     <a href="#by-keyword">by keyword</a> |
     <a href="#by-author">by author</a> |
     <a href="#by-category">by category</a>
  </p>
```

Example 16–49 is the easiest of the indexes. We select all the RFCs, order them by number, create an internal link to the RFC, and add a separator after each one, except the last.

Example 16–50 is perhaps the most difficult of all indexes, for here we need to first create a list of all the standards mentioned (without

Example 16–49. The RFC index to HTML stylesheet (3 of 7)

```
<h2><a name="by-number">RFCs by number</a></h2>
<xsl:for-each select = "category / rfc">
  <xsl:sort select="number" data-type="number"
            order="ascending"/>

  <a href="#{number}"><xsl:value-of select="number"/></a>
  <xsl:if test="not(position() = last())"> | </xsl:if>
</xsl:for-each>
```

duplicates), and then list the RFCs that mention each standard. The key trick is the use of the predicate expression that tests whether the current standard has appeared before in the list of standards. Note also the use of the `standard` variable to store the name of the standard, since that will otherwise not be available to the XPath expression in the inner `xsl:for-each`.

Example 16–50. The RFC index to HTML stylesheet (4 of 7)

```
<h2><a name="by-standard">RFCs by standard</a></h2>

<table>
<tr><th>Standard</th>   <th>RFCs</th></tr>
<xsl:for-each select = "category / rfc /
                        standard [not(preceding::standard = .)]">
  <xsl:sort select="." order="ascending"/>
  <xsl:variable name = "standard" select = "." />

  <tr>
  <td><xsl:value-of select = "." /></td>
  <td>
  <xsl:for-each select = "//rfc [standard = $standard]">
    <xsl:sort select="number" data-type="number"
              order="ascending"/>

    <a href="#{number}"><xsl:value-of select="number"/></a>
    <xsl:if test="not(position() = last())"> | </xsl:if>
  </xsl:for-each>
  </td></tr>
</xsl:for-each>
</table>
```

Example 16–51. The RFC index to HTML stylesheet (5 of 7)

```
<h2><a name="by-keyword">RFCs by keyword</a></h2>
<table>
<tr><th>Keyword</th>  <th>RFCs</th></tr>
<xsl:for-each select = "category / rfc / keywords /
                        keyword [not(preceding::keyword = .)]">
  <xsl:sort select="." order="ascending"/>
  <xsl:variable name = "keyword" select = "." />

  <tr>
  <td><xsl:value-of select = "." /></td>
  <td>
  <xsl:for-each select="//rfc [keywords / keyword = $keyword]">
    <xsl:sort select="number" data-type="number"
              order="ascending"/>

    <a href="#{number}"><xsl:value-of select="number"/></a>
    <xsl:if test="not(position() = last())"> | </xsl:if>
  </xsl:for-each>
  </td></tr>
</xsl:for-each>
</table>

<h2><a name="by-author">RFCs by author</a></h2>
<table>
<tr><th>Author</th>   <th>RFCs</th></tr>
<xsl:for-each select = "category / rfc /
                        author [not(preceding::author = .)]">
  <xsl:sort select="." order="ascending"/>
  <xsl:variable name = "author" select = "." />

  <tr>
  <td><xsl:value-of select = "." /></td>
  <td>
  <xsl:for-each select = "//rfc [author = $author]">
    <xsl:sort select="number" data-type="number"
              order="ascending"/>

    <a href="#{number}"><xsl:value-of select="number"/></a>
    <xsl:if test="not(position() = last())"> | </xsl:if>
  </xsl:for-each>
  </td></tr>
</xsl:for-each>
</table>
```

```
<h2><a name="by-category">RFCs by category</a></h2>
<xsl:for-each select = "category">
  <h3><xsl:value-of select="name"/></h3>

  <dl>
  <xsl:for-each select="rfc">
    <xsl:sort select="number" data-type="number"
              order="ascending"/>

    <dt><a name="{number}">
        <a href="{$prefix}{number}{$suffix}">RFC
          <xsl:value-of select = "number"/></a></a></dt>
    <dd><xsl:call-template name="rfc-description"/>
        <xsl:if test="@obsoleted-by">
          <i>Obsoleted by
          <a href="#{@obsoleted-by}">
            <xsl:value-of select="@obsoleted-by"/></a>. </i>
        </xsl:if>
    </dd>
  </xsl:for-each>
  </dl>
</xsl:for-each>
</body>
</html>
</xsl:template>
```

The index in Example 16–51 is relatively simple compared to the previous one; this is where we present full descriptions for each index. Note the use of a named template to create a description of the RFC. This was done to keep the source more readable.

In Example 16–52, we present the information we want to know about each RFC, depending on what has been made available.

Running this stylesheet produces the HTML document as shown in the two screenshots in Figures 16–4 and 16–5; the first screenshot showing the upper part of the document, the second the lower part.

16.3.2.2 Index to XBEL conversion

In addition to having the RFC index available as an HTML document, it would be convenient to have it as part of my bookmarks. I use the

Example 16–52. The RFC index to HTML stylesheet (6 of 7)

```
<xsl:template name = "rfc-description">
  <xsl:choose>
    <xsl:when test = "title">
      <xsl:value-of select = "title" />.
    </xsl:when>
    <xsl:when test = "nickname">
      <xsl:value-of select = "nickname" />.
    </xsl:when>
  </xsl:choose>

  <xsl:choose>
    <xsl:when test = "count(author) = 1">
      By: <xsl:value-of select = "author"/>.
    </xsl:when>
    <xsl:when test = "author">
      By: <xsl:apply-templates select = "author"/>
    </xsl:when>
  </xsl:choose>

  <xsl:apply-templates select = "date"/>
</xsl:template>
```

Example 16–53. The RFC index to HTML stylesheet (7 of 7)

```
<xsl:template match = "number | nickname | keywords | standard"/>

<xsl:template match = "date">
  <xsl:apply-templates/>.
</xsl:template>

<xsl:template match = "author">
  <xsl:apply-templates/>,
</xsl:template>

<xsl:template match = "author [ position() = last() ]">
  and <xsl:apply-templates/>.
</xsl:template>

</xsl:stylesheet>
```

Opera browser almost exclusively, so I would prefer Opera bookmarks that I could just import into the browser bookmarks. Creating an Opera

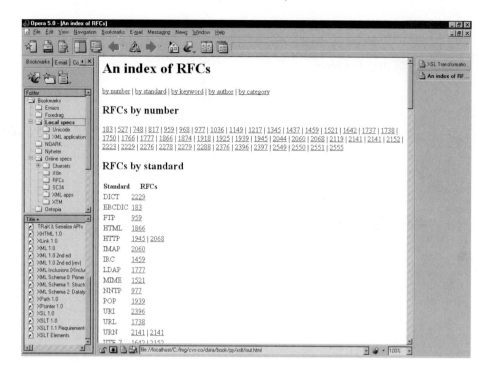

Figure 16–4   The top of the RFC index

bookmarks file with XSLT is tricky, since it has a non-XML notation, and in any case, that would only be useful for Opera users.

The solution to this problem is of course to translate the bookmarks to XBEL, and then use XBEL software to do the translation to the browser-specific formats. Doing this translation with XSLT is relatively easy, as we will see. We will create a folder for each category, and then add individual bookmarks for each RFC in the folder.

As you can see in Example 16–54, this XML to XML translation was entirely straightforward, and converting to XML is really no different from converting to HTML when using XSLT.

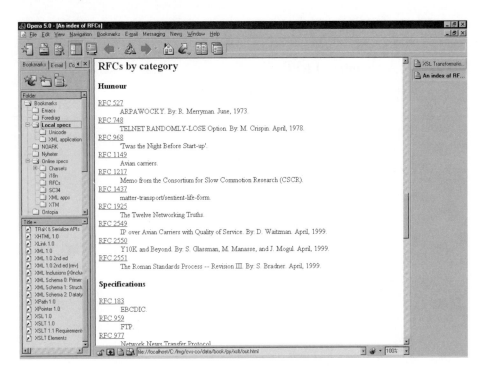

Figure 16–5   The lower part of the RFC index

16.4 | XSLT performance

In general, there are two ways to achieve good performance with XSLT: designing the larger processing application correctly and writing efficient XSLT stylesheets.[1] The first approach has to do with how you configure your processor, which processor you use, and how you choose to put together the entire processing application. The second one has to do with making sure that you write your stylesheets in such a way that they execute efficiently.

---

1.   This section owes much to Michael Kay's posting to the XSL mailing list about XSLT performance on 2000–06–02.

Example 16–54. The RFC index to XBEL translator

```
<xsl:stylesheet xmlns:xsl="http://www.w3.org/1999/XSL/Transform"
                version="1.0">

  <xsl:output indent="yes" doctype-system=
            "http://www.python.org/topics/xml/dtds/xbel-1.0.dtd"
    doctype-public="+//IDN python.org//DTD XML Bookmark Exchange
                    Language 1.0//EN//XML" />

  <xsl:template match = "rfc-index">
    <xsl:variable name = "prefix"
                  select = "string(sites / site / prefix)" />

    <xsl:variable name = "suffix"
                  select = "string(sites / site / suffix)" />

    <xbel>
      <title>RFCs</title>
      <desc>Collection of useful RFCs</desc>

      <xsl:for-each select = "category">
        <folder>
          <title><xsl:value-of select = "name" /></title>

          <xsl:for-each select = "rfc">
            <bookmark href="{$prefix}{number}{$suffix}">
              <title>RFC <xsl:value-of select = "number" />
              <xsl:choose>
                <xsl:when test = "nickname">
                - <xsl:value-of select = "nickname" />
                </xsl:when>
                <xsl:when test = "title">
                - <xsl:value-of select = "title" />
                </xsl:when>
              </xsl:choose></title>
            </bookmark>
          </xsl:for-each>
        </folder>
      </xsl:for-each>
    </xbel>

  </xsl:template>

</xsl:stylesheet>
```

This two-sided approach is not all that different from how one approaches performance in general. You start by creating a general architecture that can achieve good performance, and when this has been done, you make sure that the critical parts of your code are as efficient as they can be.

Below follows a general list of rules of thumb that may help you to design efficient XSLT-based applications. Few of these rules are really XSLT-specific, and most of them really apply to all kinds of systems, but have here been applied to XSLT to make them more concrete.

- Use a fast XSLT processor. Of course, other considerations than the speed of the processor are usually important, but this is the easiest way to improve performance.

- One thing that tends to cause problems for XSLT processors is that they must build the entire document tree before they start processing. With big documents this often causes the computer to start thrashing,[1] which generally results in very bad performance. One way to avoid this can be to split your documents into smaller pieces and process each piece by itself. Since this avoids thrashing it can be much faster than doing it all at once.

- Keep the size of the output document down, if possible. One elegant (and practical!) way of achieving this with HTML output is to produce HTML documents that use CSS stylesheets for their layout. This can dramatically reduce the size of the HTML,

---

1.   This refers to something that happens when the virtual memory of a computer is overloaded. All modern operating systems allow applications to allocate more memory than is physically available in the hardware. Any excess memory is then kept on disk, and much ingenuity is expended on making sure that the operating system only puts little-used memory on disk. As long as the memory is indeed little-used this works fine, but sometimes applications allocate so much memory and access so much of it so often that the algorithm fails. This is called *thrashing*, because the result is that the computer spends most of its time swapping memory back and forth between memory and the disk.

make the stylesheet much more readable, and make it easier for other people to customize certain aspects of the presentation.

■ It may be difficult to write very complex translations efficiently, and this may result in inefficient stylesheets. One way to avoid this problem (and at the same time to make the task easier) is to do the translation in several stages, since this will often result in the stylesheets for each stage becoming simpler.

■ When many translations are performed in series, various tricks can be used to improve performance. One is to keep the XSLT processor in memory throughout the series of translations instead of reloading it for each run. Another is to compile the stylesheet (if the processor allows this), or at least to keep it loaded between runs.

If you designed your processing application according to the guidelines above but its performance still isn't good enough, the rules below can be helpful in making your stylesheets more efficient.

■ Template matching is generally costly, so try to avoid it by using `xsl:value-of` and `xsl:for-each` where this seems natural. Note that this has the side benefit of making your stylesheets more readable.

A corollary to this rule is that you should try to avoid complex and expensive tests in template selectors. Instead, make a more general template rule and then use `xsl:choose` inside it.

■ Avoid computing the same results more than once. For example, when computing an expensive XPath expression several times within the same template rule, do it once and assign the result to a variable instead. You can then refer to this variable whenever you need the results.

A related trick is to avoid sorting more than once. Instead, create a sorted result tree fragment and then convert it back to source tree nodes using the `node-set` extension function.

- Using `xsl:key` to look up values can speed up your stylesheet considerably.

- Don't use `xsl:number` unless you have to. It is generally much more expensive than, for example, the `position()` function.

- Avoid `//foo`, since this requires the XSLT engine to search through the entire XML document to find all `foo` elements in it.

- Be careful when using the `preceding[-sibling]` and `following[-sibling]`, since if you traverse the entire length of the axis for every node in a set, this will generally have $O(n^2)$ performance. This is very similar to the text accumulation problem described in 9.6, "Speed," on page 322.

Using XSLT in applications

X SLT is not very well integrated with programming languages used to build applications, something that sets it apart from the event- and tree-based processing approaches. XSLT stylesheets do one thing, and one thing only: transformation. This, however, they do far better than its competitors, and because of this, it is often desirable to use XSLT in larger software systems that need to do transformations.

A natural way to do this would be to integrate XSLT with the programming language used to build the larger software system, so that XSLT and, say, Python code could be freely mixed. However, current programming languages (except Lisp, of course) have no means of extending the features of the language itself, which means that other solutions must be found. In the non-extensible languages, the solution is to integrate an XSLT engine with other applications through its API.

Some situations where it may be attractive to embed an XSLT engine in a larger application are:

- Web publishing. Often, an XML data source needs to be translated into HTML for publishing on the Web, whether statically or dynamically. Typically, the publishing application is a larger system which does many things besides just translating XML to HTML, and the XSLT engine will thus be only one component among many.

■ All kinds of transformation programs may use an XSLT engine to do parts of the transformation, but perhaps control the processing from software, depending on configuration. In some cases the transformation program may also convert the input to XML or serialize the output to something other than XML.

■ Applications that wish to support several different XML formats for the same application area may use an XSLT engine to transform the formats into a common notation. This avoids having to write many different structure builders, and may also make it easier for third parties to add support for new formats.

There are already several XSLT-based frameworks for building dynamic XML-based Web applications, the best-known of which is probably Cocoon. Some of these are rather thin wrappers around XSLT that basically associate various types of XML documents with specific XSLT stylesheets and automatically run the conversions whenever the XML documents are requested. Others provide much more functionality in addition to setting up and running XSLT transformations.

Most of the XSLT processors have APIs which can be used to embed the processors in other applications. In general, these APIs usually have some or all of the following functionality:

■ Allowing client software to set up, run, and control a transformation by specifying the input, the stylesheet(s), any parameters, and by capturing the output.

■ Allowing stylesheets to be reused between runs, either by caching the parsed stylesheet structure or by compiling the stylesheet into source code.

■ Allowing third parties to implement extension functions and element types which can then be used in stylesheets.

■ Controlling input and output, by building the source tree from a data source and capturing the result as a tree to either serialize it in a particular way or use it directly without serialization.

17.1 | The XSLT processor APIs

This section describes the APIs of some of the most important XSLT processors, showing how to embed them in your own applications. It covers the two processors available in Python: 4XSLT and Sablotron, leaving the Java processors for Chapter 21, "Using XSLT in Java applications," on page 794. In Python, there is no standardized API to XSLT processors, but in Java there is the JAXP API, the XSLT parts of which are described in 21.1, "Using JAXP," on page 796.

17.1.1 Using 4XSLT

The 4XSLT processor consists of three main conceptual components: the reader, the processor, and the writer, as shown in Figure 17–1.

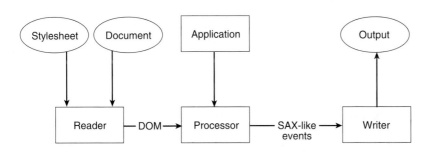

Figure 17–1   The anatomy of 4XSLT

The `Processor` class is the XSLT engine itself, and this is the class that the application using 4XSLT will interact with. The `Processor` uses a `Reader` to read in the stylesheet and the input document. It has a default reader implementation, which creates DOM trees in the

Domlette DOM implementation written specially for 4XSLT (it has been mentioned before). 4DOM will use cDomlette if available, otherwise pDomlette will be used. Applications can provide their own `Reader` implementations.

The `Processor` will, after having read in the input document and the stylesheet(s), do the XSLT processing and produce output that is passed to the `Writer` object, in the form of SAX-like events. The default `Writer` will serialize the output to a file object, but applications can provide their own `Writer` implementations.

The next sections will present the `Processor`, `Writer`, and `Reader` interfaces.

In addition to embedding 4XSLT in applications, it is possible to write extension functions and element types that can be used from XSLT stylesheets. Sections 17.1.1.4, "Writing extension functions," on page 650 and 17.1.1.5, "Writing extension element types," on page 652 describe how to do this.

17.1.1.1 The `Processor` class

The 4XSLT engine itself is represented by the `Processor` class in the `xml.xslt.Processor` module. This is the class you use to set up and run transformations. Note that the `Processor` uses two readers: one for the stylesheet(s) and one for the input document.

The `Processor` class has the following methods:

`__init__()`
    Instantiates a new processor ready for use.

`appendStylesheetUri(uri)`
    This method makes the processor load the stylesheet from the given `uri` and use it when running a transformation. The method can be called several times, and the processor will use the union of the stylesheets.

`appendStylesheetString(string, baseUri = "")`

Registers a stylesheet with the processor, the stylesheet being represented as a string in the `string` parameter. The optional `baseUri` argument can hold the base URI of the stylesheet.

`appendStylesheetNode(node, baseUri = "")`

This method also registers a stylesheet with the processor, but the `node` parameter holds the stylesheet represented as a DOM tree. This can be useful when the stylesheet is dynamically created or loaded from a source that is not addressable by a URI.

`runUri(uri, ignorePis = 0, topLevelParams = {},`
`writer = None, outputStream = sys.stdout)`

Runs a transformation with the registered stylesheets on the document referred to by the `uri` parameter. If `ignorePis` is `true`, the processor will not load stylesheets referred to by `xsl-stylesheet` PIs in the source document. The `topLevelParams` parameter holds a dictionary that maps `(namespace uri, local name)` parameter names to parameter values. Parameters that have no namespace will have a namespace URI of `' '`.

The result tree will be passed to the `writer` parameter as a series of events. The `writer` object must implement the `Writer` interface, which is defined below. The output will be written to the `outputStream`, which must be a file-like object.

The function will also return the result tree as a string.

`runString(string, ignorePis = 0,`
`topLevelParams = {}, writer = None,`
`baseUri = '', outputStream = sys.stdout)`

Just as `runUri`, except that the source document is now held in the `string` parameter as a string. The `baseUri` holds the base URI of the document.

```
runNode(node, ignorePis = 0, topLevelParams = {},
    writer = None, baseUri = '',
    outputStream = sys.stdout)
```
Just as `runString`, except that the source document is represented as a DOM node.

`setStylesheetReader(reader)`
Sets the `Reader` implementation used to read stylesheets.

`setDocumentReader(reader)`
Sets the `Reader` implementation used to read documents.

`registerExtensionModules(modules)`
Registers a set of Python modules containing implementations of extension element types and functions with the processor, so that the element types and functions are made available to stylesheets. The `modules` parameter is a list of module names. The modules are loaded and their contents registered. For more details on this, see 17.1.1.5, "Writing extension element types," on page 652.

Example 17–1 is a tiny application that takes two command-line arguments: the source document and the stylesheet file name, and runs an XSLT transformation with these, sending the output to standard out.

Example 17–1. A simple 4XSLT wrapper

```
import sys
from xml.xslt.Processor import Processor

proc = Processor()
proc.appendStylesheetUri(sys.argv[1])
print proc.runUri(sys.argv[2])
```

This example can be used from the command line in this way:
`python run4xslt.py style.xslt input.xml`.

17.1.1.2 The `Writer` interface

The `Writer` interface is implemented by a handler that receives the result tree as it is being built by the XSLT processor. The tree is received as a set of SAX-like events, but the events are relatively XSLT-specific and therefore are rather SAX-inspired than really SAX-conformant. Just as with SAX, it is the order of the events that defines the structure of the tree.

There is no default base class for `Writer` implementations, so all the methods below must be implemented.

`text(text, escapeOutput=1)`
> Represents a text node in the result tree. The `escapeOutput` parameter controls whether the content should be escaped or not.

`attribute(name, value, namespace='')`
> Represents an attribute node in the result tree. The attributes of an element, if any, will arrive as the first calls after the `startElement` event, before all other calls.
>
> The `name` parameter is the qualified name of the attribute, `value` is the value of the attribute, and `namespace` is the namespace URI of the attribute.

`startElement(name, namespace='', extraNss={})`
> Signals the beginning of an element node in the result tree. The `name` parameter is the qualified name of the element, `namespace` is the namespace URI of the element, and `extraNss` is a dictionary of the namespace declarations in effect at this point.

`endElement(name)`
> Signals the end of an element node in the result tree. The `name` parameter is the qualified name of the element. Namespace information is not available in the parameter list, so it must have been stored away internally in the `Writer` in order to be accessible.

`processingInstruction(target, data)`

    Represents a processing instruction in the result tree. The `target` and `data` parameters hold the PI target and data as strings.

`comment(body)`

    Represents a comment in the result tree, the content of the comment being held in the `body` parameter as a string.

As you can see, the interface is a bit different from SAX, but not so different for it to be impossible to map from one to the other. Example 17–2 shows a simple `Writer` implementation that writes out a trace of the method calls it receives, and a simple test program.

When this application is run with the stylesheet from Example 16–8, the output is as shown in Example 17–3.

4XSLT contains a number of `Writer` implementations in the `xml.xslt` package, which are listed below. The arguments listed for each are their constructor arguments.

`DomWriter.DomWriter(ownerDoc = None)`

    This writer builds a DOM tree from the events passed to it. By default it builds a 4DOM tree, but this can be modified by passing `Document` nodes from other implementations. (Written by Alexandre Fayolle.)

`HtmlWriter.HtmlWriter(outputParams, stream = None)`

    Writes HTML output to the file-like argument `stream`, which must support both the `write` and the `flush` methods. The `stream` parameter defaults to a `cStringIO` object. The `outputParams` parameter holds the parameters to the `xsl:output` element in an `OutputParameters` object. This class is described below.

`NullWriter.NullWriter(outputParams = None,`
    `stream = None)`

    This writer does nothing, and is merely useful as a default base class for writers and as a writer that does nothing.

Example 17–2. A simple `Writer` implementation

```
import sys
from xml.xslt.Processor import Processor

class TraceWriter:

    def text(self, text, escapeOutput=1):
        print "text('%s', %s)" % (text, escapeOutput)

    def attribute(self, name, value, namespace=''):
        print "attribute('%s', '%s', '%s')" % \
              (name, value, namespace)

    def processingInstruction(self, target, data):
        print "processingInstruction('%s', '%s')" % (target, data)

    def comment(self, body):
        print "comment('%s')" % body

    def startElement(self, name, namespace='', extraNss=None):
        print "startElement('%s', '%s', %s)" % \
              (name, namespace, extraNss)

    def endElement(self, name):
        print "endElement('%s')" % name

    def getResult(self):
        return None

proc = Processor()
proc.appendStylesheetUri(sys.argv[1])
print proc.runUri(sys.argv[2], 1, {}, TraceWriter())
```

`PlainTextWriter.PlainTextWriter(outputParams, stream = None)`
Writes plain text output to the `stream` argument.

`XmlWriter.XmlWriter(outputParams, stream = None)`
Writes the events it receives out as XML output to the `stream` argument.

Example 17–3. `TraceWriter` output

```
startElement('title', '', {})
text('An example HTML document', 1)
endElement('title')
startElement('script', '', {})
text('
    if (1 < 2)
        document.write("You have an old browser!");
    ', 1)
endElement('script')
startElement('p', '', {})
text('
    This is just a simple document.', 1)
startElement('br', '', {})
endElement('br')
text('
    Wow! A second line!
    ', 1)
endElement('p')
None
```

In addition to these `Writer` implementations, the `xml.saxtools.xsltutils` package contains a `SAXTextWriter(content_handler)` class, which takes a single `ContentHandler` in its constructor and then passes events to it.

The `OutputParameters` class lives in the `xml.xslt` module and has the attributes listed below, all of which contain string values from the attributes of the `xsl:output` element.

- method
- version
- encoding
- omitXmlDeclaration
- standalone
- doctypeSystem
- doctypePublic
- mediaType

- `cdataSectionElements`, which holds a list of the element-type names
- `indent`

17.1.1.3 The Reader interface

As mentioned above, the `Reader` is used by the `Processor` class to read documents and stylesheets into the processor. There is a default base class called `Reader` in the `Ft.Lib.ReaderBase` package, which has the methods listed below. Note that this `Reader` architecture is a close relative of the DOM reader described in 12.1.2, "Loading an XML document," on page 438.

`clone()`
> Returns a copy of the reader.

`fromStream(stream, ownerDoc=None)`
> Reads a document from the file-like object `stream` and returns the `Document` node representing it.

`releaseNode(dom)`
> Called by the processor in Python 1.5 to tell the reader that it can now dismantle this document, so that its memory is released. In Python 2.0, this is handled by garbage collection.

`fromString(st, ownerDoc=None)`
> The same as `fromStream`, but reads from a string instead of a file-like object.

`fromUri(uri, ownerDoc=None)`
> The same as `fromStream`, but reads from the given URI instead of a file-like object.

Example 17–4 shows a reader implementation that builds 4DOM trees.

Example 17–4. A 4DOM reader

```
from Ft.Lib.ReaderBase import Reader
from xml.dom.ext.reader.Sax2 import Reader
from xml.dom.ext import ReleaseNode

class DOMReader:

    def fromStream(self, stream, ownerDoc=None):
        return Reader().fromStream(stream, ownerDoc)

    def releaseNode(self, dom):
        ReleaseNode(dom)
```

Only the `fromStream` and `releaseNode` methods need to be implemented, since the default base class implements `fromString` and `fromUri` based on `fromStream`.

17.1.1.4 Writing extension functions

To add support for extension functions, write a Python module that contains the functions and has a variable named `ExtFunctions`, which maps XPath function names to the Python functions that implement them. The names must be tuples of the form `(nsuri, localname)`.

The Python functions will have the same arguments as their XPath counterparts, except that a first argument named `context`, holding the XPath context, is added. The functions also return the same values as their XPath counterparts. In 4XPath, numbers are represented as Python numbers, strings as Python strings, booleans using the `BooleanType` class in the `xml.xpath.Boolean` package, and node sets as Python lists of DOM nodes.

Example 17–5 gives the source code for a simple module implementing the `get-current-date` function, which returns the current date as a `'YYYY-MM-DD'` string.

In order to create XPath functions (and XSLT elements) that make use of the context, it is necessary to use the `context` object. This object

Example 17–5. An XPath extension function module

```
import time

def get_current_date(context):
    return time.strftime("%Y-%m-%d", time.localtime(time.time()))

LMG_NS_URI = 'http://garshol.priv.no/symbolic/'

ExtFunctions = {
    (LMG_NS_URI, 'get-current-date') : get_current_date
}
```

has a number of attributes, in which the various properties of the XPath context can be found, as well as one method. These are listed below.

`node`
This is the context node, as a DOM object. Modify this attribute in order to change the context node.

`position`
This is the context position, as a Python integer.

`size`
This is the context size, as a Python integer.

`varBindings`
This is a dictionary that maps variable names, in the form of `(nsuri, lname)` tuples, to variable values.

`processorNss`
This is a dictionary that maps the namespace prefixes currently in scope to namespace URIs. What this is depends on the context in which XPath is used.

`nss()`
This method returns a dictionary holding the namespace prefixes in effect at the context node.

The `xml.xpath.CoreFunctions` module contains all the built-in XPath functions as Python functions. All are named using camel case instead of hyphens, so that `string` becomes `String`, and `namespace-uri` becomes `NamespaceUri`. These functions can be very useful to support implementing extension functions, especially the functions used to convert values from one type to another.

17.1.1.5 Writing extension element types

Similar to XPath extension functions, extension element types must be defined in a module that has an attribute named `ExtElements`. This attribute must hold a dictionary mapping element-type names, as `(nsuri, localname)` pairs, to classes derived from `xml.xslt.XsltElement`. This class is derived from the Domlette element class, so each element will be a DOM `Element` node, in addition to being an XSLT extension element type. This means that the element implementation can use itself as a starting point for traversals of the stylesheet tree.

Extension element types must implement the following API:

`__init__(doc, uri, localName, prefix, baseUri)`

The constructor receives a number of parameters that must be passed on to the `xml.xslt.XsltElement` constructor. The `doc` argument holds the stylesheet `Document` node, the `uri` argument holds the namespace URI, the `localName` is the local name of the element type, `prefix` is the namespace prefix, and `baseUri` is the base URI of the element node.

Note that when the constructor is called, the DOM structure has not been fully built yet, so it is not yet safe to attempt to pull information out of the DOM tree.

`setup()`

This method is called after the DOM structure has been fully built and before the processor has started processing. It is mainly useful for pulling information out of the DOM tree and storing it internally for use in the `instantiate` method.

The method should always contain the statement `self.__dict__['_nss'] = xml.dom.ext.GetAllNs(self)` so that the `instantiate` method can update the set of namespace declarations in the XSLT context.

In order to support attribute value templates, the method should instantiate objects of the `AttributeValueTemplate` class from the `xml.xslt` package to represent them. Examples of how to do this are found below.

`instantiate(context, processor)`

This method is called to instantiate the element types as nodes in the result tree. The `context` argument holds the XSLT context object, while `processor` holds the XSLT processor. Before passing the context on to its children, the method should make a copy and do `the_copy.setNamespaces(self._nss)` in order to update the set of namespaces in effect in the XSLT context.

The method must return a tuple containing the original `context` in unmodified form as the first item. The rest of the tuple can contain anything, which allows you to define sets of related element types that collect information for one another.

Note that classes derived from `XsltElement` can have a class attribute `legalAttrs` holding the names of the allowed attributes of that element. The XSLT processor will use this to verify that no illegal attributes appear on the element.

Example 17–6 shows an extension element type called `debug`, which appends the string value of an XPath expression to a file given by name. This can be used to produce debug information from stylesheets without having to put it into the output.

Just as with XPath functions, some XSLT element types may wish to access the context. In 4XSLT, this is represented using a context object of a class that is derived from the 4XPath context class, so it has

Example 17–6. An XSLT extension element type

```
import string, os
import xml.dom.ext
from xml.xslt import XsltElement, XSL_NAMESPACE
from xml.xslt.AttributeValueTemplate import AttributeValueTemplate
from xml.xpath import CoreFunctions, XPathParser

class DebugElement(XsltElement):

    legalAttrs = ('select', 'filename')

    def setup(self):
        fname = self.getAttributeNS('', 'filename')
        select = self.getAttributeNS('', 'select')
        self.__dict__['_nss'] = xml.dom.ext.GetAllNs(self)
        self.__dict__['_filename'] = AttributeValueTemplate(fname)
        parser = XPathParser.XPathParser()
        self.__dict__['_select'] = parser.parseExpression(select)

    def instantiate(self, context, processor):
        orig_state = context.copy()
        context.setNamespaces(self._nss)

        filename = self._filename.evaluate(context)
        value = CoreFunctions.String(context,
                                     self._select.evaluate(context))

        outf = open(filename, 'a')
        outf.write(value + '\n')
        outf.close()

        context.set(orig_state)
        return (context,)

ExtElements = {
    ('http://garshol.priv.no/symbolic/', 'debug'): DebugElement
    }
```

all the attributes and methods of the 4XPath context object, adding those listed below.

`currentNode`

> Holds the XSLT current node, which, as mentioned earlier, is distinct from the XPath context node.

`stylesheet`

> This holds a reference to the `Document` node of the stylesheet that instantiated the current instruction.

`mode`

> The mode with which the template currently being instantiated was matched.

`documents`

> A dictionary mapping URIs to document nodes. This is used by the `document` XPath function.

`rtfs`

> A list holding all result tree fragments created during processing. This is used to release them after the stylesheet has been fully processed, so if you create any result tree fragments, make sure you put them in this list.

17.1.2 *Sablotron*

Sablotron is an XSLT processor written in C++ by the Ginger Alliance and released as open source. The processor is available as C++ source with a C API, as a standalone binary on many platforms, as well as integrated into many programming languages. At the time of writing there are two modules available that provide Python APIs to Sablotron. This section only covers the one known as Sab-pyth, written by Günther Radestock, since that was the most mature at the time of writing.

The author of Sab-pyth has explained that he made Sab-pyth's APIs mimic the Sablotron APIs as directly as possible, because he did not fully understand the Sablotron APIs and found this the easiest approach.

This explains the strangeness of some of the APIs, and this is also why I have been unable to fully explain all parts of the interfaces.

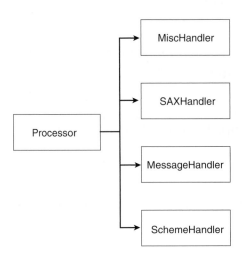

Figure 17–2   The anatomy of Sab-pyth

Sab-pyth provides a rather complete API, whose structure is outlined in Figure 17–2. The different objects shown in the diagram are explained below. Sab-pyth has no provisions for implementing XPath extension functions or XSLT extension element types.

Processor
 This class represents the Sablotron XSLT processor itself, and is used by applications to set up and run transformations.

SAXHandler
 This is the handler that receives the result tree from the processor and serializes it somehow. The result tree is passed in the form of SAX-like events, which are nearly, but not quite, SAX-conformant.

MessageHandler
 This handler receives error and log messages from the processor.

SchemeHandler
> This handler is used by the processor to read URL schemes it cannot handle internally. It defaults to use the Python `urllib`, so normally there is no need to use this handler. It is very useful, however, for supporting protocols not supported by `urllib`.

MiscHandler
> This handler is used for various callbacks that do not belong in the other interfaces. At the moment it only receives information about the document after it has been fully processed.

17.1.2.1 The Processor class

As noted above, the `Processor` class represents the XSLT processor and is the starting point of the API. It lives in the `Sablot` module, together with the other classes of the API. `Processor` instances are created using the `CreateProcessor` function, taking no arguments, and have the methods listed below.

run(stylesheet, input, result, params, args)
> This method runs an XSLT transformation with the given stylesheet, input document, and result file. The `stylesheet`, `input`, and `result` arguments all contain URIs specifying the location of the stylesheet, input document, and result, respectively.
>
> The processor has built-in support for the `file` URI scheme as well as for a scheme known as `arg`, which works by means of the `args` parameter. This parameter holds a list of (name, buffer) values. Thus, if the first argument is `arg:style`, it will cause the processor to look through the `arg` list to find the buffer with the name `style`.
>
> The `params` argument is a list of (name, value) tuples specifying the values of XSLT parameters.

regHandler(type, handler)

This method is used to register handler objects on the `Processor`. The first argument, `type`, holds an integer constant defining the handler type, while the second, `handler`, holds the handler object itself. The list of handler type constants is given below.

unregHandler(type, handler)

This method unregisters a handler. I am uncertain as to what purpose this method serves. It may have to do with memory management.

clearError()

Clears error flags set internally in the processor after an error has occurred.

setBase(base)

Sets the default base URI used to resolve relative URIs.

setBaseForScheme(scheme, base)

Seems to be used to set the default base URI for a specific URI scheme.

setLog(filename, level)

This method can be used to make Sablotron produce a log of its activities in a log file. The log mainly contains a brief summary of the files involved in the run and some simple performance statistics. Its purpose is not clear to me, and as far as I can tell, the `level` parameter has no effect.

The handler type constants are defined at the top level of the `Sablot` module:

- HLR_MESSAGE for the message handler,
- HLR_MISC for the miscellaneous handler,
- HLR_SCHEME for the scheme handler,
- HLR_SAX for the SAX handler.

Example 17–7 shows a little application that wraps Sab-pyth in a simple command-line application which simply runs a stylesheet writing output to a file.

Example 17–7. A simple Sablotron runner

```
import sys
import Sablot

def fileurl(filename):
    return "file://" + filename

class TestHandler:

    def makeCode(self, severity, facility, code):
        print "makeCode", severity, facility, code

    def log(self, code, level, fields):
        print "log", code, level, fields

    def error(self, code, level, fields):
        print "error", code, level, fields

processor = Sablot.CreateProcessor()
processor.regHandler(Sablot.HLR_MESSAGE, TestHandler())
processor.run(fileurl(sys.argv[1]), fileurl(sys.argv[2]),
            fileurl(sys.argv[3]), [], [])
```

17.1.2.2 The SAXHandler interface

This interface can be used to intercept the Sablotron output and do something else with it besides simply writing it to a file. Although the interface is called SAXHandler, it is not fully SAX compliant, though it is close. The SAXHandler interface consists of the methods listed below.

startDocument()
    This method is called when output starts, before any of the other methods in the interface. Like its SAX counterpart, it is mostly useful for initialization of reusable handler implementations.

`endDocument()`

This is `startDocument()`'s twin that is called when processing is complete and the entire document has been output. It is mostly used for clean-up actions and possibly also for resolution of references in the output.

`startElement(name, atts)`

This method is called to signal the beginning of an element. Names that have no namespace are reported as simple strings, while those that have are reported as `'nsuri`lname'`, using a backquote character as the separator.

`endElement(name)`

This method signals the end of an element.

`characters(data)`

This event represents character data nodes in the result tree.

`processingInstruction(target, data)`

This method is used to pass on processing instruction nodes in the result tree.

`startNamespace(prefix, uri)`

This method is called before a `startElement` event in order to signal that a new namespace prefix is declared within the element. The `prefix` argument holds the namespace prefix, while the `uri` argument holds the corresponding namespace URI.

`endNamespace(prefix)`

This method is called after an `endElement` event to signal the end of a namespace prefix mapping.

`comment(content)`

This method is called to pass on comments in the result tree.

Example 17–8 gives the source code for a `SAXHandler` that translates `SAXHandler` events into SAX 2.0 `ContentHandler` events.

Example 17–8. A SAX adapter

```
import string

class SAXHandler2ContentHandler:

    def __init__(self, content_handler, lex_handler = None):
        self._content_handler = content_handler

        # shortcuts
        self.startDocument= self._content_handler.startDocument
        self.endDocument  = self._content_handler.endDocument
        self.characters   = self._content_handler.characters
        self.endNamespace = self._content_handler.endPrefixMapping
        self.startNamespace=self._content_handler.startPrefixMapping
        self.processingInstruction = \
                        self._content_handler.processingInstruction

        if lex_handler:
            self.comment = lex_handler.comment

    def startElement(self, name, atts):
        self._content_handler.startElementNS(self.makeName(name),
                                             None, atts)

    def endElement(self, name):
        self._content_handler.endElementNS(self.makeName(name),None)

    def comment(self, content):
        pass

    def makeName(self, name):
        pair = string.split(name, "`")
        if len(pair) == 1:
            return (None, name)
        else:
            return tuple(pair)
```

17.1.2.3 The `SchemeHandler` interface

As mentioned earlier, this interface is used by Sab-pyth to read URLs that use schemes Sablotron does not understand. The default implementation that uses the Python `urllib` may be instructive to look at. The interface has the methods listed below.

`open(scheme, rest)`
> Opens a URI and returns a unique numeric identifier that serves as a handle to this specific URI. Sab-pyth will use this handle as an argument in later calls to this handler. The `scheme` argument is the URI scheme, for example `'http'`, while the `rest` argument is the rest of the URI, minus the colon, for example `'//www.garshol.priv.no/'`.

`getAll(scheme, rest, bytecount)`
> Opens the given URI and returns its entire contents as a string. This does not require a handle of any sort. It seems that `bytecount` can be safely ignored.

`get(handle, bytecount)`
> Reads the given number of bytes from the URI represented by the given handle and returns the data as a string.

`put(handle, buffer)`
> Writes data back to the URI if at all possible.

`close(handle)`
> Closes the connection to the URI represented by the given handle.

If any errors occur, the `Sablot.SchemeHandlerError` exception can be raised with an appropriate error code. The `Sablot` module contains a number of constants with error codes of different kinds.

17.1.2.4 The `MessageHandler` interface

This interface receives various kinds of notifications from the processor. The methods of the interface are listed below.

`makeCode(severity, facility, code)`
   This method is called by Sab-pyth to create an external code that is then passed on to the other two methods. It seems that its primary use is to allow applications to map internal Sablotron codes to codes that they themselves prefer.

`log(code, level, fields)`
   Used by Sab-pyth for logging messages. Sab-pyth produces a large number of messages during runs, most of which seem to relate to performance statistics. The `code` argument is the value returned by the previous `makeCode` call. The `level` argument indicates the importance of the log message; 1 seems to be the most common value.

   The `fields` argument is a list of strings containing log message fields as strings of the form `'field:contents'`, where contents may well contain colons. Common fields are `msgtype`, `code`, `module`, `URI`, `line`, `node`, and `msg`.

`error(code, level, fields)`
   This is the same as the `log` method, except that it is used to report errors that occur during stylesheet execution.

17.1.2.5 The `MiscHandler` interface

This interface has a single callback: `documentInfo(contentType, encoding)`, which is called after processing is complete. It holds the content type of the output and the character encoding used in the output. This defaults to UTF-8, but can be overridden by the `xsl:output` method of stylesheets.

17.2 | Larger examples of XSLT programming

17.2.1 Some XPath utility functions

In this module we present some simple XPath functions that can be quite useful in many contexts. These functions are also provided by the Saxon XSLT engine, which gave the inspiration for them. The functions provided by this module are:

`distinct(nodeset)`

   This function accepts a node set and filters it, so that after filtering it only contains nodes that have string values different from one another. With this function available, writing the RFC index stylesheet of Examples 16–47 to 16–53 would have required much less ingenuity, because the `distinct` function could have been used to filter the standards, keywords, and authors.

`split(string, delim?)`

   The `split` function splits its `string` argument by the delimiter contained in its optional `delim` argument. If `delim` is not provided, the string is split by whitespace. The return value is a node set consisting of text nodes that each hold one part of the string. The text nodes are created by the function in order to be able to represent a list of strings in XPath.

`range(low, high)`

   This function returns a node set containing the numbers from `low`, inclusive, to `high`, exclusive. It is mainly intended to be used for looping, as in `<xsl:for-each select="range(1, 10)"/>`.

`if(condition, v1, v2)`

   This function can be used inside XPath expressions to return different values depending on the result of a condition. If `condition` is `true`, `v1` is returned, otherwise, `v2` is returned. The function will evaluate all three of its arguments, but can still be a useful shorthand in many cases.

One of the major advantages of if is that it can often be used to avoid having to write xsl:if instructions, thus making stylesheets much shorter and more readable.

These four functions are all implemented by the module in Examples 17–9 to 17–14. They should illustrate the major principles of writing XPath functions that work with node sets, strings, booleans, and numbers.

Example 17–9. The xpathutils module (1 of 6)

```
import string
from xml.dom.Text import Text
from xml.xpath.CoreFunctions import String, Number, Boolean

def distinct(context, nodeset):
    if type(nodeset) != type([]):
        raise Exception("'distinct' parameter must be of type "
                        "node-set!")

    nodes = {}
    for node in nodeset:
        nodes[String(context, node)] = node

    return nodes.values()
```

The nodeset argument (Example 17–9) must be a list of DOM nodes, so we simply check whether it is a list and raise an Exception if it is not. This is the style used by 4XPath in its built-in functions. If it is indeed a list, we loop over it using for. The nodes are hashed on their string values, produced using the XPath String function, available from the CoreFunctions module. The nodes are then easily produced from the nodes dictionary using the values method.

The function in Example 17–10 does not need to verify the type of its argument, since it converts it to a string using the String function, which will always produce some string representation. Since we need the Document node of the document in order to be able to create Text nodes belonging to the correct document, we loop upwards from the context node. The rest is simple; we split using the built-in Python function of the same name and accumulate the nodes in a list as we go.

Example 17–10. The xpathutils module (2 of 6)

```
def split(context, str, delim = None):
    doc = context.node
    while doc.parentNode:
        doc = doc.parentNode

    nodeset = []
    for token in string.split(String(context, str), delim):
        nodeset.append(doc.createTextNode(token))

    return nodeset
```

The function in Example 17–11 is so similar to split that there seems little point in commenting on it. Note, however, that numbers must be converted to strings before they are used to create nodes.

Example 17–11. The xpathutils module (3 of 6)

```
def range(context, lo, hi):
    doc = context.node
    while doc.parentNode:
        doc = doc.parentNode

    lo = Number(context, lo)
    hi = Number(context, hi)

    nodeset = []
    for number in xrange(lo, hi):
        nodeset.append(doc.createTextNode(str(number)))

    return nodeset
```

Calling Boolean on the first argument (Example 17–12) converts it to a boolean, whatever its type may have been originally, and this value is used to determine whether v1 or v2 should be returned. Booleans, even though they are of a special class implemented as part of 4XPath, can be tested directly for their truth values.

Example 17–12. The xpathutils module (4 of 6)

```
def if_function(context, cond, v1, v2):
    if Boolean(cond):
        return v1
    else:
        return v2
```

Example 17–13 finds the position of the first occurrence of the second string inside the first string. Returns -1 if no occurrences are found.

Example 17–13. The xpathutils module (5 of 6)

```
def find(context, str, substr):
    return string.find(String(context, str),
                       String(context, substr))
```

Example 17–14. The xpathutils module (6 of 6)

```
ExtFunctions = {
    ('http://garshol.priv.no/symbolic/', 'distinct') : distinct,
    ('http://garshol.priv.no/symbolic/', 'split')    : split,
    ('http://garshol.priv.no/symbolic/', 'range')    : range,
    ('http://garshol.priv.no/symbolic/', 'if')       : if_function,
    ('http://garshol.priv.no/symbolic/', 'find')     : find
}
```

17.2.2 *The* group *and* item *element types*

The group and item elements are used to select a node set, group the nodes by some XPath expression, and then process each node in turn. Example 17–15 shows how we could have used these two element types to simplify the part of the RFC index stylesheet in Example 16–50 that lists RFCs by standard. These element types are also provided by the Saxon processor, and the idea has been shamelessly stolen from it.

Example 17–15. rfc2html using `group` and `item`

```
<h2><a name="by-standard">RFCs by standard</a></h2>

<table>
<tr><th>Standard</th>   <th>RFCs</th></tr>
<lmg:group select = "category / rfc"  group-by = "standard">
  <xsl:sort select="standard" order="ascending"/>

  <xsl:if test="standard">
  <tr>
  <td><xsl:value-of select = "standard" /></td>
  <td>
  <lmg:item>
    <xsl:sort select="number" data-type="number" order="ascending"/>
    <a href="#{number}"><xsl:value-of select="number"/></a>
    <xsl:if test="not(position() = last())"> | </xsl:if>
  </lmg:item>
  </td></tr>
  </xsl:if>
</lmg:group>
</table>
```

The index now becomes rather straightforward to produce, since we can select the RFCs directly, and group them by their `standard` elements. The contents of the `group` element are instantiated once for each group, while the contents of the `item` element are instantiated once for each item in each group. Note the `xsl:if` introduced to make sure that RFCs that have no standard are left out.

The main problem in writing this implementation is figuring out how to instantiate the contents of the `group` element correctly. Usually, instructions loop over their children calling `instantiate` on each, and that is enough. In our case, however, we need somehow to locate the `item` element among our children, and after we have found it, loop over all the items in the current group, instantiating the element contents once for each of them.

This problem, which may seem severe at first sight, is actually easy to solve through the use of the XSLT context. We simply introduce a new "magic" variable that holds the list of items. We then instantiate each of our children, and when the instantiation process reaches the item element, it picks out the list from the variable and loops over it, instantiating its contents once for each item, as shown in Examples 17–16 to 17–23.

The variable name given in Example 17–16 is used to transmit values between the group and item elements. It uses a namespace to avoid name collisions with variables defined in stylesheets.

Example 17–16. The group and item element types (1 of 8)

```
import string, os
import xml.dom.ext
from xml.dom.Node import Node
from xml.xslt import XsltElement, XSL_NAMESPACE
from xml.xpath import XPathParser
from xml.xpath.CoreFunctions import String

extension_uri = 'http://garshol.priv.no/symbolic/'
varname = (extension_uri, 'items')
```

During setup, we verify that both the group-by and select attributes are present (Example 17–17). If they are not, we raise exceptions in order to complain. Doing so is helpful to the stylesheet writer, who may otherwise forget an attribute and wonder why the XSLT engine suddenly crashes.

Once we have verified that the attributes are present, we parse the XPath expressions in group-by and select and store them in appropriately named internal attributes (Example 17–18). Doing this here saves much time, since the element may be instantiated many times during execution of a stylesheet.

We also store the xsl:sort elements found inside the element in the _sort_specs attribute so that we can access them quickly when we need them.

Example 17–17. The group and item element types (2 of 8)

```
# --- lmg:group

class GroupElement(XsltElement):

    legalAttrs = ('select', 'group-by')

    def setup(self):
        self.__dict__['_nss'] = xml.dom.ext.GetAllNs(self)
        parser = XPathParser.XPathParser()
        group_by = self.getAttributeNS('', 'group-by')
        select = self.getAttributeNS('', 'select')
        if not group_by:
            raise Exception("'group-by' attribute on <group> "
                            "required!")
        if not select:
            raise Exception("'select' attribute on <group> "
                            "required!")
```

Example 17–18. The group and item element types (3 of 8)

```
        self.__dict__['_group_by'] =parser.parseExpression(group_by)
        self.__dict__['_select'] = parser.parseExpression(select)

        self.__dict__['_sort_specs'] = []
        for child in self.childNodes:
            if (child.namespaceURI, child.localName) == \
               (XSL_NAMESPACE,'sort'):
                self._sort_specs.append(child)
```

The first thing we do in Example 17–19 is evaluate the select expression with ourselves as the context node. (This is set by 4XSLT before the instantiate method is called.) This produces a node set which we loop over. For each node, we evaluate the group-by expression with that node as the context node. The result is converted to a string and used to put the node into one of the groups. Once this process is complete, we have a dictionary mapping group keys to lists of the nodes in each group.

Example 17–19. The `group` and `item` element types (4 of 8)

```
def instantiate(self, context, processor):
    orig_state = context.copy()
    context.setNamespaces(self._nss)

    # select the nodes and group them
    groups = {}
    for node in self._select.evaluate(context):
        context.node = node
        key = String(context, self._group_by.evaluate(context))

        try:
            groups[key].append(node)
        except KeyError:
            groups[key] = [node]
```

Example 17–20. The `group` and `item` element types (5 of 8)

```
    # sort the groups
    nodelist = []
    groupmap = {}
    for (key, group_nodes) in groups.items():
        nodelist.append(group_nodes[0])
        groupmap[id(group_nodes[0])] = groups[key]

    if len(groups) > 1 and self._sort_specs:
        nodelist = self._sort_specs[0].instantiate(
                                context, processor, nodelist,
                                self._sort_specs[1 : ])[1]
        groups = []
        for node in nodelist:
            groups.append(groupmap[id(node)])
    else:
        groups = groups.values()
```

Once we have the groups, we can sort them, which is slightly tricky, since the `xsl:sort` implementation expects a node set as the third parameter to `instantiate` (Example 17–20). We solve this by representing each group by its first node, in the `nodelist` list, and creating a dictionary that maps from the ID of this node back to the node list, in `groupmap`. Note that this will cause the `select` attribute of an `xsl:sort` element to be evaluated with that node as the context node.

We can then sort `nodelist` and create our list of sorted groups. If there are no `xsl:sort` elements, we simply call `values` on the dictionary to produce the group list.

Finally, we set the context size to the number of groups and loop over each group, instantiating our contents once for each group (Example 17–21). Note how the context position is updated and how we use an XSLT variable to carry the list of nodes in the group down to the `item` element.

Example 17–21. The `group` and `item` element types (6 of 8)

```
# do the instantiation
context.size = len(groups)
for ix in range(len(groups)):
    items = groups[ix]
    context.node = items[0]
    context.position = ix + 1
    context.varBindings[varname] = items
    for child in self.childNodes:
        context = child.instantiate(context, processor)[0]
```

Note how much simpler sorting is in Example 17–22, since we only have a simple node set that we wish to sort.

17.2.3 *An XBEL conversion application*

In 16.3.2.2, "Index to XBEL conversion," on page 629 we developed an XSLT stylesheet that converted the RFC index to an XBEL document as a first stage on the road to creating browser bookmarks. Knowing the XSLT processor APIs now allows us to make the final step towards using XSLT to convert directly to the bookmark formats. To achieve this, we can assemble the components shown in Figure 17–3.

As the diagram shows, we reuse the XBEL object structure and builder we wrote back in 9.3.1, "XBEL data representation," on

Example 17–22. The group and item element types (7 of 8)

```
        context.set(orig_state)
        return (context,)


# --- lmg:item

class ItemElement(XsltElement):

    def setup(self):
        self.__dict__['_nss'] = xml.dom.ext.GetAllNs(self)

        self.__dict__['_sort_specs'] = []
        for child in self.childNodes:
            if (child.namespaceURI, child.localName) == \
            (XSL_NAMESPACE,'sort'):
                self._sort_specs.append(child)

    def instantiate(self, context, processor):
        orig_state = context.copy()
        context.setNamespaces(self._nss)

        items = context.varBindings[varname]

        # sort the items
        if len(items) > 1 and self._sort_specs:
            items = self._sort_specs[0].instantiate(
                                    context, processor, items,
                                    self._sort_specs[1 : ])[1]
```

page 286. In order to be able to do this, we need a 4XSLT Writer
that can emit SAX events, and this we have to write.[1] We also need
something that can traverse the XBEL object structure and write out
the right bookmark notation. Finally, although this is not shown in
Figure 17–3, we also need an application that will assemble all these
components into a working application.

The code that does all this is shown in Example 17–24.

---

1. This was how the SAXTextWriter class appeared in xml.saxtools.
    xsltutils.

Example 17–23. The group and item element types (8 of 8)

```
        # do instantiation
        context.size = len(items)
        for ix in range(len(items)):
            item = items[ix]
            context.node = item
            context.position = ix + 1
            for child in self.childNodes:
                context = child.instantiate(context, processor)[0]

        context.set(orig_state)
        return (context,)

# --- Mapping dictionary

ExtElements = {
    (extension_uri, 'group'): GroupElement,
    (extension_uri, 'item'):  ItemElement
    }
```

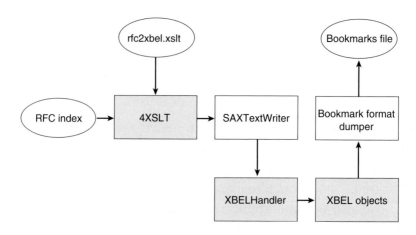

Figure 17–3   The RFC-index to bookmarks converter

Writing xbellib serializers that can be used to create output in the bookmark formats used by other browsers is left as an exercise for the reader. Attempts sent to me will be posted on the book site together with the rest of the xbellib.

Example 17–24. The RFC-index to bookmark converter

```
import sys, string
from xml.sax.saxutils import XMLGenerator
from xml.xslt.Processor import Processor
import xbellib

# --- TextWriter to SAX

class SAXTextWriter:

    def __init__(self, content_handler):
        self._handler = content_handler
        self._name = None
        self._atts = {}

    def getResult(self):
        return None

    def startDocument(self):
        self._handler.startDocument()

    def endDocument(self):
        self._handler.endDocument()

    def text(self, text, escapeOutput=1):
        if self._name:
            self._startElement()
        self._handler.characters(text)

    def attribute(self, name, value, namespace=''):
        self._atts[name] = value

    def processingInstruction(self, target, data):
        if self._name:
            self._startElement()
        self._handler.processingInstruction(target, data)

    def comment(self, body):
        pass

    def startElement(self, name, namespace='', extraNss=None):
        if self._name:
            self._startElement()

        self._name = name
        self._atts = {}
```

```python
    def endElement(self, name):
        if self._name:
            self._startElement()
        self._handler.endElement(name)

    def _startElement(self):
        self._handler.startElement(self._name, self._atts)
        self._name = None

# --- Opera bookmarks dumper

def write_opera_bookmarks(xbel, out):
    out.write("Opera Hotlist version 2.0\n\n")
    _serialize_nodes(xbel.get_nodes(), out)

def _serialize_nodes(nodes, out):
    for node in nodes:
        if isinstance(node, xbellib.Folder):
            out.write("#FOLDER\n")
            name = string.join(string.split(node.get_title()))
            out.write("\tNAME=%s\n" % name)
            if node.get_descr():
                out.write("\tDESCRIPTION=%s\n" % node.get_descr())
            out.write('\n')
            _serialize_nodes(node.get_nodes(), out)
            out.write('-\n\n')

        elif isinstance(node, xbellib.Bookmark):
            out.write('#URL\n')
            name = string.join(string.split(node.get_title()))
            out.write("\tNAME=%s\n" % name)
            out.write("\tURL=%s\n" % node.get_url())
            if node.get_descr():
                out.write("\tDESCRIPTION=%s\n" % node.get_descr())
            out.write("\n")

# --- Main program

builder = xbellib.XBELHandler()
proc = Processor()
proc.appendStylesheetUri(sys.argv[1])
writer = SAXTextWriter( builder )
proc.runUri(sys.argv[2], 0, {}, writer)

write_opera_bookmarks(builder.get_structure(), open("out.txt", "w"))
```

17.3 | Using XPath in software

Like XSLT, XPath can be used to make software development easier, but in different ways. XPath does not do transformation, but can be used for matching, selection, and computation, and it has a supremely simple and expressive syntax for this purpose. Because of this, XPath can often make parts of applications dramatically simpler and easier to configure and develop. A less obvious side to it is that it can often require quite a bit of imagination to see just what XPath can be used for.

In general, XPath implementations tend to provide three different services:

- The ability to use XPath expressions to match and select nodes in a tree representation of documents. This representation will usually be a DOM tree.
- The ability to parse XPath expressions into object structures representing those expressions and to query the object structures for information about the expressions. This is similar to how XML parsers turn XML documents into object structures that can then be queried.
- The ability to extend XPath by implementing extension functions that can be used in expressions.

Together, these services make it possible to use XPath to dispatch actions on documents that are being processed, to use it to select parts of documents, or to compute values from documents. Thus, XPath can be used to develop new processing frameworks, such as eventdom (see 22.2.2, "eventdom," on page 877), in processing applications, as well as for any number of other tasks.

This section will present the 4XPath APIs and then move on to use 4XPath to implement an XML to object mapping framework as an example application built using XPath.

17.3.1 *The 4XPath APIs*

4XPath is the XPath implementation used by 4XSLT, but it is designed to be used separately from 4XSLT as well, evaluating XPath expressions against DOM trees. It should work with any compliant DOM implementation, including minidom. 4XPath lives in the `xml.xpath` package, which provides the following functions:

`Evaluate(expr, contextNode=None, context=None)`
> Using the given context (or context node, if no context is given), the XPath expression contained in the `expr` string is evaluated and the result of the evaluation is returned.

`Compile(expr)`
> This function compiles the given XPath expression into an XPath expression object. This object can then be used to evaluate the expression in a given context, as shown below. This is useful if the expression will be used many times, since it is much more efficient to only parse the expression once.

`CreateContext(contextNode)`
> Creates a default XPath context object using the given DOM node as the context node. The interface of the context object is given in 17.1.1.4, "Writing extension functions," on page 650.

`RegisterExtensionModules(moduleList)`
> Registers a list of modules containing XPath extension functions, as described in 17.1.1.4, "Writing extension functions," on page 650.

XPath expression objects that have been created with the `Compile` function have only one method: `evaluate(context)`, which evaluates the expression in the given context and returns the result.

The interpreter dialog in Example 17–25 shows how to use these functions. The XML document that is used as input is the RSS document from Example 15–5.

Example 17–25. Using XPath expressions

```
>>> from xml.dom.ext.reader.Sax2 import Reader
>>> dom = Reader().fromStream(open("tools.rss"))
>>> dom
<XML Document at 135718944>
>>> from xml.xpath import *
>>> Evaluate("//item", dom)
[<Element Node at 135787688: Name = 'item' with 0 attributes and
5 children>, <Element Node at 135801400: Name = 'item' with
0 attributes and 7 children>]
>>> Evaluate("count(//item)", dom)
2
>>> expr = Compile("//title[starts-with(., 'New')]")
>>> expr
/descendant-or-self::node()/child::title[starts-with(self::node(),
"New")]
>>> expr.evaluate(CreateContext(dom))
[<Element Node at 135790736: Name = 'title' with 0 attributes and
1 children>, <Element Node at 135804448: Name = 'title' with
0 attributes and 1 children>]
```

17.3.2 *Creating XPath expressions*

It may sound surprising at first, but one good use of XPath may be to create XPath expressions from DOM nodes that describe their position in the XML document. This can be used in several ways, for example to show where in a document a query matches, or to analyze the structure of XML documents. In this section, we will develop a function generating XPath patterns and show how it can be used for both these purposes.

The XPath-generating function is quite straightforward: it creates an XPath pattern that essentially contains the element-type names of the parents of the node. So for the item elements in an RSS document it would generate the expression rss / channel / item. It can be told to be more precise, in which case it will generate XPath patterns of the form rss[1] / channel[1] / item[5], referring only to the specific node used to generate the expression. Example 17–26 gives the source code.

Example 17–26. The xpathgen module

```python
import string
from xml.dom import Node

def make_xpath_expr(node, add_counts = 1):
    steps = []

    if node.nodeType == Node.ATTRIBUTE_NODE:
        steps.append("@" + node.nodeName)
    elif node.nodeType == Node.DOCUMENT_NODE:
        return "/"
    elif node.nodeType != Node.ELEMENT_NODE:
        node = node.parentNode

    while node.nodeType != Node.DOCUMENT_NODE:
        name = node.nodeName

        if add_counts:
            no = 0
            while node.previousSibling:
                if node.nodeName == name:
                    no = no + 1
                node = node.previousSibling

            steps.append("%s[%d]" % (name, no))
        else:
            steps.append(name)

        node = node.parentNode

    steps.reverse()

    return string.join(steps, " / ")
```

With this function in hand, we can create a simple XPath querying
utility that searches for a text string in a document (using our XPath
extension function find) and then creates XPath expressions that tell
the user where the matches were found. Example 17–27 shows the
source code.

Querying the XML document of this book for the string 'Garshol'
gives the output shown in Example 17–28.

Example 17–27. The XPath searching utility

```
import sys, string
from xml.dom import Node
from xml.dom.ext.reader.Sax2 import Reader
from xml.xpath import Evaluate, CreateContext
from xml.xpath import RegisterExtensionModules

from xpathgen import make_xpath_expr

def print_node_set(nodeset):
    for node in nodeset:
        print "\t", make_xpath_expr(node)

RegisterExtensionModules(['xpathutils'])

text = sys.argv[1]
expr = "//text() [ lmg:find(., '%s') != -1 ]" % text
files = sys.argv[2 : ]

for file in files:
    print "===", file
    doc = Reader().fromStream(open(file))
    context = CreateContext(doc)
    context.processorNss["lmg"] = "http://garshol.priv.no/symbolic/"
    result = Evaluate(expr, None, context)

    if type(result) == type([]):
        print_node_set(result)
    else:
        print result

    print
```

Turning to the question of analyzing XML documents, we can use these XPath expressions, without the node counts, to count the number of times element types occur with different parents. Example 17–29 does just this.

Running this tool on an RSS document produces the output shown in Example 17–30.

Example 17–28. XPath query result

```
=== ../../bok.xml
  OIMBOOK[1] / FRONTM[0] / AU[1]
  OIMBOOK[1] / CHAPTER[1] / H1S[1] / H2S[1] / EXAMPLE[2] / PRE[1]
  OIMBOOK[1] / CHAPTER[1] / H1S[1] / H2S[1] / EXAMPLE[3] / PRE[1]
  OIMBOOK[1] / CHAPTER[1] / H1S[1] / H2S[4] / TABLE[1] / TBODY[1] /
    TR[1] / TD[1] / P[0]
  OIMBOOK[1] / CHAPTER[1] / H1S[2] / EXAMPLE[1] / CODE[1]
  OIMBOOK[1] / CHAPTER[6] / H1S[2] / UL[1] / LI[1] / P[0]
  OIMBOOK[1] / CHAPTER[6] / H1S[4] / H2S[2] / P[3] / IC[1]
  OIMBOOK[1] / CHAPTER[10] / H1S[4] / EXAMPLE[3] / CODE[1]
  OIMBOOK[1] / BACKM[1] / APPENDIX[0] / H1S[4] / H2S[1] / CODE[2]
  OIMBOOK[1] / BACKM[1] / APPENDIX[0] / H1S[4] / H2S[1] / CODE[3]
```

Example 17–29. A document analyzer

```python
import sys
from xml.dom import Node
from xml.dom.ext.reader.Sax2 import Reader
from xpathgen import make_xpath_expr

def analyze(node, counts):
    expr = make_xpath_expr(node, 0)
    counts[expr] = counts.get(expr, 0) + 1

    for child in node.childNodes:
        if child.nodeType == Node.ELEMENT_NODE:
            analyze(child, counts)

# === Collect results

file = sys.argv[1]

print "===", file
doc = Reader().fromStream(open(file))
counts = {}
analyze(doc, counts)

# === Print report

exprs = counts.keys()
exprs.sort()

for expr in exprs:
    print "%70s  %d" % (expr, counts[expr])
```

Example 17–30. Analysis of an RSS document

```
=== ../tools.rss
                                                          /   1
                                                        rss   1
                                              rss / channel   1
                                rss / channel / description   1
                                       rss / channel / item   4
                         rss / channel / item / description   1
                                rss / channel / item / link   4
                               rss / channel / item / title   4
                                       rss / channel / link   1
                            ,  rss / channel / title   1
```

17.3.3 *Mapping XML to objects*

Quite a few of our examples so far have been dedicated to taking XML documents conforming to a particular schema and creating an appropriate object structure from them. So far we have done it using event-based and tree-based processing, but have seen no declarative way of doing this.

As an example, we will now use 4XPath to develop a declarative system for creating object structures from XML documents. There exist several XML applications that can represent object structures using fixed schemas, but what we will develop here is something that will allow us to create an object structure for any schema (or very nearly so). The system will use a mapping document describing how to create the object structure from source documents. Such a mapping document for RSS is shown in Example 17–31.

This example creates one root object, which has the fields defined by the `field` elements. All XPath expressions inside it are evaluated with the context node selected by the XPath expression in the `context` attribute. The first four fields all get string values, while the fifth gets a list of objects. Each of these objects again has three fields, as defined by the mapping.

To complete this example, we now need to develop an object structure for representing mapping files, a structure builder for such files,

Example 17–31. An object mapping for RSS 0.9

```
<object context="rss">
  <field name="version" value="@version"/>
  <field name="title"   value="channel/title"/>
  <field name="link"    value="channel/link"/>
  <field name="descr"   value="channel/description"/>

  <field name="items">
    <list select="//item">
      <object>
        <field name="title" value="title"/>
        <field name="link"  value="link"/>
        <field name="descr" value="description"/>
      </object>
    </list>
  </field>
</object>
```

and an interpreter for the mappings. The implementation is given in Examples 17–32 to 17–37.

The class in Example 17–32 is used to represent `object` elements in the mapping document. It has an optional `_context` attribute and a list of fields. If the `get_context_node` method is called with the current node as a parameter, the method will return what the mapping selects as the context node for its contents. This defaults to the node itself, but the `_context` attribute can override this. The `get_fields` method can be called to get the list of field objects that define all fields.

The class in Example 17–33 is used to represent fields of the simple kind, represented by empty `field` elements. When `get_value` is called in a given context, the XPath expression in the `value` attribute is evaluated. The result cannot be a node set, so if it is, the node set is converted to a string using the built-in XPath function.

Each `field` element with contents is represented by an object of the `ComplexField` class (Example 17–34). The `_object` attribute contains an `ObjectMapping` object representing the `object` child. The `get_value` method here will use the `select` attribute to make a list of DOM nodes. For each of these, the `build_objects` function

Example 17–32. The xml2obj module (1 of 6)

```
from xml.sax.handler import ContentHandler
from xml.dom.ext.reader.Sax import Reader
from xml.xpath import Compile, CreateContext
from xml.xpath.CoreFunctions import String


# ===== OBJECT STRUCTURE

class ObjectMapping:

    def __init__(self, context = None):
        if context:
            context = Compile(context)
        self._context = context

        self._fields = []

    def add_field(self, field):
        self._fields.append(field)

    def get_context_node(self, current):
        if self._context:
            value = self._context.evaluate(CreateContext(current))
            if type(value) == type([]):
                value = value[0]
            return value
        else:
            return current

    def get_fields(self):
        return self._fields
```

is used to build the data object. (That function is defined in Example 17–36.)

The MappingBuilder (Example 17–35) is the SAX Content-Handler that builds the object structure representing the mapping document.

Example 17–36 is the code that takes a DOM document and a mapping object structure and builds the object structure defined by the mapping. The build_objects function simply starts with the root object and creates it as if it were an ordinary object. The built-in Python function setattr is used to define new attributes on the

Example 17–33. The xml2obj module (2 of 6)

```
class BasicField:

    def __init__(self, name, value):
        self._name = name
        self._value = Compile(value)

    def get_name(self):
        return self._name

    def get_value(self, context):
        value = self._value.evaluate(context)
        if type(value) == type([]):
            value = String(CreateContext(value))
        return value
```

Example 17–34. The xml2obj module (3 of 6)

```
class ComplexField:

    def __init__(self, name):
        self._name = name

    def set_type(self, type):
        self._type = type

    def set_select(self, select):
        self._select = Compile(select)

    def set_object(self, object):
        self._object = object

    def get_name(self):
        return self._name

    def get_value(self, context):
        objs = []
        for node in self._select.evaluate(context):
            obj = build_objects(self._object, node)
            objs.append(obj)

        return objs
```

Example 17–35. The xml2obj module (4 of 6)

```
# ===== BUILDER

class MappingBuilder(ContentHandler):

    def __init__(self):
        self._objstack = []
        self._curfield = None

    def get_root_object(self):
        return self._objstack[-1]

    def startElement(self, name, attrs):
        if name == "object":
            ctxt = attrs.get("context")
            self._objstack.append(ObjectMapping(ctxt))

            if self._curfield:
                self._curfield.set_object(self._objstack[-1])

        elif name == "field":
            if attrs.has_key("value"):
                field = BasicField(attrs.get("name"),
                                   attrs.get("value"))
            else:
                field = ComplexField(attrs.get("name"))
                self._curfield = field

            self._objstack[-1].add_field(field)

        elif name == "list":
            self._curfield.set_type("list")
            self._curfield.set_select(attrs.get("select"))


    def endElement(self, name):
        if name == "object" and len(self._objstack) > 1:
            del self._objstack[-1]
```

objects. The DataObject class is used to represent data objects, and has quite simply no attributes at all. These are all provided by the mapping.

Example 17–36. The xml2obj module (5 of 6)

```
# ===== INTERPRETER

class DataObject:
    pass

def build_objects(mapping, document):
    context = CreateContext(mapping.get_context_node(document))
    object = DataObject()
    for field in mapping.get_fields():
        name = field.get_name()
        value = field.get_value(context)

        setattr(object, name, value)

    return object
```

To make the module a little easier to use, we provide two utility functions in Example 17–37. The first one loads the mapping from an XML document; the second one uses the loaded mapping to build an object structure from a file.

Example 17–37. The xml2obj module (6 of 6)

```
# ===== UTILITIES

def load_mapping(file):
    from xml.sax import make_parser

    builder = MappingBuilder()
    parser = make_parser()
    parser.setContentHandler(builder)
    parser.parse(file)

    return builder.get_root_object()

def load_objects(mapping, file):
    document = Reader().fromStream(open(file))
    return build_objects(mapping, document)
```

Now that we have an implementation of the mapping system, we can take the RSS document in Example 15–5 and load it, using the example mapping document. This we do in the interpreter dialog in Example 17–38.

Example 17–38. Using `xml2obj`

```
>>> import xml2obj
>>> mapping = xml2obj.load_mapping("rssmap.xml")
>>> rss = xml2obj.load_objects(mapping, "tools.rss")
>>> rss.version
'0.91'
>>> rss.title
'Free XML tools'
>>> rss.link
'http://www.garshol.priv.no/download/xmltools/'
>>> rss.items
[<xml2obj.DataObject instance at 813b268>,
 <xml2obj.DataObject instance at 813b280>]
>>> item = rss.items[0]
>>> item.title
'New product: tDOM.'
>>> item.link
'http://www.garshol.priv.no/download/xmltools/prod/tDOM.html'
>>> item.descr
' '
```

17.4 | The future of XSLT

At the time of writing, W3C has released the first working draft of the XSLT 1.1 specification, which gives some idea of what will appear in XSLT 1.1. The main goal of this specification was to solve the growing problem of XSLT stylesheet portability. As described earlier, many XSLT processors provide built-in extension element types and functions to give users functionality that XSLT itself does not have. This means that stylesheets which depend on these extensions will not be portable to other XSLT processors.

The current XSLT 1.1 draft provides two counter-measures to this problem. One is to directly support the two most common extensions, which are:

- support for multiple output documents, and
- support for converting result tree fragments to node sets.

The first is provided through the `xsl:document` element type, which has a `href` attribute holding a reference to the file into which all the children of the `xsl:document` will be written. In addition, this element type has all the attributes of `xsl:output`, allowing output settings to be defined for this file.

The second is provided by simply removing the result tree fragment type from XSLT and letting `xsl:variable` create node sets directly. This of course begs the question of why the result tree fragment type was introduced in the first place, and I have to admit that I just don't know.

Another counter-measure to improve stylesheet portability is the `xsl:script` element type, which can be used to define extension functions. It can include the source code to the functions directly, or it can provide references to libraries containing several functions.

In addition to the `xsl:script` element type, the XSLT 1.1 working draft contains language bindings for Java and JavaScript that specify how to write these extension functions. The language bindings also describe how to interpret external references. At the time of writing this information has been public for 5 days, so there is as yet no Python language binding, nor any initiative to create one.

In addition to making stylesheets more portable, XSLT 1.1 fixes errors, makes some small adjustments to existing element types, and makes some other small changes. The two most important are:

- There is now a formalized process of creating namespace nodes in the result tree, known as *namespace fixup*. This basically consists of traversing the tree to create missing namespace nodes.

- There is now support for XBase. This means that the base URI of a node can now be influenced through the use of the `xml:base` attribute.

In general, stylesheets that worked with XSLT 1.0 should work just fine with XSLT 1.1 as well.

Architectural forms

I magine that you want to define a number of general element types for hyperlinks that schema designers will be able to reuse in their application-specific DTDs. Schema-independent applications, such as editors, browsers, and document management systems, should be able to recognize these linking element types and provide a special behavior for them. At the same time, schema designers should be able to choose their own names for the link element types when they appear in application-specific DTDs. How do you solve this problem?

This was the question faced by the ISO committee that developed the HyTime standard (described in 14.2.1, "What groves are," on page 507). HyTime defines a small number of very general element types that could be used to define links in SGML documents. However, this was problematic because DTDs which used HyTime would have to use these element types with the names defined in the HyTime standard, something that might not fit very well into the specific DTD.

The solution the HyTime committee adopted a mechanism called *architectural forms*, which is a standardized way of stating that an element type is a specialized form of a more general one. This allowed DTD designers to use the names they wanted for links, but still allowed them to map their own link types onto the general HyTime link types. With this solution, for example, the link and url element types of RSS could be defined as HyTime links with only minor modifications to the RSS schema.

The same is not possible with the XLink linking standard from the W3C, since this requires that the element-type names defined in the XLink specification be used directly. Instead, it relies on namespaces for the recognition of the element types as XLink element types. It may seem as though architectural forms and namespaces are competitors, but in fact they could well have been designed to supplement each other. Namespaces provide unique naming of element types and attributes by placing them in a globally unique namespace. Architectural forms provide a sub-typing and processing mechanism, which at the same time places element types in a schema that, through public identifiers, has a globally unique name.

When the HyTime standard was published in 1992, it included the formal definition of architectural forms in an annex. This allowed HyTime to use architectural forms to define its own element types, as well as allowed others to derive new element types from the standard ones. It is of course also possible to define entirely new architectural element types that have nothing to do with HyTime or linking at all, and many people have done so.

At the time of writing, there are two proposals that intend to add name independence to the XLink specification, in order to avoid the problems caused by the requirement that names be as specified in XLink. These are the XLink Naming and CLink proposals, the first based on XML Schema and the second, on CSS. The weakness of both is that they are specific to linking.

18.1 | Introduction to architectural forms

When using architectures in XML, the first thing you need to do is to specify that architectures are in use. An *architecture* is a collection of architectural forms, and can be seen as a kind of a base DTD, from which other DTDs can be derived. Identifying the architectures used is done by inserting an architecture use declaration in the documents and DTDs that use architectures. The architectural DTD itself does not have to be modified in any way to allow others to use architectural forms; it is the users' DTDs that must specify that they can be architecturally mapped to the architectural DTD. The declaration in Example 18–1 says that the document or DTD that it appears in uses the rss architecture.

Example 18–1. An architecture use declaration

```
<?IS10744:arch name="rss"?>
```

To an architectural engine, the declaration above would give the attribute rss a special meaning in documents that carried the declaration. The rss attribute would be used to find the names of element types in the rss architecture that element types in the using document would be mapped to.

Example 18–2 shows a document in the backslash DTD used by the Slashdot news site[1] as a basis for news syndication. It is very similar to RSS, but with some minor differences. The document uses the RSS architecture, as the architecture use declaration shows.

In this example, it is hard to see how the document can be mapped to the rss architecture, since all that has any connection to RSS in the document is the architecture use declaration. In this case, as in most others, the mapping attributes are declared as #FIXED attributes in the

---

1.   Slashdot, also known as /., is a well-known news site for technical people (or *nerds*, as Slashdot itself calls its audience). See http://slashdot.org/.

Example 18–2. A backslash document using the RSS architecture

```
<?IS10744:arch name="rss"?>
<!DOCTYPE backslash SYSTEM "backslash.dtd">
<backslash>
  <story>
    <title>Microsoft to be split?</title>
    <url>http://slashdot.org/stuff</url>
    <time>stuff</time>
    <author>CmdrTaco</author>
  </story>

  <story>
    <title>RMS pissed at ESR</title>
    <url>http://slashdot.org/stuff</url>
    <time>stuff</time>
    <author>RobLimo</author>
  </story>
[...]
```

DTD, to avoid having to repeat them in the documents. The DTD, with the mapping attributes, is shown in Example 18–3 (the architectural parts have been added by me).

Example 18–3. The backslash DTD using the rss architecture

```
<!ELEMENT backslash (story*)>

<!ELEMENT story (title, url, time, author)>
<!ATTLIST story rss CDATA #FIXED "item">

<!ELEMENT title (#PCDATA)>
<!ATTLIST title rss CDATA #FIXED "title">

<!ELEMENT url (#PCDATA)>
<!ATTLIST url rss CDATA #FIXED "link">

<!ELEMENT time (#PCDATA)>
<!ELEMENT author (#PCDATA)>
```

If the first document is parsed with this DTD, the parser will give most elements an attribute named rss, and this would be used by the architectural engine to map the backslash document into an RSS document. The elements that do not have the `rss` attribute do not belong to the rss architecture at all, and will be left out. The result of the mapping is shown in Example 18–4.

Example 18–4. The backslash document in the rss architecture

```
<rss>
  <item>
    <title>Microsoft to be split?</title>
    <link>http://slashdot.org/stuff</link>
  </item>
  <item>
    <title>RMS pissed at ESR</title>
    <link>http://slashdot.org/stuff</link>
  </item>
</rss>
```

Architectural forms have many more features than this. They can, for instance, map element content to attribute values and vice versa. You can also change the name of the document element type, the mapping attribute, and many other aspects of how the architectural form works.

However, in this book I want to focus on the concept rather than the technical details, so those who would like to know more are referred to David Megginson's *Structuring XML Documents* in this series. Chapters 9 to 11 of that book cover architectural forms very understandably and in great detail. An online tutorial by Eliot Kimber can be found at `http://www.isogen.com/papers/archintro.html`.

18.2 | Uses of architectural forms

Architectural forms have many uses, most of which relate to mapping between DTDs. This is similar to what XSLT does, but architectural forms differ in that they are much simpler and that they are more of a schema feature than a processing language. That is, architectural forms can rarely be used to map between DTDs that were not developed with this in mind. They are generally seen as a sub-typing feature for DTDs and not as a processing system. In general, they have been implemented as some sort of a parser filter that modifies the document to present a virtual view of the document to applications.

One of the most common uses of architectural forms has been creating local variants of well-known standardized DTDs for special users. Organizations have often used this mechanism to define their own variant of a standard DTD in the knowledge that with architectural forms, their documents can be effortlessly mapped back to the standard DTD. Adaptations could take the form of simplifications, extensions, or translations of names used.

Another common use case has been when a large organization adopts a DTD for organization-wide use. In some cases, individual departments make small changes to the common DTD in order to serve their particular needs. In such cases, architectural forms can be used to map back to the common DTD of the organization, which effectively serves as a common subset for all departments.

A third use case is that presented by HyTime: the definition of very general element types for reuse in many different kinds of DTDs. The W3C XInclude and XBase applications could very well have been designed with architectural forms rather than with namespaces.

XSDL has sub-typing features that are similar to what architectural forms do, but this sub-typing only specifies the derivation relationship. XSDL is silent about how documents in derived schemas could work in applications that only understand the base schema.

18.3 | Architectural forms software

At the time of writing there are three main implementations of architectural forms available. These are:

SP

> This is James Clark's general SGML parser written in C++. SP has a built-in architectural forms engine that implements most of the features of architectural forms. This engine can be invoked to make SP present a virtual architectural view to its application.

XAF

> This is David Megginson's architectural engine written as a SAX filter in Java. It can be used to automatically map the output from a parser to a base architecture before processing applications ever see the document contents.

xmlarch

> This is Geir Ove Grønmo's engine, which is very similar to XAF, but written in Python. It was actually used to produce the output document in Example 18–4.

18.4 | An example

Examples 18–5 and 18–6 show how an architectural engine could be used as a parser filter to add support for the backslash DTD (derived from the RSS architecture). Since the architectural engine does the transformation from one DTD to another for us, hardly any programming is required at all. The example uses xmlarch to do the transformation.

Note how we have fixed all the attributes of the channel in the top template (Example 18–5), since these are known in advance and not given in the document.

Note that the channel metadata is added statically (Example 18–6), since the information is not available in the document at all. The `ArchDocHandler` from xmlarch is used as a parser filter. The `RSSHandler` from `rsslib` is set up to receive events in the rss architecture from the parser, and then pass them on to the `RSSHandler`.

Example 18–5. Adding backslash support to rsslib (1 of 2)

```
import sys
from xml.sax import handler, make_parser

from xml.arch.xmlarch import ArchDocHandler
from xml.sax.saxexts import make_parser
from xml.sax.saxutils import ErrorRaiser, XMLGenerator
from xml.sax.handler import feature_external_pes, feature_namespaces

# --- Templates

top = \
"""
<!DOCTYPE HTML PUBLIC "-//W3C//DTD HTML 4.0 Transitional//EN">
<HTML>
<HEAD>
  <TITLE>Slashdot news</TITLE>
</HEAD>

<BODY>
<A HREF="http://slashdot.org"><H1>Slashdot news</H1></A>

<p>
News for nerds.
</p>
"""
```

Note that we require xmlproc to be used and then set the fea-
ture_external_pes on. This is necessary to make the parser read
the backslash DTD and insert the mapping attributes in the document.
If this step were omitted, the mapping attributes would not be in the
document and the architectural document would be empty apart from
the document element.

Example 18–6. Adding backslash support to rsslib (2 of 2)

```python
# --- Conversion function

def htmlconv(infile, out):
    outf = open(out, "w")

    arch_handler = ArchDocHandler()
    arch_handler.add_content_handler('rss', RSS2HTMLHandler(outf))

    parser = make_parser("xml.sax.drivers2.drv_xmlproc")
    parser.setFeature(feature_external_pes, 1)
    parser.setFeature(feature_namespaces, 0)
    parser.setContentHandler(arch_handler)
    parser.parse(infile)

    outf.close()

# --- Main program

if __name__ == "__main__":
    import sys
    htmlconv(sys.argv[1], sys.argv[2])
```

XML development in Java

- XML and Java

- Java XML parsers

- Java SAX

- Java DOM

- Java XSLT

Part Five

In this part of the book we discuss how to use Java tools to perform the same tasks that the three previous parts have shown how to do in Python.

SAX in Java

I n this book, the intention has been to give the reader a thorough grasp of the concepts relevant to developing XML applications, rather than to show the reader how to use specific versions of specific tools and standards. Python has been used as a vehicle for presenting examples, but the intention always was that the book should be useful to developers no matter in what language they chose to do their XML development.[1] This part of the book is included to make it easier for Java programmers to apply the concepts taught in this book to Java development.

As programming languages, Python and Java are much alike and much different at the same time. They are both mainstream object-oriented languages with a very similar package structure, a small number

---

1. Well, this is not entirely true. Developers working in functional or logic programming languages will probably have a hard time applying much of the material presented after the first part of the book to their languages, but since these languages require fundamentally different approaches to XML development, this was unavoidable.

of features, and a leaning towards platform independence. The differences, however, are many and as important as the similarities. And these differences are, to a large extent, what defines the experience of developing in each language. Java is statically typed and scoped; Python takes dynamic approaches to both. Java has mostly low-level features, with no built-in support for data structures; Python offers dictionaries, dynamic-length lists, and tuples well integrated into the core language. Java is strictly object-oriented and has a far stricter object model, while Python does not enforce object-orientation on the developer and has a more flexible object model.

Despite their differences, writing software in these two languages does not require the programmer to apply concepts that are too different, so writing XML-aware software in Java is easy for someone who knows how to do it in Python, and vice versa. The main things it may be useful for the Python XML developer to know when writing Java software is:

- what familiar XML APIs, such as SAX and DOM, look like in Java,
- what XML software there is in Java and how to use it, and
- what are Java's techniques for safe, efficient, and convenient programming.

It is these three things that this part of the book will concentrate on, since the previous parts already have covered the main concepts involved in XML application development.

19.1 | XML and Java

XML and Java have been used together from the very beginning, ever since Norbert Mikula released the first XML parser (NXP, written in Java) in January 1997. Nearly all early XML software was written in Java, and Java has since remained the main language for XML development. The reasons for this have much to do with Java's reputation as a platform-independent language for Internet development, and probably also with the head start Java got as an XML development language.

In some senses Java was also ideally placed to make use of the XML "revolution" in the sense that it was a language easy to learn for most developers, with the right amount of speed and static control, Unicode support, Internet support, and many other useful features.

19.2 | Java XML parsers

The first XML parser to be released was NXP, as mentioned above, and since then, quite a number of XML parsers have been written in Java — and like NXP, quite a few of them have been discontinued. Main parsers still being developed at the moment are described in this section.

This section only presents the parsers, their history and features, but does not describe their internals or interfaces. This is so done because all of the parsers have SAX drivers and since a SAX interface is generally the only interface these parsers have.

19.2.1 *Xerces-J*

This parser originally started its life as the XML for Java parser (usually called XML4J) developed by two researchers at IBM Japan. In November 1999, however, it was donated to the Apache Software Foundation to start an effort concentrating on developing XML tools in Java. The Apache Software Foundation grew out of a group of developers working on the Apache Web server, but has since also taken on other kinds of projects. Since it was donated to the Apache Foundation, the parser has been through many releases, and the result of all this effort is a parser that is fast, highly conformant, feature-complete, and also quite big. Among its features are validation, SAX and DOM support, and budding support for XSDL schema validation.

Today, this is the main XML parser in Java, and it really only has two drawbacks: its size and the fact that if your application throws an exception, the traceback will not show where in your application the problem occurred. This means that during application development it may be useful to use a different parser in order to get proper tracebacks, and then to switch to Xerces for production use.

In April 2000, the Sun XML parser, released from Sun as Java Project X, was donated to the Apache Project as well. It has been maintained as a separate parser known as Crimson within the Xerces project. If you download Xerces today, you will also get Crimson as part of the same download. Crimson mainly differs from Xerces in that it has a smaller code footprint, and in that it lacks some features like XSDL schema validation and DOM 2 support.

In addition to the Java Xerces (or Xerces-J), there is an implementation of much the same design in portable C++ called Xerces-C++. Xerces-C++ is also available as a module that can be compiled into Perl.

Unlike the Python parsers we covered in Chapter 7, "Using XML parsers," on page 160, Xerces-J does not have a native interface. Instead, Xerces implements the SAX 2.0 (and 1.0!) interfaces directly as its native interfaces. In addition to this interface, Xerces-J has an interface that is very much like SAX 2.0, but where the parser builds a DOM tree instead of emitting SAX events. We'll return to the DOM interface in 20.3.1, "Accessing Xerces directly," on page 781.

19.2.2 *Ælfred*

This parser was originally written by David Megginson at MicroStar with the goal of making it the smallest possible XML parser in terms of code size. The intention was that this would make it usable in Java applets, but it has turned out to be useful in other contexts as well.[1] The result was a small and conformant parser consisting only of a couple of classes taking up 26 Kb as a JAR file. Since then Megginson has left MicroStar, which has itself been acquired by OpenText Corp, but Ælfred has remained available from their pages. The official release has not been updated for a long time, however.

David Brownell has updated the parser and includes the updated version in his XML Utilities package. This version of the parser is faster, more conformant, validating, and supports namespaces and SAX 2, so it is recommended over the original version. Michael Kay has taken an early version of Brownell's modified Ælfred, fixed some bugs in it, and bundled it with his Saxon XSLT processor (see 21.2, "The Saxon XSLT processor," on page 817).

The original version had both a native API and a SAX driver, while the extended versions use SAX 2.0 as the native interface.

19.2.3 *XP*

XP was one of the first XML parsers to be announced. It was written by James Clark, who also wrote expat and SP. This parser has not been updated for a long time and probably is no longer in active development, but it still remains one of the fastest and most conformant XML parsers there are, together with Xerces-J.

XP is an old parser that had begun before the SAX effort was started, so it has both a native interface (as shown in 7.5, "Working in Jython," on page 226) and a SAX driver that wraps the native interface in a SAX 1.0 interface.

---

1. There is, for example, an Ælfred version ported to the kvm environment, which means that it can be used on Palm PDAs.

19.3 | The Java version of SAX

As described in 8.1, "Background and history," on page 235, the Java version of SAX was the one originally developed and the Python version presented earlier in this book is a translation of this original version to Python. The Python translation followed the original version rather closely, but diverged in areas where it was felt that problems could be solved better in Python by making use of Python-specific features than by exactly following the original design. The result is that for someone who knows Python SAX, Java SAX is easy to learn, and vice versa. The differences to be aware of are sometimes rather subtle; the main ones are listed below:

- representation of expanded names,
- the signatures of the `characters` and `ignorableWhitespace` methods,
- the helper classes and functions provided around the core interfaces,
- some extensions provided in Python, like the `Incremental-Parser` interface and extra capabilities of the `Attributes` interface.

Apart from these differences, the APIs are more or less the same. SAX development in Java is still not quite the same as SAX development in Python. This is due mainly to language differences, API differences, and differences in what is provided around the APIs. This chapter therefore presents an introduction to Java SAX for those who already know Python SAX.

19.4 | JAXP

Sun is understandably eager to see Java retain its position as one of the main languages for XML development, and to this end they have developed the Java API for XML Parsing (JAXP) using their Java Community Process (JCP), and made it part of the Java platform. The JAXP API reuses the already-developed SAX, DOM, and TRaX (see 21.1, "Using JAXP," on page 796) interfaces, but provides mechanisms for implementation-independent use of the facilities. We will only cover the SAX part of JAXP here, and leave the DOM and XSLT parts for the chapters on those subjects.

The straightforward way to create a SAX parser is to simply instantiate the class that implements the `XMLReader` interface in that parser and use it. Just like in Python, the problem with this is that it makes the application depend on a particular parser. What the SAX part of JAXP provides is a mechanism for code to create a SAX parser without having a connection to a particular parser hard-wired in the code.

JAXP consists of two parts: the first is the classes in the `javax.xml.parsers` package, which are JAXP-specific, and the second is the original SAX classes, which live in the `org.xml.sax` package. JAXP 1.1 is based on SAX 2.0, but provides some backwards compatibility with SAX 1.0.

19.4.1 *How to create a parser*

There are several ways to create a parser through JAXP, but the easiest way is to call a static method on the `SAXParserFactory` class, which returns a `SAXParser` object. This object has an interface very similar to a SAX `XMLReader` and you can either use it directly, or get the `XMLReader` wrapped by the `SAXParser`. The `SAXParserFactory` and `SAXParser` are JAXP-specific, while the `XMLReader` interface belongs to SAX 2.0.

When a parser is requested through JAXP, JAXP goes through the steps below in the order given to find out which parser to create.

1. First, JAXP will see if the `javax.xml.parsers.SAXParser-Factory` system property has been set. It should be set to the class name of a class that is derived from the `SAXParser-Factory` class.

2. Failing that, JAXP will read the `lib/jaxp.properties` file in the JRE directory. This file is an ordinary Java properties file, and should contain an assignment to the above-mentioned property.

3. Failing that, it will use the Services API (as detailed in the JAR specification), if available, to determine the class name. The Services API will look for the class name in the file `META-INF/services/javax.xml.parsers.SAXParserFactory` in jars available to the Java VM runtime.

4. If all these methods fail, the system will use the platform default, which is the default for the JRE or JDK version the application runs on. At the moment, this will usually be the XML parser known as Crimson.

Once a `SAXParserFactory` has been created, it can be used to create a `SAXParser`.

Table 19–1 shows the class names of the `SAXParserFactory` implementations of the different parsers that currently support JAXP.

It seems that at the moment there are only three parsers supporting this part of JAXP: Xerces, Saxon's version of Ælfred, and the platform default parser shipped with Java. David Brownell's Ælfred and XP do not support JAXP, nor does the Oracle XML parser. This is somewhat disappointing, perhaps, but probably reflects the fact that while JAXP is useful, it is relatively complex compared to the small benefit it provides for SAX parser creation. SAX itself has, after all, a similar service, although somewhat simpler.

Table 19–1 `SAXParserFactory` implementations

Parser	Class name
Xerces	`org.apache.xerces.jaxp.SAXParserFactoryImpl`
Crimson	`org.apache.crimson.jaxp.SAXParserFactoryImpl`
Saxon Ælfred	`com.icl.saxon.aelfred.SAXParserFactoryImpl`

19.4.2 *The JAXP APIs*

The JAXP classes are found in the `javax.xml` package, and the parts relevant to SAX are in `javax.xml.parsers`. Essentially, the SAX-related part of the API consists of the two classes, `SAXParserFactory` and `SAXParser`, as well as the two exceptions, `FactoryConfigurationError` and `ParserConfigurationError`.

19.4.2.1 The `SAXParserFactory` class

This class is where the process of creating an XML parser starts, and it provides several different means of creation, as well as some mechanisms for configuring the created parser. The class is abstract, so it cannot be created directly. The intention is that there will be a subclass implementation of this class for each SAX parser, and that that factory will create the SAX parser it belongs to.

It is also the intention that the JAR file the parser is distributed in will contain the necessary file, so that if the JAR file is on the classpath, the factory will automatically be created. This is why the third step in the factory location process explained above is there. The two steps before this step are there to ensure that if there are more parser JARs on the classpath, there is a way to control which of these get created.

`SAXParserFactory` has the following methods, all of which are public.

`static SAXParserFactory newInstance()`
> Finds a class derived from `SAXParserFactory`, instantiates it, and returns the resulting object. The procedure for finding the class to instantiate is the one explained in the previous section. If the creation fails, a `FactoryConfigurationException` will be thrown.

`SAXParser newSAXParser()`
> Returns an instance of the parser the factory has been configured to create. If creation fails, a `ParserConfigurationException` will be thrown. The most likely cause of failure is that the factory

is unable to create a parser with the specific configuration it has been asked to find.

`void setNamespaceAware(boolean awareness)`
Sets the internal flag that controls whether the created parser will provide support for XML namespaces.

`void setValidating(boolean validating)`
Sets the internal flag that controls whether the created parser will validate documents when they are parsed.

`boolean isNamespaceAware()`
Is used to determine whether or not the factory is configured to produce namespace-aware parsers.

`boolean isValidating()`
Is used to determine whether or not the factory is configured to produce validating parsers.

`void setFeature(java.lang.String name, boolean value)`
Sets a SAX feature on the `XMLReader` that will be created by the factory. You can find a list of the core SAX features in 10.1.7, "SAX 2.0 extensibility support," on page 346.

`boolean getFeature(java.lang.String name)`
Returns the value of the named SAX feature.

19.4.2.2 The `SAXParser` interface

The `SAXParser` class is what is instantiated by `SAXParserFactory` instances, and it wraps `XMLReader` objects in an interface that provides both some convenience methods and a reference to the `XMLReader` object itself. Whether one prefers to use the `SAXParser` to start parsing or to just use it to get an `XMLReader` is up to each developer's preference.

In JAXP 1.0 this class wrapped SAX 1.0 `Parser` objects, but in JAXP 1.1 it has been extended to also wrap `XMLReader` objects. Listed below are the public methods of this class that do not relate to the SAX 1.0 support. Note that the class is abstract.

`void parse(java.io.InputStream is, DefaultHandler dh)`

Configures the underlying `XMLReader` to send events to the given `DefaultHandler` and parses the document read from the `InputStream`. The `DefaultHandler` class is a common base class for SAX applications that implements all the handler interfaces, in order to make subclassing easier (see below for more information).

`void parse(java.io.InputStream is, DefaultHandler dh, String systemId)`

Same as the previous method, but now providing a system identifier so that the XML parser knows the base URI of the document.

`void parse(String uri, DefaultHandler dh)`

Parses the document at the given URI with the given `DefaultHandler`.

`void parse(java.io.File f, DefaultHandler dh)`

Parses the given file.

`void parse(InputSource is, DefaultHandler dh)`

Parses the document referred to by the given `InputSource`.

`XMLReader getXMLReader()`

Returns the wrapped `XMLReader`.

`boolean isNamespaceAware()`

Is used to find out if the wrapped `XMLReader` is namespace-aware.

`boolean isValidating()`

Is used to find out if the wrapped `XMLReader` is validating.

```
void setProperty(String name, Object value)
```
Equivalent to calling the same method on the underlying XMLReader object. You can find a list of the core SAX 2.0 properties in 10.1.7, "SAX 2.0 extensibility support," on page 346.

```
Object getProperty(String name)
```
Equivalent to calling the same method on the underlying XMLReader object.

19.4.3 *JAXP examples*

To illustrate how to use the JAXP API, Example 19–1 shows how to create a parser and prints some information about the parser.

Example 19–1. A JAXP demo

```java
import javax.xml.parsers.SAXParserFactory;
import javax.xml.parsers.SAXParser;
import javax.xml.parsers.ParserConfigurationException;
import org.xml.sax.SAXException;

public class JAXPDemo {

  public static void main(String[] args) {
    try {
      SAXParserFactory factory = SAXParserFactory.newInstance();
      SAXParser parser = factory.newSAXParser();

      System.out.println("Parser: " + parser.getClass());
      System.out.println("Namespace-aware: " +
                        parser.isNamespaceAware());
      System.out.println("Validating: " + parser.isValidating());
    }
    catch (ParserConfigurationException e) {
      System.err.println("ERROR: " + e);
    }
    catch (SAXException e) {
      System.err.println("ERROR: " + e);
    }
  }
}
```

As you can see, all the program does is create a `SAXParserFactory` and then get a `SAXParser` from it.

Example 19–2 shows the results of running this program from the command line with different configurations. Note that the `$` is the command-line prompt.

Example 19–2. Running the JAXPDemo

```
$ java JAXPDemo
Parser: org.apache.crimson.jaxp.SAXParserImpl@19c082
Namespace-aware: false
Validating: false
$ java -Djavax.xml.parsers.SAXParserFactory=org.apache.xerces.jaxp.
                                SAXParserFactoryImpl JAXPDemo
Parser: org.apache.xerces.jaxp.SAXParserImpl@1664a1
Namespace-aware: false
Validating: false
```

19.5 | Java SAX APIs

In Java, the SAX API is divided into two parts: the core API defined in the `org.xml.sax` package, and the helpers API, containing utility classes, found in the `org.xml.sax.helpers` package. Some of the classes in these packages are from SAX 1.0; these are now deprecated and will not be described here. Figure 19–1 shows an overview diagram of the SAX interfaces, which is repeated from the Python SAX chapter in order to help you remember the roles of the different interfaces.

Handling namespace processing is the main difference between the Java and Python versions of SAX. In Java, the same `startElement` and `endElement` methods are used regardless of whether namespace processing is performed or not. Names are passed to these methods as three different parameters: the namespace URI, the localname, and the unprocessed XML 1.0 name. This is also how names are represented in the `Attributes` interface. The values of these parameters are defined

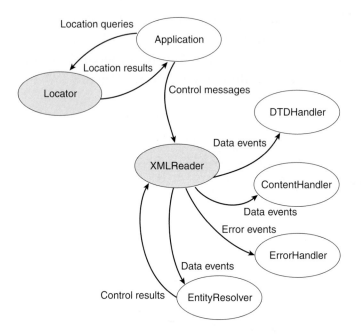

Figure 19–1   Overview of the SAX interfaces

by the values of the SAX features `namespaces` and `namespace-prefixes`.

Table 19–2 shows how SAX behaves for different combinations of these two features. Note that it is not allowed for both features to be `false`, so the table has no row for that state.

Table 19–2   The effect of the namespace features

namespaces	*namespace-prefixes*	*URIs and localnames*	**PrefixMapping events*	*Qnames*	*xmlns attributes*
`true`	`false`	reported	reported	may be reported	not reported
`true`	`true`	reported	reported	reported	reported
`false`	`true`	may be reported	may be reported	reported	reported

The default state of XML parsers is the topmost row, and all parsers must support this state. The other states may or may not be supported, and as can be seen, there is no way to force XML parsers to turn namespace processing off. This is rather different from how this is treated in the Python version of SAX.

Note that in Java SAX, the null namespace URI, that is, the namespace URI of names that have no namespace, is represented by an empty string, rather than by `null`. This was done because it makes life easier for applications in that they can always use the `equals` method to compare names, without having to check first whether the URI is a string or `null`. In Python, `None` was used for this situation, since `==` will be used for comparison regardless of which representation is chosen.

19.5.1 *The* XMLReader *interface*

As in Python SAX, the XML parser is represented by `XMLReader`, which in Java is an interface. Its public methods are listed below.

`void parse(String systemId)`
Makes the parser parse the XML document referred to. The reference must, unlike in Python, always be a URI, even when referring to files on the local disk. References to files using the file naming scheme of the local system will give an exception. The easiest way to turn a file name into a syntactically correct URL is to use the `toURL` method of the `java.io.File` class.[1]

`void parse(InputSource input)`
Parses the document referred to by the `InputSource`.

`void setErrorHandler(ErrorHandler handler)`
Sets the `ErrorHandler` to which errors will be reported.

---

1.   Note that this method only exists in JDK 1.2 and later. To handle this in earlier Java versions, see `http://www.jclark.com/xml/XMLTest.java`, the `fileToURL` method.

`ErrorHandler getErrorHandler()`
    Returns the current `ErrorHandler`.

`void setContentHandler(ContentHandler handler)`
    Sets the `ContentHandler` to which document events will be sent.

`ContentHandler getContentHandler()`
    Returns the current `ContentHandler`.

`void setDTDHandler(DTDHandler handler)`
    Sets the `DTDHandler` to which unparsed entity DTD declarations will be sent.

`DTDHandler getDTDHandler()`
    Returns the current `DTDHandler`.

`void setEntityResolver(EntityResolver resolver)`
    Sets the `EntityResolver` which will be used to resolve references to external entities.

`EntityResolver getEntityResolver()`
    Returns the current `EntityResolver`.

`void setProperty(String name, Object value)`
    Sets a value for the named SAX property.

`Object getProperty(String name)`
    Returns the current value of the named SAX property.

`void setFeature(String name, boolean value)`
    Turns the named feature either off or on.

`boolean getFeature(String name)`
    Returns the current state of the named feature.

The core features and properties are the same as those in Python SAX (see 10.1.7, "SAX 2.0 extensibility support," on page 346). Some parsers also define their own features and properties.

19.5.2 *The* ContentHandler *interface*

Just as in Python, the ContentHandler interface is the interface of the handler that receives events with document content. It has the following public methods:

void setDocumentLocator(Locator locator)
> This method is called by the XMLReader to provide the ContentHandler with a Locator that can tell it where in the document it is at all times, if the XMLReader has this information. If called, this method is the first to be called.

void startDocument()
> This method is the first data event to be invoked, and is used to tell the ContentHandler that parsing of a new document has begun. It is often used by applications for initialization purposes.

void endDocument()
> This method is the last that is called, and tells the application that the entire document has been parsed. It is often used by applications to perform operations that can only be performed after the entire document has been parsed.

void startPrefixMapping(String prefix, String uri)
> For every element that has a namespace declaration, this method will be called to provide the application with the information in that declaration, if the parser is in namespace-aware mode. This is useful so that applications can know at all points in a document what prefix-to-URI mappings are in effect, in case they need to interpret prefixes appearing in document content.

The `startPrefixMapping` method will be called before the corresponding `startElement` method.

`void endPrefixMapping(String prefix)`
> After the `endElement` method of an element that held namespace declarations, this method will be called to tell the application that it is now moving out of the scope of this particular declaration.

`void startElement(String namespaceURI,`
`    String localName, String qName, Attributes atts)`
> Is called upon encountering the start-tag of an element. The parameters are as explained above.

`void endElement(String namespaceURI,`
`    String localName, String qName)`
> Is called to inform the application that the end-tag of an element has been reached.

`void characters(char ch[], int start, int length)`
> Is called to pass character data in the document to the application. Note that the character data is not passed as a string, since the parser is working on an array of `chars` for performance reasons, and instantiating a `String` object is not a lightweight operation. Hence, the application is left to do this itself if it wants to, and quite often it may not want to.
>
> The `characters` event was designed differently in the Python version of SAX. The rationale for this was that of the parsers available in Python, only xmlproc made use of this, the performance benefit was much smaller than in Java while the awkwardness was greater.
>
> Just as in Python, what is one continuous block of character data in the document may be reported in several calls to this method.

```
void ignorableWhitespace(char ch[], int start,
    int length)
```
Is used to inform applications of whitespace appearing in element content. Validating parsers must call this method when appropriate,[1] and non-validating parsers may call it if they have enough information to do so.

```
void processingInstruction(String target,
    String data)
```
Is called to pass processing instructions on to the application.

```
void skippedEntity(String name)
```
Non-validating parsers are not required to read entities for which they have not seen a declaration (nor can they), and all parsers are allowed to skip whichever entities they please. The XML Recommendation requires parsers to tell applications of entities they skip, and this method is provided for that purpose.

19.5.3 *The* ErrorHandler *interface*

The ErrorHandler interface is used to pass information about errors to the application so that the application can decide what to do about the errors. The interface is exactly the same as in Python, but is repeated here for completeness.

```
void warning(SAXParseException exception)
```
Is called to inform the application of something that is not strictly an error, according to the XML Recommendation, but which may still be troublesome.

---

1.   See the XML Recommendation, Section 2.10.

```
void error(SAXParseException exception)
```
Is called to inform the application of errors that are not fatal errors. This will generally be what the XML Recommendation calls validity errors.

```
void fatalError(SAXParseException exception)
```
This method is called to inform the application that a fatal error, according to the XML Recommendation, has occurred. The parser may choose whether or not to continue after such an error, but it should ordinarily stop passing data events to the application, except for further error events. This means that there should be no more calls to any events other than those on the `ErrorHandler` interface.

19.5.4 *The* DTDHandler *interface*

The `DTDHandler` interface is used to pass information about unparsed entities to the application. It is exactly the same as in Python.

```
void notationDecl(String name, String publicId,
    String systemId)
```
Is called to inform the application of a notation declaration.

```
void unparsedEntityDecl(String name, String
    publicId, String systemId, String notationName)
```
Is called to inform the application of the declaration of an unparsed entity.

19.5.5 *The* EntityResolver *interface*

This interface is very nearly, but not exactly, the same as in Python. It is still used to resolve references to external entities, but in Java it can only return `InputSource` objects and not string URIs.

```
InputSource resolveEntity(String publicId,
    String systemId)
```
Is called for each reference to an external entity that the parser intends to read and must return either an `InputSource` from which the entity can be read, or `null` to indicate that the original `systemId` should be used.

19.5.6 *The* `Attributes` *interface*

As in Python, this interface is used to represent sets of attribute value assignments, most commonly those that occur on an element together. Unlike in Python, however, Java has a single interface for both namespace and non-namespace mode. Because of this, the interface is rather different in places, and since Java does not have built-in dictionaries, the methods used to do dictionary emulation are missing in Java.

```
int getLength()
```
Returns the number of attributes.

```
String getURI(int index)
```
Returns the namespace URI of the attribute at the given index. An empty string is used to represent attributes that have no namespace, and `null` is returned if the index is out of range.

```
String getLocalName(int index)
```
Returns the local name of the attribute with the given index. If namespace processing is not on, an empty string will be returned, or, if the index is out of range, `null`.

```
String getQName(int index)
```
Returns the full qualified name of the attribute, as it appeared in the XML document. In namespace mode, this may not be available, and if it is not, an empty string is returned. If the index is out of range, `null` is returned.

```
String getType(int index)
```
Returns the type of the attribute if known, or `'CDATA'` if not known. When `index` is out of range, `null` is returned. The type is represented by one of the strings `'CDATA'`, `'ID'`, `'IDREF'`, `'IDREFS'`, `'NMTOKEN'`, `'NMTOKENS'`, `'ENTITY'`, `'ENTITIES'`, or `'NOTATION'`. Enumeration attributes will be represented by `'NOTATION'` if they are notation attributes, and `'NMTOKEN'` otherwise. This means that the information that the attribute is an enumeration attribute is lost, as is the information on what the legal values are.

```
String getValue(int index)
```
Returns the value of the attribute, or `null` if the `index` is out of range.

```
int getIndex(String uri, String localPart)
```
Returns the index of the attribute with the given URI and local name, if it appears in the list, or `-1` if it does not.

```
int getIndex(String qName)
```
Returns the index of the attribute with the given qualified name, or `-1` if it does not exist.

```
String getType(String uri, String localName)
```
Returns the type of the attribute with the given expanded name, or `null` if the attribute cannot be found.

```
String getType(String qName)
```
Returns the type of the attribute with the given qualified name, if known.

```
String getValue(String uri, String localName)
```
Returns the value of the attribute with the given expanded name, or `null` if no such attribute is known.

```
String getValue(String qName)
```
Returns the value of the attribute with the given qualified name, or `null` if it is not in the set.

19.5.7 *The* `Locator` *interface*

This interface serves the same purpose as in Python: it is the interface of something that can provide a reference to a specific point in a document. It is often used to provide information about where in the document a particular event originated. The interface, as shown below, is exactly the same as in Python.

```
String getPublicId()
```
Returns the public identifier of the resource, if known.

```
String getSystemId()
```
Returns the system identifier of the resource, if known.

```
int getLineNumber()
```
Returns the line number in the resource, or -1 if it is not available.

```
int getColumnNumber()
```
Returns the column number in the line, or -1 if it is not known.

19.5.8 *The* `XMLFilter` *interface*

This is the interface of parser filters, just as `XMLFilterBase` is in Python SAX. And just as in Python, it extends `XMLReader`, but adds methods to manage the `XMLReader` it gets its events from.

```
void setParent(XMLReader parent)
```
Gives the filter the `XMLReader` from which it will be getting its events. Filters will usually get the reader in their constructor, but this method provides a way to set it common to all filters.

728 CHAPTER 19 | SAX IN JAVA

```
XMLReader getParent()
```
Returns the `XMLReader` the filter will read its events from, if one has been set.

19.5.9 *The* `InputSource` *class*

Instances of this class represent a resource from which an XML document can be read, just as in Python. It supports many different kinds of input, so as to not restrict an XML parser's possible sources of input. Note that in order for the parser to be able to resolve relative URL references in documents, the system identifier property must be set. The interface is the same as in Python, as shown below.

```
InputSource()
```
Creates an empty object.

```
InputSource(String systemId)
```
Creates an `InputSource` with the given system identifier.

```
InputSource(InputStream byteStream)
```
Creates an `InputSource` with the given byte stream. If no encoding name is given, standard XML rules for inferring it will be applied.

```
InputSource(Reader characterStream)
```
Creates an `InputSource` with the given character stream.

```
void setPublicId(String publicId)
```
Sets the public identifier of the resource represented by this `InputSource`.

```
String getPublicId()
```
Returns the public identifier.

```
void setSystemId(String systemId)
```
Sets the system identifier of this object.

```
String getSystemId()
```
Returns the system identifier.

```
void setByteStream(InputStream byteStream)
```
Sets the byte stream of this object.

```
InputStream getByteStream()
```
Returns the byte stream.

```
void setEncoding(String encoding)
```
Sets the name of the encoding used in the resource represented by this object. If a character stream is given, this property has no significance, since the parser already has the contents of the resource available in Unicode and therefore needs no assistance in converting it to Unicode.

As in Python and elsewhere, the list of allowed character encodings includes those defined by IANA in its publicly maintained registry at `http://www.isi.edu/in-notes/iana/assignments/character-sets`.

```
String getEncoding()
```
Returns the name of the encoding used in this resource, if set.

```
void setCharacterStream(Reader characterStream)
```
Sets the character stream of the resource.

```
Reader getCharacterStream()
```
Returns the character stream.

19.5.10 *The* SAXException *exception*

This is the generic exception raised by SAX parsers and SAX applications alike. It has no semantics, and merely signals that something went wrong somewhere. Other exceptions may be encapsulated in a SAX-Exception. The methods of the exception class are listed below.

```
SAXException(String message)
```
This constructor creates a `SAXException` with a string message and no embedded exception.

```
SAXException(Exception e)
```
This constructor creates a `SAXException` that wraps another exception and takes its message from that exception.

```
SAXException(String message, Exception e)
```
Creates a `SAXException` that has both a message of its own and an encapsulated exception.

```
Exception getException()
```
Returns the exception embedded in this `SAXException` or `null` if there is none.

19.5.11 *The* SAXParseException *exception*

This class is derived from `SAXException` and is used to indicate an error during parsing. Because of this, it may contain information about where the error occurred. It adds the methods shown below to those of the `SAXException`.

```
SAXParseException(String message, Locator locator)
```
Creates an exception with the given message and location information.

```
SAXParseException (String message, Locator locator,
    Exception e)
```
Creates an exception with a message, location information, and an embedded exception.

```
SAXParseException (String message, String publicId,
    String systemId, int lineNumber,
    int columnNumber, Exception e)
```
Creates an exception with the same information as above.

```
String getPublicId()
```
Returns the public identifier of the resource, if known.

```
String getSystemId()
```
Returns the system identifier of the resource, if known.

```
int getLineNumber()
```
Returns the line number in the resource, or -1 if it is not available.

```
int getColumnNumber()
```
Returns the column number in the line, or -1 if it is not known.

19.5.12 *The* `SAXNotSupportedException` *exception*

This exception is used to indicate that something has been attempted which is not supported by the `XMLReader` or whichever class threw this exception. It is primarily used by `XMLReaders` to indicate that they don't support particular values for `setProperty` or `setFeature`, but can also be used for other purposes.

The class is derived from `SAXException` and provides no extra methods. The constructor only takes a single string message.

19.5.13 *The* `SAXNotRecognizedException` *exception*

This exception is thrown to show that an identifier was given that was not recognized. It is usually thrown by `XMLReaders` who have been given SAX property or feature names they do not recognize, but it may also be used for other purposes.

The class is derived from `SAXException` and provides no extra methods. The constructor only takes a single string message.

19.5.14 *The* `org.xml.sax.helpers` *package*

In addition to the classes and interfaces presented so far, the Java version of SAX contains a number of helper classes in the `org.xml.sax.helpers` package. These classes provide various useful pieces of functionality that can make it easier to develop SAX applications or write SAX drivers.

19.5.14.1 The `AttributesImpl` class

This class implements the `Attributes` interface described in 19.5.6, "The `Attributes` interface," on page 725 as an attribute set container. It adds support for copying the contents of other `Attributes` objects and for directly modifying the contents of the object. All the methods from the `Attributes` interface are provided, and the methods listed below are added. (The source code of this class, by the way, is both easy and interesting to read, and novice developers may learn a thing or two from it.)

`AttributesImpl()`
    Creates an empty set.

`AttributesImpl(Attributes atts)`
    Creates a new instance containing a copy of the data from the given `Attributes` object. If the object given as a parameter is later modified, this is not reflected in the new object.

`void clear()`
    Removes all data in the object, making it empty.

`void setAttributes(Attributes atts)`
    Clears the object, then copies all information from the given `Attributes` object.

`void addAttribute(String uri, String localName, String qName, String type, String value)`
Adds a new attribute to the object with the given values. Note that none of these strings can be `null`. The values must follow the rules described in the section on namespace processing above.

`void setAttribute(int index, String uri, String localName, String qName, String type, String value)`
Sets the information about a specific attribute in the object. If the given `index` does not refer to an attribute that is actually in the set, a `java.lang.ArrayIndexOutOfBoundsException` is thrown.

`void removeAttribute(int index)`
Removes the attribute at the given index, shifting all attributes at higher indexes down by one. If the given `index` does not refer to an attribute that is actually in the set, a `java.lang.ArrayIndex-OutOfBoundsException` is thrown.

`void setURI(int index, String uri)`
Sets the URI of the attribute with the given index, throwing a `java.lang.ArrayIndexOutOfBoundsException` if there is no such attribute.

`void setLocalName(int index, String localName)`
Sets the local name of the attribute with the given index, throwing a `java.lang.ArrayIndexOutOfBoundsException` if there is no such attribute.

`void setQName(int index, String qName)`
Sets the qualified name of the attribute with the given index, throwing a `java.lang.ArrayIndexOutOfBoundsException` if there is no such attribute.

```
void setType(int index, String type)
```
Sets the type of the attribute with the given index, throwing a `java.lang.ArrayIndexOutOfBoundsException` if there is no such attribute.

```
void setValue(int index, String value)
```
Sets the value of the attribute with the given index, throwing a `java.lang.ArrayIndexOutOfBoundsException` if there is no such attribute.

19.5.14.2 The `DefaultHandler` class

This class implements all the event methods of the `ContentHandler`, `ErrorHandler`, `EntityResolver`, and `DTDHandler` interfaces with methods that do nothing. There is one exception: the `fatalError` method throws the exception it is given. This makes it a convenient base class of applications that implement some, but not all, methods on the event handler interfaces.

Note that even though the class implements all the event handler interfaces, objects of the class must be registered as handlers of a specific type to be used as such. That is, registering a `DefaultHandler` object as a `ContentHandler` does not mean it can be used as an `Error-Handler` unless it is explicitly registered as such.

19.5.14.3 The `LocatorImpl` class

This little class implements the `Locator` interface, storing all the data provided by that interface directly in instances of the class, and allowing client code to use it. This is mainly useful for copying information from the `Locator` provided by the parser and storing it to be used later, when the parser's `Locator` will be returning other values. It implements all the methods of the `Locator` interface, adding those listed below.

```
LocatorImpl()
```
Creates an empty object.

```
LocatorImpl(Locator locator)
```
Creates an object containing a copy of the information from the given `Locator`.

```
void setPublicId(String publicId)
```
Sets the stored public identifier.

```
void setSystemId(String systemId)
```
Sets the stored system identifier.

```
void setLineNumber(int lineNumber)
```
Sets the stored line number.

```
void setColumnNumber(int columnNumber)
```
Sets the stored column number.

19.5.14.4 The `NamespaceSupport` class

This class encapsulates the logic of namespace processing, and is useful for working with namespace prefix mapping contexts which nest inside each other and override each other. This is mainly useful for those writing SAX drivers and parsers, so this class is not covered here. If you are interested in using it, see the SAX 2.0 javadoc.

19.5.14.5 The `ParserAdapter` class

This is an implementation of the `XMLReader` interface which takes a SAX 1.0 `Parser` object and makes it behave as if it were an `XMLReader` with full namespace support. This can be used to use SAX 1.0 parsers in SAX 2.0, which may occasionally be useful if one wants to use a specific parser because it has features not provided by other parsers. (It is hard to imagine something that would make this useful, but at least the possibility is there.) The class has two constructors:

`ParserAdapter()`

    Creates a `ParserAdapter` that wraps the default SAX 1.0 parser, which is defined by the value of the `org.xml.sax.parser` system property. This must hold the name of a SAX 1.0 `Parser` implementation, or the constructor will fail.

`ParserAdapter(Parser parser)`

    Creates an adapter around the given `Parser`.

19.5.14.6 The `XMLFilterImpl` class

This class is a default implementation of the `XMLFilter` interface, which passes on all events unchanged from the four event handlers of its parent to the handlers given to it. This is mainly useful as a base class for parser filter implementations. The class has two constructors.

`XMLFilterImpl()`

    Creates a filter with no parent.

`XMLFilterImpl(XMLReader parent)`

    Creates a filter with the given parent.

19.5.14.7 The `XMLReaderAdapter` class

This class performs the opposite function of what the `ParserAdapter` class does, in that it wraps a SAX 2.0 `XMLReader` in the `Parser` interface, making it behave like a SAX 1.0 `Parser`. This is mainly useful when you need to embed a SAX 2.0 parser in a framework or application that expects a SAX 1.0 parser. This might be useful to get the latest and fastest versions of parsers, and perhaps also updates for the XML 1.0 second edition specification. The class has two constructors, listed below.

`XMLReaderAdapter()`

    Creates a `XMLReaderAdapter` that wraps the default SAX 2.0 parser, which is defined by the value of the `org.xml.sax.driver` system property. This must hold the name of a SAX 2.0 `XMLReader` implementation, or the constructor will fail.

`XMLReaderAdapter(XMLReader parser)`
Creates an adapter around the given `XMLReader`.

19.5.14.8 The `XMLReaderFactory` class

This class provides a mechanism for creating `XMLReader` implementations without hard-wiring the connection to the specific implementation class into the application code. This is much the same functionality that was later duplicated in the JAXP APIs developed by Sun.

The factory has two methods:

`static XMLReader createXMLReader()`
Creates an instance of the class referred to by the `org.xml.sax.driver` property, if any.

`static XMLReader createXMLReader(String className)`
Creates an instance of the named class, which must be an implementation of the `XMLReader` interface.

19.6 | Java SAX examples

In this section we go through a number of examples of SAX applications written in Java, to show how to do SAX development in this language. As it turns out, Java lacks many of the features that make SAX development in Python easy, so different techniques must be used to keep development painless. This section will present those techniques.

19.6.1 *RSS conversion*

In this section we revisit the by now familiar example of converting RSS documents to HTML. The first version of the converter is written much in the style of the initial Python converter, that is, without supporting objects of any kind, and the result is not very nice. The program is long, awkward, and difficult to read, as you can see for yourself in Examples 19–3 to 19–5.

Example 19–3. RSS to HTML, in Java (1 of 3)

```java
import java.io.File;
import java.io.FileWriter;
import java.io.IOException;
import java.io.Writer;
import java.util.Stack;
import javax.xml.parsers.SAXParserFactory;
import javax.xml.parsers.SAXParser;
import javax.xml.parsers.ParserConfigurationException;
import org.xml.sax.XMLReader;
import org.xml.sax.Attributes;
import org.xml.sax.SAXException;
import org.xml.sax.helpers.DefaultHandler;

public class SAXRSS2HTML {

  public static void main(String[] args) {
    try {
      convert(args[0], args[1]);
    }
    catch (ParserConfigurationException e) {
      System.err.println("ERROR: " + e);
    }
    catch (SAXException e) {
      System.err.println("ERROR: " + e);
    }
    catch (java.net.MalformedURLException e) {
      System.err.println("ERROR: " + e);
    }
    catch (IOException e) {
      System.err.println("ERROR: " + e);
    }
  }
```

```
public static void convert(String infile, String outfile)
throws java.net.MalformedURLException, IOException, SAXException,
       ParserConfigurationException {
  XMLReader parser = getXMLReader();
  parser.setContentHandler(new RSSHandler(outfile));
  parser.parse(new File(infile).toURL().toString());
}

private static XMLReader getXMLReader()
  throws SAXException, ParserConfigurationException {
  SAXParserFactory factory = SAXParserFactory.newInstance();
  SAXParser parser = factory.newSAXParser();
  return parser.getXMLReader();
}
```

This is the class that implements the command-line interface, sets up and starts parsing. The SAX application itself is written as a ContentHandler in an internal class, shown in Example 19–4.

A stack of elements is used to keep track of what container elements title, link, and description elements belong to, so they can be handled correctly. The keepContent attribute is a flag that is used to tell whether we are currently inside an element whose content we wish to record in the content buffer.

The firstItem flag is used to tell whether the item we are about to write out will be the first or not, so that we can start the ul element in the HTML output correctly. The title attribute is used to keep titles until we have the corresponding link value.

Example 19–4. RSS to HTML, in Java (2 of 3)

```
// --- Internal classes

static class RSSHandler extends DefaultHandler {
  private Writer   out;

  private Stack elements;
  private boolean keepContent;
  private StringBuffer content;
  private boolean firstItem;
  private String title;
```

Example 19–5. RSS to HTML, in Java (3 of 3)

```java
public RSSHandler(String outfile) throws IOException {
  out = new FileWriter(outfile);
  elements = new Stack();
  firstItem = true;
}


public void startElement(String nsuri, String lname,
                         String qname, Attributes attrs) {

  keepContent = lname.equals("title") ||
                lname.equals("link") ||
                lname.equals("description");

  elements.push(lname);

  if (keepContent)
    content = new StringBuffer();
}

public void endElement(String nsuri, String lname, String qname)
throws SAXException {
  try {
    keepContent = false;
    elements.pop();

    if (elements.isEmpty())
      return;

    String parent = (String) elements.peek();

    // CHANNEL
    if (parent.equals("channel")) {
      if (lname.equals("title"))
        title = content.toString();

      else if (lname.equals("link")) {
        out.write("<title>" + title + "</title>\n");
        out.write("<h1><a href=\"" + content + "\">" + title +
                  "</a></h1>\n");
      } else if (lname.equals("description"))
        out.write("<p>" + content + "</p>\n");
```

```
         // ITEM
       } else if (parent.equals("item")) {
         if (firstItem) {
           out.write("\n<ul>");
           firstItem = false;
         }

         if (lname.equals("title"))
           title = content.toString();

         else if (lname.equals("link"))
           out.write("\n<li><a href=\"" + content + "\">" + title +
                     "</a>");

         else if (lname.equals("description"))
           out.write(content.toString());


       } else if (lname.equals("channel"))
         out.write("\n</ul>\n");
     }
     catch (IOException e) {
       throw new SAXException(e);
     }
   }

   public void characters(char[] chars, int start, int length) {
     if (keepContent)
       content.append(chars, start, length);
   }

   public void endDocument() throws SAXException {
     try {
       out.close();
     }
     catch (IOException e) {
       throw new SAXException(e);
     }
   }
 }
}
```

Example 19–5 is fairly straightforward given the previous explanations and should thus require no further comment.

The structure of RSS documents is relatively simple, so the most obvious way to improve on this code is to create a `SAXTracker` class like the one designed in the Python chapters. This would take away much of the pain of tracking state and make the code easier to write and read.

To be able to reuse it in other applications, we first develop the Java `SAXTracker` as a separate class. Its source code is shown in Example 19–6.

Example 19–6. The Java `SAXTracker`

```
import java.util.HashSet;
import java.util.Set;
import java.util.Stack;
import org.xml.sax.Attributes;
import org.xml.sax.SAXException;
import org.xml.sax.helpers.DefaultHandler;

public abstract class SAXTracker extends DefaultHandler {
  protected Set          keepContentsOf;
  protected StringBuffer content;
  private   boolean      keepContents;
  protected Stack        openElements;

  // --- Configuration interface

  public SAXTracker() {
    keepContentsOf = new HashSet();
  }

  public void keepContentsOf(String elementName) {
    keepContentsOf.add(elementName);
  }

  // --- Utility interface

  public boolean isParent(String localName) {
    return !openElements.isEmpty() &&
           openElements.peek().equals(localName);
  }
```

```
// --- ContentHandler interface

public void startElement(String nsuri, String lname, String qname,
                         Attributes attrs) throws SAXException {
  openElements.push(lname);

  keepContents = keepContentsOf.contains(lname);
  if (keepContents)
    content = new StringBuffer();
}

public void characters(char[] chars, int start, int length)
  throws SAXException {
  if (keepContents)
    content.append(chars, start, length);
}

public void endElement(String nsuri, String lname, String qname)
  throws SAXException {
  keepContents = false;
  openElements.pop();
}
}
```

The interface and implementation of this SAXTracker is very similar to its Python counterpart, so little comment is needed. It is noteworthy that the isParent method is a useful shorthand since checking the name of the parent element type is rather awkward in Java.

Using the SAXTracker, the application becomes somewhat simpler and a bit easier to read. The application itself remains exactly the same, but the RSSHandler class is simplified. Example 19–7 shows the source code to the RSSHandler class.

The main difference is that much of the state tracking variables and machinery is now gone, so we only need to implement endElement and endDocument. The endElement method is also simplified somewhat, since it needs to do less, and it can also use the isParent method to check the name of the current parent element type.

Example 19–7. A simpler `RSSHandler`

```java
static class RSSHandler extends SAXTracker {
  private Writer  out;

  private boolean firstItem;
  private String title;

  public RSSHandler(String outfile) throws IOException {
    out = new FileWriter(outfile);
    firstItem = true;
    keepContentsOf("title");
    keepContentsOf("link");
    keepContentsOf("description");
  }

  public void endElement(String nsuri, String lname, String qname)
  throws SAXException {
    super.endElement(nsuri, lname, qname);

    try {
      // CHANNEL
      if (isParent("channel")) {
        if (lname.equals("title"))
          title = content.toString();

        else if (lname.equals("link")) {
          out.write("<title>" + title + "</title>\n");
          out.write("<h1><a href=\"" + content + "\">" + title +
                  "</a></h1>\n");

        } else if (lname.equals("description"))
          out.write("<p>" + content + "</p>\n");

      // ITEM
      } else if (isParent("item")) {
        if (firstItem) {
          out.write("\n<ul>");
          firstItem = false;
        }

        if (lname.equals("title"))
          title = content.toString();

        else if (lname.equals("link"))
          out.write("\n<li><a href=\"" + content + "\">" + title +
                  "</a>");
```

```
          else if (lname.equals("description"))
            out.write(content.toString());

      } else if (lname.equals("channel"))
        out.write("\n</ul>\n");
    }
    catch (IOException e) {
      throw new SAXException(e);
    }
  }

  public void endDocument() throws SAXException {
    try {
      out.close();
    }
    catch (IOException e) {
      throw new SAXException(e);
    }
  }
}
```

19.6.2 *XBEL conversion*

To provide another angle on SAX development in Java, we here show how to convert XBEL to HTML using an object model. We begin with the object model, which has classes for representing the abstract structure of XBEL documents, then go on to write the code that builds such structures from XML documents. (If you haven't read the book sequentially and don't know what XBEL is, see 9.1, "An introduction to XBEL," on page 269.)

This is the recommended way to develop SAX applications in Java, since this is the only way to build complex data structures in that language. In Python, you can handle many cases simply by using combinations of dictionaries, lists, and tuples, but in Java this quickly becomes either impossible or unbearably complex.

Example 19–8 shows the source code of the classes used to represent the XBEL object structure once it has been built, whether from an XBEL document or from some other source. Note that each class must be stored in a separate file, but here they are given in a single listing.

Example 19–8. The XBEL object structure classes

```
/**
 * Common base class for all nodes in a bookmark collection.
 */

public abstract class Node {
  protected Node parent;

  public Node(Node parent) {
    this.parent = parent;
  }

  public Node getParent() {
    return parent;
  }
}


/**
 * A common base class for the xbel, folder, and bookmark elements,
 * representing a node with ID, title, and description.
 */

public abstract class NodeWithTitle extends Node {
  protected String id;
  protected String title;
  protected String description;

  public NodeWithTitle(Node parent, String id) {
    super(parent);
    this.id = id;
  }

  public String getId() {
    return id;
  }

  public void setId(String id) {
    this.id = id;
  }

  public String getTitle() {
    return title;
  }
}
```

```
  public void setTitle(String title) {
    this.title = title;
  }

  public String getDescription() {
    return description;
  }

  public void setDescription(String description) {
    this.description = description;
  }

}

/**
 * Extends NodeWithTitle to support a list of children. Used
 * for the xbel and folder elements.
 */

public abstract class NodeWithChildren extends NodeWithTitle {
  protected List children;

  public NodeWithChildren(Node parent, String id) {
    super(parent, id);
    children = new ArrayList();
  }

  public List getChildren() {
    return children;
  }

  public void addChild(Node child) {
    children.add(child);
  }

  public void removeChild(Node child) {
    children.remove(child);
  }
}

/**
 * This represents an entire collection of bookmarks, that is,
 * an entire XBEL document.
 */
```

```java
public class BookmarkCollection extends NodeWithChildren {
  protected String baseUrl;
  protected Map    idmap;

  public BookmarkCollection(String baseUrl) {
    super(null, null);
    this.baseUrl = baseUrl;
    idmap = new HashMap();
  }

  public String getBaseUrl() {
    return baseUrl;
  }

  public void setBaseUrl(String baseUrl) {
    this.baseUrl = baseUrl;
  }

  public void registerNode(NodeWithTitle node) {
    idmap.put(node.getId(), node);
  }

  public void unregisterNode(NodeWithTitle node) {
    idmap.remove(node.getId());
  }

  public NodeWithTitle getNodeById(String id) {
    return (NodeWithTitle) idmap.get(id);
  }

}

/**
 * Represents a single bookmark.
 */

public class Bookmark extends NodeWithTitle {
  protected String url;
  protected long   visited;
  protected long   modified;

  public Bookmark(Node parent, String id) {
    super(parent, id);
    visited = -1;
    modified = -1;
  }
```

```java
  public String getUrl() {
    return url;
  }

  public void setUrl(String url) {
    this.url = url;
  }

  public long getVisited() {
    return visited;
  }

  public void setVisited(long visited) {
    this.visited = visited;
  }

  public long getModified() {
    return modified;
  }

  public void setModified(long modified) {
    this.modified = modified;
  }

}

/**
 * Represents a folder.
 */

class Folder extends NodeWithChildren {
  protected boolean isfolded;

  public Folder(Node parent, String id) {
    super(parent, id);
    isfolded = false;
  }

  public boolean getIsFolded() {
    return isfolded;
  }

  public void setIsFolded(boolean isfolded) {
    this.isfolded = isfolded;
  }

}
```

```
/**
 * Represents a separator element. It does not extend any of the
 * subclasses of Node, since separators have no properties.
 */

public class Separator extends Node {
  public Separator(Node parent) {
    super(parent);
  }
}

/**
 * Represents an alias element. The node property holds the node
 * referred to by the element.
 */

public class Alias extends Node {
  protected NodeWithTitle node;

  public Alias(Node parent) {
    super(parent);
  }

  public NodeWithTitle getNode() {
    return node;
  }

  public void setNode(NodeWithTitle node) {
    this.node = node;
  }

}
```

This, however, is only half of the equation. The next important part is to be able to build such structures from XBEL documents. The classes in Example 19–9 are used to do this.

The only part that now remains is to build a useful application with these classes. The most obvious one is an XBEL to HTML converter, but this is left as an exercise for the reader, since that task really holds no new challenges.

Example 19–9. The XBEL structure builder

```java
import java.io.*;
import javax.xml.parsers.*;
import org.xml.sax.*;

public class XBELUtilities {

  public static BookmarkCollection read(String uri)
  throws SAXException, IOException, java.net.MalformedURLException,
       ParserConfigurationException{
    XBELContentHandler handler = new XBELContentHandler(uri);
    XMLReader parser = getXMLReader();
    parser.setContentHandler(handler);
    parser.parse(uri);
    return handler.getBookmarkCollection();
  }

  public static void main(String[] args) {
    try {
      BookmarkCollection bookmarks =
        read(new File(args[0]).toURL().toString());
      System.out.println("title: " + bookmarks.getTitle());
      System.out.println("descr: " + bookmarks.getDescription());
    }
    catch (Exception e) {
      e.printStackTrace();
      System.err.println("ERROR: " + e);
    }
  }

  private static XMLReader getXMLReader()
    throws SAXException, ParserConfigurationException {
    SAXParserFactory factory = SAXParserFactory.newInstance();
    SAXParser parser = factory.newSAXParser();
    return parser.getXMLReader();
  }
}

import java.util.HashMap;
import java.util.Iterator;
import java.util.Map;
import org.xml.sax.*;
```

```java
public class XBELContentHandler extends SAXTracker {
  protected BookmarkCollection bookmarks;
  protected Map aliasRefs;

  protected Node currentNode;

  public XBELContentHandler(String uri) {
    bookmarks = new BookmarkCollection(uri);
    keepContentsOf("title");
    keepContentsOf("desc");
    currentNode = bookmarks;
  }

  public BookmarkCollection getBookmarkCollection() {
    return bookmarks;
  }

  public void startElement(String nsuri, String lname, String qname,
                           Attributes attrs) throws SAXException {
    if (lname.equals("folder"))
      currentNode = new Folder(currentNode, attrs.getValue("id"));
    else if (lname.equals("bookmark"))
      currentNode = new Bookmark(currentNode, attrs.getValue("id"));
    else if (lname.equals("separator"))
      currentNode = new Separator(currentNode);
    else if (lname.equals("alias")) {
      currentNode = new Alias(currentNode);
      aliasRefs.put(currentNode, attrs.getValue("ref"));
    }

    if (lname.equals("folder") || lname.equals("bookmark") ||
        lname.equals("alias") || lname.equals("separator")) {
      NodeWithChildren parent =
                      (NodeWithChildren) currentNode.getParent();
      parent.addChild(currentNode);

      if (lname.equals("folder") || lname.equals("bookmark"))
        bookmarks.registerNode((NodeWithChildren) currentNode);
    }

    super.startElement(nsuri, lname, qname, attrs);
  }
```

```
public void endElement(String nsuri, String lname, String qname)
  throws SAXException {
  NodeWithTitle node = ((NodeWithTitle) currentNode);

  if (lname.equals("title"))
    node.setTitle(content.toString());
  else if (lname.equals("desc"))
    node.setDescription(content.toString());

  else if (lname.equals("folder") || lname.equals("bookmark") ||
           lname.equals("alias") || lname.equals("separator"))
    currentNode = currentNode.getParent();

  super.endElement(nsuri, lname, qname);
}

public void endDocument() {
  Iterator it = aliasRefs.keySet().iterator();
  while (it.hasNext()) {
    Alias alias = (Alias) it.next();
    String id = (String) aliasRefs.get(alias);
    alias.setNode(bookmarks.getNodeById(id));
  }
}
}
```

When the XML structures get even more complex than those of XBEL documents, defining an object structure for the SAX application to build may not be enough, either. Tracking document context and interpreting document information may in itself be challenging in these cases. The recommended solution is to build a specialized state tracking class that is manipulated by the SAX application and used by it to decide what actions to perform when building the domain-specific object structure.

No examples of such applications are provided here, since the explanation of a sufficiently complex XML DTD, its object model, and object model builder implementation would necessarily be unacceptably long.

DOM in Java

- DOM in Java and Python

- Java DOM APIs

- Using Java DOM

- JDOM

# Chapter 20

s mentioned earlier, DOM[1] is specified by the W3C using a language-independent interface specification language called IDL, and both the Java and Python versions of the DOM follow this closely. In the case of Python, there are some extensions to make use of features specific to Python, but not so in Java, which is much closer to the kind of language IDL was designed to be used with. One difference, however, lies in how IDL declarations are translated into Java APIs compared to the mapping from IDL to Python. Note also that the Java binding is specified by the W3C, while the Python one is not.

In Java, the following rules are followed when translating IDL declarations into Java APIs:

- IDL interfaces become interfaces in Java as well,

---

1. If you haven't read the book sequentially, please see Chapter 11, "DOM: an introduction," on page 396 to find out what DOM is.

- IDL attributes become pairs of get/set methods (though set methods are skipped for read-only attributes), so that the attribute `nodeType` gives rise to the methods `getNodeType` and `setNodeType`,

- IDL methods become methods, and

- IDL `DOMString` objects are mapped to Java `String` objects. (This would not happen if the standardized OMG IDL mapping rules were followed, and is an extra rule added by the W3C.)

There are quite a few Java implementations of the DOM API. The most important of these are listed below.

Xerces-J

The Xerces parser includes a DOM implementation that supports levels 1 and 2 of the core DOM, the HTML DOM, the WML DOM, as well as the traversal, events, and ranges DOM modules.

DOM2

David Brownell's DOM2 is an independent open source DOM implementation that, when used together with his XML Utilities, is a complete DOM 2 implementation, supporting the core, XML, events, and traversal features.

MonsterDOM

This is a DOM implementation distributed as part of the Ozone object-oriented database. Both the database and the DOM implementation are written in Java, and the DOM implementation stores the DOM document in the database.

Java Project X

The Sun XML parser, now known as Crimson, also includes a DOM implementation.

Java HTML Tidy

As described in 24.1.1.3, "Tidy and JTidy," on page 935, the Java version of HTML Tidy also contains an HTML DOM implementation. Java HTML Tidy can build a DOM tree even from fairly broken HTML documents.

Oracle XML Parser

Oracle has made a freely available XML development kit that can be downloaded from their Web site by anyone who registers there. The kit contains a parser, a DOM 1 implementation, an XSLT processor, and some useful utilities. These tools can be used in conjunction with the Oracle database (and have extra features for this), but can also be used independently.

20.1 | JAXP and the DOM

JAXP, which was introduced in the previous chapter, can be used not only with SAX but also with DOM. JAXP is more useful when used with DOM than with SAX, since DOM, unlike SAX, has no mechanisms for loosely coupled implementation creation. JAXP is also useful because DOM itself (at least prior to level 3) does not provide any mechanisms for loading XML documents into DOM trees. In addition, the JAXP DOM interfaces offer fairly good control over the DOM-building process, allowing applications to configure various aspects of how DOM documents are built.

As mentioned earlier, DOM level 3 also adds functionality in this area, so there is a slight conflict between these two specifications on this point. This will most likely be resolved in a future version of JAXP, once DOM level 3 has been finalized.

Just as with the SAX part of the DOM, the relevant package is the `javax.xml.parsers` package, and there are two separate classes here that can be used to create and configure DOM builders. These are the `DocumentBuilderFactory` and the `DocumentBuilder`. The interfaces of these two classes are given below.

20.1.1 *The* `DocumentBuilderFactory` *class*

The `DocumentBuilderFactory` can be used to create an instance of the `DocumentBuilder` class, which can then be used to build DOM documents. The factory can be configured so that it creates the kind of builder the client application wants to use.

When instantiating a `DocumentBuilderFactory`, JAXP follows the procedure described below:

1. If the `javax.xml.parsers.DocumentBuilderFactory` property is set, try instantiating an object of the class named in the property value.

2. Alternatively, look in the file `lib/jaxp.properties` in the Java runtime directory for a key with the property name given above.

3. Alternatively, use the Services API (as detailed in the JAR specification), if available, to determine the class name. The Services API will look for the class name in the file `META-INF/services/javax.xml.parsers.DocumentBuilder-Factory` in jars available to the runtime.

4. If all these methods fail, use the platform default, which at the moment will usually be the Sun XML parser known as Crimson.

The `DocumentBuilderFactory` has the methods listed below.

`static DocumentBuilderFactory newInstance()`
Calling this static method causes the factory designated by the configuration (as described above) to be instantiated and returned.

`DocumentBuilder newDocumentBuilder()`
Calling this method on a factory causes it to create `Document-Builder` according to its current configuration settings.

`void setNamespaceAware(boolean awareness)`
This method is used to tell the factory whether to create a namespace-aware builder or not.

```
void setValidating(boolean validating)
```
   This method is used to tell the factory whether to create a validating builder or not.

```
setIgnoringElementContentWhitespace(boolean
   whitespace)
```
   This method is used to tell the factory whether to create a builder that ignores ignorable whitespace or not. (Ignorable whitespace was defined in 2.4.2.1, "How the DTD affects the document," on page 69.)

```
void setExpandEntityReferences(boolean
   expandEntityRef)
```
   This method is used to tell the factory whether to create a builder that expands entity references or not.

```
void setIgnoringComments(boolean ignoreComments)
```
   This method is used to tell the factory whether to create a builder that ignores comments in XML documents or not.

```
void setCoalescing(boolean coalescing)
```
   This method is used to tell the factory whether to create a builder that creates Text nodes from CDATA marked sections or not.

```
boolean isNamespaceAware()
```
   This method is used to tell whether the created builder will be namespace-aware or not.

```
boolean isValidating()
```
   This method is used to tell whether the created builder will be validating.

```
boolean isIgnoringElementContentWhitespace()
```
   This method is used to tell whether the created builder will be ignoring ignorable whitespace.

`boolean isExpandEntityReferences()`
> This method is used to tell whether the created builder will expand entity references or not.

`boolean isIgnoringComments()`
> This method is used to tell whether the created builder will be creating comment nodes or not.

`boolean isCoalescing()`
> This method is used to tell whether the created builder will create CDATA marked section nodes.

`void setAttribute(String name, Object value)`
> This method is used to set specific attributes on the underlying implementation. This mechanism is used for JAXP extensions, which can be defined both by Sun and by individual vendors. No such extensions have yet been defined.

`Object getAttribute(String name)`
> This method is used to get the values of attributes set on the underlying implementation.

20.1.2 *The* DocumentBuilder *class*

The `DocumentBuilder` class represents the XML parser and DOM tree builder in combination, and is used to build DOM trees from XML documents. Like the factory, it provides mechanisms for controlling the process of DOM tree building.

`Document parse(InputStream is)`
> Parses the content of the `InputStream` and returns the `Document` node of the corresponding DOM tree.

`Document parse(InputStream is, String systemId)`
> Also parses from the given stream, but now knowing the base URI of the XML document, which is useful for resolving relative URIs in the document.

`Document parse(String uri)`
> Builds a DOM tree of the XML document at the given URI.

`Document parse(java.io.File f)`
> Builds a DOM tree from the XML document in the given file.

`Document parse(org.xml.sax.InputSource is)`
> Builds a DOM tree from the XML document represented by the given SAX `InputSource`.

`boolean isNamespaceAware()`
> This method is used to find out whether the builder is namespace-aware or not.

`boolean isValidating()`
> This method is used to find out if the builder will validate during building.

`void setEntityResolver(org.xml.sax.EntityResolver er)`
> Sets the SAX `EntityResolver` to be used by the DOM builder when building the DOM tree. This provides control over the entity resolution process during DOM building.

`void setErrorHandler(ErrorHandler eh)`
> Sets the SAX `ErrorHandler` to which the DOM builder will report errors during building. This provides applications with control over the error handling of the builder.

`Document newDocument()`
> Creates an empty DOM `Document` node, for applications that wish to build their own DOM tree programmatically.

```
DOMImplementation getDOMImplementation()
```
Creates a `DOMImplementation` object, which can be used to query the capabilities of the DOM implementation represented by the `DocumentBuilder` object.

20.2 | The Java DOM APIs

DOM itself has already been explained earlier in the book, but in order to help you understand how to use DOM in Java, here is a reference guide to the Java version of the DOM APIs. Since the translation from IDL to Java and Python is mechanical, the differences between the Java and Python versions are highly systematic. Since the translation is automated, we don't give the full APIs here, only as much of them as you need to understand what the DOM looks like in Java.

Note that all IDL interfaces become interfaces in Java as well, so that any objects you come across will be instances of other classes that implement these interfaces. This also means that to get started with using DOM one must instantiate a class that is not defined by DOM. This is why JAXP is useful, and for this purpose it will remain useful even after the DOM level 3 has been defined, since with IDL, there is no way to overcome this particular difficulty.

All the interfaces listed here are found in the `org.w3c.dom` package.

20.2.1 *The* DOMImplementation *interface*

The `DOMImplementation` interface is implemented by objects that represent a specific DOM implementation, and is used to find out what features the DOM implementation supports. It has the methods listed below.

```
boolean hasFeature(String feature, String version)
```
Tests if the DOM implementation supports the given version of the named feature. Versions can be `"1.0"` and `"2.0"`, or `null`.

```
DocumentType createDocumentType(String
    qualifiedName, String publicId, String systemId)
```
Creates an empty `DocumentType` node representing a `DOCTYPE` declaration with the given values. The `qualifiedName` is the name of the document element type.

```
Document createDocument(String namespaceURI,
    String qualifiedName, DocumentType doctype)
```
Creates a `Document` node with the given document element and `DOCTYPE` declaration. The `doctype` parameter can be `null` if no declaration is wanted.

Table 20–1 shows the various DOM implementations and the values they return for the different possible parameters to the `hasFeature` method. (The values listed in the table are the precise values given to the method in method calls.)

Table 20–1   Java DOM `hasFeature` values

Feature	*Version*	*Xerces*	*Crimson*	*DOM2*
Core	none	true	false	false
Core	1.0	true	false	false
Core	2.0	true	false	false
XML	none	true	true	true
XML	1.0	true	true	true
XML	2.0	true	true	true
Views	none	false	false	false
Views	1.0	false	false	false
Views	2.0	false	false	false
StyleSheets	none	false	false	false
StyleSheets	1.0	false	false	false
StyleSheets	2.0	false	false	false
CSS	none	false	false	False

Table 20–1   Java DOM `hasFeature` values

Feature	Version	Xerces	Crimson	DOM2
CSS	1.0	false	false	false
CSS	2.0	false	false	false
CSS2	none	false	false	false
CSS2	1.0	false	false	false
CSS2	2.0	false	false	false
Events	none	true	false	true
Events	1.0	false	false	false
Events	2.0	true	false	true
UIEvents	none	false	false	true
UIEvents	1.0	false	false	false
UIEvents	2.0	false	false	true
MouseEvents	none	false	false	false
MouseEvents	1.0	false	false	false
MouseEvents	2.0	false	false	false
MutationEvents	none	true	false	true
MutationEvents	1.0	false	false	false
MutationEvents	2.0	true	false	true
HTMLEvents	none	false	false	true
HTMLEvents	1.0	false	false	false
HTMLEvents	2.0	false	false	true
Range	none	false	false	false
Range	1.0	false	false	false
Range	2.0	false	false	false
Traversal	none	true	false	true
Traversal	1.0	false	false	false
Traversal	2.0	true	false	true

This table, by the way, was produced using a Jython script that queried the different DOM implementations and produced SGML output that was then pasted into the document manuscript. The source code to this script is given in Example 20–1.

Example 20–1. Jython script for producing the features table

```
from org.apache.xerces.dom import DOMImplementationImpl
xerces = DOMImplementationImpl()
from org.apache.crimson.tree import DOMImplementationImpl
crimson = DOMImplementationImpl()
from org.brownell.xml.dom import DomDocument
brownell = DomDocument().getImplementation()

bool = ["False", "True"]
features = ["Core", "XML", "Views", "StyleSheets", "CSS", "CSS2",
            "Events", "UIEvents", "MouseEvents", "MutationEvents",
            "HTMLEvents", "Range", "Traversal"]
versions = [None, "1.0", "2.0"]

for feature in features:
  for version in versions:
    print "<tr><td>%s</td> <td>%s</td>" % (feature, version)
    print "<td>%s</td>" % bool[xerces.hasFeature(feature, version)]
    print "<td>%s</td>" % bool[crimson.hasFeature(feature, version)]
    print "<td>%s</td>" % bool[brownell.hasFeature(feature,version)]
    print "</tr>"
```

20.2.2 *The* Node *interface*

The Node interface is the base interface for all the interfaces that represent parts of an XML document. It has generic methods for accessing node data, as well as methods for navigating around the tree and some other purposes besides.

```
String getNodeName()
```
Returns the name of the node; precisely what this is depends on the type of the node. Note that the XPath node names and the DOM node names do not match.

```
String getNodeValue()
```
Returns the value of the node, though what that is depends on the node type. It may also be `null` for some node types.

```
void setNodeValue(String nodeValue)
```
Sets the node value to the given value. When the value is defined to always be `null` for the node type, setting the value has no effect.

```
short getNodeType()
```
Returns a number representing the type of the node. Constants representing the possible values are listed below.

```
Node getParentNode()
```
Returns the parent node, or `null` if there is none.

```
NodeList getChildNodes()
```
Returns the children of this node as a `NodeList` object. If this node has no children, the list will be empty.

```
Node getFirstChild()
```
Returns the first child of the node, or `null` if there are none.

```
Node getLastChild()
```
Returns the last node in the child list, or `null` if the list is empty.

```
Node getPreviousSibling()
```
Returns the node before this node in the child list of the parent of this node, if there is one.

```
Node getNextSibling()
```
Returns the node after this node in the child list this node appears in, if there is one.

```
NamedNodeMap getAttributes()
```
Returns a `NamedNodeMap` representing the attribute assignments of this node. If it is not an `Element` node, the map will be empty.

`Document getOwnerDocument()`
Returns the `Document` node the node belongs to.

`Node insertBefore(Node newChild, Node refChild)`
Inserts the `newChild` node before the `refChild` node in the child list, or as the last node if `refChild` is null. If the node already is in the tree, it will first be removed. If the node cannot have any children, a `DOMException` will be raised.

`Node replaceChild(Node newChild, Node oldChild)`
Replaces the `oldChild` node with the `newChild` node. If `newChild` is already in the tree, it is first removed. A `DOMException` is raised if `oldChild` is not a child of this node.

`removeChild(Node oldChild)`
Removes the node from the list of children, raising `DOMException` if it is not in the list.

`Node appendChild(Node newChild)`
Inserts the node last in the list of children, so this is equivalent to `insertBefore(newChild, null)`.

`boolean hasChildNodes()`
Returns `true` if the node has children.

`Node cloneNode(boolean deep)`
Returns a copy of the node. If `deep` is `true`, the subtree under the node will be copied recursively. The cloned node will have no parent.

`void normalize()`
Normalizes the subtree under this node by merging together adjacent `Text` nodes.

`boolean isSupported(String feature, String version)`
This method is a shorthand for the `hasFeature` method of the `DOMImplementation` interface and returns the same values.

```
String getNamespaceURI()
```
Returns the namespace URI that is part of the expanded name of this node.

```
String getLocalName()
```
Returns the localname that is part of the expanded name of this node.

```
String getPrefix()
```
Returns the namespace prefix used in the name of this node in the XML document.

```
void setPrefix(String prefix)
```
Sets the namespace prefix of this node.

```
boolean hasAttributes()
```
Returns true if the node has attributes.

In addition to these methods, the Node interface declares integer constants representing the various node types. The full list of these constants is given in Example 20–2.

Example 20–2. The Node constants

```
public static final short ELEMENT_NODE                = 1;
public static final short ATTRIBUTE_NODE              = 2;
public static final short TEXT_NODE                   = 3;
public static final short CDATA_SECTION_NODE          = 4;
public static final short ENTITY_REFERENCE_NODE       = 5;
public static final short ENTITY_NODE                 = 6;
public static final short PROCESSING_INSTRUCTION_NODE = 7;
public static final short COMMENT_NODE                = 8;
public static final short DOCUMENT_NODE               = 9;
public static final short DOCUMENT_TYPE_NODE          = 10;
public static final short DOCUMENT_FRAGMENT_NODE      = 11;
public static final short NOTATION_NODE               = 12;
```

These constants are all accessible through the Node interface.

20.2.3 *The* NodeList *interface*

Since the languages that IDL is meant to be used with do not have features like dynamic-length lists built in, neither does IDL. This requires the DOM to represent such lists using a specialized interface, and this is the role of NodeList. Java has classes for representing such lists that are part of the core API, but for some reason it was decided not to translate NodeLists into Vector or List objects. One could argue that this would have been consistent, since DOMString was mapped to String, but apparently the DOM designers felt otherwise.

The NodeList interface only represents a list of nodes, but does not support modification, so it is very simple. All methods for manipulating the contents of the list are available on the parent Node interface. The NodeList interface has the following methods.

Node item(int index)
> Returns the node with the given index, using 0-based indexing. If there is no node with the given index, null is returned.

int getLength()
> Returns the number of nodes in the list.

20.2.4 *The* NamedNodeMap *interface*

The NamedNodeMap interface is intended to make up for the lack of built-in dictionaries in IDL, and the issues with this interface are similar to those with NodeList. Interestingly, NamedNodeMap does support modification, while NodeList does not.

NamedNodeMap provides lookup by simple string names as well as by expanded names consisting of namespace URIs and local names. It also supports enumeration of the nodes in the map through integer-based indexing. The interface has the methods listed below.

Node getNamedItem(String name)
> Returns the node with the given name, or null if no node has the given name.

`Node setNamedItem(Node arg)`

Inserts the node into the map, causing it to be indexed under the value returned by its `getNodeName` method. The return value will be the previous node with the same name if there was one, otherwise it will be `null`.

`Node removeNamedItem(String name)`

Removes the node with the given name from the map and returns it. If there is no node with the given name, a `DOMException` is raised.

`Node item(int index)`

Returns the node at the given index, or `null` if there is no such node. This method is primarily intended to be used to traverse all the nodes in the map, and makes no guarantees as to what order the nodes will be returned in. The index is 0-based, just like its cousin in `NodeList`.

`int getLength()`

Returns the number of nodes in the map.

`Node getNamedItemNS(String namespaceURI, String localName)`

Returns the node with the given expanded name, or `null` if there is no such node.

`Node setNamedItemNS(Node arg)`

Inserts the given node into the map, where it will be accessible by its expanded name. The return value will be the previous node with the same name if there was one, otherwise it will be `null`.

`Node removeNamedItemNS(String namespaceURI, String localName)`

Removes the node with the given expanded name from the map and returns it. If there is no node with the given expanded name, a `DOMException` is raised.

20.2.5 *The* Document *interface*

This is the interface of the object that represents the entire XML document, and which is also used as a factory object for creating new nodes. It is derived from the Node interface and adds the following methods:

DocumentType getDoctype()
> Returns the DocumentType node of the document, or null if the document does not have one. Note that this node can never be altered or modified in any way.

DOMImplementation getImplementation()
> Returns the DOMImplementation object that represents the DOM implementation.

Element getDocumentElement()
> Returns the document element of the document.

Element createElement(String tagName)
> Creates a new Element node of the named type, bound to this Document object, but without any parent node.

DocumentFragment createDocumentFragment()
> Creates an empty DocumentFragment node.

Text createTextNode(String data)
> Creates a Text node with the given content.

Comment createComment(String data)
> Creates a Comment node with the given content.

CDATASection createCDATASection(String data)
> Creates a CDATASection node with the given content.

ProcessingInstruction
    createProcessingInstruction(String target,
    String data)
    Creates a ProcessingInstruction node with the given target
    and data.

Attr createAttribute(String name)
    Creates an Attr node with the given name.

EntityReference createEntityReference(String name)
    Creates an EntityReference node with the given name. If the
    name is that of an entity declared in the document's DTD, the
    contents of that entity will be parsed and inserted into the returned
    node.

NodeList getElementsByTagName(String tagname)
    Returns all elements in the document with the given element-type
    name in the order they are encountered during a pre-order traversal
    of the document. The elements are returned in a NodeList object.
    Note that the special value '*' matches all elements.

Node importNode(Node importedNode, boolean deep)
    This method is used when nodes are moved from one document
    to another. This cannot be done by simply inserting the nodes into
    another document, because nodes are bound to the document they
    originate in. This method creates a copy of the given node that
    belongs to this document, and if deep is true, it recursively copies
    the subtree under importedNode.
        The returned node is the copy of the imported node, and this
    node has no parent. The original imported node is not changed in
    any way.

Element createElementNS(String namespaceURI,
    String qualifiedName)
    Creates a new element node with the given expanded name.

```
Attr createAttributeNS(String namespaceURI,
    String qualifiedName)
```
Creates a new `Attr` node with the given expanded name.

```
NodeList getElementsByTagNameNS(String
    namespaceURI, String localName)
```
Returns a list of all elements matched, just like `getElementsBy-TagName`. The special name `'*'`, which matches all names, can be used both in `namespaceURI` and in `localName`.

```
Element getElementById(String elementId)
```
Looks up and returns an `Element` node by its ID. The ID is the value of an attribute on the element which has been declared in the DTD to be of the type `ID`. In order to support this method, the DOM implementation must know the types of the attributes in the document. If no such element is found, `null` is returned.

20.2.6 *The* DocumentType *interface*

The `DocumentType` interface represents the `DOCTYPE` declaration of a document and the DTD it refers to. It can be used to find information about the contents of the DTD, but does not allow to modify those contents. It has the methods listed below.

```
String getName()
```
Returns the name of the document element type as given in the `DOCTYPE` declaration.

```
NamedNodeMap getEntities()
```
Returns a map containing the general entities declared in the DTD, represented by `Entity` nodes.

```
NamedNodeMap getNotations()
```
Returns a map of the notations declared in the DTD.

```
String getPublicId()
```
Returns the public identifier given in the DOCTYPE declaration, or null if none were given.

```
String getSystemId()
```
Returns the system identifier given in the DOCTYPE declaration.

```
String getInternalSubset()
```
Returns the internal subset of the DTD as a string.

20.2.7 *The* Element *interface*

The Element interface is implemented by objects that represent the elements in a document, and as such, it is one of the central DOM interfaces. The interface is derived from Node and adds the following methods:

```
String getTagName()
```
Returns the element-type name. Note that the method name is really a misnomer, as the XML Recommendation calls this the element-type name, as does the SGML standard.

```
String getAttribute(String name)
```
Returns the value of the attribute with the given name, or an empty string if the attribute is not found. Note that this makes it impossible to use this method to discover whether an attribute is present or not, since an empty string is a perfectly legal attribute value. To check for the presence of an attribute, the hasAttribute method should be used instead.

```
void setAttribute(String name, String value)
```
Sets the value of the named attribute, whether it is already present or not.

`void removeAttribute(String name)`
> Removes the attribute with the given name. If the attribute does not exist, the method will just return.

`Attr getAttributeNode(String name)`
> Returns the node representing the named attribute, or `null` if there is no such attribute.

`Attr setAttributeNode(Attr newAttr)`
> Inserts the given attribute node on the element. If there already is an attribute node with the same name, it is replaced by the new node. If a node was indeed replaced, it is returned, otherwise `null` is returned.

`Attr removeAttributeNode(Attr oldAttr)`
> Removes the given attribute node from the element and returns it. If the node is not attached to the element, a `DOMException` is raised.

`NodeList getElementsByTagName(String name)`
> Works just like the `getElementsByTagName` on the `Document` interface, except that it only searches the subtree under the element node.

`String getAttributeNS(String namespaceURI,`
  `String localName)`
> Returns the value of the attribute with the given expanded name, or an empty string if there is no such attribute.

`void setAttributeNS(String namespaceURI,`
  `String qualifiedName, String value)`
> Sets the value of the attribute with the given expanded name, overriding any value that may be present already.

```
void removeAttributeNS(String namespaceURI,
     String localName)
```
Removes the attribute with the given expanded name from the element. If there is no such attribute, the method just returns.

```
Attr getAttributeNodeNS(String namespaceURI,
     String localName)
```
Returns the attribute node with the given expanded name, or `null` if there is no such node.

```
Attr setAttributeNodeNS(Attr newAttr)
```
Inserts the given attribute node into the element. If the element already has an attribute with the same expanded name, it is replaced and returned by the method, otherwise `null` is returned.

```
NodeList getElementsByTagNameNS(String
     namespaceURI, String localName)
```
Returns a list of all elements matched, just like `getElementsBy-TagNameNS` on `Document`. The special name `'*'`, which matches all names, can be used both in `namespaceURI` and in `localName`.

```
boolean hasAttribute(String name)
```
Returns `true` if the element has an attribute with the given name.

```
boolean hasAttributeNS(String namespaceURI,
     String localName)
```
Returns `true` if the element has an attribute with the given namespace name.

20.2.8 *The* Attr *interface*

An `Attr` node represents an attribute, or, more precisely, an assignment of a value to an attribute of a particular element. Note that `Attr` nodes can also represent namespace declarations, which the XML Infoset does not consider to be attributes at all.

Note that `Attr` nodes are somewhat different from other DOM nodes in that they are not considered to be children of the element they belong to, and therefore have no parent. The interface is derived from `Node` and adds the following methods:

`String getName()`
>Returns the name of the attribute. This is exactly equivalent to `getNodeName`.

`boolean getSpecified()`
>Returns `true` if the attribute was specified in the original source document, but `false` if the attribute was defaulted from the DTD. Since most DOM implementations are based on substrates that do not provide this information, this method is not reliable in most DOM implementations.

`String getValue()`
>Returns the value of the attribute.

`void setValue(String value)`
>Sets the value of the attribute.

`Element getOwnerElement()`
>Returns the element to which the attribute belongs. This method is necessary since attributes do not have elements as their parents, therefore the elements must be reachable by other means.

20.2.9 *The* `CharacterData` *interface*

This is the common interface for all nodes that contain character data, regardless of their semantics. This interface is never instantiated. The name is somewhat ill-chosen, since character data in XML terminology is the data that remains when all markup in a document has been removed. In DOM, however, the `Comment` interface is also derived from `CharacterData`. The interface is derived from `Node` and adds the following methods.

`String getData()`
> Returns the string data held by the node. This is precisely the same as `getNodeValue`.

`void setData(String data)`
> Sets the string data of the node.

`int getLength()`
> Returns the length of the string data held by the node, counted as UTF-16 code units but not as abstract Unicode characters. Unicode surrogates will therefore count as 2 characters rather than 1, despite the fact that they represent a single character.
>
> Note that this behavior is the same as that exhibited by the `length` method of the Java `String` class. If you want to count the number of actual characters in the string, the easiest way to do that is to create an array of `chars` and run through it, counting all `chars` except those in the `DC00` to `DFFF` interval. These are the lower surrogates, so by skipping them, you make sure that in each surrogate pair only the high surrogate will be counted. If the string is well-formed (from the Unicode point of view), the resulting number will be exactly the number of characters in the string.

`String substringData(int offset, int count)`
> Returns an extract of the data held by the node, starting at the given `offset` and continuing for `count` UTF-16 code units. If the `offset` is outside the range of characters held by the node, a `DOMException` is thrown. If `count` specifies more characters than are actually found in the node after the given `offset`, the rest of the string is returned.

`void appendData(String arg)`
> Appends the given string to the data held by the node.

```
void insertData(int offset, String arg)
```
Inserts the given string in the existing data at the given offset (again in UTF-16 units), moving data at that offset so that it appears after the given string.

```
void deleteData(int offset, int count)
```
Deletes the specified number of code numbers, starting from the given offset. If the `offset` is outside the range of characters held by the node, a `DOMException` is thrown. If `count` specifies more characters than are actually found in the node after the given `offset`, the rest of the string is deleted.

```
void replaceData(int offset, int count, String arg)
```
This is equivalent to calling `deleteData(offset, count)` followed by `insertData(offset, arg)`.

20.2.10 *The* Text *interface*

The `Text` interface represents character data in the document, and is another ill-chosen interface name, since in XML terminology, the `Text` of a document is its unprocessed content. In most implementations, `Text` nodes also represent CDATA marked sections. `Text` nodes may be split anywhere, at the whim of DOM tree builders. (For a discussion on how to solve this and more about the problems with `CDATASection` nodes, see 11.6.1, "The `CDATASection` interface," on page 427.)

The `Text` interface is derived from `CharacterData` and adds only a single method:

```
Text splitText(int offset)
```
Truncates the node at the given offset, creating a new node for the data after the offset. This new node is inserted after this node in the tree and is also returned by the method. If the `offset` is negative or larger than the actual number of 16-bit code units in the data, a `DOMException` is thrown. If the offset is equal to the length of the node, the new node is empty.

20.2.11 *The* Comment *interface*

The Comment interface is derived from the CharacterData interface and represents comments in the document. The interface adds no new methods, but represents a separate node type. Many DOM implementations do not create Comment nodes, and some can be configured not to do so.

20.2.12 *The* CDATASection *interface*

The CDATASection interface represents character data in the document that was contained in CDATA marked sections, and is derived from the Text interface. It has a node type of its own, but the semantics of CDATA marked sections and ordinary character data are the same, so this is usually an unwanted complication. In Java, most DOM implementations create CDATA marked section nodes, although some of those that do can be configured not to do so. CDATA nodes generally cause quite a few problems, about which you can read more in 11.6.1, "The CDATASection interface," on page 427.

No new methods are added in this interface.

20.2.13 *The* ProcessingInstruction *interface*

The ProcessingInstruction interface is implemented by nodes which represent processing instructions. The interface is derived from Node and adds the following methods:

String getTarget()
> Returns the target of the processing instruction, which is the XML name before the first whitespace inside the instruction. This is the same as what is returned by getNodeName.

```
String getData()
```
Returns the data of the processing instruction, which is the string contained after the first whitespace inside the instruction. This is the same as what `getNodeValue` returns.

```
void setData(String data)
```
Sets the data of the processing instruction.

20.3 | Using some Java DOMs

Now that you have seen an overview of the DOM interfaces, we will go through some examples that show how to use these interfaces to create actual applications. We show how to do this for each DOM implementation separately, since each one has its own way of creating the `Document` object and its own API for loading XML documents as DOM trees. This problem, however, is what JAXP is there to help you with. We'll look at how to use JAXP to solve this problem later in this section.

20.3.1 *Accessing Xerces directly*

When using Xerces to work with XML documents, there are two access points, one for parsing XML documents and another for creating empty documents. To parse XML documents, the `org.apache.xerces.parsers.DOMParser` class is used. This class uses the Xerces SAX parser to build a DOM tree and can be configured using SAX 2.0 features and properties, which can also be set on the underlying parser. The supported features and properties are listed below, following the list of methods.

```
DOMParser()
```
This constructor creates an empty parser ready for use.

`boolean getCreateEntityReferenceNodes()`
> Returns `true` if the builder has been configured to create entity reference nodes.

`Document getDocument()`
> Returns the `Document` node created by the last parse.

`boolean getFeature(String featureId)`
> Returns the state of the named feature in the underlying SAX 2.0 parser, or on the DOM builder.

`String[] getFeaturesRecognized()`
> Returns an array containing the names of the features recognized by the underlying SAX 2.0 parser and the DOM builder.

`boolean getIncludeIgnorableWhitespace()`
> Returns `true` if the builder has been configured to create `Text` nodes for ignorable whitespace in the document.

`String[] getPropertiesRecognized()`
> Returns an array containing the names of the SAX 2.0 properties recognized by the underlying parser and the DOM builder.

`Object getProperty(String propertyId)`
> Returns the value of the named SAX 2.0 property as set on the underlying parser or on the DOM builder.

`void parse(String systemId)`
> Parses the XML document with the given system identifier and builds the corresponding DOM tree, which can then be retrieved by a call to `getDocument`.

`void reset()`
> Resets the parser.

```
void setFeature(String featureId, boolean state)
```
Sets the state of the named feature on the underlying parser or on the DOM builder.

```
void setIncludeIgnorableWhitespace(boolean include)
```
Tells the builder whether to include nodes representing ignorable whitespace in the tree or not.

```
void setProperty(String propertyId, Object value)
```
Sets a SAX 2.0 property on either the underlying parser or on the DOM builder.

The `DOMParser` will intercept the set and get calls for the SAX 2.0 features and properties defined for itself, and pass all other calls on to the underlying SAX 2.0 parser. The features supported by the DOM builder are:

```
http://apache.org/xml/features/dom/
    defer-node-expansion
```
If this feature is set, the `parse` call will simply load the XML source of the document without processing it and then return immediately. The tree that is returned by `getDocument` will then be constructed lazily, that is, as the document tree is traversed. This costs memory in that the entire text of the XML document will be held in memory as the tree is created, but will allow much faster access to the first parts of the tree.

```
http://apache.org/xml/features/dom/
    create-entity-ref-nodes
```
Controls whether `EntityReference` nodes are created or not.

```
http://apache.org/xml/features/dom/
    include-ignorable-whitespace
```
Controls whether `Text` nodes are created for ignorable whitespace nodes or not.

In addition to the features listed above, the Xerces DOM builder also supports a property shown below.

```
http://apache.org/xml/properties/dom/
    current-element-node
```
> Holds the last element node created during XML parsing. This property is mainly useful for finding out where XML parsing stopped in the case of errors.

Creating an empty document in Xerces is easy; all it takes is to instantiate the `org.apache.xerces.dom.DocumentImpl` class, which has a zero-parameters constructor.

20.3.1.1 RSS to HTML conversion

To show how to use Xerces, we here implement the by now familiar RSS to HTML conversion example using Xerces. Example 20–3 shows the source code of the application.

Example 20–3. RSS to HTML with Xerces

```java
import java.io.*;
import org.xml.sax.SAXException;
import org.w3c.dom.*;
import org.apache.xerces.parsers.DOMParser;

public class DOMRSS2HTML {

  public static void main(String[] args) {
    try {
      convert(args[0], args[1]);
    }
    catch (SAXException e) {
      System.err.println("ERROR: " + e);
    }
    catch (IOException e) {
      System.err.println("ERROR: " + e);
    }
  }
```

```
public static void convert(String infile, String outfile)
  throws IOException, SAXException {
  Document doc = buildDocument(infile);
  FileWriter out = new FileWriter(outfile);

  Element root = doc.getDocumentElement();
  Element channel = getFirstChild("channel", root);
  String title = getData(getFirstChild("title", channel));
  String link = getData(getFirstChild("link", channel));
  String descr = getData(getFirstChild("description", channel));

  out.write("<title>" + title + "</title>\n");
  out.write("<h1><a href='" + link + "'>" + title +"</a></h1>\n");
  if (descr != null)
    out.write("<p>" + descr + "</p>\n");

  // loop over item elements
  out.write("<ul>\n");
  NodeList children = channel.getChildNodes();

  for (int ix = 0; ix < children.getLength(); ix++) {
    Node node = children.item(ix);
    if (node.getNodeType() == Node.ELEMENT_NODE &&
        node.getNodeName().equals("item"))
      convertItem(out, (Element) node);
  }
  out.write("</ul>\n");

  out.close();
}

public static void convertItem(Writer out, Element item)
  throws IOException {
  String title = getData(getFirstChild("title", item));
  String link = getData(getFirstChild("link", item));
  String descr = getData(getFirstChild("description", item));

  out.write("  <li><a href=\"" + link + "\">" + title + "</a>");
  if (descr != null) out.write(" " + descr);
  out.write("</li>\n");
}

// --- DOM access utilities
```

```java
public static Element getFirstChild(String name, Node parent) {
  NodeList children = parent.getChildNodes();
  for (int ix = 0; ix < children.getLength(); ix++) {
    Node node = children.item(ix);
    if (node.getNodeType() == Node.ELEMENT_NODE &&
    node.getNodeName().equals(name))
      return (Element) node;
    if (node.getNodeType() == Node.ENTITY_REFERENCE_NODE) {
      node = getFirstChild(name, node);
      if (node != null)
        return (Element) node;
    }
  }

  return null;
}

public static String getData(Element parent) {
  if (parent == null)
    return null;

  StringBuffer content = new StringBuffer();
  NodeList children = parent.getChildNodes();
  for (int ix = 0; ix < children.getLength(); ix++) {
    Node node = children.item(ix);
    if (node.getNodeType() == Node.TEXT_NODE ||
      node.getNodeType() == Node.CDATA_SECTION_NODE)
      content.append(node.getNodeValue());
  }
  return content.toString();
}

// --- DOM tree building

private static Document buildDocument(String infile)
  throws SAXException, IOException {
  DOMParser builder = new DOMParser();
  try {
    builder.parse(new File(infile).toURL().toString());
  }
  catch (java.net.MalformedURLException e) {
    throw new RuntimeException("Impossible error: " + e);
  }
  return builder.getDocument();
}

}
```

We catch this exception here, since it should never occur. In order to make sure we are not mistaken, we rethrow it as a `RuntimeException`, which need not be declared.

As you can see, writing this simple application using DOM in Java requires quite a bit of code. This is both because of the Java language itself and because of the fact that the DOM was not designed for convenience.

20.3.2 *Accessing DOM through JAXP*

The problem with the RSS to HTML converter given above is that it is hard-wired to use a particular DOM implementation. In order to make it work with a different implementation, the code has to be changed. As discussed earlier, JAXP can help solve this problem, and it is in fact very easy to do so. Example 20–4 shows the `buildDocument` method of Example 20–3, reimplemented using JAXP. Note that an `import java.xml.parsers.*` statement has been added to the example.

Example 20–4. Reimplementing the `buildDocument` method using JAXP

```
private static Document buildDocument(String infile)
  throws ParserConfigurationException, SAXException, IOException {
  DocumentBuilderFactory factory =
                          DocumentBuilderFactory.newInstance();
  DocumentBuilder builder = factory.newDocumentBuilder();
  return builder.parse(new File(infile));
}
```

20.4 | JDOM

Dissatisfaction with the Java version of the DOM has prompted a group of developers to join forces to develop an alternative interface that is intended to be easier to use and more Java-like. Unlike DOM,

JDOM (see http://www.jdom.org/) is not intended to be language-independent, nor is it intended to cover all possible uses. The JDOM APIs also are much more focused on convenience compared to the DOM APIs.

Note that JDOM has been submitted to Sun for inclusion in the Java platform using the Java Community Process. At the time of writing it seems not unlikely that JDOM may be accepted as part of Java, although the process is not yet completed. Whether, and how, the JDOM interfaces will change during this process is not clear.

As this chapter was going through its final edits before submission to the publishers, an effort similar to JDOM, called dom4j, was released. This happened too late to be included in this chapter, but you may wish to go to http://dom4j.org to check it out.

The approach taken by JDOM also differs from that taken by DOM in that the JDOM APIs are defined by a set of classes, while the DOM ones are defined by a set of Java interfaces. This means that there can be any number of implementations of the DOM APIs, while JDOM is effectively defined by the classes that make up its APIs. Since the APIs are classes rather than interfaces, they are the only implementations there can be of those classes, except for derived classes. This means that JDOM does not work well as the basis for, say, the API to an XML database.

JDOM consists of four packages:

org.jdom
Contains the data classes that represent XML documents and the exceptions used by JDOM.

org.jdom.input
Contains classes for reading XML documents into JDOM object structures, as well as for converting DOM structures to JDOM structures.

`org.jdom.output`
>   Contains classes for creating XML documents, SAX event streams, and DOM trees from JDOM structures.

`org.jdom.adapters`
>   Contains adapters to existing DOM implementations that are used by the input and output packages.

The JDOM object structure has much the same structure as all the other tree structures used to represent XML documents. The top object is a `Document` object, which represents the entire XML document, while `Elements`, `Attributes`, and `ProcessingInstructions` have their own objects. One distinguishing feature of JDOM is that there are no JDOM-specific objects that represent character data. Instead, character data is represented using `String` objects.

Example 20–5. An example XML document

```
<doc>
<title>Example</title>
<p>This example has <term>mixed content</term> in it.</p>
</doc>
```

The document in Example 20–5 would be represented in JDOM as shown in Figure 20–1.

The JDOM API is relatively large because of all the conveniences provided, so no attempt to provide a reference for it will be made here. Instead, you are referred to the copious JDOM javadoc. An example below will show what JDOM is like in use and will help you get started, should you want to look at JDOM.

20.4.1 *A JDOM example application*

We here turn to the well-worn RSS to HTML conversion example, and implement it in JDOM to give you an impression of what JDOM

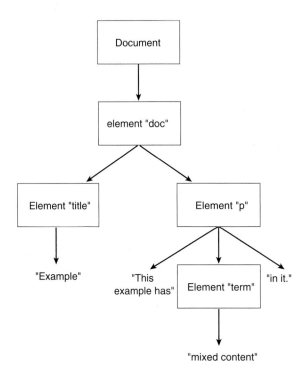

Figure 20–1   How JDOM represents documents

is like. As can be seen, the code in Example 20–6 is much easier and more natural than Example 20–3 written with DOM, and no new convenience methods were needed in order to implement the application. My conclusion is that JDOM is a very useful alternative to DOM for this kind of applications.

Example 20–6. JDOM RSS to HTML converter

```
import java.io.File;
import java.io.FileWriter;
import java.io.IOException;
import java.util.Iterator;
import org.jdom.*;
import org.jdom.input.SAXBuilder;
```

```
public class JDOMRSS2HTML {

  public static void main(String[] args) {
    try {
      convert(args[0], args[1]);
    }
    catch (JDOMException e) {
      System.err.println("ERROR: " + e);
    }
    catch (IOException e) {
      System.err.println("ERROR: " + e);
    }
  }

  public static void convert(String infile, String outfile)
    throws JDOMException, IOException {
    FileWriter writer = new FileWriter(outfile);

    SAXBuilder builder = new SAXBuilder();
    Document doc = builder.build(new File(infile));
    Element rss = doc.getRootElement();
    Element channel = rss.getChild("channel");
    String title = channel.getChildText("title");
    String link = channel.getChildText("link");
    Element descr = channel.getChild("description");

    writer.write("<html>\n");
    writer.write("<title>" + title + "</title>\n");
    writer.write("<h1><a href=\"" + link + "\">" + title +
                 "</a></h1>\n");

    if (descr != null)
      writer.write("<p>" + descr.getText()  + "</p>\n");

    writer.write("<ul>\n");
    Iterator it = channel.getChildren("item").iterator();
    while (it.hasNext()) {
      Element item = (Element) it.next();
      writer.write("  <li><a href=\"" + item.getChildText("link") +
                   "\">" + item.getChildText("title") + "</a>");

      descr = item.getChild("descr");
      if (descr != null)
        writer.write(" " + descr.getText() + "</li>\n");
      else
        writer.write("</li>\n");
    }
```

```
    writer.write("</ul>\n");

    writer.write("</html>\n");
    writer.close();
  }

}
```

Using XSLT in Java applications

- JAXP
- Saxon
- Xalan

X
SLT and XPath both have the advantage of being truly independent of programming language, in the sense that regardless of what language you use, XSLT and XPath stay the same. This chapter will therefore concentrate on how to integrate Java applications with XSLT processors, since XSLT and XPath have already been described in detail.

When integrating XSLT processors with your Java applications, you essentially have two options: you can either pick a specific processor and integrate with it, or you can use a general interface implemented by several processors and write the integration against that. This chapter will first discuss the general JAXP interfaces and then go on to examine the APIs of two specific XSLT processors: Saxon and Xalan.

It should be noted that for Web development purposes, the Cocoon development framework provides many interesting features for using XSLT in a Web environment. That framework is rather large, however, so it is not covered here. For more information about it, you may wish to see Brett McLaughlin's *Java & XML* at `http://www.oreilly.com/catalog/javaxml/chapter/ch09.html`.

21.1 | Using JAXP

The JAXP APIs, in addition to their SAX and DOM support, also provide general interfaces for running XSLT processors. This interface supports creating XSLT processors in an implementation-independent way and provides basic support for starting and controlling transformations run by the processor.

The JAXP APIs for running XSLT transformations are based on the earlier work done by a group of individual XSLT implementors, who put together a similar specification they called TRaX. TRaX was implemented by some XSLT processors, but has now been completely subsumed by JAXP and no longer leads a separate existence from it, unlike SAX and DOM. The XSLT processors that used to support the original TRaX now support the JAXP version of it. Note that people sometimes refer to the XSLT part of JAXP as TRaX, even though this is not strictly correct.

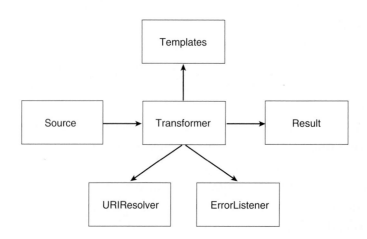

Figure 21–1   Anatomy of a JAXP XSLT transformation

Figure 21–1 shows the anatomy of an XSLT transformation process as set up using JAXP. JAXP uses an implementation of the Source interface to represent the source tree being transformed by the XSLT processor as well as the raw XSLT stylesheet used to describe the transformation. This is fed into an instance of the `Transformer` class, which represents the combination of an XSLT stylesheet and an XSLT processor.

The `Transformer` is given an instance of the `Result` interface, which it uses to write out the result of the transformation. When running the transformation, the `Transformer` also has a `Templates` object available, which represents the XSLT stylesheet. The `Templates` object can be created anew for each transformation, or reused between transformations, thus saving computational effort.

During processing, the `Transformer` is supported by two helper objects: the `URIResolver`, which resolves URI references (much the same as `EntityResolver` in SAX), and the `ErrorListener`, to which errors are reported.

Instances of the `Transformer` class are created using the `TransformerFactory` class, which works in much the same way as the DOM and SAX factories already explained.

The APIs themselves are organized into four different packages:

`javax.xml.transform`
> This is the heart of JAXP's support for XSLT transformations. It contains the core interfaces and classes used to set up and run transformations.

`javax.xml.transform.stream`
> This package contains `Source` and `Result` implementations built on Java IO streams, making it possible to run transformations that read from streams or write to streams.

`javax.xml.transform.sax`
> This package contains `Source` and `Result` implementations based on SAX event streams, as well as some helper interfaces used to map from event streams to the object structures JAXP uses.

`javax.xml.transform.dom`

> This package holds `Source` and `Result` implementations based on DOM, allowing the source tree to be given as a DOM tree and the result tree to be created as a DOM tree.

Note that the differences between the different `Source` and `Result` implementations are not hidden by the interfaces they implement, which is unusual in Java. The interfaces do not provide sufficient information for implementations to be able to access the XML documents represented by the objects, so processors must specifically implement support for each kind of `Source` and `Result`.

In other words, `Source` and `Result` are not abstractions of their implementations, they are just convenient "union types" that make the API somewhat simpler. If these types were not present, there would need to be one `transform` method for each source and result combination, which would require nine methods for the current set of sources and results.

It may be that some processors do not support all types, although the stream types should always be supported.

21.1.1 *JAXP API reference*

We will go through the JAXP APIs package by package, starting with `javax.xml.transform`, which is the central package of the API. This package defines the structure of the JAXP APIs, and the other packages mainly add useful implementations of the interfaces in this package.

21.1.1.1 The `javax.xml.transform` package

The place to start looking at the JAXP APIs is the `Transformer-Factory` class, which is where one creates `Transformer` instances, and also where one loads XSLT stylesheets into a parsed object structure (`Templates`). The `TransformerFactory` has the following methods.

`static TransformerFactory newInstance()`

Creates a `TransformerFactory` instance according to the procedure given below. If something goes wrong, a `Transformer-FactoryConfigurationException` will be thrown.

`Transformer newTransformer(Source source)`

Given a `Source` object referring to an XSLT stylesheet XML document, creates a `Transformer` object bound to that XSLT stylesheet. This is the most common way to create a `Transformer`. If something goes wrong while parsing the XSLT stylesheet, a `TransformerConfigurationException` will be thrown.

Note that if you intend to run many transformations using the same stylesheet, first creating a `Templates` object and then creating processors from it is likely to be faster, since it avoids reparsing the stylesheet for each transformation.

`Transformer newTransformer()`

Creates a new `Transformer` that will perform the identity transformation. That is, its stylesheet is fixed and the output it produces will be logically the same as the input it gets.

This method is much more useful than it seems at first glance, since it can be used to convert documents from one representation to another (that is, stream to DOM, DOM to stream, and so on).

`Templates newTemplates(Source source)`

Parses the XSLT stylesheet referred to by the `Source` object into a `Templates` object, which is returned. This can be used to create different `Transformers` bound to the same stylesheet without having to parse the stylesheet more than once. This can be useful when using multiple threads each running a transformation at the same time, or when one wants to use different configurations with different `Transformers`. It is also good for performance in that it avoids parsing the stylesheet more than once if you cache the `Templates` object.

If something goes wrong with parsing the XSLT stylesheet, a `TransformerConfigurationException` will be thrown.

`Source getAssociatedStylesheet(Source source,`
    `String media, String title, String charset)`
This method will, given a `Source` representing a source XML document, return a `Source` object representing the XSLT stylesheet referred to by the stylesheet PI in the XML document. (This is the `<?xml-stylesheet ... ?>` PI.) Since there may be several such PIs, the preferred values for the `media`, `title`, and `charset` attributes can be given. All of these can be `null`, in which case any PI will do. The JAXP specification does not specify which PI is selected when more than one matches. If something goes wrong, a `TransformerConfigurationException` is thrown.

`void setURIResolver(URIResolver resolver)`
Sets the `URIResolver` that will be used by `Transformers` created by this factory.

`URIResolver getURIResolver()`
Returns the `URIResolver` that the factory has been configured to use.

`boolean getFeature(String name)`
Returns the state of a JAXP feature. The `name` will be an absolute URI. No such URIs are defined by the JAXP specification.

`void setAttribute(String name, Object value)`
Sets the value of a named attribute, where the attribute is a configuration option provided by the implementation. In other words, the attributes supported by a `Transformer` are implementation-specific. `IllegalArgumentException` is thrown if the name or the value is not accepted.

`Object getAttribute(String name)`
Returns the value of the named attribute.

```
void setErrorListener(ErrorListener listener)
```
Sets the `ErrorListener` to be used by the `Transformer`s created by this factory.

```
ErrorListener getErrorListener()
```
Returns the `ErrorListener` of the factory.

The procedure followed by the `TransformerFactory` when creating `Transformer` objects is very similar to that followed by the other JAXP factories. It consists of the following steps.

1. If the `javax.xml.transform.TransformerFactory` property is defined and contains the name of a class derived from the factory class, that class will be loaded and instantiated.

2. If not, JAXP will look in the file `lib/jaxp.properties` in the JRE directory to see if this file sets a value for the property mentioned above.

3. If not, the Services API will be used to see if the file `META-INF/services/javax.xml.transform.TransformerFactory` exists in any of the jar files available to the system. If it does the class name will be taken from it.

4. If all of this fails, the platform default will be created.

Now that we know how to create `Templates` and `Transformer` objects, the next step is to learn how to use those objects. We'll start with the `Templates` interface, since that is the smallest. The role of the `Templates` interface is to represent XSLT stylesheets that have been parsed and will be reused by several different `Transformer`s. The interface provides no mechanisms for introspecting the contents of the stylesheet, except the properties defined by it, so it is quite simple. It has only the methods listed below.

```
Transformer newTransformer()
```
Creates and returns a `Transformer` object bound to the stylesheet this `Templates` object represents. The transformations done with

the `Transformer` will all use this stylesheet, as there is no way to change the stylesheet of a `Transformer`.

`Properties getOutputProperties()`

Returns a `Properties` object containing the attribute assignments of the `xsl:output` element in the stylesheet, if any. See 16.2.2, "Output methods," on page 590 for a description of this element type. The object is a copy of the object held by the `Templates` object, so modifications to it do not affect the `Templates` object at all.

Note that the names of the keys in this `Properties` object can be expanded names, which are then represented as described below.

The next class to consider is the `Transformer` class, which represents a specific transformation. That is, it does not represent just the XSLT processor, but the XSLT processor bound to a particular XSLT stylesheet.

Before we continue, it is necessary to understand how the XSLT part of JAXP represents expanded names. As you have seen throughout this book expanded names are troublesome creatures in that they are awkward to represent in most programming languages, and this affects the JAXP API as well. The solution that has been chosen is to completely ignore the prefixes, which are in any case irrelevant for JAXP's purposes, and represent the expanded names as strings of the form `"{nsuri}localname"`, or `"localname"` if the name has a null URI.

This solution was originally proposed by James Clark for use with SAX, but was rejected there. It has been revived for use in JAXP, and works well here. It has the useful properties that names are represented by single objects, which are nonetheless built-in to Java, equality can be tested for using the `equals` method, and you can easily check whether a name has a namespace URI by testing if the first character is `'{'`.

The `Transformer` class has the methods listed below.

```
void transform(Source xmlSource,
    Result outputTarget) throws TransformerException
```
Calling this method runs the transformation represented by this object on the XML document represented by the xmlSource object, passing the output to the outputTarget object. If the transformation fails, a TransformerException will be thrown.

```
void setParameter(String name, Object value)
```
Sets a parameter to be used during the transformation. This can be used to override the assignment of a parameter value by an xsl:parameter element in the stylesheet. Note that this method has no effect if there is no xsl:parameter element with this name in the stylesheet.

The name is an expanded name represented according to the rules given above.

```
Object getParameter(String name)
```
Returns the value of a parameter explicitly set through the set-Parameter method. Parameters defined in the stylesheet are not returned by this method.

```
void clearParameters()
```
Clears all parameters set with the setParameter method.

```
void setURIResolver(URIResolver resolver)
```
Sets the URIResolver to be used by this Transformer.

```
URIResolver getURIResolver()
```
Returns the URIResolver used by this Transformer.

```
void setOutputProperties(Properties oformat) throws
    IllegalArgumentException
```
Sets the output properties to be used by the Transformer when doing its transformation. The values set here will override those held by the Templates object. The keys in the Properties object

will be expanded names. Note that if the `oformat` argument is `null`, all previously set properties will be cleared.

`Properties getOutputProperties()`

Returns the current properties held by the `Transformer`. The `Properties` object will hold the properties as they will be applied by the `Transformer`, regardless of whether the values have been set using `setOutputProperties`, whether they come from the stylesheet, or whether they are the defaults defined by the XSLT Recommendation.

Note that the `Properties` object returned will be a copy of that held by the `Transformer`, so modifying it will have no effect on the `Transformer`.

`void setOutputProperty(String name, String value)` `throws IllegalArgumentException`

Sets the value of a particular property. If the property name has no namespace and is not recognized, an `IllegalArgumentException` will be thrown.

`String getOutputProperty(String name) throws IllegalArgumentException`

Returns the effective value of the named output property, regardless of where that value comes from. An exception will be thrown if the name has no namespace and is not recognized.

`void setErrorListener(ErrorListener listener)`

Sets the `ErrorListener` to be used by this `Transformer`.

`ErrorListener getErrorListener()`

Returns the `ErrorListener` used by this `Transformer`, which can never be `null`.

The only piece missing now before we have enough information to be able to run an XSLT transformation is what the `Source` and `Result` interfaces look like. We'll start by listing the methods of the `Source` interface, since it is logically the first of the two. `Source` objects represent XML documents, either source documents or XSLT stylesheets, and have the methods listed below.

`String getSystemId()`
> Returns the system identifier of the XML document, which may be `null` if it is not known.

`void setSystemId(String systemId)`
> Sets the system identifier of the document. In some `Source` implementations, this URI may be used to retrieve the XML document, while in others it may not. It should always be set if possible, however, since it will be used to resolve relative URI references from the XML document.

This is the entire `Source` interface, and as can be seen, it does not provide enough information for the JAXP implementation to be able to actually get hold of the XML document represented by the object. This means that JAXP implementations have to determine what particular implementation of this interface they are given (three are defined in other packages), and use this information to get hold of the document. This is not very elegant, but difficult to avoid since the different `Source` implementations represent the XML document differently.

The `Result` interface is in a similar position: it does not provide enough information in itself for the processor to know where to write the results of the transformation or how to do it. Instead, the processor must look at which particular `Result` implementation it is given. The methods of the `Result` interface are the same as those of the `Source` interface, but they are repeated below in any case.

`String getSystemId()`
> Returns the URI that the result is written to, which may be `null` if it is not known or if the output location has no particular URI. The output may be written to an `OutputStream` bound to a socket or a `StringBuffer`, or it may be turned into an object structure, and in these cases there can be no URI.

```
void setSystemId(String systemId)
```
Sets the URI of the location the result will be written to. This has no particular importance for the result, but it may still be useful to provide it in some contexts.

The actual implementations of the `Source` and `Result` interfaces are found in other JAXP packages, and we will present them when we get to those packages. The next interfaces that need to be presented are those of the supporting objects used by the `Transformer` during its transformations.

The `URIResolver` interface is implemented by objects which control how the `Transformer` and `TransformerFactory` objects resolve URI references into `Source` objects. As such it is similar in function to the `EntityResolver` interface of SAX, but it also performs an additional function in that it decides which of the three methods for representing XML documents will be used by the `Transformer`.

It is worth noting that `URIResolvers` are used to control the resolution of three kinds of URI references: in `xsl:include` elements, in `xsl:import` elements, and in calls to the `document` function. The first two are the most common, and they are resolved when parsing the XSLT stylesheet, that is, by the `TransformerFactory`. The last is resolved during stylesheet execution — that is, by the `Transformer` — since the URI may be created at runtime using an XPath expression.

The `URIResolver` interface has the methods listed below.

```
Source resolve(String href, String base) throws
    TransformerException
```
This method is called by the `Transformer` or `Transformer-Factory` to resolve external references from the XSLT stylesheet. The `href` parameter holds the URI reference as given in the stylesheet, and the `base` holds the base URI that the `href` is to be resolved against. This means that the `URIResolver` has to compute the absolute URI itself.

The return value must be an implementation of the `Source` interface, or `null` if the `URIResolver` wishes the processor to resolve the URI. A `TransformerException` is thrown if errors are encountered when resolving the URI reference.

The `ErrorListener` interface is used to control how XSLT processors react to errors. If no `ErrorListener` is given, error messages will be written to the `System.err` stream. When an `ErrorListener` has been set, the `Transformer` is required to call the `ErrorListener` when errors occur rather than to raise exceptions.

Generally, when an error has occurred, and the listener has not raised an exception to stop processing, the processor will continue in order to find more errors, but not actually produce any output.

The `ErrorListener` interface has the methods listed below.

`void warning(TransformerException exception) throws`
  `TransformerException`
  Used for conditions that are not errors, but which may still be troublesome. The default action is to ignore the call. If no exception is thrown by the `ErrorListener`, the processor must continue processing.

`void error(TransformerException exception) throws`
  `TransformerException`
  Called to notify the listener of an error from which the processor may recover. If the method does not throw an exception, the processor must continue processing.

`void fatalError(TransformerException exception)`
  `throws TransformerException`
  Informs the listener of a fatal error. If the listener does not throw an exception, the processor is required to continue processing, although there is no guarantee that the output after this point will be usable in any way.

We have now covered the most important classes and interfaces in the base package, leaving out some not very important interfaces and classes, as well as the exceptions. For more information on these, please consult the JAXP javadoc or specification.

21.1.1.2 The `javax.xml.transform.stream` package

This package contains implementations of the `Source` and `Result` interfaces based on Java IO streams. These are the most fundamental implementations that are generally used when transformations are run on serialized XML documents, whether read from files or from streams, or when they are intended to produce serialized output. Note that if no system identifier is provided the processor will not be able to resolve relative URI references.

The `Source` implementation is called `StreamSource` and has the methods listed below. Note that this is not an abstract class, but one that can be used directly.

```
StreamSource()
```
   This is a default constructor creating an empty `Source`.

```
StreamSource(java.io.InputStream inputStream)
```
   Creates a `Source` that reads from the given stream.

```
StreamSource(java.io.InputStream inputStream,
    String systemId)
```
   Creates a `Source` reading from the given stream, using the given base URI.

```
StreamSource(java.io.Reader reader)
```
   Creates a `Source` reading from the given character stream.

```
StreamSource(java.io.Reader reader,
    String systemId)
```
   Creates a `Source` reading from the given character stream, using the given base URI.

```
StreamSource(String systemId)
```
Creates a `Source` that reads from the given URI using the normal XML rules.

```
StreamSource(java.io.File f)
```
Creates a `Source` that reads from the given file, using the URI of the file as the base URI.

```
void setInputStream(java.io.InputStream
     inputStream)
```
Sets the `InputStream` of the `Source`. The XML parser will use the normal XML rules to detect the character encoding used. Note that if the character encoding is known, a `Reader` should be used instead.

```
java.io.InputStream getInputStream()
```
Returns the `InputStream` used by the `Source`. This may be `null` if the `Source` is reading from a `Reader` instead.

```
void setReader(java.io.Reader reader)
```
Sets the `Reader` to be used by the `Source`. Note that if the character encoding is not known, it is better to use an `InputStream`, since this lets the XML parser figure out the character encoding on its own.

```
java.io.Reader getReader()
```
Returns the `Reader` used by the `Source`.

```
void setPublicId(String publicId)
```
Sets the public identifier of the `Source`. This information is optional, and it is mainly useful for the end user.

```
String getPublicId()
```
Returns the public identifier of the XML document, if known.

```
void setSystemId(java.io.File f)
```
Sets the system identifier of the `Source` from a `File` object.

The StreamResult class is very similar to the StreamSource class, and implements a Result that can write the output of an XSLT transformation to a Java IO stream. This is generally used when the desired output of the transformation is a serialized representation. This is the most common case, but by no means the only possibility. The StreamResult class has the methods listed below.

StreamResult()
>   This is a default constructor which creates an empty Result object.

StreamResult(java.io.OutputStream outputStream)
>   Creates a StreamResult which writes its output to the given OutputStream. The character encoding used will be determined using the rules specified by the XSLT Recommendation. This alternative should be used when the application wishes the stylesheet and output properties to determine the output encoding.

StreamResult(java.io.Writer writer)
>   Creates a StreamResult that writes to the given Writer. This means that the Transformer cannot control the output encoding and is useful when the application wishes to control the output encoding.

StreamResult(String systemId)
>   Creates a StreamResult that writes its output to the given URI. Note that not all URIs can be written to.

StreamResult(java.io.File f)
>   Creates a StreamResult that writes its output to the given file, using a character encoding determined using the rules given in the XSLT Recommendation.

void setOutputStream(java.io.OutputStream
    outputStream)
>   Sets the byte stream that the result will be written to.

`java.io.OutputStream getOutputStream()`
Returns the byte stream that the result will be written to, if any.

`void setWriter(java.io.Writer writer)`
Sets the character stream to which output will be written.

`java.io.Writer getWriter()`
Returns the character stream to which output will be written.

`void setSystemId(java.io.File f)`
Sets the URI to which output will be written to that of the `File` object.

This is the entire contents of this package. In general, JAXP XSLT implementations can be expected to support this package.

21.1.1.3 The `javax.xml.transform.sax` package

This package contains `Source` and `Result` implementations which represent XML documents and transformation output as sequences of method calls. As was shown in earlier chapters, this can be exploited in many ways to control what is done to the input to the XSLT processor as well as what is done to its output. If such control is not needed, it is generally simpler to use the stream package. This package also provides the best mechanism for chaining together `Transformer` objects so that one acts on the output of another.

The package also contains interfaces that can be used to control how to build `Templates` objects and serialize transformation results. It also has an extended version of the `TransformerFactory` class with support for SAX-based `Transformers`. These are intended to allow XSLT transformations to be run as SAX parser filters, so that XSLT stylesheets can be run as part of SAX pipelines. These classes are not documented here, however, and you are referred to the JAXP specification for more information on them.

The `SAXSource` represents an XML document as a sequence of SAX events, and has the following methods.

`SAXSource()`
Creates an empty `SAXSource`.

`SAXSource(XMLReader reader,`
`    InputSource inputSource)`
Creates a `SAXSource` that uses the given `XMLReader` to read from the given `InputSource`. Note that the `XMLReader` does not need to be an XML parser, but can be an object implemented by the application to create SAX events from some other data source, or it can be an `XMLFilter`.

`SAXSource(InputSource inputSource)`
Creates a `SAXSource` object that reads from the given `Input-Source`. The `XMLReader` used by the `SAXSource` will be created using the JAXP `XMLReaderFactory`. (Note that Saxon 6.2.2 does not do this, although Michael Kay indicates that it may soon do so.)

`void setXMLReader(XMLReader reader)`
Sets the `XMLReader` to be used by the source.

`XMLReader getXMLReader()`
Returns the `XMLReader` set by the constructor or the `setXML-Reader` method.

`void setInputSource(InputSource inputSource)`
Sets the `InputSource` from which input will be read.

`InputSource getInputSource()`
Returns the `InputSource` used by the `SAXSource`.

The `SAXResult` is used to turn the result of an XSLT transformation into a series of method calls, in exactly the same way a SAX parser represents the document it parses as method calls. As mentioned earlier, this is mainly useful if the application wants to control what happens to the result of the transformation beyond a simple serialization of the result. The class has the methods listed below.

`SAXResult()`
  Creates an empty result.

`SAXResult(ContentHandler handler)`
  Creates a `SAXResult` object that passes the output to the given `ContentHandler` object.

`void setHandler(ContentHandler handler)`
  Sets the `ContentHandler` to which output will be passed.

`ContentHandler getHandler()`
  Returns the handler to which the result object will pass the output.

`void setLexicalHandler(LexicalHandler handler)`
  Since not all of the output can be represented as method calls to the `ContentHandler` interface (DOCTYPE declarations and comments, for example, cannot be handled by it), this method has been provided so that applications can tell the transformer where to send these events.
  Note that the `LexicalHandler`, if set, will generally be the same object as the `ContentHandler`.

`LexicalHandler getLexicalHandler()`
  Returns the `LexicalHandler` set using `setLexicalHandler`.

21.1.1.4 The `javax.xml.transform.dom` package

This package contains `Source` and `Result` implementations to be used when the input or output need to be represented as DOM trees. It also contains an interface used to represent locations in XML documents; for more information on this interface, please see the JAXP specification.

The `DOMSource` class is used to pass a DOM tree to the XSLT processor to be used as its input. This should generally only be used when the input already exists as a DOM tree, whether because it was built by the application, or for some other reason. When reading the input from a serialized XML document, the `stream` package should be used, in order to let the XSLT processor use whatever method is most efficient for it. The `DOMSource` class has the methods listed below.

`DOMSource()`
 Creates an empty `DOMSource` object.

`DOMSource(Node n)`
 Creates a `DOMSource` that operates on the subtree contained by this `Node`, which need not be a `Document` node. Note that the root of the XSLT source tree will be the root of the DOM tree that the `Node` belongs to, so the XPath expression / will evaluate to the root node of the DOM tree rather than to the `Node` given here.
 What this means is that you can process a part of an XML document, and yet have the entire document available if you need it. This can be very useful if you wish to process only part of a very large document.

`DOMSource(Node node, String systemID)`
 Creates a `DOMSource` rooted at the given `Node`, but with the given base URI.

`void setNode(Node node)`
 Sets the `Node` where processing starts.

`Node getNode()`
 Returns the start node.

The `DOMResult` class should be used when the output is wanted as a DOM tree for some reason. This is generally only useful when the application wishes to work on the output as a DOM tree after the transformation has been run. There are relatively few occasions on which this is useful, since if the application does transformations, those might be more easily expressed using XSLT. The class has the methods listed below.

`DOMResult()`

Creates an empty `DOMResult`.

`DOMResult(Node node)`

Creates a `DOMResult` with a particular DOM `Node` into which the output from the transformation will be written. This should be a `Node` which accepts children, since otherwise the `Transformer` will have a hard time writing its output.

`DOMResult(Node node, String systemID)`

Creates a result with a target `Node` and a base URI.

`void setNode(Node node)`

Sets the target node of the result object. Note that if no target node is set, the `Transformer` will create a `Document` node and write the results into it.

`Node getNode()`

Returns the node to which the output is (or was) written. After the transformation, this method can be used to get the root node of the output if no target node had been set beforehand.

21.1.2 *A JAXP example*

To make it easier to see how to make use of JAXP, we develop a simple JAXP application here (Example 21–1). The application will allow users to run XSLT transformations on XML files from the command line, producing the output as another file.

Example 21–1. An XSLT runner using JAXP

```java
import java.io.File;
import javax.xml.transform.*;
import javax.xml.transform.stream.*;

public class XSLTRunner {

  public static void main(String[] args) {
    if (args.length != 3) {
      System.err.println("Wrong number of arguments.");
      System.err.println("Usage:");
      System.err.println("  java XSLTRunner <infile> <xsltfile> "+
                         "<outfile>");
      return;
    }

    try {
      run(args[0], args[1], args[2]);
    }
    catch (TransformerConfigurationException e) {
      System.err.println("ERROR: " + e);
    }
    catch (TransformerException e) {
      System.err.println("ERROR: " + e);
    }
  }

  public static void run(String infile, String xsltfile,
                         String outfile)
    throws TransformerConfigurationException, TransformerException {
    TransformerFactory factory = TransformerFactory.newInstance();
    Transformer processor =
      factory.newTransformer(new StreamSource(new File(xsltfile)));
    processor.transform(new StreamSource(new File(infile)),
                        new StreamResult(new File(outfile)));
  }

}
```

As you can see, the basics of running an XSLT transformation are quite simple and require little programming. A `TransformerFactory` is created and used to create a `Transformer` object for a particular stylesheet. This object is then used to run the transformation, and that's that.

21.2 | The Saxon XSLT processor

The Saxon XSLT processor was written by Michael Kay, initially as a framework based on SAX for writing XML-to-HTML/XML transformation applications. Saxon has since developed into one of the best XSLT processors currently available, with advanced extension APIs. Saxon can still be used without using XSLT, but this has become rare, since most tasks are much easier to do using XSLT. Since Saxon has very good support for writing extensions, there is little one cannot achieve through a combination of XSLT and Java development.

The name was originally a double pun, in that Saxon was built on SAX (SAX-on), and in that the Ælfred parser was distributed with the framework. The Ælfred parser was named after the famous Saxon king Ælfred, also known as Alfred the Great, who ruled parts of what is now southwestern England in the 9th century.

Saxon is generally known as a fast and reliable processor, with very good conformance and a number of useful extensions to its XSLT 1.0 support. The only Java-based processor that is known to be faster than Saxon is James Clark's XT. Saxon has continually been improved, however, and is beginning to overtake XT. The author makes no predictions about the relationship between these two processors at the time when you read this.

If you are interested in more information about the internals of Saxon, I recommend that you read an article Michael Kay wrote for IBM developerWorks, which can be found at `http://www-106.ibm.com/developerworks/library/x-xslt2/`.

Saxon supports the JAXP API, so for using Saxon to run XSLT transformations, the JAXP API should be used.

21.2.1 *Writing extension functions*

Saxon has its own convention for how to call Java methods from XSLT stylesheets as if they were extension functions. The name of the function (as given in the XSLT stylesheet) must have a prefix, and the prefix must map to a URI that tells SAXON what Java class to find the function in. This can be either a URL with the fully qualified Java class name after the last / in the URL, or the fully qualified Java class name prefixed by `java:`. That is, if the class containing the method is `java.lang.Object` the namespace URI can be `/java.lang.Object`, `foo/java.lang.Object`, `http://www.foo.com/bar/baz/java.lang.Object`, or `java:java.lang.Object`. Method names are matched by ignoring hyphens and case, so that `to-string` will match `toString`. If there is more than one candidate method, one will be chosen that has the correct number of arguments, ignoring the types of the arguments.

What this means is that in many cases there is no need to write a specific XPath extension function in order to be able to do what you want in Saxon. Instead, you can quite often use the methods of existing classes in your stylesheet. You can of course also write methods designed to be called by stylesheets if desired, and below you'll see how to write methods that make use of the XSLT context.

When calling Java methods as XPath functions, there are three different cases to consider:

Static methods

These can be called directly. For example, if the `math` prefix is declared to map to `http://java.sun.com/java.lang.Math` (or, for that matter, `/java.lang.Math`), the expression `math:sqrt(25)` will produce the result 5.

Instance methods

These are called by giving an object of the class as the first parameter to the extension function, and the prefix of the function name must still identify a class. This can be compared to writing method calls as `method(obj, arg)` instead of `obj.method(arg)`. To see how to create object instances, see below.

Constructors

Constructors can be called by using the method name `new`, which can never exist in a Java class, given that `new` is a reserved keyword. Objects created by this method can only be passed to other extension functions or converted to values of the basic XSLT types.

Saxon will convert the arguments needed by the methods as best it can, following these rules:

- If the first argument of the method is of the class `com.icl.saxon.Context`, Saxon's current `Context` object will be passed. You can also use the `org.w3c.xsl.Context` object defined by the XSLT 1.1 Working Draft. This is useful for writing extension functions that somehow make use of the XSLT context.

- Booleans, numbers, and strings are converted as one would expect.

- If the value passed to the method is an XPath node set and the declared argument is a DOM `NodeList`, the node set will be converted into a `NodeList` object.

To show how to use this, Example 21–2 demonstrates a simple XSLT stylesheet template rule that inserts the current date and time into the document output.

Example 21–2. Calling Java methods in Saxon

```
<xsl:template match="/">
  <p>
  <xsl:value-of xmlns:date="/java.util.Date"
                select="date:to-string(date:new())"/>
  </p>
</xsl:template>
```

The Saxon XSLT context is represented by the `Context` class mentioned above, which has the methods listed below.

`Node getContextNode()`
> Returns the context node, where `Node` is the DOM `Node` interface.

`int getContextPosition()`
> Returns the context position.

`int getContextSize()`
> Returns the context size.

`Outputter getOutputter()`
> Returns the `Outputter` object to which the output of processing is being written. Since this is only relevant for extension element types, this object is explained in that section.

`Node getCurrentNode()`
> Returns the current node. See 16.1.1, "The context," on page 566 for an explanation of how this is different from the context node.

`void setContextNode(NodeInfo node)`
> Sets the context node; used by element types which change the context node. `NodeInfo` is a Saxon interface derived from the DOM `Node` interface. All nodes in the Saxon tree implement this interface, so any node picked from tree traversal can be pushed in here.
>
> Note that this method does not update the context position or size, which must be updated separately. Note also that it is not intended for application use, although it is necessary in order to be able to modify the context node. Use with care.

`void setPosition(int pos)`
> Sets the current context position. Note that it is not intended for application use, although it is necessary in order to be able to modify the context position. Use with care.

```
void setLast(int last)
```
Sets the context size. Not intended for application use, but necessary to change the context size. Note that if you do use this, you should also change the context node list, which I don't know how to do. Use with care.

```
void setCurrentNode(NodeInfo node)
```
Sets the current node. Not intended for application use, but necessary to change the current node. If you do use this, be careful to get the interplay between the current node and the context node right.

```
Context newContext()
```
Returns a copy of the `Context` object.

21.2.2 *Writing extension element types*

A class that implements an XSLT extension element type must implement the `com.icl.saxon.style.ExtensionElementFactory` class. To use the element type in an XSLT stylesheet, a namespace prefix must be declared that maps to a URI identifying the implementing class in the same manner as with extension functions. The namespace prefix must also be listed in an `extension-element-prefixes` attribute, as required by XSLT.

The `ExtensionElementFactory` interface has only a single method: `Class getExtensionClass(String localname)`, which, given the local name of an element type in the extension namespace, returns a `Class` object representing the class that implements the element type. This means that the class identified by the namespace prefix represents the namespace itself rather than any of the individual element types in that namespace.

The classes that implement extension element types must be derived from the class `com.icl.saxon.style.StyleElement`. Like in 4XSLT, this class is derived from the class that represents element nodes in the document tree. Since this class implements the DOM `Element` interface, the contents of the element can be accessed as in the DOM. The class has a large number of methods, but listed below are only those most relevant to implementing extension element types. The rest can be found in the Saxon javadoc.

`boolean isInstruction()`

Must be defined to return `true`, so that Saxon knows that this element represents an instruction. The default returns `false`.

`boolean isTopLevel()`

If the element type is a top-level element type, this must be redefined to return `true`. The default returns `false`.

`boolean mayContainTemplateBody()`

If the element type may contain a template body, this method must be redefined to return `true`.

`void prepareAttributes() throws TransformerConfigurationException`

This method is called during stylesheet compilation to prepare the attributes of the element so that they are ready when the element is executed. Since this only needs to be done once, while the element may be executed many times, doing this in a separate method saves time. Note that this method is abstract and must be defined in all element type implementations.

The `TransformerConfigurationException` can be thrown if there is something wrong with the attributes specified on the element. If an attribute is missing, the `void report-Absence(String attrname)` method can be called to throw the correct exception.

`ExtendedAttributes getAttributeList()`

Returns the attributes of the element in an `ExtendedAttributes` object. `ExtendedAttributes` takes the SAX 2.0 `Attributes` interface and extends it with some Saxon-specific methods for faster access to the attributes.

```
void validate() throws
    TransformerConfigurationException
```
This method is called after the entire stylesheet tree has been built to verify that the element type is being used correctly. It need not check the attributes, since this is more properly the task of `prepareAttributes`, but it should verify that the element is being used in the correct context and that its contents are reasonable.

```
void process(Context context) throws
    TransformerException
```
This is the method that is called to execute or instantiate the element. It is abstract and must be defined for every element type.

```
void processChildren(Context context) throws
    TransformerException
```
Processes the children of this element in the given context. The context is not changed in any way.

```
void checkEmpty()
```
This is a convenience method that checks whether the element is empty and raises an appropriate exception if it is not.

```
void checkTopLevel()
```
This is a convenience method that checks whether the element is at the top level and raises an appropriate exception if it is not.

```
void checkNotTopLevel()
```
This is a convenience method that verifies that the element is not at the top level and raises an appropriate exception if it is.

```
void checkWithinTemplate()
```
This is a convenience method that verifies that the element appears within a template rule and raises an appropriate exception if it does not.

`Expression makeExpression(String expr)`
Parses and creates an object structure representing a parsed XPath expression in the context of this element. Very useful for attributes containing XPath expressions.

`Expression makeAttributeValueTemplate(String expression)`
Creates an object structure representing an attribute value template.

`NamePool getNamePool()`
Returns a `NamePool` object, which can be used to get the name code for specific element and attribute names. Its use is documented below.

Extension element types write their output to the `Outputter` object which they get from the `Context` object. It has the following methods.

`void setEscaping(boolean escaping)`
Tells the `Outputter` whether escaping should be performed or not.

`void write(String s) throws TransformerException`
Writes out the string argument with no escaping.

`void writeContent(String s) throws TransformerException`
Writes out the given string, escaping it if configured to do so.

`void writeContent(char[] chars, int start, int len) throws TransformerException`
Writes out `len` characters from the `chars` array, starting with index `start`, escaping them if configured to do so.

`void writeContent(StringBuffer chars, int start, int len) throws TransformerException`
Writes out `len` characters from the given buffer, starting with character number `start`, escaping them if configured to do so.

```
void writeStartTag(int nameCode) throws
    TransformerException
```
Writes out the start-tag of the element with the given name code. The name code of an element type can be looked up using the `NamePool` object.

```
void writeAttribute(int nameCode, String value)
    throws TransformerException
```
Writes an attribute. Must be called after the corresponding `writeStartTag` and before the first content call of the element.

```
void writeAttribute(int nameCode, String value,
    boolean noEscape) throws TransformerException
```
Writes out an attribute, controlling explicitly whether its value should be escaped or not.

```
void writeEndTag(int nameCode) throws
    TransformerException
```
Writes out the end-tag of the element with the given name code.

```
void writeComment(String comment) throws
    TransformerException
```
Writes out the given comment.

```
void writePI(String target, String data) throws
    TransformerException
```
Writes out the given processing instruction.

The `NamePool` class is used by Saxon in order to be able to represent names as numbers instead of as compound objects consisting of three strings. This is much more efficient, so Saxon does this everywhere internally, as well as in the `Outputter`, as documented above. The `NamePool` has a quite large interface that is rarely used, so a method reference is not given here; see the Saxon javadoc for a full method listing.

The last class that is important to know when writing extension element types is the `com.icl.saxon.expr.Expression` class, which represents parsed XPath expressions. Its methods are listed below.

`Value evaluate(Context context)`
Evaluates the expression in the given context, returning an XPath value.

`boolean evaluateAsBoolean(Context context)`
Evaluates the expression as a boolean within the given context. This is more convenient than the default method, and this also allows Saxon to optimize special cases.

`NodeSetValue evaluateAsNodeSet(Context context)`
Evaluates the expression as a node-set expression.

`double evaluateAsNumber(Context context)`
Evaluates the expression as a number expression, allowing certain optimizations.

`String evaluateAsString(Context context)`
Evaluates the expression to a string, with certain optimizations.

`NodeEnumeration enumerate(Context context,`
`    boolean sorted)`
This method returns an enumeration of the nodes in the node set that the expression evaluates to in the given context. If `sorted` is `true`, the nodes will be in document order.

`static Expression make(String expression,`
`    StaticContext env)`
Parses the given XPath expression in the given context and returns an `Expression` object representing it.

As an example, we will write a class that implements an extension namespace consisting of a number of little utility extension element types (Example 21–3).

Example 21–3. Saxon extension element types

```java
import java.io.FileWriter;
import java.io.IOException;
import java.text.SimpleDateFormat;
import javax.xml.transform.TransformerException;
import javax.xml.transform.TransformerConfigurationException;
import com.icl.saxon.style.*;
import com.icl.saxon.Context;
import com.icl.saxon.expr.Expression;
import com.icl.saxon.output.Outputter;
import com.icl.saxon.om.ExtendedAttributes;

public class SAXONExtensions implements ExtensionElementFactory {

  public Class getExtensionClass(String localname) {
    try {
      if (localname.equals("debug"))
        return Class.forName("SAXONExtensions$DebugElement");
      else if (localname.equals("insert-time"))
        return Class.forName("SAXONExtensions$InsertTimeElement");
      else if (localname.equals("time"))
        return Class.forName("SAXONExtensions$TimeElement");
    }
    catch (ClassNotFoundException e) {
    }

    return null;
  }

  /**
   * An element type that appends the string value
   * of a specified XPath expression to a named file.
   * The expression must be in the attribute 'select'
   * and the file name in the attribute 'file'.
   */

  public static class DebugElement extends StyleElement {
    private String filename;
    private Expression select;

    public boolean isInstruction() {
      return true;
    }
```

```
public void prepareAttributes()
  throws TransformerConfigurationException {

  ExtendedAttributes atts = getAttributeList();
  filename = atts.getValue("file");
  if (filename == null)
    reportAbsence("file");
  String selectValue = atts.getValue("select");
  if (selectValue == null)
    reportAbsence("select");
  select = makeExpression(selectValue);
}

public void validate()
  throws TransformerConfigurationException {

  checkEmpty();
  checkWithinTemplate();
}

public void process(Context context)
  throws TransformerException {

  try {
    FileWriter out = new FileWriter(filename, true);
    out.write(select.evaluateAsString(context));
    out.close();
  }
  catch (IOException e) {
    throw new TransformerException(e);
  }
}
}

/**
 * An element type that inserts the current time, formatted using
 * an optional format expression.
 * The expression, if given, is given in the 'format' attribute.
 */

public static class InsertTimeElement extends StyleElement {
  private SimpleDateFormat format;

  public boolean isInstruction() {
    return true;
  }
```

```
    public void prepareAttributes()
                throws TransformerConfigurationException {
      ExtendedAttributes atts = getAttributeList();
      String formatValue = atts.getValue("format");
      if (formatValue != null)
        format = new SimpleDateFormat(formatValue);
    }

    public void validate()
                throws TransformerConfigurationException {
      checkEmpty();
      checkWithinTemplate();
    }

    public void process(Context context)
                throws TransformerException {
      String date;
      if (format != null)
        date = format.format(new java.util.Date());
      else
        date = new java.util.Date().toString();

      Outputter out = context.getOutputter();
      out.writeContent(date);
    }
  }

/**
 * An element type that can be used to measure the performance of
 * XSLT stylesheets. It measures the time it takes to execute
 * its contents and outputs this to the standard output.
 * In case there are several time elements in the stylesheet
 * the element can be given a name in the 'name' attribute.
 */

public static class TimeElement extends StyleElement {
  private String name;
  private int times;
  private double timeTotal;

  public boolean isInstruction() {
    return true;
  }

  public boolean mayContainTemplateBody() {
    return true;
  }
```

```
public void prepareAttributes()
  throws TransformerConfigurationException {

  ExtendedAttributes atts = getAttributeList();
  name = atts.getValue("name");
}

public void validate()
  throws TransformerConfigurationException {

  checkWithinTemplate();
}

public void process(Context context)
  throws TransformerException {

  double start = System.currentTimeMillis();
  processChildren(context);
  double time = System.currentTimeMillis() - start;

  timeTotal += time;
  times++;
  System.out.println("Executed " + name + " in " + (time / 1000)
                     + "seconds");
  System.out.println("Average: " + (timeTotal / times)
                     + " (" + times + ")");
  }
 }


}
```

21.3 | The Xalan XSLT processor

The Xalan XSLT processor was created by the Apache XML Project,
which also created the Xerces XML parser. It is generally known as a
conformant processor. Note that there is also a parallel C++ implementation of Xalan, known as Xalan-C, while the Java version is known as
Xalan-J.

Xalan supports the JAXP API for setting up and running XSLT
transformations, so to embed Xalan in an application, JAXP should be
used. There is also an internal API that exposes more functionality than

JAXP does, but this is really only of interest for very special uses. This API can be found in the packages `org.apache.xalan.processor`, `org.apache.xalan.templates`, and `org.apache.xalan.transformer`, where it is to some extent mixed up with internal code and things unrelated to embedding the processor.

The tree structure Xalan uses to represent the source is a DOM tree, but with an implementation that is specially geared towards Xalan's needs.

Like Saxon, Xalan has clearly defined extension mechanisms. This allows you to create extension element types and functions in Java, but also, through the Bean Scripting Framework (BSF), to write them in other languages, including Jython. We will omit the BSF here and concentrate on how to write extensions in Java.

21.3.1 *Writing extension functions*

In general, calling Java methods from XSLT stylesheets in Xalan is similar to what it is in Saxon, but the mechanisms used have some differences. Any Java method can be called as an XPath function from Xalan, with the namespace prefix and the local name used to locate the method. Xalan will automatically map the types used in the method signature from and to the types used to represent XSLT types.

If the method has `org.apache.xalan.extensions.Expression-Context` as the type of its first parameter, Xalan will automatically supply such an object as the first parameter. This object represents the XSLT context, but is not needed by all extension functions. The rest of the arguments will then be taken from the XPath function call.

Table 21–1 shows which Java types are acceptable for which XSLT types. When the value given in the XPath function call is of the type in the left-hand column, this can be converted to any of the types in the right-hand column in the same row. This also applies to the return value, with the conversion going then in the opposite direction.

Table 21–1 Xalan type conversions

XSLT type	Java types
node set	`org.w3c.dom.traversal.NodeIterator,` `org.w3c.dom.NodeList, org.w3c.dom.Node` or its subclasses, `java.lang.String, java.lang.Object, char, [double, float, long, int, short, byte], boolean`
string	`java.lang.String, java.lang.Object, char, [double, float, long, int, short, byte], boolean`
boolean	`boolean, java.lang.Boolean, java.lang.Object, java.lang.String`
number	`double, java.lang.Double, float, long, int, short, char, byte, boolean, java.lang.String, java.lang.Object`
result tree fragment	`org.w3c.dom.traversal.NodeIterator,` `org.w3c.dom.NodeList, org.w3c.dom.Node` or its subclasses, `java.lang.String, java.lang.Object, char, [double, float, long, int, short, byte], boolean`

The most complex part of calling Java methods from XSLT with Xalan is actually understanding how to create namespace prefixes that map to the correct methods. In Xalan there are three different ways of doing this:

Class format

With this format, the namespace URI takes the form `xalan://FQCN`, where `FQCN` is the fully qualified class name of the class. So to create a prefix that maps to the class `java.lang.Object` you should use the URI `xalan://java.lang.Object`.

To call a static method using this format is easy. With the prefix `integer` mapping to the URI `xalan://java.lang.Integer`, you can simply say `integer:toHexString(200)` to call the static method `toHexString`.

To call a constructor is also easy: `integer:new(20)` will create a new `Integer` object. This can then be used as if it were an ordinary XPath value, for example by calling one of its instance methods: `integer:hashCode(integer:new(20))`. Note that we here pass an object to the instance method as the first argument, just as we did in Saxon.

Package format

This format is exactly like class format, except that only a partial package name is used. That is, a prefix mapping to the package `java.lang` can be created by binding a namespace prefix to the URI `xalan://java.lang`.

This format works exactly like class format, except that now the class (and the missing parts of the package name, if any) must be specified in the local name. So if `lang` maps to `xalan://java.lang`, the expression `lang:Integer.toHexString(200)` will also call the static method `toHexString`.

Java format

This format is unlike the others, as it only tells the processor that the localname is a Java name. The namespace URI is the fixed URI `http://xml.apache.org/xslt/java`. This format moves the entire specification of the method name into the localname. If the `java` prefix is mapped to this fixed URI, then to call the `toHexString` method we must say `java:java.lang.Integer.toHexString(200)`.

Since Java supports overloading, the result of matching a combination of a namespace URI and a localname can be more than just one method. To figure out which one to call, Xalan will rank all the methods with matching names. This is done using the types in Table 21–1, where for each actual argument given in the XPath function call, its type is matched with that of the Java method. Java types that come earlier in the list for a particular XSLT type yield higher scores for the Java method arguments with those types. The method eventually called is the one with the highest score. If two methods have the same score, an exception is thrown.

Example 21–4 shows how to call Java methods from XSLT stylesheets using Xalan.

Example 21–4. Calling Java methods from Xalan

```
<xsl:stylesheet xmlns:xsl="http://www.w3.org/1999/XSL/Transform"
                xmlns:date="xalan://java.util.Date"
                xmlns:format="xalan://java.text.SimpleDateFormat"
                version="1.0">

  <xsl:template match="/">
    <xsl:value-of select="format:format(format:new('yyyy-MM-dd'),
                                         date:new())"/>
  </xsl:template>

</xsl:stylesheet>
```

This stylesheet creates a new `Date` object and a new `SimpleDate-Formatter`, then calls the `format` method on the formatter, giving it the `Date` object. The result is that it prints the current date to the output in the format `'yyyy-MM-dd'`. When I wrote this, the output was `2001-04-29`.

This example should show that simply by using existing Java methods, XSLT stylesheets can perform quite advanced tasks.

As mentioned above, Java methods that have `org.apache.xalan.extensions.ExpressionContext` as the type of their first argument will have this object passed to them when called as XPath functions. This makes it possible to write XPath functions that make use of the XPath context to do their work. The methods of the `Expression-Context` interface are listed below.

`Node getContextNode()`
    Returns the current XPath context node.

`NodeIterator getContextNodes()`
    Returns the current context node list, in the form of an iterator over that list.

```
double toNumber(Node n)
```
This is a convenience method that returns the value of a node as a number.

```
String toString(Node n)
```
Another convenience method, this time returning the string value of a node.

Note that this class does not provide access to the entire XPath context as it is defined by the XPath Recommendation. Why this is so is not clear to me.

21.3.2 *Writing extension element types*

In Xalan, extension element types are implemented in a manner very different from that used in 4XSLT and Saxon: They are implemented by methods. These methods must have the following signature: `public type foo(XSLProcessorContext context, ElemExtensionCall elem)`. The `XSLProcessorContext` provides access to the processing context, holding information such as the XSLT processor, the XML source tree, the stylesheet and so on. The `ElemExtensionCall` represents the extension element type in the stylesheet tree and provides all necessary information about it.

Note that the return value from the method is inserted in the result tree. If this is not wanted, simply return `null` or declare the method as being `void`. There are also other ways to insert output in the result tree, to which we will return shortly.

The easiest way to use an extension element type from an XSLT stylesheet is to define a prefix that maps to the class name, and then use the name of the method implementing the extension as the local name. This means that each namespace effectively becomes one class, which may well make sense. Other namespace prefix formats can also be used, but this is the most natural one.

The `XSLProcessorContext` object has the following methods:

`Node getContextNode()`
> Returns the current XSLT context node.

`QName getMode()`
> Returns the name of the mode currently being processed, or `null` if there is no current mode. The `QName` class is used to represent expanded names.

`Node getSourceTree()`
> Returns the root node of the source tree currently being processed.

`Stylesheet getStylesheet()`
> Returns the `Stylesheet` currently being used. The `Stylesheet` class is Xalan's representation of XSLT stylesheets that provides complete access to the stylesheet.

`TransformerImpl getTransformer()`
> Returns an object representing the XSLT processor. `Transformer-Impl` is the class that implements the JAXP `Transformer` interface, providing a number of extra methods.

`void outputToResultTree(Stylesheet stylesheetTree, Object obj)`
> This method is used to write to the result tree. The `obj` parameter is converted according to Xalan's type conversion rules.

The `ElemExtensionCall` class is derived from the DOM `Element` interface, but provides a number of additional methods. Listed below are the most important methods of this class.

`String getAttribute(String rawName)`
> Returns the value of the named attribute of the extension element, or `null` if it is not found.

```
String getAttribute(String rawName,
    Node sourceNode, TransformerImpl transformer)
```
Returns the contents of the named attribute of the extension element interpreted as an attribute value template. That is, any XPath expressions in curly braces will be interpreted and their values inserted.

The other interesting methods in the class are those on the DOM `Element` interface, which you have already seen listed elsewhere.

To make this discussion a little more concrete, we implement the three extension element types, already implemented for Saxon, for Xalan, to allow you to compare the implementations and see how to write Xalan extension element types.

Example 21–5. Extension element types implemented in Xalan

```
import java.io.FileWriter;
import java.io.IOException;
import java.text.SimpleDateFormat;
import javax.xml.transform.TransformerException;
import javax.xml.transform.TransformerConfigurationException;
import org.apache.xalan.templates.ElemExtensionCall;
import org.apache.xalan.extensions.XSLProcessorContext;
import org.apache.xpath.XPathContext;
import org.apache.xpath.XPath;
import org.apache.xpath.objects.XObject;

public class XalanExtensions {

  /**
   * An element type that appends the string value of a specified
   * XPath expression to a named file. The expression must be in the
   * attribute 'select' and the file name in the attribute 'file'.
   */
```

```
public void debug(XSLProcessorContext context,
                  ElemExtensionCall elem)
  throws TransformerException {
  String filename = elem.getAttribute("file",
                                      context.getContextNode(),
                                      context.getTransformer());
  if (filename == null)
    throw new TransformerException("file attribute missing!");

  String select = elem.getAttribute("select");
  if (select == null)
    throw new TransformerException("select attribute missing!");

  XPathContext xctxt = context.getTransformer().getXPathContext();
  XPath myxpath = new XPath(select, elem,
                            xctxt.getNamespaceContext(),
                            XPath.SELECT);
  XObject xobj = myxpath.execute(xctxt, context.getContextNode(),
                                 xctxt.getNamespaceContext());

  try {
    FileWriter out = new FileWriter(filename, true);
    out.write(xobj.str());
    out.close();
  }
  catch (IOException e) {
    throw new TransformerException(e);
  }
}

/**
 * An element type that inserts the current time, formatted using
 * an optional format expression.
 * The expression, if given, is given in the 'format' attribute.
 */

public String insertTime(XSLProcessorContext context,
                         ElemExtensionCall elem)
  throws TransformerException {

  String formatValue = elem.getAttribute("format");
  if (formatValue != null) {
    SimpleDateFormat format = new SimpleDateFormat(formatValue);
    return format.format(new java.util.Date());
  } else
    return new java.util.Date().toString();
}
```

```
/**
 * An element type that can be used to measure the performance of
 * XSLT stylesheets. It measures the time it takes to execute
 * its contents and outputs this to the standard output.
 * In case there are several time elements in the stylesheet
 * the element can be given a name in the 'name' attribute.
 */

public void time(XSLProcessorContext context,
                 ElemExtensionCall elem)
  throws TransformerException {

  String name = elem.getAttribute("name");
  if (name == null) name = "";

  double start = System.currentTimeMillis();
  context.getTransformer().executeChildTemplates(elem,
                                   context.getContextNode(),
                                   null, true);
  double time = System.currentTimeMillis() - start;

  System.out.println("Executed " + name + " in " + (time / 1000)
                     + " seconds.");
}


}
```

As you can see, the extensions end up being shorter in Xalan, but also somewhat less elegant and harder to write.

XML processing in depth

- Other processing approaches
- Schemas and validation
- Generating XML
- XML from databases: an example
- An RSS application suite

Part Six

In this part we go into more depth on XML processing, showing some more processing approaches. We will discuss how to make use of schemas and how to generate XML, and will also present some more complete and in-depth examples of XML-based applications.

Other approaches to processing

- Pull APIs
- Hybrid approaches
- Simplified approaches

Chapter

22

This chapter discusses processing frameworks that are neither purely event-based or tree-based, nor declarative. Some of the frameworks are presented mainly as illustrations of other possible ways to process XML documents, while others are very useful and in many cases actually preferable to the pure approaches. So while the book does not devote all that much space to these approaches, one should not make the mistake of assuming that they are not useful or important. They just require less explanation.

22.1 | Pull APIs

In 3.1, "Documents viewed as events," on page 81, event-based APIs were discussed, and a variation of such APIs called pull APIs was mentioned. As described there, pull APIs are at the same level of abstraction as event-based APIs, but have some minor differences. The main difference is that in a pull API, the client application has the driving loop and controls parsing by "pulling" the document from the parser piece by piece. These pieces typically correspond to the events in event-based parsers, but are instead represented by token objects. That is, each kind of event (start-tag, end-tag, data, PI, etc.) has its own kind of token which the parser may return. The code snippet in Example 22–1 illustrates how one might write an adapter from a pull API to an event-based API.

Example 22–1. How to convert from a pull API to an event-based API

```
parser.parse("mydocument.xml")

cnt_handler.startDocument()
while parser.has_more_tokens():
    token = parser.get_next_token()

    if token.type == starttype:
        cnt_handler.startElement(token.name, token.attrs)
    elif token.type == endtype:
        cnt_handler.endElement(token.name)
    elif token.type == texttype:
        cnt_handler.characters(token.contents)
    # and so on...

cnt_handler.endDocument()
```

As this example shows, the essential difference between a pull API and an event-based API is really that the driving loop is in the client application, and that events must be represented by explicit objects, rather than method/function calls with parameters.

The pull approach is intuitive and easy to understand, but rather inconvenient in that the application needs to dispatch on the various token types before it can make use of the information in the tokens. This is necessary because it is impossible (in general, at least) for the application to know what type of token it will receive from a get_next_token call before it makes the call.

As the pseudo-code in Example 22–1 shows, it is very easy to write an adapter from a pull API to an event-based API. However, going the other way is very difficult, because it requires the flow of control to move in a way that event-based APIs are not designed for. Imagine implementing the `get_next_token()` function. This function would have to make the XML parser parse one more event into the document, turn that event into a token object, and return control to the pulling application. The problem is that event-based parsers require having the controlling loop in their own code, while a pulling application requires a similar loop in its code.

One way to implement this would be to use a feature of programming languages known as *coroutines*. These allow control to be transferred between different places in programs in a way that would allow two controlling loops to run in parallel. However, hardly any programming languages support this. Simula 67, the first object-oriented programming language, is the only example I can think of. There is also a modified version of the standard Python interpreter, known as Stackless Python, developed by Christian Tismer, that supports coroutines. (Note that coroutines can be implemented using threads, although this is not recommended.)

Few people use languages that support coroutines, however, so other solutions to this problem are needed. Most of the Python XML parsers (Pyexpat, xmllib, xmlproc, and sgmlop) are incremental, and this provides an alternative mechanism. The idea is due to Fredrik Lundh, who posted it on the Python XML-SIG mailing list. Example 22–2 shows pseudo-code for such a solution.

22.1.1 *RXP*

RXP was written by Richard Tobin of the Language Technology Group (LTG) at the University of Edinburgh. It is the only parser available in Python that has a pull-based interface, and this is why it is described in this section, rather than in Chapter 7, "Using XML parsers," on page 160 with the other parsers. RXP is a complete parser that supports quite a few character encodings and can validate. RXP is used by the

Example 22–2. An adapter from an event-based to a pulling interface

```
class EventToPullAdapter:

    def __init__(self, parser, file):
        self._parser = parser
        self._tokens = []
        self._file   = file

    def get_next_token(self):
        if self._tokens == []:
            self._parser.feed(file.read(BUFFER_SIZE))

        token = self._tokens[0]
        self._tokens = self._tokens[1 : ]
        return token

    # --- event handlers

    def startElement(name, attrs):
        self._tokens.append(StartTagToken(name, attrs))

    # more handlers...
```

LTG's XML processing framework LTXML.[1] LTXML is written in C, as is the parser.

RXP is also used by the XED XML editor, which is written in Python using Tkinter for the GUI. To develop XED, the LTG had to wrap RXP as a Python module so that they could access it from Python, and this module wrapper has also been made available separately. This means that there is actually a C-based validating parser available in Python.

22.1.1.1 The RXP API

RXP has a relatively simple interface, which supports only the contents of the XML documents and does not provide DTD information. It

---

1. Note that there is also a version of LTXML known as LTSGML which supports SGML.

also provides quite a bit of lexical information, but most of it is provided in a non-obtrusive fashion, so that applications can easily ignore it. The parser is also relatively configurable in what information it provides, and it can validate documents. RXP lives in the `XMLinter` module.

To parse a document, one must create an object that represents the data source from which the document is read. This is done using one of the three functions below. Note that there is nothing in the API that represents the parser itself, except perhaps the module.

`Open(filename, flags)`
> This makes the parser read from a file in the file system, by providing the name of the file as the first argument. The second argument is used to set parsing options. The various options are described below.

`FOpen(fileobj, flags)`
> This function can be used to make RXP read from a file-like object rather than from a named file.

`OpenString(string, flags)`
> With this function it is possible to make RXP read the document from a string. Note that this string must contain the entire document, since there is no incremental parsing API.

The `flags` argument has two main values: `NSL_read`, which means non-validating parsing, and `NSL_read | NSL_read_validate`, which means validating parsing. The `flags` argument is a bit mask, which is why `|`, the binary `or` operator, was used to combine the two values.

All these three functions return an object that represents the data source being read from, and this object is used to pull the data from the data source with the `GetNextBit` function, which either returns a token object, called a *bit* in RXP, or `None` if parsing is complete. Example 22–3 shows the structure of a typical RXP application.

What now remains is mainly to understand how to interpret the bits returned by `GetNextBit`. When interpreting a bit, one more or less

Example 22–3. Pseudo-code for an RXP application

```
from XMLinter import *

file = Open('doc.xml', NSL_read)

while 1:
    bit = GetNextBit(file)
    if bit is None: break

    # interpret bit and do something useful with it
```

always starts with its `type` attribute, which contains a string that gives the bit (or token) type. The possible values for this are listed below.

`'start'`

This means that the bit represents a start-tag. The element-type name can be found in the `label` attribute, and the attributes, in the `item` attribute. (More about `item` below.)

`'end'`

This means that the bit represents an end-tag, and the element-type name can be found in the `label` attribute. The other attributes will be empty.

`'empty'`

This value is used for empty-element tags and should be interpreted as a start-tag followed immediately by an end-tag. The element-type name is in `label` and the attributes are in `item`. Note that this bit type makes things a bit awkward, since empty elements can also be legally represented using both a start-tag and an end-tag, which means that applications must test for both cases.

`'text'`

This value is used for pieces of character data. The actual data can be found in `body`. If the data came from a CDATA marked section, the `isCData` attribute will be `true`. If it came from an entity reference, the `isERef` attribute will be `true`.

'pi'
> This value is used for processing instructions, with the entire PI contents (both target and data) in the `body` attribute. Bits of this type will only be returned if the `NSL_read_all_bits` flag is set.

'comment'
> This value is used for comments, with the comment contents in the `body` attribute. Bits of this type will only be returned if the `NSL_read_all_bits` flag is set.

'doctype'
> This bit represents the DOCTYPE declaration, with the entire contents of the declaration from (but not including) `'<!DOCTYPE '` up to (but not including) the final `'>'` in the `body` attribute.

Decoding the attributes of an element requires a bit more work by the client application. The `item` attribute of the start-tag or empty-element bit contains an object of type `item`. The information in this object can be extracted using the following functions:

ItemActualAttributes(item)
> This function returns the attributes as a list of name/value tuples.

GetAttrVal(item, name)
> Returns the value of the attribute named `name` as a string. It returns `None` if the attribute does not exist.

The PyXML package has more functionality than just an interface to the RXP parser. It also has functionality for generating XML documents as output and a query processor interface. In the interests of brevity I will not describe these interfaces here.

22.1.1.2 An example application

Here we revisit the RSS to HTML converter, this time implementing it as a pull application (Examples 22–4 to 22–7). The style of the application is somewhere between the event-based and tree-based styles. The application controls the flow of execution, but in the same way as event-based applications it can only see a part of the document at a time. This leads to state-tracking similar to that of event-based applications.

As usual, we start with importing the necessary modules, and define the templates (Example 22–4). Note that this time we finish the UL list of items in the bottom template, rather than in the code.

Example 22–4. The RSS to HTML converter using RXP (1 of 4)

```
import sys
from XMLinter import *

# --- Templates

top = \
"""
<!DOCTYPE HTML PUBLIC "-//W3C//DTD HTML 4.0 Transitional//EN">
<HTML>
<HEAD>
  <TITLE>%s</TITLE>
</HEAD>

<BODY>
<A HREF="%s"><H1>%s</H1></A>
"""

bottom = \
"""
</UL>

<HR>

<ADDRESS>
Converted to HTML using RXP.
</ADDRESS>

</BODY>
</HTML>
"""
```

Example 22–5 is the top-level function that does the conversion. It takes a file name and a file-like object and reads from the file, writing to the object.

Example 22–5. The RSS to HTML converter using RXP (2 of 4)

```
# --- Conversion

def convert_file(filename, outf):
    convert(Open(filename, NSL_read), outf)
```

The function in Example 22–6 does the conversion. It keeps the name of the currently open element in the `parent` variable, and puts the channel title into `title`. The `parent` variable is used to figure out what kind of element the `'text'` bits belong to, and act accordingly. When the end of the `rss` element is reached, the function returns.

Note how the function calls `convert_item` to handle `item` elements. This means that we don't need a variable to track the parent of the `title`, `link`, and `description` elements. Instead, we know how to handle them from which function we are in. This approach is possible because the controlling loop is in the application code.

The `convert_item` function (Example 22–7) is very similar to the other function. The main difference is that it accumulates all the information it needs about the item before returning. Since it knows that this function only needs to handle a single item, it can collect all its information first and not produce any output until after it is finished. Again, this is an approach that is made possible by the fact that the controlling loop is in the application.

22.2 | Hybrid event/tree-based approaches

So far we have only discussed processing frameworks which are either purely event-based or purely tree-based (or something else altogether), but some of the most useful tools available take a hybrid approach that

Example 22–6. The RSS to HTML converter using RXP (3 of 4)

```python
def convert(file, outf):
    parent = None
    title  = None
    first_item = 1

    while 1:
        bit = GetNextBit(file)

        if bit.type == 'start':
            parent = bit.label

            if bit.label == 'item':
                if first_item:
                    outf.write('<ul>\n')
                    first_item = 0

                convert_item(file, outf)

        elif bit.type == 'text':
            if parent == 'title':
                title = bit.body
            elif parent == 'link':
                outf.write(top % (title, bit.body, title))
            elif parent == 'description':
                outf.write('<p>%s</p>\n' % bit.body)

        elif bit.type == 'end':
            parent = None

            if bit.label == 'rss':
                outf.write(bottom)
                break
```

combines the positive aspects of each approach. Most of these tools do event-based processing, but also provide access to the document tree in some form. Some tools will build the entire tree and then traverse over it firing events, whereas others will only build parts of the tree at a time and discard one fragment before building the next.

This approach gives you all the convenient aspects of event-based processing, without requiring you to give up the convenient sides of tree-based processing. Some of these tools require full trees to be built,

Example 22–7. The RSS to HTML converter using RXP (4 of 4)

```
def convert_item(file, outf):
    parent = None
    title  = None
    link   = None
    descr  = ""

    while 1:
        bit = GetNextBit(file)

        if bit.type == 'start':
            parent = bit.label

        elif bit.type == 'text':
            if parent == 'title':
                title = bit.body
            elif parent == 'link':
                link = bit.body
            elif parent == 'description':
                descr = bit.body

        elif bit.type == 'end':
            parent = None

            if bit.label == 'item':
                outf.write('  <li><a href="%s">%s</a> %s</li>\n' %
                           (link, title, descr))
                break
```

thus being just as resource-intensive as ordinary tree-based processing, while others can employ different kinds of tricks to avoid having to keep the entire document tree in memory at the same time. The result is a set of tools that are both powerful and easy to use.

22.2.1 *Pyxie*

Pyxie is a pure-Python framework built by Sean McGrath to support his own many XML processing projects. He described the framework in detail in his *XML Processing with Python* book, published in this series. When the book was published, Sean also released Pyxie as an open source project, and it is still being maintained as one.

Pyxie supports tree-based, event-based, and hybrid processing and can also build partial document trees. It is somewhat peculiar in that it does not read XML at all, but only a simplified XML syntax called *PYX*. To make Pyxie read an XML document, it must first be converted to PYX. This is a straightforward operation, however, as Pyxie includes utilities that can convert XML to PYX using either Pyexpat (directly) or any parser (through SAX 1.0 and 2.0). It also means that any data source that can be translated to a PYX file can be accessed using Pyxie. PYX essentially becomes the internal data representation of Pyxie, and anything that can be translated to it can be used by Pyxie.

Figure 22–1 shows a possible anatomy of a Pyxie application. It must have some data source, whether an XML document or something else, that is used to create a PYX file. This file is then read by Pyxie's `xDispatch` or `xTree` class, and the chosen class will make the information available to the Pyxie application. `xDispatch` is used for event-based processing, while `xTree` is used for tree-based and hybrid processing.

22.2.1.1 The PYX notation

The PYX notation is essentially a subset of the ESIS syntax (ESIS was described on 7.1.2.2, "The `Application` interface," on page 170). PYX files are line-oriented, and each line starts with a character that makes it clear what type of construct is found on that line. There are five different types of constructs shown in the list below.

(name
>   Signals a start-tag of the element type name. The attributes, if any, will be on the lines immediately following the start-tag line.

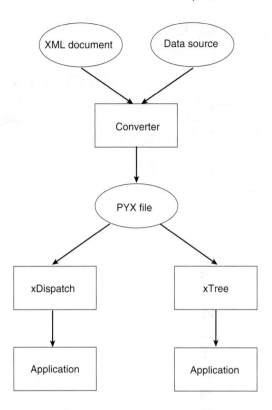

Figure 22–1 The anatomy of Pyxie

`Aname value`

Contains an attribute assignment and will appear immediately
following a start-tag line. Line ends in attribute values will be
represented as `\n` and tabs as `\t`.

`)name`

Signals an end-tag.

`-chardata`

Represents a piece of character data in the document. Just as with
attribute values, line ends and tabs will be escaped.

`?target data`
> Represents a processing instruction. The data will be escaped.

As mentioned above, Pyxie does not really care how a PYX file is created as long as it gets a file-like object from which it can be read. Pyxie provides a number of convenience functions for creating PYX notation, all of which return a file-like object from which the PYX file can be read. These functions are all found in the `pyxie` module, and are listed below:

`String2PYX(str)`
> Parses the XML document found in the string `str` with Pyexpat and returns a file-like object from which the PYX data can be read.

`File2PYX(filename)`
> Parses the XML document found in the named file with Pyexpat and returns a file-like object from which the PYX data can be read.

`PYExpat2PYX(fo)`
> Parses the XML document that can be read from the file-like object `fo` with Pyexpat and returns a new file-like object holding the resulting PYX.

`SAX2PYX(fo, driver=None)`
> Parses the XML document in the file-like object `fo` with SAX 1.0 and returns a file-like object from which the PYX data can be read. It is possible to select parser driver with the `driver` argument, which Pyxie will prefix with `"xml.sax.drivers."` before using it.

`SAX22PYX(fo, driver=None)`
> Parses the XML document in the file-like object `fo` with SAX 2.0 and returns a file-like object from which the PYX data can be read. It is possible to select parser driver with the `driver` argument, which must be the full package name of a SAX 2.0 driver. The driver will use the `make_parser` function by default.

Note that all these functions will use the Python `tempfile.mktemp` function to create a temporary file name and write the PYX data there. This may cause problems in certain circumstances, and may also be a security problem in some cases.

It should also be noted that Pyxie will write PYX files in UTF-8 when using Pyexpat, and in whatever encoding the SAX driver gives it when using SAX. In Python 2.0, this is easily fixed by wrapping the PYX file object in a codec, but in Python 1.5 this is less trivial to handle. Another potential problem is that Pyxie will split character events and nodes just like SAX and DOM do. One should also be aware that attribute values, character data, and processing instruction data reported to applications by Pyxie will contain character data in escaped form. Pyxie itself does not convert escaped character data back to unescaped form, and applications must use the `PYXDecoder` function to do this.

22.2.1.2 Event-based development

In Pyxie, event-based applications are written as classes derived from the `xDispatch` class, and the approach used is very similar to that of xmllib. The application can implement generic methods for the start-tags and end-tags of elements, for character data and processing instructions, or it can implement methods that are specific to certain element types (as with xmllib). The generic methods are listed below.

`characters(data)`
> Called for character data in the document.

`default_start(name, attrs)`
> Called for the start-tag of an element, with the element-type name in `name` and the attributes as a dictionary in `attrs`.

`default_end(name)`
> Called for the end-tag of an element.

```
processinginstruction(target, data)
```
Called for processing instructions.

In addition to these methods, xDispatcher will note any methods with names of the form start_* and end_* and call these for the start-tags and end-tags of elements with matching names. So, start_foo and end_foo will be called for the start-tag and end-tag of a foo element. The default_start and default_end methods are, as the names indicate, just default fallbacks. In other words, the start_* methods will work even if you implement default_start.

In addition to these methods, xDispatcher makes life a little easier for the developer by keeping a stack of open elements as a list in the Ancestors attribute. For each open element this list contains a (name, attrsdict) tuple. This means that keeping track of this part of the document context is done by Pyxie so you do not need to write your own utilities for this.

One little detail worthy of note is that element-type names containing '.' are mapped to names containing '_' instead of the period, in order to make Pyxie's name mapping support more element-type names.

As an example, the RSS to HTML converter in Examples 22–8 and 22–9 is implemented using xDispatch. As you can see, writing this program with Pyxie is easy and straightforward.

Example 22–8. Pyxie RSS to HTML converter (1 of 2)

```
import sys, codecs
from pyxie import xDispatch, File2PYX, PYXDecoder

# --- Templates

top = \
"""
<!DOCTYPE HTML PUBLIC "-//W3C//DTD HTML 4.0 Transitional//EN">
<HTML>
<HEAD>
  <TITLE>%s</TITLE>
</HEAD>
```

```
<BODY>
<A HREF="%s"><H1>%s</H1></A>
"""

bottom = \
"""
</UL>

<HR>

<ADDRESS>
Converted to HTML using Pyxie.
</ADDRESS>

</BODY>
</HTML>
"""

# --- xDispatch application

class RSS2HTML(xDispatch):

    def __init__(self, out = None):
        xDispatch.__init__(self)
        self._out = out or sys.stdout

        self._title = None
        self._link = None
        self._descr = None
        self._top_written = 0

    def characters(self, data):
        parent = self.Ancestors[-1][0]

        if parent == "title":
            self._title = PYXDecoder(data)
        elif parent == "link":
            self._link = PYXDecoder(data)
        elif parent == "description":
            self._descr = PYXDecoder(data)
```

Note that this `characters` implementation is not really safe, as Pyxie may split these events. Note also how we use `PYXDecoder` to unescape the character data.

Example 22–9. Pyxie RSS to HTML converter (2 of 2)

```
    def start_item(self, name, attrs):
        if not self._top_written:
            self._out.write(top % (self._title, self._link,
                                    self._title))
            if self._descr:
                self._out.write("<p>%s</p>\n" % self._descr)
            self._out.write("<ul>\n")
            self._top_written = 1

        self._title = None
        self._link = None
        self._descr = ""

    def end_item(self, name):
        self._out.write('<li><a href="%s">%s</a> %s\n' %
                        (self._link, self._title, self._descr))

    def end_rss(self, name):
        self._out.write(bottom)

# --- Main program

pyxfile = File2PYX(sys.argv[1])

handler = RSS2HTML(codecs.open(sys.argv[2], "w", "iso-8859-1"))
handler.Dispatch(pyxfile)
```

22.2.1.3 Tree-based development

As mentioned earlier, Pyxie supports tree-based development through the xTree class. This is actually a full object model of XML documents, just like DOM, but with many more utilities and much simpler. The model consists of four classes:

xTree
   Represents the entire document, and is usually the interface through which one works with the entire tree. It has a concept of the current node, which is used to navigate around the tree.

xNode
> This is the abstract base class of the classes that represent constructs in the tree, but not of xTree itself.

xElement
> Represents elements in the tree.

xData
> Represents character data in the tree.

These are in fact all the classes used to represent XML documents. Processing instructions are left out, as are all lexical details. The nodes in the tree have the attributes listed below:

Up
> The parent of the node, if any.

Down
> The first child of the node, if any.

Left
> The previous sibling of the node, if any.

Right
> The following sibling of the node, if any.

Data
> The character data of the node. This attribute only exists on xData nodes; xElement nodes do not have it.

ElementTypeName
> The element-type name of the node. Only exists on xElement nodes.

AttributeValues
> The attributes of the node as a dictionary. Only exists on xElement nodes.

As mentioned earlier, an xTree object has a concept of the current position, which means that it can be used as the "peephole" through which we look at the document. We can move the peephole around, perform operations relative to its current position, as well as set bookmarks and return to them. When the xTree is first populated, the current position is at the document element.

The xTree class has a large number of methods, which are all listed below. In addition to these it supports access to the nodes in the tree through index notation on the tree itself in document order. Thus, for node in tree: will access all the nodes in the tree in document order. It also supports accessing the attributes of xNode objects on the tree itself. So, tree.ElementTypeName will give the element-type name of the current node (which must be an xElement).

ZapTree()
> Breaks all cyclic references in the tree to ensure that all nodes are garbage-collected.

PushPos()
> Pushes the current node on an internal stack of current nodes. This is useful for storing the current position, doing something else for a while, and then calling PopPos to get back to the previous position. Since this is a stack, this process can be nested arbitrarily deeply.

PopPos()
> Returns to the previous current node.

AtElement(name = None)
> If called with no arguments, returns true if the current node is an element node. If called with an element-type name as the argument, returns true if the current node is an element node of that type.

AtData()
> Returns true if the current node is an xData node.

`Home()`
Sets the current node to the root node.

`Seek(node)`
Sets the current node to the given node.

`Down()`
Moves the current position down, that is, to the first child of the current node.

`HasDown()`
Returns `true` if the current node has children.

`Up()`
Sets the current node to the parent of the current node.

`HasUp()`
Returns `true` if the current node has a parent.

`GetUp()`
Returns not what the alarm clock says, but the parent of the current node.

`Left()`
Sets the current node to the previous sibling of the current node.

`HasLeft()`
Returns `true` if the current node has a previous sibling.

`Right()`
Sets the current node to the following sibling of the current node.

`HasRight()`
Returns `true` if the current node has a following sibling.

`Walk(func)`

Takes a function of two arguments and calls it twice for each node in the tree, once before the node's children are processed and once after the node's children are processed. The first argument is the tree itself (that is, the `xTree` object), and the second is `true` before the children of the node have been walked and `false` after.

`WalkData(func)`

Like `Walk`, but only calls `func` for `xData` nodes.

`WalkElements(func)`

Like `Walk`, but only calls `func` for `xElement` nodes.

`Dispatch(handler)`

Used to trigger the first hybrid processing mode described in the next section. The method is also described there and is only mentioned here for completeness.

`PYX2Tree(fo)`

Empties the tree and re-populates it with the XML document it reads in PYX notation from the `fo` file-like object.

`Cut()`

Removes the current node (and all its descendants) from the current tree and returns it. The new current node in this tree becomes the parent of the previous current node.

`PasteDown(tree)`

Pastes the given `xTree` into this tree as the first child of the current node.

`PasteRight(tree)`

Pastes the given tree as the following sibling of the current node.

`Descendants(node = None)`

Returns a list of the descendants of the given node, or of the current node if none is given, in document order.

`JoinData(sep, node = None)`

> Returns the character data content of all descendants of the current node, or of the given node if none is given, with the `sep` string as the separator. Use `sep` = `' '` if you do not want a separator.

`Children(node = None)`

> Returns the children of the given node, or of the current node if none is given, as a list.

`Ancestors(node = None)`

> Returns the ancestors of the given node, or of the current node if none is given, as a list, with the parent first and the document element last.

As an example of how to use this abundance of utility methods, we implement the RSS to HTML translator as an `xTree` application in Examples 22–10 to 22–13. As you can see, the resulting program is short and requires only one simple utility function.

The function in Example 22–10 runs as far to the right in the tree it can get, while looking for an element with the given type name. It returns when either there are no more following siblings or when it has found an element with the matching type name.

The function in Example 22–11 is called when the current node is an `item` or `channel` and returns its `title`, `link`, and `description`.

Example 22–12 is the function that receives the tree and writes out the HTML rendition to the file-like object in the `out` parameter. The comments should explain what happens inside the function.

22.2.1.4 Hybrid processing with full tree

In addition to the pure event-based and tree-based processing modes we have seen so far, Pyxie also has two hybrid processing modes that combine the advantages of both methods. The one presented in this section works by first building the entire tree and then traversing over it, firing events as it goes, but making the tree available to the event

Example 22–10. Pyxie xTree RSS to HTML translator (1 of 4)

```
import sys, codecs
from pyxie import xTree, File2PYX, PYXDecoder

# --- Templates

top = \
"""
<!DOCTYPE HTML PUBLIC "-//W3C//DTD HTML 4.0 Transitional//EN">
<HTML>
<HEAD>
   <TITLE>%s</TITLE>
</HEAD>

<BODY>
<A HREF="%s"><H1>%s</H1></A>
"""

bottom = \
"""
</UL>

<HR>

<ADDRESS>
Converted to HTML using Pyxie.
</ADDRESS>

</BODY>
</HTML>
"""

# --- xTree application

def find_right(tree, elem_name):
    while tree.HasRight() and not tree.AtElement(elem_name):
        tree.Right()
```

handlers. The approach presented in the next section only builds tree fragments for selected parts of the tree.

The method described here first builds an xTree in the usual way. It then calls the Dispatch method with a handler object, and the tree then traverses the sub-tree under the current node calling event methods

Example 22–11. Pyxie xTree RSS to HTML translator (2 of 4)

```python
def extract_fields(tree):
    find_right(tree, "title")
    title = PYXDecoder(tree.JoinData(""))

    find_right(tree, "link")
    link  = PYXDecoder(tree.JoinData(""))

    find_right(tree, "description")
    if tree.AtElement("description"):
        descr = PYXDecoder(tree.JoinData(""))
    else:
        descr = ""

    return (title, link, descr)
```

Example 22–12. Pyxie xTree RSS to HTML translator (3 of 4)

```python
def convert(tree, out = None):
    out = out or sys.stdout

    tree.Down() # set current node to first <rss> child
    find_right(tree, "channel")
    tree.Down() # set current node to first <channel> child
    tree.PushPos() # remember this position

    (title, link, descr) = extract_fields(tree)
    out.write(top % (title, link, title))
    if descr:
        out.write("<p>%s</p>" % descr)
    out.write("<ul>\n")

    tree.PopPos() # go back, in case find_right took us too far
    find_right(tree, "item")
    while tree.AtElement("item"):
        tree.Down() # go to first child of <item>
        (title, link, descr) = extract_fields(tree)
        out.write('<li><a href="%s">%s</a> %s\n' %
                   (link, title, descr))
        tree.Up() # come back up
        tree.Right() # step one past this <item>
        find_right(tree, "item")

    out.write(bottom)
```

Example 22–13. Pyxie `xTree` RSS to HTML translator (4 of 4)

```
# --- Main program

pyxfile = File2PYX(sys.argv[1])

tree = xTree()
tree.PYX2xTree(pyxfile)

convert(tree, codecs.open(sys.argv[2], "w", "iso-8859-1"))
```

as it goes. For each node the appropriate handler method will be called twice, once before the node's children, with the `before` flag set to `1`, and once after, with the flag set to `0`.

Note that this approach can be freely combined with ordinary tree-based processing in the sense that once the tree has been built, the application is free to do as it wishes. It can first do ordinary processing, then call `Dispatch`, and afterwards do more ordinary tree-based processing if it so wishes.

The event methods do not receive any information about the node that triggered the event, but this node will be the current node of the tree and can be accessed if the handler object has a reference to the tree. The event methods are of three kinds, listed below. Note that the methods will be called twice, first with `before` set to `true`, and then with `before` set to `false`.

`characters(before)`
    Called for `xData` nodes in the tree.

`default_handler(before)`
    Called for `xElement` nodes that have no `handle_*` method.

`handle_*(before)`
    The method `handle_foo` will be called for elements of the type `foo`, just as with `start_*` and `end_*`.

Using this approach we can somewhat simplify the RSS to HTML converter implemented in the previous examples, as Examples 22–14 to 22–16 show.

Example 22–14. RSS to HTML translator using `Dispatch` (1 of 3)

```
import sys, codecs
from pyxie import xTree, File2PYX, PYXDecoder


# --- Templates

top = \
"""
<!DOCTYPE HTML PUBLIC "-//W3C//DTD HTML 4.0 Transitional//EN">
<HTML>
<HEAD>
  <TITLE>%s</TITLE>
</HEAD>

<BODY>
<A HREF="%s"><H1>%s</H1></A>
"""

bottom = \
"""
</UL>

<HR>

<ADDRESS>
Converted to HTML using Pyxie.
</ADDRESS>

</BODY>
</HTML>
"""

# --- xTree application

class DispatchHandler:

    def __init__(self, tree, out):
        self._cur = tree
        self._out = out
```

```
def handle_channel(self, before):
    if not before:
        return

    (title, link, descr) = extract_fields(self._cur)
    self._out.write(top % (title, link, title))
    if descr:
        self._out.write("<p>%s</p>" % descr)
    self._out.write("<ul>\n")

def handle_item(self, before):
    if not before:
        return

    (title, link, descr) = extract_fields(self._cur)
    self._out.write('<li><a href="%s">%s</a> %s\n' %
                    (link, title, descr))
```

We now do all our processing from the DispatchHandler (Example 22–14). The application now becomes much simpler, since we don't need to move around the tree to find the parts we want to work with. Instead, the events come to us. Once we know where we are, we extract the information we need from the tree, use it, and move on.

The extract_fields method (Example 22–15) has had to change a little. It now goes down into the list of children by itself, and it also remembers the current position (and goes back to it), so that the Dispatch method of the xTree will not be confused.

22.2.1.5 Hybrid processing with sparse trees

In addition to the pure event-based and tree-based processing modes we have seen so far, Pyxie also has a hybrid processing mode that combines the advantages of these two methods. To use this method, one writes xDispatch applications, but uses a service provided by xDispatch that has not yet been mentioned: the ability to build tree fragments.

With xDispatch, it is possible to process data in event-based mode, but request xTree building for some elements. If you want to build a

Example 22–15. RSS to HTML translator using `Dispatch` (2 of 3)

```
def find_right(tree, elem_name):
    while tree.HasRight() and not tree.AtElement(elem_name):
        tree.Right()

def extract_fields(tree):
    tree.PushPos()
    tree.Down()

    find_right(tree, "title")
    title = PYXDecoder(tree.JoinData(""))

    find_right(tree, "link")
    link  = PYXDecoder(tree.JoinData(""))

    find_right(tree, "description")
    if tree.AtElement("description"):
        descr = PYXDecoder(tree.JoinData(""))
    else:
        descr = ""

    tree.PopPos()
    return (title, link, descr)
```

Example 22–16. RSS to HTML translator using `Dispatch` (3 of 3)

```
# --- Main program

pyxfile = File2PYX(sys.argv[1])

tree = xTree()
tree.PYX2xTree(pyxfile)

outf = codecs.open(sys.argv[2], "w", "iso-8859-1")
tree.Dispatch(DispatchHandler(tree, outf))
sys.stdout.write(bottom)
```

tree fragment for an element, you catch its start-tag event and push that back into the xDispatch object with the `PushElement(name, attrs)` method. Then, the `PYX2xTree(xdisp)` function is used to build an `xTree` for the element. Once that is done, processing can continue as usual.

To illustrate this, the Shakespeare's plays application is re-implemented in Examples 22–17 to 22–22 as a hybrid Pyxie application.

Example 22–17. The plays application implemented with Pyxie (1 of 6)

```
import sys
from pyxie import xDispatch, File2PYX, PYX2xTree, PYXDecoder

# --- HTML templates

top = \
"""
<!DOCTYPE HTML PUBLIC "-//W3C//DTD HTML 4.0 Transitional//EN">

<HTML>
<HEAD>
  <TITLE>%s</TITLE>
  <LINK REL=stylesheet HREF="play.css" TYPE="text/css">
</HEAD>

<BODY>

<H1>%s</H1>
"""

bottom = \
"""
<HR>

<ADDRESS>
Converted from Jon Bosak's XML to HTML with Pyxie.
</ADDRESS>

</BODY>
</HTML>
"""

# --- Utilities

def find_right(tree, elem_name):
    while tree.HasRight() and not tree.AtElement(elem_name):
        tree.Right()
```

```
# --- The xDispatch application

class PlayHandler(xDispatch):

    def __init__(self, out = None):
        xDispatch.__init__(self)
        self._out = out or sys.stdout
        self._data = ""

    def characters(self, data):
        self._data = self._data + PYXDecoder(data)

    def default_start(self, name, attrs):
        self._data = ""
```

We use the `_data` attribute to store the character data inside each element, so it must be reset at the beginning of each element.

Example 22–18. The plays application implemented with Pyxie (2 of 6)

```
    def end_TITLE(self, name):
        parent = self.Ancestors[-1][0]

        if parent == "PLAY":
            self._out.write(top % (self._data, self._data))

        elif parent == "PERSONAE":
            self._out.write("<h2>%s</h2>\n" % self._data)
            self._out.write("<ul>\n")

        elif parent == "ACT":
            self._out.write("<h2>%s</h2>\n" % self._data)

        elif parent == "SCENE":
            self._out.write("<h3>%s</h3>\n" % self._data)

    def end_P(self, name):
        self._out.write("<p>%s</p>\n" % self._data)

    def end_PERSONAE(self, name):
        self._out.write("</ul>\n")

    def end_PERSONA(self, name):
        self._out.write("  <li>%s\n" % self._data)
```

The end element handlers in Example 22–18 handle the titles in the plays as well as the P elements in the front matter and the dramatis personae. The only thing that is not handled is the PGROUPs, since we would like to display these by using two levels of lists, something that requires storing all the people in the groups and outputting the description (which appears last) before them.

In order to display the PGROUP elements the way we want, we build xTrees to represent the PGROUP elements. We then loop over the tree picking out the PERSONA contents and the group description. Finally, once we have collected the information we need, we write out our rendering of the element (Example 22–19).

Example 22–19. The plays application implemented with Pyxie (3 of 6)

```
def start_PGROUP(self, name, attrs):
    self.PushElement(name, attrs)
    cur = PYX2xTree(self)

    persons = []
    descr = None

    cur.Down()
    while cur.HasRight():
        if cur.AtElement("PERSONA"):
            persons.append(cur.JoinData(""))
        elif cur.AtElement("GRPDESCR"):
            descr = cur.JoinData("")

        cur.Right()

    cur.ZapTree()

    self._out.write("  <li><b>%s</b>\n" % descr[ : -1])
    self._out.write("  <ul>\n")
    for person in persons:
        self._out.write("  <li>%s\n" % person)
    self._out.write("  </ul>\n")
```

The contents of the play itself are handled by the handlers in Example 22–20, except for the lines, which are difficult because they can contain STAGEDIRs. To handle these correctly, we must think of some tricks, since an element appearing inside another element with character data content will split the content because of the way we accumulate character data.

Example 22–20. The plays application implemented with Pyxie (4 of 6)

```
def end_STAGEDIR(self, name):
    self._out.write('<p class="stagedir">%s</p>\n' % self._data)

def end_SPEAKER(self, name):
    self._out.write('<p class="speaker">%s</p>\n' % self._data)

def end_PLAY(self, name):
    self._out.write(bottom)
```

To avoid the problem described above, we build xTrees for the LINEs (Example 22–21), loop over them and output the data as we go.

Example 22–21. The plays application implemented with Pyxie (5 of 6)

```
def start_LINE(self, name, attrs):
    self.PushElement(name, attrs)
    cur = PYX2xTree(self)
    cur.Down()

    self._out.write('<p class="line">')
    while 1:
        if cur.AtElement("STAGEDIR"):
            self._out.write("<i>%s</i>" % cur.JoinData(""))
        else:
            self._out.write(cur.Data)

        if cur.HasRight():
            cur.Right()
        else:
            break

    self._out.write("</p>\n")
    cur.ZapTree()
```

Example 22–22. The plays application implemented with Pyxie (6 of 6)

```
# --- Main program

pyxfile = File2PYX(sys.argv[1])
handler = PlayHandler()
handler.Dispatch(pyxfile)
```

22.2.1.6 Conclusion

As this section should make clear, Pyxie is a relatively large framework, despite its very simple model of XML, because it provides a large number of utilities, conveniences, and processing modes. This makes it easy to work with and also makes it a very good tool for XML processing. Its main weaknesses are perhaps the use of PYX notation and the way it uses temporary files. The last problem can be avoided with some simple modifications to Pyxie itself. The first is rather more difficult, as I'll explain below.

The four different processing modes of Pyxie each have their advantages and disadvantages, as described below.

The pure event-based mode
> This one is both the fastest and the least memory-intensive. It is also the most awkward to program in.

The pure tree-based mode
> This is the slowest mode, together with the hybrid-with-full-tree mode, but easier to program than the event-based approach. It is also very memory-intensive.

The sparse tree mode
> This strikes a middle ground between the two previous approaches, being a little slower than the event-based mode, but at least as convenient as the pure tree-based mode. The memory consumption is not a problem if the application is written correctly.

Hybrid with full tree mode

This mode is perhaps the most convenient of all the alternatives, and no less efficient than the pure tree-based mode, in terms of speed and memory use.

Which of these modes is the best for a given task is a matter of personal preference and the nature of the task at hand.

As for removing the PYX dependency, this can be done by providing an `xDispatch` handler that translates directly from events of one type to `xDispatch` events, with no need to write an intermediate PYX file. With `xTree`, one could easily write a tree builder that used events directly, rather than going through PYX. The only problem is the sparse tree mode, which, through the `PushElement` method, is very much interwoven with PYX. I believe that this too could be implemented without using PYX, however. Whether this will ever be done is another matter.

22.2.2 *eventdom*

Paul Prescod built eventdom to fill the role of the default Python tool for more convenient and higher-level XML processing than what SAX can provide. As such, it can be seen as a competitor to Pyxie, and the two fill much the same ecological niche. The eventdom framework is built on top of SAX and uses minidom to provide DOM capabilities. It goes beyond DOM as well, however, by using XPath to dispatch event handler methods, and it also builds sparse trees, like Pyxie.

The eventdom framework has a simple, yet powerful interface that for the most part reuses the DOM. It is event-based like SAX, but events are represented as DOM nodes that are partially connected to each other, and eventdom can build DOM tree fragments for parts of an XML document. Event handlers are registered using XPath expressions (only a subset of the full language, though) and will be called for all nodes that match the expression.

Applications are written by defining a handler class subclassed from `eventdom.eventdom.EventDOMHandler`. This class may define handler methods that receive eventdom events, and these are identified by their documentation strings. The documentation strings take the form `'keyword: XPath-expr'`. The keyword can be `start` (call when encountering start-tag), `process` (build DOM tree for children, then call), or `end` (call when encountering end-tag). In all cases, the handler method takes a single argument, which is the DOM node representing the element that fired the event. The difference is that when the keyword is `start` or `end`, the node will have parents, but not be connected to any other nodes. When it is `process`, the node will also have children.

Inside `process` handlers, one often first performs some initial actions and then wants to process the rest of the current element in the usual eventdom way. Since `process` handlers receive the entire sub-tree of the descendants of the node, eventdom does not dispatch events for the descendants. Applications may, however, cause this to happen themselves by calling the `processChildren(node)` method with the parent node as the only argument. In addition to this, there is the `parse_file(filename, handler, error = saxutils.Error-Printer())` function, which does parsing. This is the entire API that you need to know.

Only partial DOM trees can be built by eventdom. That is, nodes that are passed to handlers have parents, but no siblings, and have children only if the handler method is a `process` handler. This keeps memory usage low and also lowers the time needed to instantiate and set up the nodes.

22.2.2.1 The RSS to HTML converter

The eventdom framework being so simple, and having so little in the way of an ordinary API, it is perhaps best explained through examples. This section revisits the tried-and-true RSS to HTML translation example and implements it as an eventdom application (Examples 22–23 to 22–27). Of all the versions shown so far in the book, this is perhaps the simplest and cleanest implementation.

Example 22–23. The RSS to HTML converter as an eventdom application (1 of 5)

```
import sys
from eventdom.eventdom import *
from domutils import *

# --- Templates

top = \
"""
<!DOCTYPE HTML PUBLIC "-//W3C//DTD HTML 4.0 Transitional//EN">
<HTML>
<HEAD>
  <TITLE>%s</TITLE>
</HEAD>

<BODY>
<H1><A HREF="%s">%s</A></H1>
"""

bottom = \
"""
<HR>

<ADDRESS>
Converted from RSS to HTML with eventdom.
</ADDRESS>

</BODY>
</HTML>
"""
```

Note that we use the `domutils` module to simplify the application (Example 22–23). Even though eventdom builds on minidom instead of 4DOM, the `domutils` work with this DOM implementation as well.

Example 22–24 is the application handler class. It derives from the `EventDOMHandler` of eventdom, and it is very important to remember to call the constructor. If this is forgotten, none of the handler functions will be registered, since it is the constructor that looks at the defined methods and registers the handlers.

Example 22–24. The RSS to HTML converter as an eventdom application (2 of 5)

```
# --- Handler class

class RSSHandler(EventDOMHandler):

    def __init__(self, out = None):
        EventDOMHandler.__init__(self)
        self._out = out or sys.stdout
```

Example 22–25 is the handler method for the `channel` element. It starts out by extracting the metadata and writing it out. Since the `item` elements should be child elements of the `channel`, it then calls `processChildren` to process those as well.

Example 22–25. The RSS to HTML converter as an eventdom application (3 of 5)

```
    # handler methods

    def channel(self, node):
        ' process: channel '

        title = data(find_first_elem(node, 'title'),
                     '<no title>')
        link  = data(find_first_elem(node, 'link'),
                     '<no link>')
        descr = data(find_first_elem(node, 'description'), None)

        self._out.write(top % (title, link, title))
        if descr:
            self._out.write("<p>%s</p>\n" % descr)

        self._out.write("<ul>\n")
        self.processChildren(node)
        self._out.write("</ul>\n")

        self._out.write(bottom)
```

It should be noted that defining a `process` method for the `channel` element will cause the tree to be built for the entire RSS document. This does not matter for RSS, however, since RSS documents are invariably small. For larger applications this might have been troublesome.

In Example 22–26, we handle the `item` elements, in a manner very similar to what we have done before.

Example 22–26. The RSS to HTML converter as an eventdom application (4 of 5)

```
def item(self, node):
    ' process: item '
    title = data(find_first_elem(node, 'title'), '<no title>')
    link  = data(find_first_elem(node, 'link'), '<no link>')
    descr = data(find_first_elem(node, 'description'), '')

    self._out.write('  <li><a href="%s">%s</a> %s</li>\n' %
                    (link, title, descr))
```

Example 22–27 shows how the conversion is started: by calling the `parse_file` convenience function provided by eventdom.

Example 22–27. The RSS to HTML converter as an eventdom application (5 of 5)

```
# --- Main program

def _test(file):
    parse_file(file, RSSHandler())

if __name__ == "__main__":
    _test(sys.argv[1])
```

22.2.2.2 The XBEL to HTML converter

This section revisits the XBEL to HTML converter, to show how an application can handle potentially very large documents (Examples 22–28 to 22–36). This application also demonstrates how to handle recursion and shows some of the benefits of having the tree available.

Example 22–28. The XBEL to HTML converter with eventdom (1 of 9)

```
import sys
from eventdom.eventdom import *
from domutils import *

# --- HTML templates

top = \
"""
<!DOCTYPE HTML PUBLIC \"-//W3C//DTD HTML 4.0 Transitional//EN\">
<HTML>
<HEAD>
  <TITLE>%s</TITLE>
</HEAD>

<BODY>
<H1>%s</H1>
"""

bottom = \
"""
<HR>

<ADDRESS>
Converted by xbel2html.py using eventdom.
</ADDRESS>

</BODY>
</HTML>
"""
```

Example 22–28 shows the usual imports and templates.

The handler class in Example 22–29 needs to track some state, because XBEL documents are not required to have titles or descriptions. That means that we can't print the top template in the handler for the `title` element, because we may never find one. The same applies to the `desc` element. Instead, we define variables to store the values in, make a default for the `title`, and print the values in the first `folder` or `bookmark` we find.

The two handlers in Example 22–30 merely store the top-level title and description.

Example 22–29. The XBEL to HTML converter with eventdom (2 of 9)

```
# --- Handler class

class XBEL2HTML(EventDOMHandler):

    def __init__(self, out = None):
        EventDOMHandler.__init__(self)
        self._out = out or sys.stdout
        self._title = "XBEL bookmark collection"
        self._desc = None
```

Example 22–30. The XBEL to HTML converter with eventdom (3 of 9)

```
    def title(self, node):
        ' process: xbel/title '
        self._title = data(node)

    def desc(self, node):
        ' process: xbel/desc '
        self._desc = data(node)
```

Bookmarks are easy to handle (Example 22–31). We tell eventdom to build the subtree and easily extract the information from there, then print it out. The first two lines handle the top template.

Example 22–31. The XBEL to HTML converter with eventdom (4 of 9)

```
    def bookmark(self, node):
        ' process: bookmark '
        if self._title:
            self._write_top()

        title = data(find_first_elem(node, 'title'), '<none>')
        link  = node.getAttribute('href')
        desc = data(find_first_elem(node, 'desc'), '')

        self._out.write('  <li><a href="%s">%s</a> %s</li>\n' %
                        (link, title, desc))
```

Folders have to be treated differently, since they can potentially be very large, so we do not build subtrees for them. Instead, we build one for the `title` element only and extract the title element (Example 22–32). This is used to create the markup at the beginning of the folder. Since we don't build the subtree, we can't list bookmarks first and then sub-folders. Instead, they are all output where they appear in the source.

This means that we can only create headers for the folders on the top level, so we check the depth and act accordingly. The `_find_depth` method is defined further on.

Example 22–32. The XBEL to HTML converter with eventdom (5 of 9)

```
def folder_title(self, node):
    ' process: folder/title '
    if self._title:
        self._write_top()

    depth = self._find_depth(node)
    title = data(node)

    if depth == 0:
        self._out.write('<h1>%s</h1>' % title)
        self._out.write('<ul>\n')

    else:
        self._out.write('   <li><b>%s</b>\n' % title)
        self._out.write('   <ul>\n')
```

The `folder` handler closes the UL list started for the folder earlier. The `xbel` handler writes out the bottom template (Example 22–33).

The method in Example 22–34 simply writes out the top template, and adds the description if there was one. Note that the `_title` attribute is set to `None` afterwards, so that handlers will know that the top template has been written out.

In the first line of Example 22–35 we set `node` to the parent of the `folder` element. Note that we have to go two steps up, since we start

Example 22–33. The XBEL to HTML converter with eventdom (6 of 9)

```
def end_folder(self, node):
    ' end: folder '
    self._out.write('</ul>\n')

def end_xbel(self, node):
    ' end: xbel '
    self._out.write(bottom)
```

Example 22–34. The XBEL to HTML converter with eventdom (7 of 9)

```
# internal methods

def _write_top(self):
    self._out.write(top % (self._title, self._title))
    if self._desc:
        self._out.write("<p>%s</p>\n" % self._desc)

    self._title = None
```

Example 22–35. The XBEL to HTML converter with eventdom (8 of 9)

```
def _find_depth(self, node):
    node = node.parentNode.parentNode # must get out of title...
    depth = 0

    while node.nodeName != 'xbel':
        depth = depth + 1
        node = node.parentNode

    return depth
```

Example 22–36. The XBEL to HTML converter with eventdom (9 of 9)

```
# --- Main program

def _test(file):
    parse_file(file, XBEL2HTML())

if __name__ == "__main__":
    _test(sys.argv[1])
```

from the `title` child. Then we loop, counting the number of nodes we must pass until we reach the `xbel` element.

22.2.2.3 The Shakespeare to HTML converter

Examples 22–37 to 22–41 show how to convert Shakespeare's plays to HTML using eventdom, to give a feel for more document-oriented applications. Since the mapping from input to output is rather simple, the result is a very simple and straightforward application.

The P elements in the FM element are easily mapped to elements of the same kind on output (Example 22–37).

The title is required, so we use that to trigger the writing of the top template (Example 22–38).

The two handlers in Example 22–39 take care of most of the dramatis personae, except for closing the UL list and dealing with the PGROUP elements.

In Example 22–40, we handle the PGROUP differently from what we have done before. We create a bolded list item with the description (note that we uppercase the first letter and cut away the final period). Then we turn the children into list items in a sub-list.

The rest of the application (Example 22–41) should be more or less self-explanatory.

22.3 | Simplified approaches

XML has a relatively complicated data model, with many different kinds of constructs. The most complex part of it is perhaps the contents of elements, where character data, other elements, and processing instructions can be mixed together. As you've seen, this is typically represented in tree-based APIs as lists of nodes that may be either element, character data, or processing instruction nodes. For data-oriented applications, one usually only needs either character data or elements

Example 22–37. A Shakespeare to HTML converter with eventdom (1 of 5)

```python
import sys, string

from eventdom.eventdom import *
from domutils import *

# --- Templates

top = \
"""
<!DOCTYPE HTML PUBLIC "-//W3C//DTD HTML 4.0 Transitional//EN">
<HTML>
<HEAD>
  <TITLE>%s</TITLE>
  <LINK REL=stylesheet HREF="play.css" TYPE="text/css">
</HEAD>

<BODY>
<H1>%s</H1>
"""

bottom = \
"""
<HR>
<ADDRESS>
Converted to HTML from Jon Bosak's XML by play2html using eventdom.
</ADDRESS>

</BODY>
</HTML>
"""

# --- Handler class

class PlayHandler(EventDOMHandler):

    def __init__(self, out = None):
        EventDOMHandler.__init__(self)
        self._out = out or sys.stdout

    # front matter

    def fm_para(self, node):
        "process: P"
        self._out.write("<p>%s</p>" % data(node))
```

Example 22–38. A Shakespeare to HTML converter with eventdom (2 of 5)

```
def play_title(self, node):
    "process: PLAY/TITLE"
    title = data(node)
    self._out.write(top % (title, title))
```

Example 22–39. A Shakespeare to HTML converter with eventdom (3 of 5)

```
def personae_title(self, node):
    "process: PERSONAE/TITLE"
    self._out.write("<h2>%s</h2>\n" % data(node))
    self._out.write("<ul>\n")

def persona(self, node):
    "process: PERSONA"
    self._out.write("  <li>%s</li>\n" % data(node))
```

Example 22–40. A Shakespeare to HTML converter with eventdom (4 of 5)

```
def pgroup(self, node):
    "process: PGROUP"

    descr = data(find_first_elem(node, "GRPDESCR"))
    if descr[-1] == ".":
        end = -1
    else:
        end = len(descr)
    descr = string.upper(descr[0]) + descr[1 : end]
    self._out.write("  <li><b>%s:</b>\n<ul>" % descr)

    for person in filter(predicate(ELEMENT_NODE, "PERSONA"),
                          node.childNodes):
        self._out.write("  <li>%s</li>\n" % data(person))

    self._out.write("</ul></li>\n")
```

inside elements, and for this reason APIs that simplify XML can often be useful for such applications.

One such API is RAX, which was created by Sean McGrath. RAX is an abbreviation for Record API for XML, and as the name indicates it takes a record-oriented view of XML documents. It can be configured

Example 22–41. A Shakespeare to HTML converter with eventdom (5 of 5)

```
    def personae(self, node):
        "end: PERSONAE"
        self._out.write("</ul>\n")

    # structure

    def act_title(self, node):
        "process: ACT/TITLE"
        self._out.write("<h2>%s</h2>\n" % data(node))

    def scene_title(self, node):
        "process: SCENE/TITLE"
        self._out.write("<h3>%s</h3>\n" % data(node))

    # content

    def speaker(self, node):
        "process: SPEAKER"
        self._out.write("<p class=speaker>%s</p>" % data(node))

    def line(self, node):
        "process: LINE"
        self._out.write("<p class=line>%s</p>" % data(node))

    def speech_stagedir(self, node):
        "process: SPEECH/STAGEDIR"
        self._out.write("<p class=line>%s</p>" % data(node))

    def line_stagedir(self, node):
        "process: LINE/STAGEDIR"
        self._out.write("<i>%s</i>" % data(node))

    # end

    def play_end(self, node):
        "end: PLAY"
        self._out.write(bottom)
```

to consider elements of a particular type record containers and will then treat all sub-elements as fields containing string values. Attributes, comments, processing instructions, and mixed content are all ignored.

Example 22–42. A backslash document

```
<?IS10744:arch name="rss"?>
<!DOCTYPE backslash SYSTEM "backslash.dtd">
<backslash>
  <story>
    <title>Microsoft to be split?</title>
    <url>http://slashdot.org/stuff</url>
    <time>stuff</time>
    <author>CmdrTaco</author>
  </story>

  <story>
    <title>RMS pissed at ESR</title>
    <url>http://slashdot.org/stuff</url>
    <time>stuff</time>
    <author>RobLimo</author>
  </story>
[...]
```

The result is that for structures like that in Example 22–42 (which is in the backslash DTD mentioned in 18.1, "Introduction to architectural forms," on page 695) RAX is the perfect tool. For more complicated structures it cannot really be used.

Example 22–43. Using RAX

```
>>> import rax
>>> import os
>>> fo = os.popen("xmln cvs-co\\data\\book\\py\\backslash-doc.xml")
>>> reader = rax.RAX(fo)
>>> reader.SetRecord("story")
>>> rec = reader.ReadRecord()
>>> rec.GetField("title")
'Microsoft to be split?'
>>> rec.GetField("url")
'http://slashdot.org/stuff'
>>> rec = reader.ReadRecord()
>>> rec.GetField("title")
'RMS pissed at ESR'
>>> rec.GetField("url")
'http://slashdot.org/stuff'
```

In this document, the record container element type is `story`, and the child elements clearly contain single values. So for this structure RAX is a perfect match. The interpreter dialog in Example 22–43 shows how RAX can be used.

A peculiarity of RAX is that it does not read XML documents as one would expect. Instead, it uses the C application xmln to create PYX, just like Pyxie, which it then reads. The Pyxie utilities for converting XML to PYX can be used in addition to the approach shown here.

Schemas

A s first mentioned in 1.1.4, "Data models," on page 16, a schema formally defines the information model of an application in terms of the underlying data model. In XML this is done by describing the possible element types and attributes and how these may be combined. One of the benefits of making a schema for an application is the one you have already seen: it makes it much easier to explain the structure of the XML documents used by the application.

Schemas can also be used by software applications to automatically verify that a document follows its schema, to generate skeleton code for applications, and to guide the user when editing XML. Other uses are of course also possible.

This chapter will look at XML's schema languages, some available software for working with schemas, and some of the ways they can be used by software.

23.1 | Schemas and XML

This section describes the various XML schema languages, both official ones created by the W3C and unofficial ones created by third parties. Due to space limitations, the languages are only described in outline and data modeling techniques are not touched at all.

23.1.1 *Schema languages*

The XML 1.0 Recommendation includes a schema language that is usually known as DTDs, or Document Type Definitions, although DTDs are what is written in the language, and not the language itself. The correct term for the syntax used to define DTDs is *markup declarations*. This syntax is not the same as that used for XML documents themselves, and this has caused much controversy.

The success of XML caused it to be taken up by entirely new groups of users, which had never used it (or its predecessor SGML) before. These groups had backgrounds in areas other than markup languages and brought certain values, expectations, and priorities with them. The result was a clash of cultures, and this was especially keenly felt in the area of schema languages.

These new groups levelled three main criticisms against DTDs, and because of how important they felt these issues were they wanted DTDs replaced by a new schema language for XML that would solve these issues, as they perceived them.

The first criticism was that the syntax for XML instance documents and the syntax for constraints on these documents were not the same. This meant that when developing XML parsers one effectively had to develop two parsers: one for the XML syntax, and one for the markup declaration syntax. This was seen as causing unnecessary work for implementors, as well as being simply The Wrong Thing.

In hindsight it seems clear that this was more of an emotional or esthetic issue than anything else. The syntax used for DTDs is much more readable (and writable) than that for XSDL, but on the other hand XSDL schemas can be processed with ordinary XML software (such as XSLT), which DTDs cannot. So there are certain tradeoffs, but it is not clear that the one is obviously more desirable than the other.

The argument that implementing DTDs is more work because you have to write a parser for one more syntax is clearly a red herring. XSDL requires no extra parser, but it has a very complex structure and a large feature set, and so is far more work to implement than are DTDs, which are quite easy to parse, and even easier to implement. (It is interesting to note that RELAX-NG, one of the latest schema languages, in fact includes an alternative non-XML syntax for readability.)

The second criticism was that DTDs provide no control over the character data in documents, that is, character data cannot be constrained. The fact is that DTDs do provide a mechanism for declaring that the character data in an element type must be of a certain type. This one of the things NOTATION declarations are intended to be used for.

The problem is that although you can declare the type of the element's content there is no standardized way of connecting these declarations with any standardized data types or syntactical constraints. So while part of the machinery is there it was never made use of in any standard[1]. The critics of DTDs could have solved this problem by extending the NOTATION mechanism, but as they had rejected DTDs anyway (because of the syntax) this approach was rejected.

The third criticism was that DTDs have weak support for what Tim Bray has called "DTD engineering". That is, for a DTD to be specified in such a way that it can be extended, customized, and modified by third parties without changing the DTD files themselves. DTDs *do* support this, through the use of parameter entities, but these are essentially macros, and work on the lexical level.

---

1.   There exists a W3C NOTE, called DT4DTD, which does this, but it was never adopted.

Some consider this a weakness in that there is a limit to the complexity this mechanism can support and the flexibility it allows. On the other hand, the mechanism is easy to use, trivial to understand, and quite simple to implement. XSDL provides a more structural solution, but at the cost of increased complexity.

In order to satisfy these new user groups, the W3C started a process to produce a new schema language for XML which would have an XML syntax. During this process many proposals were submitted to the W3C as input to the design process. It is from this phase that many schema languages are known, such as SOX, DDML, DCD, XML Data, and XDR. This has caused much confusion, since many assumed they were competing proposals from vendors out to make everyone use their schema language. This was not the case, and these proposals were only used as design input into what eventually became the XML Schema Recommendation.

The end result of this clash of cultures is that XML now has two standardized schema languages. One that is simple and easy to use, but less powerful, and one that is harder to understand and use, but which provides greater power and flexibility. Time will show what users will prefer in the long run.

One criticism that XML Schema did not address, perhaps because it did not come from the new user groups mentioned above, was the charge that DTDs have poor support for contextual constraints. That is, it is impossible to create structural rules that depend on the context in the document. For example, you cannot require an element to have an attribute if it is inside one element, but make it optional inside others. It is equally impossible to make the allowed contents of an element depend on one of its attribute values. We will briefly look at some languages besides DTDs and XML Schema that address this problem.

This book has so far assumed that the reader has at least a basic understanding of DTD syntax and semantics, since the explanations of several XML applications used in examples have used DTDs. I will therefore not give a DTD tutorial here.

23.1.2 *XML Schema*

The XML Schema definition language and datatypes are described in the following three Recommendations issued by the W3C:

XML Schema Part 0: Primer
This document is not normative, which in standards-speak means it's actually not part of the definition of the schema language at all. It is just a tutorial introduction to schemas provided to make it easier to learn XSDL.

XML Schema Part 1: Structures
This document defines the XML Schema definition language, which is used to define constraints on the structure of XML documents.

XML Schema Part 2: Datatypes
This document defines the mechanisms available for constraining character data and attribute values. This is done through defining data types that are then assigned to element and attributes. The data types can also be used with schema languages other than XSDL.

The syntax used in XSDL is XML. This means that unlike DTDs, XSDL documents can be processed using XML tools. It does not mean, however, that they are easier to implement than DTDs. In fact, quite the contrary. The capabilities of XSDL are a superset of those of DTDs, and XSDL has a much larger feature set, making it much more complex to use. It also means that XSDL is much harder to read than DTDs, since it requires many more bytes to express the same things than DTDs.

The main things that XML Schema provides that DTDs do not are:

- standardized support for expressing constraints on the character data in a document, through the use of data types,
- support for abstracting common patterns in schemas that is cleaner and more powerful than the macro-like parameter entities,

- support for requiring that all the content particles in a content model be included *in any order*,[1]

- support for requiring that certain values in a document be unique, as well as support for controlled references to such values, and,

- support for XML namespaces.

As an example, Example 23–1 gives a simple schema for RSS 0.9 documents.

Example 23–1. An RSS 0.9 schema

```
<xs:schema xmlns:xs="http://www.w3.org/2001/XMLSchema"
           xmlns:rdf="http://www.w3.org/1999/02/22-rdf-syntax-ns#">

  <xs:element name="rdf:RDF">
    <xs:complexType>
      <xs:sequence>
        <xs:element ref="channel" />
        <xs:element minOccurs="0" ref="image" />
        <xs:element maxOccurs="unbounded" ref="item" />
        <xs:element minOccurs="0" ref="textinput" />
      </xs:sequence>
    </xs:complexType>
  </xs:element>

  <xs:element name="channel">
    <xs:complexType>
      <xs:sequence>
        <xs:element ref="title" />
        <xs:element ref="description" />
        <xs:element ref="link" />
      </xs:sequence>
    </xs:complexType>
  </xs:element>

  <xs:element name="title" type="xs:string" />
  <xs:element name="description" type="xs:string" />
  <xs:element name="link" type="xs:string" />
```

---

1.   This is a feature of SGML that was rejected for XML...

```
<xs:element name="image">
  <xs:complexType>
    <xs:sequence>
      <xs:element ref="title" />
      <xs:element ref="url" />
      <xs:element ref="link" />
    </xs:sequence>
  </xs:complexType>
</xs:element>

<xs:element name="url" type="xs:string" />

<xs:element name="item">
  <xs:complexType>
    <xs:sequence>
      <xs:element ref="title" />
      <xs:element ref="link" />
    </xs:sequence>
  </xs:complexType>
</xs:element>

<xs:element name="textinput">
  <xs:complexType>
    <xs:sequence>
      <xs:element ref="title" />
      <xs:element ref="description" />
      <xs:element ref="name" />
      <xs:element ref="link" />
    </xs:sequence>
  </xs:complexType>
</xs:element>

<xs:element name="name" type="xs:string" />
</xs:schema>
```

Note that the language defined in this example is not exactly identical to RSS 0.9. The last element type defined is named as `rdf:RDF` here, but an XSDL validator will accept any RSS document whose document element type has local name `RDF` and the same namespace URI. So `foo:RDF` will validate equally well, provided the `foo` prefix maps to the right namespace URI.

Those who defined the RSS 0.9 language intended the document element type to be named `rdf:RDF` and did not intend for other alternatives to be possible. This cannot be expressed with XSDL, since namespace support is built into it and cannot be turned off.

23.1.3 *Other languages*

In addition to DTDs, XML Schema, and the languages created as input to the XML Schema standardization process, there are a number of languages created to be alternatives to these. Some have been created more or less in protest, while others have been created to serve as supplements. The three most important of these schema languages are perhaps the ones listed below.

RELAX-NG

This schema language is a combination of TREX, developed by James Clark, and RELAX, which was created by Murata MAKO-TO[1] based on his mathematical theory of hedge automata. It is a relatively simple and straightforward language with XML syntax, designed to be used together with DTDs. Through the use of hedge automata, RELAX-NG provides for context-dependent constraints. It has already been published as JIS TR 0029:2000, a technical report issued by the Japanese national standards body. More information can be found at `http://www.xml.gr.jp/relax/`.

DSD

DSD was created by researchers at the University of Aarhus in Denmark. It was clearly born out of frustration with the W3C's XML Schema specification and intended to be a counter-proposal to it. Like RELAX-NG, it provides context-dependent constraints. It is simple and has been explicitly designed to be able to express the assumptions made by XSLT stylesheets about their input.

---

1. Murata-san prefers to write his name this way: family name first, then given name in uppercase.

Schematron

This schema language was created by Rick Jelliffe and takes an approach that is completely different from all other schema languages. It uses XML syntax with embedded XPath expressions to express constraints on XML documents. It is defined in such a way that XSLT stylesheets can be used to perform validation and produce validation reports with error messages defined in the schema. The Schematron is supremely simple and easy to understand, yet powerful, which makes it a very interesting contender in the schema languages race.

23.2 | Validating documents

The reasons to validate documents and the challenges inherent in this task were presented in 4.3, "Validation," on page 104. Generally, XML applications will want to validate their input when they have reasons to believe that the input they receive may not conform to the schema of the application. This may be if the documents were written by humans or perhaps if they have been transmitted across the network or received from untrusted sources. Validation is also useful as a method for testing that the output from translations is correct.

23.2.1 *Why validate?*

Any program that processes XML documents that are specific to some XML application makes certain assumptions about those documents. Typically, the program will assume that certain elements and attributes are used, that they carry specific information, and that they appear in specific places in the documents. For example, the play application assumes that SCENE elements will appear inside ACT elements, and also that an ACT represents a component at a higher level of granularity than a SCENE.

If such an application receives documents that violate these assumptions, it should ideally detect this and report it to the user. However, detecting and handling such schema violations gracefully is generally very difficult and requires much extra work. For example, if the RSS to HTML converter shown in Example 8–3 is fed the XML representation of *Hamlet*, it produces the output as in Example 23–2.

Example 23–2. *Hamlet* converted to HTML by the RSS to HTML converter

```
</ul>

<HR>

<ADDRESS>
Converted to HTML using SAX 2.0.
</ADDRESS>

</BODY>
</HTML>
```

This is the only output. No complaints are produced by the program, because it does not verify its input in any way. None of the elements the program expects ever show up, and the only reason any output is produced at all is that the endDocument event triggers printing of the bottom template. Obviously, this level of robustness would be unacceptable for many programs.

The question is how to extend an application so that it can detect when it receives bad input. Writing code to verify that all title elements appear inside channel or item elements, that the version attribute only appears on the rss elements and so on is a lot of work, and better left to a validating parser. There are also certain things a validating parser does not check, and these must be verified by the application itself.

23.2.2 *Using a validating parser*

The easiest way to detect schema violations in documents is to use a validating parser when reading in the document. The parser will then detect whether the document follows the DTD and complain if it does not, allowing the application to handle the error. However, a validating parser will *not* complain in the example case above. The reason is that `hamlet.xml` contains a `DOCTYPE` declaration that refers to a DTD which the document does indeed follow. This is all the parser verifies; it cannot know that this DTD is in fact the wrong DTD for our application.

The most obvious way to guard against this problem is to verify that the `DOCTYPE` declaration of the document states what one expects it to. This, however, also has its pitfalls. Can the application know where the correct DTD is stored? And if the correct public identifier is used, can the application be sure that it is mapped to the right DTD? The safest thing to check can in fact be the name of the document element type. A better approach may be for the application itself to load the DTD and perform the validation. This will ensure that the right DTD is used.

The main problem here is not the design of DTDs, but the way people are used to thinking about them. It is useful for documents to have a `DOCTYPE` declaration, as it will make it clear to any human reader what DTD they were written to. This, however, does not mean that applications can just run the document through a validating parser, and be satisfied. Instead, they should have their own DTD that enforces the structure the applications expect, and set validation up in such a way that this DTD is always the one used. The unfortunate thing is that little available software allows validation to be performed in this way.

XML Schema allows documents to contain an attribute on their document element that plays the same role as the `DOCTYPE` declaration, but does not require documents to use this in order to be validated. In practice, XSDL validators allow applications to specify the DTD, rather than just validate against whatever the document declares. So while the schema languages are technically equivalent in this regard, their implementations differ.

In Examples 23–3 to 23–9 we rewrite the SAX-based RSS to HTML converter from Example 8–3 to make it validate the RSS it receives.

The import statements and the templates are unchanged from the previous version, so they are not repeated here.

The `ContentHandler` implementation has been somewhat extended (Example 23–3). It now takes an `ErrorHandler` object in the `err` parameter to which errors are reported. It also uses the attribute `_first_elem` to decide whether the current `startElement` event is that of the document element or not.

Example 23–3. The SAX RSS translator, now with error handling (1 of 7)

```
# --- ContentHandler

class RSS2HTMLHandler(handler.ContentHandler):

    def __init__(self, out, err):
        self._out = out
        self._err = err

        # tracking state
        self._data = ""
        self._first_item = 1
        self._first_elem = 1

        self._title = None
        self._link = None
        self._descr = None
```

In Example 23–4, we verify that the document element is in fact the `rss` element of RSS, and also that the `version` attribute holds the expected version number. Both errors are reported to the `Error-Handler` object for greater flexibility. We want a version mismatch to only produce a warning, since we do not know what results it may have. Providing a warning has the benefit that if the mismatch does cause problems, the user will know what the problem was.

Example 23–4. The SAX RSS translator, now with error handling (2 of 7)

```
def startElement(self, name, attrs):
    if self._first_elem:
        if name != "rss":
            exc = SAXException("Document element must be 'rss',"
                               " not '%s'" % name)
            self._err.error(exc)

        self._first_elem = 0

        if attrs.get("version") != "0.91":
            exc = SAXException("Unknown RSS version: %s" %
                               attrs.get("version"))
            self._err.warning(exc)
```

The rest of the `startElement` method is as before (Example 23–5).

Example 23–5. The SAX RSS translator, now with error handling (3 of 7)

```
        self._data = ""

    if name == "item":
        if self._first_item:
            self._out.write(top % (self._title, self._link,
                                   self._title))

            if self._descr != None:
                self._out.write("<p>%s</p>" % self._descr)

            self._out.write("\n<ul>\n")

        self._descr = None # reset for this item
        self._first_item = 0
```

The other methods are also unchanged (Example 23–6).

The error handler (Example 23–7) is relatively simple. For fatal and validity errors it writes out warnings to the HTML output and stops parsing by raising the exception. For warnings, it merely writes to `sys.stderr`. Writing to `sys.stderr` has the benefit that the environment knows that what appears there are error messages. For example,

Example 23–6. The SAX RSS translator, now with error handling (4 of 7)

```
def endElement(self, name):
    if name == "title":
        self._title = self._data

    elif name == "link":
        self._link = self._data

    elif name == "description":
        self._descr = self._data

    elif name == "item":
        self._out.write('  <li><a href="%s">%s</a> %s\n' %
                        (self._link, self._title, self._descr or ""))

def endDocument(self):
    self._out.write("</ul>\n")
    self._out.write(bottom)

def characters(self, chars):
    self._data = self._data + chars
```

Example 23–7. The SAX RSS translator, now with error handling (5 of 7)

```
# --- Error handler

class RSSErrorHandler(handler.ErrorHandler):

    def __init__(self, outf):
        self._out = outf

    def fatalError(self, exception):
        self._out.write("<p class=error>Input was not well-formed: "
                        "%s</p>\n" % exception)
        raise exception

    def error(self, exception):
        self._out.write("<p class=error>Input was not valid: "
                        "%s</p>\n" % exception)
        raise exception
```

on Windows and Unix error messages will still appear on the console, even if the output is redirected. Under Unix it is also possible to redirect sys.stderr specifically. For these reasons it is better to write to sys.stderr than to just use print.

In Java you can write to System.err, while in C++ you can write to the cerr stream.

The function in Example 23–8 does the conversion and writes the output to a file-like object. Note that it creates a specific parser, since xmlproc is the only validating parser currently available in Python. Note also that validation is turned on, using the SAX 2.0 feature for it. The function handles SAXExceptions and returns true if none occur, false otherwise.

Example 23–8. The SAX RSS translator, now with error handling (6 of 7)

```
# --- Conversion function

def htmlconv_to_stream(infile, stream):
    err = RSSErrorHandler(stream)
    p = make_parser("xml.sax.drivers2.drv_xmlproc")
    p.setContentHandler(RSS2HTMLHandler(stream, err))
    p.setErrorHandler(err)
    p.setFeature(handler.feature_validation, 1)

    try:
        p.parse(infile)
        return 1
    except _exceptions.SAXException, e:
        sys.stderr.write("ERROR: Conversion aborted\n")
        sys.stderr.write(str(e) + "\n")
        return 0
```

A problem with the previous version of this program was that it would start writing the output and then stop if errors occurred. By that time the previous contents of the output file would already be destroyed. This could be awkward if the program was, for example, generating files on a Web server, since this would leave the output file in a broken state. Since the output from RSS documents is relatively small, this program solves that by writing the output to a StringIO object and then writing it to disk only if no errors were detected.

Example 23–9. The SAX RSS translator, now with error handling (7 of 7)

```
import cStringIO

def htmlconv(infile, out):
    io = cStringIO.StringIO()
    if htmlconv_to_stream(infile, io):
        outf = open(out, "w")
        outf.write(io.getvalue())
        outf.close()

if __name__ == "__main__":
    htmlconv(sys.argv[1], sys.argv[2])
```

23.2.3 *Other approaches to validation*

As described above, another possible approach to validation may be to validate the document by your application, instead of using a validating parser. This has the benefit that you know which DTD the document is being validated against, and it does not require the document that is being validated to refer correctly to the DTD, whether by URL or public identifier.

The best way to do this is to use a SAX parser filter that passes all events through unchanged, but performs validation first. This approach has the added benefit that none of the DOM or XSLT implementations currently available in Python can perform validation on the source document.

23.3 | DTD programming

In some cases it may be useful to be able to write programs that read a DTD and use the information in it. It is relatively rare, but it happens when one wants to auto-generate code from the DTD, perform some kind of analysis, list all defined elements or entities, or use it for some other task. The most common use case is of course validating a document against the DTD, but since validating parsers do this, there is hardly ever any need to implement this.

There are very few libraries available for working with DTDs today. There is one by Mark Wutka in Java and some others in Perl (by Earl Hood and Norm Walsh). In Python, there is only one alternative: the DTD APIs of xmlproc. This section will show how to use those.

23.3.1   *The xmlproc DTD APIs*

The xmlproc parser has APIs for parsing DTDs as well as for representing a DTD as an object structure. The `xml.parsers.xmlproc.xmldtd` module has a function `load_dtd(filename)` that parses the DTD in the given file into a DTD object. DTD objects support the methods listed below.

`resolve_ge(name)`
> Returns the entity object (see below) that represents the named general entity. If the entity is not declared, `KeyError` is raised.

`resolve_pe(name)`
> Returns the entity object (see below) that represents the named parameter entity. If the entity is not declared, `KeyError` is raised.

`get_general_entities()`
> Returns a list of the names of all declared general entities.

`get_parameter_entities()`
> Returns a list of the names of all declared parameter entities.

`get_elem(name)`
> Returns an element object (see below) representing the named element type. Raises `KeyError` if the element is unknown.

`get_elements()`
> Returns a list of all declared element-type names.

`get_notation(name)`
> Returns a `(pubid, sysid)` tuple representing the named notation. Raises `KeyError` if the notation does not exist.

`get_notations()`
> Returns a list of the names of all declared notations.

`get_root_elem()`
> Returns the name of the document element, if declared in a `DOCTYPE` declaration, or `None` if none were declared.

The objects that represent element types support the methods listed below.

`get_name()`
> Returns the name of the element type.

`get_attr_list()`
> Returns a list of the names of all declared attributes on this element type.

`get_attr(name)`
> Returns an attribute object (see below) representing the named attribute. If no such attribute exists on this element type, `KeyError` is raised.

`get_start_state()`
> Returns a token representing the start state of the element's content model. This token is meant to be an opaque value. Applications should not make any assumptions about its type or meaning, but only pass it back to the element object in the methods below. This is because the type and value may change in future releases.

`final_state(state)`
> Returns `true` if the `state` token represents a final state, that is, a state in which the content model permits the element to finish.

`next_state(state, name)`
> Returns a state token representing the state we come to from `state` after reading an element of the type `name`. Character data is represented as the string `'#PCDATA'`. If the `state` is unknown or the given element is not allowed, `0` is returned.

`get_valid_elements(state)`
> Returns a list of the type names of all elements that are allowed in this state of the content model.

`get_content_model()`
> Returns the content model of the element as tuple (`separator`, `content`, `modifier`), where `separator` is the separator used in this content model group, which can be `','` or `'|'`, and `content` is a list of tuples representing the content of the content model group. Single names become (`name`, `modifier`) tuples, while parentheses become (`separator`, `content`, `modifier`) tuples. Finally, `modifier` is the Kleene operator `'*'`, `'+'`, or `'?'` that controls how many times the content particle may be repeated.
>
> `ANY` content models are represented by `None` and `EMPTY` content models by (`""`, `[]`, `""`).

Attribute objects support the methods listed below.

`get_name()`
> Returns the name of the attribute.

`get_type()`
> Returns the type of the attribute. This can be `'CDATA'`, `'ID'`, `'IDREF'`, etc. Enumerated types are represented as lists of the allowed values.

`get_decl()`
> Returns the default declaration of the attribute. This can be either `'#IMPLIED'`, `'#REQUIRED'`, `'#FIXED'`, or `'#DEFAULT'`.

`get_default()`
> Returns the declared default value of the attribute, or `None` if none has been declared.

Entities are represented by objects that support the methods listed below.

`is_internal()`
> Returns `true` if the entity is an internal entity, `false` otherwise.

`get_value()`
> Returns the replacement text of the entity. This method is only supported for internal entities.

`is_parsed()`
> Returns `true` if the entity is a parsed entity.

`get_pubid()`
> Returns the public identifier of the entity, or `None`. This method is only supported for external entities.

`get_sysid()`
> Returns the system identifier of the entity, or `None`. This method is only supported for external entities.

`get_notation()`
> Returns the name of the notation associated with the entity, or `None`. This method is only supported for external entities.

In addition to having an API for representing parsed DTDs, xmlproc has an API that allows applications to parse DTDs themselves. This API follows more or less the same model as the XML parsing API. There is a DTD parser object, and this DTD parser has a listener object that receives callbacks with parser events. Normally, the listener builds the DTD objects just described, but applications can implement their own handlers if they wish.

The DTD parser is implemented by the `DTDParser` class in the `xml.parsers.xmlproc.dtdparser` module. This class supports the methods listed below.

`__init__()`
Instantiates a parser ready for use.

`set_dtd_consumer(consumer)`
Registers the DTD application (or event handler) with the parser. The `DTDConsumer` interface that DTD applications must implement is described below.

`set_error_handler(handler)`
Registers an error handler with the parser. This object must follow the ordinary xmlproc `ErrorHandler` interface described in 7.1.2.4, "The `ErrorHandler` interface," on page 173.

`set_internal(yesno)`
Tells the parser whether to follow the rules for internal DTD subsets (`true`) or external subsets (`false`). The default is external subsets.

`set_inputsource_factory(factory)`
Registers an `InputSourceFactory` with the parser. This interface is described in 7.1.2.6, "The `InputSourceFactory` interface," on page 177.

`parse_resource(sysid, bufsize = 16384)`
Parses the DTD with the given system identifier.

`feed(data)`
Makes the DTD parser parse the `data` block incrementally.

`close()`
Tells the DTD parser that the final block has been passed to it and that it must finish up parsing.

`reset()`
> Resets the parser to process another DTD.

`set_error_language(lang)`
> Tells the parser which language to report errors in; `lang` must be an ISO 639 language identifier. If the language is not supported, `KeyError` will be thrown. Currently supported are `'en'` (English), `'no'` (Norwegian), and `'sv'` (Swedish).

`get_current_sysid()`
> Returns the system identifier of the current entity.

`get_offset()`
> Get the current offset (number of bytes[1]) from the start of the current entity. All location information points to the beginning of the construct that triggered the current event.

`get_line()`
> Returns the current line number.

`get_column()`
> Returns the current column position on the current line.

`deref()`
> During configuration, the parser creates circular data structures. To ensure that these are freed this method must be called. When this method has been called, the parser is no longer usable.

The interface that DTD applications must implement contains the methods listed below. In `xml.parsers.xmlproc.xmldtd`, there is a class `CompleteDTD` which implements both this interface and the DTD interface. This class can be used to build the DTD object structure from a DTD file.

---

1.   At the moment xmlproc does not distinguish between bytes and characters. Once it does, this will most likely change to the number of characters.

`dtd_start()`
> This method is called when DTD parsing begins, before any of the other data callbacks.

`dtd_end()`
> This method is called when the entire DTD has been parsed as the final callback.

`handle_comment(contents)`
> This method is called to pass comments to the application.

`handle_pi(target, data)`
> Notifies the application of processing instructions.

`new_general_entity(name, repltext)`
> Notifies the application of the declaration of a new internal general entity. The name is in the `name` parameter and the literal entity replacement text is in the `repltext` parameter.

`new_external_entity(name, pubid, sysid, ndata)`
> Notifies the application of the declaration of an external entity named `name`. The `pubid` holds the public identifier (or `None` if there was none), while the `sysid` holds the system identifier. The `ndata` parameter holds the name of the associated notation, or `None` if it is a parsed entity.

`new_parameter_entity(name, repltext)`
> Notifies the application of the declaration of an internal parameter entity.

`new_external_pe(name, pubid, sysid)`
> Notifies the application of the declaration of an external parameter entity.

```
new_notation(name, pubid, sysid)
```
Notifies the application of the declaration of a notation. The `pubid` and `sysid` parameters may both be `None`, since none of them are required to be present in the DTD.

```
new_element_type(name, cont_model)
```
Notifies the application of an element type declaration; `name` holds the name of the element type, while `cont_model` holds the content model as a three-tuple such as that returned by the `get_content_model` method of the `ElementType` interface described above.

```
new_attribute(elem, attr, atype, adecl, adef)
```
Notifies the application of an attribute declaration. The `elem` argument holds the name of the associated element type, `attr` is the name of the attribute, `atype` is the attribute type, `adecl` is the attribute default declaration, and `adef` is the default value (or `None`).

23.3.2 *DTD normalization*

Most real XML DTDs make heavy use of parameter entities in order to simplify maintenance and to make it easier for other DTDs to include and extend them. However, this use of parameter entities can make them harder to read, since you constantly have to look up the definitions of parameter entities to see what declarations mean. The application in Examples 23–10 to 23–19 translates DTDs to new DTDs that have all parameter entity references expanded.

The application does not build a DTD object structure, but instead uses the event-based interface, since it is simply reading in the DTD to write it straight back out again. (The parser does the parameter entity expansion for us.)

The program starts off with a number of functions that are used by the normalizer implementation. The `content_model_to_string` function takes a tuple-encoded content model and produces a string representing the original content model (Example 23–10).

Example 23–10. A DTD normalizer (1 of 10)

```
"""
Normalizes an XML DTD by parsing it and writing it back out.
"""

import string, sys
from xml.parsers.xmlproc import dtdparser, xmlapp

# --- Utilities

def content_particle_to_string(cp):
    if len(cp) == 2:
        return cp[0] + cp[1]
    else:
        return content_model_to_string(cp)

def content_model_to_string(cm):
    if type(cm) == type(""):
        return cm

    (sep, cont, mod) = cm
    return "(%s)%s" % (string.join(map(content_particle_to_string,
                       cont), sep), mod)
```

The three functions in Example 23–11 create string representations of the attribute type, default declaration, and default value respectively.

The two functions in Example 23–12 escape entity and attribute values respectively. Two functions are needed because entity values may contain markup, so the < character should not be escaped there.

The DTDWriter class implements the DTDConsumer interface in order to write the normalized DTD back out (Example 23–13). The _attlist attribute contains a list of attribute declarations. It is used because the new_attribute method only passes a single attribute per call. In order to put all attributes that belong to a single ATTLIST declaration back into a single declaration, this list is used as temporary storage.

Example 23–11. A DTD normalizer (2 of 10)

```
def atype_to_string(atype):
    if type(atype) == type([]):
        return "(%s)" % string.join(atype, " | ")
    else:
        return atype

def adecl_to_string(adecl):
    if adecl == "#DEFAULT":
        return ""
    else:
        return adecl

def adef_to_string(adef):
    if adef == None:
        return ""
    else:
        return "'%s'" % attr_escape(adef)
```

Example 23–12. A DTD normalizer (3 of 10)

```
def entity_escape(value):
    return string.replace(string.replace(value, "&", "&amp;"),
                          "'", "&apos;")

def attr_escape(value):
    return string.replace(string.replace(
                    string.replace(value, "&", "&amp;"),
                          "'", "&apos;"), "<", "&lt;")
```

Example 23–13. A DTD normalizer (4 of 10)

```
# --- The DTD application

class DTDWriter(xmlapp.DTDConsumer):

    def __init__(self, outf):
        self._out = outf
        self._attlist = []
```

The `new_attribute` method merely accumulates declarations in the `_attlist` list. For all other declaration types, the `_empty_attlist` method is called before anything else is done to write out the accumulated attribute list, if any. This allows the writer to handle the attribute declarations together.

Example 23–14. A DTD normalizer (5 of 10)

```
def new_general_entity(self, name, val):
    self._empty_attlist()
    self._out.write("<!ENTITY %s '%s'>\n" %
                    (name, entity_escape(val)))

def new_external_entity(self, name, pubid, sysid, ndata):
    self._empty_attlist()
    if pubid:
        self._out.write("<!ENTITY %s PUBLIC '%s' '%s'" %
                        (name, pubid, sysid))
    else:
        self._out.write("<!ENTITY %s SYSTEM '%s'" %
                        (name, sysid))

    if ndata:
        self._out.write(" NDATA %s>\n" % ndata)
    else:
        self._out.write(">\n")
```

The handling of general entities is relatively simple (Example 23–14).

Example 23–15. A DTD normalizer (6 of 10)

```
def new_parameter_entity(self, name, val):
    self._empty_attlist()
    self._out.write("<!ENTITY %% %s '%s'>\n" %
                    (name, entity_escape(val)))

def new_external_pe(self, name, pubid, sysid):
    self._empty_attlist()
    if pubid:
        self._out.write("<!ENTITY %% %s PUBLIC '%s' '%s'>\n" %
                        (name, pubid, sysid))
    else:
        self._out.write("<!ENTITY %% %s SYSTEM '%s'>\n" %
                        (name, sysid))
```

It could be debated whether parameter entity declarations should be retained or not, but in this case they have been included for reference (Example 23–15).

Notations, elements, attributes, comments, and processing instructions are all easy to handle (Example 23–16).

Example 23–16. A DTD normalizer (7 of 10)

```python
def new_notation(self, name, pubid, sysid):
    self._empty_attlist()
    if pubid and sysid:
        self._out.write("<!NOTATION name PUBLIC '%s' '%s'>\n" %
                        (name, pubid, sysid))
    elif pubid:
        self._out.write("<!NOTATION name PUBLIC '%s'>\n" %
                        (name, pubid))
    else:
        self._out.write("<!NOTATION name SYSTEM '%s'>\n" %
                        (name, sysid))

def new_element_type(self, name, cont):
    self._empty_attlist()
    self._out.write("<!ELEMENT %s %s>\n" %
                    (name, content_model_to_string(cont)))

def new_attribute(self, elem, attr, a_type, a_decl, a_def):
    self._attlist.append((elem, attr, a_type, a_decl, a_def))

def handle_comment(self, contents):
    self._empty_attlist()
    self._out.write("<!-- %s -->\n" % contents)

def handle_pi(self, target, data):
    self._empty_attlist()
    self._out.write("<?%s %s?>" % (target, data))
```

The _empty_attlist method ensures that attributes are written out correctly (Example 23–17). Note that it also handles the case where the accumulated attributes belong to more than one element type.

Example 23–17. A DTD normalizer (8 of 10)

```
# internal methods

def _empty_attlist(self):
    prev = None
    for (elem, attr, a_type, a_decl, a_def) in self._attlist:
        if elem != prev:
            if prev != None:
                self._out.write(">\n")

            self._out.write("<!ATTLIST %s " % elem)
            prev = elem

        self._out.write("\n          %s %s %s %s" %
                        (attr, atype_to_string(a_type),
                         adecl_to_string(a_decl),
                         adef_to_string(a_def)))

    if self._attlist != []:
        self._out.write(">\n")
        self._attlist = []
```

The function in Example 23–18 can normalize a DTD in one file to another by setting up a DTDParser with the DTDWriter as its application and parsing the DTD.

Example 23–18. A DTD normalizer (9 of 10)

```
# --- Main functions

def normalize_dtd_file(dtdfile, outfile):
    outf = open(outfile, "w")

    parser = dtdparser.DTDParser()
    parser.set_dtd_consumer(DTDWriter(outf))
    parser.parse_resource(dtdfile)

    outf.close()
```

Example 23–19. A DTD normalizer (10 of 10)

```
# --- Main program

if __name__ == "__main__":
    normalize_dtd_file(sys.argv[1], sys.argv[2])
```

Running this program on the XBEL DTD presented in 9.1.1, "The structure of XBEL documents," on page 270 gives the output shown in Example 23–20.

Example 23–20. The normalized XBEL DTD

```
<!-- This is the XML Bookmarks Exchange Language, version 1.0.
It should be used with the formal public identifier:

+//IDN python.org//DTD XML Bookmark Exchange Language 1.0//EN//XML

One valid system identifier at which this DTD will remain
available is:

  http://www.python.org/topics/xml/dtds/xbel-1.0.dtd

More information the on the DTD, including reference
documentation, is available at:

  http://www.python.org/topics/xml/xbel/

Attributes which take date/time values should encode the value
according to the W3C NOTE on date/time formats:

  http://www.w3.org/TR/NOTE-datetime
-->
<!-- Customization entities.  Define these before "including"
this DTD to create "subclassed" DTDs.
-->
<!ENTITY % local.node.att ''>
<!ENTITY % local.url.att ''>
<!ENTITY % local.nodes.mix ''>
<!ENTITY % node.att 'id       ID    #IMPLIED
                     added    CDATA #IMPLIED
                 '>
```

```
<!ENTITY % url.att 'href       CDATA #REQUIRED
                        visited  CDATA #IMPLIED
                        modified CDATA #IMPLIED
                        '>
<!ENTITY % nodes.mix 'bookmark|folder|alias|separator
                        '>
<!ELEMENT xbel (title?,info?,desc?,
              (bookmark|folder|alias|separator)*)>
<!ATTLIST xbel
        id ID #IMPLIED
        added CDATA #IMPLIED
        version CDATA #FIXED '1.0'>
<!ELEMENT title (#PCDATA)>
<!-- ================== Info ================================= -->
<!ELEMENT info (metadata+)>
<!ELEMENT metadata EMPTY>
<!ATTLIST metadata
        owner CDATA #REQUIRED >
<!-- ================== Folder =============================== -->
<!ELEMENT folder (title?,info?,desc?,
                (bookmark|folder|alias|separator)*)>
<!ATTLIST folder
        id ID #IMPLIED
        added CDATA #IMPLIED
        folded (yes | no)  'yes'>
<!-- ================== Bookmark ============================= -->
<!ELEMENT bookmark (title?,info?,desc?)>
<!ATTLIST bookmark
        id ID #IMPLIED
        added CDATA #IMPLIED
        href CDATA #REQUIRED
        visited CDATA #IMPLIED
        modified CDATA #IMPLIED >
<!ELEMENT desc (#PCDATA)>
<!-- ================== Separator ============================ -->
<!ELEMENT separator EMPTY>
<!-- ================== Alias ================================ -->
<!--   <alias> elements correspond to Netscape bookmark aliases.  The
     required "ref" attribute must refer to a <bookmark> or <folder>
     element.  Note that MSIE aliases can refer to folders, so that
     is supported in XBEL.  Applications must be careful about
     traversing aliases to folders to avoid improper recursion
     through circular data structures.
  -->
<!ELEMENT alias EMPTY>
```

23.3.3 *Producing test documents*

One DTD-aware application that people sometimes ask for is an application that will read a DTD and generate random documents valid according to this DTD. In Examples 23–21 to 23–25 is the source code of an application that will do just that.

Given the type of an attribute, represented as xmlproc represents attribute types (for example, in the return value of `Attribute.get_type`), the function in Example 23–21 returns a value valid for such an attribute. If the type is an enumeration, one of the alternatives is chosen. If it is an ID, a unique ID is generated. If it is an IDREF, an existing ID is referred to. Otherwise, the string `'attrval'` is returned.

Example 23–21. DTD-based random document generator (1 of 5)

```
import sys
import xmlgen
import random
from xml.parsers.xmlproc import xmldtd

used_ids = []

def generate_value(attr_type):
    if type(attr_type) == type([]):
        return random.choice(attr_type)
    elif attr_type == "ID":
        id = "id%d" % len(used_ids)
        used_ids.append(id)
        return id
    elif attr_type == "IDREF":
        if used_ids == []:
            return "id0"
        else:
            return random.choice(used_ids)

    else:
        # missing: handling of ENTITY, ENTITIES and NOTATION
        return "attrval" # always a valid value
```

This function does not handle attributes of the types ENTITY, ENTITIES, and NOTATION correctly, but it is hard to see how it could do so.

Note that the random.choice function takes a sequence as its parameter and returns a random member of the sequence.

Given an element-type declaration object, the function in Example 23–22 returns a dictionary containing attribute values. It loops over the list of declared attributes, inserting fixed ones, defaulted ones, required ones, and maybe also the #IMPLIED attributes.

Example 23–22. DTD-based random document generator (2 of 5)

```
def generate_attributes(elemdef):
    attrs = {}
    for aname in elemdef.get_attr_list():
        attr = elemdef.get_attr(aname)
        include = random.choice([0, 1])

        if attr.get_decl() == "#FIXED":
            value = attr.get_default()
        elif attr.get_decl() == "#DEFAULT":
            if include:
                value = attr.get_default()
            else:
                value = generate_value(attr.get_type())
        elif attr.get_decl() == "#REQUIRED" or include:
            value = generate_value(attr.get_type())
        else:
            continue

        attrs[aname] = value

    return attrs
```

The function in Example 23–23 generates an element with its contents. First the start-tag is generated. Then the start state is extracted from the compiled content model. Then a loop is started that stops only with the probability of 25% when the content model is found in a final state. If it is not in a final state, the loop continues.

Example 23–23. DTD-based random document generator (3 of 5)

```
def generate_element(name, dtd, gen):
    elemdef = dtd.get_elem(name)
    gen.startElement(name, generate_attributes(elemdef))

    state = elemdef.get_start_state()
    while (not elemdef.final_state(state)) or \
          random.choice([0, 1, 1, 1]):

        valid = elemdef.get_valid_elements(state)
        if valid == []:
            break

        next = random.choice(valid)
        if next == "#PCDATA":
            gen.characters("This is text. ")
        else:
            generate_element(next, dtd, gen)
        state = elemdef.next_state(state, next)

    gen.endElement(name)
```

Inside the loop, a random element is chosen from the list of valid elements. That element is then generated recursively, and finally, when we escape the loop, the end-tag is generated.

Setting up the document generation is simple (Example 23–24). First, we load the DTD, then we instantiate an XML generator, then we generate the document element, and finally we close the generator.

Example 23–24. DTD-based random document generator (4 of 5)

```
def generate_document(dtdfile, doc_elem, outfile):
    dtd = xmldtd.load_dtd(dtdfile)
    gen = xmlgen.file_writer(outfile)

    generate_element(doc_elem, dtd, gen)

    gen.close()
```

Example 23–25. DTD-based random document generator (5 of 5)

```
if __name__ == "__main__":
    generate_document(sys.argv[1], sys.argv[2], sys.argv[3])
```

Running this program with the XBEL DTD produces the result shown in Example 23–26.

Example 23–26. Random document output

```
<xbel version="1.0">
<bookmark href="attrval">
  <info>
    <metadata owner="attrval"></metadata>
    <metadata owner="attrval"></metadata>
    <metadata owner="attrval"></metadata>
  </info>
</bookmark>

<folder added="attrval" folded="yes">
</folder>
</xbel>
```

Some whitespace has been inserted to make the output more readable.

Creating XML

928

A s discussed earlier, XML is much used for exchanging information, which often involves first creating XML from some non-XML data source and later converting from XML to some other non-XML data format. We have already discussed in depth how to read XML documents and do something with them, but so far we have looked very little at how to create XML documents from other data sources. That is what this chapter is all about.

The non-XML data sources can be almost anything conceivable, from documents in some rendering notation, text files, HTML documents, SGML documents, databases, or something completely different. In all these different cases, the main problems are those outlined in 4.2, "Transformation," on page 98, that is: moving the data from one syntax or basic storage form to another, from one data model to another, and from one ontology to another. This chapter will mainly deal with the issues of syntax and basic storage form.

The task of creating XML from non-XML sources begins with mapping the non-XML data into the XML data model. Once that is done, the application may create the resulting document as a stream of SAX events or a DOM tree. The conversion will quite often stop there and use the XML document directly, or it may continue by serializing the XML document to a sequence of bytes in the XML syntax. The example presented in 17.2.3, "An XBEL conversion application," on page 672 has already showed one way in which the XML document can be used directly rather than being written out to a file first.

24.1 | Creating XML from HTML

Today, HTML is perhaps the world's most common document rendering notation, and there are vast amounts of data currently available both online and offline in HTML. Much of this information has been created from highly abstract sources, and could often be used for more than just display if only that structure were apparent in the Web pages. HTML, however, is a rendering notation, so any structural information in the original data source is lost in publication. RSS is perhaps the most obvious example of this, since RSS documents are really a reformulation of news pages. The news pages have structure, but it is not apparent in the markup. RSS documents have structure, and that structure *is* apparent in the markup.

The first obstacle one runs into when working with HTML is that although the HTML syntax is clearly defined by the W3C HTML Recommendation,[1] very few applications and authors actually follow this specification and instead produce all kinds of strange variations on the basic HTML syntax. In effect, HTML as a language is defined by what the author's version of Netscape or Internet Explorer displays correctly on the author's platform and with the author's configuration. This is of course not the same everywhere, and the result is that effectively HTML becomes the union of all these variants.

---

1. Which in fact describes HTML as an SGML application, conformant with ISO 8879.

What this means is that developing software that can accept all the HTML documents on the net, or even a large fraction of them, and interpret them the way that Netscape/Internet Explorer do is exceedingly difficult. In fact, the main developers of the Opera browser once told me that in the first years of development they spent more than half their development time on supporting non-standard HTML.

24.1.1 *How to read HTML documents*

Partly because it is so difficult to correctly interpret all the invalid HTML documents out there, there are rather few solutions available for parsing HTML documents. In general, these solutions can be divided into three groups: SGML parsers that require documents to follow the standard; tools that expect the input to be broken, but do their best to fix it; and string-hacking based on regular expressions.

Using an SGML parser is the best solution if you can trust that your data providers have tried to follow the standard, since SGML parsers will inform you of errors and make it easier to detect data corruption. Such data providers, however, are relatively rare, and one usually ends up with having to use the best-effort tools or regular expressions.

This section presents some of the tools and techniques that are available to Python programmers for reading HTML documents. The HTML DOM tools were described in 13.2, "The HTML part of the DOM," on page 474, so they will not be covered here. How to use an SGML parser is left for the section on SGML (24.2, "Creating XML from SGML," on page 954).

24.1.1.1 The Python library

The Python distribution contains a simple best-effort SGML parser known as sgmllib. The library also has an application built on it, known as htmllib. The latter, however, is not really very interesting, since all it adds to sgmllib is functionality for formatting HTML. This is very rarely wanted, so this module is not really very useful. However, sgmllib itself is very useful for parsing HTML. It can handle omitted tags and many of SGML's abbreviations, but does not infer omitted tags and elements, since it does not read the DTD.

The sgmllib interface is very similar to that of xmllib, without being exactly the same. In fact, the xmllib interface was originally based on that of sgmllib, but eventually departed from it, because of the need to support XML Namespaces. In addition to sgmllib, there is a very useful module known as `htmlentitydefs`, which contains a dictionary called `entitydefs` mapping HTML entity names to the characters they represent.

The sgmllib library defines a single class, `SGMLParser`. Just like with xmllib (see 7.3, "xmllib," on page 204), the interface of this class can be divided into sections for parser control, general methods, a mapping interface, and a static DTD interface. The interface sections will be covered in this order.

The parser control interface has the following methods:

`__init__()`
> Instantiates the parser. Note that the parser is intended to be sub-classed to create applications by inheritance.

`feed(data)`
> Feeds the parser a possibly incomplete block of data for parsing. The block will be parsed as far as possible and the remainder left in an internal buffer for the next call.

`close()`
> Makes the parser process data left over from previous `feed` calls and tells it that the parse is now over.

`reset()`
> Resets the parser so that it is ready to parse again. All unprocessed data will be lost.

General methods are used to handle generic parsing events, just like those in the XML parsers. Note that like xmllib, sgmllib mixes lexical and logical events. Below are the methods for logical events.

`unknown_starttag(name, attrs)`
    This method is called for the start-tags of all elements that have no methods in the mapping interface (see below). The `name` is the name of the element type, and the `attrs` parameter holds the attributes as a list of `(name, value)` tuples.

`unknown_endtag(name)`
    This method is called for the end-tags of unknown elements.

`handle_data(data)`
    This method is called for character data in the document.

`handle_pi(data)`
    This method is called for processing instructions.

In addition to the logical events, there is a number of lexical events, listed below.

`handle_charref(charref)`
    This method is called for character references. The `charref` argument holds the character reference as a string. The default implementation calls `handle_data` with the correct character as the data.

`handle_entityref(entity)`
    This method is called for entity references. The default implementation uses the `entitydefs` attribute to map the entity name to a value that is then reported to the application with the `handle_data` method. If no entity is found in the dictionary, the `unknown_entityref` method is called.

`handle_comment(contents)`
> This method is called for comments.

There is a more convenient interface in sgmllib designed for applications specific to a particular DTD. Methods with signatures like those below will be called automatically by sgmllib for instances of the element types they represent.

`start_*(attributes)`
> If a method with a name of this form exists, it will be called when an element type with the given type name (replacing the *) is found. For elements of this type the parser expects to find an end-tag.

`do_*(attributes)`
> If a method with a name of this form exists and no `start_*` method for the same name exists, it will be called for the start-tags of elements of this type. No end-tags will be expected for these elements.

`end_*()`
> This method is called for the end-tags of the elements.

Just as with xmllib and Pyxie, this interface makes it much more convenient to develop sgmllib applications, since it requires less dispatching code to be written.

The static DTD interface of sgmllib is very simple and only consists of the special attribute `entitydefs`, which is a dictionary that maps entity names to entity values. This is used by sgmllib to provide support for entity references, even though it does not read the DTD at all. For HTML, the `htmlentitydefs` module provides all the entities. This makes it very easy to support the HTML entities, as Example 24–1 demonstrates.

The `from htmlentitydefs import entitydefs` statement creates an attribute of the class named `entitydefs` that contains the HTML entities. This makes the `SGMLParser` use this dictionary to resolve entity references.

Example 24–1. Pseudo-code for an HTML application of sgmllib

```
class MyHTMLApplication(sgmllib.SGMLParser):

    from htmlentitydefs import entitydefs

    def __init__(self, ...):
        # ...
```

24.1.1.2 Regular expressions

In some cases, the HTML you have may be very poor or extremely unreliable, or the job at hand may be quite simple. In these cases it may be better to simply use regular expressions and match these against the document contents to locate the important parts of the document and extract information from these. Using this approach to processing SGML and HTML is not recommended, however, since both specifications contain many subtleties that are better left to well-tried software such as that described above.

Example 24–2 shows a script that uses regular expressions to extract all the links from an HTML document. If you do not already know Python's regular expression syntax, it is the same as that of Perl, and is documented in the *Python Regular Expression HOWTO*, available from `http://www.python.org/doc/howto/`.

24.1.1.3 Tidy and JTidy

Tidy is an HTML parser written in C++ by Dave Raggett of the W3C, who has been the editor for the past few versions of the HTML Recommendation. Tidy does its best to clean up poor HTML and can infer omitted tags, as well as repair much broken HTML. It can be used both as a parser and to convert broken HTML documents into valid HTML documents. Not even Tidy can handle all the poor HTML out there, but at the moment it is the best alternative that is freely available. Tidy also supports XML, except for CDATA marked sections and the internal DTD subset, and can to some extent fix up broken XML. It can also convert HTML to XHTML.

Example 24–2. Regular expression link extractor

```
import sys, re, string
from pprint import pprint

# find start of link
reg_link_start = re.compile("<a\s+", re.IGNORECASE)

# find URL
reg_link_url   = re.compile("href\s*=[\"']?([^\"'> ]*)",
                                re.IGNORECASE)

def find_links(doc):
    links = {}

    pos = 0
    match = reg_link_start.search(doc, pos)
    while match:
        pos = match.end()
        match = reg_link_url.search(doc, pos)
        tagend = string.find(doc, ">", pos)
        if match and match.start() < tagend:
            link = match.group(1)
            if link:
                links[link] = link

        match = reg_link_start.search(doc, pos)

    return links.keys()

if __name__ == "__main__":
    pprint(find_links(open(sys.argv[1]).read()))
```

While Tidy does a great job of cleaning up bad HTML, you should be aware that it can't handle all the bad HTML there is. Second-guessing what authors meant when they wrote their bad HTML, and turning it into something that is both valid HTML and displays the same way in the major browsers is truly difficult. In most cases, however, Tidy does its job correctly.

In addition to Tidy, there is a Java port of Tidy called JTidy, written by Andy Quick. JTidy can be run from the command line, or it can be integrated into other software. Both Tidy and JTidy build a parse tree representing the document structure, and in fact JTidy can build a DOM tree from its internal tree. This makes it possible to use JTidy as a smart HTML parser from Jython.

The easiest way to use JTidy API in Jython is to load DOM using the JTidy API and then wrap the DOM using the javadom DOM implementation presented in 13.1.1, "Using Java DOMs," on page 469. The heart of the JTidy API is the `org.w3c.tidy.Tidy` class, whose methods are listed below.

`Tidy()`
> The constructor takes no arguments and simply creates a `Tidy` object.

`parseDOM(InputStream in, OutputStream out)`
> This method reads an HTML or XML document from `in` and builds a DOM tree. The `Document` node of that tree is returned. If the `out` parameter is not `None`, the tidied document will be written out to it.

`pprint(Document doc, OutputStream out)`
> Pretty-prints the document in `doc` to `out`.

`setErrFile(PrintWriter errout)`
> Calling this method with a `PrintWriter` makes JTidy write its warnings and error messages to it. If it is not called, JTidy will write them to `System.err` instead.

`setXHTML(boolean xHTML)`
> If set to `true`, JTidy will write the output as XHTML rather than as ordinary HTML.

`setXmlTags(boolean XmlTags)`
> If set to `true`, JTidy will treat the input as XML.

The `Tidy` class has many more methods, mostly dealing with the details of how bad HTML is cleaned up. These have not been listed

here, but can be found in the javadoc documentation that comes with
JTidy.

As mentioned before, JTidy is supported by javadom (see
13.1.1, "Using Java DOMs," on page 469) through the `TidyDom-`
`Implementation` class. This class supports the following methods:

`buildDocumentUrl(url, errstream = None)`
> Reads an HTML document from the given `url` and returns the
> corresponding DOM `Document` object. The optional `errstream`
> object can hold a Java `PrintWriter` to which error messages and
> warnings will be written. If it is not given, these messages will be
> silently swallowed.

`buildDocumentFile(file, errstream = None)`
> Reads an HTML document from the given file name and returns
> the corresponding DOM `Document` object. The optional
> `errstream` object can hold a Java `PrintWriter` to which error
> messages and warnings will be written. If it is not given, these
> messages will be silently swallowed.

24.1.2 *Monitoring a Web page*

Like many people who work with XML on a daily basis, I feel the need
to keep an eye on what is going on at the W3C. The most important
part of this is to know when new specifications are published and when
specifications have been updated. Luckily for me and many others, a
list of the current versions of all W3C specifications and technical notes
is available as an HTML document from `http://www.w3.org/TR/`.

The main problem with this list is that to see if there is anything
new you have to load it in your browser and look at it. It would of
course be much more convenient if the list could somehow be moni-
tored automatically by a piece of software that could notify me whenever something was updated. If the list were available as abstract XML
it would be easy to do this, and quite likely other uses for it could also
be invented.

In this section we create an application that reads the rendered HTML, extracts information about all specifications currently available from the W3C, and uses this to send a notification email with a change report every time something has changed.

24.1.2.1 Analyzing the data

The first step is to examine the data to see what information is there and what actual form it takes, to enable us to develop something that extracts the information and makes it available in some more useful form. In this case, the first thing to note is that the page can be divided into three distinct parts, each shown in a separate screenshot below.

The upper part of the page (Figure 24–1) is simply some introductory information, followed by a list of recent updates to the specifications, to make it easier for the people monitoring the list to see what's new.

The middle part (Figure 24–2) is where the real information is. Here we find the complete list of specifications, and for each specification, its title, a link to the specification, the date of the last update, and the list of authors. This pattern is repeated all the way down the list.

The last part of the document (Figure 24–3) consists of information about the page itself, how to get printed versions, and so on. So clearly the interesting part for our purposes is the middle part, since that is where we find the complete list of specifications with metadata. The rest of the document can be ignored for our purposes. So the next questions is: How can we tell where the middle part starts and where it ends? And what is the structure of the middle part?

Conveniently, there is a link from the top part of the page to the "Recommendations" header at the beginning of the middle part. This link uses the anchor `#Recommendations`, which tells us that as soon as we see an A element with the NAME attribute set to `'Recommendations'`, we have found the beginning of the middle section. Until that, we can just ignore everything. Similarly, there is a link from the top part to the "About W3C Technical Reports" header that starts the bottom part of the page, and this link uses the anchor `#About`. This

W3C Technical Reports and Publications

W3C Publications:
> Recommendations · Proposed Recommendations · Candidate Recommendations · Working Drafts · Notes · About W3C Publications

Related:
> How to Release a W3C Technical Report · Translations of W3C documents · Acknowledged Submissions · W3J
> **Member only:** Newsletter · Newswire

Recent Recommendations

- 3 February 2000: Authoring Tool Accessibility Guidelines 1.0
- 26 January 2000: XHTML™ 1.0: The Extensible HyperText Markup Language - A Reformulation of HTML 4 in XML 1.0
- 24 December 1999: HTML 4.01 Specification This document supersedes the HTML 4.0 Recommendation, first issued 18 December 1997, revised 24 April 1998.
- ...more Recommendations

Proposed Recommendations

- 10 March 2000: User Agent Accessibility Guidelines 1.0 - Proposed Recommendation Phase Ends 7 April 2000

Candidate Recommendations

- 27 March 2000: Resource Description Framework (RDF) Schema Specification 1.0 - Candidate Recommendation Phase Ends 15 June 2000

Figure 24–1   The upper part of the page

enables us to tell when we are done with parsing and can stop the process.

The remaining question is, exactly what data is listed in the middle section, and how to extract it. To find out we have to take a look at the HTML source of the document. The markup fragment in Example 24–3 shows the entries for three specifications.

From this we can see that for each specification, there is a DT element that contains the title and the link, and a DD element that contains the date and the list of authors. Each specification has one such pair.

Recommendations

A Recommendation is work that represents consensus within W3C and has the Director's stamp of approval. W3C considers that the ideas or technology specified by a Recommendation are appropriate for widespread deployment and promote W3C's mission.

Authoring Tool Accessibility Guidelines 1.0
    3 February 2000, Jutta Treviranus, Charles McCathieNevile, Ian Jacobs, Jan Richards
XHTML™ 1.0: The Extensible HyperText Markup Language - A Reformulation of HTML 4 in XML 1.0
    26 January 2000, Steve Pemberton *et al.*
HTML 4.01 Specification
    24 December 1999. Dave Raggett, Arnaud Le Hors, Ian Jacobs
    This specification is the latest version of HTML 4. It supersedes the HTML 4.0 Recommendation first published as HTML 4.0 on 18 December 1997 and revised as HTML 4.0 on 24 April 1998.
XSL Transformations (XSLT) Version 1.0
    16 November 1999, James Clark
XML Path Language (XPath) Version 1.0
    16 November 1999, James Clark, Steve DeRose
Mathematical Markup Language (MathML™) 1.01 Specification
    7 April 1998, revised 7 July 1999. Patrick Ion, Robert Miner, Stephen Buswell, Nico Poppelier
Associating Style Sheets with XML documents
    29 June 1999, James Clark
Web Content Accessibility Guidelines 1.0
    5 May 1999, Wendy Chisholm, Gregg Vanderheiden, Ian Jacobs
Resource Description Framework (RDF) Model and Syntax Specification
    22 February 1999, Ora Lassila, Ralph R. Swick
WebCGM Profile
    21 January 1999, David Cruikshank, John Gebhardt, Lofton Henderson, Roy Platon, Dieter Weidenbrueck
Namespaces in XML
    14 January 1999, Tim Bray, Dave Hollander, Andrew Layman

Figure 24–2   The middle part of the page

Inside the DT element, there is the title of the specification as the content of the innermost A element, the URL as the value of the HREF attribute, and an anchor name in the NAME attribute. Since the value of the NAME attribute has to be unique, this can probably be used as an ID of the specification, provided that it remains stable. There is no way to know if it does, though. Also, while we want every recommendation to have an ID, we see that in Example 24–3, MathML does not have a NAME attribute in its A element.

The structure of the DD element is very simple. The contents seem to be the date followed by a comma and then the list of authors separated by commas. However, a closer look reveals an exception to this

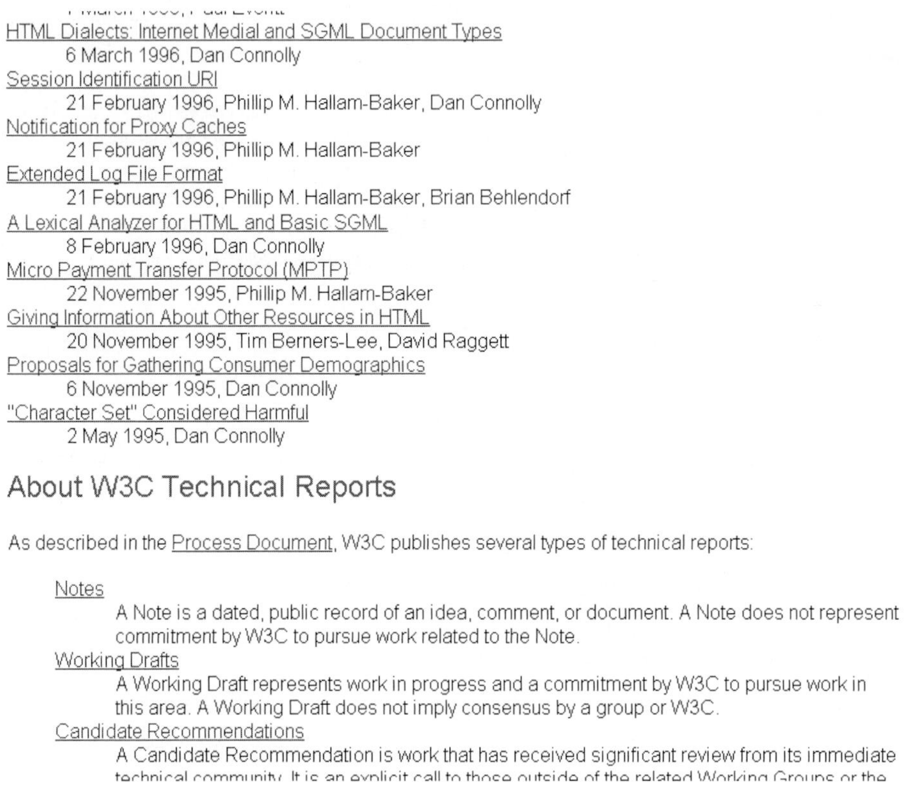

About W3C Technical Reports

As described in the Process Document, W3C publishes several types of technical reports:

Notes
        A Note is a dated, public record of an idea, comment, or document. A Note does not represent
        commitment by W3C to pursue work related to the Note.
Working Drafts
        A Working Draft represents work in progress and a commitment by W3C to pursue work in
        this area. A Working Draft does not imply consensus by a group or W3C.
Candidate Recommendations
        A Candidate Recommendation is work that has received significant review from its immediate
        technical community. It is an explicit call to those outside of the related Working Groups or the

Figure 24–3   The bottom part of the page

Example 24–3. The markup of the W3C reports page

```
<dt><b><i><a href="http://www.w3.org/TR/xslt" name="xslt">XSL
Transformations (XSLT) Version 1.0</a></i></b></dt>
<dd>16 November 1999, James Clark</dd>

<dt><b><i><a href="http://www.w3.org/TR/xpath" name="xpath">XML Path
Language (XPath) Version 1.0</a></i></b></dt>
<dd>16 November 1999, James Clark, Steve DeRose</dd>

<dt><b><i><a href="http://www.w3.org/TR/REC-MathML">Mathematical
Markup Language (MathML<sup>&#8482;</sup>) 1.01
Specification</a></i></b></dt>
<dd>7 April 1998, revised 7 July 1999. Patrick Ion, Robert Miner,
Stephen Buswell, Nico Poppelier</dd>
```

rule: the last specification has the date followed by a comma, another date, a period, and then the list of authors.

This means two things: first, that the structure of the DD element is actually rather complex, and second, that the data on the page is not 100% consistent. (The lack of a NAME for MathML hints at the same thing.) This lack of consistency is rather serious, as it means that not only can there be more exceptions lurking in the data, but more surprises may also be introduced in future updates.

In general, we run into this problem because we try to impose an abstract structure on a data source which only has a very loose rendered structure. A close study of the page shows more inconsistencies like the two described above, which means that the page is almost certainly edited by hand.

After this example was first written, another inconsistency was indeed introduced: the DOM level 2 specifications were placed into a single UL list inside a single DT/DD pair, which caused the script to fail with the new versions of the page from November 13 2000 onwards. The Recommendations in question were written as in Example 24–4.

How this is handled will be explained below as we go through the source code of the script.

24.1.2.2 An information model for the specification list

Now that we have a broad idea of the structure of the source data, we are ready to take the next step (despite the fact that we still do not know if there are any exceptions to the above rules), which is to create an information model. In this case we do it in the form of a Python class definition, shown in Example 24–5.

An object of this class contains the information about one specification, using the anchor, i.e. the NAME attribute, as the ID, or the URL if no anchor is given. Note how the title and other information items are normalized by first splitting the strings on whitespace and then rejoining them using spaces as separators, effectively replacing all whitespace sequences with single spaces.

Example 24–4. Specification page inconsistency

```
<dt>Document Object Model (DOM) Level 2 Specifications</dt>
<dd>13 November 2000</dd>
<dd>
<ul>
<li><b><i><a id="DOM-Level-2-Core" href="DOM-Level-2-Core/"
name="DOM-Level-2-Core">Document Object Model (DOM) Level 2 Core
Specification</a></i></b><br />
Arnaud Le Hors, Philippe Le H&eacute;garet, Lauren Wood, Gavin
Nicol, Jonathan Robie, Mike Champion, Steve Byrne</li>

<li><b><i><a id="DOM-Level-2-Views" href="DOM-Level-2-Views"
name="DOM-Level-2-Views">Document Object Model (DOM) Level 2 Views
Specification</a></i></b><br />
Laurence Cable, Arnaud Le Hors</li>

<li><b><i><a id="DOM-Level-2-Events" href="DOM-Level-2-Events/"
name="DOM-Level-2-Events">Document Object Model (DOM) Level 2
Events Specification</a></i></b><br />
Tom Pixley</li>

<li><b><i><a id="DOM-Level-2-Style" href="DOM-Level-2-Style/"
name="DOM-Level-2-Style">Document Object Model (DOM) Level 2 Style
Specification</a></i></b><br />
Vidur Apparao, Philippe Le H&eacute;garet, Chris Wilson</li>

<li><b><i><a id="DOM-Level-2-Traversal-Range"
href="DOM-Level-2-Traversal-Range/"
name="DOM-Level-2-Traversal-Range">Document Object Model (DOM)
Level 2 Traversal and Range Specification</a></i></b><br />
Vidur Apparao, Mike Champion, Joe Kesselman, Jonathan Robie, Peter
Sharpe, Lauren Wood</li>
</ul>
</dd>
```

24.1.2.3 Extracting the data

The next step is now to extract the data from the HTML page and put it into the data model we defined in the previous section. Since the W3C page is actually a valid HTML document, we decide to use the sgmllib parser, which should handle the document sufficiently well to enable us to reliably extract the information we need (Examples 24–6 to 24–16).

Example 24–5. Internal data structure

```
# Object structure

class Document:

    def __init__(self, id, url, title, date, other):
        self._id = id or url
        self._url = url
        self._title = string.join(string.split(title), " ")
        self._date = date
        self._other = string.join(string.split(other), " ")

    def get_id(self):
        return self._id

    def get_url(self):
        return self._url

    def get_title(self):
        return self._title

    def get_date(self):
        return self._date

    def __repr__(self):
        return "<W3C Document %s, '%s'>" % (self._id, self._title)
```

The _specs attribute holds the list of all the specification objects, and the _in_middle attribute is a flag that tells whether we have started to parse the middle section (which contains the data) or not. The _inside attribute is another flag that is used to tell what kind of element we are inside at the moment. When we are inside an A element, _parent is used to remember whether we are inside an LI or DD element. The last five attributes hold information about each specification (Example 24–6).

The _getattr method (Example 24–7) is used by the other methods to extract attribute values from the attribute lists passed by sgmllib, which are lists of (attribute, value) tuples.

The method in Example 24–8 is called for every DT element, and when it's called we note that we are now inside a DT element.

Example 24–6. The structure builder (1 of 11)

```
# Spec page parser

reg_date = re.compile("\d\d? \w+ \d+")

class SpecParser(sgmllib.SGMLParser):

    def __init__(self):
        sgmllib.SGMLParser.__init__(self, None)
        self._specs = []
        self._in_middle = 0
        self._inside = None
        self._parent = None

        self._name   = None
        self._href   = None
        self._title  = ""
        self._date   = ""
        self._other  = ""
```

Example 24–7. The structure builder (2 of 11)

```
    def _getattr(self, attr, attrs):
        for (a, v) in attrs:
            if a == attr:
                return v

        return None
```

Example 24–8. The structure builder (3 of 11)

```
    def start_dt(self, attrs):
        self._inside = "dt"
```

The method in Example 24–9 is called for every A element, and the first thing it does it to check whether we are inside the middle section yet. If we are not, it checks to see whether this element is the A element that sets the Recommendations anchor at the start of the middle section. If it is, it notes that we are in the middle section and returns.

Example 24–9. The structure builder (4 of 11)

```
def start_a(self, attrs):
    if not self.in_middle:
        self.in_middle = \
            self._getattr("name", attrs) == "Recommendations"

        return
    else:
        return

    if self._getattr("name", attrs) == "About":
        self.in_middle = 0
        return

    if self._inside == ("dt", li"):
        self._href = self._getattr("href", attrs)
        self._name = self._getattr("name", attrs)
        self._parent = self._inside
        self._inside = "a"
```

The next thing it does is to see if this is the A element that marks the end of the middle section, and if so, sets _in_middle back to false, thus making sure that no more processing happens.

And finally, if both these tests succeed, and we are inside a DT or LI element, we know that this is a link to a specification. We immediately extract the URL of the specification and its NAME anchor, and set _inside to 'a'. Note that we record what the type of the parent was in order to be able to continue correctly after the A element.

The method in Example 24–10 is called for every DD element, and if we are in the middle section and _inside is set to 'a', we assume that the A element is now ended, and the DD that contains the specification publication date and authors list has just begun, so we set _inside to 'dd'.

Example 24–10. The structure builder (5 of 11)

```
def start_dd(self,attrs):
    if self.in_middle and self._inside == "a":
        self._inside = "dd"
```

In order to handle the DOM 2 specifications correctly, the two methods in Example 24–11 set the flags that tell us if we are inside a UL list inside a DD element.

Example 24–11. The structure builder (6 of 11)

```
def start_ul(self,attrs):
    if self._in_middle:
        self._inside = "ul"

def start_li(self, attrs):
    if self._in_middle and self._inside == "ul":
        self._inside = "li"
```

When we receive data, we check whether we are in the middle section and whether we are inside a DD or A element, and store the data accordingly (Example 24–12). If we are inside a LI element, it means that we are in the author list, so we store it in the _other field directly.

Example 24–12. The structure builder (7 of 11)

```
def handle_data(self,text):
    if self.in_middle:
        if self._inside == "dd":
            self._date = self._date + text
        elif self._inside == "a":
            self._title = self._title + text
        elif self._inside == "li":
            self._other = self._other + text
```

In order to be able to accumulate the author names correctly in the _other attribute, we need to know that we are inside the LI element after we leave the A, so we reset _inside using the _parent attribute when we leave the A (Example 24–13).

Finally, we reach the end of the DD element, and now we have parsed all the information about the specification and can create the Document object that represents it (Example 24–14). The only thing that must

Example 24–13. The structure builder (8 of 11)

```
def end_a(self):
    if self._in_middle and self._inside == "a":
        self._inside = self._parent
        self._parent = None
```

be checked is whether this is one of the two DDs for the DOM level 2 specifications, and if it is, the title will be empty, and then we do nothing. Once we know that we are in the right place, we can extract the date from the contents of the DD element, which we do with a regular expression. We then cut off the author list (and other information) from the date and create the object. Finally, we clean up some of the data-carrying attributes.

Example 24–14. The structure builder (9 of 11)

```
def end_dd(self):
    if self.in_middle and self._inside == "dd" and self._title:
        match = reg_date.match(self._date)
        date = match.group()
        other = self._date[match.end()+1 : ]
        self._title = string.strip(self._title)

        self._specs.append(Document(self._name, self._href,
                                    self._title, date, other))

        self._inside = ""
        self._date  = ""
        self._title = ""
```

Note that we set _inside to an empty string before leaving, and check whether it is 'dd' before actually doing anything inside the method. This is because there is an additional inconsistency in the data: the HTML 4.01 specification has an additional DD that explains the relationship between HTML 4.01 and HTML 4.0. This little trick works around that problem.

Example 24–15. The structure builder (10 of 11)

```
def end_li(self):
    if self._in_middle and self._inside == "li":
        date = string.strip(self._date)
        other = self._other
        self._title = string.strip(self._title)

        self._specs.append(Document(self._name, self._href,
                                    self._title, date, other))

        self._inside = "ul"
        self._title  = ""
        self._other  = ""
```

The last part of the script (Example 24–15) is the handler for the LI elements that hold the DOM level 2 specifications. This is almost identical to the DD handler, except that the date and the authors were now stored separately in two attributes rather than both being in one, thus making this handler a little simpler. Note that we do not reset the _date attribute, since the date is not repeated for each of these specifications.

The parse function takes a file-like object and parses the data read from it to create the list of specifications, which is then returned (Example 24–16). This function is used by all the following pieces of code to read the specification page.

Example 24–16. The structure builder (11 of 11)

```
def parse(inf):
    parser = SpecParser()
    while 1:
        data = inf.read(16384)
        if data == "":
            break

        parser.feed(data)

    parser.close()

    return parser._specs
```

24.1.2.4 Testing

Now that we have the code to parse the HTML page and represent the list of specifications, the first thing to do is to verify that this code does in fact do what we expect it to do. For this we write a simple function (Example 24–17) that uses the utilities above to create an HTML report containing all the data in the list.

Example 24–17. A debugging function

```
def debug_dump(specs):
    print "<TABLE>"
    for spec in parser._specs:
        print "<TR><TD>%s <TD>%s <TD>%s <TD>%s <TD>%s" % \
              (spec.get_id(), spec.get_title(), spec.get_url(),
               spec.get_date(), spec.get_other())
    print "<TABLE>"
```

The function iterates over the list of the specifications, emitting an HTML table row for each one with all the information about it. This little function is very useful for debugging and verifying that the page is being interpreted correctly.

24.1.2.5 Monitoring for changes

Now that we can read the page and interpret it, we can implement an application that monitors the page for changes and notifies interested parties of any changes. And with the library above at hand, writing the script is actually quite simple as Examples 24–18 and 24–19 demonstrate.

Example 24–18 is the configuration of the script, conveniently written as a set of variable declarations collected at the top of the script. The `datfile` is the file where the data collected during the last run is saved, `notify` is the list of addresses to send change notifications to, `smtpserver` is the mail server to use, and `send_mail` is a flag that controls whether we actually send any mails or not.

Example 24–18. The monitoring script (1 of 2)

```
# Config

datfile    = "specs.dat"
notify     = ["larsga@garshol.priv.no"]
smtpserver = "mail.garshol.priv.no"
send_mail  = 1
from_addr  = "larsga@garshol.priv.no"
```

The rest of the script (Example 24–19) is relatively simple. Old and new data are both represented as dictionaries mapping from specification IDs to Document objects. This makes it easy to test for new specifications, just as having the date of the last modification makes it easy to test for updated specifications. Note that it is possible to configure the script to print the report instead of sending it as an email. This is useful for debugging.

Example 24–19. The monitoring script (2 of 2)

```
def check_for_changes():
    # load current specs
    specs = parse(urllib.urlopen("http://www.w3.org/TR/"))
    newspecs = {}
    for spec in specs:
        newspecs[spec.get_id()] = spec

    # load data from previous run
    try:
        inf = open(datfile, "rb")
    except IOError, e:
        if e.errno == 2:
            # if datfile does not exist, just save and exit
            savedata(newspecs)
            return

        raise # some other problem; report it

    p = pickle.Unpickler(inf)
    oldspecs = p.load()
    inf.close()
```

```
        # save current data
        savedata(newspecs)

        # Compare!
        import StringIO
        out = StringIO.StringIO()

        for spec in newspecs.values():
            if oldspecs.has_key(spec.get_id()):
                old = oldspecs[spec.get_id()]
                if spec.get_date() != old.get_date():
                    out.write("Spec '%s' updated\n" % spec.get_title())
            else:
                out.write("New spec '%s' at '%s'\n" % (spec.get_title(),
                                                       spec.get_url()))

        report = out.getvalue()

        # Sending email

        msgtemp = \
        """Subject: watchw3 update
        From: %s (W3C-Watch mailer)

        %s
        --
        watchw3"""

        if report != "":
            if send_mail:
                smtp=smtplib.SMTP(smtpserver)
                smtp.sendmail(from_addr, notify, msgtemp %
                              (from_addr, report))
            else:
                print report

def savedata(specs):
    outf = open(datfile, "wb")
    p = pickle.Pickler(outf)
    p.dump(specs)
    outf.close()
```

24.2 | Creating XML from SGML

XML is a proper subset of SGML. From this it follows that SGML has all the features XML has, as well as many features XML does not have, so it may sound a bit strange that one would want to convert from SGML into the less powerful XML. However, the very fact that XML is a subset of SGML means that there is more software for XML than there is for SGML, since less effort is required to produce XML software, and also since XML has received a lot more attention. This means that it can often be useful to convert SGML data into XML in order to be able to use XML software on it.

In order to do such a conversion, it is necessary to first parse the SGML source text correctly, and this is in fact a very complex task. SGML has a large set of features and a complicated syntax for them, mainly because there are many alternative ways to express the same things. This complexity is mostly there to allow SGML to be written more compactly than would be possible otherwise. The result, however, for our purposes, is that when faced with SGML markup, you should not try to parse it yourself, but should instead use an SGML parser.

The following two sections present such an SGML parser, two Python interfaces to it, and one application that can be used to convert data to XML. Before we look at those, however, it may be useful to know about some SGML constructs that may cause problems for the conversion, since they have no obvious counterparts in XML. The most important of these are listed below.

SDATA entities

These are entities declared with the SDATA flag, which means that the contents of the entity are somehow dependent on a specific system, device, or application process. What this means is basically that if you find SDATA character data in an SGML document, you will need to look closer at it to see what it means and how it is best translated to the system where you intend to use it.

SDATA entities have most often been used to represent characters that do not exist in the application's character set. Many publishers have been using ISO 8859–1 for their text, but still wanted to be able to use special characters that did not exist in it in their documents. The preferred solution has often been to use collections of character entities, which have usually been declared as SDATA entities. This practice is really obsolete now that Unicode is here, but is often used even today, since there is much SGML software that expects things to be done this way.

Name normalization

Whether the names of element types, attributes, and so on are case-sensitive in SGML can be controlled using the SGML declaration. This means that some SGML applications may be case-sensitive, while others may be not. If names are not case-sensitive, the parser will normalize them, usually to upper-case.

When converting from HTML to, for example XHTML, this may cause problems, since XHTML names are in lower-case, so you may need to normalize the names to lower-case instead.

Processing instruction targets

In SGML, processing instructions are not required to begin with a target name, although in practice they usually do. When they do not, they can be difficult to translate sensibly to XML processing instructions.

Converting SGML DTDs to XML DTDs involves many problems in addition to those described above, since SGML DTDs have many features that their XML counterparts do not. This means that in some cases, the SGML DTD will have constraints that quite simply cannot be expressed in the same way in an XML DTD. For those DTDs, some or all of the conversion will have to be done manually.

24.2.1 *SP*

SP is a free, open source full SGML parser written by James Clark in C++. SP implements nearly all of SGML, and has been much used for years as *the* SGML parser. It is also the basis for several commercial products, such as the Balise SGML processing framework. As mentioned above, SP assumes that the documents it receives are valid, and will complain if they are not. It will usually do its best to interpret the document anyway, but it has not, like Tidy, been designed to do major repair on broken documents, and so works best when it receives good input. It can also be useful as a tool that tests that the input is valid and warns when it is not.

In Python, there are essentially four ways to use SP:

- Through spin_py, which is a wrapper module that wraps SP as a Python module and makes it accessible to Python applications. This module has quite a few features, but your humble author has been unable to understand how to use it, and therefore this book does not cover it.

- You can run NSGMLS, the command-line front-end to SP, which produces ESIS output, a notation that is very similar to PYX. You can then easily parse the ESIS output to get the contents of the SGML documents.

- You can use pysp, a simple Python module wrapper for SP that provides a very simple event-based API to it.

- You can use drv_pysp, which is a SAX driver built on the pysp module. This allows you to use SP through SAX as if it were an XML parser.

One extra way to use SP is through the command-line application SX, based on SP, which comes with the parser. It parses SGML documents and converts them to XML documents. It requires no configuration, and will usually do conversions with no problems at all. If it encounters SGML constructs that lack a direct XML equivalent, as described above, it will warn about them, but still complete the conversion. For very simple tasks where the tools below may not be attractive, SX can be an efficient means of making XML tools work with SGML documents.

24.2.1.1 pysp

The pysp module is written in C and uses the so-called generic API of SP to present a very simple API to SP that allows SGML documents to be parsed from files and events to be passed back to an application. Some simple options can also be set on the parser. The API is somewhat restricted because the underlying generic API of SP has the same restrictions.

The pysp module has the following attributes:

version
: This variable holds the current version number of the pysp module as a string.

sp_version
: This variable holds the version number of the version of SP that pysp was built against.

add_catalog(sysid)
: This function can be called to give SP a catalog file that it should read and use during parsing. Calls to this function will affect all parsers created afterwards, and there is no way to restrict an add_catalog call to only affect a single parser instance.

make_parser(sysid)
: Returns a parser object bound to the given file name.

Parser objects have the methods listed below.

run(app)
: Makes the parser start parsing and pass events to the application object passed in the app argument. The application interface is described below.

`get_byte_offset()`
>   This method can be called during parsing. It returns the number of bytes in the storage object, i.e. the entire document, before the point where the current event occurred.

`get_line_number()`
>   Returns the line number where the current event occurred.

`get_column_number()`
>   Returns the column number on the line where the current event occurred.

`get_filename()`
>   Returns the name of the file where the current event occurred. If the event occurred in an external entity, the file name of that entity will be returned.

`get_entity_name()`
>   Returns the name of the entity where the current event occurred. For the document entity, an empty string will be returned.

`get_entity_offset()`
>   Returns the number of bytes in the current entity preceding the point where the current event occurred.

`halt()`
>   Makes the parser stop parsing.

Application objects can have the methods listed below. If any methods are omitted, they will not be called and no problems will be caused by this. Thus, not having implementations of methods that are not used can give higher performance.

`start_element(name, attrs)`
>   This method is called to signal the beginning of an element, with the attributes as a dictionary in the `attrs` argument.

`data(data)`

> This method is called for character data in the document, with the data themselves as a string in the `data` argument.

`end_element(name)`

> This method is called to signal the end of an element.

`pi(data)`

> This method is called for processing instructions, with the contents of the PI in the `data` argument as a string. There is no `target` argument, since SGML processing instructions are not required to begin with a target name.

`error(msg)`

> This method is called on errors, with the error message in the `msg` parameter as a string. The error message will be of the form `[file]:[line]: [column]:[E/W]: [msg]`, where the square brackets contain pseudo-field names and in actual messages will be replaced with values.

`sdata(text, name)`

> This method is called for SDATA entities, with the entity data as a string in the `text` parameter and the entity name in the `name` parameter.

Using this simple interface, it is possible to implement most kinds of SGML processing applications in a manner very similar to the XML processing applications we have seen so far. No lexical or DTD information about SGML documents is made available in this interface, but for most applications that is no problem.

The manuscript of this book was written in SGML, using a DTD originally developed by Paul Prescod and Charles Goldfarb for their *XML Handbook* in this series. That DTD was slightly modified by me for this book and the top level of the DTD is shown in Example 24–20.

Examples 24–21 to 24–23 show the source code of a simple `pysp` application that creates a plain text table of contents for the book. I use

Example 24–20. A DTD fragment for this book

```
<!ELEMENT oimbook    O O (frontm?, (chapter|partopen)*, backm?)
        -- root element for complete book; flexible for fragments -->

<!-- ********************* FRONT MATTER ********************* -->
<!ELEMENT frontm   - O (title, au+, dedication*, fmchap*) >

[...]

<!-- ********************* BACK MATTER ********************* -->
<!ELEMENT backm    - O (appendix*) -- index is added later -->

<!ELEMENT appendix - O (title, p, (%paras;)*, (h1, h1s)*) >
[...]

<!-- ******************* CHAPTER STRUCTURE ****************** -->
<!ELEMENT partopen O O   (title, sb+) >
<!ATTLIST partopen id  ID  #REQUIRED >
[...]

<!ELEMENT chapter  - O (chapopen,(%paras;)*, (h1, h1s)*) >
<!ATTLIST chapter  id  ID  #REQUIRED>

<!ELEMENT chapopen O O (title, sb+, (cq, cqa?)?) >

<!ELEMENT h1s O O ((%paras;)*, (h2, h2s)*) -- headed section -->
<!ELEMENT h2s O O ((%paras;)*, (h3, h3s)*) -- headed section -->
<!ELEMENT h3s O O ((%paras;)*, (h4, h4s)*) -- headed section -->
<!ELEMENT h4s O O ((%paras;)*) -- headed section -->

<!ELEMENT (h1|h2|h3|h4) - O (%phrases;)* -- heading -->

[...]
```

this table of contents as an easy reference when going through comments from reviewers who refer to sections by number.

We use the `_numbers` list to hold the count on each of the section levels, that is, chapters, sections, subsections and so on. The `_contents` attribute is used to accumulate character data (Example 24–21).

The `end_element` handler is the handler that does the real work (Example 24–22). For CHAPOPEN and APPENDIX TITLEs it prints them, with the current chapter count. Note how the _numbers list is truncat-

Example 24–21. A table of contents generator for this book (1 of 3)

```
import sys, string
import pysp

# --- Utilities

def normalize(str):
    return string.join(string.split(str), " ")

# --- The application object

class ToCHandler:

    def __init__(self, out = None):
        self._out = out or sys.stdout
        self._numbers = [0]
        self._elemstack = []
        self._contents = None
```

ed so that section and subsection counts are lost and have to be restarted. For the Hx elements, we act similarly.

The main program (Example 24–23) sets up and runs the parser. Note how it takes the catalog files listed in the SGML_CATALOG_FILES environment variable and notifies the parser of them. This environment variable is supported by the command-line applications of SP, so it makes sense to also use it for this application.

24.2.1.2 drv_pysp

The drv_pysp is a SAX driver based on the pysp module that makes it possible to use pysp as if it were an ordinary XML parser. The driver supports one SAX property, http://garshol.priv.no/symbolic/ properties/catalogs, which must be a list of catalog file names.

Example 24–24 is the table of contents application rewritten using the SAX driver. It is nearly identical to the version that is built directly on top of pysp, but is given here for reference.

Example 24–22. A table of contents generator for this book (2 of 3)

```
def error(self, msg):
    sys.stderr.write(msg + "\n")

def start_element(self, name, attrs):
    self._elemstack.append(name)
    if name in ("TITLE", "H1", "H2", "H3", "H4"):
        self._contents = ""

def data(self, data):
    if "TITLE" in self._elemstack or \
        "H1" in self._elemstack or \
        "H2" in self._elemstack or \
        "H3" in self._elemstack or \
        "H4" in self._elemstack:
        self._contents = self._contents + data

def end_element(self, name):
    del self._elemstack[-1]

    level = 0
    if name == "TITLE" and \
        self._elemstack[-1] in ("CHAPOPEN", "APPENDIX"):
        self._numbers = [self._numbers[0] + 1]
        self._out.write("\n%d. %s\n" % (self._numbers[0],
                                        normalize(self._contents)))

    elif name == "H1":
        level = 1
    elif name == "H2":
        level = 2
    elif name == "H3":
        level = 3

    if level:
        if len(self._numbers) == level:
            self._numbers = self._numbers[ : level] + [1]
        else:
            self._numbers = self._numbers[ : level] + \
                            [self._numbers[level] + 1]

        self._out.write(("  " * level))
        for number in self._numbers[ : level + 1]:
            self._out.write("%d." % number)

        self._out.write(" %s\n" % normalize(self._contents))
```

Example 24–23. A table of contents generator for this book (3 of 3)

```python
# --- Main program

if __name__ == "__main__":
    import os
    if os.environ.has_key("SGML_CATALOG_FILES"):
        string.split(os.environ["SGML_CATALOG_FILES"], os.pathsep)
        for catalog in files:
            pysp.add_catalog(catalog)

    parser = pysp.make_parser(sys.argv[1])
    parser.run(ToCHandler())
```

Example 24–24. The table of contents generator again

```python
import sys, string
from saxtracker import SAXTracker
from xml.saxtools.drivers import drv_pysp

# --- Utilities

def normalize(str):
    return string.join(string.split(str), " ")

# --- The ContentHandler

class ToCHandler(SAXTracker):

    def __init__(self, out = None):
        SAXTracker.__init__(self, ["TITLE", "H1", "H2", "H3", "H4"])
        self._out = out or sys.stdout
        self._numbers = [0]

    def endElement(self, name):
        SAXTracker.endElement(self, name)

        level = 0
        if name == "TITLE" and \
           self._elemstack[-1] in ("CHAPOPEN", "APPENDIX"):
            self._numbers = [self._numbers[0] + 1]
            self._out.write("\n%d. %s\n" % (self._numbers[0],
                                            normalize(self._contents)))
```

```
        elif name == "H1":
            level = 1
        elif name == "H2":
            level = 2
        elif name == "H3":
            level = 3

        if level:
            if len(self._numbers) == level:
                self._numbers = self._numbers[ : level] + [1]
            else:
                self._numbers = self._numbers[ : level] + \
                                [self._numbers[level] + 1]

            self._out.write(("  " * level))
            for number in self._numbers[ : level + 1]:
                self._out.write("%d." % number)

            self._out.write(" %s\n" % normalize(self._contents))

# --- Main program

if __name__ == "__main__":
    parser = drv_pysp.create_parser()
    parser.setProperty(drv_pysp.property_catalogs, [sys.argv[2]])
    parser.setContentHandler(ToCHandler())
    parser.parse(sys.argv[1])
```

24.3 | Creating XML from other document formats

In some cases, valuable data may also be hiding in document formats different from HTML and SGML. Often this information is documents that you may want to structure in order to be able to use them more flexibly or automate some maintenance tasks. However, there might also be cases where you want to receive information from users in the form of documents, but cannot expect the users to learn an XML editor, nor can you justify the expense of developing a custom editor.

In these cases, it may be better to give the users guidelines for how to produce documents according to some conventions in the word processor and then extract the information from those documents. Software that exploits the application-specific conventions can then extract the information correctly, as long as the conventions have been followed correctly. If they have not, all manner of errors and problems may occur, and the software cannot generally be trusted to discover all problems.

At the moment, the most common source formats are these:

RTF

This is a document notation defined by Microsoft and supported by many Microsoft products as well as many other software products. The notation is character based like XML, although much less readable, and has a fixed data model geared strictly towards presentation.

The specification of the notation is freely available from Microsoft, although you cannot really trust all tools, whether produced by Microsoft or by others, to follow all parts of the specification correctly. Also, the notation changes quite often.

Many software products for extracting information from RTF documents are available.

Microsoft Word

This is the notation used by MS Word, and is a bit based notation. The notation changes with every version of Word and is not supported by nearly as many tools as RTF. Since Word can produce and accept RTF, the latter is often a better alternative.

TEX

TEX is an old and venerable typesetting system developed by computer scientist and guru Donald Knuth. It uses character based markup that is rendered by a TEX processor. Even though TEX is old, it produces output that is surpassed by few typesetting systems, especially when it comes to mathematics.

TEX can be very difficult to parse, however, because it was never designed to be an abstract notation, so there are a large number of little details for the unwary to trip over. The users can also define their own macros, and when used in the right way, these can be used to structure documents, but they can also make parsing much harder.

The paper *Parsing TₑX into Mathematics*, by Richard Fateman and Eylon Caspi, describes the development of one system designed to interpret formulas and equations from TₑX documents.

PostScript and PDF (the latter is also erroneously known as Acrobat, after the popular viewer) are also commonly used document formats. However, these are very rarely used as the basis for conversion to abstract formats, since they are very heavily geared towards presentation and it is difficult to extract information from them. In addition documents available in PostScript and PDF are nearly always maintained in some other, more accessible, notation, which can be used instead.

24.4 | Creating XML from data formats

So far we have only discussed document formats, but there are also many other formats that are slanted more towards pure data which contains information that may be usefully converted into XML. In these cases the data is usually more abstract than it is when found in documents, and often you can simply mimic the original data model more or less directly in XML.

Some of the common data formats are:

Comma-separated files

This notation is perhaps the most common data exchange notation of all, and it is sometimes also known as CSV files, where the CSV is short for "comma-separated values." It is a strictly record-based notation (very similar to a single table in a relational database) where each record fills a line and the fields are separated by some delimiter, usually comma, but other characters such as semicolons and tabs are sometimes also used.

These files can be produced by nearly any database and spreadsheet in existence as well as by many other kinds of applications. Extracting data from them is usually straightforward.

Text files

In many cases data can be found in text files where they are structured according to some simple (or complex) conventions like those of comma-separated files. These conventions are usually application-specific, but there are also some standards like those for email messages (RFC 822 and MIME).

How easy it is to extract data from text files varies with the specific text file and application. Some are easy to parse and have a very regular and reliable structure, while others may be more complex or less regular.

DBF files

This is a bit based file notation used by many older pseudo-relational databases such as dBase and FoxPro. They are not found all that often any more, but one can still come across them, and software that can process DBF files can also be found.

The data model is more or less the same as in relational databases. I call the databases pseudo-relational because they did not really have all the features required from true relational database systems, such as concurrent access (many were DOS products), transactions, security, and so on.

Handling comma-separated files, DBF files, and databases is covered in more detail in the following chapter.

The tabproc framework

I
n this chapter we develop a general processing framework called tabproc for converting data from various forms of tabular data into XML. This is not an application with a command-line or GUI interface, but rather a framework consisting of many different components. These components can be plugged together in various ways to create applications, as well as to implement parts of other applications. Hopefully, this chapter will help you turn many of the abstract and general ideas discussed so far into more concrete understanding. The source of the framework can be found in the `py/tabproc.py` file on the CD-ROM.

In this chapter we will develop support for the following kinds of input:

- Comma-separated files. These will be supported in various forms, allowing client code to configure the CSV file reader somewhat.

- Relational databases. Python has a general database interface, and tabproc will allow client code to access RDBMSs through it and use an SQL statement to produce tabular data.

- DBF files. These are files used by old pseudo-relational databases such as dBase and FoxPro, and tabproc will support getting data from DBF files.

Of course, tabproc will also be designed so that new kinds of tabular data generators can be plugged into the framework. This is achieved by giving the data generators a common interface that is sufficiently general to support any tabular data source.

The generated XML will be configurable, since developers are likely to require that the XML output they get matches the schemas of their applications. This will be done by wrapping the table readers in different XML generators that can generate a standard generic XML representation as well as various forms of customized output.

There is of course also the question of how the XML should be represented once it has been generated. The obvious alternatives are SAX events, DOM trees, and byte streams. Since SAX events are the most efficient, tabproc uses these as the representation of its output, but provides mechanisms for building the other representations from the SAX events.

With these initial decisions out of the way, we have a rough initial design of the framework as shown in Figure 25–1.

25.1 | Input handling

The first step in the development process is to define the interface used to read tabular data into the framework. It seems suitable to define an interface, which we might call `TableReader`, for this. Obviously, this interface should support getting data from the reader. However, data sources may make available not only data, but also schema information. This raises the question if perhaps there should be some means of

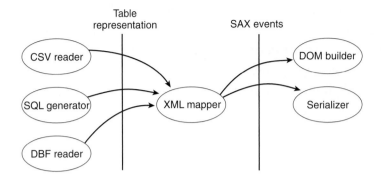

Figure 25–1   Outline of the tabproc architecture

representing schema information from a data source. If we represent the schema information as a separate object, the interface below seems reasonable for the TableReader.

get_rows(no = 10)
>   Calling this method returns a list of rows, where each row is represented as a tuple. Getting more than one row at a time is good for speed reasons, since it limits the necessary number of method calls.

get_schema()
>   This method returns the object that represents the schema information from the data source. The interface of the schema object is described below.

close()
>   This method is used to tell the TableReader that we are finished with it, so it can release whatever resources it is holding.

This interface does not define how to tell a TableReader where to get its data from, since this will be so different for the three readers that it seems better to make it specific to each reader.

Before designing the interface of the schema object, it is necessary to find out what the schema information consists of. The following items seem reasonable: table name, record name, field names, and field types. With this in mind, the name `TableSchema` and the interface below seems reasonable.

Since the schema information provided by a data source will in many cases be inadequate, or may need to be modified, we provide the schema object with methods for modifying the information. We also make a default implementation that the different `TableReaders` can instantiate and fill with data.

`get_table_name()`
> Returns the table name. This will be the name of the entire table of data generated by the reader.

`set_table_name()`
> Sets the table name.

`get_record_name()`
> Returns the name of the record type. This will be the name of the individual rows or records of data that make up the table.

`set_record_name()`
> Sets the name of the record type.

`get_field_data()`
> This method returns a list of (name, type) tuples, where both names and types are strings. The list can be modified by clients, thus removing the need for a set method.

The following type names are used by table readers:

`'STRING'`
> This means that the field is of the string type. If the field has a maximum length, that information is simply not available.

`'BINARY'`
> Used for binary data.

`'NUMBER'`
Used for numeric types of all kinds.

`'DATETIME'`
Used for date, time, datetime, and timestamp types.

The next step is then to develop the three readers.

25.1.1 *The CSV file reader*

Comma-separated files have very simple structure, although it may have many variations. Each row occupies one line, and the values in each row are separated by a delimiter character, usually semicolon. Some generators make files where strings are enclosed in quotes to avoid problems in case they contain the delimiter character. In some cases the first line contains the field names. In order to limit the complexity of this example to what is relevant for XML, our CSV reader does not accept quoted strings, but it does handle field names on the first line. Example 25–1 shows the source of the `CSVFileReader`.

25.1.2 *The DB-API reader*

All relational databases are very similar in that they use the same data model mostly with the same data types and very similar query languages and APIs. However, they are also different enough so that two different Python modules created to access two different databases are unlikely to have the same APIs. To deal with this problem, the Python community has defined a Python database API that standardizes the interface to relational databases, just like ODBC and JDBC do. This interface exists in two versions: 1.0 and 2.0, where 2.0 extends and clarifies 1.0 and also makes some small incompatible changes.

The full DB-API is not relevant for this book, so only an outline will be given here. The full specification can be found at `http://www.python.org/sigs/db-sig/`. There are implementa-

Example 25–1. Source of the CSVFileReader class

```
class CSVFileReader:
    "This class can read comma-separated files."

    def __init__(self, inf, sep = ";", field_names_included = 0):
        self._inf = inf
        self._sep = sep
        self._schema = TableSchema() # create empty schema

        if field_names_included:
            field_data = self._schema.get_field_data()
            for field_name in \
                string.split(self._inf.readline()[ : -1], sep):
                field_data.append((field_name, None))

            # table and record names are not provided,
            # so we cannot set them

    def get_schema(self):
        return self._schema

    def get_rows(self, no = 10):
        rows = []
        sep = self._sep
        line = self._inf.readline()

        while line != "" and len(rows) < no:
            rows.append(tuple(string.split(line[ : -1], sep)))
            line = self._inf.readline()

        return rows

    def close(self):
        self._inf.close()
```

tions for most databases out there, including DB2, Informix, Interbase, MySQL, any ODBC database, any JDBC database (for Jython), Oracle, and Sybase.

A central concept in the interface is the Connection object, which represents a connection to a database. The Connection object can be used to execute SQL queries and control transactions. The two methods that matter to us are cursor() that creates a Cursor object (see below) and `close()` that closes the connection. Closing the connection is important because database connections are generally heavy-weight objects and databases usually have an upper limit on the number of open connections. Forgetting to close connections can therefore have quite serious consequences.

`Cursor` objects are the objects through which SQL queries are executed. This is done through the `execute(query)` method. The resulting rows can then be retrieved with the `fetchone()` method, which returns the next row as a sequence and `None` when no more rows are available. The `close()` method closes the cursor object.

The `DBAPIReader` will take a database connection and an SQL query as parameters, and generate the table that corresponds to the results of the SQL query. The schema is generated from the information provided by the database module in the `description` attribute.

The implementation is shown in Example 25–2.

Example 25–2. The `DBAPIReader` implementation

```
class DBAPIReader:
    "This class can generate tables from SQL queries."

    def __init__(self, cur, sql, module = None):
        self._cur = cur
        self._cur.execute(sql)
        self._module = module or __import__(self._cur.__module__,
                                            globals(), locals())

        self._schema = TableSchema()
        if self._cur.description:
            field_data = self._schema.get_field_data()
            print self._cur.description
            for descr in self._cur.description:
                name = descr[0]
                type = descr[1]
                field_data.append((name, self._get_type(type)))

            # table and record name not available

    def get_schema(self):
        return self._schema
```

```
def get_rows(self, no = 10):
    rows = []
    row = self._cur.fetchone()

    while row != None and len(rows) < no:
        rows.append(tuple(row))
        row = self._cur.fetchone()

    return rows

def close(self):
    self._cur.close()

# internal methods

def _get_type(self, type):
    # we use a method rather than a dictionary because type
    # objects may compare equal to more than one other type
    # object

    if type == self._module.STRING:
        return 'STRING'
    elif type == self._module.BINARY:
        return 'BINARY'
    elif type in (self._module.NUMBER, self._module.ROWID):
        return 'NUMBER'
    elif type == self._module.DATETIME:
        return 'DATETIME'
    else:
        raise TypeError("Unknown database type '%s'" % type)
```

25.1.3 *The DBF file reader*

DBF files that were mentioned in 24.4, "Creating XML from data formats," on page 966 also contain tabular information. Each DBF file contains a single table, making the mapping to the tabproc API relatively straightforward. The files are read using the dbfreader module, whose source is not given here but can be found in py/dbfreader.py. This module also provides access to the schema information contained in a DBF file, which is used to generate schema information inside tabproc as well.

The implementation for DBF file reader is given in Example 25–3.

Example 25–3. A `TableReader` for DBF files

```
class DBFReader:
    "This class can generate tables from DBF files."

    typemap = {"Character"  : 'STRING',
               "Numeric"    : "NUMBER",
               "Logical"    : "NUMBER",
               "Memo field" : "STRING",
               "Object"     : "BINARY",
               "Date"       : "DATETIME",
               "Float"      : "NUMBER",
               "Picture"    : "BINARY"}

    def __init__(self, dbf):
        self._dbf = dbf

        self._schema = TableSchema()
        field_data = self._schema.get_field_data()
        for field in self._dbf.get_fields():
            field_data.append((field.get_name(),
                        DBFReader.typemap[field.get_type_name()]))

    def get_schema(self):
        return self._schema

    def get_rows(self, no = 10):
        rows = []
        record = self._dbf.get_next_record()

        while record != None and len(rows) < no:
            row = []
            for field in self._dbf.get_fields():
                row.append(record[field.get_name()])

            rows.append(tuple(row))
            record = self._dbf.get_next_record()

        return rows

    def close(self):
        self._dbf.close()
```

25.2 | Generating XML from tables

Now that we can read the three forms of source data through a common API, we are ready to map the tables to XML. In this section we develop three implementations of a common `XMLGenerator` interface. Each generator can use any table reader.

- The `GenericXMLGenerator` uses a fixed generic schema for representing tables.
- The `SimpleXMLGenerator` generates XML according to a schema that can be slightly modified, but not much.
- The `XSLTGenerator` uses an XSLT stylesheet and the 4XSLT engine to map from either the generic or the simple schema to whatever is desired.

The `XMLGenerator` interface has only one method, `generate`, which is used to generate XML. After a generator has been instantiated, it is intended to be configured before generation starts. The interface for configuration is not specified, since it will be different for each generator. The `generate(handler)` method generates XML based on the current configuration, passing it as SAX 2.0 events to the `handler`, which must be a `ContentHandler` implementation.

One problem we have not yet looked at is that some fields in the database may contain binary data. These will be delivered to us as strings, and if we just put them straight through into the generated XML, they will almost certainly violate XML syntax and data model rules. This could be solved by automatically re-encoding them with base64 encoding. For simplicity, we do not do this here, but in a proper framework we should have done that.

25.2.1 *The generic XML representation*

The easiest representation is perhaps to use one element type for rows (`row`), another for cells (`cell`), and a container element type for the entire table (`table`). Null values can be represented with a dedicated element type (`null`). If there is schema information available, it can be included in a `schema` element before the first `row`. The `schema` element can hold `table-name`, `record-name`, and `fields` elements, where `fields` contains `field` elements with `name` and `type` children.

With this representation, the DOM loading performance data in Example 25–4, taken from page 495, will be mapped to XML as shown in Example 25–5.

The code that does the conversion is very simple as Example 25–6 shows.

Example 25–4. The DOM loading performance data as CSV

```
DOM;Subsystems;Othello;WD-XSLT;Xmltools;airports
4DOM;Pyexpat;46;18;61;149
4DOM;xmlproc;59;24;83;184
PyDOM;Pyexpat;73;46;63;
minidom;Pyexpat;59;32;64;210
javadom;Sun DOM;1.4;2.4;2.1;4.0
javadom;Xerces;1.5;1.7;1.7;3.0
javadom;DOM2;4.1;3.2;7.5;22
javadom;Indelv DOM;1.9;1.5;1.7;5.0
javadom;SXP;4.6;;4.4;15
javadom;OpenXML;1.9;;1.9;5.0
4DOM;cPickle;16;6.7;25;
minidom;cPickle;16;10;22;
```

Example 25–5. The DOM loading performance data as XML

```
<?xml version="1.0" encoding="iso-8859-1"?>
<table>
<schema>
  <fields>
    <field><name>DOM</name></field>
    <field><name>Subsystems</name></field>
    <field><name>Othello</name></field>
    <field><name>WD-XSLT</name></field>
    <field><name>Xmltools</name></field>
    <field><name>airports</name></field>
  </fields>
</schema>
</schema>
```

```
<row><cell>4DOM</cell><cell>Pyexpat</cell><cell>46</cell>
     <cell>18</cell><cell>61</cell><cell>149</cell></row>
<row><cell>4DOM</cell><cell>xmlproc</cell><cell>59</cell>
     <cell>24</cell><cell>83</cell><cell>184</cell></row>
<row><cell>PyDOM</cell><cell>Pyexpat</cell><cell>73</cell>
     <cell>46</cell><cell>63</cell><cell></cell></row>
[...]
</table>
```

Example 25–6. The `GenericXMLGenerator` class

```python
class GenericXMLGenerator(XMLGenerator):

    def __init__(self, reader):
        self._reader = reader

    def generate(self, handler):
        emptyatts = AttributesImpl({})

        handler.startDocument()
        handler.startElement('table', emptyatts)

        schema = self._reader.get_schema()
        if schema.get_table_name() or schema.get_record_name() or \
           schema.get_field_data():
            self._generate_schema(schema, handler)

        rows = self._reader.get_rows(100)
        while rows != []:
            for row in rows:
                handler.startElement('row', emptyatts)

                for value in row:
                    handler.startElement('cell', emptyatts)

                    if value == None:
                        handler.startElement('none', emptyatts)
                        handler.endElement('none')
                    else:
                        handler.characters(str(value))

                    handler.endElement('cell')

                handler.endElement('row')
```

```
            rows = self._reader.get_rows(100)

        handler.endElement('table')
        handler.endDocument()

    def _generate_schema(self, schema, handler):
        "Generates the schema part of the XML."
        emptyatts = AttributesImpl({})

        handler.startElement('schema', emptyatts)
        if schema.get_table_name():
            handler.startElement('table-name', emptyatts)
            handler.characters(schema.get_table_name())
            handler.endElement('table-name')

        if schema.get_record_name():
            handler.startElement('record-name', emptyatts)
            handler.characters(schema.get_record_name())
            handler.endElement('record-name')

        if schema.get_field_data():
            handler.startElement('fields', emptyatts)
            for (name, type) in schema.get_field_data():
                handler.startElement('field', emptyatts)
                if name:
                    handler.startElement('name', emptyatts)
                    handler.characters(name)
                    handler.endElement('name')

                if type:
                    handler.startElement('type', emptyatts)
                    handler.characters(type)
                    handler.endElement('type')

                handler.endElement('field')

            handler.endElement('fields')

        handler.endElement('schema')
```

25.2.2 *The simple XML mapping*

The next step is to decide how client code could map the data to XML of its choice. The easiest way to do this is to use the schema information to generate the element-type names, but otherwise keep the structure. Thus the table name becomes the document element-type name, the record type becomes the row element type, and the field names are used as the cell element-type names. Of course, it is possible that some of these names may not be acceptable as XML element-type names, but in that case the client code may adjust the schema.

Example 25–7. Using the simple XML mapping

```
handler = ContentGenerator()
reader = CSVFileReader(open("domload.csv"), ";", 1)

schema = reader.get_schema()
schema.set_table_name("domload-data")
schema.set_record_name("implementation")

gen = SimpleXMLGenerator(reader, handler)
gen.generate()
reader.close()
```

With this solution, we can use the code in Example 25–7 to generate the XML output shown in Example 25–8.

The `SimpleXMLGenerator` class source is shown in Example 25–9.

25.2.3 *The XSLT generator*

This generator uses an XSLT stylesheet, interpreted using 4XSLT, to map the generated XML into the wanted XML structure. The idea is that with a sub-generator, we make XML that can then be mapped into the desired form using an XSLT stylesheet.

In order to be able to use 4XSLT for our purposes, we must map the tabular data into a source tree acceptable to 4XSLT, and we must map the output into a stream of SAX events. The `SAXTextWriter` from `saxtools` does the second job for us, but we still need something that will build the source tree from one of our `XMLGenerators`. Close study of the 4XSLT source showed how to create such a piece of code,

Example 25–8. The output of the simple XML mapping

```
<?xml version="1.0" encoding="iso-8859-1"?>
<domload-data>

<implementation>
  <DOM>4DOM</DOM>
  <Subsystems>Pyexpat</Subsystems>
  <Othello>46</Othello>
  <WD-XSLT>18</WD-XSLT>
  <Xmltools>61</Xmltools>
  <airports>149</airports>
</implementation>

<implementation>
  <DOM>4DOM</DOM>
  <Subsystems>xmlproc</Subsystems>
  <Othello>59</Othello>
  <WD-XSLT>24</WD-XSLT>
  <Xmltools>83</Xmltools>
  <airports>184</airports>
</implementation>

[...]

</domload-data>
```

and its source is given in Examples 25–10 and 25–11 together with the XSLT generator itself.

4XSLT uses implementations of the `Reader` interface described in 17.1.1.3, "The `Reader` interface," on page 649 to build the source tree. Looking at the default implementation, I have been able to build one that accepts a tabproc `XSLTGenerator` and uses it to build the source tree. The details of why the code in Example 25–10 works are omitted for brevity.

Example 25–11 is the entire `XSLTGenerator` implementation. To do its job it needs the URI of an XSLT stylesheet and a reference to another `XSLTGenerator` that generates the source tree. Using these, `generate` creates a processor by giving it the `Reader` implementation above. It then loads the stylesheet, the source tree, and runs the transformation.

Example 25–9. The `SimpleXMLGenerator` class

```python
class SimpleXMLGenerator(XMLGenerator):

    def __init__(self, reader):
        self._reader = reader

    def generate(self, handler):
        emptyatts = AttributesImpl({})

        schema = self._reader.get_schema()
        table = schema.get_table_name() or "table"
        record = schema.get_record_name() or "record"
        fields = map(lambda tuple: tuple[0] or "cell",
                     schema.get_field_data())

        handler.startDocument()
        handler.startElement(table, emptyatts)

        rows = self._reader.get_rows(100)
        while rows != []:
            for row in rows:
                handler.startElement(record, emptyatts)

                ix = 0

                for value in row:
                    cell = fields[ix]
                    handler.startElement(cell, emptyatts)

                    if value == None:
                        handler.startElement('none', emptyatts)
                        handler.endElement('none')
                    else:
                        handler.characters(str(value))

                    handler.endElement(cell)

                    ix = ix + 1

                handler.endElement(record)

            rows = self._reader.get_rows(100)

        handler.endElement(table)
        handler.endDocument()
```

Example 25–10. The XSLTGenerator (1 of 2)

```
from Ft.Lib import FtException, Error
from Ft.Lib.pDomlette import PyExpatReader
from xml.xslt.Processor import Processor
from xml.saxtools.xsltutils import SAXTextWriter
from xml.sax._exceptions import SAXException

class TabprocDocumentReader(PyExpatReader, ContentHandler):
    """A StylesheetReader that can be used with a tabproc
    XMLGenerator."""

    def __init__(self):
        # telling the base that it is overriden
        PyExpatReader.__init__(self, 1)

    def fromGenerator(self, generator):
        self.initState()

        try:
            generator.generate(self)
        except SAXException, e:
            if self._rootNode: self.releaseNode(self._rootNode)
            if self._ownerDoc: self.releaseNode(self._ownerDoc)
            raise FtException(Error.XML_PARSE_ERROR, (-1,-1,str(e)))

        self._completeTextNode()
        return self._rootNode or self._ownerDoc
```

Example 25–11. The XSLTGenerator (2 of 2)

```
class XSLTGenerator(XMLGenerator):

    def __init__(self, sheet_uri, subgen):
        self._sheet_uri = sheet_uri
        self._subgen = subgen

    def generate(self, handler):
        proc = Processor(TabprocDocumentReader())
        proc.appendStylesheetUri(self._sheet_uri)
        doc = proc._docReader.fromGenerator(self._subgen)
        proc.runNode(doc, writer = SAXTextWriter(handler))
        proc._docReader.releaseNode(doc)
```

25.3 | A SAX XMLReader interface

In order to make it possible to use XMLGenerators as SAX XMLReaders we make a simple TabprocXMLReader (Example 25–12) that wraps the generators as SAX parsers. This makes it possible to use them as if they were ordinary SAX parsers.

I chose a simple design for this XMLReader, giving it one property, XMLGenerator, which it uses to generate its XML. This really was the easiest way to do things, since the only alternative was to make one reader for each generator, and it is not clear if there would be much gain in that.

25.4 | Handling the XML output

Now we can read in tabular data, and we can map it to XML in the form of SAX events. The next step is to support turning those SAX events into other XML representations. The two other most common standardized representations are byte streams and DOM trees, so these are the two representations that tabproc will support.

Building the DOM tree that corresponds to the generated XML is relatively straightforward. All that is needed is to make the generator feed its SAX events into the DOM tree builder of the DOM implementation. For tabproc we will use minidom. The implementation is given in Example 25–13.

Generating a stream of bytes written to a file object turns out to be even simpler. The XMLGenerator from xml.sax.saxutils can be reused for this purpose, yielding the implementation in Example 25–14.

Example 25–12. The `TabprocXMLReader`

```python
from xml.sax._exceptions import *

namespace = "http://garshol.priv.no/symbolic/tabproc/"
property_generator = namespace + "generator"

class TabprocXMLReader(XMLReader):

    def __init__(self):
        XMLReader.__init__(self)
        self._generator = None
        self._parsing = 0

    def parse(self, source = None):
        if not self._generator:
            raise SAXException("Can't generate XML without an "
                               "XMLGenerator!")

        try:
            self._parsing = 1
            self._generator.generate(self._cont_handler)
        finally:
            self._parsing = 0

    def getProperty(self, name):
        if name == property_generator:
            return self._generator

        raise SAXNotRecognizedException(("Property '%s' not "
                                         "recognized" % name))

    def setProperty(self, name, value):
        if self._parsing:
            raise SAXNotSupportedException(
                "Cannot change property '%s' while parsing" % name)

        if name == property_generator:
            self._generator = value

        raise SAXNotRecognizedException(
                            "Property '%s' not recognized" % name)
```

Example 25–13. Generating a DOM tree

```
def build_dom(generator):
    from xml.dom.pulldom import SAX2DOM

    handler = SAX2DOM()
    generator.generate(handler)

    return handler.document
```

Example 25–14. Generating a byte stream

```
def make_xml(generator, outfile = None):
    handler = XMLGenerator(outfile or sys.stdout)
    generator.generate(handler)
```

25.5 | Examples of use

In this section we give two examples of how tabproc can be used to generate output, either as XML or via XML, from tabular data sources.

25.5.1 *Making an RSS document*

Most RSS channels consist of a fixed header and a variable list of headings and links. An easy way to keep such a channel up to date may be to have a CSV file containing the headings and links and then write a simple application that uses tabproc to generate the RSS document from the CSV file. By putting the column names in the CSV file and setting the table element-type name (channel) and the record element-type name (item) on the schema, the entire RSS document can be trivially generated, except for the channel header.

The easiest way to insert a channel header and the document element (rss) into the XML document is to use the DOM. RSS documents are so small in any case that there are no memory or performance concerns that might make this unattractive.

The implementation is given in Example 25–15.

Example 25–15. Using tabproc to generate RSS

```python
from xml.dom.minidom import parseString
from domutils import find_first_elem

from tabproc import CSVFileReader, build_dom, SimpleXMLGenerator

header = \
"""
<rss>
  <channel>
    <title>Infotek-nytt</title>
    <link>http://www.infotek.no/</link>
    <descr>Nytt fra STEP Infotek</descr>
  </channel>
</rss>
"""

reader = CSVFileReader(open("rss.csv"), ";", 1)
schema = reader.get_schema()
schema.set_table_name("channel")
schema.set_record_name("item")

doc1 = build_dom(reader, SimpleXMLGenerator(reader))

doc2 = parseString(header)
channel = find_first_elem(doc2.documentElement, "channel")

for item in doc1.documentElement.childNodes:
    channel.appendChild(item)

print doc2.toxml()
```

25.5.2 *Making a Web page*

The DOM performance data is something that might have general interest, so publishing it on the Web might be useful. This could be done by creating a simple single-rule XSLT stylesheet that contains the static text and uses an `xsl:for-each` element to convert the tabular XML data into an XHTML table for display purposes. To do this, we need two pieces of code: an XSLT stylesheet and a little driver program that sets up the transformation and runs it, shown in Example 25–16.

Example 25–16. The XSLT transformation driver

```
import sys
from tabproc import *
from xml.sax import saxutils

(csvfile, sheet_uri, outfile) = sys.argv[1 : ]

subgen = GenericXMLGenerator(CSVFileReader(open(csvfile), ";", 1))
gen = XSLTGenerator(sheet_uri, subgen)
gen.generate(saxutils.XMLGenerator(open(outfile, "w")))
```

The code is relatively straightforward in this case, especially since we completely omit all kinds of error checking.

The stylesheet used is shown in Example 25–17.

Figure 25–2 shows the result of this transformation as viewed in a browser.

Example 25–17. The XSLT stylesheet

```
<xsl:stylesheet xmlns:xsl="http://www.w3.org/1999/XSL/Transform"
                version="1.0">

<xsl:template match="table">
<html>
  <head>
    <title>DOM performance data</title>
  </head>

  <h1>DOM performance data</h1>

  <p>
  Here are the times needed to load a set of XML documents in a
  collection of DOM implementations, given in seconds.
  </p>

  <table>
  <tr><th>Implementation</th>
      <th>Subsystems used</th>
      <th>Othello</th>
      <th>WD-XSLT</th>
      <th>xmltools</th>
      <th>airports.rdf</th></tr>

  <xsl:for-each select = "row">
  <tr>
    <xsl:for-each select = "cell">
      <td><xsl:apply-templates/></td>
    </xsl:for-each>
  </tr>
  </xsl:for-each>
  </table>
</html>
</xsl:template>

</xsl:stylesheet>
```

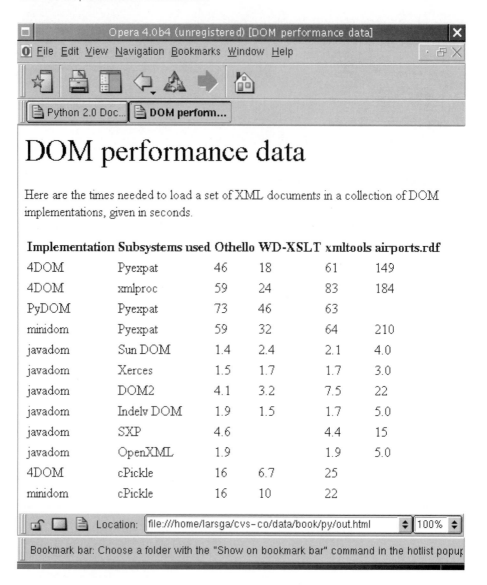

DOM performance data

Here are the times needed to load a set of XML documents in a collection of DOM implementations, given in seconds.

Implementation	Subsystems used	Othello	WD-XSLT	xmltools	airports.rdf
4DOM	Pyexpat	46	18	61	149
4DOM	xmlproc	59	24	83	184
PyDOM	Pyexpat	73	46	63	
minidom	Pyexpat	59	32	64	210
javadom	Sun DOM	1.4	2.4	2.1	4.0
javadom	Xerces	1.5	1.7	1.7	3.0
javadom	DOM2	4.1	3.2	7.5	22
javadom	Indelv DOM	1.9	1.5	1.7	5.0
javadom	SXP	4.6		4.4	15
javadom	OpenXML	1.9		1.9	5.0
4DOM	cPickle	16	6.7	25	
minidom	cPickle	16	10	22	

Location: file:///home/larsga/cvs-co/data/book/py/out.html   100%

Bookmark bar: Choose a folder with the "Show on bookmark bar" command in the hotlist popup

Figure 25–2   The transformation result

The RSS development kit

Chapter

26

R SS is being used by large numbers of people for many different purposes, and so it seems worthwhile to develop a toolkit of software that could make it easier for Python developers to produce RSS output and use RSS in their own applications. The RSS kit is, like tabproc, a general framework of components, but it is also, unlike tabproc, a set of end-user applications built from that set of components.

Figure 26–1 shows the relationships between the individual components that make up the kit. Software components are shown as boxes, while input and output is shown as ovals. The heart of the kit is the RSS object structure, which is basically a set of classes for representing RSS documents. Also central are the structure builder component, which can create RSS object structures from RSS documents, and the serializer components, which can create RSS documents from RSS object structures.

Since there are several different RSS formats, one for each version, the structure builder will have to be written in such a way that it can accept all of these. Similarly, it must be possible to serialize the object

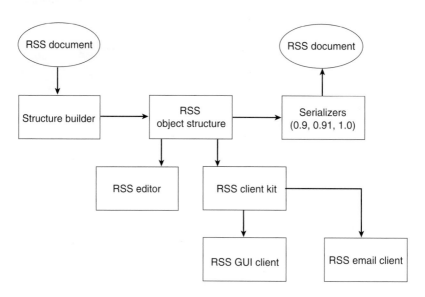

Figure 26–1   Overview of the RSS kit components

structure in documents following any one of the three versions of the notation.

On top of these three base components we will build a graphical RSS document editor and a general kit for making RSS clients. RSS clients here mean programs that can monitor RSS channels and keep end users informed of new headings as they appear. On top of the general client kit we will build two specific clients: an RSS client with a graphical interface and an RSS email client.

The source code to the RSS kit is found in the `py/rsskit` directory on the CD-ROM.

26.1 | The RSS object structure

The object structure should hold all the information about an RSS channel that is found in its RSS document, and should be general enough that it can be implemented in different ways with the same interface. It should also support all the three different versions of RSS

(0.9, 0.91, and 1.0), which means that it must support all the fields that exist in all of these versions. Ideally, the structure should also be extensible with new fields, but we do not implement that here. This chapter will be long enough as it is.

The statement that the structure should hold all the information in an RSS document leaves something important unsaid: that this only refers to information in the RSS information model. Lexical information about the document is not part of this, nor is information that in many other applications is considered significant, such as the order of elements. The item elements have an ordering that is part of the information model, but whether the title appeared before or after the link we really don't care about.

The RSS DTDs have four container element types, which we will here represent as classes. These classes are listed below.

SiteSummary
   Represents the entire RSS document.

Item
   Represents an individual news item.

Image
   Represents the image element type, which is used to add logos to RSS channels.

TextInput
   Represents the textinput element type, which is used to create a form for feedback to an RSS channel.

Since all these classes have title, link, and descr attributes, we use a common abstract base class (named TitleLink) to avoid having to repeat code needlessly. The code is shown in Example 26–1.

Example 26–1. The rsskit object structure

```
# --- Abstract base

class TitleLink:
    """Abstract convenience base class for things with title and
    link props."""

    def get_title(self):
        return self._title

    def set_title(self, title):
        self._title = title

    def get_link(self):
        return self._link

    def set_link(self, link):
        self._link = link

    def get_description(self):
        return self._descr

    def set_description(self, descr):
        self._descr = descr

# --- SiteSummary

class SiteSummary(TitleLink):
    "Represents an RSS document."

    def __init__(self, baseurl):
        self._baseurl = baseurl
        self._title = None
        self._link = None
        self._descr = None
        self._items = []
        self._image = None
        self._text = None

        # 0.91 properties
        self._language = None
        self._copyright = None
        self._managing_editor = None
        self._web_master = None
        self._rating = None
        self._pub_date = None
```

```python
        self._last_build_date = None
        self._docs = None
        self._skip_days = None
        self._skip_hours = None

    def get_baseurl(self):
        return self._baseurl

    def set_baseurl(self, baseurl):
        self._baseurl = baseurl

    def get_items(self):
        return self._items

    def add_item(self, item):
        self._items.append(item)

    def get_image(self):
        return self._image

    def set_image(self, image):
        self._image = image

    def get_textinput(self):
        return self._text

    def set_textinput(self, text):
        self._text = text

    def get_language(self):
        return self._language

    def set_language(self, language):
        self._language = language

    def get_copyright(self):
        return self._copyright

    def set_copyright(self, copyright):
        self._copyright = copyright

    def get_managing_editor(self):
        return self._managing_editor

    def set_managing_editor(self, managing_editor):
        self._managing_editor = managing_editor
```

```
def get_web_master(self):
    return self._web_master

def set_web_master(self, web_master):
    self._web_master = web_master

def get_rating(self):
    return self._rating

def set_rating(self, rating):
    self._rating = rating

def get_pub_date(self):
    return self._pub_date

def set_pub_date(self, pub_date):
    self._pub_date = pub_date

def get_last_build_date(self):
    return self._last_build_date

def set_last_build_date(self, last_build_date):
    self._last_build_date = last_build_date

def get_docs(self):
    return self._docs

def set_docs(self, docs):
    self._docs = docs

def get_skip_days(self):
    return self._skip_days

def set_skip_days(self, skip_days):
    self._skip_days = skip_days

def get_skip_hours(self):
    return self._skip_hours

def set_skip_hours(self, skip_hours):
    self._skip_hours = skip_hours
```

```python
# --- Item

class Item(TitleLink):
    "Represents an item element in an RSS channel."

    def __init__(self, title, link):
        self._title = title
        self._link = link
        self._descr = None

# --- Image

class Image(TitleLink):
    "Represents an image element in an RSS channel."

    def __init__(self, title, link, url):
        self._title = title
        self._link = link
        self._descr = None
        self._url = url

        # 0.91 properties
        self._width = None
        self._height = None

    def get_url(self):
        return self._url

    def set_url(self, url):
        self._url = url

    def get_width(self):
        return self._width

    def set_width(self, width):
        self._width = width

    def get_height(self):
        return self._height

    def set_height(self, height):
        self._height = height
```

```
# --- TextInput

class TextInput(TitleLink):
    "Represents a textinput element in an RSS channel."

    def __init__(self, title, descr, name, link):
        self._title = title
        self._descr = descr
        self._name = name
        self._link = link

    def get_name(self):
        return self._name

    def set_name(self, name):
        self._name = name
```

The object structure should be self-explanatory, since it consists of nothing but get and set methods, and closely follows the DTD.

Now that we have the structure defined, we are ready to create code that can build such structures from RSS documents.

26.1.1   *The structure builder*

The builder must be based on some XML representation, and the only real choices seem to be SAX and DOM. Given that SAX is the simplest of these, but is sufficient for such a simple application, we will use it as the basis for our structure builder. The main challenge for the builder lies in the fact that it has to support three different formats, versions 0.9, 0.91, and 1.0.

The builder is based on the SAXTracker class developed earlier, and is implemented as shown in Examples 26–2 and 26–3.

The RSS 1.0 specification requires the RSS 0.91 elements to use the rss091 prefix in RSS 1.0 documents, which means we must cater specifically for this case. This is done by mapping them to the same class attributes as those used for the ordinary 0.91 elements.

Example 26–2. The RSS kit structure builder (1 of 2)

```
class RSSHandler(SAXTracker):

    def __init__(self, baseurl, ss = None):
        SAXTracker.__init__(self, {
            "title"                  : "title",
            "link"                   : "link",
            "description"            : "description",
            "name"                   : "name",
            "url"                    : "url",

            # 0.91
            "language"               : "language",
            "copyright"              : "copyright",
            "managingEditor"         : "managing_editor",
            "webMaster"              : "web_master",
            "rating"                 : "rating",
            "pubDate"                : "pub_date",
            "lastBuildDate"          : "last_build_date",
            "docs"                   : "docs",
            "skipDays"               : "skip_days",
            "skipHours"              : "skip_hours",
            "width"                  : "width",
            "height"                 : "height",

            # 0.91 properties in 1.0
            "rss091:language"        : "language",
            "rss091:copyright"       : "copyright",
            "rss091:managingEditor"  : "managing_editor",
            "rss091:webMaster"       : "web_master",
            "rss091:rating"          : "rating",
            "rss091:pubDate"         : "pub_date",
            "rss091:lastBuildDate"   : "last_build_date",
            "rss091:docs"            : "docs",
            "rss091:skipDays"        : "skip_days",
            "rss091:skipHours"       : "skip_hours",
            "rss091:width"           : "width",
            "rss091:height"          : "height"})

        self._site = ss or SiteSummary(baseurl)
```

With this in the toolkit, it becomes an easy task to read RSS documents into an object structure and access their contents. Example 26–4 shows an example document, and an interpreter dialog in Example 26–5 shows how the document appears through the rsskit interface.

Example 26–3. The RSS kit structure builder (2 of 2)

```python
def startElement(self, name, attrs):
    SAXTracker.startElement(self, name, attrs)

    if (name == "item" and self._site.get_items() == []) or \
        name == "image":
      self._site.set_title(self.title)
      self._site.set_link(self.link)

      if self.description:
          descr = string.join(string.split(self.description),
                                " ")
          self._site.set_description(descr)
      if self.language:
          self._site.set_language(self.language)
      if self.copyright:
          self._site.set_copyright(self.copyright)
      if self.managing_editor:
          self._site.set_managing_editor(self.managing_editor)
      if self.web_master:
          self._site.set_web_master(self.web_master)
      if self.rating:
          self._site.set_rating(self.rating)
      if self.pub_date:
          self._site.set_pub_date(self.pub_date)
      if self.last_build_date:
          self._site.set_last_build_date(self.last_build_date)
      if self.docs:
          self._site.set_docs(self.docs)
      if self.skip_days:
          self._site.set_skip_days(self.skip_days)
      if self.skip_hours:
          self._site.set_skip_hours(self.skip_hours)

    if name in ["channel", "item", "image", "textinput"]:
        for attribute in self._field_elements.values():
            setattr(self, attribute, None)
```

```
    def endElement(self, name):
        SAXTracker.endElement(self, name)

        if name == "item":
            item = Item(self.title, self.link)
            if self.description:
                item.set_description(self.description)

            self._site.add_item(item)

        elif name == "image":
            image = Image(self.title, self.link, self.url)
            if self.description:
                image.set_description(self.description)
            if self.width:
                image.set_width(self.width)
            if self.height:
                image.set_height(self.height)
            self._site.set_image(image)

        elif name == "textinput":
            text = TextInput(self.title, self.description,
                             self.name, self.link)
            self._site.set_textinput(text)

def load_rss(sysid):
    handler = RSSHandler(sysid)
    sax.parse(sysid, handler)
    return handler._site
```

Example 26–4. An example RSS document

```
<?xml version="1.0" encoding="ISO-8859-1"?>
<rss version="0.91">
   <channel>

   <title>xmlhack</title>
   <link>http://www.xmlhack.com</link>
   <description>Developer news from the XML community</description>
   <language>en-us</language>
   <copyright>Copyright 1999, xmlhack team.</copyright>
   <managingEditor>editor@xmlhack.com</managingEditor>
   <webMaster>webmaster@xmlhack.com</webMaster>
```

```
<image>
  <title>xmlhack</title>
  <url>http://www.xmlhack.com/images/mynetscape88.gif</url>
  <link>http://www.xmlhack.com</link>
  <width>88</width>
  <height>31</height>
  <description>News, opinions, tips and issues concerning XML
               development</description>
</image>

<item>
<title>XML::RAX: Record-oriented XML API for Perl</title>
<link>http://www.xmlhack.com/read.php?item=472</link>
<description>Sean McGrath's RAX proposal, featured
on XML.com last week, has already attracted a Perl
implementation, by Robert Hanson.</description>
</item>
<item>
<title>IBM posts SOAP implementation on alphaWorks</title>
<link>http://www.xmlhack.com/read.php?item=471</link>
<description>IBM has released a Java implementation of the
new SOAP 1.1 specification. IBM-SOAP is described as a "reference
implementation" for SOAP 1.1.</description>
</item>
<item>
<title>XML for Web developers</title>
<link>http://www.xmlhack.com/read.php?item=470</link>
<description>The O'Reilly Network has published a selection of
articles aimed at introducing XML to Web developers, including
an Introduction to XHTML and an online HTML Tidy processor.
</description>
</item>
</channel>
</rss>
```

26.1.2 *The serializers*

Since there are three different RSS versions, and it is conceivable that RSS producers may want to produce RSS conforming to a specific version, one serializer has been provided for each version (Examples 26–6 to 26–9). Since one may want not only to store the documents in files, but perhaps also to transmit them to other applications or transform them using XSLT, the serializers generate SAX events

Example 26–5. Using the `rsslib` from the interpreter

```
>>> import rsslib
>>> site = rsslib.load_rss("xmlhack.rss")
>>> site
<rsslib.SiteSummary instance at 0077B34C>
>>> site.get_title()
u'xmlhack'
>>> site.get_link()
u'http://www.xmlhack.com'
>>> site.get_description()
u'News, opinions, tips and issues concerning XML development'
>>> site.get_web_master()
u'webmaster@xmlhack.com'
>>> site.get_image()
<rsslib.Image instance at 00A2BEBC>
>>> len(site.get_items())
3
>>> item = site.get_items()[0]
>>> item.get_title()
u'XML::RAX: Record-oriented XML API for Perl'
>>> item.get_link()
u'http://www.xmlhack.com/read.php?item=472'
>>> item.get_description()
u"Sean McGrath's RAX proposal, featured\012on XML.com last week,
has already attracted a Perl\012implementation, by Robert Hanson."
```

rather than write directly to a file-like object. To do this, the XML generator from 9.4.2, "An XML generator," on page 300 is reused.

The utility function in Example 26–6 is used to generate the triple of `title`, `link`, and `description` elements, since they appear again and again in all RSS documents.

Example 26–6. The RSS kit serializers (1 of 4)

```
def generate_triple(holder, gen):
    gen.fieldElement('title', holder.get_title())
    gen.fieldElement('link', holder.get_link())
    gen.fieldElementOptional('description',
                             holder.get_description())
```

The two functions in Example 26–7 quite straightforwardly generate RSS 0.9 and RSS 0.91 output, respectively.

Example 26–7. The RSS kit serializers (2 of 4)

```python
def generate_rss_09(site, gen):
    nsdecls = {
        "xmlns:rdf" : "http://www.w3.org/1999/02/22-rdf-syntax-ns#",
        "xmlns"     : "http://my.netscape.com/rdf/simple/0.9/" }
    gen.startElement('rdf:RDF', nsdecls)
    gen.startElement('channel')
    generate_triple(site, gen)

    if site.get_image():
        image = site.get_image()
        gen.startElement('image')
        generate_triple(image, gen)
        gen.fieldElement('url', image.get_url())
        gen.endElement('image')

    for item in site.get_items():
        gen.startElement('item')
        generate_triple(item, gen)
        gen.endElement('item')

    if site.get_textinput():
        text = site.get_textinput()
        gen.startElement('textinput')
        generate_triple(text, gen)
        gen.fieldElement('name', text.get_name())
        gen.endElement('textinput')

    gen.endElement('channel')
    gen.endElement('rdf:RDF')

def generate_rss_091(site, gen):
    version = {"version" : "0.91"}
    gen.startElement('rss', xmlreader.AttributesImpl(version))
    gen.startElement('channel')
    generate_triple(site, gen)
    gen.fieldElementOptional('language', site.get_language())
    gen.fieldElementOptional('copyright', site.get_copyright())
    gen.fieldElementOptional('managingEditor',
                             site.get_managing_editor())
    gen.fieldElementOptional('webMaster', site.get_web_master())
```

```
gen.fieldElementOptional('rating', site.get_rating())
gen.fieldElementOptional('pubDate', site.get_pub_date())
gen.fieldElementOptional('lastBuildDate',
                         site.get_last_build_date())
gen.fieldElementOptional('docs', site.get_docs())
gen.fieldElementOptional('skipDays', site.get_skip_days())
gen.fieldElementOptional('skipHours', site.get_skip_hours())

if site.get_image():
    image = site.get_image()
    gen.startElement('image')
    generate_triple(image, gen)
    gen.fieldElement('url', image.get_url())
    gen.fieldElementOptional('height', image.get_height())
    gen.fieldElementOptional('width', image.get_width())
    gen.endElement('image')

for item in site.get_items():
    gen.startElement('item')
    generate_triple(item, gen)
    gen.endElement('item')

if site.get_textinput():
    text = site.get_textinput()
    gen.startElement('textinput')
    generate_triple(text, gen)
    gen.fieldElement('name', text.get_name())
    gen.endElement('textinput')

gen.endElement('channel')
gen.endElement('rss')
```

The function in Example 26–8 generates RSS 1.0 output. Note the use of namespaces, and the way certain elements are put into an explicit RSS 0.91 namespace. The RSS 0.91 namespace is declared regardless of whether any parts of the document actually use it.

In addition to these functions, convenience functions for writing to files are also provided, as shown in Example 26–9.

Example 26–8. The RSS kit serializers (3 of 4)

```
def generate_rss_10(site, gen):
    nsdecls = {
      "xmlns:rdf"    : "http://www.w3.org/1999/02/22-rdf-syntax-ns#",
      "xmlns"        : "http://purl.org/rss/1.0/",
      "xmlns:rss091": "http://purl.org/rss/1.0/modules/rss091/"}
    gen.startElement('rdf:RDF', nsdecls)

    gen.startElement('channel', {"rdf:about" : site.get_baseurl()})
    generate_triple(site, gen)
    gen.fieldElementOptional('rss091:language', site.get_language())
    gen.fieldElementOptional('rss091:copyright',
                             site.get_copyright())
    gen.fieldElementOptional('rss091:managingEditor',
                             site.get_managing_editor())
    gen.fieldElementOptional('rss091:webMaster',
                             site.get_web_master())
    gen.fieldElementOptional('rss091:rating', site.get_rating())
    gen.fieldElementOptional('rss091:pubDate',
                             site.get_pub_date())
    gen.fieldElementOptional('rss091:lastBuildDate',
                             site.get_last_build_date())
    gen.fieldElementOptional('rss091:docs', site.get_docs())
    gen.fieldElementOptional('rss091:skipDays',
                             site.get_skip_days())
    gen.fieldElementOptional('rss091:skipHours',
                             site.get_skip_hours())
    gen.endElement('channel')

    if site.get_image():
        image = site.get_image()
        gen.startElement('image', {"rdf:about" : image.get_url()})

        gen.emptyElement('inchannel',
                         {"rdf:resource" : site.get_baseurl()})
        generate_triple(image, gen)
        gen.fieldElement('url', image.get_url())
        gen.fieldElementOptional('rss091:height',
                                 image.get_height())
        gen.fieldElementOptional('rss091:width', image.get_width())
        gen.endElement('image')
```

```
    for item in site.get_items():
        gen.startElement('item')
        gen.emptyElement('inchannel',
                        {"rdf:resource" : site.get_baseurl()})
        generate_triple(item, gen)
        gen.endElement('item')

    if site.get_textinput():
        text = site.get_textinput()
        gen.startElement('textinput')
        gen.emptyElement('inchannel',
                        {"rdf:resource" : site.get_baseurl()})
        generate_triple(text, gen)
        gen.fieldElement('name', text.get_name())
        gen.endElement('textinput')

    gen.endElement('rdf:RDF')
```

Example 26–9. The RSS kit serializers (4 of 4)

```
def write_rss_09(site, filename):
    generate_rss_09(site, xmlgen.file_writer(filename))

def write_rss_091(site, filename):
    generate_rss_091(site, xmlgen.file_writer(filename))

def write_rss_10(site, filename):
    generate_rss_10(site, xmlgen.file_writer(filename))
```

26.1.3 *The* rsslib *module*

These components together make up the rsslib module, which is the heart of the toolkit. The rest of the toolkit will be built on top of rsslib and rely on it for crucial parts of their own functionality. The parts of this module that are used by applications built on it are:

- the load_rss function;
- the SiteSummary, Item, Image, and TextInput classes;
- the generate_rss_09, generate_rss_091, gener-ate_rss_10 and the corresponding write_* functions.

26.2 | The client kit

The client kit consists of utilities that are useful for writing applications monitoring RSS channels, such as the clients. In general, RSS clients will need two things: to be able to load and save their configuration data, and to maintain a cache of which stories the user has already read. The kit has two main components, corresponding to these two needs:

- The `config` module. This module knows where to find important files, and it reads and writes the user's configuration settings.
- The `clientlib` module. This module has the story cache and other supporting classes. The story cache has functionality for keeping track of which stories the clients have and have not seen and for remembering stories between runs of the applications.

26.2.1 *The* `config` *module*

Examples 26–10 to 26–16 contain the code to the `config` module.

The functions in Example 26–10 are responsible for telling the RSS kit where to find its files. There are essentially three locations: those of the story cache, of the configuration file, and of the bitmaps used for icons in the GUI client. The cache and config files are either in the user's home directory (as defined by the HOME environment variable) or in the code directory. The bitmaps are in a sub-directory of the code directory.

The variables in Example 26–11 hold the configuration and are accessed through functions defined further down. They are also used internally in the module. (This module behaves in many respects like a singleton class.[1])

---

1.   The singleton pattern is one where a class is designed to have only a single instance in any program.

Example 26–10. The config module implementation (1 of 7)

```
"""Functionality for finding important files and user configuration.

$Id: config.py,v 1.3 2001/01/12 08:16:54 larsga Exp $
"""

from socket import gethostbyaddr, gethostname
import os, string
import rsslib

# ===== File location logic

def code_location():
    path = os.path.split(rsslib.__file__)[0]
    if path == "": path = "."
    return path + os.sep

def cache_file_location():
    if os.environ.has_key("HOME"):
        return os.environ["HOME"] + os.sep + ".rss-cache.mar"
    else:
        return code_location() + "rss-cache.mar"

def config_file_location():
    if os.environ.has_key("HOME"):
        return os.environ["HOME"] + os.sep + ".rssconfig.xml"
    else:
        return code_location() + "rss-config.xml"

def bitmap_file_location():
    return code_location() + "icons" + os.sep
```

The class in Example 26–12 is used to store information about an RSS channel the user wants to monitor. Instances are stored in the sources list.

The function in Example 26–13 stores the configuration into the configuration file. The configuration uses an XML syntax specially designed to be easy to parse with SAX (that is, all information is in attributes).

Example 26–14 contains the functions for accessing the internal configuration variables.

Example 26–11. The `config` module implementation (2 of 7)

```
# ===== User configuration

# --- Global variables

sources = []
use_threading = 0
show_errors = 1
expiry_wait = 28 # days
list_size = 80 # percent of full window

mail_server = "localhost"
host = gethostbyaddr(gethostname())[0]
recipients  = ["%s@%s" % (os.environ["USER"], host]
from_addr   = "%s@%s" % (os.environ["USER"], host)
```

Example 26–12. The `config` module implementation (3 of 7)

```
# --- Useful classes

class Source:
    "Represents an RSS channel."

    def __init__(self, url, title = "", descr = ""):
        self._url = url
        self._title = title
        self._descr = descr

    def get_title(self):
        return self._title

    def get_url(self):
        return self._url

    def get_descr(self):
        return self._descr

    def set_title(self, title):
        self._title = title

    def set_descr(self, descr):
        self._descr = descr
```

Example 26–13. The `config` module implementation (4 of 7)

```
# --- Function interface

def save():
    outf = open(config_file_location(), "w")
    outf.write('<rssconfig version="1.0">\n')

    for source in sources:
        outf.write('  <source url="%s"' % source.get_url())
        if source.get_title():
            outf.write(' title="%s"' % source.get_title())
        if source.get_descr():
            outf.write(' descr="%s"' % source.get_descr())
        outf.write('/>\n')


    outf.write(('  <clientconfig show-errors="%s" '
                '                 use-threading="%s" '
                '                 expiry-wait-days="%s" '
                '                 list-size="%s"/>\n\n') %
               (get_show_errors(),
                get_use_threading(),
                expiry_wait,
                get_list_size()))

    outf.write(('  <emailconfig mail-server="%s" recipients="%s" '
                '                 from-addr="%s"/>\n\n') %
               (get_mail_server(),
                string.join(get_recipients(), " "),
                get_from_addr()))

    outf.write('</rssconfig>\n')
    outf.close()
```

Example 26–15 is the code that loads the configuration from the config file. It is run when the module is imported.

In Example 26–16, we clean up the module namespace by removing names that are no longer needed. This makes the module contents a bit cleaner when inspected from within Python.

Example 26–14. The `config` module implementation (5 of 7)

```
def get_sources():
    return sources

def get_show_errors():
    return show_errors

def get_use_threading():
    return use_threading

def get_expiry_wait():
    return expiry_wait * 86400

def get_list_size():
    return list_size

def set_list_size(size):
    global list_size
    list_size = size

def get_mail_server():
    return mail_server

def get_recipients():
    return recipients

def get_from_addr():
    return from_addr
```

26.2.2 *The* `clientlib` *module*

With the config module in place, we can access the stored list of RSS channels and find out how the user would like the client to behave. The next step is to implement the story cache and other utilities useful for the clients. The story cache is the main part of the functionality, and it must fulfill the following requirements:

- it must remember between runs whether a specific story has been read by the user or not,

- it must remember old stories that the user has not read and that are no longer available from the RSS site,

Example 26–15. The `config` module implementation (6 of 7)

```
# --- Internal

from xml.sax.handler import ContentHandler

class ConfigHandler(ContentHandler):

    def startElement(self, name, attrs):
        global show_errors, use_threading, expiry_wait, list_size
        global mail_server, global recipients, from_addr

        if name == "source":
            sources.append(Source(attrs["url"],
                                   attrs.get("title"),
                                   attrs.get("descr")))

        elif name == "clientconfig":
            show_errors = attrs.get("show-errors", 1)
            use_threading = attrs.get("use-threading", 0)
            expiry_wait = attrs.get("expiry-wait", 28)
            list_size = int(attrs.get("list-size", 80))

        elif name == "emailconfig":
            mail_server = attrs.get("mail-server", mail_server)
            recipients  = string.split(attrs.get("recipients",
                                          string.join(recipients, " ")))
            from_addr   = attrs.get("from-addr", from_addr)

def _load():
    from xml.sax import parse
    try:
        parse(config_file_location(), ConfigHandler())
    except IOError, e:
        if e.errno == 2:
            pass  # no config file, that is, use defaults
        else:
            raise # some other error; notify user

_load()
```

Example 26–16. The `config` module implementation (7 of 7)

```
del _load, ContentHandler, ConfigHandler
```

- it must automatically remove old stories after a certain time period so that the cache does not just keep growing without limit,

- and, finally, it must be able to sort the stories by their age, so that the reader can have the newest stories at the top at all times.

The source code of the clientlib module is given in Examples 26–17 to 26–21.

In Example 26–17, we import the fastest implementation of the pickle module we can find, which is used by the story cache to store its data. We use pickle rather than the faster marshal because the cache contains instance objects, which marshal cannot handle.

Example 26–17. The clientlib module implementation (1 of 5)

```
"""Classes to simplify the development of RSS clients.

$Id: clientlib.py,v 1.2 2001/01/12 08:16:53 larsga Exp $
"""

try:
    import cPickle
    pickle = cPickle
except ImportError:
    import pickle
```

The class in Example 26–18 is used to represent a single story from an RSS channel. It is used both by the story cache and by the clients to represent stories. The class holds references to both the channel and the item. Note the timestamp in the _time attribute. This is used for two purposes: to keep items sorted by the time order in which they showed up and to let items expire from the story cache.

Example 26–19 is the story cache implementation. Essentially this class can perform two actions: tell us which stories are already in the cache that we haven't read (get_old_unread) and tell us whether a story is in the cache or not (show). There is also support for loading

Example 26–18. The clientlib module implementation (2 of 5)

```python
import time
from xml.sax._exceptions import SAXException
import config, rsslib

# --- Useful classes

class Story:

    def __init__(self, site, item):
        self._site = site
        self._item = item
        self._time = time.time()

    def get_title(self):
        return self._item.get_title()

    def get_site_title(self):
        return self._site.get_title()

    def get_link(self):
        return self._item.get_link()

    def get_description(self):
        return self._item.get_description()

    def get_item(self):
        return self._item

    def get_characteristic(self):
        return self.get_title() + " " + self.get_link()

    def get_time(self):
        return self._time

    def __cmp__(self, other):
        if isinstance(other, Story):
            res = cmp(self.get_site_title(), other.get_site_title())
            if res == 0:
                res = cmp(self.get_time(), other.get_time())
            if res == 0:
                res = cmp(self.get_title(), other.get_title())
            return res
        else:
            return -1
```

the cache from disk (__init__), writing it back to disk (save), and for telling the cache that the user has read a story (read).

Example 26–19. The clientlib module implementation (3 of 5)

```
class StoryCache:

    def __init__(self, file):
        try:
            inf = pickle.Unpickler(open(file, "rb"))
            self._read = inf.load()
            self._unread = inf.load()

            self._expire(self._read)
            self._expire(self._unread)
        except IOError:
            self._read = {}
            self._unread = {}

    def save(self, file):
        pickler = pickle.Pickler(open(file, "wb"))
        pickler.dump(self._read)
        pickler.dump(self._unread)

    def get_old_unread(self):
        return self._unread.values()

    def show(self, story):
        if self._read.has_key(story.get_characteristic()) or \
            self._unread.has_key(story.get_characteristic()):
            return 0
        else:
            self._unread[story.get_characteristic()] = story
            return 1

    def read(self, story):
        del self._unread[story.get_characteristic()]
        self._read[story.get_characteristic()] = story

    def _expire(self, stories):
        now = time.time()
        for (key, story) in stories.items():
            if story.get_time() + config.get_expiry_wait() < now:
                del stories[key]
```

In order to keep the cache from filling up with old stories that just accumulate forever, old items are expired every time the cache is created. The timestamps in the story objects are used to implement this.

The class in Example 26–20 is used by the clients to collect errors that occur during the downloading and parsing of RSS documents.

Example 26–20. The `clientlib` module implementation (4 of 5)

```
# --- ErrorRecorder

class ErrorRecorder:

    def __init__(self):
        self._errors = []

    def error(self, exception):
        self._errors.append(str(exception))

    def fatalError(self, exception):
        self._errors.append(str(exception))

    def warning(self, exception):
        self._errors.append(str(exception))
```

Example 26–21 is the implementation of the external interface of this module. Essentially, it consists of a story cache object, a function for storing internal state, and a convenience function for getting site summary objects for each RSS channel in the `sources` list.

26.3 | The RSS email client

The idea behind this client is to make a small Python script that can be run automatically every now and then to send email about new stories to its users (Example 26–22). A typical way to deploy this client would be to put it on a Unix machine somewhere with a permanent Internet connection. The cron daemon could then be configured to run the script once every two hours during the day, for example. Every

Example 26–21. The `clientlib` module implementation (5 of 5)

```
# --- Function interface

def save():
    cache.save(config.cache_file_location())

def get_summaries(error_handler):
    summaries = []

    for source in config.get_sources():
        try:
            summary = rsslib.load_rss(source.get_url())
            source.set_title(summary.get_title())
            source.set_descr(summary.get_description())
            summaries.append(summary)
        except Exception, e:
            error_handler.fatalError(SAXException(str(e), e))

    return summaries

def get_sources():
    return config.get_sources()

# --- Global variables

cache = StoryCache(config.cache_file_location())
```

time new stories appear on the channels the client has been configured to monitor, emails about these would go out automatically.

Example 26–22. The RSS email client code

```
#!/usr/bin/python
"""
This RSS client informs listed users of new stories via email every
time it is run.

$Id: rss-email.py,v 1.3 2001/01/12 08:16:54 larsga Exp $
"""

import smtplib, StringIO, sys
import clientlib, config
```

```
# --- Main program

errors = clientlib.ErrorRecorder()
summaries = clientlib.get_summaries(errors)

stories = []

for summary in summaries:
    for item in summary.get_items():
        story = clientlib.Story(summary, item)
        if clientlib.cache.show(story):
            clientlib.cache.read(story)
            stories.append(story)

if stories == [] and errors._errors == []:
    sys.exit()

stories.sort()

smtp = smtplib.SMTP(config.get_mail_server())
for recipient in config.get_recipients():
    email = StringIO.StringIO()
    email.write(("From: rss-email client <%s>\n"
                 "To: %s\n"
                 "Subject: New RSS stories\n\n") %
                (config.get_from_addr(), recipient))

    for story in stories:
        email.write(("---%s:\n  %s\n") %
                    (story.get_title(), story.get_link()))
        if story.get_description():
            email.write("\n" + story.get_description() + "\n")

        email.write("\n")

    if errors._errors != []:
        email.write("===== ERRORS =====\n\n")
        for error in errors._errors:
            email.write("   " + error + "\n")

    email.write("\n-- \nThe RSS email client")

    smtp.sendmail(config.get_from_addr(), [recipient],
                  email.getvalue())

smtp.quit()
```

Example 26–23 shows an email sent by the email client.

Example 26–23. An RSS email

```
To: larsga@garshol.priv.no
Subject: New RSS stories

---New product: rsskit:
  http://www.garshol.priv.no/download/xmltools/prod/rsskit.html


--
The RSS email client
```

26.4 | The GUI RSS client

The first end-user application we develop with this toolkit is an RSS client with a graphical user interface. To create the user interface we use the wxPython toolkit. This toolkit is based on the C++ wxWindows GUI framework by Julian Smart and has been wrapped as a Python module by Robin Dunn. Both wxPython and wxWindows have been ported to Windows and Unix, and on Unix they can use any one of several widget toolkits, such as Qt and GTK. The reasons for choosing wxPython are the ease of development (compared to, say, Tkinter) and portability (compared to, say, PyGTK). I will not attempt to give a wxPython introduction here, since that is a topic large enough to merit a book of its own. Those who are interested can refer to the wxPython home page at `http://www.wxpython.org/`.

The idea behind this client is to create a simple desktop client that can be used to read news from different RSS channels in a convenient way. The user gives the URLs of the channels s/he wants to monitor, and the client will then download new items from these channels when asked to do so. The client remembers which stories the user has read, and will not show stories the user has read before (using the story cache). It will also remember stories the user has *not* read, and show these, even if they are no longer available from the channels. The user can remove uninteresting stories without reading them, or open a story in the browser of the user's choice. Opening a story can be done either by telling the client to do so, or by copying the URL to the clipboard and pasting it into the browser.

The interface of the client can be seen in Figure 26–2, which shows how the unread stories are displayed. Note the area at the bottom of the window, which is used for displaying story descriptions. At bottom right of the window there is a little light used to indicate whether the client is busy getting new news or it has finished.

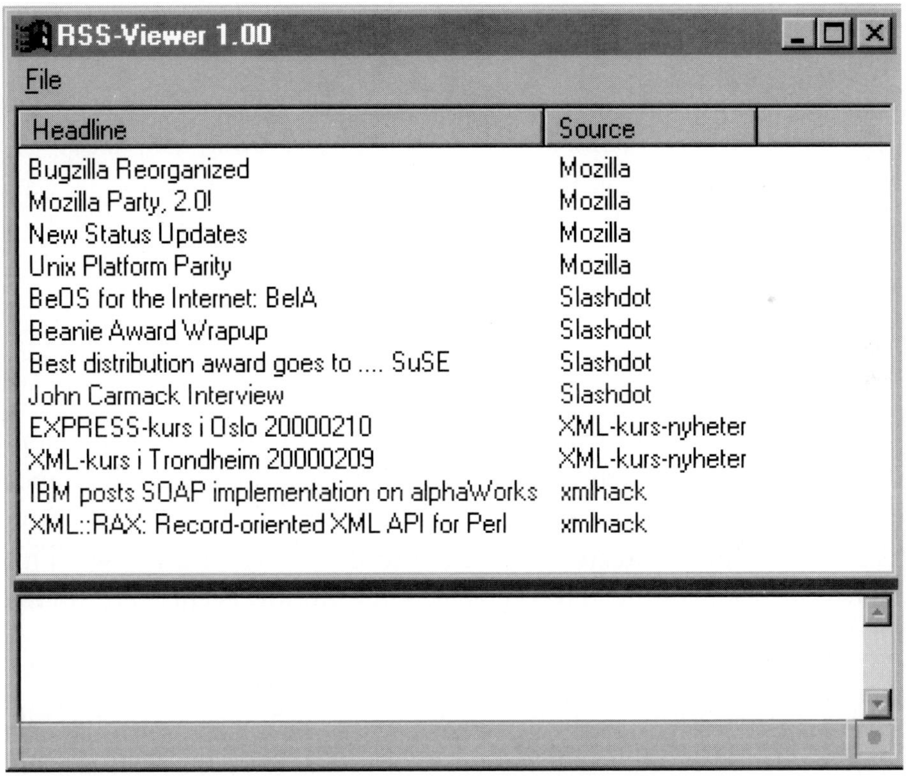

Headline	Source
Bugzilla Reorganized	Mozilla
Mozilla Party, 2.0!	Mozilla
New Status Updates	Mozilla
Unix Platform Parity	Mozilla
BeOS for the Internet: BeIA	Slashdot
Beanie Award Wrapup	Slashdot
Best distribution award goes to .... SuSE	Slashdot
John Carmack Interview	Slashdot
EXPRESS-kurs i Oslo 20000210	XML-kurs-nyheter
XML-kurs i Trondheim 20000209	XML-kurs-nyheter
IBM posts SOAP implementation on alphaWorks	xmlhack
XML::RAX: Record-oriented XML API for Perl	xmlhack

Figure 26–2   The RSS viewer main window

26.4.1 *Client application utilities*

Examples 26–24 to 26–27 show the first part of the client source code, which contains the top part as well as some utilities used in later parts of the code.

Example 26–24. The first part of the RSS client (1 of 4)

```
#!/usr/bin/python
"""
A GUI RSS client built on wxPython.

$Id: rss-viewer.py,v 1.4 2001/01/18 17:09:26 larsga Exp $
"""

from wxUtils import *
import clientlib, config, time, sys, rsslib, string

try:
    if not config.get_use_threading(): raise ImportError()
    import thread

except ImportError:
    import thread_dummy
    thread = thread_dummy
```

Getting news items from the network can often take a while, and during this time the entire application will just hang, since it cannot process any incoming window events. To avoid this, we use the Python `thread` module to create a separate thread for getting the news. This allows the original thread to keep receiving window events and run the application as usual. If the user does not want to use this module, or if it is not there, the `thread_dummy` module is used in its stead. (On some Unix platforms Python does not build with the `thread` module by default.) This allows us to hide the difference between threading and non-threading from the rest of the program.

Example 26–25 is the wxPython application class. It is a construct required by wxPython which we do not use much in this program. All

Example 26–25. The first part of the RSS client (2 of 4)

```
version = "1.00"

# --- Application

class RSSViewer(wxApp):

    def OnInit(self):
        frame = MainWindow(NULL, -1, "RSS-Viewer " + str(version))
        frame.Show(true)
        self.SetTopWindow(frame)
        return true
```

Example 26–26. The first part of the RSS client (3 of 4)

```
# --- A cooler status bar

# This class was stolen from the Slashdot 1.2 applet by Harm van der
# Heijden (H.v.d.Heijden@phys.tue.nl) and modified a little to show
# a bitmap instead of a button

class BitmapStatusBar(wxStatusBar):

    def __init__(self, parent):
        wxStatusBar.__init__(self, parent, -1)
        self.SetFieldsCount(2)
        self.SetStatusWidths([-1, 22])
        EVT_SIZE(self, self.OnSize)

        path = config.bitmap_file_location()
        if sys.platform[ : 5] == "win32":
            self.busy_img = wxBitmap(path + "busy.bmp",
                                     wxBITMAP_TYPE_BMP)
            self.free_img = wxBitmap(path + "free.bmp",
                                     wxBITMAP_TYPE_BMP)

        elif sys.platform[ : 5] in ("linux", "sunos"):
            self.busy_img = wxBitmap(path + "busy.xpm",
                                     wxBITMAP_TYPE_XPM)
            self.free_img = wxBitmap(path + "free.xpm",
                                     wxBITMAP_TYPE_XPM)
```

it does here is create the main window and tell wxPython that this is the main window.

Since the Windows variant of wxPython only supports BMP bitmaps, while the Linux GTK version only supports X bitmaps, we must have two different sets of icons and set them up differently (Example 26–26).

Example 26–27 is a wxPython status bar that not only displays the status text, but also has a bitmap in the right-hand corner. In this program, we use the bitmap to show the little light in the lower right corner that indicates whether the client is busy downloading new items or not.

Example 26–27. The first part of the RSS client (4 of 4)

```
        self.busy = wxStaticBitmap(self, NewId(), self.free_img)
        self.OnSize(None)

    def logprint(self,x):
        self.SetStatusText(x, 0)

    def set_state(self, busy):
        if busy:
            self.busy.SetBitmap(self.busy_img)
        else:
            self.busy.SetBitmap(self.free_img)

    def OnSize(self, event):
        rect = self.GetFieldRect(1)
        self.busy.SetPosition(wxPoint(rect.x+2, rect.y+2))
        self.busy.SetSize(wxSize(rect.width-4, rect.height-4))
```

26.4.2 *The main window*

Examples 26–28 to 26–47 contain the source code to the main window of the client application, which is where most of the application logic is implemented.

Example 26–28 is the constructor of the main window class. So far we have set up our fancy status bar and created the main menu.

Example 26–28. The RSS client main window (1 of 20)

```
# --- Main window

ID_ABOUT   = 101
ID_EXIT    = 102
ID_SOURCES = 103
ID_STORIES = 104
ID_GOTO    = 105
ID_READ    = 106
ID_COPYURL = 107

class MainWindow(wxFrame):
    def __init__(self, parent, ID, title):
        wxFrame.__init__(self, parent, ID, title,
                         wxDefaultPosition, wxSize(550, 450))

        # --- Status bar

        self.statusbar = BitmapStatusBar(self)
        self.SetStatusBar(self.statusbar)
        self.SetAutoLayout(true)

        # --- Menu

        menu = wxMenu()
        menu.Append(ID_SOURCES,  "&Source list",
                    "Show the list of RSS sources")
        menu.Append(ID_STORIES,  "&New stories",
                    "Gets new RSS stories")

        menu.Append(ID_GOTO,  "&Goto story",
                    "Loads the selected story in your browser")
        menu.Append(ID_COPYURL,  "&Copy URL",
                    "Copies the URL of the selected story onto the "
                    "clipboard")
        menu.Append(ID_READ,  "&Mark as read",
                    "Marks the selected stories as read")
        menu.AppendSeparator()
        menu.Append(ID_ABOUT, "&About",
                    "More information about this program")
        menu.Append(ID_EXIT, "E&xit", "Terminate the program")

        menuBar = wxMenuBar()
        menuBar.Append(menu, "&File");

        self.SetMenuBar(menuBar)
```

Example 26–29. The RSS client main window (2 of 20)

```
# --- Splitter control

splitter = wxSplitterWindow(self, -1)
lc = wxLayoutConstraints()
lc.height.SameAs(self, wxHeight, 0)
lc.top.SameAs(self, wxTop, 0)
lc.left.SameAs(self, wxLeft, 0)
lc.right.SameAs(self, wxRight, 0)
splitter.SetConstraints(lc)
```

Example 26–30. The RSS client main window (3 of 20)

```
# --- Story list

list_id = NewId()
list = wxListCtrl(splitter, list_id, wxDefaultPosition,
                  wxDefaultSize,
                  wxLC_REPORT | wxSUNKEN_BORDER)

list.InsertColumn(0, "Headline")
list.InsertColumn(1, "Source")

lc = wxLayoutConstraints()
lc.top.SameAs(splitter, wxTop, 0)
lc.left.SameAs(splitter, wxLeft, 0)
lc.right.SameAs(splitter, wxRight, 0)
list.SetConstraints(lc)

EVT_MENU(self, ID_ABOUT,    self.OnAbout)
EVT_MENU(self, ID_EXIT,     self.TimeToQuit)
EVT_MENU(self, ID_SOURCES,  self.ShowSources)
EVT_MENU(self, ID_STORIES,  self.ShowStories)
EVT_MENU(self, ID_GOTO,     self.GotoStory)
EVT_MENU(self, ID_COPYURL,  self.CopyURL)
EVT_MENU(self, ID_READ,     self.MarkAsRead)

self.tracker = ListSelectionTracker(list, self)
```

Wrapping the window contents in the wxSplitterWindow object shown in Example 26–29 allows us to create a window split in two with a moveable sash. This is useful to let users modify the layout of the window.

In Example 26–30, we create the list control that holds the story headlines. The EVT_MENU statements hook up window methods with menu IDs, which makes wxPython call the window methods when users select the menu items. The last statement creates an object that tracks what selections the user makes in the list control.

In Example 26–31, we create the text box that holds the descriptions in the bottom of the window. We also store the percentage of the window that it covers, so that we can keep that constant when the window is resized.

Example 26–31. The RSS client main window (4 of 20)

```
# --- Description box

descr = wxTextCtrl(splitter, -1, "", wxDefaultPosition,
                   wxDefaultSize,
                   wxTE_MULTILINE | wxTE_READONLY)
lc = wxLayoutConstraints()
lc.top.Below(list, 0)
lc.bottom.SameAs(splitter, wxBottom, 0)
lc.left.SameAs(splitter, wxLeft, 0)
lc.right.SameAs(splitter, wxRight, 0)
descr.SetConstraints(lc)

splitter.SplitHorizontally(list, descr)
pos = self.GetSizeTuple()[1] * config.get_list_size() / 100
splitter.SetSashPosition(pos)
self.splitter = splitter
self.percent = config.get_list_size()
```

And finally, we round off by storing interesting information in attributes (Example 26–32). The call to _update_story_list is made so that old unread stories from previous runs will be in the story list when the window is first displayed.

Example 26–32. The RSS client main window (5 of 20)

```
# --- Internal data

self.list = list
self.descr = descr
self._update_story_list(clientlib.cache.get_old_unread())
self.checking = 0
```

In Example 26–33, we tell wxPython to call our `OnCloseWindow` method when the window is closed, and `MyOnSize` when it is resized. We also want to know when the splitter is resized.

Example 26–33. The RSS client main window (6 of 20)

```
EVT_CLOSE(self, self.OnCloseWindow)
EVT_SIZE(self, self.MyOnSize)
EVT_SPLITTER_SASH_POS_CHANGED(self.splitter,
                              self.splitter.GetId(),
                              self.MyOnSplitterSize)
```

Example 26–34 contains the method that implements the "Goto story" command. It uses the Python 2.0 `webbrowser` module to open the URL in the user's default browser. This module will use a platform-specific and configurable method for contacting a running browser, or starting a new one if required, and loading the story in it.

Example 26–34. The RSS client main window (7 of 20)

```
def GotoStory(self,event):
    if self.stories == [] or self.tracker.current_ix == None:
        return

    import webbrowser
    link = self.stories[self.tracker.current_ix].get_link()
    webbrowser.open(link)
    self.__read(self.tracker.current_ix)
```

The method in Example 26–35 copies the URL of the currently selected story to the clipboard so that the user can paste it into the URL field of a browser, or do something else with it. Note the call to `str` that is used to turn what may be a Unicode string object into a byte string, since wxPython does not handle Unicode strings.

Example 26–35. The RSS client main window (8 of 20)

```
def CopyURL(self,event):
    if self.stories == [] or self.tracker.current_ix == None:
        return

    link = str(self.stories[self.tracker.current_ix].get_link())
    txt = wxTextDataObject(link)
    if wxTheClipboard.Open():
        wxTheClipboard.SetData(txt)
        wxTheClipboard.Close()

    self.__read(self.tracker.current_ix)
```

The method in Example 26–36 is called by wxPython every time a story in the list control is selected. It sets the URL of the story in the status bar and puts the description in the description box.

Example 26–36. The RSS client main window (9 of 20)

```
def OnItemSelected(self, event):
    story = self.stories[event.m_itemIndex]
    self.SetStatusText(str(story.get_link()))
    descr = str(story.get_description() or "")
    self.descr.SetValue(string.join(string.split(descr)))
```

Example 26–37 is the implementation of the "About" command, which creates a simple dialog with a little information about the program.

Example 26–37. The RSS client main window (10 of 20)

```
def OnAbout(self, event):
    dlg = wxMessageDialog(self, "A simple tool for watching RSS"
                          " news\nsources for updates.\n\n" +
                          "Version: " + version + "\n" +
                          "rsslib version: %\n" %rsslib.version,
                          "About RSS-Viewer",
                          wxOK | wxICON_INFORMATION)
    dlg.ShowModal()
    dlg.Destroy()
```

The method in Example 26–38 is called when the window is resized, and we take the opportunity to resize the description box so that its percentage of the window remains constant.

Example 26–38. The RSS client main window (11 of 20)

```
def MyOnSize(self, event):
    self.splitter.SetSize(self.GetClientSize())
    pos = self.GetSizeTuple()[1] * self.percent / 100
    self.splitter.SetSashPosition(pos)
```

When the splitter moves, we must also record the new position (Example 26–39).

Example 26–39. The RSS client main window (12 of 20)

```
def MyOnSplitterSize(self, event):
    self.percent = int(float(event.GetSashPosition()) /
                       float(self.GetSizeTuple()[1]) * 100) + 1
```

The method in Example 26–40 is called when the user selects the "Exit" command in the menu. It closes the main window of the program, thus exiting the wxPython main loop and leaving the entire program.

Example 26–40. The RSS client main window (13 of 20)

```
def TimeToQuit(self, event):
    self.Close(true)
```

The method in Example 26–41 is called by wxPython when the window is closed. We then store the current size of the list control back into the config module, so that it can write the setting into the config file. This is done by the main program code that also creates the wxPython application.

Example 26–41. The RSS client main window (14 of 20)

```
def OnCloseWindow(self, event):
    list_height = float(self.list.GetSizeTuple()[1])
    win_height = float(self.GetSizeTuple()[1])
    config.set_list_size(int(list_height / win_height * 100) +1)
    self.Destroy()
```

Example 26–42 is the implementation of the "Source list" menu item, which opens the RSS channel list window.

Example 26–42. The RSS client main window (15 of 20)

```
def ShowSources(self, event):
    frame = SourceListWindow(NULL)
    frame.Show(true)
```

The method in Example 26–43 is called on startup and every time new stories have been downloaded to update the list control. Note that the stories are sorted in order to display them in a consistent order.

Example 26–44 is the method that downloads new stories. It starts with all the old unread stories, then downloads all the summaries in the source list. For each item in each summary it adds a story to the list, provided it has not been seen before. The _update_story_list method is then called to update the list control. Finally, if there were

Example 26–43. The RSS client main window (16 of 20)

```
def _update_story_list(self, stories):
    self.stories = stories
    self.stories.sort()
    self.list.DeleteAllItems()
    for ix in range(len(self.stories)):
        self.list.InsertStringItem(ix,
                        str(self.stories[ix].get_title()))

    for ix in range(len(self.stories)):
        self.list.SetStringItem(ix, 1,
                        str(self.stories[ix].get_site_title()))

    self.list.SetColumnWidth(0, wxLIST_AUTOSIZE)
    self.list.SetColumnWidth(1, wxLIST_AUTOSIZE)
```

any errors, those are displayed in a separate window, and the status bar goes back to non-busy mode. We turn off the flags in a `finally` block to make sure they come off even if something goes wrong.

Example 26–44. The RSS client main window (17 of 20)

```
def get_stories(self):
    try:
        stories = clientlib.cache.get_old_unread()
        err_handler = clientlib.ErrorRecorder()
        summaries = clientlib.get_summaries(err_handler)
        for summary in summaries:
            for item in summary.get_items():
                story = clientlib.Story(summary, item)
                if clientlib.cache.show(story):
                    stories.append(story)

        self._update_story_list(stories)

        if config.get_show_errors():
            if err_handler._errors != []:
                errwin = ErrorWindow(err_handler._errors, self)
                errwin.Show(true)
    finally:
        self.checking = 0
        self.statusbar.set_state(0)
```

Example 26–45 is the method that actually implements the "New stories" menu item. If the client is already checking for news items, nothing is done. If it is not, internal flags are set, the status bar is set to busy mode (red light), and a new thread is started to read the stories. However, if threading is off, we use `thread_dummy`, which will not start a new thread, but just call the function and wait for it to return.

Example 26–45. The RSS client main window (18 of 20)

```
def ShowStories(self, event):
    if self.checking:
        return

    self.checking = 1
    self.statusbar.set_state(1)
    thread.start_new_thread(self.get_stories, ())
```

Since we set the flags here, we should really have used `try`/`finally` to turn them off again as well, but when threading is on, the `start_new_thread` function will return immediately. So catching whatever exceptions may be raised must be left to the other thread. (See `get_stories` above.)

The method in Example 26–46 is called whenever a story is considered to have been read, to update the cache and the list control.

Example 26–46. The RSS client main window (19 of 20)

```
def __read(self, ix):
    self.tracker.selected.clear()
    clientlib.cache.read(self.stories[ix])
    self.list.DeleteItem(ix)
    del self.stories[ix]
```

The method in Example 26–47 implements the "Mark as read" menu item. Notice how it supports marking of multiple stories by marking them from the bottom up. This is necessary, since the stories

Example 26–47. The RSS client main window (20 of 20)

```
def MarkAsRead(self, event):
    if self.stories == [] or self.tracker.current_ix == None:
        return

    mark = self.tracker.selected.keys()
    mark.sort()
    mark.reverse() # ensure that we delete stuff bottom-up
    for ix in mark:
        self.__read(ix)
```

are identified by indexes, which would otherwise be invalidated when stories are removed.

26.4.3   *The error and source list windows*

Examples 26–48 to 26–54 contain the last two windows of the RSS client application, which are the window used to show errors, as well

Example 26–48. The error window and the source list window (1 of 7)

```
# --- Error window

class ErrorWindow(wxFrame):
    def __init__(self, errors, parent):
        wxFrame.__init__(self, parent, NewId(), "Errors",
                         wxDefaultPosition, wxSize(550, 250))

        list_id = NewId()
        list = wxListCtrl(self, list_id, wxDefaultPosition,
                          wxDefaultSize,
                          wxLC_REPORT|wxSUNKEN_BORDER)

        list.InsertColumn(0, "Error message")

        ix=0
        for error in errors:
            list.InsertStringItem(ix, str(error))
            ix = ix + 1

        list.SetColumnWidth(0, wxLIST_AUTOSIZE)
```

as the window used to show the RSS channels the user has subscribe to. At the very end is also the code that sets up the entire client application and starts it.

The error window in Example 26–48 is relatively simple: it just displays a list of error messages in a list control in a window.

In Example 26–49, we set up the "Add" and "Delete" buttons of the source list window, and hook them up to the methods that implement the actions.

Example 26–49. The error window and the source list window (2 of 7)

```
# --- Sources list window

class SourceListWindow(wxFrame):

    def __init__(self, parent):
        wxFrame.__init__(self, parent, -1, "Sources list",
                         wxDefaultPosition, wxSize(750, 250))
        self.SetAutoLayout(true)

        # --- Buttons

        add_id = NewId()
        addbtn = wxButton(self, add_id, "Add")
        lc = wxLayoutConstraints()
        lc.height.AsIs()
        lc.width.AsIs()
        lc.top.SameAs(self, wxTop, 5)
        lc.left.SameAs(self, wxLeft, 5)
        addbtn.SetConstraints(lc)
        EVT_BUTTON(self, add_id, self.AddButton)

        del_id = NewId()
        delbtn = wxButton(self, del_id, "Delete")
        lc = wxLayoutConstraints()
        lc.top.SameAs(self, wxTop, 5)
        lc.height.AsIs()
        lc.width.AsIs()
        lc.left.RightOf(addbtn, 5)
        delbtn.SetConstraints(lc)
        EVT_BUTTON(self, del_id, self.DelButton)
```

Example 26–50 creates the URL text control and the list control holding the information about the current RSS channels.

Example 26–50. The error window and the source list window (3 of 7)

```
# --- URL field

url = wxTextCtrl(self, -1)
lc = wxLayoutConstraints()
lc.top.SameAs(self, wxTop, 5)
lc.height.AsIs()
lc.left.RightOf(delbtn, 5)
lc.right.SameAs(self, wxRight, 5)
url.SetConstraints(lc)

# --- List

list_id = NewId()
list = wxListCtrl(self, list_id, wxDefaultPosition,
                  wxDefaultSize,
                  wxLC_REPORT|wxSUNKEN_BORDER)

list.InsertColumn(0, "Title")
list.InsertColumn(1, "Description")
list.InsertColumn(2, "URL")

lc = wxLayoutConstraints()
lc.top.Below(addbtn, 5)
lc.left.SameAs(self,wxLeft)
lc.bottom.SameAs(self,wxBottom)
lc.right.SameAs(self,wxRight)
list.SetConstraints(lc)
```

Example 26–51 gets the RSS channel information from `clientlib` and fills it into the list control.

The method in Example 26–52 is called when the "Add" button is activated. Note how it returns immediately if there is no URL. Insertion into `self.sources` also inserts into the `sources` list in `clientlib`, since these two variables actually refer to the same list object.

Example 26–53 is the implementation of the "Delete" button. We use the same trick here that we used when marking stories as read.

Example 26–51. The error window and the source list window (4 of 7)

```
# --- Loading data

sources = clientlib.get_sources()
for ix in range(len(sources)):
    list.InsertStringItem(ix,
                          str(sources[ix].get_title() or ""))
    list.SetStringItem(ix, 1,
                          str(sources[ix].get_descr() or ""))
    list.SetStringItem(ix, 2, str(sources[ix].get_url()))

list.SetColumnWidth(0, wxLIST_AUTOSIZE)
list.SetColumnWidth(1, wxLIST_AUTOSIZE)
list.SetColumnWidth(2, wxLIST_AUTOSIZE)

self.tracker = ListSelectionTracker(list)
```

Example 26–52. The error window and the source list window (5 of 7)

```
# --- Storing internal data

self.sources = sources
self.url = url
self.list = list

def AddButton(self, event):
    url = string.strip(self.url.GetValue())
    if url == "": return
    src = config.Source(url)
    ix = len(self.sources)

    self.list.InsertStringItem(ix, str(src.get_title()))
    self.list.SetStringItem(ix, 1, str(src.get_descr()))
    self.list.SetStringItem(ix, 2, str(src.get_url()))

    # force a resize
    self.list.SetColumnWidth(0, wxLIST_AUTOSIZE)
    self.list.SetColumnWidth(1, wxLIST_AUTOSIZE)
    self.list.SetColumnWidth(2, wxLIST_AUTOSIZE)

    self.sources.append(src)
```

Example 26–53. The error window and the source list window (6 of 7)

```
def DelButton(self, event):
    mark = self.tracker.selected.keys()
    mark.sort()
    mark.reverse() # ensure that we delete stuff bottom-up
    self.tracker.selected.clear()
    for ix in mark:
        self.list.DeleteItem(ix)
        del self.sources[ix]
```

In Example 26–54, we create the wxPython application and enter the wxPython main loop. When we emerge from the main loop, we store our configuration and the clientlib data (essentially the story cache).

Example 26–54. The error window and the source list window (7 of 7)

```
# --- Main program

app = RSSViewer(0)
app.MainLoop()

config.save()
clientlib.save()
```

26.5 | The RSS editor

This is a GUI program, written using wxPython, which allows a user to edit RSS documents. It can load RSS documents, create new RSS documents, and allows documents to be saved. Essentially, what it does is make all possible fields of an RSS document available to the user for editing and saves the results. New items can be added and old ones removed. The code of the application is shown in Examples 26–55 to 26–58.

This application is slightly different from the RSS client, since it accepts a filename as its argument (Example 26–55). This is done so that the editor can accept a file name on the command line and open it directly.

Example 26–55. The RSS editor code (1 of 4)

```
"""A wxPython-based RSS editor.

$Id: rss-editor.py,v 1.3 2001/01/12 08:16:54 larsga Exp $
"""

from wxPython.wx import *
from wxUtils import *
from xml.sax._exceptions import SAXException, SAXParseException
import rsslib, sys

on_windows = sys.platform == "win32"
version    = "0.01"

# --- Application

class RSSEditor(wxApp):

    def __init__(self, arg, file = None):
        self.file = file
        wxApp.__init__(self, arg)

    def OnInit(self):
        frame = EditorWindow(NULL, -1, "RSS-Editor " + str(version))
        frame.Show(true)
        self.SetTopWindow(frame)

        if self.file != None:
            frame.open_file(self.file)

        return true
```

The channel_book (Example 26–56) is the control that is used to create several panels with labels that can be switched between. The "main", "contacts", and "metadata" sections in Example 26–57 each make up one panel.

Example 26–56. The RSS editor code (2 of 4)

```python
# --- Editor window

ID_NEW     = NewId()
ID_OPEN    = NewId()
ID_SAVE    = NewId()
ID_SAVE_AS = NewId()
ID_ABOUT   = NewId()
ID_EXIT    = NewId()


ID_NEW_ITEM = NewId()
ID_DEL_ITEM = NewId()
ID_UP_ITEM  = NewId()
ID_DN_ITEM  = NewId()


ID_ITEM_LIST = NewId()

class EditorWindow(wxFrame):
    def __init__(self, parent, ID, title):
        wxFrame.__init__(self, parent, ID, title,
                         wxDefaultPosition, wxSize(550, 450))

        self.CreateStatusBar()
        self.SetAutoLayout(true)

        # --- Menu

        menu = wxMenu()
        menu.Append(ID_NEW,   "&New file",
                    "Open a file for editing")
        menu.Append(ID_OPEN,  "&Open file...",
                    "Open a file for editing")
        menu.Append(ID_SAVE,  "&Save",
                    "Save the current file")
        menu.Append(ID_SAVE_AS,  "Save &as...",
                    "Save the current file in a specified location")
        menu.AppendSeparator()
        menu.Append(ID_ABOUT, "&About",
                    "Information about the editor")
        menu.Append(ID_EXIT, "E&xit", "Terminate the editor")

        menuBar = wxMenuBar()
        menuBar.Append(menu, "&File");

        self.SetMenuBar(menuBar)
```

```
EVT_MENU(self, ID_NEW,     self.NewDocument)
EVT_MENU(self, ID_OPEN,    self.Open)
EVT_MENU(self, ID_SAVE,    self.Save)
EVT_MENU(self, ID_SAVE_AS, self.SaveAs)
EVT_MENU(self, ID_ABOUT,   self.OnAbout)
EVT_MENU(self, ID_EXIT,    self.TimeToQuit)


# --- File controls

# channel controls
channel_book = wxNotebook(self,-1)
item_panel = wxPanel(self,-1)
lc = wxLayoutConstraints()
lc.top.SameAs(self, wxTop)
lc.height.Absolute(125)
lc.left.SameAs(self, wxLeft)
lc.right.SameAs(self, wxRight)
channel_book.SetConstraints(lc)
```

Example 26–57. The RSS editor code (3 of 4)

```
# main
main_panel = wxPanel(channel_book, -1)
main_panel.SetAutoLayout(true)
putter = RowPairPutter(main_panel)

ctrl = wxTextCtrl(putter.get_parent(), -1, "")
self.title = putter.add_pair("Title: ", ctrl)
ctrl = wxTextCtrl(putter.get_parent(), -1, "")
self.link  = putter.add_pair("Link: ", ctrl)
ctrl = wxTextCtrl(putter.get_parent(), -1, "")
self.descr = putter.add_pair("Description: ", ctrl)

channel_book.AddPage(main_panel, "Main")

# contacts
contacts_panel = wxPanel(channel_book, -1)
contacts_panel.SetAutoLayout(true)
putter = RowPairPutter(contacts_panel)

ctrl = wxTextCtrl(putter.get_parent(),-1,"")
self.editor = putter.add_pair("Editor: ", ctrl)
ctrl = wxTextCtrl(putter.get_parent(),-1,"")
self.webmaster = putter.add_pair("Webmaster: ", ctrl)
```

```
channel_book.AddPage(contacts_panel, "Contacts")

# metadata
meta_panel = wxPanel(channel_book, -1)
meta_panel.SetAutoLayout(true)
putter = RowPairPutter(meta_panel)

ctrl = wxTextCtrl(putter.get_parent(),-1,"")
self.lang = putter.add_pair("Language: ", ctrl)
ctrl = wxTextCtrl(putter.get_parent(),-1,"")
self.rating = putter.add_pair("Rating: ", ctrl)
ctrl = wxTextCtrl(putter.get_parent(),-1,"")
self.copyright = putter.add_pair("Copyright: ", ctrl)

channel_book.AddPage(meta_panel, "Metadata")

# item controls
# item_panel created higher up
item_panel.SetAutoLayout(true)
lc = wxLayoutConstraints()
lc.top.SameAs(channel_book, wxBottom)
lc.bottom.SameAs(self, wxBottom)
lc.left.SameAs(self, wxLeft)
lc.right.SameAs(self, wxRight)
item_panel.SetConstraints(lc)

items = wxListCtrl(item_panel, ID_ITEM_LIST,
                   wxDefaultPosition, wxDefaultSize,
                   wxLC_REPORT | wxSUNKEN_BORDER)
items.InsertColumn(0, "Title")
text_panel = wxPanel(item_panel, -1)
lc = wxLayoutConstraints()
lc.top.SameAs(item_panel, wxTop)
lc.bottom.SameAs(text_panel, wxTop)
lc.left.SameAs(item_panel, wxLeft)
lc.right.SameAs(item_panel, wxRight)
items.SetConstraints(lc)

# text_panel created above
button_panel = wxPanel(item_panel, -1)
text_panel.SetAutoLayout(true)
lc = wxLayoutConstraints()
lc.height.Absolute(70)
lc.bottom.SameAs(item_panel, wxBottom)
lc.left.SameAs(item_panel, wxLeft)
lc.right.SameAs(button_panel, wxLeft)
text_panel.SetConstraints(lc)
```

```
putter = RowPairPutter(text_panel)
ctrl = wxTextCtrl(putter.get_parent(),-1,""))
title = putter.add_pair("Title: ", ctrl)
ctrl = wxTextCtrl(putter.get_parent(),-1,"")
link = putter.add_pair("Link: ", ctrl)
ctrl = wxTextCtrl(putter.get_parent(), -1, "",
                  wxDefaultPosition, wxDefaultSize,
                  wxTE_MULTILINE))
descr  = putter.add_pair("Description: ", ctrl)

# button_panel created above
button_panel.SetAutoLayout(true)
lc=wxLayoutConstraints()
lc.height.SameAs(text_panel, wxHeight)
lc.bottom.SameAs(item_panel, wxBottom)
lc.width.Absolute(70)
lc.right.SameAs(item_panel, wxRight)
button_panel.SetConstraints(lc)
put = RowPutter(button_panel).put
new = put(wxButton(button_panel, ID_NEW_ITEM, "New"))
delete = put(wxButton(button_panel, ID_DEL_ITEM, "Delete"))
up = put(wxButton(button_panel, ID_UP_ITEM, "Up"))
down = put(wxButton(button_panel, ID_DN_ITEM, "Down"))

EVT_BUTTON(new, ID_NEW_ITEM, self.NewItem)
EVT_BUTTON(delete, ID_DEL_ITEM, self.DelItem)
EVT_BUTTON(up, ID_UP_ITEM, self.UpItem)
EVT_BUTTON(down, ID_DN_ITEM, self.DownItem)

# --- Internal data
self.file = None

self.ss = rsslib.SiteSummary(None)
TMC = TextMethodConnector # short-hand
self.titlec = TMC(self.ss, "title", self.title)
self.linkc = TMC(self.ss, "link", self.link)
self.descrc = TMC(self.ss, "description", self.descr)
self.editorc = TMC(self.ss, "managing_editor", self.editor)
self.masterc = TMC(self.ss, "web_master", self.webmaster)
self.langc = TMC(self.ss, "language", self.lang)
self.ratingc = TMC(self.ss, "rating", self.rating)
self.copyrightc = TMC(self.ss, "copyright", self.copyright)
```

The connector objects are objects that link an attribute in an object (the first two parameters) with an editing control, handling the events and updates automatically (Example 26–58).

Example 26–58. The RSS editor code (4 of 4)

```
        # pub_date
        # last_build_date
        # docs
        # skip_days
        # skip_hours

        item = rsslib.Item("", "")
        self.itemc = ListConnector(self.ss.get_items(), items,
          lambda c,ix,it: c.InsertStringItem(ix,str(it.get_title())))

        self.itemc.subconnectors = \
            [TextMethodConnector(item, "title", title, self.itemc),
             TextMethodConnector(item, "link", link),
             TextMethodConnector(item, "description", descr)]

    # --- Actions

    def NewDocument(self, event):
        self.connect(rsslib.SiteSummary(None))

    def NewItem(self, event):
        self.itemc.add(0, rsslib.Item("[New]", "", ""))

    def DelItem(self, event):
        self.itemc.delete_selected()

    def UpItem(self, event):
        ix = self.itemc.tracker.current_ix
        if ix == None or ix < 1:
            return

        self.itemc.exchange(ix,ix-1)
        self.itemc.select(ix-1)
        self.itemc.unselect(ix)
```

```
def DownItem(self, event):
    ix = self.itemc.tracker.current_ix
    if ix == None or ix+1 >= len(self.ss.items):
        return

    self.itemc.exchange(ix,ix+1)
    self.itemc.select(ix+1)
    self.itemc.unselect(ix)

def Open(self, event):
    if on_windows:
        wildcards = "RSS documents (*.rss)|*.rss|" \
                    "RSS documents (*.rdf)|*.rdf|" \
                    "RSS documents (*.xml)|*.xml|" \
                    "All files (*.*)|*.*"
    else:
        wildcards = "*.rss"

    file = wxFileSelector("Choose a file to open", "", "", "",
                          wildcards, wxOPEN | wxHIDE_READONLY)
    if file == "": return
    self.open_file(file)

def SaveAs(self, event):
    if self.ss == None: return
    file = wxFileSelector("Choose a file to save in", "", "",
                          "", "", wxSAVE | wxOVERWRITE_PROMPT)
    if file == "": return
    self.file = file
    self.Save(None)

def Save(self, event):
    if self.ss == None: return
    file = self.file or wxFileSelector(
                          "Choose a file to save in", "", "",
                          "", "", wxSAVE | wxOVERWRITE_PROMPT)
    if file == "":
        return

    rsslib.write_rss_091(self.ss, self.file)

    self.file = file
```

```
def OnAbout(self, event):
    dlg = wxMessageDialog(self, "A simple RSS file editor.\n\n"+
                          "Version: " + version + "\n" +
                          "rsslib version: " + rsslib.version +
                          "\n",
                          "About RSS-Editor",
                          wxOK | wxICON_INFORMATION)
    dlg.ShowModal()
    dlg.Destroy()

def TimeToQuit(self, event):
    self.Close(true)

# --- Internal functions

def connect(self, ss):
    self.ss = ss
    self.titlec.set_object(self.ss)
    self.linkc.set_object(self.ss)
    self.descrc.set_object(self.ss)
    self.editorc.set_object(self.ss)
    self.masterc.set_object(self.ss)
    self.langc.set_object(self.ss)
    self.ratingc.set_object(self.ss)
    self.copyrightc.set_object(self.ss)

    self.itemc.set_list(self.ss.get_items())

def open_file(self, file):
    try:
        self.connect(rsslib.load_rss(file))
        self.file = file
    except SAXParseException, e:
        wxMessageBox("Parse error: %s on %s:%s"
                     % (e.getMessage(),
                        e.getLineNumber(),
                        e.getColumnNumber()),
                        "Error")
    except Exception, e:
        wxMessageBox(str(e), "Error")
```

```
# --- Main program

if len(sys.argv) > 1:
    file = sys.argv[1]
else:
    file = None

app = RSSEditor(0, file)
app.MainLoop()
```

Figure 26–3 shows a screenshot of the editor under wxGTK on Linux.

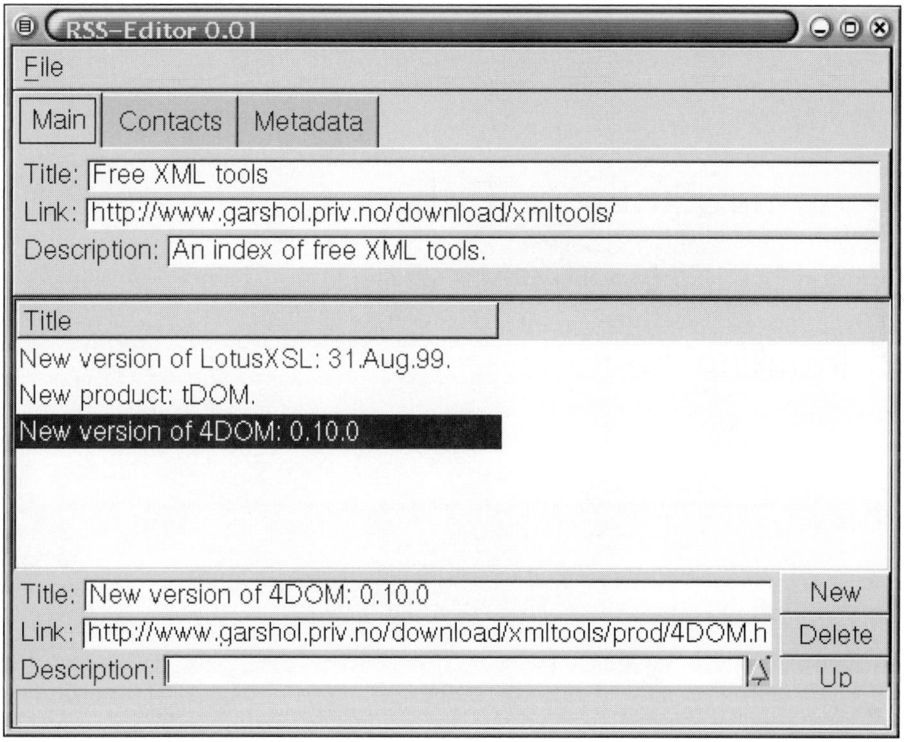

Figure 26–3   The RSS editor

Appendices

- An introduction to Python

- An XML glossary

- Installing the tools

Part Seven

A lightning introduction to Python

- Introducing Python
- Classes and objects
- Useful APIs

Appendix
A

S ince Python is not familiar to most programmers, and we consider this book to be useful even for developers who do not intend to do their programming in Python, this appendix provides an introduction to Python for readers unfamiliar with the language. The intention is that they should learn enough of the language to at least understand the Python examples in this book.

Since it is the principles and concepts described in this book that are really important, this appendix provides enough information to make it possible for non-Python programmers to understand the book. Anyone interested in learning more about Python is referred to the Python book list at `http://www.python.org/psa/bookstore/`. The Python interpreter comes with a tutorial as part of its documentation collection that can also be useful.[1]

This book takes into account that you may be using any of versions 1.5.2, 1.6, 2.0, or 2.1, and describes the differences where they are important.

---

1.   This was how I learned Python myself, way back in 1997.

A.1 | A quick introduction

Python is in many ways an unusual language, combining as it does many features of the traditional scripting languages with those from more respected full-scale programming languages. The result is a language that is extraordinarily easy to program in and that, at the same time, scales very well. Most likely this has to do with Python's ancestry. Python is based on ABC, which was a programming language designed for use in teaching, so readability and predictability have always been important design principles in the evolution of Python. This keeps the language simple and contributes to making it easy to program in.

Python has a very simple syntax and a rather simple execution model where the same principles have been applied everywhere, which has led to a language with remarkable orthogonality. What you can do with variables you can also expect to do with functions, classes, and modules, in exactly the same way. This lack of surprises is perhaps one of the nicest things about the language.

As for making the language scale to large programs, that seems to be a natural consequence of the fact that Python has all the features full programming languages have, but at a higher level of abstraction. This, combined with the overall clean design and readability, makes large-scale development much easier than in many other scripting languages.

The Python execution model is similar to that of many other so-called scripting languages in that Python is an interpreted language. Programs are compiled to byte-code for a stack-based virtual machine and afterwards executed on it, something that gives reasonable performance and makes the language extraordinarily dynamic. A somewhat unusual feature about Python is that it can be used interactively through the interpreter. It is possible to start the interpreter and execute statements directly in it, as shown in Example A–1.

While unusual, this feature is extremely convenient since it makes it possible to quickly test how Python and Python modules work by just starting the interpreter and trying them out. I strongly recommend that when reading this tutorial you keep the Python interpreter available so that you can try out what you read immediately. That will enable

Example A–1. Interaction with the Python interpreter

```
Python 1.5.2 (#0, Jul 11 1999) [MSC 32 bit (Intel)] on win32
Copyright 1991-1995 Stichting Mathematisch Centrum, Amsterdam
>>> 1 + 2
3
>>> a = 3 * (4 + 5)
>>> a + 2
29
```

you at once to get answers to many of the questions you are likely to have. An explanation of how to install Python is found in C.1, "The Python interpreter," on page 1111.

Finally, an extremely important feature of the language is the standard libraries that come with the interpreter. These contain almost unbelievable riches for any programmer. Anything from HTTP servers to file compression and Python byte-code decompilation can be found in this library. Before writing anything that is not meant to be a purely educational exercise in Python, you should read through the list of library modules, and you should revisit it regularly. This *will* save you much effort later on.

A.2 | Basic building blocks

Unlike many programming languages, Python does not require the source code of programs to be "wrapped" in any form of "container." Pascal, for example, requires PROGRAM statement, C, a function, and Java, a class with a method. In Python, the code can just be written directly, which means that the line `print "Hello, world!"` is an entire program in itself.

To run it, write the program in your favorite text editor[1] and save it in a file, which you may call for example `hello.py`.

How to run this program is platform-dependent, and several development environments have easier ways to run programs, but on Windows and Unix a common way is to use the command line. Go to the directory where the hello.py script resides, make sure Python is on your path, say `python hello.py` and watch your first Python script greet the world.

Note that the IDLE development environment, which comes with the Python interpreter, can be very useful as a Python development environment. Emacs is, of course, also a very good alternative.[2]

A.2.1   *Variables, values, and types*

In Python, variables do not have types, but values do. In other words, the type is a property of a value, and any variable can refer to any value, regardless of the type of that value. Also, variables are dynamic and can be created and deleted at will. Unlike most other programming languages, Python does *not* have static scoping. This can be slightly awkward at times, but also has its benefits, and one quickly learns to adapt to it.

The interpreter dialog in Example A–2 may illustrate this.

This example shows how the variable a is not initially defined, so trying to use it results in an error. Assigning the value 2 to it creates the variable, so that trying to evaluate it again yields the value 2. It is then deleted with the `del a` statement, which causes later accesses to the variable to fail.

---

1. Note that Python comes with a development environment called IDLE that also has a text editor. This environment can be found in the Tools/IDLE directory of the Python distribution. Another editor much used for Python programming is Emacs, for which there is a major mode on the CD-ROM.

2. This book was written entirely in Emacs.

Example A–2. Using variables

```
>>> a
Traceback (innermost last):
  File "<stdin>", line 1, in ?
NameError: a
>>> a = 2
>>> a
2
>>> a + 2
4
>>> del a
>>> a
Traceback (innermost last):
  File "<stdin>", line 1, in ?
NameError: a
>>>
```

A.2.2 *Numeric types*

Python has four numeric types:

- *integers*, which are in reality C `longs`, with the same limitations on size. On 32-bit machines these can generally hold numbers in the range `-2147483648` to `2147483647`;
- *floats*, which are C `doubles`, with the same precision limits as C `doubles`;
- *long integers*, whose size is in theory unlimited. They work exactly like the numeric types, but long integer literals are written with a trailing `L`, as in `42L`;
- *complex numbers*, which also work like the other numbers and are written `1 + 2j`. The imaginary component is stored in `number.imag`, while the real component is stored in `number.real`. Complex numbers are not used in this book, so I will not speak any more about them here.

Numeric expressions in Python are as in most other programming languages (Example A–3). Parentheses and the operators +, -, *, and

/ work as you would expect them to in most other languages, with one exception: if both arguments to / are integers the result will also be a truncated integer. The ** operator is the power operator, while % is modulo.

Example A–3. Using numbers in Python

```
>>> 1 + 2 * 3
7
>>> 1.0 + 1
2.0
>>> 2 / 3
0
>>> 3 ** 2
9
>>> 271 % 2
1
>>> 2L ** 70
1180591620717411303424L
>>> (1 + 2j) * 3
(3+6j)
```

Below are the most important built-in functions that are used with numbers:

abs(x)
   Returns the absolute value of the number.

float(x)
   Converts x to a float; x can be a number or a string.

int(x)
   Converts x to an integer; x can be a number or a string.

long(x)
   Converts x to a long integer; x can be a number or a string.

```
round(x, n = 0)
```
Rounds x to n decimals. The n = 0 in the function signature means that the n parameter is optional, and defaults to 0.

See also the `math` library module, which has many useful mathematical functions and constants. The `random` library module has functionality for generating and using random numbers. On some platforms, the `mpz` module provides fast unlimited-precision integers and floats.

A.2.3 *Strings*

Python prior to version 2.0 had only one string type, which is immutable. This means that the value of a string can never be changed, just like in Java. Instead, string variables must be made to refer to a new string object[1] if they are to change. The expression a = a + b will, if a and b are both strings, cause a new string object containing a followed by b to be created and a to be made to refer to the new object.

In version 2.0 Unicode strings were introduced. These can hold Unicode data. There are several different string literal syntaxes:

`"..."`

Ordinary string literals, which may not span lines. Escape sequences like \n, \\, \", and \t may be used in these strings.

`'...'`

Ordinary string literals, just like the `"..."` variety. Useful for strings that contain double quotes, but not single ones.

`"""..."""` **or** `'''...'''`

Long string literals, which may span any number of lines. Escape sequences work normally, and single and double quotes can freely

---

1. Note that in Python the term *object* refers to any value, while the term *instance object* is used for objects that are instances of a class.

be used inside these literals. Long string literals are mostly used for documentation strings (see A.5.7, "Documentation strings," on page 1095) and various kinds of large string templates.

u"..." **or** u'...'

Unicode string literals, which may not span lines. Escape sequences work normally, but in addition \u*XXXX* escape sequences may be used. These refer to Unicode characters by code point, where *XXXX* is a hexadecimal number.

r"..." **or** r'...'

Raw string literals, where backslash escape sequences do not work. This is useful for strings that contain backslashes, such as Windows directory paths or regular expressions.

Note that Python does not have a distinct type for single characters. Instead, these are represented as strings of length 1. In fact, strings behave as sequences (see the next section) of such single-character strings. This means that the + operator, the slice operator, and all the other machinery for sequences described in the next section also work for strings.

Two very important functions for working with strings are str(x) and repr(x). These take any object and convert it to a string. The str function creates a human-friendly version, while repr creates a representation that shows more clearly the raw details of the object's composition, which may be useful for debugging.

One very convenient operator for strings is the % operator, which can be used to fill in string templates in a manner similar to that of the C printf function. The expression a % b evaluates to a string by using a as a template where values from b are filled in; b is usually a tuple, but can also be a dictionary. Example A–4 shows how to use this operator.

Example A–4. The Python % string operator

```
>>> "%s expects %s" % ("Nobody", "The Spanish Inquisition")
'Nobody expects The Spanish Inquisition'
>>> "%s is %d years old" % ("LMG", 25)
'LMG is 25 years old'
>>> "%s is %d years old" % ("LMG", "25")
Traceback (innermost last):
  File "<stdin>", line 1, in ?
TypeError: illegal argument type for built-in operation
>>> "Dear %(recip)s, please send %(amount)s to %(address)s ASAP. " \
    "Thank you" % \
... {"address" : "larsga@garshol.priv.no", "amount" : "NOK 25000",
... "recip" : "reader"}
'Dear reader, please send NOK 25000 to larsga@garshol.priv.no ASAP.
Thank you'
```

Below is a list of the main functions used with strings:

chr(i)

Creates a single-character string that contains the character with the given code point in the system default character set. See also ord and unichr.

intern(s)

Enters the string in the global string interning table, if it is not there already, and returns the table entry. Calling this function on two strings with the same value will always return the exact same object.

len(s)

Returns the length of the string s. This is a general sequence function that also happens to work for strings.

ord(c)

Returns the code point in the system default character set of the single character in the string c. This is the reverse of chr, but also works for Unicode strings.

```
unichr(i)
```
Returns a single-character Unicode string that contains the Unicode character with the given code point.

```
unicode(str, encoding = 'utf-8')
```
Converts `str` to a Unicode string, assuming that it is in the character encoding specified by the `encoding` argument.

The `string` library module contains many extremely useful functions, especially `split` and `join`. It is described in A.5.1, "The `string` module," on page 1086. The `re` module contains the regular expression library. Note also the `StringIO` module.

A.2.4   *No value*

Python has a special value called `None`, which is used to represent the concept of "no value". A variable that exists, but has no value yet, will usually be set to `None`. This value is written `None` in programs, and is exactly the same as `null` in Java, `NULL` in C/C++, and `nil` in Scheme and Common Lisp.

A.2.5   *Truth values*

One type that may seem to be missing is the boolean type. This does not exist in Python, and instead any kind of object can be evaluated to see whether it evaluates as `true` or `false`. `None`, 0, an empty string, an empty list, an empty dictionary, and an empty tuple all count as `false`, and all other values as `true`.

There are no truth value literals (like the `true` and `false` of Java), but you can always define your own if you so wish. Traditionally, 0 has been used to mean `false`, and 1 to mean `true`.

The comparison operators in Python are the same as in C: <, >, <=, >=, != (meaning inequality), and ==, meaning equality, as distinct from =, which is used for assignment. The `is` operator checks whether two objects are identical (rather than merely equal). A little interpreter dialog in Example A–5 may help make this clearer.

Example A–5. Identity versus equality

```
>>> "ab" == "a" + "b"
1
>>> "ab" is "a" + "b"
0
>>> intern("ab") is intern("a" + "b")
1
```

A.2.6   *Sequence types*

In Python there is a general concept of *sequence types*. Sequence types are containers that may contain values of any type in a specific order. Python has two sequence types: lists and tuples, and it is possible for the developer to define new ones. Sequences can be accessed by a numeric index, just like an array. Neither lists nor tuples are exactly like arrays, however. Lists differ from arrays in that they can grow and shrink dynamically, and so are very similar to the `java.util.Vector` class of Java. Tuples differ in that once created they cannot be modified at all. Note that you can also define your own kinds of sequences using objects (see below).

List literals are written in square brackets: `[1, 2, 3, 4]`. When accessing a specific index in a list, the index is given using the same square brackets: `list[index]`. In addition to accessing single indexes it is possible to use slices to extract parts of a list: `list[first_index : last_index]`. This creates a new list, consisting of the items from the first index (inclusive) to the last index (exclusive). Negative indexes are considered to refer to elements starting with the last one. So `list[-1]` is the last element, `list[-2]` the second last, and so on.

All sequence types in Python, including lists, tuples, and strings, use zero-based indexes. This means that `list[0]` refers to the first element in a list, while `list[1]` refers to the second.

The `in` operator can be used to check whether a value occurs in a list or not, as in: `5 in list`. It returns `true` if the value is found, `false` otherwise.

The `del` statement is used to remove elements from sequences that support it, which tuples do not, but lists do.

Example A–6 demonstrates how to use Python lists.

Example A–6. How to use Python lists

```
>>> list = [1, 2, 3, "hello", 5, "Python", -200]
>>> list[0]
1
>>> list[1]
2
>>> list[-1]
-200
>>> list[-2]
'Python'
>>> list[200]
Traceback (innermost last):
  File "<stdin>", line 1, in ?
IndexError: list index out of range
>>> list[2 : 3]
[3]
>>> list[1 : -1]
[2, 3, 'hello', 5, 'Python']
>>> list[3] = 4
>>> list
[1, 2, 3, 4, 5, 'Python', -200]
>>> del list[1]
>>> list
[1, 3, 4, 5, 'Python', -200]
```

Lists, like objects, also have methods that can be called using ordinary method call syntax: `list.method(para1, para2)`. These methods are:

`append(value)`

Inserts the value at the end of the list, growing it by one element.

`count(value)`
> Counts the number of occurrences of the given value in the list.

`index(value)`
> Returns the index of the first occurrence of the given value in the list, raising an exception if no such value is found.

`insert(index, value)`
> Inserts the given value in front of the value at `index`.

`pop()`
> Removes the last value of the list and returns it.

`remove(value)`
> Removes the first occurrence of `value` in the list, raising an exception if the value is not found in the list.

`reverse()`
> Reverses the contents of the list.

`sort([cmpfunc])`
> Sorts the contents of the list. The optional `cmpfunc` argument is a comparison function that takes two values and returns -1, 0, or 1 if the first value is smaller than, equal to, or larger than the second.

Except from the fact that they cannot be modified in any way, tuples behave nearly identically to lists. The literal syntax uses ordinary parentheses: `(5, 7)`. Tuples are perfect for representing a group of objects that belong together in a single place, such as in the return value from a function or a value in a list. Indexes and slices work exactly the same way on tuples as on lists.

A very useful feature with sequences is unpacking: `(x, y) = (1, 2)` will result in x being set to 1 and y being set to 2. This works with all kinds of sequences and can even be nested: `(x, (y, z)) = (1, (2, 3))`. Note, however, that the number of variables and elements must match exactly, or the unpacking will fail with an exception.

There are a number of useful functions that work on sequences:

`filter(function, list)`
> Takes a function and a list and returns a list consisting of only those elements in the original list that the function returned `true` for.

`len(s)`
> Returns the number of elements in the sequence.

`list(s)`
> Returns a list containing the elements of the sequence. This can be used to turn a tuple or another kind of sequence into a list.

`map(function, list)`
> Takes a function and a list and returns a new list where each element in the original list is replaced with the result of calling the function on that element. For example, `map(str, [1, 2, 3])` will produce `['1', '2', '3']`.

`range([start,] stop[, step])`
> Creates a list of integers, beginning with `start` (or 0 if `start` is omitted) and ending with the last element smaller than `stop`. The `step` value, which defaults to 1, gives the increments. Thus `range(2)` produces `[0, 1, 2]` and `range(1,3)` produces `[1, 2]`, while `range(1, 10, 3)` gives `[1, 4, 7]`.

`reduce(function, list)`
> Takes a function of two parameters and a list and returns the result of using the function to combine the elements of the list. For example, the `operator` module contains the function `add`, which adds together its two parameters. Thus, `reduce(operator.add, [1, 2, 3])` returns 6, which is the sum of the elements of the list. This can also be seen as the result of doing `operator.add(operator.add(1, 2), 3)`.

`tuple(sequence)`
> Returns a tuple containing the elements of the sequence. This can be used for converting lists and other kinds of sequences into tuples.

`xrange([start,] stop [,step]`
> This function has the exact same semantics as `range`, except that it does not create the list all at once. Instead, it creates an object that mimics a sequence by calculating the numbers when they are accessed, instead of storing them all at the same time. The advantage is that it saves memory when the sequence is very large, and especially when not all elements are accessed.

The `operator` module contains a number of functions that are very useful in combination with `map` and `reduce`.

A.2.7 *Dictionaries*

Python also supports *dictionaries*, known as hashes to Perl hackers and associative arrays to language theorists, which map *keys* to *values*. This is an extremely useful feature that makes programming much easier by making it easy to create maps from one set of values to another. Dictionary literals are written using curly braces, and access uses square brackets, just like sequences. The `del` statement is used to remove values.

Example A–7 shows how to use dictionaries in Python.

Example A–7. Using dictionaries in Python

```
>>> dict = {"no" : "Norway", "uk" : "United Kingdom",
... "tv" : "Tuvalu"}
>>> dict["tv"]
'Tuvalu'
>>> del dict["uk"]
>>> dict
{'no': 'Norway', 'tv': 'Tuvalu'}
```

Like lists, dictionaries also have methods that allow different kinds of access to their contents:

`clear()`
> Empties the dictionary by removing all items from it.

`copy()`
> Creates a copy of the dictionary with the exact same contents. That is, the contents of the original dictionary are not copied, just referenced again from the new dictionary.

`get(key, alternative = None)`
> Returns the value associated with the `key` if it is found in the dictionary, otherwise the `alternative` is returned.

`has_key(key)`
> Returns `true` if the key is found in the dictionary, `false` otherwise.

`items()`
> Returns a list of tuples of the form `(key, value)` for each key, value pair in the dictionary. The order is unpredictable.

`keys()`
> Returns a list of keys in unpredictable order.

`update(b)`
> Writes all the key, value pairs in `b` (which must be a dictionary) into the dictionary, overwriting old values if necessary.

`values()`
> Returns a list of all the values in the dictionary, again in unpredictable order.

An interpreter dialog showing how to use these methods is given in Example A–8.

Example A–8. Using Python dictionary methods

```
>>> dict.has_key("zz")
0
>>> dict.get("zz", "Unknown")
'Unknown'
>>> dict.items()
[('no', 'Norway'), ('tv', 'Tuvalu')]
>>> dict.keys()
['no', 'tv']
>>> dict.values()
['Norway', 'Tuvalu']
>>> dict.copy()
{'no': 'Norway', 'tv': 'Tuvalu'}
>>> dict.clear()
>>> dict
{}
```

A.2.8 *Statements*

Python has all the traditional statements, like `if`, `while`, and `for`. In
Python, the syntax of `if` is as shown in Example A–9.

Example A–9. The Python `if` statement

```
if condition:
  block
elif condition:
  block
else:
  block
```

A peculiarity of the Python syntax is that unlike most other languages,
the block structure is given by indentation. This means that a statement
like the one in Example A–10 is complete and perfectly legal.

There are several advantages to this way of doing things, the most
obvious being that there is less to type. Another is that everyone is
forced to write things the same way, thus avoiding the interminable
debates about where to put the curly braces.

Example A–10. Python block structure

```
if hungry:
    food = Steak()
    food.prepare()
    food.eat()
```

One problem with the indentation-based syntax is that if tabs are used in source code, confusion may occur if there is disagreement as to how many spaces each tab is equivalent to. When resolving indentation, Python will replace each tab character from left to right by looking at the spaces before the first tab and making sure that the number of spaces after replacement is a multiple of eight. This means that `' \t\t'` (one space, two tabs) and `' \t \t'` (two spaces, one tab, one space, one tab) are both equivalent to 16 spaces when the interpreter reads the source.

You are recommended to not mix tabs and spaces at all in your source code, but to stick strictly to one or the other. If you think you may have problems of this kind with your source, you can use the `tabnanny` module in the standard Python library to check your source files. If you use IDLE or Emacs for development, you will generally be safe, since these interpret tabs in exactly the same way as Python.

Python also has the familiar `while` statement, which allows us to improve the above example somewhat, as shown in Example A–11.

Example A–11. The Python `while` loop

```
food = Dinner()
while self.hungry() and not food.all_eaten():
  piece = food.get_piece()
  piece.eat()
```

The `for` statement also exists in Python, but has somewhat unusual semantics: it can only iterate over a sequence, assigning each element in the sequence to the controlled variable for each iteration, as Example A–12 demonstrates. This may sound inconvenient, but in practice it has turned out not to be.

Example A–12. The Python `for` loop

```
for dish in dishwasher.contents():
  cupboard.put_inside(dish)
```

To make these loop statements more convenient to use, Python provides the two statements, `break` (which terminates the innermost loop) and `continue` (which jumps immediately to the next iteration of the loop).

Note that `if`, `for`, and `while` all require at least one statement in their body parts, which can be inconvenient during development if one wants to comment out the body of one of these statements or don't know what to write there just yet. Hence, the code in Example A–13 is invalid and will cause a syntax error.

Example A–13. Illegal `for` statement

```
for dish in dishwasher.contents():
  # cupboard.put_inside(dish)
```

Python has the `pass` statement, which has the same meaning as the `empty;` statement of C, C++, and Java, specifically to avoid this problem. It does nothing, so the illegal code fragment above can be legally rewritten as shown in Example A–14.

Example A–14. Using the `pass` statement

```
for dish in dishwasher.contents():
  # cupboard.put_inside(dish)
  pass
```

A.2.9 *Functions*

Functions are the most basic means of abstraction provided by Python, and many simple programs do not use anything more than what has been explained so far, plus functions. In Python, functions are defined with the def keyword, as shown in Example A–15.

Example A–15. Function definition

```
def square(x):
  return x * x
```

This defines a function named square of one argument named x that returns the square of x. If x is not a number, the function will fail with an exception. The return keyword is used to return a value from a function at any point in its body. If return does not appear in the function or if it appears with no value after it the function will not return any value at all.[1] Many languages (especially descendants of Algol 60) do not consider such functions to be functions at all, but call them procedures. Python makes no such distinction. Example A–16 shows a function that returns no values.

Example A–16. A function with no return value

```
def error(message):
  print "ERROR:", message
  sys.exit(1) # causes the Python interpreter to stop execution
```

In Python, functions can have optional arguments, which can be a very convenient way of simplifying function signatures for their users by specifying sensible defaults for arguments that are often not needed. This can be done by listing the parameter as follows: param =

---

1. At least that is the common way to think of the situation. In reality, the interpreter will cause None to be returned.

`default`. In Example A–16 we might want the user of the function to be able to specify the error code returned to the operating system by `exit` in the rare cases where that is wanted, without requiring it.

Example A–17 shows how to specify a Python function with optional parameters.

Example A–17. A Python function with optional parameters

```
def error(message, code = 1):
  print "ERROR:", message
  sys.exit(code) # causes the Python interpreter to stop execution
```

Python's scope rules are a bit peculiar and may require some explanation. When a variable name is used, it will first match the local variable with that name if there is one, and the global variable with the same name if there is not. However, apart from function parameters there is no way to declare a variable to be local, but assigning to it within the function (even after its first use) will make Python consider it local. Since this would otherwise make it impossible to assign to global variables inside functions, the `global` statement can be used to declare a variable to have global scope inside a function. Example A–18 demonstrates the scope rules.

These scope rules may sound complex, but in general you will find that you hardly ever need to think about them. The only problem is that sometimes forgetting `global` statements may cause long bug hunts before you realize your mistake.

In line with Python's principle of orthogonality, functions are values just like anything else. Just using the name of a function without the parentheses behind it will give you a reference to the function. This can then be stuffed into a variable, a list, a tuple, a dictionary, or passed as a parameter to a function, just like any other kind of value.

Example A–18. Python's scope rules

```
a = 0

def test1():
    a = 1
    print "test1, a:", a

def test2():
    print "test2, a:", a

def test3():
    print "test2, a:", a
    a = 14

def test4():
    global a
    print "test2, a:", a
    a = 14

test1() # prints 1, because a is local due to the assignment
test2() # prints 0, because a is global (no assignment)
# test3() fails with a NameError exception, because a is local (due
#         to the assignment in the second line), but used before it
#         is initialized
test4() # prints 0, because a is declared to be global, also sets
        # global a to 14
test1() # prints 1, since a is local
test2() # prints 14, since a is global and global a has been
        # modified
```

A.3 | An example program

Now that we have covered the fundamentals of Python, you are probably struggling to digest all the information you have absorbed in the last few pages. In this section we develop a small Python program using the constructs explained so far in order to help you understand how all these pieces fit together. The example I have chosen is to parse a Web server log. Nearly all Web servers can be configured to write a log showing what they are doing. Web servers that produce the log notation we will parse here (known as the NCSA log format) simply write one line to a file every time it receives a request from some Web client. Our application will parse this file and count the number of hits to each page, producing an HTML report with statistics.

The NCSA log notation contains one line per request, as shown in Example A–19. (Note that the lines have been broken where the \ has been inserted to make this example readable.)

Example A–19. An NCSA log extract

```
195.0.222.227 - - [02/Sep/1999:06:44:40 +0200] "GET / \
   HTTP/1.0" 200 1441
195.0.222.227 - - [02/Sep/1999:06:44:40 +0200] "GET /p_/ZopeButton \
   HTTP/1.0" 200 9491
195.0.222.227 - - [02/Sep/1999:06:44:46 +0200] "GET /QuickStart/ \
   HTTP/1.0" 200 3253
195.0.222.227 - - [02/Sep/1999:06:44:46 +0200] "GET /p_/pl \
   HTTP/1.0" 200 1068
```

The first part is the address of the host from which the request came, followed by date and time (with time zone) inside square brackets. After that comes the first line of the request inside double quotes (this is the part that contains the reference to the document the client requested), followed by the HTTP response code (200 means that the request was successful) and the number of bytes transmitted from server to client.

The high-level structure of the program will be as shown in Example A–20.

The main program (Examples A–21 to A–25) is the easiest part to write. It will simply get the file name of the log file from the command line and pass it to read_logfile. To do this we use the sys module, which has the command-line arguments used to invoke the Python script as a list in its argv variable (Example A–21).

With this in hand we can write the read_logfile function (Example A–22).

Now that read_logfile has been taken care of, we can write process_request to handle the updating of the global variables with

Example A–20. A Web server log reader

```
# --- Global variables

total_hits   = 0
hits_by_page = {}   # maps a document URL to the hit count
                    # for that document

# --- Functions

def read_logfile(filename):
    pass # reads the log file, calling process_request for each line

def process_request(host, user, passwd, date, timezone, method, url,
                    protocol, code, bytes):
    pass # updates the global variables based on the request data

def produce_report():
    pass # prints the HTML report

# --- Main program

read_logfile(filename)
produce_report()
```

Example A–21. Counting page hits (1 of 5)

```
import sys

if len(sys.argv) != 2:  # script name is sys.argv[0]
    print "Usage: %s <log file name>" % sys.argv[0]
    sys.exit(1)

read_logfile(sys.argv[1])
produce_report()
```

the information from the current request (Example A–23). The pro-cess_request function must first of all check whether the request was successful. Only HTTP response codes of the form "2xx" or "3xx" signal successful requests. Also, many requests will be for server-side scripts, and in these cases the URL may contain the parameters to the scripts (a ? character will separate the URL from the parameters).

Example A–22. Counting page hits (2 of 5)

```
def read_logfile(filename):
    inf = open(filename)     # open file, set inf to file object

    line = inf.readline()    # read first line of file
    while line != "":        # readline() gives "" at end-of-file

        # string.split returns a list of whitespace-separated
        # fragments
        fields = string.split(line)

        # here we call process_request,
        # passing on the interesting fragments
        process_request(fields[0], fields[3], fields[4], fields[5],
                        fields[6], fields[7], fields[8], fields[9])

        line = inf.readline()

    inf.close()
```

Example A–23. Counting page hits (3 of 5)

```
def process_request(host, date, timezone, method, url, protocol,
                    code, bytes):
    global total_hits        # is assigned to, so decl. is needed

    if code > "399": return  # request was not successful,
                             # so don't count it

    total_hits = total_hits + 1

    # split url string on "?", and set url to first fragment, thus
    # discarding script parameters, if any
    url = string.split(url, "?")[0]

    if hits_by_page.has_key(url):
        hits_by_page[url] = hits_by_page[url] + 1
    else:
        hits_by_page[url] = 1
```

However, we want to consider the script a single "page" or "document," so process_request must strip out any script parameters.

If we run the program at this stage it will correctly accumulate its statistics in the global variables, but produce no output. Shown in Examples A–24 and A–25 are the `produce_report` function and a string template used by it.

Example A–24. Counting page hits (4 of 5)

```
report_top = \
"""
<title>Web server statistics</title>
<h1>Web server statistics</h1>
<table>
<tr><th>Total number of hits:  <td>%d
<tr><th>Total number of pages: <td>%d
</table>
"""
```

This template makes up the first part of the report, containing headings and some summary information. Note the `%d`s that will be filled in by the function.

Example A–25. Counting page hits (5 of 5)

```
def produce_report():
    print report_top % (total_hits, len(hits_by_page))

    pages = []
    for (url, hits) in hits_by_page.items():
        pages.append((hits, url))
    pages.sort()
    pages.reverse()

    print "<table>"
    print "<tr><th>Page    <th>Hits"
    for (hits, url) in pages:
        print "<tr><td>%s <td>%d" % (url, hits)
    print "</table>"
```

A.4 | Classes and objects

Classes provide another means of abstraction in Python, slightly higher-level than functions. Classes and objects in Python are very much like classes and objects in mainstream languages such as C++ and Java, with some minor variations. The main differences are caused by the fact that Python is much more dynamic than C++ and Java.

A.4.1 *Defining classes*

Class definitions in Python are rather simple: they consist of a named block starting with the `class` keyword containing function and attribute definitions. Example A–26 shows an incomplete definition of a class that could represent contacts in an address database.

Example A–26. Python class definition

```
class Person:

  def __init__(self):
    self.givenname = None
    self.surname   = None
    self.addresses = {}
    self.phones    = {}
    self.emails    = []

  def get_name(self):
    return self.givenname + " " + self.surname

  def add_phone(self, name, number):
    self.phones[name] = number
```

Methods in Python are essentially functions whose first argument is a reference to the object the method is being called on. This argument is called `self` by universal convention. Most object-oriented languages hide this first argument (it is still there under the covers), but make it available through a keyword (`this` in Java and C++). The first method, named __init__, is not an ordinary method, but the constructor, which is called automatically during object creation to initialize the object. The second method, get_name, is straightforward; it just returns the name of the person. The third method is just as simple, it simply adds a new phone number to the phones dictionary.

With this class definition loaded into Python we can interact with the interpreter as shown in Example A–27. Note that to instantiate an object of a class, you must call the class as if it were a function, passing the necessary arguments to the constructor.

Example A–27. Using objects in Python

```
>>> Person
<class __main__.Person at 797e50>
>>> me = Person()
>>> me
<__main__.Person instance at 7971b0>
>>> me.givenname
>>> me.givenname = "Lars Marius"
>>> me.surname = "Garshol"
>>> me.get_name()
'Lars Marius Garshol'
```

Note that unlike statically scoped languages, in Python the attributes of an object are not fixed once and for all in its class definition. Instead, attributes are created when they are assigned to, which means that the list of attributes given in the constructor of the Person need not necessarily be the complete list of attributes supported by that class. However, it is strongly recommended to initialize all attributes in the constructor for the sake of readability.

Another feature of Python that may seem surprising is that the implementation makes very little distinction between attributes and methods. Both can be accessed with the dot notation, both for getting and setting. However, it should be noted that when a method is accessed in this way, the value that is returned is essentially a function bound to the instance from which the method was retrieved. The dialog in Example A–28 may illustrate this.

Example A–28. Python's dynamic scoping

```
>>> me.age = 26
>>> me.age
26
>>> me.add_email
<method Person.add_email of Person instance at 7971b0>
>>> me.add_email = 5
>>> me.add_email
5
>>> me.what_is_my_name = me.get_name
>>> me.what_is_my_name()
'Lars Marius Garshol'
>>> get_name = me.get_name
>>> get_name()
'Lars Marius Garshol'
```

A.4.2 *Inheritance and scoping*

In Python, a class inherits from others by listing the base classes in parentheses after the class name. Note that there may be more than one base class, since Python supports multiple inheritance. An aside for C++ programmers: unlike in C++, all methods in Python are implicitly virtual, so there is no need to, or indeed any way to, declare them to be virtual.

Example A–29 shows the definition of a Contact class, which extends the Person class with information one might want to store about a professional contact in an address database.

Example A–29. Subclassing in Python

```
class Contact(Person):

  def __init__(self):
    Person.__init__(self)
    self.company  = None
    self.position = None
```

Note the first line of the constructor, which calls the constructor of the `Person` base class. If this method were not called, the extra attributes of `Person` would not be defined on `Contact` objects at creation time, only the methods from `Person`.

In class methods there are essentially three levels of scope: local, class, and global. Variables will be searched for first in the local and then in the global scope, just as in functions. To access a variable with class scope one must use dot notation either via the class name or via a reference to an instance object. Methods always have class scope, and only values with class scope are inherited. Simple variables can also be given class scope, by placing them inside the class definition.

The interpreter dialog in Example A–30 illustrates some of these things.

Note that by convention, attribute and method names beginning with an underscore are private and not intended to be accessed directly from outside the class. They may be accessed from subclasses, however. Names beginning with two underscores are even more private, and Python will protect these against access from the outside and also from subclasses. In general, single-underscore names are the most useful and most often used.

A.4.3   *The magic methods*

Python classes can define methods with "magic" names in order to add special capabilities to the class. Using these methods, classes can customize the string representation of the class, control attribute access, emulate sequences and dictionaries, and emulate numeric types. There are many such methods, but only string representations and sequence and dictionary emulation are relevant to this book, so only these are explained here. The rest can be found in Chapter 3.3 of the *Python Reference Manual*.

Example A–30. Python's scope rules

```
>>> class A:
...      a = 10
...      def test(self):
...              print a
...
>>> a = A()
>>> a.a
10
>>> A.a
10
>>> a.test()
10
>>> class B(A):
...      pass
...
>>> b = B()
>>> b.test
10
>>> b.a
10
>>> b.test()
10
>>> test = A.test
>>> test
<unbound method A.test>
>>> test(a)
10
>>> test(b)
10
```

__repr__()

When the repr function is called on an object, it first tries to use this method to generate the string, and if that fails it creates a much less useful default string.

__str__()

This is called by the str function to create a string representation of the object, in the same way as __repr__.

`__len__()`
   Used for classes that want to emulate lists or dictionaries. Should return the number of items held by the object.

`__getitem__(index)`
   Used by classes that want to emulate lists of dictionaries to handle `self[index]`. Classes that emulate lists should accept integers,[1] and raise `IndexError` when the index is outside the set of indexes. Classes that emulate dictionaries must decide for themselves what they wish to accept.

`__setitem__(index, value)`
   Used by classes to implement assignment to `self[index]`. By not implementing this method one gets immutable objects.

`__delitem__(index)`
   Used to implement `del self[index]`.

A.5 | Various useful APIs

A.5.1   *The* `string` *module*

The `string` module contains useful functions and variables for working with strings. Most of the programs in this book use at least some of the functions in this module. The most important ones are listed below.

`find(str, sub, start = (first), end = (last))`
   Finds the first occurrence of the string `sub` within `str` and returns the index where it begins. The `start` and `end` arguments can be used to limit the search to the substring that would have been created by `str[start : end]`.

---

1.   And slice objects! See *Python Reference Manual* for more information on these.

`rfind(str, sub, start = (first), end = (last))`
  Like `find`, but finds the last occurrence instead.

`lower(s)`
  Returns `s` with all characters converted to lower case. This function only understands ASCII.

`translate(str, table, delete = '')`
  Returns a copy of `str` that has been translated using the `table` and where all characters found in the `delete` string have been deleted. The `table` must contain exactly 256 characters, and each character in `str` that is not deleted will be replaced by `table[ord(char)]`.

`maketrans(from, to)`
  Returns a translation table suitable for use with `translate`, where each character `from[i]` is set up to be replaced by `to[i]`.

`split(str, sep = None, maxsplit = 0)`
  Returns a list of fragments from `str` that were separated by the `sep` string. If `sep` is None, any sequence of whitespace will serve as a separator. If `maxsplit` is nonzero, no more than `maxsplit` splits will occur, and after the last split the remainder of the string will be the last fragment.

`join(fragments, sep = " ")`
  Takes a list of strings and returns a single string where the fragments have been concatenated and separated by `sep`.

`strip(str)`
  Returns a copy of `str` without leading or trailing whitespace.

`lstrip(str)`
  Returns a copy of `str` without leading whitespace.

`rstrip(str)`
  Returns a copy of `str` without trailing whitespace.

upper(str)

> Returns a copy of str where all characters have been converted to uppercase. Only understands ASCII.

replace(str, old, new, maxrep = 0)

> Replaces all occurrences of old in str by new. If maxrep is nonzero only the first maxrep occurrences of old are replaced.

There are more functions than these in the string module, and for these, see the Python library documentation.

A.5.2   *The* sys *module*

The sys module is very useful because it provides information about the interpreter itself, the platform it runs on, and functionality for interacting with it. The most important variables and functions are listed below, but as with string the list is not complete.

argv

> The command-line arguments that were passed to the interpreter on start-up represented as a list of strings. The file name of the script will always be the first element, if the script was run directly.

exit(status = 0)

> Calling this function causes the Python interpreter to terminate, returning the status argument to the environment to indicate why Python terminated. Zero generally means successful termination, while non-zero statuses tend to be interpreted as abnormal termination. Note that many systems only accept values in the range 0-127.

hexversion

> The current version number of the Python interpreter encoded as a single integer. For each release, including non-production releases, the size of this number will increase. When viewed as a hexadecimal

number the relation between the interpreter version and this number is apparent.[1]

path
>   The list of directories that will be searched for modules as a list of strings. Can be modified, but you are not encouraged to do so.

platform
>   A string containing a platform identifier. Under RedHat Linux 7.0 with Python 1.5.2 it contains `'linux-i386'`.

stdin
>   A file-like object representing standard input. Can be modified. The original value will be held in `__stdin__`.

stdout
>   A file-like object representing standard output. Can be modified. The original value will be held in `__stdout__`.

stderr
>   A file-like object representing standard error. Can be modified. The original value will be held in `__stderr__`.

version
>   A string containing the version number of the Python interpreter. My Python 1.5.2 interpreter on RedHat Linux 7.0 held `'1.5.2 (#1, Aug 25 2000, 09:33:37) [GCC 2.96 20000731 (experimental)]'`.

A.5.3 *File handling*

To read and write files in Python, the built-in `open` function can be used. It has the signature `open(filename, mode = 'r')` and returns

---

1.   Using the built-in function `hex` in version 1.5.2 gives `'0x10502f0'`.

a file object which can be used to read from and write to the file. If it fails for some reason, an `IOError` is raised. Filenames are written in the notation of the operating system, which means `'c:\autoexec.bat'` on Windows/DOS and `'/etc/inetd.conf'` on Unix. Note that on Windows Python can also accept forward slashes.

The mode is used to tell Python (and the operating system) what kinds of operations you plan to perform on the file. The default, `'r'`, simply means reading. As one would expect, `'w'` means writing, while `'a'` means appending to the end of the file. Note that Python represents the line terminators used on the local platform as single `'\n'` characters, and invisibly converts back and forth.

File objects support the following methods (somewhat shortened and simplified for brevity):

`close()`
> Closes the file, flushing buffers to disk and releasing the file. After this call the object cannot be used any more. This function is called automatically when the file object is garbage-collected.

`flush()`
> Flushes the internal buffers to disk.

`read(size = all)`
> Read a number of bytes from the file as a string. The `size` argument gives the maximum number of bytes to read, and if it is not given the entire file will be read in. If the end of the file has been reached an empty string is returned.

`readline()`
> Reads a line from the file, returning it with the trailing `'\n'` character.

`readlines()`
> Returns a list of all the lines in the file.

```
write(str)
```
Writes `str` to the file, *without* adding a trailing line separator.

```
writelines(list)
```
Writes a list of strings to the file, *without* adding line separators.

Example A–31 shows a simple function that reads a comma-separated file into a list of tuples.

Example A–31. Reading in a file

```
import string

def parse_csv(filename):
    rows = []
    inf = open(filename)

    for line in inf.readlines():
        line = line[ : - 1] # remove newline
        rows.append(tuple(string.split(line, ",")))

    inf.close()

    return rows
```

A.5.4 *Modules and packages*

A crucial feature for large-scale programming is the ability to partition applications into separate modules that can be maintained separately and which also have separate namespaces. This simplifies the management of the development process and at the same time prevents problems caused by name collisions. Or, to put it another way, it means that you do not have to mutilate every function and class name in your program with ugly prefixes.

Python has this feature, through what it calls modules and packages. In Python, any Python source file can be used as a module. The statement `import foo` will make Python search all the directories on the Python path (set from the PYTHONPATH environment variable) for a file named `foo.py`. If such a file is found it will be executed, and the top-level name bindings in it will be accessible through the dot notation, as in `foo.bar`. (If it is not found an `ImportError` will be raised.)

Example A–32 shows a simple module.

Example A–32. A simple Python module (`ostest.py`)

```
import sys

def platform_is_java():
    return sys.platform[ : 4] == "java"

def platform_is_win32():
    return sys.platform[ : 5] == "win32"

def platform_is_linux():
    return sys.platform[ : 5] == "linux"
```

When this module is imported with `import ostest`, code can access the functions as `ostest.platform_is_java`, `ostest.platform_is_win32`, and `ostest.platform_is_linux`. Since the `import sys` statement in the module creates a `sys` variable bound to the `sys` module (inside the `ostest` module) this is also visible from the outside as `ostest.sys`, as any other variable in the top level module would be.

When loading a module, Python parses the code in it, compiles it to Python byte-code and then executes it. Since an application may (and quite often does) load a large number of modules on start-up, Python saves time by storing the byte-code in a `.pyc` file of the same name as the module. When attempting to load a module which has a `.pyc` file, Python load the `.pyc` file directly, unless the `.py` file is newer. The result is faster program loading, with no loss in convenience for the developer.

In addition to simple modules Python also supports several levels of nesting through the package system. A directory is turned into a package by placing a file named `__init__.py` in it. All the modules in the directory will then be visible as sub-modules of the package. So if we place the `ostest` module in a directory on the `PYTHONPATH` called `lmgexts` and create an `__init__.py` file in the directory, we can make `ostest` available with `from lmgexts import ostest`.

A.5.5 *Exception handling*

Exceptions are an indispensable feature for robust programming, since they allow programs to be written without requiring every part of a program to test for possible error conditions that may have arisen somewhere else. Instead, when an error condition occurs, an exception can be raised, causing a jump upwards on the call stack to the first caller capable of handling it. This avoids tedious and error-prone checking of error flags.

In Python exceptions are (usually) objects, from classes with names that (usually) end in `Error`. They are raised, or thrown, with the keyword `raise`, as in `raise TotalConfusionError()`. The statement above creates an object of the `TotalConfusionError` class, which is non-existent and invented for this example, and raises it as an exception.

Code that wants to catch exceptions can use `try`/`except` clauses, as in Example A–33, which is an application that uses the `parse_csv` function defined in Example A–31.

Example A–33. Using Python exceptions

```
import sys

from csv import parse_csv

try:
  csv_structure = parse_csv(sys.argv[1])
except IOError, e:
  print "Error on reading file:", e
  sys.exit(1)

# do something useful with csv_structure
```

The parse_csv function does not test for or handle error conditions in any way, but since Python has exceptions, this becomes a feature rather than a bug. If something goes wrong with the file reading (file does not exist, user does not have read access, corrupt disk sector hit during file reading, etc.) Python will raise an IOError exception.

Since parse_csv does not know what context it is called in, it cannot handle such an error in a meaningful way. Therefore it does not attempt to catch IOErrors with a try/except, so the exception moves up the stack to the caller, which in this case *does* have an except IOError clause. That clause is then executed, with the exception object assigned to the e variable. If no exception (or an exception of a different class) had been raised the clause would not have been executed.

A.5.6   *Memory management*

In general, programming languages take two different approaches to memory management: either the programmer must explicitly allocate and deallocate memory, or the language will handle this transparently. C and C++ are examples of the former, while Java, Smalltalk, and Common Lisp are examples of the latter. Languages that have transparent memory management are said to have garbage collection, since they have a subsystem (known as the garbage collector) that steps into action now and then to see which objects can no longer be reached from existing values and deletes these.

Python took a middle road with respect to memory management prior to version 2.0, in that all objects and values in Python keep a count of how many references there are to them from elsewhere. Once the count goes to zero the object is immediately deallocated. This has the benefit of predictable behavior and also has better performance than naive garbage collection implementations. However, the disadvantage is that the reference counts of cyclic structures will never reach zero (even when they become garbage), so one must explicitly break the cycles to reclaim these structures.

Example A–34. Creating cyclic references

```
>>> a = {}
>>> b = {}
>>> a["a"] = 0
>>> a["b"] = b
>>> b["a"] = 0
>>> b["b"] = b
>>> a
{'b': {'b': {...}, 'a': 0}, 'a': 0}
>>> b
{'b': {...}, 'a': 0}
>>> a = None
>>> b = None
```

For example, in Example A–34 the dictionary a will be reclaimed when the a variable is set to None, while the b dictionary will not be.

Python 2.0 solves this by introducing full garbage collection, which means that even cyclic structures will be collected once there are no references to them. This garbage collector is relatively advanced, using generational scavenging and dividing objects into three generations. The gc module can be used to interact with and tune the garbage collector, but will not be available if Python was built without garbage collection.

Python 2.0 still retains the reference counting, however, since this causes objects to disappear immediately when there are no references to them. This feature is exploited by many programs, so removing it would cause hard-to-detect failures.

Detecting and removing cycles in programs that will run under Python 1.5.2 and 1.6 is still necessary and can be very difficult. The plumbo and cyclops modules, not in the standard library, but still available on the net, can be used to track down cycles.

A.5.7   Documentation strings

One feature of Python that may seem confusing to the uninitiated are the documentation strings. These are simply strings that appear in the source and which only serve as documentation. These strings are available inside programs and can be looked at when using the interpreter interactively or used to automatically generate documentation for modules and scripts.

In general, any string appearing before any other code inside a module, class, or function will be considered a documentation string. This string will be placed in the __doc__ attribute of the module, class, or function. Example A–35 demonstrates this.

Example A–35. Using documentation strings

```
>>> def square(x):
...     'square(x): returns the square of its argument'
...     return x * x
...
>>> square(5)
25
>>> square
<function square at 80ce058>
>>> square.__doc__
'square(x): returns the square of its argument'
>>> import string
>>> print string.__doc__
Common string manipulations.

Public module variables:

whitespace -- a string containing all characters considered
  whitespace
lowercase -- a string containing all characters considered
  lowercase letters
uppercase -- a string containing all characters considered
  uppercase letters
letters -- a string containing all characters considered letters
digits -- a string containing all characters considered
  decimal digits
hexdigits -- a string containing all characters considered
  hexadecimal digits
octdigits -- a string containing all characters considered
  octal digits
```

Adding documentation strings to reusable modules is considered good practice.

A.5.8   *Unicode support*

In Python 1.6, Unicode support was introduced, as explained above. In general, Unicode strings are just like ordinary strings and can freely be mixed with them. The only aspect of the Unicode support that is not really intuitive is how to read and write files to and from Unicode. This capability is provided by the `codecs` module, which provides functionality for handling both files and file-like objects. Listed below are the main functions provided by this module.

`open(filename, mode, encoding = None)`
> Opens the named file in the given mode, interpreting it according to the given character `encoding` name. Returns a file-like object that returns Unicode strings instead of ordinary strings.

`lookup(encoding)`
> Looks up the named encoding in Python's internal registry of codecs. It is not found, a `LookupError` is raised. The return value is a `(encoder, decoder, reader, writer)` tuple. The two first are functions that are mostly used by Python itself. The really interesting part are the two last arguments, which are factory functions that can be used to wrap ordinary file-like objects. If you have a file-like object `fo` that you wish to read Unicode data from, calling `reader(fo)` will give you such an object. The `writer` function works the same way, but is used to wrap files for writing.

With this module, it is trivial to read files in all kinds of encodings and have them converted to Unicode. The interpreter dialog in Example A–36 demonstrates this.

Parts of the Unicode character database are also available through the `unicodedata` module.

Example A–36. Using the `codecs` module

```
Python 2.0 (#1, Oct 16 2000, 18:10:03)
[GCC 2.95.2 19991024 (release)] on linux2
Type "copyright", "credits" or "license" for more information.
>>> inf = open("dssslref.txt")
>>> inf.readline()
'\012'
>>> inf.readline()
'FUNCTIONS:\012'
>>> import codecs
>>> uni_inf = codecs.open("py/sax/mailreader.py", "r", "iso-8859-1")
>>> uni_inf.readline()
u'import rfc822\012'
>>> uni_inf.readline()
u'from xml.sax.xmlreader import XMLReader, AttributesImpl\012'
>>> (enc, dec, reader, writer) = codecs.lookup("iso-8859-1")
>>> reader
<class encodings.latin_1.StreamReader at 0x80dda24>
>>> inf2 = reader(inf)
>>> inf2.readline()
u'\012'
>>> inf2.readline()
u' - (ancestor gi node)\012'
>>> inf2.readline()
u'\012'
```

A.5.9   *A useful idiom*

One thing it may be useful to be aware of is that in any Python source file the global namespace always contains the variable __name__, which contains the name of the module. When a script is run from the command line it does not have a module name, since it is used as a script and not as a module. In this case __name__ will be set to '__main__'.

This is often exploited by Python modules to provide testing code, or even a command-line interface, that is only run when the module is run as a script, but otherwise not run at all. Example A–37 demonstrates this.

Example A–37. The ostest module again

```
import sys

def platform_is_java():
    return sys.platform[ : 4] == "java"

def platform_is_win32():
    return sys.platform[ : 5] == "win32"

def platform_is_linux():
    return sys.platform[ : 5] == "linux"

if __name__ == "__main__":
    if platform_is_java():
        print "Running under Java"
    elif platform_is_win32():
        print "Running under Windows 32"
    elif platform_is_linux():
        print "Running under Linux"
    else:
        print "Running on an unknown platform!"
```

The module can now be used as before, but when run as a script it will print out a message saying which platform it thinks it is running on. This is of course inappropriate when it is being used by a program, so we have inserted the if test that makes sure that this will not happen when it is used as a module.

Glossary of terms

- Definitions of useful XML terms
- Definitions from the XML Recommendation
- Enhanced with explanations

T
his appendix contains a glossary of terms used in the book
that may be unfamiliar to readers who do not know XML
well. Rather than turn the text proper into an XML tutorial,
the material has been moved here, where it can be found
by those who need it.

B.1 | CDATA marked sections

The XML Recommendation, Section 2.7

CDATA sections may occur anywhere character data may occur; they
are used to escape blocks of text containing characters which would
otherwise be recognized as markup. CDATA sections begin with the
string "<![CDATA[" and end with the string "]]>".

Note that the terms CDATA sections and CDATA marked sections
mean the same and are often used interchangeably.

B.2 | Character data

The XML Recommendation, Section 2.4
> Text consists of intermingled character data and markup. [...] All text that is not markup constitutes the character data of the document.

Thus, the character data of a document is those parts of the document that are not markup, such as the content that occurs between the start-tag and end-tag of an element.

B.3 | Character references

These are references to individual characters by number, for example `&#65;` (decimal) or `&#x41;` (hexadecimal). They are also erroneously known as numeric character entities, and correctly as numeric character references. The XML Recommendation defines them as shown below.

The XML Recommendation, Section 4.1
> A character reference refers to a specific character in the ISO/IEC 10646 character set, for example one not directly accessible from available input devices.

B.4 | Document element

The XML Recommendation, Section 2.1
> There is exactly one element, called the root, or document element, no part of which appears in the content of any other element.

In other words, the document element of an XML or SGML document is the root element, the element that contains the entire document.

B.5 | Document entity

This is the entity that begins the XML or SGML document. Many people think of it as being the same as the file that contains the document, which is correct, except that it does not have to be a file, and that the entire document need not be in the file. The definition from the XML Recommendation, given below, is perhaps more telling in what it does not say than it what it says.

The XML Recommendation, Section 4.8
> The document entity serves as the root of the entity tree and a starting-point for an XML processor.

B.6 | Document order

When speaking of nodes in a document, this is quite simply the order in which the text corresponding to the nodes originally appeared in the source document. This term is widely used in the XML family of specifications, but is not, as far as I can tell, formally defined anywhere.

B.7 | Mixed content

The XML Recommendation, Section 3.2.2
> An element type has mixed content when elements of that type may contain character data, optionally interspersed with child elements.

This essentially means that the element may contain character data, and that some of the character data may be marked up. This is universal in document-oriented applications and rare in data-oriented applications.

B.8 | Processing instruction

The XML Recommendation, Section 2.6.2
Processing instructions (PIs) allow documents to contain instructions for applications.

A PI is a markup construct in XML that cannot be controlled by the DTD or a schema. It can appear anywhere in a document except within tags or other markup. The processing instruction used to include stylesheets in XML documents is one example of this.

Processing instructions have a target and associated data, as in: `<?target data?>`, where the target must be an XML name, but the data can take any form. The target gives the meaning of the processing instruction (just as namespaces do for elements).

B.9 | Replacement text

The full story of how entity values are produced and interpreted is long and rather complex, and uses quite a few specialized terms. One of them is replacement text, which is defined by XML as follows.

The XML Recommendation, Section 4.5
The replacement text is the content of the entity, after replacement of character references and parameter-entity references.

B.10 | Standalone declaration

A pseudo-attribute that may appear on the *XML declaration*, as in `<?xml version="1.0" standalone="yes"?>`. It tells parsers whether reading the external subset will affect the parsing of the document. See 2.4.2.1, "How the DTD affects the document," on page 69 for more details.

The XML Recommendation, Section 2.9
> Markup declarations can affect the content of the document, as passed from an XML processor to an application [...]. The standalone document declaration, which may appear as a component of the XML declaration, signals whether or not there are such declarations which appear external to the document entity or in parameter entities.

B.11 | Text

In XML and SGML, this has a very specific meaning: it means all the characters that a document consists of. This includes both markup and *character data*.

The XML Recommendation, Section 2.4
> Text consists of intermingled character data and markup.

B.12 | Text declaration

External entities, as opposed to *document entities*, may also contain *XML declarations*, but since these cannot have a *standalone declaration*, they are called text declarations to separate them from XML declarations.

B.13 | XML declaration

This is the `<?xml version="1.0" ...?>`, a pseudo-*processing instruction*[1] that appears at the beginning of most XML documents. It is used to give content processors information about the document as well as to help them identify what the document contains. See also *text declaration*.

---

1. According to the Infoset, zit is not a processing instruction, however suspiciously it may resemble one.

Python XML packages

- Installation instructions
- Python tools
- Java packages

Appendix
C

This appendix contains information about how to find and install the tools used in the examples in this book. These packages can also be found on the CD-ROM that accompanies the book, but URLs are included in this chapter in case you wish to install newer versions than those on the CD-ROM.

Explanations of how to install the tools are given for Windows and Linux only. Other Unix systems should be similar enough to Linux that you can see how to install on them given the Linux instructions. I would have liked to have Macintosh instructions as well, but do not know the platform well enough to be able to provide any.

Installing software is notoriously difficult, because of the infinite number of possible and likely combinations of platforms, installed versions, and configurations. So please do forgive me if in this appendix I make the very difficult sound easy. The instructions given here worked for me, although I cannot guarantee that they will for you. Mistakes and pitfalls pointed out to me via email to `larsga@garshol.priv.no` will be incorporated into the errata at `http://www.garshol.priv.no/download/text/ph1/`.

In general, when installing Python packages on your system there are two ways to make sure that Python can find the packages. One is to set the PYTHONPATH environment variable to point to the directory that contains the packages. This environment variable is an ordinary path variable like the PATH and the CLASSPATH and uses the same separators (: on Unix and ; on Windows).

The second possibility is to put the Python packages into the lib/site-packages directory, inside the directory where Python was installed. Python always looks for packages here, regardless of what is on the PYTHONPATH. For many packages this may be the easiest way to install them.

Note that compiled C extensions, in the form of .so, .dll, or .pyd files, can be placed in the same places as ordinary Python source code, and will be found and imported by the Python interpreter.

If you are completely new to Python development, you should give some thought to what editor you wish to write Python code in. Below are some suggestions:

Emacs

If you are an Emacs user, the choice is simple.[1] There is a good Python mode for Emacs available from http://www.python.org/.

IDLE

IDLE is a graphical IDE for Python that comes with the Python distribution (from 2.0 onwards). You can find it in the tools directory in the Python distribution. It is quite nice and has some very useful features. It's based on Tk, and so works on most platforms.

---

1. All the source code in this book was written in Emacs as was the XML Recommendation itself. See http://www.dina.dk/~abraham/religion/ to find out why this was inevitable.

UltraEdit

If you work on Windows and want something that looks and works like an ordinary Windows application, UltraEdit may be what you want. It has a Python mode, and can be downloaded from `http://www.ultraedit.com`.

C.1 | The Python interpreter

The first thing you will need is the Python interpreter itself. You can use version 1.5.2 with the examples and software in this book, and do not need to upgrade if this is what you have on your system. I recommend, however, that a Python 2.x version be used, because it will have the distutils, which make installing the rest of the needed software much easier. (You can use distutils with 1.5.2 as well, more about that below.)

Linux

Most Linux distributions come with Python already installed. You can verify this by typing `python` at the command line and seeing if Python starts up. If it does, you have it, although it is quite likely that you have Python 1.5.2.

If you do not have Python installed, you can look for packages from your distribution (most distributions provide Python packages), or you can go to `http://www.python.org/download/` and download the C sources.

If you have 1.5.2 and want to install 2.1 from C sources, that is entirely possible, and the two versions can coexist. (Achieving coexistence with distribution packages, like `.rpms` or `.debs`, is harder.) To install from source, simply unpack the sources into a directory. Then enter the directory and give the command `./configure`, followed by `make`. Then, become superuser (`su`), and say the magic words `make install`.

Note: If you do this on RedHat Linux 7.0 you will get this error message: "LONG_BIT definition appears wrong for platform (bad gcc config?).” This is due to a problem in the glibc shipped with RedHat Linux 7.0. Upgrade to glibc-2.2–9 or newer, and all should go well.

Windows

Windows users should go to `http://www.python.org/download/` and download the newest Windows installer. This is a graphical installer which will guide you through the installation process and install like any other Windows software.

C.I.I   *Jython*

Some of the examples in this book use Jython, and in any case Jython is a great tool to have when working with Java, so I recommend that you install it. You can get it from the Jython Web site at `http://www.jython.org/`. Jython is distributed as a Java application that is run to be installed, presenting a graphical interface similar to that used by Windows installers.

To be able to install, and indeed make use of, Jython you must have a Java environment installed. This can be downloaded from `http://java.sun.com/`, where you will find packages that are easy to install. Once you have a Java environment you can simply download the Jython installer, go to the directory you placed it in on the command line, and give the command `java jython-20`. On Linux you should be superuser when doing this, at least if you intend to install under `/usr`.

Note that Jython does *not* use the PYTHONPATH environment variable. Instead, there is a file named `registry` in the Jython directory. In it you can set the `python.path` setting, which is analogous to the PYTHONPATH.

C.2 | The Python XML-SIG package

In order to create XML processing tools for Python, a number of volunteers have formed a Special Interest Group (SIG) for Python XML processing. This group has created a package that contains a large part of the software you need to work with the examples in this book. The package is usually known as PyXML.

The package contains:

- A more complete SAX package than what comes with Python 2.x,
- xmlproc,
- 4DOM,
- qp_xml,
- javadom,
- sgmlop,
- 4XPath,
- 4XSLT, and
- minidom.

The package can be downloaded from the SIG pages at `http://www.python.org/sigs/xml-sig/`. The package has a distutils installer, and can be installed with the command `python setup.py install`. On Windows, it is better to download the Windows installer, since the distutils installation requires a C compiler to compile the extensions.

C.3 | 4Suite

The 4Suite package is a collection of XML processing tools developed by Fourthought. It contains 4XSLT as well as a number of things beyond what the XML-SIG package has. It requires the XML-SIG package to work, so you should install that before continuing with 4Suite.

You can download 4Suite from `http://www.4suite.org/`. The distribution contains a distutils installer, so it should be easy to install. There is also a graphical Windows installer for Windows environments. Note that the site also has copious installation instructions. These contain a number of steps that are not strictly necessary, but which may be useful if you run into trouble.

C.4 | Sab-pyth

Sab-pyth requires that you already have Sablotron installed. You can download it from `http://www.gingerall.com/charlie-bin/ get/webGA/act/sablotron.act`, where you can find `.rpm` packages, source packages, and zipped Windows binaries. Sab-pyth itself can be downloaded from `http://www.ubka.uni-karlsruhe.de/ ~guenter/Sab-pyth/`, where you can find a source package and a package with Windows binaries. Installation should be relatively straightforward.

Windows
The Windows Sablotron and Sab-pyth binaries can just be unzipped into a directory. After that you can install the package in the usual way. Note that you may need to copy the `.dlls` from the Sablotron distribution into the same directory as the Sab-pyth packages so that Python can find them.

Linux with `.rpms`
Under Linux, Sablotron is packaged rather awkwardly, so installing it is not easy. If you can use `.rpms` I suggest that you do so. You will need to get both the expat, expat-devel, sablot and sablot-devel `.rpms`. (There are links to the expat packages on the Sablotron site, luckily.)

Once the `.rpms` are in place, you will be ready to compile and install Sab-pyth. It comes with a distutils installer, but you will need to tweak it a little. The `setup.py` file in the Sab-pyth wants the xmlparse and xmltok libraries (that is, `lib*.a` files), but expat-devel does not have those. This is solved by editing `setup.py` to replace `'xmlparse'`, `'xmltok'` with `'expat'`.

Now, all you need to do is say `python setup.py install` and Sab-pyth will build and install. (At least, it did for me.)

Unix, with sources

First, download and unpack both the expat and Sablotron sources. Go into the expat directory and do the usual `./configure`, `make`, and `make install` dance. You should now have a compiled version of expat. Note that you must install expat, or the Sablotron configure script will not find expat.

The next step is to compile Sablotron itself, and this is done with the same `./configure`, `make`, `make install` spell.

Now you have built and installed expat and Sablotron, and all that remains is Sab-pyth, which will build and install if you say `python setup.py install`.

C.5 | RXP

RXP is mainly available for Python under Windows and Unix (although it could probably be made to work elsewhere too).

Under Windows, the easiest way to get RXP to work is to download XED from `http://www.ltg.ed.ac.uk/~ht/xed.html` and install it. After installing, you can take the `XMLinter.dll` file from the `PyXML` subdirectory in the XED installation and put it in the `DLLs` subdirectory of your Python installation, so that Python can find it. After that you will be all set and ready to use it.

This may sound somewhat surprising, but for Windows you don't need to download the RXP/PyXML distribution at all, unless you want the C source or the (rather sparse) documentation for it. If you do, you can get it from `ftp://www.ltg.ed.ac.uk/pub/ht/PyXML.tar.gz`.

Under Unix the easiest way to do this is to get the LTXML distribution from `http://www.ltg.ed.ac.uk/software/xml/` and install the sources somewhere. After that you can download RXP/PyXML and install it in a separate directory. Then you can edit the RXP/PyXML makefile and set the references at the top to point into the Python and LTXML sources.

Then you can go into the LTXML directory and say `make`, wait until it has compiled, go into the RXP/PyXML directory and say `make` there, whereafter you should have the `XMLintermodule.so` file ready for use. That file can then be placed on the `PYTHONPATH` or in `site-packages`.

C.6 | pysp

pysp can be downloaded from `http://www.garshol.priv.no/download/software/pysp/`. It requires that you already have SP installed, which you can get from `http://www.jclark.com/sp/`. There is no binary distribution of pysp, so Windows users must have a C++ compiler to install it. (You can check the Web pages to see if anyone has contributed Windows binaries.)

The install is relatively straightforward. First, download SP and compile it. (`make` is all that is required on Linux.) Then, edit the `setup.cfg` file in the pysp directory to point to the SP directory and its `lib/` subdirectory. Now you should be able to say `python setup.py install`, and everything should work.

Note that an older distutils version had a bug which kept the setup script from working. Python 2.1 and newer has a working distutils.

C.7 | The easy ones

A number of packages are easy to install, mostly because they are sources only and thus only need to be unpacked and copied into the right directories. Instructions for these have been collected below.

GPS

You can download GPS from `http://www.ontopia.net/~grove/software/gps/`. The package has no installer, but all you need to do is either put the Python files on your `PYTHONPATH` or put them in the `site-packages` directory.

Pyxie

Pyxie is blessedly easy to install: go to `http://pyxie.source-forge.net/`, download `pyxie.py`, and place it where Python can find it. (Note that you must have the Python XML-SIG package already.)

eventdom

A package containing the Python sources can be downloaded from `http://www.prescod.net/python/eventdom/`. The `.zip` file has Python sources that must be placed where Python can find them.

xmlarch

You can download xmlarch from `http://www.ontopia.net/~grove/software/xmlarch/`. The package contains only Python source files, and no distutils installer; you can place these on the `PYTHONPATH` or in `site-packages`.

wxPython

Graphical Windows installers and `.rpms` can be downloaded from `http://www.wxpython.org/`. If you need to build from sources, there are distutils packages on the site as well, together with good instructions for building.

6.8 | Java packages

Luckily, the Java packages are all easy to install. They generally either have graphical installers, or contain `.jar` files, which you can put on Java's CLASSPATH. Once that is done, you should be able to use them without further complications.

SAX 2.0

This is included in most other packages, but if you want it and its documentation, you can get this from `http://www.megginson.com/SAX/`.

Xerces-J

This can be downloaded from `http://xml.apache.org/dist/xerces-j/`.

Ælfred

An improved version is contained in the SAXON package, so I recommend that you simply use the version in that package.

XP

Can be downloaded from `http://www.jclark.com/xml/xp/`.

JAXP

This is generally included in the packages that use it, but you can get the specification and reference implementation from `http://java.sun.com/xml/xml_jaxp.html`.

JDOM

JDOM can be downloaded from the JDOM site at `http://www.jdom.org/`.

Saxon

Saxon can be found at `http://saxon.sourceforge.net`.

Xalan-J

Can be downloaded from `http://xml.apache.org/xalan/`.

If any of these URLs have changed, or if you simply want to find more Java XML tools, you can go to my Free XML tools site at `http://www.garshol.priv.no/download/xmltools/` where you can find links to all the generic free XML software I know of.

Index

▌ *Numbers*

0 (zero)
  binary digit, 6
  in Python, 1064
  in XPath, 576, 578
1 (one)
  binary digit, 6
  in Python, 1064
  in XPath, 578
4DOM, DOM implementation,
    400–401, 409, 430, 435–441, 443,
    470, 474, 477, 484, 488, 490–491,
    495–497, 530, 533, 536, 642, 1113
  speed of, 496
4ODS, database, 401
4Suite, toolkit, 401, 438, 1113
4XPath, XPath implementation, 530,
    533, 650, 653, 667, 683, 1113
  APIs of, 677–679
  built-in functions in, 665
4XSLT, XSLT processor, 439, 530, 534,
    536, 607, 641, 670, 678, 821, 978,
    982–983, 1113
  extension element types in, 652–655
  extension functions in, 650–652

▌ *Symbols*

!=, operator
  in Python, 1064
  in XPath, 575
" (quote)
  in attributes, 317
  in Python, 1061
  in XPath, 575
(number sign), in DOM, 408
$ (dollar sign), in XPath, 581
€ (euro sign), 118
% (percent sign)
  in entity names, 358, 360
  in Python, 1059, 1062
  in URLs, 594

& (ampersand)
  during parsing, 60
  in URLs, 67
  in XML, 590
  in XSLT, 536
  serialized from DOM, 419
  treatment by SAX, 263
&#, in entity references, 1102
&, entity reference (ampersand),
    419, 590
<, entity reference (less than), 55, 590
 , entity reference (no-break
    space), 55
' (apostrophe)
  in Python, 1061
  in XPath, 575
( ) (parentheses)
  in DTDs, 360
  in Python, 1059, 1067, 1075, 1083
  in PYX, 854
* (asterisk)
  in DOM, 416, 418, 772–773, 776
  in DTDs, 360, 911
  in Python, 1059
  in regular expressions, 576
  in XPath, 572, 574–575
  in XSLT, 597
**, operator (Python), 1059
+ (plus sign)
  in DTDs, 360, 911
  in Python, 1059
  in UTF-7, 123
  in XPath, 575
, (comma)
  in CSV files, 966
- (minus sign, hyphen)
  in Python, 1059, 1065
  in PYX, 855
  in UTF-7, 123
  in XPath, 575
  in XPath function names, 652
--, character sequence (XSLT), 588
. (period)
  in Python, 1084
  in Pyxie, 858
  in XPath, 584
.., character sequence (XPath), 568, 584

A

G